DM567

How do you view the
challenge and benefit of
IT? CHAP 5

Q 3,4,7,8 CH 3

Q 4,8,10 CH 4

Supply Chain Logistics Management

The McGraw-Hill/Irwin Series Operations and Decision Sciences

OPERATIONS MANAGEMENT

Burt, Dobler, and Starling
Purchasing and Supply Management
Seventh Edition

Chase, Jacobs, and Aquilano
Operations Management for Competitive Advantage
Eleventh Edition

Davis and Heineke
Operations Management: Integrating Manufacturing and Services
Fifth Edition

Davis and Heineke
Managing Services
First Edition

Finch
Operations Now
Second Edition

Flaherty
Global Operations Management
First Edition

Fitzsimmons and Fitzsimmons
Service Management
Fifth Edition

Gehrlein
Operations Management Cases
First Edition

Gray and Larson
Project Management
Third Edition

Harrison and Samson
Technology Management
First Edition

Hill
Manufacturing Strategy: Text & Cases
Third Edition

Hopp and Spearman
Factory Physics
Second Edition

Jacobs and Whybark
Why ERP?
First Edition

Knod and Schonberger
Operations Management
Seventh Edition

Lambert and Stock
Strategic Logistics Management
Third Edition

Leenders, Johnson, Flynn, and Fearon
Purchasing and Supply Chain Management
Thirteenth Edition

Melnyk and Swink
Value-Driven Operations Management
First Edition

Moses, Seshadri, and Yakir
HOM Operations Management Software
First Edition

Nahmias
Production and Operations Analysis
Fifth Edition

Nicholas
Competitive Manufacturing Management
First Edition

Olson
Introduction to Information Systems Project Management
Second Edition

Pinto and Parente
SimProject: A Project Management Simulation for Classroom Instruction
First Edition

Schroeder
Operations Management: Contemporary Concepts and Cases
Third Edition

Seppanen, Kumar, and Chandra
Process Analysis and Improvement
First Edition

Simchi-Levi, Kaminsky, and Simchi-Levi
Designing and Managing the Supply Chain
Second Edition

Stevenson
Operations Management
Eighth Edition

Vollmann, Berry, Whybark, and Jacobs
Manufacturing Planning & Control Systems
Fifth Edition

Supply Chain Logistics Management

Second Edition

Donald J. Bowersox
David J. Closs
M. Bixby Cooper
Michigan State University

Boston   Burr Ridge, IL   Dubuque, IA   Madison, WI   New York   San Francisco   St. Louis
Bangkok   Bogotá   Caracas   Kuala Lumpur   Lisbon   London   Madrid   Mexico City
Milan   Montreal   New Delhi   Santiago   Seoul   Singapore   Sydney   Taipei   Toronto

McGraw-Hill
Irwin

SUPPLY CHAIN LOGISTICS MANAGEMENT

Published by McGraw-Hill/Irwin, a business unit of The McGraw-Hill Companies, Inc., 1221 Avenue of the Americas, Now York, NY, 10020. Copyright © 2007 by The McGraw-Hill Companies, Inc. All rights reserved. No part of this publication may be reproduced or distributed in any form or by any means, or stored in a database or retrieval system, without the prior written consent of The McGraw-Hill Companies, Inc., including, but not limited to, in any network or other electronic storage or transmission, or broadcast for distance learning.

Some ancillaries, including electronic and print components, may not be available to customers outside the United States.

This book is printed on acid-free paper.

2 3 4 5 6 7 8 9 0 QPD/QPD 0 9 8 7 6

ISBN 978-0-07-294788-5
MHID 0-07-294788-8

Editorial director: *Brent Gordon*
Executive editor: *Scott Isenberg*
Editorial assistant: *Lee Stone*
Senior marketing manager: *Douglas Reiner*
Senior media producer: *Victor Chiu*
Project manager: *Jim Labeots*
Senior production supervisor: *Rose Hepburn*
Coordinator freelance design: *Artemio Ortiz Jr.*
Media project manager: *Cathy Tepper*
Cover design: *Chris Bowyer*
Typeface: *10/12 Times New Roman*
Compositor: *Interactive Composition Corporation*
Printer: *Quebecor World Dubuque Inc.*

Library of Congress Cataloging-in-Publication Data

Bowersox, Donald J.
    Supply chain logistics management / Donald J. Bowersox, David J. Closs, M. Bixby Cooper.–2nd ed.
        p. cm. – (McGraw-Hill/Irwin series operations and decision sciences)
    Includes bibliographical references and indexes.
    ISBN-13: 978-0-07-294788-5 (alk. paper)
    ISBN-10: 0-07-294788-8 (alk. paper)
    1. Business logistics. I. Closs, David J. II. Cooper, M. Bixby. III. Title. IV. Series.

HD38.5.B697 2007
658.7–dc22   2005049643

www.mhhe.com

This book is dedicated to our wives and families for their time, encouragement, and patience for it is the authors' families who ultimately pay the dearest price.

About the Authors

Donald J. Bowersox is the John H. McConnell Chaired University Professor at Michigan State University where he also served as Dean of the Eli Broad College of Business. He received his Ph.D. at Michigan State and has worked in industry throughout his career. He is the author of numerous articles in publications such as the *Harvard Business Review, Journal of Marketing, Journal of Business Logistics,* and *Supply Chain Management Review.* Dr. Bowersox has led a number of industry-supported research studies investigating the best practices of logisticians in North America and around the world. He is a frequent speaker at industry and academic meetings.

David J. Closs is the John H. McConnell Chaired Professor of Business Administration at Michigan State University. He received his Ph.D. in marketing and logistics from Michigan State. Dr. Closs is the author and coauthor of many publications in journals, proceedings, and industry reports. He was also a principal researcher for *World Class Logistics: The Challenge of Managing Continuous Change* and *21st Century Logistics: Making Supply Chain Integration a Reality.* Dr. Closs is a frequent speaker at industry and academic conferences and presenter at executive education programs. Dr. Closs formerly served as the editor of the *Journal of Business Logistics* and is currently the executive editor of *Logistics Quarterly.*

M. Bixby Cooper is an Associate Professor in the Department of Marketing and Supply Chain Management at Michigan State University. He is coauthor of three texts on distribution and logistics, including *World Class Logistics: The Challenge of Managing Continuous Change* and *Strategic Marketing Channel Management.* He also served for 4 years on the Executive Board of the International Customer Service Association as Head of the Research and Education Committee.

Preface

Over the last six decades, the discipline of business logistics has advanced from the warehouse and transportation dock to the boardroom of leading global enterprises. We have had the opportunity to be actively involved in this evolution through research, education, and advising. *Supply Chain Logistics Management* encompasses the development and fundamentals of the logistics discipline within a supply chain structure. It also presents our vision of the future of business logistics and supply chain management and their role in enterprise competitiveness.

Although individually and collectively the three authors have written extensively on various aspects of logistics, the decision to initially write and subsequently revise *Supply Chain Logistics Management* represents the synthesis of many years of research, augmenting and, in many ways, supplanting earlier works of the authors published by McGraw-Hill. The union of ideas presented in this text provides an integrated supply chain framework for the study of logistics, serves to expand the treatment of supply chain management by placing it firmly in the context of integrated business strategy, and highlights the increasing importance of logistics in the supply chains supporting a global economy.

Logistics includes all the activities required to move product and information to, from, and between members of a supply chain. The supply chain provides the framework for businesses and their suppliers to jointly deliver goods, services, and information efficiently, effectively, and relevantly to customers. *Supply Chain Logistics Management* presents the mission, business processes, and strategies needed to achieve integrated logistical management. We hope the text achieves three fundamental objectives: (1) presents a comprehensive description of existing logistical practices in a global economy, (2) describes ways and means to apply logistics principles to achieve competitive advantage, and (3) provides a conceptual approach for integrating logistics as a core competency within enterprise supply chain strategy.

It would be impossible to list all the individuals who have made significant contributions to the contents of this book. Special thanks are due to Robert W. Nason, Chair of the Department of Marketing and Supply Chain Management at Michigan State University, for maintaining a collegial environment that fosters creativity. We also express our gratitude to Professor Emeritus Donald A. Taylor of Michigan State University, who has been a guiding force throughout our careers. In addition, for their specific suggestions regarding the manuscript, our appreciation goes to Hugh Turner, University of Maryland; Soonhung Min, University of Oklahoma; Ted Stank, University of Tennessee; Robert Novack, Penn State University; David Borst, Concordia University; Charles Peterson, Northern Illinois University; and John Mawhinney, Duquesne University, all of whom provided detailed reviews and offered numerous suggestions for improving the presentation.

We also wanted to acknowledge the staff at McGraw-Hill/Irwin for their guidance and efforts on behalf of the book: Brent Gordon, Publisher; Scott Isenberg, Executive Editor; Lee Stone, Editorial Coordinator Assistant; Jim Labeots, Project Manager; Rose Hepburn, Production Supervisor; Artemio Ortiz, Designer; and Victor Chiu, Media Producer. Also assisting us was Beth Baugh, Developmental Editor with Carlisle Publishers Services.

As active members of the Council of Supply Chain Management Professionals, we have been the fortunate recipients of contributions by many council members to the development of this manuscript. In particular, we wish to acknowledge the assistance of

George Gecowets, former executive director, Maria McIntyre, current executive director, and the CSCMP staff who maintain an open door to the academic community.

Over the past 40 years, the business executives who have attended the annual Michigan State University Logistics Management Executive Development Seminar have been exposed to the basic concepts presented in the text and have given freely of their time and experience. We also acknowledge the long-standing support to Michigan State logistics, through the funding of the endowed chairs, provided by John H. McConnell, founder of Worthington Industries.

The number of individuals involved in teaching logistics around the world expands daily. To this group in general, and in particular to our colleagues at Michigan State University, whose advice and assistance made it possible to complete and enhance this text, we express our sincere appreciation.

Teachers receive continuous inspiration from students over the years, and in many ways the day of judgment in an academic career comes in the seminar or classroom. We have been fortunate to have the counsel of many outstanding young scholars who currently are making substantial impact on the academic and business worlds. In particular, we appreciate the input of students who have used this text in manuscript form and made suggestions for improvement. We also acknowledge the contributions of current and former doctoral students, particularly Drs. Judith Whipple and Thomas Goldsby, who participated extensively in case development and editorial support. Student Research Assistant John Bowersox provided valuable assistance throughout manuscript preparation and managed the complex process of obtaining publication permissions. Appreciation is extended to Major G. Scott Webb, who assististed in updating materials for this edition.

We wish to acknowledge the contributions of Felicia Kramer and Pamela Kingsbury, for manuscript preparation on several earlier versions of this text. Cheryl Lundeen, who prepared many drafts of the manuscript, provided outstanding support for the last two editions. Without Felicia, Pam, and Cheryl, this long published text in its many variations would not be a reality.

With so much able assistance, is it difficult to offer excuses for any shortcomings that might appear. Any faults are solely our responsibility.

Donald J. Bowersox

David J. Closs

M. Bixby Cooper

Brief Contents

Contents

PART ONE

Supply Chain Logistics Management

Part 1 establishes the strategic importance of logistics to achieving business success by creating value throughout domestic and global supply chains. The initial chapter scopes the current business attention to supply chain management. The supply chain provides the framework within which logistical strategies are developed and executed. Logistics, the primary topic of this book, is introduced in Chapter 2. The concept of lean logistics is developed by discussing the ways specific work tasks combine to support customer accommodation, manufacturing, and procurement. Chapter 3 describes the importance of customer accommodation to successful logistics. The value created by logistics can serve as a powerful driver of customer success. Chapter 4 introduces procurement and manufacturing. The combination of customer accommodation, procurement, and manufacturing represents the supply chain operational areas that are linked and supported by logistics. Chapter 5, the final chapter in Part 1, presents an overview of information technology that is specifically applicable to supply chain logistics. A framework is developed to serve as a format for presenting specific technology applications in supply chain logistics operation and design.

21st-Century Supply Chains

Chapter Outline

As recently as the 1990s, the average time required for a company to process and deliver merchandise to a customer from warehouse inventory ranged from 15 to 30 days, sometimes even longer. The typical order-to-delivery process involved order creation and transfer, which was usually via telephone, fax, electronic data interchange (EDI), or public mail; followed by order processing, which involved the use of manual or computer systems, credit authorization, and order assignment to a warehouse for processing; followed by shipment to a customer. When everything went as planned, the average time for a customer to receive items ordered was lengthy. When something went wrong, as it often did, such as inventory out-of-stock, a lost or misplaced work order, or a misdirected shipment, total time to service customers escalated rapidly.

To support this lengthy and unpredictable time to market, it became common practice to accumulate inventory. For example, inventories of identical products were typically stocked by retailers, wholesalers, and manufacturers. Despite such extensive inventory, out-of-stocks and delayed deliveries were common due in part to the large number of product variations.

These accepted business practices of the 20th century, as well as the distribution channel structure used to complete delivery, evolved from years of experience dating from the industrial revolution. Such long-standing business practices remained in place and unchallenged because no clearly superior alternative existed. The traditional distribution process was designed to overcome challenges and achieve benefits that long ago ceased to be important. The industrialized world is no longer characterized by scarcity. Consumer affluence and desire for wide choice of products and services continue to grow. In fact, today's consumers want a wide range of product and source options they can configure to their unique specifications. The desires of customers have shifted from passive acceptance to active involvement in the design and delivery of specific products and services. Transportation capacity and operational performance have increasingly become more economical and reliable. Today's transportation is supported by sophisticated information systems that facilitate predictable and precise delivery.

Massive change has occurred as a result of available information technology. During the decade of the 1990s, the world of commerce was irrevocably impacted by computerization, the Internet, and a range of inexpensive information transmission capabilities. Information characterized by speed, accessibility, accuracy, and most of all relevancy became the norm. The Internet has become a common and economical way to complete business-to-business (B2B) transactions. Driven by these fundamental forces, a global economy rapidly emerged.

What began during the last decade of the 20th century and will continue to unfold well into the 21st century is what historians will characterize as the dawning of the **information** or **digital age.** In the information age the reality of business connectivity continues to drive a new order of relationships called **supply chain management.** Managers are increasingly improving traditional marketing, manufacturing, purchasing and logistics practices. In this new order of affairs, products can be manufactured to exact specifications and rapidly delivered to customers at locations throughout the globe. Logistical systems exist that have the capability to deliver products at precise times. Customer order and delivery of product assortments can be performed in hours. The frequent occurrence of service failures that characterized the past is increasingly being replaced by a growing managerial commitment to zero defect or what is commonly called **six-sigma** performance.[1] **Perfect orders**— delivering the desired assortment and quantity of products to the right location on time, damage-free, and correctly invoiced—once the exception, are now becoming the expectation. Perhaps most important is the fact that such high-level performance is being achieved at lower total cost and with the commitment of fewer financial resources than was characteristic of the past. All of this fundamental change in business enterprise structure and strategy is primarily being driven by information technology.[2]

In this initial chapter, the supply chain management business model and value proposition is introduced as a growing strategic posture of contemporary firms. The chapter reviews the development of the supply chain revolution in business practice. Next, the supply chain concept is presented in a strategic framework. The chapter then examines integrative management, responsiveness, financial sophistication, globalization, and digital transformation as forces driving the emergence of supply chain logic. The overall objective of Chapter 1 is to position the logistical challenges of supporting a 21st century supply chain strategy. The supply chain is positioned as the strategic framework within which logistical requirements are identified and related operations managed.

---

[1] Six-sigma performance reflects a level of achievement having an error rate of 3.4 defects per million, or 99.99966 percent perfect.

[2] For a discussion and examples of supply chain agility, adaptability, and alignment, see Hau L. Lee, "The Triple A Supply Chain," *Harvard Business Review* (October 2004), pp. 102–12.

The Supply Chain Revolution

What managers are experiencing today we choose to describe as the **supply chain revolution** and a related **logistical renaissance.** These two massive shifts in expectation and practice concerning best-practice performance of business operations are highly interrelated. However, they are significantly different aspects of contemporary strategic thinking.

Supply chain management consists of firms collaborating to leverage strategic positioning and to improve operating efficiency. For each firm involved, the supply chain relationship reflects a strategic choice. A supply chain strategy is a channel arrangement based on acknowledged dependency and collaboration. Supply chain operations require managerial processes that span functional areas within individual firms and link trading partners and customers across organizational boundaries.

In contrast to supply chain management, logistics is the work required to move and position inventory throughout a supply chain. As such, logistics is a subset of and occurs within the broader framework of a supply chain. Logistics is the process that creates value by timing and positioning inventory. Logistics is the combination of a firm's order management, inventory, transportation, warehousing, materials handling, and packaging as integrated throughout a facility network. Integrated logistics serves to link and synchronize the overall supply chain as a continuous process and is essential for effective supply chain connectivity. While the purpose of logistical work has remained essentially the same over the decades, the way the work is performed continues to radically change.

The fundamental focus of this book is integrated logistics management. However, to study logistics, a reader must have a basic understanding of supply chain management. Supply chain decisions establish the operating framework within which logistics is performed. As will be reviewed shortly, dramatic change continues to evolve in supply chain practice. Accordingly, logistics best practice, as described in this book, is presented as a work in progress, subject to continuous change based on the evolving nature of supply chain structure and strategy. Chapter 2, Logistics, scopes the renaissance taking place in logistics best practice and sets the stage for all chapters that follow.

At first blush, supply chain management may appear to be a vague concept. A great deal has been written on the subject without much concern for basic definition, structure, or common vocabulary. Confusion exists concerning the appropriate scope of what constitutes a supply chain, to what extent it involves integration with other companies as contrasted to integrating internal operations, and how to best implement it in terms of competitive practices and legal constraints. For most managers, the supply chain concept has intrinsic appeal because it visions new business arrangements offering the potential to improve competitiveness. The concept also implies a highly efficient and effective network of business relationships that serve to improve efficiency by eliminating duplicate and nonproductive work. Understanding more specifically what constitutes the supply chain revolution starts with a review of traditional distribution channel practice.

To overcome challenges of commercial trading, firms developed business relationships with other product and service companies to jointly perform essential activities. Such acknowledged dependency was necessary to achieve benefits of specialization. Managers, following the early years of the industrial revolution, began to strategically plan core competency, specialization, and economy of scale. The result was realization that working closely with other businesses was essential for continued success. This understanding that no firm could be totally self-sufficient contrasted to some earlier notions of vertical ownership integration.[3] Acknowledged dependence between business firms created the study of what became known as **distribution** or **marketing channels.**

Because of the high visibility of different types of businesses, the early study of channel arrangements was characterized by classification based on specific roles performed during the distributive process. For example, a firm may have been created to perform the value-added services called wholesaling. Firms doing business with a wholesaler had expectations concerning what services they would receive and the compensation they would be expected to pay. In-depth study of specific activities quickly identified the necessity for leadership, a degree of commitment to cooperation among all channel members, and means to resolve conflict. Scholars who conduct research in channel structure and strategy developed typologies to classify observable practice ranging from a single transaction to highly formalized continuous business relationships.[4]

The bonding feature of channel integration was a rather vague concept that all involved would enjoy benefits as a result of cooperating. However, primarily due to a lack of high-quality information, the overall channel structure was postured on an adversarial foundation. When push came to shove, each firm in the channel would first and foremost focus on its individual goals. Thus, in final analysis, channel dynamics were more often than not characterized by a dog-eat-dog competitive environment.

During the last decade of the 20th century, channel strategy and structure began to shift radically. Traditional distribution channel arrangements moved toward more collaborative practice that began with the rapid advancement of computers and information transfer technology and then accelerated with the advent of digital business transformation. The connectivity potential of the Internet served to facilitate a new vision.

Generalized Supply Chain Model

The general concept of an integrated supply chain is typically illustrated by a line diagram that links participating firms into a coordinated competitive unit. Figure 1.1 illustrates a generalized model adapted from the supply chain management program at Michigan State University.

The context of an integrated supply chain is multifirm collaboration within a framework of key resource flows and constraints. Within this context, supply chain structure and strategy results from efforts to operationally align an enterprise with customers as well as the supporting distributive and supplier networks to gain competitive advantage. Business operations are therefore integrated from initial material purchase to delivery of products and services to customers.[5]

Value results from the synergy among firms composing the supply chain with respect to five critical flows: information, product, service, financial, and knowledge (see the bidirectional arrow at the top of the Figure 1.1). Logistics is the primary conduit of product and service flow within a supply chain arrangement. Each firm engaged in a supply chain is

---

[3] Henry Ford, *Today and Tomorrow* (New York: Doubleday, Page, and Company, 1926). Reprinted by Productivity Press (Portland, OR, 1988).

[4] For example, see Anne T. Coughlan, Erin Anderson, Louis W. Stern, and Adel I. El-Ansary, *Marketing Channels*, 6th ed. (Upper Saddle River, NJ: Prentice Hall, 2001).

[5] Customers are defined as destination points in a supply chain. Customers either consume a product or use it as an integral part or component of an additional process or product. The essential point is that the original product loses its unique configuration when consumed. Business entities that purchase products from manufacturers for resale, for example, wholesalers and retailers, are referred to as intermediate customers.

FIGURE 1.1 **The Integrated Supply Chain Framework**

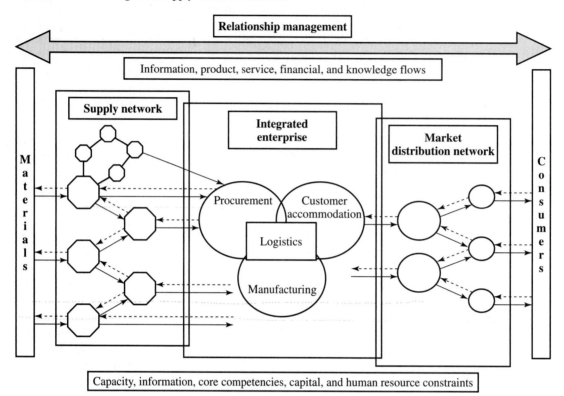

involved in performing same aspects of overall logistics. Achievement of logistical integration and efficiency is the focus of this text.

The generalized supply chain arrangement illustrated in Figure 1.1 logically and logistically links a firm and its distributive and supplier network to customers. The message conveyed by the figure is that the integrated value-creation process must be aligned and managed from material procurement to end-customer product/service delivery.

The integrated supply chain perspective shifts traditional channel arrangements from loosely linked groups of independent businesses that buy and sell inventory to each other toward a managerially coordinated initiative to increase market impact, overall efficiency, continuous improvement, and competitiveness. In practice, many complexities serve to cloud the simplicity of illustrating supply chains as directional line diagrams. For example, many individual firms simultaneously participate in multiple and competitive supply chains. To the degree that a supply chain becomes the basic unit of competition, firms participating in multiple arrangements may confront loyalty issues related to confidentiality and potential conflict of interest.

Another factor that serves to add complexity to understanding supply chain structure is the high degree of mobility and change observable in typical arrangements. It's interesting to observe the fluidity of supply chains as firms enter and exit without any apparent loss of essential connectivity. For example, a firm and/or service supplier may be actively engaged in a supply chain structure during selected times, such as a peak selling season, and not during the balance of a year.

The overarching enabler of supply chain management is information technology. In addition to information technology, the rapid emergence of supply chain arrangements is being driven by five related forces: (1) integrative management, (2) responsiveness,

(3) financial sophistication, (4) globalization, and (5) digital transformation. These forces will continue, for the foreseeable future, to drive supply chain structure and strategy initiatives across most industries. A brief discussion of each supply chain driver provides a foundation to understand the challenges supply chain management places on exacting logistical performance.

Integrative Management

Across all aspects of business operations, attention is focused on achieving improved integrative management. The challenge to achieving integrated management results from the long-standing tradition of performing and measuring work on a functional basis. Since the industrial revolution, achieving best practice has focused managerial attention on functional specialization.[6] The prevailing belief was the better the performance of a specific function, the greater the efficiency of the overall process. For well over a century, this fundamental commitment to functional efficiency has driven best practice in organization structure, performance measurement, and accountability.

In terms of management, firms have traditionally been structured into departments to facilitate work focus, routinization, standardization, and control. Accounting practices were developed to measure departmental performance. Most performance measurement focused on individual functions. Two examples of common functional measurement are the cost per unit to manufacture and the cost per hundredweight to transport. Cross-functional measurements and allocations were typically limited to costs common to all functional areas of work, such as overhead, labor, utilities, insurance, interest, and so on.

The fundamental challenge of integrated management is to redirect traditional emphasis on functionality in an effort to focus on process achievement. Over the past few decades, it has become increasingly apparent that functions, individually performed best in class, do not necessarily combine or aggregate to achieve lowest total cost or highly effective processes. Integrative process management seeks to identify and achieve lowest total cost by capturing trade-offs that exist between functions. To illustrate using a logistical example, a firm might be able to reduce total cost to serve a customer as a result of spending more for faster, dependable transportation because the overall cost of inventory associated with the process may be reduced by an amount greater than that being spent for premium transportation. The focus of integrated management is **lowest total process cost,** which is not necessarily the achievement of the lowest cost for each function included in the process.

The concept of trade-off and the goal of lowest total cost have logical appeal. While deceptively simple, managers continue to find the identification, measurement, and implementation of a process to minimize total cost a difficult task in day-to-day operations. The unavailability of process performance data and cost measures capable of quantifying cross-functional trade-offs served to stimulate development of such integrative tools as Total Cost Analysis, Process Engineering, and Activity-Based Costing (ABC).

Three important facets of supply chain logic resulted from increased attention to integrated management: (1) collaboration, (2) enterprise extension, and (3) integrated service providers.

Collaboration

As discussed earlier, the history of business has been dominated by a desire to cooperate but always couched within a competitive framework. Whereas competition remains the

[6] Frederick W. Taylor, *Scientific Management* (New York: W. W. Norton, 1967).

dominant model guiding free market economies, the increasing importance of collaboration has positioned the supply chain as a primary unit of competition. In today's global economy, supply chain arrangements compete with each other for customer loyalty. Supply chains dominated by Sears Holding, Target, and Wal★Mart are direct competitors in many markets. Similar supply chain alignments can be observed in industries ranging from entertainment to food to automobiles to chemicals. The global strategic reach of Limited Logistics Services is an example of the complexity of modern supply chain management. Garments are manufactured throughout the world and are sold in all fashion seasons to U.S. consumers.

The general impetus to institutionalized collaborative working arrangements was the 1984 enactment of the National Cooperative Research and Development Act which was expanded in scope by the Production Amendments of 1993 and 2004.[7] This national legislation and its subsequent modification signaled fundamental change in traditional Justice Department antitrust philosophy. The basic legislation, as supplemented by administrative rulings, encouraged firms to develop collaborative initiatives in an effort to increase the global competitiveness of U.S.-based firms. Widespread realization that cooperation is both permissible and encouraged served to stimulate formation of supply chain arrangements.

While all forms of price collusion remain illegal, the collaborative legislation served to facilitate cross-organizational sharing of operating information, technology, and risk as ways to increase competitiveness. The response was a wide variety of new and innovative operating arrangements. One such development was the growing vision of the extended enterprise.

Enterprise Extension

The central thrust of enterprise extension expanded managerial influence and control beyond the ownership boundaries of a single enterprise to facilitate joint planning and operations with customers and suppliers. The fundamental belief is that collaborative behavior between firms that integrate processes will maximize customer impact, reduce overall risk, and greatly improve efficiency. Enterprise extension builds on two basic paradigms: information sharing and process specialization.

The **information sharing paradigm** is the widespread belief that achieving a high degree of cooperative behavior requires that supply chain participants voluntarily share operating information and jointly plan strategies. The scope of cross-enterprise collaboration should span beyond sales history to include plans detailing promotion, new product introduction, and day-to-day operations. It's important to emphasize that information sharing to support collaboration must not be limited to historical or even accurate current sales data. Of greater importance is a willingness to share information about future strategic initiatives to facilitate joint operations. The guiding principle is that information sharing is essential among supply chain participants to collectively do the things customers demand faster and more efficiently.

[7] On October 11, 1984, President Reagan signed into law the National Cooperative Research Act of 1984 (Public Law 98-462) in an effort "to promote research and development, encourage innovation, stimulate trade, and make necessary and appropriate modifications in the operation of the antitrust laws." This law enables research and development activities to be jointly performed up to the point where prototypes are developed. The law further determined that antitrust litigation would be based on the rule of reason, taking into account all factors affecting competition. An extension to this act was signed into law by President Clinton on June 10, 1993. The extension, National Cooperative Production Amendments of 1993 (Public Law 103-42), allows joint ventures to go beyond just research to include the production and testing of a product, process, or service. This created a new act called the National Cooperative Research and Production Act of 1993 to replace the 1984 act. Furthermore, this new act established a procedure for businesses to notify the Department of Justice and the Federal Trade Commission of their cooperative arrangement in order to qualify for "single-damages limitation on civil antitrust liability." In 2004 President Bush signed into law the Standards Development Organization Advancement Act (SDOAA, H. R. 1086) which amended the 1993 act to include immunity for standards development organizations and thereby further validated the collaborative doctrine.

The **process specialization paradigm** is commitment to focusing collaborative arrangements on planning joint operations with a goal of eliminating nonproductive or non-value-adding redundancy by firms in a supply chain. The basic idea is to design the overall supply chain processes in a manner that identifies a specific firm's competencies along with the responsibility and accountability to perform each element of essential work in a manner that maximizes overall results.

Firms participating in a supply chain have specific roles and share strategic goals. Sharing information and joint planning can reduce risk related to inventory positioning. Collaboration can eliminate duplicative or redundant work, such as repetitive quality inspection, by designating and empowering a specified member of the supply chain to be fully responsible and accountable. Such extended enterprise integration introduces new challenges regarding measurement, benefit and risk sharing, trust, leadership, and conflict resolution. It is clear that the challenges of collaboration and enterprise extension constitute new managerial horizons. A third contributing force to supply chain development is the rapidly changing managerial attitude toward integrated service providers.

Integrated Service Providers

As noted earlier, the origins of contemporary business were grounded in functional specialization. It is not surprising that firms developed the practice of outsourcing work to businesses that are specialists in the performance of specific functions. The two traditional logistics service providers are transportation and warehousing specialists.

The for-hire transportation industry consists of thousands of carriers who specialize in product movement between geographic locations. Over the years, a comprehensive carrier network has emerged, providing shippers a broad assortment of services, utilizing all available forms or modes of transportation and related technology. The value proposition of for-hire transportation is based on specialization, efficiency, and scale economies. Value is generated by a carrier's capability to provide shared transportation services for multiple shippers. The transport alternatives for shippers are either to invest capital in transportation equipment and operations or to engage the services of for-hire carriers. Naturally, a large number of firms develop transportation solutions that combine benefits of these alternatives.

In addition to transportation, a large number of service companies have traditionally provided warehouse services. Traditionally called **public warehouses,** these firms provide product storage supplemented with other specialized services. Two significant benefits are gained when shippers use public warehouses. First is elimination of capital investment in warehouse buildings. The second is the ability to consolidate small shipments for combined delivery with products of other firms that use the same public warehouse. Such multishipper consolidation achieves transportation efficiency not typically available when a firm ships from its own warehouse. Many firms combine private and public warehouses into a go-to-market distribution network.

In 1980 the landscape of for-hire services in the United States changed dramatically. Within a few short months, the economic and political regulatory infrastructure of transportation in the United States shifted from economic to social regulation as a result of the passage of the Motor Carrier Regulatory Reform and Modernization Act (MCA-80) and the Staggers Rail Act.[8] These regulatory changes served to initiate a trend toward an open transportation market that ultimately resulted in less government economic regulation for all forms of transportation. Over time, this trend extended worldwide to deregulate transportation in most free-market industrialized nations.

---

[8] Public Laws 96-296 and 96-488, respectively. These laws, as well as others briefly noted here, are discussed in greater detail in Chapter 7.

In contrast to transportation, firms engaged in public warehousing were not operationally regulated by federal or state governments. Most warehouse firms did not offer transportation services so as to avoid regulation. However, with the deregulation of transportation, that practice soon changed. Overnight, warehousing firms began to offer transportation services. Likewise, many transport carriers began to offer customers integrated warehouse services.

What occurred in the logistics service industry was a radical shift from single function to multifunctional outsourcing. **Integrated service providers** (ISPs) began to market a range of logistics services that included all work necessary to accommodate customers, ranging from order entry to product delivery. In many situations the foundation of transportation and warehouse services was augmented by the performance of a wide range of special services. These customized services are typically described as **value-added services.** For example, United Parcel Service (UPS) stocks Nike shoes and warm-ups at its Louisville warehouse and processes orders hourly. All related communication and financial administration are handled by a UPS call center. Thus, Nike has effectively outsourced basic logistics and related value-added service to UPS.[9]

The common name used throughout industry to describe ISPs is **third-party and fourth-party logistics service providers.** In a general sense, ISPs are commonly classified as being either **asset-** or **nonasset-based,** the distinction being that asset-based (third-party) firms own and operate transportation equipment and warehousing buildings. In contrast, nonasset service (fourth-party) firms specialize in providing comprehensive information services that facilitate supply chain arrangements. Such fourth-party service providers arrange services, often integrating third-party asset operators on behalf of their customers.

The 2003 logistics service market was estimated to be $76.9 billion.[10] The growth of integrated service providers makes both the formation and dismantling of supply chain arrangements easier. Thus, supply chain participants have the opportunity to engage the capabilities of what amounts to a virtual logistics network. Such outsourcing helps facilitate process-focused integrative management.

As discussed, the advent of collaboration, extended enterprise visioning, and the increased availability of integrated service providers combined to drive radically new supply chain solutions. The notion of shared and synergistic benefits served to solidify the importance of relationships between firms collaborating in a supply chain. The extended enterprise logic stimulated visions of increased efficiency, effectiveness, and relevance as a result of sharing information, planning, and operational specialization between supply chain participants. The deregulation of transportation served as a catalyst for the development of integrated service providers. This development served to redefine and expand the scope of specialized services available to facilitate supply chain operations. In combination, these three drivers helped create integrated supply chain management. They served to identify and solidify the strategic benefits of integrated management. They combined to reinforce the value of core-competence specialization and cast the challenges and opportunity of creating virtual supply chains.

Responsiveness

One could argue that the challenges and benefits of integrative management offered sufficient reason for the supply chain revolution. However, other basic drivers continue to make supply chain arrangements even more appealing. A fundamental paradigm shift in strategic

---

[9] Kelly Barron, "Logistics in Brown," *Forbes,* January 10, 2000, p. 78.

[10] Rosalyn Wilson, 16th Annual "State of Logistics Report," Council of Supply Chain Management Professionals, Oak Brook, IL, June 2005.

thinking occurred as a direct impact of information technology. Information connectivity creates the potential for developing responsive business models. To elaborate the far-reaching implications of this major development, it is useful to contrast traditional or **anticipatory** business practice to the emerging time-based **responsive** business model. Strategies related to incorporation of postponement are also developed. Postponement is a major strategy in contemporary supply chain management.

Anticipatory Business Model

Since the industrial revolution, the dominant business model has required anticipation of what customers will demand in the future. Because information concerning purchase behavior was not readily available and firms loosely linked together in a channel of distribution did not feel compelled to share their plans, business operations were driven by forecasts. The typical manufacturer produced products based upon a market forecast. Likewise, wholesalers, distributors, and retailers purchased inventory based on their unique forecasts and promotional plans. Since the forecast results were more often than not wrong, considerable discontinuities existed between what firms planned to do and what they, in fact, ended up doing. Such discontinuity typically resulted in unplanned inventory. Because of high cost and risk associated with conducting business on an anticipatory basis, the prevailing relationship between trading partners was adversarial; each firm needed to protect its own interest.

Figure 1.2 illustrates the typical stages in the anticipatory business model: forecast, purchase materials, manufacture, warehouse, sell, and then deliver. In nonmanufacturing firms, operations involved anticipatory purchase of inventory assortments to accommodate expected sales. The key point is that almost all essential work was performed in anticipation of future requirements. The likelihood of misgauging customer requirements rendered the anticipatory business model highly risky. In addition, each firm in the distribution channel duplicated the anticipatory process.

Responsive Business Model

The fundamental difference in anticipatory and responsive supply chain arrangements is timing. The responsive business model seeks to reduce or eliminate forecast reliance by joint planning and rapid exchange of information between supply chain participants.

The availability of low-cost information has created *time-based competition.* Managers are increasingly sharing information to improve both the speed and accuracy of supply chain logistics. To illustrate, managers may share information to improve forecasting accuracy or even eliminate forecasts in an effort to reduce anticipatory inventory deployment. This transformation from anticipatory toward responsive business is possible because today's managers have the technology to rapidly obtain and share accurate sales information and exercise improved operational control. When all members of the supply chain synchronize their operations, opportunities exist to reduce overall inventory and eliminate costly duplicate practices. More important, customers can be provided with products they want, fast.

FIGURE 1.2 **Anticipatory Business Model**

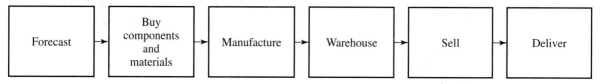

FIGURE 1.3
Responsive Business Model

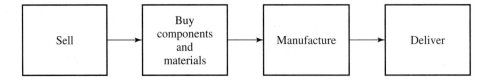

Figure 1.3 illustrates a responsive business model that manufactures or assembles products to customer order. The fundamental difference in responsive models is the sequence of events that drive business practice. Also notable, in comparison to Figure 1.2, are the fewer steps required to complete the responsive process. Fewer steps typically equate to less cost and less elapsed time from order commitment to delivery. The responsive sequence is initiated by a sale followed by a sequence of material purchase, custom manufacturing, and direct customer delivery.

In many ways, the responsive business model is similar to the traditional build-to-order manufacturing. The primary differences between modern responsive operations and traditional build-to-order are the time to execute and the degree of potential customization. While response-based examples are observable in many different industries, a high degree of attention has focused on the operational model developed by Dell Corporation. In 2004 Dell perfected a responsive distribution model wherein computers sold in the United States were built to order in China and delivered to United States consumers within a five-day order-to-delivery cycle.

In terms of time to execute the order to delivery, the contemporary responsive system is substantially faster than the traditional build-to-order manufacturing. It is becoming common practice to replenish retail store inventories of consumer products on a daily basis. Custom-built automobiles are being promised for delivery within 10 working days, with the goal to even further reduce the order-to-delivery cycle. Such compressed order-to-delivery cycles were not even imaginable a few years ago.

Perhaps an even more appealing attribute of responsive supply chains is their potential to uniquely customize products on smaller orders than was typical of traditional build-to-order lot size manufacturing. Direct connectivity with customers via Internet-based communications is accelerating customization. In most traditional anticipatory distribution systems, the customer is a passive participant. About the only power the customer has in the traditional process is the decision to buy or not buy. Direct involvement of customers in a responsive process has at least three benefits. First, involvement provides comprehensive search capabilities that serve to expand the range of sources and choices a customer can consider when selecting a product or service. Second, customers are better informed about prices and, in some situations, are able to drive price advantage by virtue of bids and/or auctions. Finally, information-intense responsive systems provide innovation such as a **customer choiceboard** wherein customers design or customize their own product configuration.[11]

Postponement

At the heart of time-based competition is the capability to postpone customization and the timing of logistical fulfillment. The concept of **postponement** has long been discussed in business literature.[12] However, practical examples involving postponement are directly

---

[11] Adrian J. Slywotzky, "The Age of the Choiceboard," *Harvard Business Review* (January/February 2000), pp. 40–41; and Jarrus D. Pagh and Martha C. Cooper, "Supply Chain Postponement and Speculation Strategies: How to Choose the Right Strategy," *Journal of Business Logistics* 19, no. 2 (1998), pp. 13–28.

[12] Wroe Alderson, *Marketing Behavior and Executive Action* (Homewood, IL: Richard D. Irwin, Inc., 1957), p. 426. For a more contemporary discussion of postponement, see B. Joseph Pine II, Bart Victor, and Andrew C. Boynton, "Making Mass Customization Work," *Harvard Business Review* (September/October 1993), pp. 108–19.

related to advancements in information technology. Postponement strategies and practices serve to reduce the anticipatory risk of supply chain performance. As noted earlier, anticipatory arrangements require most inventory to be produced and deployed on the basis of forecasts or planned requirements. Working arrangements, which allow postponement of final manufacturing or distribution of a product until receipt of a customer order, reduce the incidence of wrong manufacturing or incorrect inventory deployment. Two types of postponement are common in highly responsive supply chain operations: (1) manufacturing, or **form postponement;** and (2) geographic, or **logistics postponement.**

Manufacturing Postponement

The global competitive climate of the 21st century is facilitating the development of new manufacturing techniques designed to increase flexibility and responsiveness while maintaining unit cost and quality. Traditional practice has focused on achieving economy of scale by planning long manufacturing runs. In contrast, flexible and lean manufacturing logic is driven by a desire to increase responsiveness to customer requirements.

Responsive manufacturing stresses flexibility. The vision of **manufacturing,** or **form postponement** is one of products being manufactured one order at a time with no preparatory work or component procurement until exact customer specifications are fully known and purchase confirmation is received. This dream of building to customer order is not new. What is new is the expectation that flexible manufacturing can achieve such responsiveness without sacrificing efficiency. To the degree technology can support market-paced flexible manufacturing strategies, firms are freed from forecast-driven anticipatory operations.

In practice, manufacturing lot size economics cannot be ignored. The challenge is to quantify cost trade-offs between procurement, manufacturing, and logistics. At this point, it is sufficient to understand that the trade-off is between the cost and risk associated with anticipatory manufacturing and the loss of economy of scale resulting from introducing flexible procedures. Manufacturing lot size reduction requires a trade-off between line setup, switchover, and associated procurement expense balanced against cost and risk associated with stockpiling finished inventory. In the traditional functional style of management, manufacturing schedules were established to realize the lowest unit cost of production. From an integrative management perspective, the goal is to achieve desired customer satisfaction at the lowest total cost. This may require manufacturing postponement at some per-unit-cost sacrifice to achieve overall supply chain efficiency.

The operative goal of manufacturing postponement is to maintain products in a neutral or noncommitted status as long as possible. The ideal application of form postponement is to manufacture a standard or base product in sufficient quantities to realize economy of scale while deferring finalization of features, such as color or accessories, until customer commitment is received. Given a postponement-driven manufacturing scenario, economy of scope is introduced into the logistics equation by producing a standard or base product to accommodate a wide range of different customers. One of the first commercially viable examples of manufacturing postponement was mixing paint color at retail stores to accommodate individual customer request. Perfecting the in-store mixing process dramatically reduced the number of stockkeeping units required at retail paint stores. Instead of trying to maintain inventories of premixed color paint, retail stores stock a base paint and customize the color to accommodate specific orders.

In other industries, manufacturing practice is to process and store product in bulk, postponing final packaging configuration until customer orders are received. In some situations products are processed and packed in cans with brand identification labeling being postponed until specific customer orders are received. Other examples of manufacturing postponement include the increased practice of installing accessories at automobile, appliance, and motorcycle dealerships, thereby customizing products to customer request at the time of purchase.

These manufacturing postponement examples have one thing in common: They reduce the number of stockkeeping units in logistical inventory while supporting a broad-line marketing effort and retaining mass manufacturing economies of scale. Until the product is customized, it has the potential to serve many different customers.

The impact of manufacturing postponement is twofold. First, the variety of differentiated products, moved in anticipation of sale, can be reduced, and therefore the risk of logistics malfunction is lower. The second, and perhaps the more important, impact is the increased use of logistical facilities to perform light manufacturing and final assembly. To the extent that a degree of specialized talent or highly restrictive economy of scale does not exist in manufacturing, product customization may be best delegated and performed near the customer destination market. The traditional mission of logistical warehouses in some industries has changed significantly to accommodate manufacturing postponement.

Geographic Postponement

In many ways **geographic,** or **logistics postponement** is the exact opposite of manufacturing postponement. The basic notion of geographic postponement is to build and stock a full-line inventory at one or a few strategic locations. Forward deployment of inventory is postponed until customer orders are received. Once the logistical process is initiated, every effort is made to accelerate the economic movement of products directly to customers. Under the concept of geographic postponement, the anticipatory risk of inventory deployment is completely eliminated while manufacturing economy of scale is retained.

Many applications of geographic postponement involve service supply parts. Critical and high-cost parts are maintained in a central inventory to assure availability for all potential users. When demand occurs, orders are electronically transmitted to the central service center and expedited shipments are made direct to the service center, using fast, reliable transportation. The end result is highly reliable customer service with reduced overall inventory investment.

The potential for geographic postponement has been facilitated by increased logistical system capability to process, transmit, and deliver precise order requirements with a high degree of accuracy and speed. Geographic postponement substitutes accelerated delivery of precise order requirements for the anticipatory deployment of inventory to local market warehouses. Unlike manufacturing postponement, systems utilizing geographic postponement retain manufacturing economies of scale while meeting customer service requirements by accelerating direct shipments.

In combination, manufacturing and geographic postponement offer alternative ways to refrain from anticipatory distribution by waiting until customer commitments are received. The factors favoring one or the other form of postponement hinge on volume, value, competitive initiatives, economies of scale, and desired customer delivery speed and consistency. In a growing number of supply chains, both types of postponement are combined to create a highly flexible strategy.

Barriers to Implementing Responsive Systems

In reality, today's best supply chain practices do not reflect either extreme anticipatory or responsive design. Most established firms remain, to a significant degree, committed to anticipatory practices. However, responsive strategies are rapidly emerging. Perhaps the greatest barrier to adopting responsive arrangements is the need for publicly held corporations to maintain planned quarterly profits. This accountability creates expectations concerning continued sales and financial results. Such expectations often drive promotional and pricing strategies to "load the channel" with inventory to create timely sales. Conversely, it is never timely to make a major reduction in channel inventory. Efforts to lean or deload inventory to implement a more responsive operating posture require the ability to absorb a one-time sale reduction among supply chain partners. Start-up ventures are ideally positioned to implement responsive fulfillment systems because they do not face the deload challenge.

A second barrier to implementing responsive operations is the need to establish collaborative relationships. Most business managers simply do not have training or experience in development of collaborative arrangements designed to share benefits and risks. While managers generally express a high degree of belief in the long-term potential for responsive alliances, they typically confront considerable frustration concerning how to implement such supply chain arrangements.

For the foreseeable future, most firms will continue to implement strategies that combine anticipatory and responsive supply chain arrangements. The trend toward increased involvement in responsive arrangements with specific customers and suppliers will continue to expand.

Financial Sophistication

Few managers question the benefits of applying the time-based strategies discussed above to supply chain operations. However, a valid question is, How fast is fast enough? Speed simply for the sake of being fast has little, if any, enduring value.[13] The answer concerning how much speed is desirable is found in the financial impact. The process of creating value dictates that faster, more flexible, and more precise ways of servicing customers are justified as long as they can be provided at competitive prices. A third force driving competitive supply chain strategy is the ability to manage in a more timely manner to achieve financially attractive working arrangements.

The financial benefits of timely response are straightforward. Fast delivery translates to less inventory and reduced need for distribution facilities. Faster to customers means less working capital is required to support supply chain operations. Three aspects of financial sophistication are cash-to-cash conversion, dwell time minimization, and cash spin.

Cash-to-Cash Conversion

The time required to convert raw material or inventory purchases into sales revenue is referred to as **cash-to-cash conversion.** Cash conversion is generally related to inventory turn: The higher the inventory turn, the quicker the cash conversion. A goal of supply chain design is to reduce and control order receipt-to-delivery time in an effort to accelerate inventory turns.

In traditional business arrangements, benefits related to cash-to-cash conversion have typically been enjoyed at the expense of business partners. Given typical purchase discounts and invoicing practices, it is operationally possible for firms to rapidly sell merchandise and still qualify for prompt payment discounts. To illustrate, terms of sale offering a 2 percent discount net 10-day payment (2% net 10) means that a prompt payment discount is earned if the invoice is paid within 10 days from time of delivery. Thus, if the invoice is $1000, a payment made within 10 days will earn a $20 discount. If the firm sells

---

[13] George Stalk, Jr., and Alan M. Webber, "Japan's Dark Side of Time," *Harvard Business Review* (July/August 1993), pp. 93–102.

the product for cash before the invoice payment date, it, in effect, enjoys free inventory and may even earn interest by investing cash while awaiting the payment date.

In responsive systems, cash-to-cash conversion benefits can be shared by managing inventory velocity across the supply chain. This ability to manage inventory velocity from origin to final destination has the potential to achieve greater overall efficiencies than are attainable by a single firm. Coordinated operations may require that a designated firm in the supply chain serve as the principal inventory stocking location. Such practice means that risk and benefits related to inventory need to be shared by participating firms. To facilitate such arrangements, supply chain members often replace the discounts with **dead net pricing.**[14]

Dead net pricing means that all discounts and allowances are factored in the selling price. Thus, incentives for timely payment are replaced by detailed performance commitments at a specified net price. Invoice payment, based on negotiated net price, is completed upon verification of physical receipt. Such payment is typically in the form of Electronic Funds Transfer (EFT), thereby streamlining both the flow of physical goods and cash among supply chain partners. Managing supply chain logistics as a continuous synchronized process also serves to reduce dwell time.

Dwell Time Minimization

Traditional distribution arrangements typically involve independent business units loosely linked together on a transaction-to-transaction basis. Traditional business operations are driven by a series of **independent** transactions buffered by inventory. In contrast, a supply chain has the potential to function as a synchronized series of **interdependent** business units.

At the heart of supply chain operating leverage is the willingness to transfer inventory on an as-needed basis, taking advantage of as much collaboration and information as possible. Such collaboration and information can be focused on maintaining the continued flow and velocity of inventory moving throughout the supply chain. The potential of such synchronization is a key benefit of supply chain connectivity.

A significant measure of supply chain productivity is **dwell time.** Dwell time is the ratio of time that an asset sits idle to the time required to satisfy its designated supply chain mission. For example, dwell time would be the ratio of the time a unit of inventory is in storage to the time that it is moving or otherwise contributing to achieving sales or operational objectives.

To reduce dwell time, firms collaborating in a supply chain need to be willing to eliminate duplicate and non-value-added work. For example, if three different firms perform identical processes as a product flows along a supply chain, dwell times will accumulate. Designating a specific firm to perform and be accountable for the value-added work can serve to reduce overall dwell.

Likewise, timely arrival and continuous inventory flow between supply chain partners reduces dwell. When a product flows from a supplier through a retailer's cross-dock sortation process without coming to rest or being diverted to warehouse storage, overall dwell time is minimized. A collateral benefit of reducing dwell time and the associated logistics cost is the ability to reduce investment in inventory and related assets.

Cash Spin

A popular term for describing the potential benefits of reducing assets across a supply chain is **cash spin,** sometimes referred to as **free cash spin.**[15] The concept is to reduce

---

[14] Logistical pricing is discussed in Chapter 11.

[15] Gene Tyndall et al., *Supercharging Supply Chains* (New York: John Wiley & Sons, 1988), p. 1.

overall assets committed to supply chain performance. Thus, a dollar of inventory or the investment in a warehouse, if eliminated by a reengineered supply chain, spins cash for redeployment. Such free capital can be reinvested in projects that might otherwise have been considered too risky.

Naturally, cash spin opportunity is not unique to the supply chain. The potential to spin cash applies to all areas of a firm. What makes the potential of supply chain cash spin so attractive is the opportunity to collaborate between firms.

The benefits flowing from fast cash-to-cash conversion, reduced dwell time, and cash spin combine to increase the financial attractiveness of effective collaboration. Another major force driving expansion of supply chain management is the growing involvement of most firms in international operations.

Globalization

A conservative estimate is that as much as 90 percent of global demand is not fully satisfied by local supply. Current demand coupled with a world population projected to increase by an average over 200,000 persons per day for the next decade equate to substantial market opportunity. The range of product/service growth potential varies greatly between industrialized and emerging economies. In industrialized sectors of the global economy, opportunities focus on upscale consumer products. These more advanced economies offer substantial opportunities for the sale of products combined with value-added services. While it is true that consumers in developing nations enjoy relatively less purchasing power than those in their industrialized counterparts, demand in such economies for basic products and necessities is huge. Consumers in developing nations are more interested in quality of basic life than in fashion or technology. For example, the growing populations of India and China offer huge market opportunities for basic products like food, clothing, and consumer durables such as refrigerators and washing machines. Firms with aggressive growth goals cannot neglect the commercialization of the global marketplace.

In addition to sales potential, involvement in global business is being driven by significant opportunities to increase operating efficiency. Such operational efficiencies are attainable in at least three areas. First, the global marketplace offers significant opportunity to strategically source raw material and components. Second, significant labor advantages can be gained by locating manufacturing and distribution facilities in developing nations ("offshoring"). Third, favorable tax laws can make the performance of value-adding operations in specific countries highly attractive.

The decision to engage in global operations to achieve market growth and enjoy operational efficiency follows a natural path of business expansion. Typically, firms enter the global marketplace by conducting import and export operations. Such import and export transactions constitute a significant portion of global international business. The second stage of internationalization involves a firm's establishment of local presence in foreign nations and trading areas. Such presence can range from franchise and licensing of local businesses to the establishment of manufacturing and distribution facilities. The important distinction between import/export involvement and establishment of local presence is the degree of investment and managerial involvement characteristic of stage 2. The third stage of internationalization is the full-fledged conduct of business operations within and across international boundaries. This most advanced phase of international engagement is typically referred to as **globalization.**

The logistics of internationalization involves four significant differences in comparison to national or even regional operations. First, the **distance** of typical order-to-delivery operations is significantly longer in international as contrasted to domestic business. Second, to accommodate the laws and regulations of all governing bodies, the required **documentation** of business transactions is significantly more complex. Third, international logistics operations must be designed to deal with significant **diversity** in work practices and local operating environment. Fourth, accommodation of cultural variations in how consumers **demand** products and services is essential for successful logistical operations.

Finally, 21st-century commerce is conducted within a constant threat of terrorism, which requires increased security. The intensity and severity of terrorist disruption involves both the shipment itself and the exposure to using the logistics infrastructure as a means to deliver explosive and chemical devices. The security aspects of global logistics are further discussed in Chapter 12. It is important to understand that successfully going supply chain global requires mastering the associated logistical challenges.

While logistics principles and the ideals of supply chain integration are essentially the same globally as they are domestically, the above characteristics make operating environments more complex and costly. The cost of logistics on a global basis is estimated to exceed $6 trillion a year.[16] Such expenditure is justified in terms of potential market expansion and operating efficiencies. However, risk exposure related to capitalizing on international supply chain management and its logistical components requires integrated operating strategies and tactics.

Digital Business Transformation[17]

The 21st century is witnessing a growing adoption of a new and extensive form of change management referred to as **Digital Business Transformation** (DBT). The basic premise of DBT involves a complete assessment and reinvention of a firm's overall operation to assure that the benefits of modern information technology are being fully deployed. DBT is about reinventing and positioning business operations, processes, and relationships to fully exploit information technology and to facilitate supply chain collaboration to achieve unprecedented levels of operational excellence.

Focusing on information technology, DBT seeks to simultaneously meet the challenges and exploit the inherent opportunities of integrative management, responsiveness, financial sophistication, and globalization. Expanding Internet capabilities provide an information framework that can replace traditional one-to-one, one-to-many, or many-to-one communication with Web-based, simultaneous many-to-many connectivity. The potential exists for all firms participating in a supply chain to simultaneously have access to the same strategic and operational information. The potential of DBT is the synchronized distribution of information and knowledge across the supply chain. In essence, DBT is the forward-looking model for a business that is transitioning from the Industrial Age to the Information Age.

Figure 1.4 provides a summary of DBT in the form of key paradigms. The six paradigms speak to the mindset leaders must adopt as they navigate the DBT journey. It should be clear that DBT is not a consulting project or a one-time improvement initiative. It is the process of reinventing a business to digitize operations and formulate extended supply chain collaboration.

---

[16] Donald J. Bowersox, Roger J. Calantone, and Alexander M. Rodriguez, "Estimation of Global Logistics Expenditures Using Neural Networks," *Journal of Business Logistics* 26, no. 2 (2005), pp. 1–16.

[17] The following discussion is based on Donald J. Bowersox, David J. Closs, and Ralph Drayer, "The Digital Transformation: Technology and Beyond," *Supply Chain Management Review* (January 2005), pp. 22–29.

FIGURE 1.4
The "6 F's" of Going Digital

Source: Reprinted with permission from Donald J. Bowersox, David J. Closs, and Ralph Drayer, "The Digital Transformation: Technology and Beyond," *Supply Chain Management Review,* January 2005, pp. 22–29.

Six paradigms seem to frame the challenge of digitally transforming business. We call these paradigms the "Six Fs" of going digital. They speak to the mindset that leaders must adopt as they begin to reconfigure every aspect of their organization to contribute economic value.

1. Fact-Based Management: Fact-based management is a commitment to—even an obsession with—developing precise information on every facet of what the organization does and needs to do. Fact-based management provides answers to questions such as, Why do we provide this service? What value does it add to customers? What are our precise performance expectations? How exactly do we meet and measure these expectations? Facts are not averages. Facts deal with specific performance results in terms of specific customers. Managers must learn to understand and rapidly act on these results at the specific product level and customer purchase location.

2. Flexible: Driven by facts, successful firms demonstrate an inherent ability to rapidly adapt operations to pursue a new course of action. Confronted with a breakthrough opportunity, they are agile enough to make adjustments quickly and commit the resources necessary to capitalize on the opportunity.

3. Focus on Cash: A business exists to generate cash. Quarterly or annual earnings are not the fuel of long-term success. The only meaningful measure at the end of any day, week, month, or year is the cash balance. As they make the digital transformation, companies must remember that cash pays bills, cash pays salaries and wages, and cash pays shareholder dividends. The focus must be cash first, cash second, and cash always.

4. Fast Return on Investment (ROI): A business needs to make continuous investments in new products, services, technology, people, and facilities. All investments are made with an expectation of financial return. The new mandate, however, is not just high rates of return but high rates of return *fast.* Payback periods need to be short and rapidly yield positive returns—which translates to cash.

5. Fungible: Fungible means that business processes are modular in design with maximum interchangeability. Modularity allows flexibility in process design and maximum incorporation of the principles of postponement and acceleration. The operational characteristics of agility, flexibility, sustainability, scale, scope and responsiveness are all attributes of fungible organizations.

6. Frugal: Capital investment, cash velocity, and a flat organizational structure with focused human resources are characteristics of a frugal enterprise. Frugal enterprises are lean in every conceivable way. Overhead is minimal. Operations are focused on cash generation. Lean is an enterprisewide attribute that must permeate every facet of every process. In frugal enterprises, the real benefits are cash and dividends, not fringe benefits or luxurious environments. At the end of the day, employees work for income and owners invest for dividends. With business success, both constituents will benefit from the enterprise's success.

Summary

The development of integrated management skill is critical to continued productivity improvement. Such integrative management must focus on quality improvement at both functional and process levels. In terms of functions, critical work must be performed to the highest degree of efficiency. Processes that create value occur both within individual firms and between firms linked together in collaborative supply chains. Each type of process must be continuously improved.

The idea that all or even most firms will link together to form highly collaborative end-to-end supply chain initiatives at any time in the foreseeable future is quite unlikely. The dynamics of a free competitive market system will serve to harness such an end state. However, initiatives aimed at cross-enterprise integration along the supply chain are increasingly occurring and, to the extent successfully implemented, offer new and exciting business models for gaining competitive advantage. Once achieved, such supply chain integration is hard to maintain and is subject to continuous redefinition. What works today may not work tomorrow. Conversely, what won't work today may work tomorrow.

Thus, supply chain collaborations must be viewed as highly dynamic. Such collaborations are attractive because they offer new horizons for achieving market position and operating efficiency. Supply chain opportunities are challenges that 21st-century logistics managers must explore and exploit. However, supply chain integration is a means to increased profitability and growth and not an end in itself.

From the perspective of integrated logistics management, supply chain strategies define the relevant operating framework. What must be logistically accomplished is directly linked to supply chain structure and strategy. When such structure and strategy are internationally positioned, logistics performance must embrace challenges related to globalization. In short, the supply chain strategy or lack of strategy and its related structure serve to shape the framework for logistical requirements. Chapter 2 presents logistics in greater detail.

Challenge Questions

1. Why can the current movement toward the establishment of supply chains be characterized as a revolution?

2. Compare the concept of a modern supply chain with more traditional distribution channels. Be specific regarding similarities and differences.

3. What specific role does logistics play in supply chain operations?

4. Describe integrative management. Be specific concerning the relationship between function and process.

5. In terms of enterprise extension, describe the importance of the information sharing and process specialization paradigms.

6. Describe and illustrate an integrated service provider. How does the concept of integrated service provider differ from traditional service providers, such as for-hire transportation and warehousing?

7. Compare third-party and fourth-party integrated service providers.

8. Compare and contrast anticipatory and responsive business models. Why has responsiveness become popular in supply chain strategy and collaboration?

9. Compare and contrast manufacturing and geographic postponement.

10. Define and illustrate cash-to-cash conversion, dwell time minimization, and cash spin. How do supply chain strategy and structure impact each?

Logistics

Chapter Outline

No other area of business operations involves the complexity or spans the geography of logistics. All around the globe, 24 hours of every day, 7 days a week, during 52 weeks a year, logistics is concerned with getting products and services where they are needed at the precise time desired. It is difficult to visualize accomplishing any marketing, manufacturing, or international commerce without logistics. Most consumers in highly developed industrial nations take a high level of logistical competency for granted. When they purchase goods—at a retail store, over the telephone, or via the Internet—they expect product delivery will be performed as promised. In fact, their expectation is for timely, error-free logistics every time they order. They have little or no tolerance for failure to perform.

Although logistics has been performed since the beginning of civilization, implementing 21st-century best practices is one of the most exciting and challenging operational areas of supply chain management. Because logistics is both old and new, we choose to characterize the rapid change taking place in best practice as a **renaissance.**

Logistics involves the management of order processing, inventory, transportation, and the combination of warehousing, materials handling, and packaging, all integrated throughout a network of facilities. The goal of logistics is to support procurement, manufacturing, and customer accommodation operational requirements. Within a firm the challenge is to coordinate functional competency into an integrated operation focused on servicing customers. In the broader supply chain context, operational synchronization is essential with customers as well as material and service suppliers to link internal and external operations as one integrated process.

Logistics refers to the responsibility to **design and administer systems to control movement and geographical positioning of raw materials, work-in-process, and finished inventories at the lowest total cost.** To achieve lowest total cost means that financial and human assets committed to logistics must be held to an absolute minimum. It is also necessary to hold operational expenditures as low as possible. The combinations of resources, skills, and systems required to achieve lean logistics are challenging to integrate, but once achieved, such integrated competency is difficult for competitors to replicate.

This chapter focuses on the contribution of logistics to integrated supply chain management. First, cost and service are emphasized. Next, the logistics value proposition is developed. Then traditional business functions that combine to create the logistical process are reviewed. Finally, the importance of logistical synchronization to supply chain integration is highlighted in terms of performance cycle structure and dynamics.

The Logistics of Business Is Big and Important

It is through the logistical process that materials flow into the manufacturing capacity of an industrial nation and finished products are distributed to consumers. The recent growth in global commerce has expanded the size and complexity of logistical operations.

Logistics adds value to the supply chain process when inventory is strategically positioned to achieve sales. Creating logistics value is costly. Although difficult to measure, most experts agree that the annual expenditure to perform logistics in the United States in 2004 was approximately 8.6 percent of the $11.74 billion Gross National Product (GNP), or $1,015 billion.[1] Expenditure for transportation in 2004 was $644 billion, which represented 63.3 percent of total logistics cost. As further illustrated in Table 2.1, the logistics of business is truly big business!

Despite the sheer size of logistical expenditure, the excitement about logistics is not cost containment or reduction. The excitement generates from understanding how select firms use logistical competency to help achieve competitive advantage. Firms having world-class logistical competency enjoy competitive advantage as a result of providing their most important customers superior service. Leading performers typically utilize information technology capable of monitoring global logistical activity on a realtime basis. Such technology identifies potential operational breakdowns and facilitates corrective action prior to delivery service failure. In situations where timely corrective action is not possible, customers can be provided advance notification of developing problems, thereby eliminating the surprise of an unavoidable service failure. In many situations, working in collaboration with customers and suppliers, corrective action can be taken to prevent operational shutdowns or costly customer service failures. By performing at above industry average with respect to inventory availability, speed and consistency of delivery, and operational efficiencies, logistically sophisticated firms are ideal supply chain partners.

[1] Rosalyn Wilson, 16th Annual "State of Logistics Report," Council of Supply Chain Management Professionals, Oak Brook, IL, June 2005.

TABLE 2.1   U.S. Logistics Cost, 1980–2004: ($ Billion except GDP)

Source: Adapted from Rosalyn Wilson, 16th Annual "State of Logistics Report," Council of Supply Chain Management Professionals. Oak Brook, IL, 2005.

Year	Nominal GDP ($ trillion)	Values of All Business Inventory	Percent of Inventory Carrying Rate	Inventory Carrying Costs	Transportation Costs	Administrative Costs	Total U.S. Logistics Cost	Logistics (% of GDP)
1980	$ 2.80	692	31.8	220	214	17	451	16.1
1981	3.13	747	34.7	259	228	19	506	16.2
1982	3.26	760	30.8	234	222	18	474	14.5
1983	3.54	758	27.9	211	243	18	472	13.3
1984	3.93	826	29.1	240	268	20	528	13.4
1985	4.22	847	26.8	227	274	20	521	12.3
1986	4.45	843	25.7	217	281	20	518	11.6
1987	4.74	875	25.7	225	294	21	540	11.4
1988	5.10	944	26.6	251	313	23	587	11.5
1989	5.48	1005	28.1	282	329	24	635	11.6
1990	5.80	1041	27.2	283	351	25	659	11.4
1991	5.99	1030	24.9	256	355	24	635	10.6
1992	6.34	1043	22.7	237	375	24	636	10.0
1993	6.64	1076	22.2	239	396	25	660	9.9
1994	7.05	1127	23.5	265	420	27	712	10.1
1995	7.40	1211	24.9	302	441	30	773	10.4
1996	7.81	1240	24.4	303	467	31	801	10.3
1997	8.32	1280	24.5	314	503	33	850	10.2
1998	8.70	1317	24.4	321	529	34	884	10.1
1999	9.27	1381	24.1	333	554	35	922	9.9
2000	9.82	1478	25.3	374	594	39	1006	10.2
2001	10.13	1403	22.8	320	609	37	966	9.5
2002	10.49	1451	20.7	300	582	35	918	8.8
2003	11.00	1494	20.1	300	607	36	944	8.6
2004	11.74	1627	20.4	332	644	39	1015	8.6

The Logistical Value Proposition

Thus far it has been established that logistics should be managed as an integrated effort to achieve customer satisfaction at the lowest total cost. Logistics performed in this manner creates **value.** In this section, the elements of the logistical value proposition—service and cost minimization—are discussed in greater detail.

Service Benefits

Almost any level of logistical service can be achieved if a firm is willing to commit the required resources. In today's operating environment, the limiting factor is economics, not technology. For example, a dedicated inventory can be maintained in close geographical proximity to a major customer. A fleet of trucks can be held in a constant state of delivery readiness. To facilitate order processing, dedicated communications can be maintained on a real time basis between a customer and a supplier's logistical operation. Given this high state of logistical readiness, a product or component could be delivered within minutes of identifying a customer requirement. Availability is even faster when a supplier agrees to consign inventory on site at a customer's facility, eliminating the need to perform logistical operations when a product is needed. The logistics to support consignment are completed in advance of the customer's need for the product. While such extreme service commitment might constitute a sales manager's dream, it is costly and typically not necessary to support most customer expectations and manufacturing operations.

The key strategic issue is how to outperform competitors in a cost-effective manner. If a specific material is not available when required for manufacturing, it may force a plant shutdown resulting in significant cost, potential lost sales, and even the loss of a major customer's business. The profit impact of such failures can be significant. In contrast, the profit impact of an unexpected 1- or 2-day delay in delivering products to replenish warehouse inventory could be minimal or even insignificant in terms of impact on overall operational performance. In most situations, the cost/benefit impact of logistical failure is directly related to the importance of service to the customer. The more significant the service failure impact upon a customer's business, the greater is the priority placed on error-free logistical performance.

Creation and basic logistical performance is measured in terms of availability, operational performance, and service reliability. The term **basic logistics service** describes the level of service a firm provides all established customers.

Availability involves having inventory to consistently meet customer material or product requirements. The traditional paradigm has been the greater the desired availability, the larger the required inventory amount and cost. Information technology that facilitates system flexibility is providing new ways to achieve high availability for customers without correspondingly high capital investment in inventory. Information that facilitates flexibility with respect to inventory availability is critical to achieving lean logistics performance.

Operational performance deals with the time required to deliver a customer's order. Operational performance involves delivery **speed** and **consistency.** Naturally, most customers want fast delivery. However, fast delivery is of limited value if inconsistent from one order to the next. A customer gains little benefit when a supplier promises next-day delivery but frequently delivers late. To achieve smooth operations, firms typically focus on delivery consistency first and then seek to improve delivery speed. Other aspects of operational performance are also important. A firm's operational performance can be viewed in terms of its **flexibility** to accommodate unusual and unexpected customer requests. Another aspect of operational performance is frequency of malfunction and, when such malfunction occurs, the typical recovery time. Few firms can perform perfectly all the time. It is important to estimate the likelihood of something going wrong. **Malfunction** is concerned with the probability of logistical performance failure, such as damaged products, incorrect assortment, or inaccurate documentation. When such malfunction occurs, a firm's logistical competency can be measured in terms of **recovery time.** Operational performance is concerned with how a firm handles all aspects of customer requirements, including service failure, on a day-in and day-out basis.

Service reliability involves the **quality** attributes of logistics. The key to quality is accurate measurement of availability and operational performance. Only through comprehensive performance measurement is it possible to determine if overall logistical operations are achieving desired service goals. To achieve service reliability, it is essential to identify and implement inventory availability and operational performance measurements. For logistics performance to continuously meet customer expectations, it is essential that management be committed to continuous improvement. Logistical quality does not come easy; it's the product of careful planning supported by employee training, operational dedication, comprehensive measurement, and continuous improvement. To improve service performance, goals need to be established on a selective basis. Some products are more critical than others because of their importance to the customer and their relative profit contribution.

The level of basic logistical service should be realistic in terms of customer expectations and requirements. In most cases, firms confront situations wherein customers have significantly different purchase potential. Some customers require unique or special value-added services. Thus, managers must realize that customers are different and that services provided must be matched to accommodate unique requirements and purchase potential. In general, firms tend to be overly optimistic when committing to basic customer service performance. Inability to consistently meet an unrealistically high basic service target might result in more operating and customer relationship problems than if less ambitious goals had been attempted from the outset. Unrealistic across-the-board service commitments can also dilute a firm's capability to satisfy special requirements of high-potential customers.

Cost Minimization

The focus of logistics can be traced to relatively recent developments of total costing theory and practice. In 1956, a classic monograph describing potential airfreight economics provided a new perspective concerning logistical cost.[2] In an effort to explain conditions under which high-cost air transport could be justified, Lewis, Culliton, and Steele conceptualized the total cost logistics model. Total cost was positioned to include all expenditures necessary to perform logistical requirements. The authors illustrated an electronic parts distribution strategy wherein the high variable cost of direct factory-to-customer air transport was more than offset by reductions in inventory and field warehouse costs. They concluded that the least total cost logistical way to provide the desired customer service was to centralize inventory in one warehouse and make deliveries using air transportation.

This concept of total cost had not previously been applied to logistical operations. Probably because of the economic climate of the times and the radical departure in traditional practice, the total cost proposition generated a great deal of debate. The prevailing managerial practice, reinforced by accounting and financial control, was to focus attention on achieving the lowest possible cost for each individual function of logistics with little or no attention to integrated total cost trade-offs. Managers had traditionally focused on minimizing functional cost, such as transportation, with the expectation that such effort would achieve the lowest combined costs. Development of the total cost concept opened the door to examining how functional costs interrelate and impact each other. Subsequent refinements provided a more comprehensive understanding of logistical cost components and identified the critical need for developing functional cost analysis and activity-based costing capabilities. However, the implementation of effective logistical process costing remains a 21st-century challenge. Many long-standing practices of accounting continue to serve as barriers to fully implementing total cost logistical solutions.

Logistics Value Generation

The key to achieving logistical leadership is to master the art of matching operating competency and commitment to key customer expectations and requirements. This customer commitment, in an exacting cost framework, is the **logistics value proposition.** It is a unique commitment of a firm to an individual or selected customer groups.

The typical enterprise seeks to develop and implement an overall logistical competency that satisfies customer expectations at a realistic total cost expenditure. Very seldom will either the lowest total cost or the highest attainable customer service constitute the desirable logistics strategy. Likewise, the appropriate combination will be different for different customers. A well-designed logistical effort must have high customer impact while controlling operational variance and minimizing inventory commitment. And, most of all, it must have relevancy to specific customers.

[2] Howard T. Lewis, James W. Culliton, and Jack D. Steele, *The Role of Air Freight in Physical Distribution* (Boston: Harvard University Press, 1956).

Significant advances have been made in the development of tools to aid management in the measurement of cost/service trade-offs. Formulation of a sound strategy requires a capability to estimate operating cost required to achieve alternative service levels. Likewise, alternative levels of system performance are meaningless unless viewed in terms of overall business unit customer accommodation, manufacturing, and procurement strategies. Supply chain design is the focus of Part Three.

Leading firms realize that a well-designed and well-operated logistical system can help achieve competitive advantage. In fact, as a general rule, firms that obtain a strategic advantage based on logistical competency establish the nature of their industry's competition.

The Work of Logistics

In the context of supply chain management, logistics exists to move and position inventory to achieve desired time, place, and possession benefits at the lowest total cost. Inventory has limited value until it is positioned at the right time and at the right location to support ownership transfer or value-added creation. If a firm does not consistently satisfy time and location requirements, it has nothing to sell. For a supply chain to realize the maximum strategic benefit from logistics, the full range of functional work must be integrated. Decisions in one functional area will impact cost of all others. It is this interrelation of functions that challenges the successful implementation of integrated logistical management. Figure 2.1 provides a visual representation of the interrelated nature of the five areas of logistical work: (1) order processing; (2) inventory; (3) transportation; (4) warehousing, materials handling, and packaging; and (5) facility network. Integrated work related to these functional areas creates the capabilities needed to achieve logistical value.

Order Processing

The importance of accurate information to achieving superior logistical performance has historically been underappreciated. While many aspects of information are critical to logistics operations, the processing of orders is of primary importance. Failure to fully comprehend this importance resulted from not fully understanding how distortion and operational failures in order processing impact logistical operations.

Current information technology is capable of handling the most demanding customer requirements. When desired, order information can be exchanged between trading partners.

FIGURE 2.1
Integrated Logistics

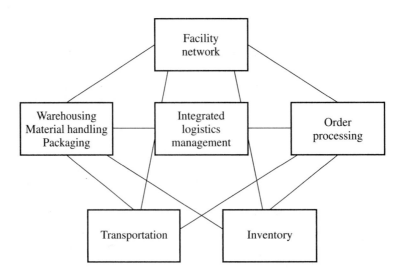

The benefit of fast information flow is directly related to work balancing. It makes little sense for a firm to accumulate orders at a local sales office for a week, mail them to a regional office, process the orders in a batch, assign them to a distribution warehouse, and then ship them via air to achieve fast delivery. In contrast, Internet communication of orders direct from the customer, combined with slower, less costly surface transportation, may achieve even faster overall delivery service at a lower total cost. The key objective is to balance components of the logistical system.

Forecasting and communication of customer requirements are the two areas of logistical work driven by information. The relative importance of each facet of operational information is directly related to the degree to which the supply chain is positioned to function on a responsive or anticipatory basis. The more responsive the supply chain design, the greater the importance is of accurate and timely information regarding customer purchase behavior. As discussed in Chapter 1, supply chains are increasingly reflecting a blend of responsive and anticipatory operations.

In most supply chains, customer requirements are transmitted in the form of orders. The processing of these orders involves all aspects of managing customer requirements, including initial order receipt, delivery, invoicing, and collection. The logistics capabilities of a firm can only be as good as its order processing competency.

Inventory

The inventory requirements of a firm are directly linked to the facility network and the desired level of customer service. Theoretically, a firm could stock every item sold in every facility dedicated to servicing each customer. Few business operations can afford such a luxurious inventory strategy because the risk and total cost are prohibitive. The objective of an inventory strategy is to achieve desired customer service with the minimum inventory commitment. Excessive inventories may compensate for deficiencies in basic design of a logistics system but will ultimately result in higher-than-necessary total logistics cost.

Logistical strategies should be designed to maintain the lowest possible financial investment in inventory. The basic goal is to achieve maximum inventory turn while satisfying service commitments. A sound inventory strategy is based on a combination of five aspects of selective deployment: (1) core customer segmentation, (2) product profitability, (3) transportation integration, (4) time-based performance, and (5) competitive performance.

Every enterprise that sells to a variety of different customers confronts uneven demand. Some customers are highly profitable and have outstanding growth potential; others do not. The profitability of a customer's business depends upon the products purchased, volume, price, value-added services required, and supplemental activities necessary to develop and maintain an ongoing relationship. Because highly profitable customers constitute the core market of every enterprise, inventory strategies need to focus on them. The key to effective logistical segmentation rests in the inventory priorities dedicated to support core customers.

Most enterprises experience a substantial variance in the volume and profitability across product lines. If no restrictions are applied, a firm may find that less than 20 percent of all products marketed account for more than 80 percent of total profit. While the so-called 80/20 rule, or **Pareto principle,** is common in business, management must avoid such outcomes by implementing inventory strategies based on fine-line product classification. A realistic assessment of the incremental value added by stocking low-profit or low-volume products is essential to avoiding excessive inventory. For obvious reasons, an enterprise wants to offer high availability and consistent delivery of its most profitable products. High-level support of less profitable items, however, may be necessary to provide full-line service to core customers. The trap to avoid is high service performance on less profitable items that are typically purchased by fringe or noncore customers. Therefore, product line profitability analysis is essential in developing a selective inventory policy.

The product stocking plan at a specific facility has a direct impact upon transportation performance. Most transportation rates are based on the volume and shipment size. Thus, it may be sound strategy to stock a sufficient range or assortment of products at a warehouse to be able to arrange consolidated shipments. The corresponding savings in transportation may more than offset the increased cost of holding the inventory.

A firm's degree of commitment to deliver products rapidly to meet a customer's inventory requirement is a major competitive factor. If products and materials can be delivered quickly, it may not be necessary for customers to maintain large inventories. Likewise, if retail stores can be replenished rapidly, less safety stock is required. The alternative to stockpiling and holding safety stock is to receive exact and timely inventory replenishment. While such time-based programs reduce customer inventory to absolute minimums, the savings must be balanced against other supply chain costs incurred as a result of the time-sensitive logistical process.

Finally, inventory strategies cannot be created in a competitive vacuum. A firm is typically more desirable to do business with than competitors if it can promise and perform rapid and consistent delivery. Therefore, it may be necessary to position inventory in a specific warehouse to gain competitive advantage even if such commitment increases total cost. Selective inventory deployment policies may be essential to gain a customer service advantage or to neutralize a strength that a competitor currently enjoys.

Material and component inventories exist in a logistical system for reasons other than finished product inventory. Each type of inventory and the level of commitment must be viewed from a total cost perspective. Understanding the interrelationship between order processing, inventory, transportation, and facility network decisions is fundamental to integrated logistics.

Transportation

Transportation is the operational area of logistics that geographically moves and positions inventory. Because of its fundamental importance and visible cost, transportation has traditionally received considerable managerial attention. Almost all enterprises, big and small, have managers responsible for transportation.

Transportation requirements can be satisfied in three basic ways. First, a private fleet of equipment may be operated. Second, contracts may be arranged with dedicated transport specialists. Third, an enterprise may engage the services of a wide variety of carriers that provide different transportation services as needed on a per shipment basis. From the logistical system viewpoint, three factors are fundamental to transportation performance: (1) cost, (2) speed, and (3) consistency.

The cost of transport is the payment for shipment between two geographical locations and the expenses related to maintaining in-transit inventory. Logistical systems should utilize transportation that minimizes **total system cost.** This may mean that the least expensive method of transportation may not result in the lowest total cost of logistics.

Speed of transportation is the time required to complete a specific movement. Speed and cost of transportation are related in two ways. First, transport firms capable of offering faster service typically charge higher rates. Second, the faster the transportation service is, the shorter the time interval during which inventory is in transit and unavailable. Thus, a critical aspect of selecting the most desirable method of transportation is to balance speed and cost of service.

Consistency of transportation refers to variations in time required to perform a specific movement over a number of shipments. Consistency reflects the dependability of transportation. For years, transportation managers have identified consistency as the most important attribute of quality transportation. If a shipment between two locations takes 3 days one time and 6 the next, the unexpected variance can create serious supply chain operational problems. When transportation lacks consistency, inventory safety stocks are required to protect against service breakdowns, impacting both the seller's and buyer's overall inventory commitment. With the advent of new information technology to control and report shipment status, logistics managers have begun to seek faster movement while maintaining consistency. Speed and consistency combine to create the quality aspect of transportation.

In designing a logistical system, a delicate balance must be maintained between transportation cost and service quality. In some circumstances low-cost, slow transportation is satisfactory. In other situations, faster service may be essential to achieving operating goals. Finding and managing the desired transportation mix across the supply chain is a primary responsibility of logistics.

Warehousing, Materials Handling, and Packaging

The first three functional areas of logistics—order processing, inventory, and transportation—can be engineered into a variety of different operational arrangements. Each arrangement has the potential to contribute to a specified level of customer service with an associated total cost. In essence, these functions combine to create a system solution for integrated logistics. The fourth functionality of logistics—warehousing, materials handling, and packaging—also represents an integral part of a logistics operating solution. However, these functions do not have the independent status of those previously discussed. Warehousing, materials handling, and packaging are an integral part of other logistics areas. For example, inventory typically needs to be warehoused at selected times during the logistics process. Transportation vehicles require materials handling for efficient loading and unloading. Finally, the individual products are most efficiently handled when packaged together into shipping cartons or other unit loads.

When distribution facilities are required in a logistical system, a firm can choose between the services of a warehouse specialist or operating its own facility. The decision is broader than simply selecting a facility to store inventory, since many value-adding activities may be performed during the time products are warehoused. Examples of such activities are sorting, sequencing, order selection, transportation consolidation, and, in some cases, product modification and assembly related to postponement strategies.

Within the warehouse, materials handling is an important activity. Products must be received, moved, stored, sorted, and assembled to meet customer order requirements. The direct labor and capital invested in materials handling equipment is a significant element of total logistics cost. When performed in an inferior manner, materials handling can result in substantial product damage. It stands to reason that the fewer the times a product is handled, the less the potential exists for product damage. A variety of mechanized and automated devices exist to assist materials handling. In essence, each warehouse and its materials handling capability represent a minisystem within the overall logistical process.

To facilitate handling efficiency, products in the form of cans, bottles, or boxes are typically combined into larger units. This larger unit, typically called the master carton, provides two important features. First, it serves to protect the product during the logistical process. Second, the master carton facilitates ease of handling, by creating one large package rather than a multitude of small, individual products. For efficient handling and transport, master cartons are typically consolidated into larger unit loads.

When effectively integrated into an enterprise's logistical operations, warehousing, materials handling, and packaging facilitate the speed and overall ease of product flow throughout the logistical system. In fact, several firms have developed processes to move product assortments from manufacturing plants directly to retail stores with limited intermediate handling and storage.

Facility Network Design

Classical economics neglected the importance of facility location and overall network design to efficient business operations. When economists originally discussed supply-and-demand relationships, facility location and transportation cost differentials were assumed either nonexistent or equal among competitors.[3] In business operations, however, the number, size, and geographical relationship of facilities used to perform logistical operations directly impacts customer service capability and cost. Facility network design is a primary responsibility of logistical management, since a firm's facility structure is used to ship products and materials to customers. Typical logistics facilities are manufacturing plants, warehouses, cross-dock operations, and retail stores.

Facility network design is concerned with determining the number and location of all types of facilities required to perform logistics work. It is also necessary to determine what inventory and how much to stock at each facility as well as the assignment of customers. The facility network creates a structure from which logistical operations are performed. Thus, the network integrates information and transportation capabilities. Specific work tasks related to processing customer orders, warehousing inventory, and materials handling are all performed within the facility network.

The design of a facility network requires careful analysis of geographical variation. The fact that a great deal of difference exists between geographical markets is easy to illustrate. The 50 largest United States metropolitan markets in terms of population account for the majority of retail sales. Therefore, an enterprise marketing consumer products on a national scale must establish a logistical network capable of servicing prime markets. A similar geographic disparity exists in typical material and component part source locations. When a firm is involved in global logistics, issues related to network design become increasingly complex.

The importance of continuously modifying the facility network to accommodate change in demand and supply infrastructures cannot be overemphasized. Product assortments, customers, suppliers, and manufacturing requirements are constantly changing in a dynamic competitive environment. The selection of a superior locational network can provide a significant step toward achieving competitive advantage. *First sentence*

Logistical Operations

The internal operational scope of integrated logistics operations is illustrated by the shaded area of Figure 2.2. Information from and about customers flows through the enterprise in the form of sales activity, forecasts, and orders. Vital information is refined into specific manufacturing, merchandising, and purchasing actions. As products and materials are procured, a value-added inventory flow is initiated, which ultimately results in ownership

[3] Alfred Weber, *Theory of the Location of Industries,* translated by Carl J. Friedrich (Chicago: University of Chicago Press, 1928); August Lösch, *Die Rümliche Ordnung der Wirtschaft* (Jena: Gustav Fischer Verlag, 1940); Edgar M. Hoover, *The Location of Economic Activity* (New York: McGraw-Hill Book Company, 1938); Melvin L. Greenhut, *Plant Location in Theory and Practice* (Chapel Hill, NC: University of North Carolina Press, 1956); Walter Isard et al., *Methods of Regional Analysis: An Introduction to Regional Science* (New York: John Wiley & Sons, 1960); Walter Isard, *Location and Space Economy* (Cambridge, MA: The MIT Press, 1968); and Michael J. Webber, *Impact of Uncertainty on Location* (Cambridge, MA: The MIT Press, 1972).

FIGURE 2.2 **Logistical Integration**

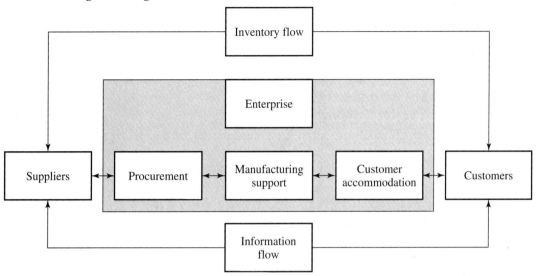

transfer of finished products to customers. Thus, the logistical process is viewed in terms of two interrelated flows: inventory and information. While internal process integration is important to success, the firm must also align and integrate across the supply chain. To be fully effective in today's competitive environment, firms must extend their enterprise integration to incorporate customers and suppliers. This extension reflects the position of logistics in the broader perspective of supply chain management. Supply chain integration is discussed later in this chapter (see Supply Chain Synchronization).

Inventory Flow

The operational management of logistics is concerned with movement and storage of inventory in the form of materials, work-in-process, and finished products. Logistical operations start with the initial shipment of a material or component part from a supplier and are finalized when a manufactured or processed product is delivered to a customer.

From the initial purchase of a material or component, the logistics process adds value by moving inventory when and where needed. Providing all goes well, materials and components gain value at each step of their transformation into finished inventory. In other words, an individual part has greater value after it is incorporated into a machine than it had as a part. Likewise, the machine has greater value once it is delivered to a customer.

To support manufacturing, work-in-process inventory must be properly positioned. The cost of each component and its movement becomes part of the value-added process. For better understanding, it is useful to divide logistical operations into three areas: (1) customer accommodation, (2) manufacturing support, and (3) procurement. These components are illustrated in the shaded area of Figure 2.2 as the combined logistics operational units of an enterprise.

Customer Accommodation

The movement of finished product to customers is customer accommodation. In customer accommodation, the customer's ship-to location represents the final destination. The availability of product is a vital part of each channel participant's marketing effort. Unless a proper assortment of products is efficiently delivered when and where needed, a great deal of overall marketing effort will be jeopardized. It is through the customer accommodation process that the timing and geographical placement of inventory become an integral part of marketing. To support the wide variety of marketing systems that exist in a highly commercialized nation, many different customer accommodations systems are available. All customer accommodation systems have one common feature: They align manufacturers, wholesalers, and retailers into supply chain arrangements to provide customers product availability.

Manufacturing Support

The area of manufacturing support concentrates on managing work-in-process inventory as it flows between stages of manufacturing. The primary logistical responsibility in manufacturing is to participate in formulating a master production schedule and to arrange for its implementation by timely availability of materials, component parts, and work-in-process inventory. Thus, the overall concern of manufacturing support is not how production occurs but rather **what, when,** and **where** products will be manufactured.

Manufacturing support is significantly different from customer accommodation. Customer accommodation attempts to service the desires of customers, and therefore must accommodate the uncertainty of demand. Manufacturing support involves scheduling movement requirements that are under the control of the manufacturing enterprise. The uncertainties introduced by random customer ordering and erratic demand that customer accommodation must expect are not typical in manufacturing operations. From the viewpoint of overall planning, the separation of manufacturing support from customer accommodation and inbound procurement activities provides opportunities for specialization and improved efficiency. The degree to which a firm adopts a responsive strategy serves to reduce or eliminate the separation of manufacturing.

Procurement

The area of procurement is concerned with purchasing and arranging inbound movement of materials, parts, and/or finished inventory from suppliers into manufacturing or assembly plants, warehouses, or retail stores. Depending on the situation, the acquisition process is commonly identified by different names. In manufacturing, the process of acquisition is typically called **purchasing.** In government circles, acquisition has traditionally been referred to as **procurement.** In retailing and wholesaling, **buying** is the most widely used term. In many circles, the process is referred to as **inbound logistics.** For the purposes of this text, the term **procurement** will include all types of purchasing. The term **material** is used to identify inventory moving inbound to an enterprise, regardless of its degree of readiness for resale. The term **product** is used to identify value-added inventory that is sold to customers. In other words, materials are involved in the process of adding value through manufacturing whereas products are ready for consumption. The fundamental distinction is that products result from the value added to material during manufacture, sortation, or assembly.

Within a typical enterprise, the three logistics operating areas overlap. Viewing each as an integral part of the overall value-adding process creates an opportunity to specialize performance and capitalize on the unique attributes of each within the overall process. Table 2.2 provides a more exacting definition of the day-to-day work involved in each subprocess of logistics. The overall challenge of a supply chain is to integrate the logistical processes of participating firms in a manner that facilitates overall efficiency.

Information Flow

Information flow identifies specific locations within a logistical system that have requirements. Information also integrates the three operating areas. Within individual logistics areas, different movement requirements exist with respect to size of order, availability of

TABLE 2.2

Specific Operating Concerns of Customer Accommodation, Manufacturing Support, and Procurement in Overall Logistics

Customer Accommodation

Activities related to providing customer service. Requires performing order receipt and processing, deploying inventories, storage and handling, and outbound transportation within a supply chain. Includes the responsibility to coordinate with marketing planning in such areas as pricing, promotional support, customer service levels, credit delivery standards, handling return merchandise, and life cycle support. The primary market distribution objective is to assist in revenue generation by providing strategically desired customer service delivery levels at the lowest total cost.

Manufacturing Support

Activities related to planning, scheduling, and supporting manufacturing operations. Requires master schedule planning and performing work-in-process storage, handling, transportation, and sortation, kilting, sequencing and time phasing of components. Includes the responsibility for storage of inventory at manufacturing sites and maximum flexibility in the coordination of geographic and assembly postponement between manufacturing and customer accommodation operations.

Procurement

Activities related to obtaining products and materials from outside suppliers. Requires performing resource planning, supply sourcing, negotiation, order placement, inbound transportation, receiving and inspection, storage and handling, and quality assurance. Includes the responsibility to coordinate with suppliers in such areas as scheduling, supply continuity, hedging, and speculation, as well as research leading to new sources or programs. The primary procurement objective is to support manufacturing or resale organizations by providing timely purchasing at the lowest total cost.

inventory, and urgency. The primary objective of information flow management is to reconcile these differentials to improve overall supply chain performance. It is important to stress that information requirements parallel the actual work performed in customer accommodation, manufacturing support, and procurement. Whereas these areas contain the actual logistics work, information facilitates coordination of planning and control of day-to-day operations. Without accurate information, the effort involved in the logistical system can be misdirected.

Logistical information has two major components: planning/coordination and operations. In-depth discussion of information technology is reserved for Chapter 5 in which the architecture of logistical information systems is developed in detail. The structure and dynamics of supply chain logistics are discussed next.

Logistical Operating Arrangements

The potential for logistical services to favorably impact customers is directly related to operating system design. The many different facets of logistical performance requirements make operational design a complex task, as an operating structure must offer a balance of performance, cost, and flexibility. When one considers the variety of logistical systems used throughout the world to service widely diverse markets, it is astonishing that any structural similarity exists. But keep in mind that all logistical arrangements have two common characteristics. First, they are designed to manage inventory. Second, the range of logistics alternatives is limited by available technology. These two characteristics tend to create commonly observed operating arrangements. Three widely utilized structures are echelon, direct, and combined.

Echelon

Classification of a logistical system as having an echeloned structure means that the flow of products typically proceeds through a common arrangement of firms and facilities as it moves from origin to final destination. The use of echelons usually implies that total cost

FIGURE 2.3 **Echelon-Structured Logistics**

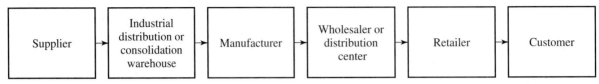

analysis justifies stocking some level of inventory or performing specific activities at consecutive levels of a supply chain.

Echelon systems utilize warehouses to create inventory assortments and achieve consolidation economies associated with large-volume transportation shipments. Inventories positioned in warehouses are available for rapid deployment to meet customer requirements. Figure 2.3 illustrates the typical echeloned value chain.

Typical echelon systems utilize either break-bulk or consolidation warehouses. A break-bulk facility typically receives large-volume shipments from a variety of suppliers. Inventory is sorted and stored in anticipation of future customer requirements. Food distribution centers operated by major grocery chains and wholesalers are examples of break-bulk warehouses. A consolidation warehouse operates in a reverse profile. Consolidation is typically required by manufacturing firms that have plants at different geographical locations. Products manufactured at different plants are stored in a central warehouse facility to allow the firm to ship full-line assortments to customers. Major consumer product manufacturers are prime examples of enterprises using echeloned systems for full-line consolidation.

Direct

In contrast to inventory echeloning are logistical systems designed to ship products direct to customer's destination from one or a limited number of centrally located inventories. Direct distribution typically uses the expedited services of premium transport combined with information technology to rapidly process customer orders and achieve delivery performance. This combination of capabilities, designed into the order delivery cycle, reduces time delays and overcomes geographical separation from customers. Examples of direct shipments are plant-to-customer truckload shipments, direct store delivery, and various forms of direct-to-consumer fulfillment required to support e-commerce shopping. Direct logistical structures are also commonly used for inbound components and materials to manufacturing plants because the average shipment size is typically large.

When the economics permit, logistic executives desire direct alternatives because they reduce anticipatory inventories and intermediate product handling. The deployment of direct logistics is limited by high transportation cost and potential loss of control. In general, most firms do not operate the number of warehouses today that were common a few years ago and have been able to modify echelon structures to include direct logistics capabilities. Figure 2.4 illustrates direct logistics capability being added to an echeloned logistics structure.

Combined

The ideal logistical arrangement is a situation wherein the inherent benefits of echeloned and direct logistics structures are combined. As noted in Chapter 1, anticipatory commitment of inventory should ideally be postponed as long as possible. Inventory strategies often position fast-moving products or materials in forward warehouses, while other, more risky or costly items, are stocked at a central location for direct delivery to customers. The

FIGURE 2.4 **Combined Echeloned and Direct Delivery**

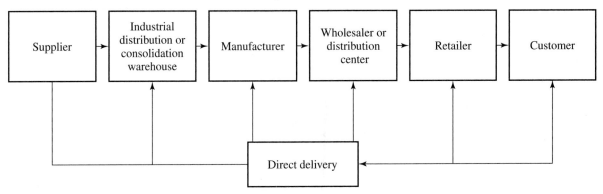

basic service commitment and order size economics determine the most desirable and economical structure to service a specific customer.

To illustrate, automobile replacement parts are typically distributed to customers by utilizing a combined logistics strategy. Specific parts are inventoried in warehouses located at various distances from dealers and retail outlets on the basis of pattern and density of demand. As a general rule, the slower the part turnover is, the more erratic the demand is, and therefore the greater the benefit is of centralized inventory. The slowest or least-demanded parts may be stocked at only one location that services customers throughout the world. Fast-moving parts that have more predictable demand are stocked in forward warehouses close to dealers to facilitate fast, low-cost delivery.

A contrasting example is an enterprise that sells machine parts to industrial firms. The nature of this business supports a completely opposite combined distribution strategy. To offer superior service to customers who experience machine failure and unexpected downtime, the firm stocks slow movers in all local warehouses. In contrast to the automotive firm, high-demand, fast-turnover parts in this industry can be accurately forecasted because of routine preventive maintenance. The least-cost logistical methods for these fast movers are to ship direct from a centralized warehouse located adjacent to the parts manufacturing plant.

These alternative strategies, both of which use different logistical capabilities, are justified on the basis of unique customer requirements, total cost to service, and intensity of competition confronted. The automotive manufacturer is the sole supplier of parts during the new-car warranty period and must provide dealers rapid delivery of parts to promptly repair customer cars. Dealers require fast replenishment of parts inventory to satisfy customers while minimizing inventory investment. As cars become older and the demand for replacement parts increases, alternative manufacturers enter the replacement parts market. During this highly competitive stage of the model's life cycle, rapid logistical response is required to be competitive. As a model ages, competition drops out of the shrinking aftermarket, leaving the original manufacturer as the sole supplier.

The industrial component supplier, in contrast to the automotive company, offers standard machine parts having a high degree of competitive substitutability. Whereas products used on a regular basis can be forecasted, slow- or erratic-demand products are impossible to forecast. This enterprise forces a situation wherein customers measure suppliers in terms of how fast unexpected machine breakdowns can be remedied. Failure to perform to the level of customer expectation can open the door for a competitor to prove its capability.

Each enterprise faces a unique customer situation and can be expected to use a different logistics strategy to achieve competitive superiority. The strategy that satisfies customer expectations at lowest attainable total cost typically utilizes a combination of echeloned and direct capabilities.

Beyond the basic channel structure, flexible capabilities can be designed into a logistical system by developing a program to service customers by using alternative facilities.

Flexible Structure

Flexible operations are preplanned contingency strategies to prevent logistical failures. A typical emergency occurs when an assigned shipping facility is out of stock or for some other reason cannot complete a customer's order. For example, a warehouse may be out of an item with no replenishment inventory scheduled to arrive until after the customer's specified order delivery date. To prevent back-ordering or delivery cancellation, a contingency operating policy may assign the total order, or at least those items not available, for shipment from an alternative warehouse. The use of flexible operations is typically based on the importance of the specific customer or the critical nature of the product being ordered.

A flexible logistics capability that has gained popularity as a result of improved communications involves procedures for serving specified situations as part of the basic logistical strategy. The flexible logistics rule and decision scenarios specify alternative ways to meet specific service requirements, such as assignment of different shipping facilities. A strategy that utilizes flexible operations is common practice in four different situations.

First, the customer-specified delivery facility might be near a point of equal logistics cost or equal delivery time from two different logistics facilities. Customers located at such indifference points offer the supplying firm an opportunity to fully utilize available inventory and logistical capacity. Orders can be serviced from the facility having the best inventory position or the available transportation capacity to achieve timely delivery. This form of flexible logistics offers a way to fully utilize system capacity by balancing workloads between facilities while protecting customer service commitments. The benefit is operating efficiency, which is transparent to the customer, who experiences no service deterioration.

A second situation justifying flexible distribution is when the size of a customer's order creates an opportunity to improve logistical efficiency if serviced through an alternative channel arrangement. For example, the lowest-total-cost method to provide small shipment delivery may be through a distributor. In contrast, larger shipments may have the lowest total logistical cost when shipped factory direct to customers. Provided that alternative methods of shipment meet delivery expectations, total logistical cost may be reduced by implementing flexible policies.

A third type of flexible operation may result from a selective inventory stocking strategy. The cost and risk associated with stocking inventory require careful analysis to determine which items to place in each warehouse. With replacement parts, a common strategy mentioned earlier is to stock selected items in specific warehouses with the total line being stocked only at a central facility. In general-merchandise retailing, a store or distribution center located in a small community may stock only a limited or restricted version of a firm's total line. When customers desire nonstocked items, orders must be satisfied from an alternative facility. The term *mother facility* is often used to describe inventory strategies that designate larger facilities for backup support of smaller restricted facilities. Selective inventory stocking by echelon level is a common strategy used to reduce overall inventory risk. The reasons for selective echelon stocking range from low product profit contribution to high per-unit cost of inventory maintenance. One way to operationalize a fine-line inventory classification strategy is to differentiate stocking policy by system echelons. In situations following such classified stocking strategies, it may be necessary to obtain advanced customer approval for split-order delivery. However, in some situations firms that use differentiated inventory stocking strategies are able to consolidate customer orders for same-time delivery, thereby making the arrangement customer transparent.

The fourth type of flexible operations results from agreements between firms to move selected shipments outside the established echeloned or direct logistics arrangements. Two special arrangements gaining popularity are flow through cross-docks and service supplier arrangements. A cross-dock operation involves multiple suppliers arriving at a designated time at the handling facility and is typically deployed in situations where storage and materials handling can be avoided. Inventory receipts are sorted across the dock and consolidated into outbound trailers for direct destination delivery. Cross-dock operations are growing in popularity in the retail industry for building store-specific assortments and are common methods of continuous inventory replenishment for mass merchants.

Another form of flexible operations is to use integrated service providers to consolidate products for delivery. This is similar to consolidation for transportation purposes discussed in the previous section of this chapter. However, as a form of flexible logistics, specialists are used to avoid storage and handling of slow-moving products through the mainstream of the echeloned logistics structure. Such service providers can also provide important value-added services. For example, Smurfit-Stone builds in-store point-of-sale displays for direct store delivery.

Figure 2.5 introduces flexibility to the logistical operating structures previously illustrated. A prerequisite to effective flexible operations is the use of information technology to monitor inventory status throughout the logistical network and provide the capability to rapidly switch methods for servicing customer orders. The use of flexible operations in emergency situations has a well-established track record. The overall improvement in information technology is resulting in flexible operations becoming a part of basic logistics strategy.

FIGURE 2.5   **Flexible Echeloned and Direct Delivery**

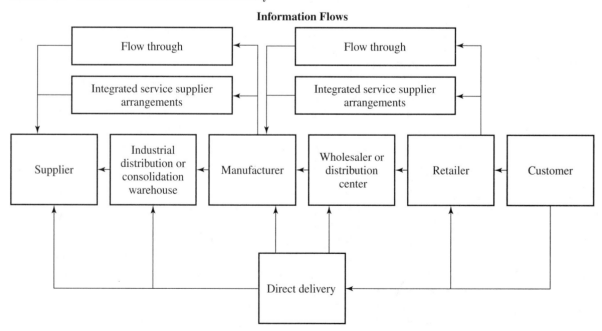

Supply Chain Synchronization

The previous discussion positioned logistics as an integrated management process within an individual firm. A challenge of supply chain management is to integrate operations across multiple firms. In an effort to facilitate logistical operations, supply chain participants must jointly plan and implement operations. Multifirm operational integration across a supply chain is referred to as **supply chain synchronization.**

Supply chain synchronization seeks to coordinate the flow of materials, products, and information between supply chain partners to reduce duplication and unwanted redundancy. It also seeks to reengineer internal operations of individual firms to leverage overall supply chain capability. Leveraged operations require a joint plan concerning the logistics work that each participating firm in a supply chain will perform and be held accountable for. At the heart of supply chain integration is the goal of leveraging member core competencies to achieve overall reduction of inventory dwell time.

As defined in Chapter 1, dwell time is the ratio of time inventory sits idle in comparison to the amount of time it is being productively moved to a desired location in the supply chain. To illustrate, a product or component stored in a warehouse is dwelling. In contrast, the same part moving in a transportation vehicle on the way to a customer is being productively deployed. Ideally, the shipment will arrive in a timely manner to be immediately used by the customer in a value-added process. The desire is to directly integrate inventory into the customer's value-adding process without product being placed in storage or otherwise restricting continuous movement. The benefits of synchronization serve to support the generalization that speed of performing a specific service or product movement is secondary to synchronizing the timing of supply with demand requirements.

Performance Cycle Structure

The performance cycle represents the elements of work necessary to complete the logistics related to customer accommodation, manufacturing, or procurement. It consists of specific work ranging from identification of requirements to product delivery. Because it integrates various aspects of work, the performance cycle is the primary unit of analysis for logistical design and synchronization. At a basic level, information and transportation must link all firms functioning in a supply chain. The operational locations that are linked by information and transportation are referred to as nodes.

In addition to supply chain nodes and links, performance cycles involve inventory assets. Inventory is measured in terms of the asset investment level allocated to support operations at a node or while a product or material is in transit. Inventory committed to supply chain nodes consists of base stock and safety stock. Base stock is inventory held at a node and is typically one-half of the average shipment size received. Safety stock exists to protect against variance in demand or operational lead time. It is at and between supply chain nodes that work related to logistics is performed. Inventory is stocked and flows through nodes, necessitating a variety of different types of materials handling and, when necessary, storage. While a degree of handling and in-transit storage takes place within transportation, such activity is minor in comparison to that typically performed within a supply chain node, such as a warehouse.

Performance cycles become dynamic as they accommodate **input/output requirements.** The **input** to a performance cycle is demand, typically an order that specifies requirements for a product or material. A high-volume supply chain will typically require a different and wider variety of performance cycles than a chain having fewer throughputs. When operating requirements are highly predictable or relatively low-volume throughput, the performance cycle structure required to provide supply chain logistical support can be simplified. The performance cycle structures required to support a large retail enterprise like Target or Wal★Mart supply chains are far more complex than the operating structure requirements of a catalog fulfillment company.

Supply chain **output** is the level of performance expected from the combined logistical operations. To the extent that operational requirements are satisfied, the combined logistical performance cycle structure of the supply chain is effective in accomplishing its mission. Efficiency of a supply chain is a measure of resource expenditure necessary to achieve such logistical effectiveness. The effectiveness and efficiency of logistical performance cycles are key concerns in supply chain management.

Depending on the operational mission of a particular performance cycle in a supply chain structure, the associated work may be under the complete control of a single enterprise or may involve multiple firms. For example, manufacturing support cycles are often under the operational control of a single enterprise. In contrast, performance cycles related to customer accommodation and procurement typically involve multiple firms.

It is important to realize that transaction frequency and intensity will vary between performance cycles. Some performance cycles are established to facilitate a one-time purchase or sale. In such a case, the associated supply chain is designed, implemented, and abolished once the transaction is complete. Other performance cycles represent long-standing operating arrangements. A complicating fact is that any operation or facility in one supply chain may simultaneously be participating in a number of other arrangements. For example, the warehouse facility of a hardware wholesaler might regularly receive merchandise from multiple manufacturers and service competing retailers. Likewise, a motor carrier may participate in numerous different supply chains, spanning a wide variety of industries.

When one considers a supply chain of national or multinational scope that is involved in marketing a broad product line to numerous customers, engaging in basic manufacturing and assembly, and procuring materials and components on a global basis, the notion of individual performance cycles linking all participating firms' operations is difficult to comprehend. It is almost mind-boggling to estimate how many performance cycles exist in the supply chain structure of General Motors or IBM.

Regardless of the number and different missions of performance cycles a specific supply chain deploys to satisfy its logistical requirements, each must be individually designed and operationally managed. The fundamental importance of performance cycle design and operation cannot be overemphasized: **The logistics performance cycle is the basic unit of supply chain design and operational control. In essence, the performance cycle structure is the framework for implementation of integrated logistics across the supply chain.**

Figure 2.6 portrays an echeloned supply chain structure illustrating basic logistics performance cycles. Figure 2.7 illustrates a network of flexible performance cycles integrated in a multiecheloned structure.

Three points are important to understanding the architecture of integrated supply chain logistical systems. First, as noted earlier, the performance cycles are the fundamental unit for integrated logistics across the supply chain. Second, the performance cycle structure of a supply chain, in terms of link and nodal arrangement, is basically the same whether one is concerned with customer accommodation, manufacturing support, or procurement. However, considerable differences exist in the degree of control that an individual firm can exercise over a specific type of performance cycle. Third, regardless of how vast and complex the overall supply chain structure, essential interfaces and control processes must be identified and evaluated in terms of individual performance cycle arrangements and associated managerial accountability.

FIGURE 2.6
Logistical
Performance Cycles

Material
source

}
Purchasing
cycle

Lead
supplier
(tier 1)

}
Manufacturing
support cycle

Manufacturing
plant

Distributors

}
Customer
accommodation
cycle

Customer

Node

Transportation
links ⟶

Communication
links ----➤

FIGURE 2.7 **Multi-echeloned Flexible Logistical Network**

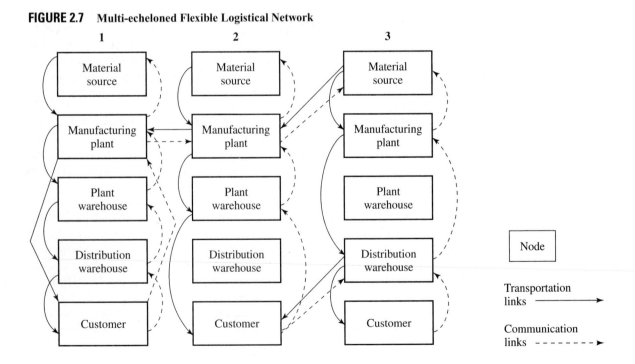

| 1 | 2 | 3 |

Material source — Material source — Material source

Manufacturing plant — Manufacturing plant — Manufacturing plant

Plant warehouse — Plant warehouse — Plant warehouse

Distribution warehouse — Distribution warehouse — Distribution warehouse

Customer — Customer — Customer

Node

Transportation
links ⟶

Communication
links ----➤

FIGURE 2.8   **Performance Cycle Uncertainty**

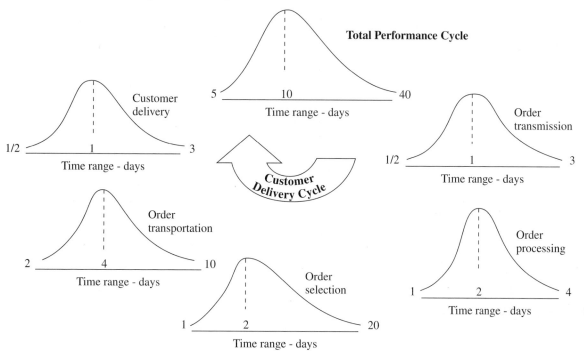

Performance Cycle Uncertainty

A major objective of logistics in all operating areas is to reduce performance cycle uncertainty. The dilemma is that the structure of the performance cycle itself, operating conditions, and the quality of logistical operations all randomly introduce operational variance.

Figure 2.8 illustrates the type and magnitude of variance that can develop in performance cycle operations. The performance cycle illustration is based on finished goods inventory delivery. The time distributions, as illustrated, statistically reflect operational history for each task of the performance cycle. The diagram illustrates the minimum to maximum time historically required to complete each task and the resultant time distribution for the overall performance cycle. The vertical dashed line reflects the average time for performing each task.

In terms of specific tasks, the variance results from the nature of the work involved. Order transmission is highly reliable when electronic transfer (EDI) or Internet communications are used and more erratic when telephone or routine mail is used. Regardless of the level of technology deployed, operational variance will occur as a result of daily changes in workload and resolution of unexpected events.

Time and variance related to order processing are a function of workload, degree of automation, and policies related to credit approval. Order selection, speed, and associated delay are directly related to capacity, materials handling sophistication, and human resource availability. When a product is out of stock, the time to complete order selection may include manufacturing scheduling or inventory purchase. The required transportation time is a function of distance, shipment size, type of transport, and operating conditions. Final delivery to customers can vary, depending on authorized receiving times, delivery appointments, workforce availability, and specialized unloading and equipment requirements.

In Figure 2.8 the history of total order-to-delivery time performance ranges from 5 to 40 days. The 5-day cycle reflects the unlikely event that each task will be performed at the minimum possible time. The 40-day cycle represents the equally unlikely opposite extreme wherein each task requires maximum time. The planned or target order-to-delivery cycle performance is to control combined variance so that actual operations are 10 days as often as possible. Whenever actual performance is more or less than 10 days, managerial action may be necessary to satisfy customer requirements. Such expediting and de-expediting require extra resources and reduce overall logistical efficiency.

The goal of performance cycle synchronization is to achieve the planned time performance. Delayed performance at any point along the supply chain results in potential disruption of operations. Such delays require that safety stocks be established to cover variances. When performance occurs faster than expected, unplanned work will be required to handle and store inventory that arrives early. Given the inconvenience and expense of either early or late delivery, it is no wonder that logistics managers place a premium on operational consistency. Once consistent operations are achieved, every effort should be made to reduce the time required to complete the performance cycle to a minimum. In other words, shorter cycles are desirable because they reduce total assets deployed. However, the importance of speed is directly related to performance consistency. Given consistency as the primary goal, faster order cycles reduce inventory risk and improve turn performance.

Summary

Logistics is the process that links supply chain participants into integrated operations. The cost of performing logistics is a major expenditure for most businesses and supply chain arrangements.

Logistical service is measured in terms of availability, operational performance, and service reliability. Each aspect of service is framed in terms of customer expectations and requirements. Logistics is all about providing the essential customer service attributes at the lowest possible total cost. Such customer commitment, in an exacting cost framework, is the logistics value proposition.

The actual work of logistics is functional in nature. Facility locations must be established to form a network, information must be formulated and shared, transportation must be arranged, inventory must be deployed, and, to the extent required, warehousing, materials handling, and packaging activities must be performed. The traditional orientation was to perform each functional task as well as possible with limited consideration given to how one work area impacted another. Because the work of logistics is extremely detailed and complex, there is a natural tendency to focus on functional performance. While functional excellence is important, it must be supportive of overall logistical competency.

The functions of logistics combine into the three primary operational processes of customer accommodation, manufacturing support, and procurement. To achieve internal integration, the inventory and information flows between these areas must be coordinated.

In supply chain synchronization, the operational focus becomes the logistics performance cycle. The performance cycle is also the primary unit of analysis in logistical design. The performance cycle structure provides the logic for combining the nodes, levels, links, and allocation of assets essential to performing customer accommodation, manufacturing support, and procurement operations. Many similarities and a number of critical differences exist between performance cycles dedicated to these logistics operating areas. Fully understanding these similarities and differences is vital to planning and controlling overall supply chain integration. The basic proposition is that regardless of size and complexity, logistical integration is best understood and evaluated by the structure and dynamics of performance cycle.

The primary goal is to achieve consistency. The challenge is to design a supply chain capable of performing the required logistical work as rapidly but, even more important, as consistently as possible. Unexpected delays, as well as faster than expected performance, can combine to increase or decrease the elapsed time required to complete a performance cycle. Both early and late delivery are undesirable and unacceptable from an operational perspective.

Chapter 2 has developed some important foundations of the logistical discipline and how it creates value in a supply chain context. These insights regarding the nature of logistics work, the importance of achieving internal operational integration through managing inventory and information flow, viewing the performance cycle structure as the basic unit of analysis, and the management of operational uncertainty combine to form a logically consistent set of concepts essential to supporting supply chain management. Chapter 3 focuses on customer accommodation, which is the primary force driving supply chain performance.

Challenge Questions

1. Illustrate a common trade-off that occurs between the work areas of logistics.

2. Discuss and elaborate on the following statement: "The selection of a superior location network can create substantial competitive advantage."

3. Why are customer accommodation operations typically more erratic than manufacturing support and procurement operations?

4. How has transportation cost, as a percentage of total logistics cost, tracked since 1980?

5. Describe the logistics value proposition. Be specific regarding specific customer accommodation and cost.

6. Describe the fundamental similarities and differences between procurement, manufacturing support, and customer accommodation performance cycles as they relate to logistical control.

7. Compare and contrast a performance cycle node and a link. Give an example of each.

8. How does the "quest for quality" affect logistical operations? Does the concept of total quality have relevancy when applied to logistics?

9. Discuss uncertainty as it relates to the overall logistical performance cycle. Discuss and illustrate how performance cycle variance can be controlled.

10. What is the logic of designing echeloned logistical structures? Can echeloned and direct structures be combined?

Customer Accommodation

While in some ways it's an insight into the obvious, it is important to establish initially that logistics contributes to an organization's success by accommodating customers' delivery and inventory availability expectations and requirements. What is not so obvious, however, is what exactly is meant by the term *customer*. The supply chain management concept requires careful consideration of just what is meant by the term and realization that there are many different perspectives.

From the perspective of the total supply chain, the ultimate customer is the end user of the product or service whose needs or requirements must be accommodated. It has historically been useful to distinguish between two types of end users. The first is a consumer, an individual or a household that purchases products and services to satisfy personal needs. When a family purchases an automobile to be used for personal transportation, that family is the consumer of the supply chain. The second type is an organizational end user. Purchases are made by organizations or institutions to allow an end user to perform a task or job in the organization. When a company buys an automobile for a salesperson or buys tools to be used by an assembly worker in a manufacturing plant, the company is considered to be a customer and the salesperson or assembly worker is the end user of the supply chain's products. A supply chain management perspective demands that all firms in the supply chain focus on meeting the needs and requirements of end users, whether they are consumers or organizational users.

Another perspective of customer exists for a specific firm within the supply chain. This perspective recognizes that intermediate organizations often exist between the firm and end users. Common terminology generally recognizes these organizations as intermediate customers. Thus, in the Procter & Gamble (P&G) supply chain that provides Tide laundry detergent to ultimate consumers, Kroger and Safeway supermarkets are intermediate customers; they purchase Tide from P&G for the purpose of reselling to consumers.

Finally, for a logistician, a customer is any delivery location. Typical destinations range from consumers' homes to retail and wholesale businesses to the receiving docks of manufacturing plants and warehouses. In some cases the customer is a different organization or individual who is taking ownership of the product or service being delivered. In many other situations the customer is a different facility of the same firm or a business partner at some other location in the supply chain. For example, it is common for the logistics manager of a retail warehouse to think of the individual stores to be served as warehouse customers, even though the stores are part of the same organization.

Regardless of the motivation and delivery purpose, the customer being served is the focal point and driving force in establishing logistical performance requirements. It is critical to fully understand customer needs that must be accommodated in establishing logistical strategy. This chapter details various approaches to accommodating customer requirements. The first section presents the fundamental concepts that underlie customer-focused marketing, with consideration of how logistics supports a firm's overall marketing strategy. The second section describes how supply chain outputs impact end users and how such outputs must be structured to meet their requirements. The sections that follow expand upon increasing levels of sophistication in accommodating customers. These levels range from traditional notions of logistics customer service to satisfaction of customers by meeting their expectations to the ultimate in accommodation, helping customers be successful by meeting their business requirements. The chapter concludes with a discussion of forecasting customer demand, the process that establishes a company's initial commitment to meeting customer requirements.

Customer-Focused Marketing

The basic principles of customer-focused marketing have their roots in the **marketing concept,** a business philosophy that suggests that the focal point of a business's strategy must be the customers it intends to serve. It holds that for an organization to achieve its goals, it must be more effective than competitors in identifying specific customer needs and focusing resources and activities on accommodating these customer requirements. Clearly, many aspects of a firm's strategy must be integrated to accommodate customers, and logistics is only one of these. The marketing concept builds on four fundamental ideas: Customer needs and requirements are more basic than products or services; different customers have different needs and requirements; products and services become meaningful only when available and positioned from the customer's perspective, which is the focus of logistics strategy; and volume is secondary to profit.

The belief that customer needs are more basic than products or services places a priority on fully understanding what drives market opportunities. The key is to understand and develop the combination of products and services that will meet those requirements. For example, if customers require a choice of only three different colored appliances, it makes little sense to offer six colors. It also makes little sense to try to market only white appliances if color selection is important from a customer's perspective. The idea is to develop sufficient insight into basic customer needs so that products and services can be matched to these opportunities. Successful marketing begins with in-depth study of customers to identify product and service requirements.

The second fundamental aspect of the marketing concept is that there is no single market for any given product or service. All markets are composed of different segments, each of which has somewhat different requirements. Effective market segmentation requires that firms clearly identify segments and select specific targets. While a comprehensive discussion of market segmentation is beyond the scope of this text, it is important to note that customers' logistical requirements frequently offer an effective basis for classification. For example, a contractor building new homes may place an order for appliances several weeks before needed for installation, while a consumer buying a replacement for a broken appliance may require immediate availability and delivery. It is unlikely that a company can operate in every market segment or profitably fulfill every possible combination of customer requirements; thus careful matching of capabilities with specific segments is an essential aspect of the marketing concept.

For marketing to be successful, products and services must be available to customers. In other words, the third fundamental aspect of marketing is that customers must be readily able to obtain the products they desire. To facilitate purchase action, the selling firm's resources need to be focused on customers and product positioning. Four economic utilities add value to customers: **form, possession, time,** and **place.** The product's form is for the most part generated during the manufacturing process. For example, form utility results from the assembly of parts and components for a dishwasher. Marketing creates possession by informing potential customers of product/service availability and enabling ownership exchange. Thus, marketing serves to identify and convey the attributes of the product or service and to develop mechanisms for buyer-seller exchange. Logistics provides time and place utility. Essentially, this means that logistics must ensure that the product is available when and where desired by customers. The achievement of time and place requires significant effort and is expensive. Profitable transactions materialize only when all four utilities are combined in a manner relevant to customers.

The fourth aspect of the marketing concept is the focus on profitability as contrasted to sales volume. An important dimension of success is the degree of profitability resulting from relationships with customers, not the volume sold. Therefore, variations in all four basic utilities, form, possession, time, and place, are justified if a customer or segment of customers values and is willing to pay for the modification. In the appliance example, if a customer requests a unique color option and is willing to pay extra, then the request can and should be accommodated, providing a positive contribution margin can be earned. A final refinement of marketing strategy is based on an acknowledgment that all aspects of a product/service offering are subject to modification when justifiable on the basis of profitability.

Transactional versus Relationship Marketing

Traditional marketing strategies focus on obtaining successful exchanges, or transactions, with customers to drive increases in revenue and profit. In this approach, termed **transactional marketing,** companies are generally oriented toward short-term interaction with their customers. The traditional marketing concept emphasizes accommodating customers' needs and requirements, something few business organizations would argue with. However, as practiced in many firms, the result is a focus on creating successful individual transactions between a supplier and its customers.

Paralleling the development of the supply chain management concept, there has been a shift in philosophy regarding the nature of marketing strategy. This shift has generally been acknowledged as **relationship marketing.** Relationship marketing focuses on the development of long-term relations with key supply chain participants such as consumers, intermediate customers, and suppliers in an effort to develop and retain long-term preference and loyalty. Relationship marketing is based on the realization that in many industries it is as important to retain current customers and gain a larger share of their purchases as it is to attract new customers.[1]

The ultimate in market segmentation and relationship marketing is to focus on the individual customer. This approach, referred to as **micromarketing** or **one-to-one marketing,** recognizes that each individual customer may indeed have unique requirements. For example, although Wal★Mart and Target are both mass merchandisers, their requirements in terms of how they desire to interact logistically with suppliers differ significantly. A manufacturer who wants to do business with both of these major retailers must adapt its logistical operations to the unique needs of each. The best way to ensure long-term organizational success is to intensely research and then accommodate the requirements of individual customers.[2] Such relationships may not be feasible with every customer. It is also true that many customers may not desire this close relationship with all suppliers. However, one-to-one relationships can significantly reduce transaction costs, better accommodate customer requirements, and move individual transactions into a matter of routine.

Supply Chain Service Outputs

Imagine a society in which every individual is totally self-sufficient: Each individual would produce and consume all of the products and services necessary for survival so there would be no need for any economic activity related to the exchange of goods and services between individuals. No such society can be found today. In reality, as individuals begin to specialize in the production of specific goods or services, a mechanism must arise for the exchange of those goods and services to satisfy the consumption needs of individuals. To do so efficiently and effectively, firms must overcome three discrepancies: discrepancy in **space,** discrepancy in **time,** and discrepancy in **quantity and assortment.**

Discrepancy in space refers to the fact that the location of production activities and the location of consumption are seldom the same. Consider, for example, the household furniture industry. Most household furniture in the United States is manufactured in a small geographic area in North Carolina and a great deal of office furniture is manufactured in western Michigan. Yet, where is furniture demanded? All over the United States! This difference between the location of production and the location of consumption is a fundamental transportation challenge that must be overcome to accomplish exchange.

Discrepancy in time refers to the difference in timing between production and consumption. Some products, agricultural commodities, for example, are produced during short time periods but are demanded by customers continuously. On the other hand, many products are manufactured in anticipation of future customer demand. Since manufacturing often does not occur at the same time products are demanded, inventory and

---

[1] Thomas O. Jones and W. Earl Sasser, Jr., "Why Satisfied Customers Defect," *Harvard Business Review* (November/December 1995), pp. 88–99.

[2] For a comprehensive discussion of the one-to-one approach, see Don Peppers and Martha Rogers, *The One-to-One Manager: Real World Lessons in Customer Relationship Management* (New York: Doubleday, 1999).

warehousing are required. It should be noted that much of the discussion in this text is devoted to the challenges firms face in more closely matching the rate of production with market consumption.

Discrepancy in quantity and assortment refers to the fact that manufacturing firms typically specialize in producing large quantities of a limited variety of items. Customers, on the other hand, typically demand small quantities of numerous items. This difference between the production and consumption sectors of the economy must somehow be reconciled to deliver the required product variety and assortment to customers.

To eliminate these discrepancies, Bucklin developed a longstanding theory that specifies four generic service outputs necessary to accommodate customer requirements: (1) spatial convenience, (2) lot size, (3) waiting or delivery time, and (4) product variety and assortment.[3] As discussed above, different customers may have different requirements regarding such services. It follows that different supply chain structures may be required to accommodate such differences.

Spatial Convenience

Spatial convenience, the first service output, refers to the amount of shopping time and effort that will be required on the part of the customer. Higher levels of spatial convenience are achieved in a supply chain by providing customers with access to its products in a larger number of places, thus reducing shopping effort. Consider, for example, the household furniture industry. Some manufacturers utilize a structure that includes department stores, mass merchandisers, and numerous chain and independent furniture specialty stores. Ethan Allen, on the other hand, restricts brand availability to a limited number of authorized Ethan Allen retail stores. This difference in the level of spatial convenience has major implications for the overall supply chain structure and for the logistics cost incurred in the supply chain. It is also clear that some customers are willing to expend greater time and effort than others as they search for a desired product or brand.

Lot Size

The second service output is lot size, which refers to the number of units to be purchased in each transaction. When customers are required to purchase in large quantities, they must incur costs of product storage and maintenance. When the supply chain allows them to purchase in small lot sizes, they can more easily match their consumption requirements with their purchasing. In developed economies, alternative supply chains frequently offer customers a choice of the level of lot-size service output. For example, consumers who are willing to purchase paper towels in a 12- or 24-roll package may buy at Sam's Club or Costco. As an alternative, they may buy single rolls at the local grocery or convenience store. Of course, the supply chain that allows customers to purchase in small quantities normally experiences higher cost and therefore demands higher unit prices from customers.

Waiting Time

Waiting time is the third generic service output. Waiting time is defined as the amount of time the customer must wait between ordering and receiving products: the lower the waiting time, the higher the level of supply chain service. Alternative supply chains offer consumers and end users choices in terms of the amount of waiting time required. In the personal computer industry, a consumer may visit an electronics or computer specialty

---

[3] Louis P. Bucklin, *A Theory of Distribution Channel Structure* (Berkeley, CA: IBER Special Publications, 1966).

store, make a purchase, and carry home a computer with literally no waiting time. Alternatively, the customer may order from a catalog or via the Internet and wait for delivery to the home or office. In a general sense, the longer the waiting time required, the more inconvenient for the customer. However, such supply chains generally incur lower costs and customers are rewarded in the form of lower prices for their willingness to wait.

Product Variety and Assortment

Product variety and assortment are the fourth service output. Different supply chains offer differing levels of variety and assortment to consumers and end users. Typical supermarkets are involved in supply chains that provide a broad variety of many different types of products and an assortment of brands, sizes, etc., of each type. In fact, supermarkets may have over 35,000 different items on the shelves. Warehouse stores, on the other hand, offer much less product variety or assortment, generally stocking in the range of 8000 to 10,000 items, and usually offer only one brand and size of an item. Convenience stores may stock only a few hundred items, offering little variety or assortment compared to supermarkets.

Supply chains provide additional service outputs to their customers. In addition to the four generic service outputs discussed above, other researchers have identified services related to information, product customization, and after-sales support as critical to selected customers.[4] The point to keep in mind is that there is no such thing as a homogeneous market where all consumers desire the same services presented in the same way. They may differ in terms of which services are most important and in terms of the level of each of the services desired to accommodate their needs. For example, some consumers may require immediate availability of a personal computer while others feel that waiting 3 days for a computer configured to their exact requirements is preferable. Additionally, customers differ in terms of how much they are willing to pay for services. Since higher levels of service generally involve higher market distribution costs, organizations must carefully assess customer sensitivity to prices relative to their desire for reduced waiting time, convenience, and other service outputs. Accommodating customer requirements for service outputs has important implications for how supply chains are ultimately configured, what types of participating companies may be included to satisfy service requirements, and the costs that are incurred in the process. Attention is now focused on more specific considerations of customer accommodation in a logistical context. Three levels of customer accommodation are discussed: customer service, customer satisfaction, and customer success.

Customer Service

The primary value of logistics is to accommodate customer requirements in a cost-effective manner. Although most senior managers agree that customer service is important, they sometimes find it extremely difficult to explain what it is and what it does. While common expressions of customer service include "easy to do business with" and "responsive to customers," to develop a full understanding of customer service, a more thorough framework is required.

Philosophically, customer service represents logistics' role in fulfilling the marketing concept. A customer service program must identify and prioritize all activities required to

---

[4] V. Kasturi Rangan, Meluia A. J. Menzies, and E. P. Maier, "Channel Selection for New Industrial Products: A Framework, Method, and Application," *Journal of Marketing* 56 (July 1992), pp. 72–3.

accommodate customers' logistical requirements as well as, or better than, competitors. In establishing a customer service program, it is imperative to identify clear standards of performance for each of the activities and measurements relative to those standards. In basic customer service programs, the focus is typically on the operational aspects of logistics and ensuring that the organization is capable of providing the seven rights to its customer: the right amount of the right product at the right time at the right place in the right condition at the right price with the right information.

It is clear that outstanding customer service adds value throughout a supply chain. The critical concern in developing a service strategy is: **Does the cost associated with achieving specified service performance represent a sound investment?** Careful analysis of competitive performance and customer sensitivity to service attributes is required to formulate a basic service strategy. In Chapter 2, the fundamental attributes of basic customer service were identified as availability, operational performance, and service reliability. These attributes are now discussed in greater detail.

Availability

Availability is the capacity to have inventory when desired by a customer. As simple as this may seem, it is not at all uncommon for an organization to expend considerable time, money, and effort to generate customer demand and then fail to have product available to meet customer requirements. The traditional practice in many organizations is to stock inventory in anticipation of customer orders. Typically an inventory stocking plan is based on forecasted demand for products and may include differential stocking policies for specific items as a result of sales popularity, profitability, and importance of an item to the overall product line and the value of the merchandise.

While the detail of establishing inventory stocking policies is covered in Chapter 6, it should be clear that achieving high levels of inventory availability requires a great deal of planning. In fact, the key is achieving these high levels of availability, while minimizing overall investment in inventory and facilities. Exacting programs of inventory availability are not conceived or managed on average; availability is based on three performance measures: stockout frequency, fill rate, and orders shipped complete.

Stockout Frequency

A stockout, as the term suggests, occurs when a firm has no product available to fulfill customer demand. Stockout frequency refers to the probability that a firm will not have inventory available to meet a customer order. For example, a study of retail supermarkets revealed that at any point in time during a week, the average supermarket is out of stock of approximately 8 percent of the items planned to be on the shelves. It is important to note, however, that a stockout does not actually occur until a customer desires a product. The aggregation of all stockouts across all products is an indicator of how well a firm is positioned to provide basic service commitments in product availability. While it does not consider that some products may be more critical in terms of availability than others, it is the starting point in thinking about inventory availability.

Fill Rate

Fill rate measures the magnitude or impact of stockouts over time. Being out of stock does not affect service performance until a customer demands a product. Then it is important to determine that the product is not available and how many units the customer wanted. For example, if a customer wants 100 units of an item and only 97 are available, the fill rate is 97 percent. To effectively consider fill rate, the typical procedure is to evaluate performance over time to include multiple customer orders. Thus, fill rate performance can be evaluated for a specific customer, product, or for any combination of customers, products, or business segments.

Fill rate can be used to differentiate the level of service to be offered on specific products. In the earlier example, if all 100 products ordered were critical to a customer, then a fill rate of 97 percent could result in a stockout at the customer's plant or warehouse and severely disrupt the customer's operations. Imagine an assembly line scheduled to produce 100 automobiles that receives only 97 of its required brake assemblies. In situations where some of the items are not critical to performance, a fill rate of 97 percent may be acceptable. The customer may accept a back order or be willing to reorder the short items at a later time. Fill rate strategies need to consider customer requirements for products.

Orders Shipped Complete

The most exacting measure of performance in product availability is orders shipped complete. It views having everything that a customer orders as the standard of acceptable performance. Failure to provide even one item on a customers order results in that order being recorded as zero in terms of complete shipment.

These three measures of availability combine to establish the extent to which a firm's inventory strategy is accommodating customer demand. They also form the basis to evaluate the appropriate level of availability to incorporate into a firm's basic logistical service program. High levels of inventory have typically been viewed as the means to increasing availability; however, new strategies that use information technology to identify customer demand in advance of actual customer orders have allowed some organizations to reach very high levels of basic service performance without corresponding increases in inventory.

Operational Performance

Operational performance deals with the time required to deliver a customer's order. Whether the performance cycle in question is customer accommodation, manufacturing support, or procurement, operational performance is specified in terms of speed of performance, consistency, flexibility, and malfunction recovery.

Speed

Performance cycle speed is the elapsed time from when a customer establishes a need to order until the product is delivered and is ready for customer use. The elapsed time required for total performance cycle completion depends on logistical system design. Given today's high level of communication and transportation technology, order cycles can be as short as a few hours or may take several weeks or months.

Naturally, most customers want fast order cycle performance. Speed is an essential ingredient in many just-in-time and quick-response logistical strategies, as fast performance cycles reduce customer inventory requirements. The counterbalance is that speed of service is typically costly: Not all customers need or want maximum speed if it means increased total cost. The justification for speed must be found in the positive trade-offs; that is, the only relevant framework for estimating the value of service speed is the customer's perceived benefits.

Consistency

Order cycle consistency is measured by the number of times that actual cycles meet the time planned for completion. While speed of service is important, most logistical managers place greater value on consistency because it directly impacts a customer's ability to plan and perform its own activities. For example, if order cycles vary, then a customer must carry safety stock to protect against potential late delivery; the degree of variability translates directly into safety stock requirements. Given the numerous activities involved in order cycle execution, there are many potential sources of inconsistency in performance (review Figure 2.8).[5]

The issue of consistency is fundamental to effective logistics operations, as it is becoming increasingly common for customers to actually specify a desired date and even specify a delivery appointment when placing orders. Such a precise specification may be made, taking into consideration a supplier's performance cycle, but that is not always the case. In fact, customers frequently place orders far in advance of their need for product replenishment. In such situations, it is very difficult for customers to understand why failure to deliver as specified occurs. Their viewpoint of supplier consistency in operational performance is whether the supplier delivered at the specified date and time. In such situations the definition of consistency must be modified. It is no longer sufficient to evaluate in terms of planned time, such as 4 days to complete the cycle. It is essential to determine whether the performance cycle was completed according to the customer's specification. Thus, in today's logistical environment, consistency is frequently viewed as a firm's performance in terms of on-time delivery.

Flexibility

Flexibility involves a firm's ability to accommodate special situations and unusual or unexpected customer requests. For example, the standard pattern for servicing a customer may be to ship full-trailer quantities to a customer's warehouse. However, from time to time, the customer may desire to have shipments of smaller quantities made direct to individual retail locations. A firm's logistical competency is directly related to how well it is able to accommodate such unexpected circumstances. Typical events requiring flexible operations are: (1) modification to basic service agreements such as a change in ship-to location; (2) support of unique sales or marketing programs; (3) new-product introduction; (4) product recall; (5) disruption in supply; (6) one-time customization of basic service for specific customers or segments; and (7) product modification or customization performed while in the logistics system, such as pricemarking, mixing, or packaging. In many ways the essence of logistical excellence rests in the ability to be flexible.

Malfunction Recovery

Regardless of how fine-tuned a firm's logistical operations, malfunctions will occur. The continuous performance of service commitments on a day-in, day-out basis is a difficult task. Ideally, adjustments can be implemented to prevent or accommodate special situations, thereby preventing malfunctions. For example, if a stockout of an essential item occurs at a warehouse that normally services a customer, the item may be obtained from an alternative facility by utilizing some form of expedited transportation. In such situations the malfunction may actually be transparent to the customer. While such transparent recoveries are not always possible, effective customer service programs anticipate that malfunctions and service breakdowns will occur and have in place contingency plans to accomplish recovery and measure compliance.

Service Reliability

Service reliability involves the combined attributes of logistics and concerns a firm's ability to perform all order-related activities, as well as provide customers with critical information regarding logistical operations and status. Beyond availability and operational performance, attributes of reliability may mean that shipments arrive damage-free; invoices are

[5] See Figure 2.8, p. 41.

correct and error-free; shipments are made to the correct locations; and the exact amount of product ordered is included in the shipment. While these and numerous other aspects of overall reliability are difficult to enumerate, the point is that customers demand that a wide variety of business details be handled routinely by suppliers. Additionally, service reliability involves a capability and a willingness to provide accurate information to customers regarding operations and order status. Research indicates that the ability of a firm to provide accurate information is one of the most significant attributes of a good service program.[6] Increasingly, customers indicate that advanced notification of problems such as incomplete orders is more critical than the complete order itself. Customers hate surprises! More often than not, customers can adjust to an incomplete or late delivery if they have advanced notification.

The Perfect Order

The ultimate in logistics service is to do everything right and to do it right the first time. It is not sufficient to deliver a complete order but to deliver it late. Nor is it sufficient to deliver a complete order on time but to have an incorrect invoice or to incur product damage during the handling and transportation process. In the past, most logistics managers evaluated customer service performance in terms of several independent measures: fill rates were evaluated against a standard for fill; on-time delivery was evaluated in terms of a percentage of deliveries made on time relative to a standard; damage rates were evaluated relative to a standard for damage; etc. When each of these separate measures was acceptable relative to standard, overall service performance was considered acceptable.

Recently, however, logistics and supply chain executives have begun to focus attention on zero-defect or six-sigma performance. As an extension of Total Quality Management (TQM) efforts within organizations, logistics processes have been subjected to the same scrutiny as manufacturing and other processes in the firm. It was realized that if standards are established independently for customer service components, even if performance met standard on each independent measure, a substantial number of customers may have order-related failures. For example, if orders shipped complete, average on-time delivery, average damage-free delivery, and average correct documentation are each 97 percent, the probability that any order will be delivered with no defects is approximately 88.5 percent. This is so because the potential occurrence of any one failure combined with any other failure is $.97 \times .97 \times .97 \times .97$. The converse of this, of course, is that some type of problem will exist on as much as 11.5 percent of all orders.

The notion of the perfect order is that an order should be delivered complete, delivered on time, at the right location, in perfect condition, with complete and accurate documentation.[7] Each of these individual elements must comply with customer specifications. Thus, complete delivery means all product the customer originally requested, on time means at the customer's specified date and time, etc. In other words, total order cycle performance must be executed with zero defects, availability and operational performance must be perfectly executed, and all support activities must be completed exactly as promised to the customer. While it may not be possible to offer zero defects as a basic service strategy across the board to all customers, such high-level performance may be an option on a selective basis.

It is clear that the resources required to implement a perfect order platform are substantial. Extremely high fill rates require high inventory levels to meet all potential

---

[6] Donald J. Bowersox, David J. Closs, and Theodore P. Stank, *21st Century Logistics: Making Supply Chain Integration a Reality* (Oak Brook, IL: Council of Logistics Management, 1999).

[7] Robert A. Novack and Douglas J. Thomas, "The Challenges of Implementing the Perfect Order Concept," *Transportation Journal* 43, no. 1 (Winter 2004), pp. 5–16.

order requirements and variations. However, such complete service cannot be achieved totally on the basis of inventory. One way of elevating logistics performance to at least near zero defects is to utilize a combination of customer alliances, information technology, postponement strategies, inventory stocking strategies, premium transportation, and selectivity programs to match logistical resources to core customer requirements. Each of these topics is the subject of detailed discussion in subsequent chapters. Suffice it to say at this time that firms achieving superior logistical customer service are well aware of the challenge related to achieving zero defects. By having a low tolerance for errors, coupled with a commitment to resolve whatever discrepancies occur, such firms can achieve strategic advantage over their competitors.

Basic Service Platforms

To implement a basic service platform, it is necessary to specify commitment level to all customers in terms of availability, operational performance, and reliability. The fundamental question, "How much basic service should the system provide?" is not easy to answer. The fact is that many firms establish their basic service platforms on the basis of two factors. The first factor is competitor or industry-acceptable practice. In most industries, levels of minimum and average service performance have emerged. These acceptable levels are generally well known by both the suppliers and the customers throughout the industry. It is not uncommon to hear logistics and supply chain executives speak of customer service commitments in terms of doing as well as competition or beating major competitors' performance. The second factor derives from the firm's overall marketing strategy. If a firm desires to differentiate from competitors on the basis of logistics competency, then high levels of basic service are required. If the firm differentiates on price, then it likely will commit to lower levels of logistical service because of the resources required and costs related to high-level commitment.

The fact is that even firms with a high level of basic customer service commitment generally do not take a total zero-defect approach across the board for all customers. The common service commitment is to establish internal performance standards for each service component. These standards typically reflect prevailing industry practice in combination with careful consideration of cost and resource commitments.

Typical service standards such as 97 percent fill rate or delivery within 3 days may be established, and then performance would be monitored relative to these internal standards. While it is generally assumed that this strategic approach results in accommodating customers as well as or better than competitors, it does not assure that customers are, in fact, satisfied with either the overall industry performance or even the performance of an organization that performs above industry standard. In fact, there is only one way to be sure customers are satisfied: ask them.

Customer Satisfaction

Customer satisfaction has long been a fundamental concept in marketing and business strategy. In building a customer satisfaction program, however, the first question that must be answered is, "What does it mean to say that a customer is satisfied?" The simplest and most widely accepted method of defining customer satisfaction is known as **expectancy disconfirmation.** Simply stated, if a customer's expectations of a supplier's performance are met or exceeded, the customer will be satisfied. Conversely, if perceived performance is less than what the customer expected, then the customer is dissatisfied. A number of companies have adopted this framework for customer satisfaction and follow a commitment to meet or exceed customers' expectations. In fact, many organizations have gone further by speaking in terms of delighting their customers through performance that exceeds expectations.

While this framework for customer satisfaction is relatively straightforward, the implications for building a customer service platform in logistics are not. To build this platform it is necessary to explore more fully the nature of customer expectations. What do customers expect? How do customers form these expectations? What is the relationship between customer satisfaction and customer perceptions of overall logistics service quality? Why do many companies fail to satisfy customers, and why are so many companies perceived as providing poor logistics quality? If a company satisfies its customers, is that sufficient? The following sections provide some insights to these critical questions.

Customer Expectations

It is clear that when customers transact business with a supplier they have numerous expectations, many of which revolve around the supplier's basic logistical service platform; that is, they have expectations regarding availability, operational performance, and service reliability. Frequently, they have in place formal programs to monitor supplier performance with respect to each of these dimensions of logistical performance. In a pioneering study Parasuraman, Zeithaml, and Berry identified 10 customer expectations that form a useful framework for evaluating logistical impact.[8] Table 3.1 uses their framework to conceptualize specific logistics-based expectations.

In a logistical and supply chain context, the notion of customer expectations is particularly complex because customers are usually business organizations made up of numerous functions and individuals. Different personnel in a customer organization may prioritize the criteria of performance differently, or they may have different levels of expectation for the criteria. For example, some personnel may be most concerned with responsiveness and rapid handling of an inquiry regarding order status, while others may be more concerned with order completeness or meeting a delivery appointment. Meeting customer expectations requires an understanding of how these expectations are formed and the reasons many companies fail to meet those expectations.

A Model of Customer Satisfaction

Figure 3.1 provides a framework for understanding the process by which customers actually form their expectations of supplier performance. It also suggests that frequently a number of gaps exist that a supplier must overcome in order to develop customer satisfaction.

There are several factors that influence customer expectations, both in terms of a prioritization of the criteria discussed above, as well as the level of expectation relative to each of the criteria. The first of these factors is very simply the customers' needs or requirements. At the heart of their own business strategies, customers have requirements that depend on the performance of their suppliers. To a major extent, customers expect that these needs can and will be met by suppliers. Interestingly, however, customers' expectations are frequently not the same as their real requirements or needs. Previous supplier performance is a major factor influencing customer expectations. A supplier who consistently delivers on time will most likely be expected to deliver on time in the future. Similarly, a supplier with a poor record concerning performance will be expected to perform poorly in the future. It is important to note that previous performance experienced with one supplier may also influence the customers' expectation regarding other suppliers. For example, when Federal Express demonstrated the ability to deliver small packages on a next-day basis, many customers began to expect a similar performance capability from other suppliers.

---

[8] A. Parasuraman, Valerie Zeithaml, and Leonard L. Berry, "A Conceptual Model of Service Quality and Its Implications for Future Research," Report No. 84-106 (Cambridge, MA: Marketing Science Institute, 1984).

TABLE 3.1
Customer
Expectations
Related to Logistical
Performance

Reliability: Reliability is one of the aspects of the firm's basic service platform. In this context, however, reliability refers to performance of *all* activities as promised by the supplier. If the supplier promises next-day delivery and delivery takes 2 days, it is perceived as unreliable. If the supplier accepts an order for 100 cases of a product, it implicitly promises that 100 cases will be delivered. The customer expects and is only satisfied with the supplier if all 100 are received. Customers judge reliability in terms of all aspects of the basic service platform. Thus, customers have expectations concerning damage, documentation accuracy, etc.

Responsiveness: Responsiveness refers to customers' expectations of the willingness and ability of supplier personnel to provide prompt service. This extends beyond mere delivery to include issues related to quick handling of inquiries and resolution of problems. Responsiveness is clearly a time-oriented concept and customers have expectations regarding suppliers' timely handling of all interactions.

Access: Access involves customer expectations of the ease of contact and approachability of the supplier. For example, is it easy to place orders, to obtain information regarding inventory or order status?

Communication: Communication means proactively keeping customers informed. Rather than waiting for customer inquiries concerning order status, customers have expectations regarding suppliers' notification of status, particularly if problems with delivery or availability arise. Customers do not like to be surprised, and advance notice is essential.

Credibility: Credibility refers to customer expectations that communications from the supplier are in fact believable and honest. While it is doubtful that many suppliers intentionally mislead customers, credibility also includes the notion of completeness in required communications.

Security: Security deals with customers' feelings of risk or of doubt in doing business with a supplier. Customers make plans based on their anticipation of supplier performance. For example, they take risks when they schedule production and undertake machine and line setups in anticipation of delivery. If orders are late or incomplete, their plans must be changed. Another aspect of security deals with customer expectations that their dealings with a supplier will be confidential. This is particularly important in supply chain arrangements when a customer has a unique operating agreement with a supplier who also services competitors.

Courtesy: Courtesy involves politeness, friendliness, and respect of contact personnel. This can be a particularly vexing problem considering that customers may have contact with numerous individuals in the organization ranging from sales representatives to customer service personnel to truck drivers. Failure by one individual may destroy the best efforts of all the others.

Competency: Competence is judged by customers in every interaction with a supplier and, like courtesy, can be problematic because it is perceived in every interaction. In other words, customers judge the competence of truck drivers when deliveries are made, warehouse personnel when orders are checked, customer service personnel when phone calls are made, and so forth. Failure by any individual to demonstrate competence affects customer perceptions of the entire organization.

Tangibles: Customers have expectations regarding the physical appearance of facilities, equipment, and personnel. Consider, for example, a delivery truck that is old, damaged, or in poor condition. Such tangible features are additional cues used by customers as indicators of a firm's overall performance.

Knowing the Customer: While suppliers may think in terms of groups of customers and market segments, customers perceive themselves as unique. They have expectations regarding suppliers' understanding their uniqueness and supplier willingness to adapt to their specific requirements.

Related to a customer's perception of past performance is word-of-mouth. In other words, customers frequently communicate with one another concerning their experiences with specific suppliers. At trade and professional association meetings, the subject of suppliers is a common topic of discussion among executives. Much of the discussion may revolve around supplier performance capabilities. Such discussions help form individual customer expectations. Perhaps the most important factor influencing customer expectations is the communications coming from the supplier itself. Promises and commitments made by sales personnel or customer service representatives, statements contained in marketing and promotional messages, even the printed policies and procedures of an organization represent communications that customers depend upon. These communications become a critical basis on which they form their expectations. The promise of meeting a delivery

FIGURE 3.1   **Satisfaction and Quality Model**

Source: Adapted from A. Parasuraman, Valerie Zeithaml, and Leonard L. Berry, "A Conceptual Model of Service Quality and Its Implications for Future Research," Report No. 84-106 (Cambridge, MA: Marketing Science Institute, 1984).

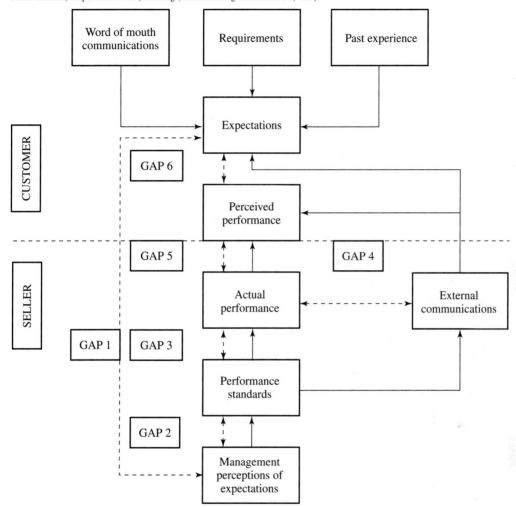

appointment or having full product availability becomes an expectation in the customer's mind. Indeed many suppliers may be guilty of setting themselves up for failure by over-committing in an attempt to influence customer expectations. Figure 3.1 also provides a framework for understanding what must be done by an organization to deliver customer satisfaction. The failure of many firms to satisfy their customers can be traced to the existence of one or more of the gaps identified in the framework.

Gap 1: Knowledge

The first and the most fundamental gap that may exist is between customers' real expectations and managers' perception of those expectations. This gap reflects management's lack of knowledge or understanding of customers. While there may be many reasons for this lack of understanding, it is clear that no beneficial customer satisfaction platform can be established without a thorough understanding of customer expectations, how they are prioritized, and how they are formed. Since sales typically has the major responsibility for customer interactions, knowledge regarding logistics expectations is often difficult to obtain.

Gap 2: Standards

Even if full understanding of customer expectations exists, it is still necessary to establish standards of performance for the organization. The standards gap exists when internal performance standards do not adequately or accurately reflect customer expectations. This is precisely the case in many organizations that develop their basic service platform from an examination of internal operating capabilities or a superficial examination of competitive service performance.

Gap 3: Performance

The performance gap is the difference between standard and actual performance. If the standard is a fill rate of 98 percent, based on research with customers regarding their expectations, and the firm actually performs at 97 percent, a performance gap exists. It should be pointed out that many firms focus their efforts to improve satisfaction by eliminating the performance gap. It may be, however, that the dissatisfaction exists as a result of a poor understanding of customer expectations in the first place.

Gap 4: Communications

The role of communications in customer satisfaction cannot be overemphasized. As discussed previously, overcommitment, or promising higher levels of performance than can actually be provided, is a major cause of customer dissatisfaction. There should be no gap between what a firm is capable of doing and what customers are told about those capabilities.

Gap 5: Perception

It is true that customers sometimes perceive performance to be lower or higher than actually achieved. In logistics, many managers frequently lament, "We're only as good as the last order." Thus, although performance over a long time period has been very good, a late or incomplete or otherwise subpar delivery may result in a customer's expression of extreme dissatisfaction.

Gap 6: Satisfaction/Quality

The existence of any one or more of the above gaps leads to customer perception that performance is not as good as expected. In other words, these gaps result in customer dissatisfaction. When building a platform for delivering customer satisfaction, a firm must ensure that these gaps do not exist.

Increasing Customer Expectations

As an important component of TQM the notion of continuous improvement has been accepted by most organizations. As a corollary of continuous improvement, there has been a continued escalation of customers' expectations concerning supplier capabilities. Performance that meets customer expectations one year may result in extreme dissatisfaction next year, as customers increase their expectations regarding acceptable performance levels.

To some extent, the increase in expectations can be traced to the dynamics of competition. As discussed previously, most industries traditionally have had explicit or implied levels of performance, which were considered to be adequate. If a firm wanted to be a serious competitor, it generally had to achieve these minimum industry service expectations. However, when one firm in the industry focuses on logistics as a core competency and provides higher performance levels, customers come to expect other suppliers to follow. Consider, for example, that after Federal Express introduced real-time tracking of shipment status, UPS and other parcel delivery firms shortly followed suit.

Does achieving perfect order performance ensure that customers are satisfied? On the surface it would seem so. After all, if all orders are delivered with no defects, what basis exists for customers to be dissatisfied? Part of the answer to this question lies in the fact that perfect orders, as important as they are, deal with the execution of individual transactions and deliveries. Customer satisfaction is a much broader concept, dealing with many other aspects of the overall relationship between suppliers and customers. For example, a customer may continuously receive perfect orders but be dissatisfied with such aspects of the relationship as difficulty in obtaining information, long delays in response to inquiries, or even the perception that some supplier personnel do not treat the customer with proper courtesy and respect. Thus, satisfaction transcends operational performance to include aspects of personal and interpersonal relationships.

Limitations of Customer Satisfaction

Because of its explicit focus on customers, a commitment to satisfaction represents a step beyond a basic service platform in an organization's efforts to accommodate its customers. It is realistic to think that a firm satisfying customer expectations better than competitors will gain some competitive advantage in the marketplace. Nevertheless, it is important to realize some of the shortcomings and limitations of the customer satisfaction emphasis.

The first limitation is that many executives make a fundamental, yet understandable, mistake in their interpretation of satisfaction. In many organizations it is assumed that customers who are satisfied are also happy, maybe even delighted, with the supplier's performance. That may or may not be the actual situation. It must be remembered that satisfaction is the customers' perception of actual performance in relation to expectation, not their requirements. Examination of Figure 3.2 may help explain this difference between satisfaction and happiness. The fact is that customers may have an expectation that a firm will not perform at a high level. If the customer has an expectation of a low level of performance and indeed perceives that the firm performs at this low level, it is clear that performance and expectation match. By definition, the customer is satisfied. The same is true at midlevel expectations and perceptions as well as high levels of each.

This notion that low levels of performance may be considered satisfactory can best be illustrated by example. Suppose a customer expects a supplier to provide, over time, a fill rate of 95 percent, or late deliveries 10 percent of the time, or damage of 2 percent. If the supplier in fact provides this level of performance, as perceived by the customer, the customer is satisfied. Performance perceived to be poorer than the expectation level results in dissatisfaction. Is the satisfied customer necessarily happy about the supplier's fill rate or late deliveries? Of course not. While expectations may be met, indeed may be met as well as or better than competition, there is still no assurance that the customer will be happy. Even performance higher than that expected, while satisfying to customers, may not actually result in happiness. The focus on customer expectations ignores the fact that expectations are not the same as needs or requirements.

The second limitation to consider is actually related to the first: Satisfied customers are not necessarily loyal customers. Even though their expectations are being met, satisfied

FIGURE 3.2
Satisfaction Is Not the Same as Happiness

		Expectation		
		LO	**MED**	**HI**
Performance	**HI**	Very Satisfied	Very Satisfied	Satisfied
	MED	Very Satisfied	Satisfied	Dissatisfied
	LO	Satisfied	Dissatisfied	Dissatisfied

customers may choose to do business with competitors. This can occur because they expect a competitor to perform at a higher level or at least as well as the organization in question. For many years, marketing and supply chain executives have assumed that satisfied customers are also loyal customers. Yet research has frequently shown that many customers who report being satisfied that their expectations have been met are likely to patronize and do business with competitors.[9] A third limitation to customer satisfaction is that firms frequently forget satisfaction lies in the expectations and perceptions of individual customers. Thus, there is a tendency to aggregate expectations across customers and neglect the basic tenets of marketing strategy related to differences among customer segments as well as individual customers. Simply stated, what satisfies one customer may not satisfy other, much less all, customers.

Despite these limitations, customer satisfaction does represent a commitment beyond basic service to accommodate customers. It provides explicit recognition that the only way to ensure that customers are being accommodated is to focus on customers themselves. Firms that focus primarily on industry and competitor standards of basic service performance are much less likely to find that their customers are very satisfied or highly satisfied with their performance.

Customer Success

In recent years, some firms have discovered that there is another commitment that can be made to gain true competitive advantage through logistical performance. This commitment is based on recognition that a firm's ability to grow and expand market share depends on its ability to attract and hold the industry's most successful customers. The real key, then, to customer-focused marketing lies in the organization's using its performance capabilities to enhance the success of those customers. This focus on customer success represents major commitment toward accommodating customers. Table 3.2 summarizes the evolution that customer-focused organizations have experienced. Notice that a customer service focus is oriented toward establishment of internal standards for basic service performance. Firms typically assess their customer service performance relative to how well these internal standards are accomplished. The customer satisfaction platform is built on the recognition that customers have expectations regarding performance and the only way to ensure that customers are satisfied is to assess their perceptions of performance relative to those expectations.

Customer success shifts the focus from expectations to the customer's real requirements. Recall from the previous discussion that customer requirements, while forming the basis for expectations, are not the same as expectations. Requirements are frequently downgraded into expectations because of perceptions of previous performance, word-of-mouth, or communications from the firm itself. This explains why simply meeting expectations may not result in happy customers. For example, a customer may be satisfied with a

---

[9] Michael J. Ryan, Robert Raynor, and Andy Morgan, "Diagnosing Customer Loyalty Drivers," *Marketing Research* 11, no. 2 (Summer 1999), pp. 18–26.

TABLE 3.2
Evolution of Management Thought

Philosophy	Focus
Customer service	Meet internal standards
Customer satisfaction	Meet expectations
Customer success	Meet customer requirements

98 percent fill rate, but for the customer to be successful in executing its own strategy, a 100 percent fill rate on certain products or components may be necessary.

Achieving Customer Success

Clearly, a customer success program involves a thorough understanding of individual customer requirements and a commitment to focus on long-term business relationships having high potential for growth and profitability. Such commitment most likely cannot be made to all potential customers. It requires that firms work intensively with customers to understand requirements, internal processes, competitive environment, and whatever else it takes for the customer to be successful in its own competitive arena. Further, it requires that an organization develop an understanding of how it can utilize its own capabilities to enhance customer performance. As an example, one major manufacturer of electronic components adopted as its logistics slogan, "We take pride in helping our customers become more profitable."

In many ways a customer success program requires a comprehensive supply chain perspective on the part of logistics executives. This is most easily explained by examining the relations depicted in Figure 3.3. The typical focus in basic service and satisfaction programs is that the firm attempts to meet standards and expectations of next-destination customers, whether they are consumers, industrial end users, or intermediate or even internal customers. How those customers deal with their customer is typically not considered to be a problem. A supply chain perspective and a customer success program explicitly recognize that logistics executives must alter this focus. They must understand the entire supply chain, the different levels of customer within that supply chain, and develop programs to ensure that next-destination customers are successful in meeting the requirements of customers down the supply chain. If all supply chain members adopt this perspective, then all members share in the success.

To ensure that a customer is successful may require a firm to reinvent the way a product is produced, distributed, or offered for sale. In fact, collaboration between suppliers and customers to find potential avenues for success may result in the greatest breakthroughs in terms of redefining supply chain processes. The general topic of collaborative relationships and alliances is further developed in Chapter 15. It is enough to say here that such arrangements are not possible without significant amounts of information exchange between the involved businesses to facilitate an in-depth understanding of requirements and capabilities. However, one important way that many firms have responded to the challenges of customer success is through the development of value-added services.

FIGURE 3.3
Moving toward
Customer Success

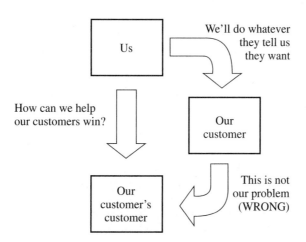

Value-Added Services

The notion of value-added service is a significant development in the evolution to customer success. By definition, value-added services refer to unique or specific activities that firms can jointly develop to enhance their efficiency, effectiveness, and relevancy. Value-added services help foster customer success. Because they tend to be customer specific, it is difficult to generalize all possible value-added services.

When a firm becomes committed to value-added solutions for major customers, it rapidly becomes involved in customized or tailored logistics. It is doing unique things to enable specific customers to achieve their objectives. IBM's ability to produce and deliver customized personal computers and networks to individual customers is one example of adding value to a rather standard product. In a logistical context, firms can provide unique product packages, create customized unit loads, place prices on products, offer unique information services, provide vendor-managed inventory service, make special shipping arrangements, and so forth, to enhance customer success.

In reality, some of the value-added services that buyers and sellers agree to involve integrated service providers that are positioned to provide such services. Transportation carriers, warehouse firms, and other specialists may become intimately involved in the supply chain to make such value-adding activities a reality. At this point, a few specific examples of how they may work within a specific supply chain to provide value-added services are sufficient. Warehouses, whether private or third-party, can be utilized to perform a number of customization activities. For example, a retail customer may desire a unique palletization alternative to support its cross-dock activities and meet the unique product requirements of its individual store units. Each store requires different quantities of specific product to maintain in-stock performance with minimum inventory commitment. In another situation, first-aid kits consisting of many different items are actually assembled in the warehouse as orders are received to meet the unique configuration of kit desired by specific customers. It is also common for warehouses to provide pick-price-repack services for manufacturers to accommodate the unique product configurations required by different customers.

Another form of value-added service involves the proper sorting and sequencing of products to meet specific customer requirements. For example, an auto assembly plant may require that components not only be received on time but also be sorted and sequenced in a particular manner to meet the needs of specific automobiles on the assembly line. The objective is to reduce assembly plant handling and inspection of incoming components. Meeting such exacting requirements for delivery is far beyond the basic service capability of many component suppliers. The use of third-party specialists is a necessity, especially when subcomponents from multiple suppliers must be integrated and then properly sequenced.

Value-added services can be performed directly by participants in a business relationship or may involve specialists. It has become more common in recent years to turn to specialists because of their flexibility and ability to concentrate on providing the required services. Nevertheless, regardless of how the specifics are organized and implemented, it is clear that logistics value-added services are a critical aspect of customer success programs.

Forecasting

Accommodating customer requirements in most supply chain arrangements inevitably requires a forecast to drive the process. The forecast is a specific definition of what is projected to be sold, when, and where. The forecast defines the requirements for which the supply chain must schedule the inventory and resources to fulfill. Since there are still many

TABLE 3.3
How Product Characteristics Influence the Need to Forecast

Source: Reprinted with permission from David J. Closs, *Forecasting and Its Use in Logistics,* Council of Supply Chain Management Professionals, Oak Brook, IL.

	Low Economies of Scale	High Economies of Scale
Long response time experienced in replenishing product	Detailed accurate forecasting is not as critical, as the firm has more production flexibility. For example, final product customization could be postponed so that it's only necessary to forecast the base units (i.e, at a higher level of aggregation) with final customization much nearer time of demand.	Accurate forecasting is critical in this case as it's necessary to forecast an extended time into the future to allow for production or transportation economies.
Short response time experienced in replenishing product	When it's possible to obtain product quickly and there are limited scale economies, the focus should shift from forecasting to the design of a responsive and flexible process.	Focus on developing an accurate short-term forecast with strong consideration of marketing and competitive tactics and less consideration of history.

logistics and supply chain activities that must be completed in anticipation of a sale, forecasting remains a critical capability for customer accommodation.

Table 3.3 illustrates how the need for forecasting is influenced by replenishment response time and economies of scale. Accurate forecasting should be a major focus for situations where there are long replenishment lead times and high economies of scale. On the other hand, accurate forecasts are not as critical when there are shorter lead times or lesser economies of scale. The implications in Table 3.3 can be applied two different ways. First, one could take the product characteristics as requiring long lead time and high economies of scale and decide to place emphasis on forecasting. Alternatively, one could evaluate the potential for developing accurate forecasts, given short life cycle and high number of variations, and decide to place primary focus for this item on reduced lead time. These situations illustrate that, while improved forecasts are often desirable, there are other ways to achieve the objectives of enhanced service or reduced inventory. One is to forecast at a higher level of aggregation. The second is to develop a flexible supply chain process that can make to order, even further reducing inventory. While firms are using these methods to reduce their reliance on forecasting, there are still many situations where forecasting is necessary to achieve service objectives or take advantage of scale economies.

With the above considerations in mind, this section focuses on forecasting needs, benefits, methods, techniques, applications, and measures. It provides background to understand logistics applications of forecasting, forecast components, forecasting process, forecasting techniques, software applications, error, and collaborative forecasting.

Forecasting Requirements

Effective logistics requires matching the product requirements of customers with the capacity capabilities of the enterprise and supply chain. Although consumer demands in terms of service level and product variations are increasing, the focus on reduced supply chain assets simultaneously requires more timely and accurate forecasts. Logistics forecasts are necessary (1) to support collaborative planning, (2) to drive requirements planning, and (3) to improved resource management.

Collaborative Planning

Without collaboration, each partner tries to plan the level and timing of demand for its customers, both individually and collectively. The result is speculative inventory positioned in anticipation of independently forecasted demand resulting in a never-ending cycle of inventory excesses and out-of-stocks. Historically, manufacturers have scheduled their promotions, price changes, new product introductions, and special events, either independently or without collaboration with their major retailers. When no single retailer accounted for a substantial proportion of a firm's sales volume, such collaboration was not critical. However, when a single major customer can account for more than 20 percent of a firm's sales, such coordination becomes essential. Without a collaborative plan, the supplier-customer combination typically results in either inventory excess or shortage. A collaborative forecast, jointly agreed to by supply chain partners, provides a common goal that can be the basis for developing effective operating plans.

Requirements Planning

Once a collaborative forecast is developed, logisticians next need forecasts to drive requirements planning. The plan determines inventory projections and resulting replenishment or production requirements for the planning horizon. The requirements planning process, called **sales and operations planning** (S&OP), integrates forecasts, open orders, available inventory, and production plans into a definition of periodic inventory availability and requirements.[10] Ideally, the requirements planning process operates collaboratively and interactively both internally across the firm's operations and externally with supply chain partners to develop a common and consistent plan for each time period, location, and item.

Resource Management

Once the plan is completed, it is can be used to manage critical supply chain processes such as production, inventory, and transportation. Accurate forecasts collaboratively developed by supply chain partners along with a consistent definition of supply chain resources and constraints enable effective evaluation of trade-offs associated with supply chain decisions. The trade-offs consider the relative costs of supply chain strategies such as maintaining extra production or storage capacity, speculative production or product movement, or outsourcing. Timely identification and evaluation of these trade-offs enable a better match of requirements to resources and better resource utilization.

Forecasting Components

The forecast is generally a monthly or weekly figure for each stockkeeping unit (SKU) and distribution location. The forecast components include: (1) base demand, (2) seasonal, (3) trend, (4) cyclic, (5) promotion, and (6) irregular. Assuming the base demand as the average sales level, the other components, except for irregular, are multiplicative factors of the base level available to support positive or negative adjustments. The resulting forecast model is:

$$F_t = (B_t \times S_t \times T \times C_t \times P_t) + I$$

where

F_t = forecast quantity for period t

B_t = base level demand for period t

S_t = seasonality factor for period t

T = trend component index reflecting increase or decrease per time period

C_t = cyclical factor for period t

P_t = promotional factor for period t

I = irregular or random quantity.

---

[10] Sales and operations planning is discussed in greater detail in Chapter 11.

While some forecasts may not include all components, it is useful to understand the behavior of each so that each component can be tracked and incorporated appropriately. For example, some forecasting techniques cannot effectively address seasonality whereas others can.

The **base demand** represents the long-term average demand after the remaining components have been removed. The base demand is the average over an extended time. The base demand is the forecast for items having no seasonality, trend, cyclic, or promotional components.

The **seasonal** component is an annually recurring upward and downward movement in demand. An example is the annual demand for toys, which reflects low demand for three-fourths of the year and then increased demand just before Christmas. It should be noted that the seasonality discussed above refers to consumer retail seasonality. Seasonality at the wholesale level precedes consumer demand by approximately one quarter of a year.

The **trend** component is the long-range shift in periodic sales. Trend may be positive, negative, or neutral in direction. A positive trend means that sales are increasing over time. For example, the trend for personal computer sales during the decade of the 1990s was increasing. Over the product life cycle, trend direction may change a number of times. For example, beer consumption changed from a neutral to an increasing trend during the past decade. Increases or decreases result from changes in overall population or consumption patterns. Knowledge of which factor is primarily influencing sales is important in making such projections. For example, a reduction in the birth rate implies that a reduction in the demand for disposable diapers will follow. However, a trend toward usage of disposable as contrasted to cloth diapers may result in increased demand of a specific product category even though overall market size is decreasing. The above are obvious examples of forecast trend. While the impact of trend on short-range logistics forecasts is subtle, it still must be considered. Unlike the other forecast components, the trend component influences base demand in the successive time periods. The specific relationship is

$$B_{t+1} = B_t \times T$$

where

B_{t+1} = base demand in period $t + 1$

B_t = base demand in period t

T = periodic trend index.

The trend index with a value greater than 1.0 indicates that periodic demand is increasing, while a value less than 1.0 indicates a declining trend.

The **cyclic** component is characterized by periodic shifts in demand lasting more than a year. These cycles may be either upward or downward. An example is the business cycle in which the economy typically swings from recession to growth cycles every 3 to 5 years. The demand for housing, as well as the resulting demand for major appliances, is typically tied to this business cycle.

The **promotional** component characterizes demand swings initiated by a firm's marketing activities, such as advertising, deals, or promotions. These swings can often be characterized by sales increases during the promotion followed by sales declines as customers sell or use inventory purchased to take advantage of the promotion. Promotions can be deals offered to consumers or trade promotions offered only to wholesalers and retailers. The promotion can be regular and thus take place at the same time each year. From a forecasting perspective, a regular promotion component resembles a seasonal component. An irregular promotion component does not necessarily occur during the same time period, so it must be tracked and considered separately. The promotional component is particularly important to track, especially for consumer industries, since it has a major influence on sales variation. In some industries, promotional activity explains 50 to 80 percent of volume variations. Thus, promotion results in demand that is more lumpy than would otherwise be the case. The promotional component is different from the other forecasting components in that its timing and magnitude are controlled, to a large extent, by the firm. Thus, it should be possible to input information from the firm's sales or marketing departments regarding the timing and likely impact of scheduled promotional plans. The benefits of coordinating such promotional offerings among channel partners provide the rationale for collaborative forecasting practices.

The **irregular** component includes the random or unpredictable quantities that do not fit within the other categories. Because of its random nature, this component is impossible to predict. In developing a forecast process, the objective is to minimize the magnitude of the random component by tracking and predicting the other components.

Forecasting Process

Logistics planning and coordination require the best possible estimate of SKU/location demand. Although forecasting is far from an exact science, the forecast management process should incorporate input from multiple sources, appropriate mathematical and statistical techniques, decision support capability, and trained and motivated individuals.

Supply chain operational forecasts are normally developed for daily, weekly, or monthly periods. An effective forecast management process requires a number of components, as illustrated in Figure 3.4. The process foundation is the forecast database, including open orders, demand history, and the tactics used to stimulate demand, such as promotions, special deals, or product changes. The forecast database is ideally part of an enterprise resource planning system (ERP) central data warehouse, although some firms maintain independent forecast databases. Other environmental data, such as the state of the economy and competitive action, is often be included in this database. To support effective forecasting, this database must include timely historical and planning information in a manner facilitating its manipulation, summarization, analysis, and reporting.

Finally, the development of an effective forecast requires a process that integrates three components: forecast technique, forecast support system, and forecast administration. The box on the right side of Figure 3.4 illustrates that it would be ideal if a firm could use a common and consistent forecast for all planning functions.

Technique

The technique component is the mathematical or statistical computation used to combine base, seasonal, and cyclical components and elements of promotion history into a forecast quantity. Techniques include time series modeling, in which sales history is a major factor, and correlation modeling, in which relationships with other independent variables are the major forecast drivers. Specific techniques are discussed in the forecast technique section

FIGURE 3.4
Forecast
Management
Process

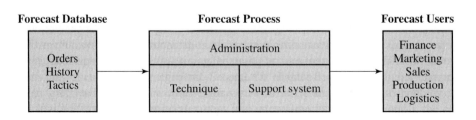

of this chapter. While techniques can easily connect historical patterns into future forecasts, they do not do as well at incorporating the input of anticipated future events. As a result, it is increasingly apparent that accuracy requires integration of the forecast techniques with appropriate support and administrative systems.

Support System

The forecast support system includes the supply chain intelligence to gather and analyze data, develop the forecast, and communicate the forecast to relevant personnel and planning systems. This component allows consideration of external factors such as the impact of promotions, strikes, price changes, product line changes, competitive activity, and economic conditions. For example, if the firm plans to promote 12-packs of a beverage, it is reasonable to assume 2-liter sales will decrease. The system must be designed not only to allow the consideration of these factors but also to encourage them. As another example, the marketing manager may know that the promotion scheduled for next month is likely to increase sales by 15 percent. However, if the forecast support system makes it difficult to adjust the forecast figures for next month, the forecast adjustments may not occur. Similarly, when a package size change is announced, it is likely that forecast history should be changed to reflect the new package size so that future forecasts will reflect correct sizes and volumes. If this is difficult to accomplish within the system constraints, the individual completing the forecast will probably not consider the adjustments. It is thus very important that an effective forecasting process include a support system to facilitate the maintenance, update, and manipulation of the historical database and the forecast.

Administration

Forecast administration includes the organizational, procedural, motivational, and personnel aspects of forecasting and its integration into the other firm functions. The organizational aspect concerns individual roles and responsibilities. It is important these impacts be specified in detail in defining the forecast administration function. If an integrated forecast is desirable, it is necessary to specifically define each organization's forecasting responsibility and then hold it accountable with specific measurements. Effective forecast administration requires that organizational responsibility and procedural guidelines are documented and measured. Effective administration also requires that forecast analysts be trained both in the process and the input of forecasts on supply chain logistics operations.

Dynamic simulation illustrates the impact of forecast inconsistency across multiple members of the supply chain. From initial stimulant to feedback, the cost of direct communication of sales or forecasts is overshadowed by the cost of a faulty message. Since a great deal of supply chain action is initiated in anticipation of future transactions, communications containing overly optimistic predictions or projections may stimulate a fever of ultimately useless work. Analysis of communications between channel members suggests that anticipation has a tendency to amplify as it proceeds between supply chain participants, particularly as the information gets further from the ultimate consumer. Each error in the interpretation of transaction requirements creates a disturbance for the total logistical channel. In a classic work, Forrester simulated channel interrelationships to demonstrate how the total channel may enter into an oscillating corrective pattern, resulting in a series of over-and-under adjustments to real market requirements.[11] Figure 3.5 illustrates the channel inventory oscillations that are stimulated when the retailer increases demand by 10 percent but does not directly inform the other members of the channel.

---

[11] Jay W. Forrester, *Industrial Dynamics* (Cambridge, MA: The MIT Press, 1961).

FIGURE 3.5
Response of a Simulated Production/Distribution System to a Sudden 10 Percent Increase in Sales at the Retail Level

Source: Reprinted with permission from Jay W. Forrester, *Industrial Dynamics* (Waltham, MA: Pegasus Communications, 1961). www.pegasuscom.com.

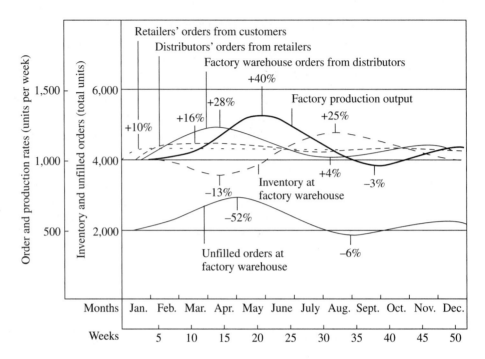

Figure 3.5 illustrates that an increase of retail demand by 10 percent without clear communication back to other members of the supply chain results in inventory swings of 16 percent for the distributor, 28 percent for the factory warehouse, and 40 percent for factory production. These swings obviously increase supply chain variance, which increases costs and diminishes asset utilization.

By the very nature of its mission, a distribution channel must respond to transaction requirements. The system must stand ready to initiate logistical action upon receipt of a message. Extreme care must be taken to structure the communication function with a high degree of reliability while retaining the flexibility required for change and adaptation.

As Figure 3.4 illustrated, it is important to realize that a meaningful forecast process requires an integrated and consistent combination of components. Historically, it was thought that intensive effort in one of the individual components such as technique could overcome problems in the other components. For example, it was thought that a "perfect" forecast technique could be identified that would overcome the need for systems support and a consistent process. There is increasing realization that all three components must work together. The design process must adequately consider the strengths and weaknesses of each individual component, and design for the optimal performance of the integrated system.

Even though the forecast technique is only one component of the overall demand management process, it is useful to understand the breadth of techniques available and the measures to evaluate them.

Forecasting Techniques

Demand forecasting requires the selection of appropriate mathematical or statistical techniques to generate periodic forecasts. The effective use of a technique requires matching the characteristics of the situation with the abilities of the technique. Some criteria for evaluating the applicability of a technique include: (1) accuracy, (2) forecast time horizon, (3) the value of forecasting, (4) data availability, (5) type of data pattern, and (6) experience of the forecaster.[12] Each alternative forecast technique must be evaluated both qualitatively and quantitatively with respect to these six criteria.

There are three categories of forecast techniques: (1) qualitative, (2) time series, and (3) causal. A qualitative technique uses data such as expert opinion and special information to forecast the future. A qualitative technique may or may not consider the past. A time series technique focuses entirely on historical patterns and pattern changes to generate forecasts. A causal technique, such as regression, uses refined and specific information regarding variables to develop a relationship between a lead event and forecasted activity.

Qualitative

Qualitative techniques rely heavily on expertise and are quite costly and time-consuming. They are ideal for situations where little historical data and much managerial judgment are required. Using input from the sales force as the basis of the forecast for a new region or a new product is an example of a supply chain application of a qualitative forecast technique. However, qualitative methods are generally not appropriate for supply chain forecasting because of the time required to generate the detailed SKU forecasts necessary. Qualitative forecasts are developed by using surveys, panels, and consensus meetings.

Time Series

Time series techniques are statistical methods utilized when historical sales data containing relatively clear and stable relationships and trends are available. Using historical sales data, time series analysis is used to identify seasonality, cyclical patterns, and trends. Once individual forecast components are identified, time series techniques assume the future will reflect the past. This implies that past demand patterns will continue into the future. This assumption is often reasonably correct in the short term, so these techniques are most appropriate for short-range forecasting.

When the rate of growth or trend changes significantly, the demand pattern experiences a turning point. Since time series techniques use historical demand patterns and weighted averages of data points, they are typically not sensitive to turning points. As a result, other approaches must be integrated with time series techniques to determine when turning points will likely occur.

Time series techniques include a variety of methods that analyze the pattern and movement of historical data to establish recurring characteristics. On the basis of specific characteristics, techniques of varying sophistication can be used to develop time series forecasts. Four time series techniques in order of increasing complexity are (1) moving averages, (2) exponential smoothing, (3) extended smoothing, and (4) adaptive smoothing.

Moving average forecasting uses an average of the most recent period's sales. The average may use any number of previous time periods, although 1-, 3-, 4-, and 12-period averages are common. A 1-period moving average results in next period's forecast being projected by last period's sales. A 12-period moving average, such as monthly, uses the average of the last 12 periods. Each time a new period of actual data becomes available, it replaces the oldest time period's data; thus, the number of time periods included in the average is held constant.

Although moving averages are easy to calculate, there are several limitations. Most significantly, they are unresponsive or sluggish to change and a great amount of historical data must be maintained and updated to calculate forecasts. If the historical sales variations are large, average or mean value cannot be relied upon to render useful forecasts. Other than the base component, moving averages do not consider the forecast components discussed earlier.

[12] Spyros Makridakis, Steven Wheelright, and Robert Hyndman, *Forecasting, Methods and Applications,* 3rd ed. (New York: John Wiley & Sons, 1997).

Mathematically, moving average is expressed as

$$F_t = \frac{\sum_{i=1}^{n} S_{t-i}}{n}$$

where

F_t = moving average forecast for time period t

S_{t-i} = sales for time period i

n = total number of time periods

For example, an April moving forecast based on sales of 120, 150, and 90 for the previous 3 months is calculated as follows:

$$F_{\text{April}} = \frac{120 + 150 + 90}{3}$$

$$= 120.$$

To partially overcome these deficiencies, weighted moving averages have been introduced as refinements. The weight places more emphasis on recent observations. Exponential smoothing is a form of weighted moving average. **Exponential smoothing** bases the estimate of future sales on the weighted average of the previous demand and forecast levels. The new forecast is a function of the old forecast incremented by some fraction of the differential between the old forecast and actual sales realized. The increment of adjustment is called the **alpha factor.** The basic format of the model is

$$F_t = \alpha D_{t-1} + (1 - \alpha) F_{t-1}$$

where

F_t = forecasted sales for a time period t

F_{t-1} = forecast for time period $t - 1$

D_{t-1} = actual demand for time period $t - 1$

α = alpha factor or smoothing constant $(0 \leq \alpha \leq 1.0)$

To illustrate, assume that the forecasts for the most recent time period were 100 and actual sales experience was 110 units. Further, assume that the alpha factor being employed is 0.2. Then, by substitution,

$$F_t = \alpha D_{t-1} + (1 - \alpha) F_{t-1}$$

$$= (0.2)(110) + (1 - 0.2)(100)$$

$$= 22 + 80$$

$$= 102$$

So the forecast for period t is for product sales of 102 units.

The prime advantage of exponential smoothing is that it permits a rapid calculation of a new forecast without substantial historical records and updating. Thus, exponential smoothing is highly adaptable to computerized forecasting. Depending on the value of the smoothing constant, it is also possible to monitor and change technique sensitivity.

The major decision when using exponential smoothing is selecting the alpha factor. If a factor of 1 is employed, the net effect is to use the most recent period's sales as the forecast for next period. A very low value, such as .01, has the net effect of reducing the forecast to almost a simple moving average. Large alpha factors make the forecast very sensitive to change and therefore highly reactive. Low alpha factors tend to react slowly to change and therefore minimize response to random fluctuations. However, the technique cannot tell the difference between seasonality and random fluctuation. Thus, exponential smoothing does not eliminate the need for judgment. In selecting the value of the alpha factor, the forecaster is faced with a trade-off between eliminating random fluctuations or having the forecast fully respond to demand changes.

Extended exponential smoothing incorporates the influence of trend and seasonality when specific values for these components can be identified. The extended smoothing calculation is similar to that of the basic smoothing model except that there are three components and three smoothing constants to represent the base, trend, and seasonal components.

Like basic exponential smoothing, extended smoothing allows rapid calculation of new forecasts with minimal data. The technique's ability to respond depends on the smoothing constant values. Higher smoothing constant values provide quick responsiveness but may lead to overreaction and forecast accuracy problems.

Adaptive smoothing provides a regular review of alpha factor validity. The alpha value is reviewed at the conclusion of each forecast period to determine the exact value that would have resulted in a perfect forecast for the previous period. Once determined, the alpha factor used to generate the subsequent forecast is adjusted to a value that would have produced a perfect forecast. Thus, managerial judgment is partially replaced by a systematic and consistent method of updating alpha. Most forecast software packages include the capability to systematically evaluate alternative smoothing constants to identify the one that would have given the best performance in the most recent time periods.

More sophisticated forms of adaptive smoothing include an automatic tracking signal to monitor error. When the signal is tripped because of excessive error, the constant is automatically increased to make the forecast more responsive to smoothing recent periods. If the recent-period sales demonstrate substantial change, increased responsiveness should decrease forecast error. As the forecast error is reduced, the tracking signal automatically returns the smoothing constant to its original value. While adaptive techniques are designed to systematically adjust for error, their weakness is that they sometimes overreact by interpreting random error as trend or seasonality. This misinterpretation leads to increased errors in the future.

Causal

Forecasting by regression estimates sales for an SKU on the basis of values of other independent factors. If a good relationship can be identified, such as between expected price and consumption, the information can be used to effectively predict requirements. Causal or regression forecasting works well when a leading variable such as price can be identified. However, such situations are not particularly common for supply chain applications. If the SKU forecast is based upon a single factor, it is referred to as **simple regression.** The use of more than one forecast factor is **multiple regression.** Regression forecasts use the correlation between a leading or predictable event and the dependent demand SKU's sales. No cause/effect relationship need exist between the product's sale and the independent event if a high degree of correlation is consistently present. A correlation assumes that the forecasted sales are preceded by some leading independent factor such as the sale of a related product. However, the most reliable use of regression forecasting of sales is based on a cause/effect relationship. Since regression can effectively consider external factors and events, causal techniques are more appropriate for long-term or aggregate forecasting. For example, causal techniques are commonly used to generate annual or national sales forecasts. From the preceding discussion, it should be clear that forecasting software offers a wide range of

TABLE 3.4   **Forecast Technique Summary**

Source: Reprinted with permission from David J. Closs, *Forecasting and Its Use in Logistics,* Council of Supply Chain Management Professionals, Oak Brook, IL.

Forecast Technique	Description	Application	Limitations
Moving average	An unweighted average of the previous periods of sales	Useful when there are only base and irregular demand components	Not useful when there is significant seasonality or trend
Exponential smoothing	An exponentially weighted moving average using smoothing constants to place greater weights on more recent demands	Useful when necessary to maintain data and generate forecasts for a large number of items that incorporate individual trend and seasonality components	Not as useful when there are other factors influencing demand, such as promotions, price changes, or competitive actions not regularly scheduled
Time series	Uses time period as the independent variable to predict future demand patterns	Useful when demand patterns repeat with some cyclic, seasonal, or trend components	Not particularly responsive to change, as it takes numerous periods for the model to identify changes in patterns and for the forecast to respond to the pattern changes; also requires judgment in selecting variables that should be included
Regression	Uses other independent variables, such as price, promotion plans, or related product volumes, to predict sales	Useful when there's a strong linear or nonlinear relationship between independent variables and demand	Not particularly responsive to change, as it takes numerous periods for the model to identify changes in patterns and for the forecasts to respond to the pattern changes; also requires judgment in selecting which variables should be included
Multivariate	Uses more complex statistical techniques to identify more complex demand history relationships; techniques include spectral analysis, Fourier analysis, transfer functions, and neural networks	Useful when there's a complex, generally nonlinear relationship, between historical patterns and demand. The analyses identify and evaluate alternative sets of parameters to determine the best fit and use it to predict future demand. These techniques are often more useful for predicting macro forecasts, such as energy consumption, economic growth, or aggregate transportation.	While there are quantitative factors for selecting the best model, there is often substantial judgment involved as well, so these techniques are often nonsuited for detailed item–location–time period forecasts.

capabilities in terms of both techniques and sophistication. Table 3.4 provides a summary of applications and limitations of available forecast techniques.

Forecasting Accuracy

Forecast accuracy refers to the difference between forecasts and corresponding actual sales. Forecast accuracy improvement requires error measurement and analysis. While forecast error can be defined generally as the difference between actual demand and forecast, a more precise definition is needed for calculation and comparison. Table 3.5 provides monthly unit demand and forecast for a specific personal computer model at a regional distribution center. This example illustrates alternative forecast error measures.

One approach for error measurement is to sum up the errors over time, as illustrated in column 4. With this approach, errors are summed over the year and a simple average is

TABLE 3.5
Monthly Personal
Computer Demand
and Forecast

(1) Month	(2) Demand	(3) Forecast	(4) Error	(5) Absolute Error
January	100	110	−10	10
February	110	90	20	20
March	90	90	0	0
April	130	120	10	10
May	70	90	−20	20
June	110	120	−10	10
July	120	120	0	0
August	90	110	−20	20
September	120	70	50	50
October	90	130	−40	40
November	80	90	−10	10
December	90	100	−10	10
Sum	1200	1240	−40	200
Mean	100	103.3	−3.3	16.7[a]
Percent (error/mean)				17.1%[b]

a = Mean absolute deviation (MAD).
b = Mean of (Monthly forecast error/monthly demand).

FIGURE 3.6
Comparative
Forecast Errors

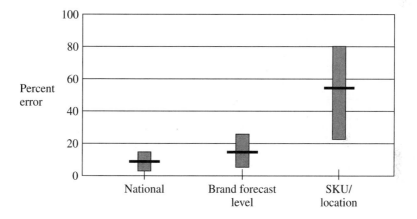

calculated. As illustrated, the average error is very near zero even though there are some months with significant error. The concern with this approach is that the positive errors cancel negative errors, masking a significant forecasting problem. To avoid this problem, an alternative approach is to ignore the "sign" and evaluate absolute error. Column 5 illustrates the computation of the absolute error and the resulting Mean Absolute Deviation (MAD). To compare forecasts, error percentages are usually calculated. Mean absolute percentage error (MAPE) is calculated by dividing mean absolute error by mean demand.

Another consideration is the measurement level or aggregation. Assuming that individual SKU detail is recorded, forecast error can be calculated for individual SKU location combinations, groups of SKUs or locations, and nationally. Generally, more aggregation results in lower relative forecast errors. For example, Figure 3.6 illustrates comparative forecast errors at the national, brand for groups of SKUs, and SKU location level. The figure illustrates the minimum, maximum, and mean relative forecast error for a sample of firms marketing consumer products. As Figure 3.6 illustrates, while a relative error of 40 percent is average for a SKU/location level of aggregation, it would reflect very poor forecasting if measured at the national level.

Collaborative Planning, Forecasting, and Replenishment

The forecasting processes and techniques described above have achieved significant benefits in providing superior logistical performance. However, there can still be costly unplanned and uncoordinated events that distort smooth flow of product throughout the supply chain. These distortions occur because individual businesses frequently fail to coordinate their individual forecasts of final consumer demand and marketing events designed to stimulate demand. Imagine, for example, that at the beginning of the month, the manufacturer forecasts sales of 100,000 cases to a particular retail customer with planned advertising and sales promotions to support that level of sales. Meanwhile, that same retailer forecasts sales of 150,000 and plans specific promotional events to achieve that forecast. Clearly, joint planning and information sharing concerning such events would increase the likelihood of a successful relationship.

Collaborative planning, forecasting, and replenishment (CPFR) is a process initiated by the consumer products industry to achieve such coordination. It does not replace replenishment strategies but supplements them by a cooperative process. In essence, CPFR coordinates the requirements planning process between supply chain partners for demand creation and demand fulfillment activities. Figure 3.7 illustrates the base CPFR relationships. The CPFR solution shares information involving promotions, forecasts, item data, and orders, using either EDI or the Internet. The collaboratively developed information is then used jointly and iteratively by planners to generate demand, determine replenishment requirements, and match production to demands.

The first step in the CPFR process is joint business planning, wherein a customer and supplier share, discuss, coordinate, and rationalize their own individual strategies to create a joint plan. The joint plan offers a common and consistent vision of what is expected to be sold, how it will be merchandized and promoted, in which marketplace, and during what time period. A joint calendar is created to share information determining product flow. A common sales forecast is created and shared between retailer and supplier based on shared knowledge of each trading partner's plan. CPFR includes an iterative process where the forecast and requirements plan is exchanged and refined between the partners until a consensus is developed. Using this consensus forecast, production, replenishment, and shipment plans are developed. Ideally, the collaborative forecast becomes a commitment between the two firms.

FIGURE 3.7
CPFR in the Retail Information Technology Environment

Source: Reprinted with permission from Matt Johnson, "Collaboration Data Modeling: CPFR Implementation Guidelines," *Proceedings of the 1999 Annual Conference of the Council of Supply Chain Management Professionals,* Oak Brook, IL, p. 17.

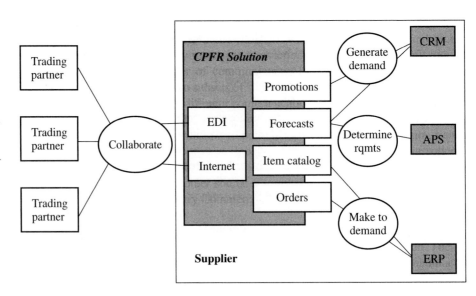

Relational distribution channels hold great promise for superior logistical performance. Conventional channels are primarily adversarial in nature, fail to acknowledge dependency, and are driven by information hoarding rather than sharing, so they cannot achieve the sophisticated logistical interfaces required by CPFR. Alliances and partnerships create long-term relationships between supply chain partnerships. When problems occur, as they inevitably will, they can be quickly resolved. Ultimately, the close-working arrangements reduce the cost of doing business for all channel members. Issues and concepts related to collaboration are discussed in Chapter 15.[13]

Customer Relationship Management

Customer relationship management (CRM) is designed to extend the functionality of the ERP sales and delivery applications, as illustrated in Figure 3.8. While traditional ERP applications focus on efficiently taking customer orders, firms are finding it necessary to

[13] For more detailed and timely information, see the CPFR Web site at **www.cpfr.org.**

FIGURE 3.8
Typical Customer Relationship Management Extension System

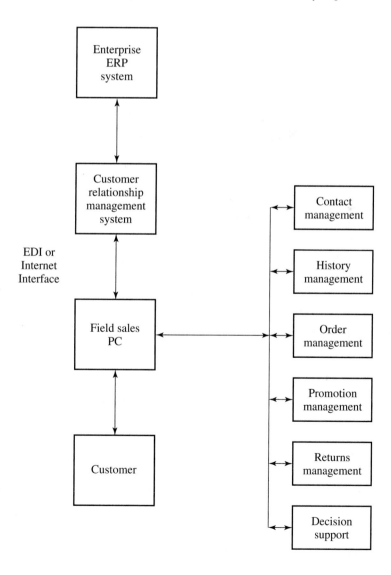

transition from treating customers as income sources to be exploited to treating customers as assets to be nurtured. While the traditional sales and delivery technology was configured to accept customer orders in a wide range of formats and allow those orders to be managed throughout the fulfillment process, a broader range of capabilities is necessary to manage the overall customer relationship. An integrated CRM system includes a combination of a server-based common database, remote PCs carried by the sales representatives, and a global synchronization process to ensure that both corporate and sales representative data are timely and consistent. Beyond this basic functionality, CRM today requires sales tracking, sales history analysis, pricing management, promotion management, product mix management, and category management. In some cases, customers expect their supplier's sales force to manage the entire category of products at the customer's facility. For example, it is becoming more common for grocers to expect their suppliers to manage both the product mix and the shelf quantities for major product categories such as beverages and specialty products. This practice, termed **category management,** requires substantial information support from the manufacturer but also facilitates information sharing.

Summary

The fundamental rationale for logistics is the need to accommodate customers, whether those customers are end users, intermediate, or even internal. The marketing concept provides the foundation for customer accommodation with its fundamental focus on customer needs rather than on products or services, the requirement to view and position products and services in a customer context, identification of market segments that differ in needs, and commitment that volume is secondary to profit.

Contemporary implementation of the marketing concept suggests that it is more important to focus on the development of relationships with customers than to perfect individual transactions. This interpretation focuses on the needs and requirements of individual customers as the core ingredient of one-to-one marketing. In a supply chain context, customer requirements related to spatial convenience, lot size, waiting time, and variety and assortment must be supported by logistical performance.

Organizations build their platform for customer accommodation on three levels of increasing commitment. The first of these is basic logistics customer service. To be competitive, a firm needs a basic service capability that balances availability, operational performance, and reliability for all customers. The level of commitment to each dimension of service requires careful consideration of competitive performance and cost/benefit analysis. The highest level of commitment is perfect order performance, which requires zero defects logistics operations. Such high-level commitment is generally reserved for a firm's key customers.

Going beyond basic service to create customer satisfaction represents the second level of customer accommodation. Where basic service focuses on the organization's internal operational performance, customer satisfaction focuses on customers, their expectations, and their perceptions of supplier performance. Customer expectations extend beyond typical logistical considerations and include factors related to communication, credibility access, responsiveness, and customer-specific knowledge as well as reliability and responsiveness of operations. A firm can provide logistics service that is equal to or even better than competitors' but still have dissatisfied customers. Failure to satisfy customers can arise from lack of knowledge about customer expectations, improper standards of performance, performance failure, poor communication, or incorrect customer or firm perception of performance. As customer expectations escalate, logistics executives must continuously monitor customer satisfaction and logistics performance.

The highest level of customer accommodation is known as customer success. Where satisfaction programs seek to meet or exceed expectations, a success platform focuses on customer needs and requirements. Customer expectations are frequently different from needs and requirements. Achieving success requires intimate knowledge of customers' needs and their operational requirements and a commitment by the service provider to enhance a customer's ability to compete more successfully in the marketplace. Value-added services represent one way logistics can contribute to customer success. While customer success is normally associated with one-to-one marketing relationships, in isolated instances it may represent the most viable approach to ensuring the long-term survival of entire categories of customers.

In most supply chains, customer requirements must be anticipated by using forecasts. Forecasts include a number of components with the major ones being level, trend, and seasonality. While these external components are significant, demand variation also results from operational actions such as promotions, price changes, and new product introductions. The forecasting process must incorporate a combination of techniques, support systems, and administration. Forecasting techniques provide a quantitative starting point, the support system refines the data in consideration of changes in the market, and forecast administration provides a management process to guide and monitor the overall effort. There are qualitative and causal forecasting techniques, but most logistics and supply chain forecasts are developed by using time series methods. While there have been some advancements in forecasting techniques and methods, the most substantial forecast improvements have been achieved through the use of collaborative techniques such as CPFR and CRM, involving multiple supply chain partners.

Challenge Questions

1. Explain the differences between transactional and relationship marketing. How do these differences lead to increasing emphasis on logistical performance in supply chain management?

2. Why are the four primary service outputs of spatial convenience, lot size, waiting time, and product variety important to logistics management? Provide examples of competing firms that differ in the level of each service output provided to customers.

3. Using the 10 categories of customer expectations in Table 3.1, develop your own examples of how customers might evaluate performance of a supplier.

4. Compare and contrast the customer service, customer satisfaction, and customer success philosophies of supply chain management.

5. What is meant by value-added services? Why are these services considered essential in a customer success program?

6. How could a company use the four-stage process of cost-effectiveness, market access, market extension, and market creation to gain competitive superiority?

7. Identify and discuss the major forecast components. Why is it important to decompose demand into these components when developing new forecasts?

8. Compare and contrast the basic logic differentiator of time series and causal forecast techniques. Under what conditions would each be appropriate?

9. Discuss how error accountability can be a major factor in improving forecast performance.

10. Discuss how a minor change in demand at the retail level can significantly impact supply chain variation at distributors, manufacturers, and suppliers.

Procurement and Manufacturing

In Chapter 2, performance cycles were presented as the framework for integrated logistics across the supply chain. Three performance cycles were identified that must be linked through effective logistics. The **procurement cycle** links an organization with its suppliers, the **manufacturing support cycle** involves the logistics of supporting production, and the **customer accommodation cycle** links a firm with its markets. As will be seen later in this chapter, manufacturing firms differ in their manufacturing strategies; thus, alternative approaches to procurement may be implemented to support specific manufacturing requirements. Of course, all of this performance must meet customer requirements for quality products. This chapter begins, with a discussion of product quality from a customer's perspective and Total Quality Management programs. Procurement and manufacturing are then each discussed with a focus on alternative strategies. The chapter concludes with a discussion of logistical interfaces necessary to support an organization's chosen procurement and manufacturing strategies.

The Quality Imperative

An overriding concern of all organizations is quality. In a competitive marketplace, no company dares fall behind in providing quality to its customers. Yet quality remains an elusive concept. In the end, quality is in the eyes of customers and how they perceive an organization, its products, and its services. Customer service quality was introduced in Chapter 3 in terms of customer expectations and requirements. Much of the focus in supply chain logistics is on helping ensure products are delivered on time, damage-free, and with all the service attributes necessary to meet customer requirements. In this chapter, dealing with procurement of materials and manufacturing processes, critical issues of **product quality** are addressed.

Dimensions of Product Quality

In the context of physical product form, quality is not as simple as it may first appear. In fact, the term *quality* means different things to different people. While everyone wants a quality product, not all may agree that a particular item or brand has all of the quality attributes desired. Quality is often viewed in terms of eight different competitive dimensions.[1]

Performance

Perhaps the most obvious aspect of quality from a customer's viewpoint is performance, or how well the product actually performs in comparison to how it was designed to perform. For example, personal computers may be judged with respect to their processing speed; audio components, in terms of sound clarity and lack of noise; or dishwashers, relative to how clean and spotless the dishes. Superior performance in a product is generally an objective attribute, which can be compared between items and brands. Of course, an item may actually have several performance dimensions, which complicates comparison. The personal computer is judged not only in terms of processing speed but also by such characteristics as internal memory, hard disk capacity, and numerous other performance features.

Reliability

Reliability refers to the likelihood that a product will perform throughout its expected life. It is also concerned with the number of breakdowns or repairs that a customer experiences after purchase. Consider, for example, Maytag's slogan "The Dependability People" and long-running advertising campaign featuring a company repairman as "the loneliest person in town." Maytag stresses its products are more reliable than those of competitors by showing that the Maytag repairman is never needed to fix a broken appliance. Like performance, reliability is a characteristic of quality that can be objectively measured.

Durability

While related to reliability, durability is a somewhat different attribute. It refers to the actual life expectancy of a product. An automobile with a life expectancy of 10 years may be judged by many consumers to be of higher quality than one with a projected 5-year life. Of course, life span may be extended through repair or preventive maintenance. Thus, durability and reliability are distinct but interrelated aspects of quality.

---

[1] David A. Garvin, "Competing on the Eight Dimensions of Quality," *Harvard Business Review* (November/December 1987), pp. 101–9.

Conformance

Conformance refers to whether a firm's products actually meet the precise description or specifications as designed. It is frequently measured by looking at an organization's scrap, rework, or rate of defects. Conformance quality measurement is usually internal in an organization. For example, if 95 percent of a firm's products meet the specifications as designed, it has a 5 percent defect rate. Defective products may be scrapped or reworked to bring them into conformance.

Features

Customers frequently judge quality of specific products on the basis of the number of functions or tasks that they perform independent of reliability or durability. For example, a television receiver with features such as remote control, picture-in-picture, and on-screen programming is typically perceived to be of higher quality than a basic model. But, in general, the more features a product contains, the greater is the likelihood that another quality attribute may be lacking, such as reliability.

Aesthetics

Aesthetics, the styling and specific materials used in a product, is used by many consumers to judge quality. In clothing, cashmere sweaters are considered of higher quality than polyester fabrics. In automobiles, the use of leather rather than cloth for seats, wood or metal rather than plastic, are aesthetics that imply quality. Included in aesthetics is the notion of fit and finish such as high-gloss paint on an automobile or seams having no overlap. Product designs that are unique or innovative are frequently regarded by customers to be of higher quality.

Serviceability

Serviceability, the ease of fixing or repairing a product that fails, is an important aspect of quality for some customers. Consider, for example, how some new appliances contain diagnostic capability, which alerts users or service technicians that a failure is about to occur. Ideally, serviceability would allow the customer to fix the product with little or no cost or time lost. In the absence of such serviceability, customers generally consider those items or brands that can be repaired quickest with least cost to have superior quality.

Perceived Quality

As noted earlier, customers are the ultimate judges of product quality through their perception of how well the product meets their requirements. Perceived quality is based on customers' experience before, during, and after they purchase a product. Total product quality is a combination of the eight dimensions, how they are blended by an organization, and how that blend is perceived by the customer. It is perfectly plausible that two different customers may perceive two different brands as each having best quality, depending upon which blend of elements each considers most critical.

Total Quality Management

It is useful to remember that total quality encompasses much more than the physical attributes of a product. Of specific concern in logistics are the quality dimensions of service, satisfaction, and success. From the customer's perspective, not only does the physical product incorporate the desired elements, but also the product must be available in a timely and suitable manner. Quality is, therefore, a major responsibility of a logistics organization.

Total Quality Management (TQM) is a philosophy supported by a managerial system focused on meeting customer expectations with respect to all needs, from all departments or functions of an organization, whether the customer is internal or external, a supply chain partner, or a consumer. While the specific tools and methodologies employed in TQM are beyond the scope of logistics, the basic conceptual elements are: (1) top management commitment and support; (2) maintaining a customer focus in product, service, and process performance; (3) integrated operations within and between organizations; and (4) commitment to continuous improvement.

Quality Standards

Establishing global quality standards is extremely difficult as a result of different circumstances, practices, and procedures around the world. As a simple example, engineering tolerances in one country might be measured in millimeters, while in another, they are measured in tenths of an inch. Nevertheless, a set of standards has emerged from the **International Organization for Standardization (ISO)** and has gained worldwide acceptance.

A series of quality standards have been issued under the name ISO 9000. Incorporating several subsets (ISO 9001, 9002, etc.), these standards provide basic definitions for quality assurance and quality management. ISO 9001, for example, deals with the quality system in place for product design, development, production, installation, and service. Several organizations around the world are authorized to perform audits of companies and their practices and procedures for TQM. A company that conforms to the ISO guidelines can receive certification. In 1998, another set of guidelines, ISO 14000, was released. ISO 14000 deals with guidelines and procedures for managing a firm's environmental impact. Certification in both ISO 9000 and ISO 14000 indicates a company conforms to both quality and environmental standards.

Procurement[2]

Every organization, whether it is a manufacturer, wholesaler, or retailer, buys materials, services, and supplies to support operations. Historically, purchasing has been perceived as a clerical or low-level managerial activity charged with responsibility to execute and process orders initiated elsewhere in the organization. The role of purchasing was to obtain the desired resource at the lowest possible purchase price from a supplier. This traditional view of purchasing has changed substantially in the past several decades. The modern focus is on total spend and the development of relationships between buyers and sellers. As a result, procurement has been elevated to a strategic activity.

The increasing importance of procurement can be attributed to several factors. The most basic of these factors has been the recognition of the substantial dollar spend for purchases of a typical organization and the potential dollar savings from a viable procurement strategy. The simple fact is that purchased goods and services are among the largest cost elements for most firms. In the average manufacturing firm in North America, purchased goods and services account for approximately 55 cents of every sales dollar.[3] By way of contrast, the average expense of direct labor in the manufacturing process accounts for about 10 cents of each sales dollar. While the percentage spent on purchased inputs varies considerably across manufacturing industries, it is clear that the potential savings from strategic management of procurement are substantial.

---

[2] This section draws on Robert Monczyka, Robert Trent, and Robert Handfield, *Purchasing and Supply Chain Management* (Mason, OH: Thomson South-Western, 2005).

[3] Shawn Tulley, "Purchasing: New Muscle," *Fortune*, February 20, 1995, p. 75.

Related to the cost of purchased inputs is a growing emphasis on outsourcing. The result is that the amount spent on procurement has increased significantly in many organizations. Firms today purchase not only raw materials and basic supplies but also complex fabricated components with very high value-added content. They spin off functions to suppliers to focus internal resources on core competencies. The result is that more managerial attention must then be focused on how the organization interfaces and effectively manages its supply base. For example, General Motors uses its first-tier supplier network and third-party logistics providers to complete subassemblies and deliver finished components as needed to their automotive assembly lines. Many of these activities were once performed internally by the General Motors organization. Developing and coordinating these relationships represent critical aspects of an effective procurement strategy. The logistical requirements related to effective procurement strategy are identified below.

Procurement Perspectives

The evolving focus on procurement as a key organizational capability has stimulated a new perspective regarding its role in supply chain management. The emphasis has shifted from adversarial, transaction-focused negotiation with suppliers to ensuring that the firm is positioned to implement its manufacturing and marketing strategies with support from its supply base. In particular, considerable focus is placed on ensuring continuous supply, inventory minimization, quality improvement, supplier development, and lowest total cost of ownership.

Continuous Supply

Stockouts of raw materials or component parts can shut down or force a change in production plans, resulting in unexpected cost. Downtime due to production stoppage increases operating costs and may result in an inability to provide finished goods as promised to customers. Imagine the chaos that would result if an automobile assembly line had all parts available but tires. Assembly of automobiles would have to be halted until tires were available. Thus, one of the core objectives of procurement is to ensure that a continuous supply of materials, parts, and components is available to maintain manufacturing operations.

Minimize Inventory Investment

In the past, downtime due to material shortages was minimized by maintaining large inventories of materials and components to protect against potential disruption in supply. However, maintaining inventory is expensive and requires scarce capital. One goal of procurement is to maintain supply continuity with the minimum inventory investment possible. This requires balancing the costs of carrying material against the possibility of a production stoppage. The ideal, of course, is to have needed materials arrive just at the moment they are scheduled to be used in the production process, in other words, **just-in-time.**

Quality Improvement

Procurement is critical to the quality requirements discussed earlier in this chapter. The quality of finished goods and services is dependent upon the quality of the materials and components used. If poor-quality components and materials are used, then the final product likely will not meet customer quality standards. Thus, both a firm and its suppliers need to be jointly committed to a continuous quality improvement initiative.

Supplier Development

In the final analysis, successful procurement depends on locating or developing suppliers, analyzing their capabilities, and selecting and working with those suppliers to achieve continuous improvement.[4] Developing good supply relationships with firms that are committed to the buying organization's success is critical in supplier development. It is important to develop close relationships with those suppliers in order to share information and resources to achieve better results. For example, a manufacturer might share a production schedule with key suppliers, which in turn allows them to better meet the buyer's delivery requirements. A retailer might share point-of-sale information and promotional plans to help suppliers meet quantity requirements at specific times. This perspective on effective procurement stands in stark contrast to the traditional focus on price alone, which inherently created adversarial relationships between a firm and its suppliers.

Lowest Total Cost of Ownership

Ultimately, the difference in perspective between a traditional adversarial and more contemporary collaborative procurement strategy can be summarized as a focus on **Total Cost of Ownership (TCO)** as contrasted to a focus on purchase price. Procurement professionals recognize that, although the purchase price of a material or item remains important, it is only one part of the total cost for their organization.[5] Service costs and life cycle costs must also be considered.

Whether established through competitive bidding, buyer-seller negotiation, or simply from a seller's published price schedule, the purchase price and discounts of an item are obviously a concern in procurement. No one wants to pay a higher price than necessary. Related to the price quote is normally a schedule of one or more possible discounts a buyer may receive. For example, quantity discounts may be offered as an inducement to encourage buyers to purchase larger quantities or cash discounts may be offered for prompt payment of invoices.

Consideration of supplier's discounts immediately takes the buyer beyond simple quoted purchase price. Other costs associated with purchasing must be considered. For the benefits of quantity discounts to be factored into the total cost, the buyer must quantify inventory holding costs. Larger purchase quantities increase average inventory of materials or supplies. Size of purchase also impacts administrative costs associated with purchasing. Lot-size techniques such as Economic Order Quantity (EOQ), discussed fully in Chapter 6, can help quantify these cost trade-offs.

Supplier terms of sale and cash discount structures also impact the total cost of ownership. A supplier offering more favorable credit terms is, in effect, impacting the purchase price from the buyer's perspective. For example, a discount for prompt payment of an invoice offered by one supplier must be compared with the offers of other suppliers.

What normally is not considered in traditional purchasing practice is the impact of pricing and discount structures on logistics operations and costs. For example, while traditional EOQ does consider inventory carrying costs, it generally does not include such factors as the impact of order quantity on transportation costs or the costs associated with receiving and handling different size shipments. Many of these logistical considerations are ignored or given cursory consideration as buyers attempt to achieve the lowest purchase price. Today there is increasing recognition of the importance of these logistics costs to the TCO.

---

[4] Daniel Krause, "Suppliers Development: Current Practices and Outcomes," *Journal of Supply Chain Management* (Spring 1997), pp. 12–20.

[5] Zeger Degraeve and Filip Roodhooft, "Effectively Selecting Suppliers Using Total Cost of Ownership," *Journal of Supply Chain Management* (Winter 1999), pp. 5–10. See also Lisa M. Ellram, "Total Cost of Ownership," *International Journal of Physical Distribution and Logistics Management* (August 1995), pp. 4–23.

Sellers typically offer a number of standard services that must be considered in procurement. Additionally, available value-added services must be evaluated as organizations seek to identify the lowest TCO. Many of these services involve logistical operations and the logistical interface between buyers and sellers.

The simplest of these services is delivery. How delivery will be accomplished, when, and at what location all impact cost structures. In many industries it is standard practice to quote a price that includes delivery. Alternatively, the seller may offer the buyer an allowance if the item being purchased is picked up at the seller's location. The buyer may be able to reduce total costs, not only through taking advantage of such allowances, but also by more fully utilizing its own transportation equipment.

In Chapter 3, value-added services were discussed, ranging from special packaging to preparation of promotional displays. Performance of subassembly operations in a supplier's plant or at an integrated service provider warehouse represents an extension of potential value-added service. The point is that each potential service has a cost to the supplier and a price to the buyer. A key aspect of determining the TCO for purchased requirements is to consider the trade-offs involved in terms of value added versus cost and price of each service. To do so, the purchase price of an item must be **debundled** from the price of services under consideration. Each of the related available services should be priced on an independent basis so that appropriate analysis can be performed. In Chapter 11, this practice will be referred to as **menu pricing.** Where traditional purchasing might overlook value-added services in seeking lowest possible price, effective procurement executives consider whether such services should be performed internally, by suppliers, or at all. Debundling allows the buyer to make the most appropriate procurement decision.

The final aspect of lowest TCO includes numerous elements known as life cycle costs. The total cost of materials, items, or other inputs extends beyond the purchase price and value-added service to include the lifetime costs of such items. Some of these costs are incurred before actual receipt of the items, others are incurred while the item is being used, and some occur long after the buyer has actually used the item.

One aspect of life cycle costs involves the administrative expense associated with procurement. Expenses related to screening potential suppliers, negotiation, order preparation, and transmission are just a few procurement administrative costs. Receiving, inspecting, and payment are also important. The costs related to defective finished goods, scrap, and rework associated with poor supplier quality must also be considered, as well as related warranty administration and repair. Even the costs associated with recycling or recovery of materials after the useful life of a finished product may have an impact on TCO.

Figure 4.1 presents a model of the various elements that TCO comprises. When each of these elements is considered in procurement, it is clear that numerous opportunities for improvement exist in most companies. Many of these opportunities arise from closer working relationships with suppliers than would be possible if adversarial price negotiation dominated the buyer-seller relationship. When buyers work cooperatively with suppliers, several strategies may be employed to reduce both the buyers' and the sellers' costs, making the total supply chain more efficient and allowing it to more effectively meet the requirements of downstream partners. Such strategies are discussed next.

Procurement Strategies

Effective procurement strategy to support supply chain operations requires a much closer working relationship between buyers and sellers than was traditionally practiced. Specifically, three strategies have emerged: volume consolidation, supplier operational integration, and value management. Each of these strategies requires substantial collaboration between supply chain partners and should be considered as stages of continuous improvement.

FIGURE 4.1 **Major Categories for the Components of Total Cost of Ownership**

Source: Reprinted with permission from Michael Leanders and Harold Fearon, *Purchasing and Supply Management,* 11th ed. (New York: McGraw-Hill Irwin, 1997) p. 334.

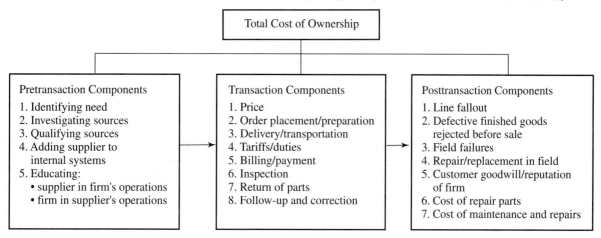

Volume Consolidation

An important step in developing an effective procurement strategy is volume consolidation through reduction in the number of suppliers. Beginning in the 1980s many firms faced the reality that they dealt with a large number of suppliers for almost every material or input used. In fact, purchasing literature prior to that time emphasized that multiple sources of supply constituted best procurement practice. First, potential suppliers were continually bidding for a buyer's business, ensuring constant pressure to quote low prices. Second, maintaining multiple sources reduced the buyer's dependence on any one supplier. This in turn served to reduce the buyer's risk should a specific supplier encounter supply disruptions such as a strike, a fire, or internal quality problems.

By consolidating volumes with a limited number of suppliers, procurement is also positioned to leverage its share of a supplier's business. At the very least, it increases the buyer's negotiating strength in relationship to the supplier. More important, volume consolidation with a reduced number of suppliers provides a number of advantages for those suppliers. The most obvious advantage of concentrating a larger volume of purchases with a supplier is that it allows the supplier to improve economies of scale by spreading fixed cost over a larger volume of output. Additionally, assured of a volume of purchases, a supplier is more likely to make investments in capacity or processes to improve customer service. When a buyer is constantly switching suppliers, no one firm has an incentive to make such investments.[6]

Clearly, when a single source of supply is used, risk increases. For this reason, supply base reduction programs are almost always accompanied by rigorous supplier screening, selection, and certification programs. In many instances, procurement executives work closely with others in their organization to develop preferred or certified suppliers. It should be noted that volume consolidation does not necessarily mean that a single source of supply is utilized for every, or any, purchased input. It does mean that a substantially smaller number of suppliers are used than was traditionally the case in most organizations. Even when a single source is chosen, it is essential to have a contingency plan.

[6] Matthew G. Anderson, "Strategic Sourcing," *International Journal of Logistics Management* (January 1998), pp. 1–13.

The savings potential from volume consolidation is not trivial. One consulting firm has estimated that savings in purchase price and other elements of cost can range from 5 to 15 percent of purchases.[7] If the typical manufacturing firm spends 55 percent of its revenue on purchased items and can save 10 percent through volume consolidation, the potential exists to deliver a $5.5 million improvement on revenue of $100 million to the bottom line.

Supplier Operational Integration

The next stage of development occurs when buyers and sellers begin to integrate their processes and activities in an attempt to achieve substantial performance improvement. Such integration typically involves alliances or partnerships with selected suppliers to reduce total cost and improve operational integration.

Such integration takes many different forms. For example, the buyer may allow the supplier to have access to sales and ordering information, thereby giving the supplier continuous knowledge of which products are selling. Detailed sales information allows the supplier to be better positioned to effectively meet buyer requirements at a reduced cost. Cost reduction occurs because the supplier has more information to plan and can reduce reliance on cost-inefficient practices, such as forecasting and expediting.

Further operational integration can result for buyers and suppliers working together to identify processes involved in maintaining supply and searching for ways to redesign those processes. Establishing direct communication linkages to reduce order time and eliminate communication errors is a common benefit of such integration. More sophisticated integrative efforts may involve eliminating redundant activities that both parties perform. For example, in some sophisticated relationships, activities such as buyer counting and inspection of incoming deliveries have been eliminated as greater reliance and responsibility are assumed by suppliers. Many firms have achieved operational integration focused on logistical arrangements, such as continuous replenishment programs and vendor-managed inventory.[8] Such integration has considerable potential for reducing TCO.

Some of the efforts in operational integration strive to reduce total cost through two-way learning. For example, Honda of America works closely with its suppliers to improve their quality management. Honda visits supplier facilities and helps identify ways to increase quality. Such improvements ultimately benefit Honda by reducing the supplier's costs of rework and by providing Honda with higher levels of quality materials.

The primary objective of operational integration is to cut waste, reduce cost, and develop a relationship that allows both buyer and seller to achieve mutual improvements. Combined creativity across organizations can create synergy that one firm, operating in isolation, would be unable to achieve. It has been estimated that operational integration with a supplier can provide incremental savings of 5 to 25 percent over and above the benefits of volume consolidation.[9]

Value Management

Achieving operational integration with suppliers creates the opportunity for value management. Value management is an even more intense aspect of supplier integration, going beyond a focus on buyer-seller operations to a more comprehensive and sustainable relationship. Value engineering, reduced complexity, and early supplier involvement in new product design represent some of the ways procurement can work with suppliers to reduce TCO.

Value engineering is a concept that involves closely examining material and component requirements at the early stage of product design to ensure that a balance of lowest total

---

[7] Matthew Anderson, Les Artman, and Paul B. Katz, "Procurement Pathways," *Logistics* (Spring/Summer 1997), p. 10.

[8] These concepts are discussed in Chapter 6.

[9] Anderson, Artman, and Katz, "Procurement Pathways," p. 10.

FIGURE 4.2
Flexibility and Cost of Design Changes

Source: Reprinted with permission from Robert M. Monczka et al., *New Product Development; Strategies for Supplier Integration* (Milwaukee: ASQ Quality Press, 2000) p. 6.

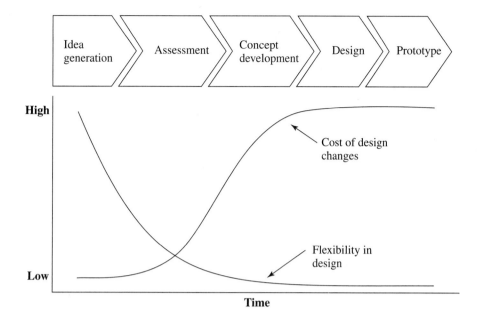

cost and quality is incorporated into new product design. Figure 4.2 shows how early supplier involvement can be critical in achieving cost reductions. As a firm's new product development process proceeds from idea generation through the various stages to commercialization, the company's flexibility in making design changes decreases. Design changes are easily accommodated in the early stages, but by the time prototypes have been developed, a design change becomes difficult and expensive. The earlier a supplier is involved in the design process, the more likely an organization is to capitalize on that supplier's knowledge and capabilities.

An example from an automobile manufacturer demonstrates the benefit of early supplier involvement. In designing the front bumper for a new model, the design engineer was completing design of the bracket assembly for the bumper. During the process, an engineer from the assembly supplier, which had already been identified even though actual production was in the future, asked if the bracket location could be moved by about $\frac{1}{2}$ inch. The design engineer, after some consideration, replied that it could be done with no impact on the final product. The design engineer was interested to know why the supplier requested the change. The answer was that by moving the bracket, the supplier would be able to use existing tools and dies to manufacture the bracket. Under the original design, major capital investment would have been required for new tooling. The result was approximately a 25 to 30 percent reduction in cost of the bracket.

Clearly, value management extends beyond procurement in an organization and requires cooperation between numerous participants, both internal and external. Teams representing procurement, engineering, manufacturing, marketing, and logistics as well as key supplier personnel jointly seek solutions to lower total cost, improve performance, or improved accomodation of customer requirements.

Purchase Requirement Segmentation

The Pareto effect applies in procurement just as it applies in almost every facet of business activity. In procurement, it can be stated simply: A small percentage of the materials, items, and services acquired account for a large percentage of the dollars spent. The point is that all procured inputs are not equal. However, many organizations use the same approach and procedures for procuring small-volume items that they do for acquiring their most strategic purchases. As a result, they spend as much in acquiring a $10,000 order of raw materials as they do for a $100 order of copy paper. Since all purchased inputs are not equal, many firms have begun to pay attention to segmented purchase requirements and prioritizing resources and expertise to handle those requirements.

It would be a mistake, though, to simply use dollar expenditure as the basis for segmenting requirements. Some inputs are strategic materials. Others are not. Some inputs have potential for high impact on the business success. Others do not. Some purchases are very complex and high risk. Others are not. For example, failure to have seat assemblies delivered to an auto assembly line on time could be catastrophic, while failure to have cleaning supplies might constitute a nuisance. The key is for an organization to apply a segmented approach to procurement. Volume consolidation and supply base reduction most likely can be justified for almost every material and service. The benefits described earlier can be enjoyed for office supplies as well as raw materials.

E-Commerce and Procurement

The explosion in technology and information systems is having a major impact on the procurement activity of most organizations. Much of the actual day-to-day work in procurement has traditionally been accomplished manually with significant amounts of paperwork, resulting in slow processes subject to considerable human error. Applying technology to procurement has considerable potential to speed the process, reduce errors, and lower acquisition cost.

Probably the most common technology used in procurement is **Electronic Data Interchange (EDI).** EDI involves the electronic transmission of data between a firm and its suppliers. This allows two or more companies to obtain and provide timely and accurate information. Using EDI there are many types of data being directly transmitted, including purchase requisitions, purchase orders, purchase order acknowledgment, order status, advanced shipment notification and tracking and tracing information. The explosion in EDI usage is a direct recognition of associated benefits, including standardization of data, more accurate information, more timely information, shortening of lead times with associated reductions in inventories, and reduced TCOs. More specifics related to EDI and related information technologies are provided in chapter 5.

Another procurement application of electronic commerce is the development of electronic catalogs. In fact, making information available about products and who can supply them is a natural application for **Internet-based** communications. Electronic catalogs allow buyers to gain rapid access to product information, specifications, and pricing, allowing buyers to quickly identify products and place orders. Many companies have developed their own online electronic catalogs and efforts have also been devoted to developing catalogs containing products from multiple suppliers, which permits buyers to rapidly compare features, specifications, and prices.

As early as 1996, several major organizations, including General Motors and Wal★Mart, announced that suppliers not capable of conducting business via the Internet would be eliminated from consideration. An advantage of the Internet relative to traditional EDI is that it overcomes some of the technical issues of computer system compatibility. The Internet provides capability for buyers and sellers to exchange files and information easily. General Electric created a "Trading Process Network" that turned a once completely manual process for procuring custom-designed parts into an electronic system. The system sends requests for quotation along with drawings and specifications to vendors worldwide.

Buying exchanges are another technology-based purchasing development. While some companies have formed their own trading networks for dealing with suppliers, buying exchanges represent cooperative efforts among companies, frequently competitors, to deal with their common base of suppliers. In the auto industry, General Motors, Ford, and DaimlerChrysler, each of which had initially formed separate trading networks, established a joint online buying exchange.[10] The auto companies allow their suppliers to view requirements for parts and supplies, look at technical specifications, and even have a limited view of planned production schedules. Since the auto manufacturers in many instances deal with common sources, the suppliers can better plan their own production and delivery requirements by having access to information concerning all of their customers available from a single location.

The potential volume of procurement activity through buying exchanges is enormous. Exchanges have been developed in the aircraft parts industry, chemicals, steel building products, food distribution, and even retailing. However, there is a potential downside. Many suppliers fear that the exchanges will become a mechanism that ultimately will reinforce past practice of buyers to focus strictly on purchase price. If buyers post their requirements and needs on the Internet primarily for the purpose of soliciting bids from alternative suppliers, or use the technology to have suppliers enter into an auctioning process, some fear many of the advances in supplier integration and value management will suffer.

In a supply chain management context, the link between a company and its external suppliers is critical. It provides for the integration of materials and resources from outside the organization into internal operations. Procurement is charged with the responsibility of ensuring that this transition is accomplished as efficiently and as effectively as possible. Much of the concern in procurement is focused on the logistical interface between the organization and its supply base. Ultimately, the purpose of procurement is to integrate material flow in accordance with requirements. It's the job of logistics to efficiently move purchases to the desired location. In the next section, alternative manufacturing strategies are discussed with a focus on identifying their logistical requirements.

Manufacturing[11]

A substantial number of firms in the supply chain are involved in manufacturing products. Manufacturers add value by converting raw materials into consumer or industrial products. They create value by producing product/service bundles for either customers or intermediate members in the supply chain. For example, retailers purchase a wide range of products from varied manufacturers to create an appealing assortment for consumers. This section reviews supply chain structure and strategy from a manufacturing perspective. As in the previous section that discussed procurement, the objective is to highlight logistics requirements and challenges necessary to integrate and support manufacturing supply chain operations.

Manufacturing Perspectives

The range of products a firm manufactures is based on its technological capability and marketing strategy. Firms perfect manufacturing competencies on the basis of market opportunity and willingness to take innovative risk. At the outset, a manufacturing firm creates or invents a new product assortment as its entry point as a value-added supply chain participant. Initial market success serves to define and clarify a firm's competency as perceived by customers and suppliers. A firm initiating manufacturing operations to produce automotive parts will be viewed by trading partners as being distinctly different from one that produces

---

[10] Robert Simson, Farn Werner, and Gregory White, "Big Three Carmakers Plan Net Exchange," *The Wall Street Journal,* February 28, 2000, p. A-3.

[11] This section draws on Steven A. Melnyk and Morgan Swink, *Value-Driven Operations Management: An Integrated Modular Approach* (New York: McGraw-Hill, 2003).

garments. While the products produced are clearly different, the real differentiator between firms is found in competencies related to knowledge, technology, process, and strategy. Once established, a manufacturing firm's image and focus are continuously modified in the eyes of supply chain partners as it conducts business, researches and develops new products, and performs agreed- to value-added services. Thus, the combinations of capabilities and competencies that are exhibited by a manufacturing firm are dynamic. In terms of supply chain participation, the combination of products, services, capabilities, and competencies represents a firm's value proposition and provides dimension to its supply chain opportunities. A firm's manufacturing competency is based on brand power, volume, variety, constraints, and leadtime requirements.

Brand Power

Many manufacturers spend a great deal of promotional money to create brand awareness and acceptance among prospective buyers. As a result, they are typically identified by their product brands. The measure of a customer's purchase preference based on a manufacturer's reputation, product quality, and supply chain capabilities is known as **brand power.**

Buyers across a supply chain range from consumers to industrial purchasing agents. Under market conditions wherein a brand has high customer awareness, acceptance, and preference, manufacturers can be expected to have a great deal of influence. As a general rule, the stronger a firm's product brand image among buyers, the more leverage the manufacturing organization will have in determining supply chain structure and strategy. For instance, Deere & Company dominates how farm machinery is sold, distributed, and maintained.

Independent of customer acceptance is the reality that a firm that brands and markets a particular line of products may not, in fact, be engaged in either the actual manufacturing/ assembly or in the performance of associated logistics services. It is common practice for an organization to outsource some or even all manufacturing and logistics operations required to market a specific product. The nature of the manufacturing process, cost, and final destination in the supply chain go a long way to determine the attractiveness of such outsourcing. Logistical requirements are created by the geographical network linking locations of manufacturing operations and those of suppliers and customers. However, the power to determine the range of value-added services, physical product movement requirements, timing, and characteristics of flow along the supply chain is directly related to brand power.

Volume

Manufacturing processes can be classified in terms of the relationship of cost per unit to volume of output. The traditional perspective is to treat volume in terms of the well-established principle of **economy of scale.** The scale principle defines a relationship wherein the average cost of producing a product declines as its manufacturing volume increases. In terms of economy of scale, product quantity should be increased as long as increases in volume decrease the average cost per unit manufactured. Economy of scale results from efficiencies generated by specialization of process, workforce, fixed asset utilization, procurement economies, and reduced need for process changeover.

Economy of scale is extremely important when high-fixed-cost machinery is used to convert raw material into finished products. Typical examples are the paper, steel, and refining industries. In fact, some petroleum processing firms have decoupled their refineries from their supply chain marketing structure and positioned them as independent external suppliers. The refineries are then able to sell in the open market to all potential buyers and fully exploit economy-of-scale advantage.

In volume-sensitive industries, high capital investment coupled with high cost of changeover tends to encourage extremely long production runs. In terms of logistical support, two considerations related to volume influence supply chain design. First, supply chain logistics must accommodate the number of times a product is manufactured during a planning period. Such manufacturing frequency has a direct impact on both inbound and outbound logistical requirements. Second, the quantity or lot size typically produced during a manufacturing run determines the subsequent volume that must be handled and warehoused in a supply chain logistics structure.

Variety

In contrast to manufacturing situations dominated by scale, other production technologies feature flexibility. These manufacturing processes are characterized by relatively frequent product runs and high repetition of small lot sizes. As contrasted to economy of scale, manufacturing processes that feature variety rapidly switch production from one product to another while retaining efficiency are referred to as having **economy of scope.** Scope means that a manufacturing process can use varied combinations of overhead support, materials, equipment, and labor to produce a variety of different products.

Variety also refers to the **range** of product variations that are capable of being manufactured by using a given process. Range may result from the sequence of routing products through a manufacturing plant as well as the use of general as contrasted to specialized equipment. The achievement of economy of scope is also directly related to the speed and cost of changeover from one product to another. In terms of logistical support, high variety translates to relatively small manufacturing lot sizes, flexible material requirements, and a broad range of product outputs. High manufacturing variety directly impacts the type of logistical transportation and warehousing services required to support flexible manufacturing.

Constraints

All manufacturing processes reflect a balance between economy of scale and economy of scope. Volume and variety drive logistical support requirements. Constraints interact with volume and variety to create realistic manufacturing plans. The three primary constraints that influence manufacturing operations are **capacity, equipment, and setup/changeover.** Each of these constraints drives compromise regarding ideal manufacturing operations. Such compromise planned in the context of forecasted sales and planned promotions creates the production plan.

Capacity, as the name implies, is a measure of how much product can be produced per unit of time. Of particular interest is a firm's demonstrated capacity of quality production. Whereas a factory, process, or machine may have a rated capacity, the relevant measure is a firm's demonstrated ability to reach and maintain a specific level of quality output in a predictable time period. A measure of manufacturing competency is the speed to which a particular process reaches demonstrated capacity, given an unplanned change in requirements.[12] Such **scalability** is achieved by a combination of manufacturing, procurement, and logistical agility.

Equipment constraints are related to flexibility concerning the use and sequencing of specific machines to perform multiple manufacturing tasks. The variety a factory can produce is constrained by the range of available equipment and the required sequence of work. However, some manufacturing requirements are more easily accommodated across a family of machines and by using variable work sequences than are others. In many situations, a specific machine or work task tends to constrain or act as a bottleneck to the overall manufacturing process. Likewise, logistical capability to accommodate different patterns of equipment utilization may serve to enhance or constrain flexibility of the manufacturing process. Manufacturing executives devote substantial time and resources to eliminating

---

[12] Thomas G. Gunn, *21st Century Manufacturing* (Essex Junction, VT: OM NEO, 1992), Chapter 8.

bottlenecks that serve to constrain operations. The structure for focusing managerial attention is captured in **theory of constraint** methodology.[13]

Setup/changeover constraints are directly related to the need for variety. Substantial progress has been made in manufacturing management to speed up both process changeover time and the time required to reach demonstrated capacity. Whereas several hours and even days were once required for changeover, today the tasks are being performed in hours. For example, modular-manufacturing units, such as paint sprayers, are being set up and calibrated offline and then being inserted ready to spray paint into assembly lines. Of course all efforts to increase setup/changeover speed are directly dependent upon supply chain logistical support.

Leadtime

Manufacturing leadtime is a measure of the elapsed time between release of a work order to the shop floor and the completion of all work necessary to achieve ready-to-ship product status. Any given manufacturing process consumes operational and interoperational time.[14]

Operational time is the combination of setup/changeover and running or actual production time. In any manufacturing situation, the greater the amount of total leadtime accounted for by actual production, the inherently more efficient is the conversion process. Efficient operational time must be traded off against the issues discussed earlier concerning volume and variety.

Manufacturing processes also encounter unexpected delays or **inoperational time.** During periods that a process, line, or machine is idle because of queuing, waiting, breakdown, or failure in logistical support, manufacturing efficiency is negatively impacted. All forms of unexpected delay represent serious bottleneck issues. For example, it is estimated that between 75 and 95 percent of all nonproductive delays result from unplanned queuing in manufacturing processes.[15] Needless to say, most senior managers have little or no tolerance for unexpected production delays that result from late or damaged arrival of critical materials or components. Logistical delay on the part of a supplier who provides parts or materials can result in manufacturing failure to meet planned output. A firm's strategic impact is directly affected by leadtime performance. As a general rule, firms that compress manufacturing leadtimes and control or eliminate unexpected performance variance exhibit greater flexibility to accommodate customer requirements while simultaneously enjoying low-cost manufacturing.

Logistical operations commitments to supporting manufacturing can impact operating efficiency in a variety of ways. The potential benefits of brand power are based on a firm's track record regarding timely accommodation of customer order-to-delivery requirements. Lot-size efficiencies related to manufacturing frequency and repetition depend on reliable logistical support. The decision to produce large manufacturing lot sizes directly creates need for logistical support. Economy of scale drives procurement best practice and average inventory investment across the supply chain. The decision to focus on variety in manufacturing impacts the logistics requirements by adding the complexity of frequent changeover. Logistical performance is also a key variable in managing constraints. Such constraints can be created or resolved on the basis of logistical flexibility. Finally, logistics is critical to achieving manufacturing leadtime. In particular, logistical failure can increase manufacturing leadtime by introducing unexpected delays.

---

[13] For origins of this logic, see Eliyahu M. Goldratt and J. Cox, *The Goal* (Croton on Hudson, NY: North River Press, 1984); and Eliyahu M. Goldratt and Robert E. Fox, *The Race* (Croton on Hudson, NY: North River Press, 1986).

[14] Steven A. Melnyk and R. T. Christensen, *Back to Basics: Your Guide to Manufacturing Excellence* (Boca Raton: St. Lucie Press, 2000), pp. 15–17.

[15] Ibid., p. 17.

Logistics, as well as all other factors that impact manufacturing performance predictability, serves to create uncertainty requiring inventory. Inventory safety stocks are required when the timing of customer demand exceeds a firm's, or a supplier's, ability to deliver the correct assortment of products to the right place at the right time.

Manufacturing Strategies

The unique nature of each manufacturing process and customer requirements limit the practical range of alternative manufacturing strategies. Manufacturing strategic range is constrained by both marketing and technological forces. Prevailing marketing practices serve to ground manufacturing strategy in terms of customer acceptability. Technology drives strategy to a manufacturing model that is competitive. For example, a manufacturer having a process dominated by economy of scale may desire to improve process flexibility. However, significant investment will typically be required to increase frequency and repetition.

Over time, the changing nature of the market and available technology serve to alter a firm's strategic posture. Consider, for example, the steel industry, which was long dominated by processes highly dependent on economy of scale. Recent years have witnessed market acceptance of a wide range of new steel-based materials combined with value-added services. The Steel Service Center introduced cutting and shaping postponement to steel distribution as a way to increase customer accommodation. The nature of basic steel production has also undergone dramatic change. New process methods are being perfected that reduce long-time dependence on high-scale manufacturing processes. The combined impact of these changes in market and process has shifted the strategic posture of steel producers.

Matching Manufacturing Strategy to Market Requirements

In Chapter 3, typical marketing strategies were classified as being mass, segmental and focused, or one-on-one. These strategies are differentiated, in part, in terms of the desired degree of product and service accommodation. Mass marketing requires limited product/service differentiation. In contrast, one-on-one marketing strategy builds on unique or customized product/service offerings for each and every customer. A firm's strategic marketing posture concerning flexibility and agility to accommodate specific customer requirements is directly related to manufacturing capability. To a significant degree, a firm's manufacturing capability drives the feasible range of effective marketing strategy. For a manufacturing firm to effectively compete, it must be able to integrate manufacturing capability into a meaningful marketing value proposition.

Alternative Manufacturing Strategies

The most common manufacturing strategies are **make-to-plan (MTP), make-to-order (MTO),** and **assemble-to-order (ATO).** It is also common to refer to MTP as **make-to-stock (MTS).**

As a general rule, MTP strategies are characteristic of industries exploiting economy of scale gained from long production runs. Significant finished goods inventory is typically manufactured in anticipation of future customer requirements. The logistical requirement to support MTP is warehousing capacity to store finished product and to facilitate product assortment to meet specific customer requirements. When flexible manufacturing is introduced to speed up switchover, the inventory lots produced are typically smaller in quantity. However, warehouses are still required for temporary storage and to facilitate product assortment.

In contrast, MTO manufacturing strategies seek to manufacture to customer specification. While MTO may not be as limited as the traditional job shop, exact quantities and configurations are produced in relatively small quantities. Logistical capacity may be required for temporary storage and to achieve outbound transportation consolidation, but most product produced in an MTO environment is shipped direct to customers.

In ATO situations, base products and components are manufactured in anticipation of future customer orders; however, the products are not fully assembled or customized until a customer's order is received. Such final assembly reflects implementation of the principle of manufacturing or form postponement. The need for logistical capacity is critical in ATO operations. In fact, an increasing amount of ATO product finalization is being performed in supply chain logistics warehouses. The attractiveness of an ATO manufacturing strategy is that it has the potential to combine some facets of economy of scale typical of MTP with a degree of flexibility characteristic of MTO. Full implementation of an ATO strategy requires that warehouse operations be integrated in the value creation process to perform customizing and assembly operations.

Total Cost of Manufacturing

The marketing and manufacturing strategies of a firm drive logistical service requirements. For example, MTO manufacturing strategies typically require less finished goods inventory than MTP and ATO strategies. However, MTO strategies typically require significant component inventory and may result in high-cost customer accommodation. In light of such cost trade-offs, the design of a logistics support system should be based on the **Total Cost of Manufacturing (TCM).**

Total cost of manufacturing consists of production/procurement, inventory/warehousing, and transportation. All of the above costs are impacted by manufacturing strategy. As such, TCM represents the foundation for formulating a customer accommodation strategy. Figure 4.3 represents a generalized model of the TCM **per unit** ranging across strategic alternatives from MTO to ATO to MTP. Naturally, exact cost relationships will depend upon specifics related to individual business situations. The design objective is to identify the manufacturing strategy that best fits the marketing opportunity confronted.

In Figure 4.3, the per unit cost of manufacturing and procurement declines as quantity increases, reflecting economy of scale associated with MTP. Inventory and warehousing costs increase, reflecting the impact of larger manufacturing lot sizes. Transportation cost per unit decreases as a result of shipment consolidation. In contrast, MTO strategies reflect high per unit manufacturing and procurement costs which are, in part, offset by lower inventory and warehousing costs. In the MTO strategy, transportation cost per unit is higher, reflecting small shipment and/or premium transportation. The value of Figure 4.3 is to generalize

FIGURE 4.3
Total Cost of
Manufacturing

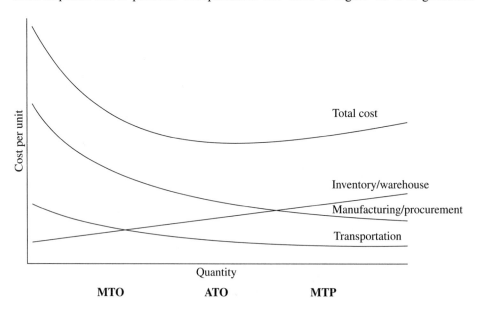

relationships and visualize important cross functional trade-offs. The TCM results from functional integration of manufacturing, procurement, and logistics. From a perspective of integrated management it is important for manufacturing firms to design a supply chain strategy that achieves lowest total cost of manufacturing across the entire process.

Logistical Interfaces

The efficient and effective coordination of manufacturing strategy with the procurement of materials and components ultimately depends on logistics. Resources must be procured and positioned as needed to support manufacturing operations. Whether the manufacturing strategy is MTO, ATO, or MTP, logistics links suppliers and customers with manufacturing processes. Clearly, the more seamless the interface, the better the opportunity is for achieving lowest total cost of ownership and, ultimately, lowest total cost of manufacturing. Such operations only emerge when there is high-level supplier integration in both operations and in design. Just-in-Time, Materials Requirements Planning, and Design for Logistics represent three approaches to achieving desired coordination.

Just-in-Time

Just-in-Time (JIT) techniques have received considerable attention and discussion in recent years in all areas related to supply chain management. Sometimes referred to as just-in-time production, often called just-in-time purchasing, and frequently referred to as just-in-time delivery, the goal of JIT is to time-phase activities so that purchased materials and components arrive at the manufacturing or assembly point just at the time they are required for the transformation process. Ideally, raw material and work-in-process inventories are minimized as a result of reducing or eliminating reserve stocks. The key to JIT operations is that demand for components and materials depends on the finalized production schedule. Requirements can be determined by focusing on the finished product being manufactured. Once the production schedule is established, just-in-time arrival of components and materials can be planned to coincide with those requirements, resulting in reduced handling and minimal inventories.

The implications of JIT are numerous. Obviously, it is necessary to deal with suppliers who have high and consistent levels of quality, as their components will go directly into the finished product. Absolutely reliable logistical performance is required and eliminates, or at least reduces, the need for buffer stocks of materials. JIT generally requires more frequent deliveries of smaller quantities of purchased inputs, which may require modification of inbound transportation. Clearly, to make JIT work, there must be very close cooperation and communication between a manufacturer's purchasing organization and suppliers. In JIT operations, companies attempt to gain the benefits of backward vertical integration but avoid the formal tie of ownership. They achieve many of the same ends through coordination and process integration with suppliers.

Originally, JIT was applied to manufacturing processes characterized as MTP, since the effective functioning of the system is dependent upon a finalized production schedule. However, as manufacturing strategies have evolved with more emphasis on flexibility, reduced lot-size production quantities, and quick changeovers, JIT concepts have evolved to accommodate ATO and MTO manufacturing as well. In many situations, lead suppliers are used by manufacturers to sort, segregate, and sequence materials as they flow into assembly operations. The goal is to reduce handling and facilitate continuous JIT.

Some organizations, seeing the benefits of JIT systems and recognizing the benefits of supplier integration, have gone so far as to bring their suppliers' personnel into their production plants. The supplier personnel are empowered to use the customer's purchase orders, have full access to production schedules, and have responsibility for scheduling arrival of materials. Originally introduced by the Bose Corporation, the term **JIT II** has been applied to these efforts to reduce leadtimes and cost.

Requirements Planning

In complex manufacturing organizations a process known as **Materials Requirements Planning (MRP)** is frequently used to aid in the interface between purchaser and supplier. MRP systems attempt to gain benefits similar to those of JIT, minimize inventory, maintain high utilization of manufacturing capacity, and coordinate delivery with procurement and manufacturing activities. Implementation of MRP systems, discussed in Chapters 6 and 11, requires a high level of technological sophistication. Software applications such as advanced planning and scheduling systems deal with the complexity of information required, such as leadtimes, quantities on-hand and on-order, and machine capacities for literally thousands of materials across multiple manufacturing locations.

Design for Logistics

The logistics interface with procurement and manufacturing, as well as with engineering and marketing, can be greatly enhanced by incorporating a concept known as **Design for Logistics** into the early phases of product development. Recall that the objectives of JIT and MRP are to minimize inventories and handling, with materials and components being ready for assembly or transformation as they are needed. How a product is designed and design of the components and materials themselves can have a significant impact on this process. In particular, product packaging and transportation requirements need to be incorporated into the design process. For example, if inbound components are packaged in containers with a standard quantity of 50 but only 30 components are needed to meet production requirements, then waste will occur. Additionally, product and component design must have consideration of transportation and internal materials handling methods to ensure that cost-efficient, damage-free logistics performance can be achieved. Similar design considerations must be made for the finished product itself.

Table 4.1 summarizes the critical relationships between customer accommodation, manufacturing/procurement, and logistical requirements. The framework is useful in positioning how logistical requirements flow from the customer accommodation, manufacturing, and procurement strategies.

TABLE 4.1 **Strategic Integration Framework**

Customer Accommodation	Manufacturing	Procurement	Logistics
Focused:	Make-to-Order (MTO):	B2B	Direct Fulfillment:
One-on-one strategies	Maximum variety	Discrete quantities	Time postponement
Unique product/service offerings	Unique configuration	Supplier-managed inventory	Small shipment
Response-based	Flexible manufacturing		
	High variety		
			Form and Time
Segmental:	Assemble-to-Order (ATO):	B2B	Postponement:
Limited size	Wide variety	JIT	Warehouse ATO
Customer groups	Quick changeover		Combination direct and
Differentiated products	Product customization		warehouse fulfillment
Mixed response and anticipatory	High variety and volume		Consolidated shipment
Mass Marketing:	Make-to-Plan (MTP):	B2B	Warehouse Fulfillment:
Anticipatory	Long product runs	Commodity	Full stocking strategy
Little product differentiation	Focus low cost	Auction	Assortment mixing
	High volume/low variety	E-procurement	Volume shipment

Summary

Managing logistics in the supply chain requires an interface between logistics, procurement, and manufacturing strategies.

A primary concern of procurement and manufacturing is product quality, a prerequisite for any firm that desires to be a global competitor. In fact, product quality has several different dimensions. It can mean reliability, durability, product performance, and conformance to engineered specifications. From a customer's perspective it may also include aspects of product features, aesthetics, or serviceability. World-class companies have implemented Total Quality Management programs in all their activities in an effort to achieve quality from their customer's perspective.

Procurement in an organization is charged with responsibility for obtaining the inputs required to support manufacturing operations. The focus is multidimensional, attempting to maintain continuous supply, minimize leadtimes from suppliers and inventory of materials and components, and develop suppliers capable of helping the organization achieve operating goals. Procurement professionals are focused on the Total Cost of Ownership as contrasted solely on purchase price. This requires careful consideration of trade-offs between purchase price, supplier services and logistical capability, quality of material, and how the material impacts costs over the life cycle of the finished product.

Procurement strategies require consolidation of purchase volumes into a small number of reliable suppliers. Such strategies include efforts to integrate supplier and buyer operations to achieve better and lower-cost overall performance. Supplier integration in new product design represents an important strategy to reduce Total Cost of Ownership.

In Chapters 3 and 4, strategic considerations related to customer accommodation, procurement, and manufacturing have been discussed in terms of their combined impact on logistical requirements. A number of important trade-offs were identified. The fundamental point is that isolated optimization of any specific functional area without considering cross-functional impact and requirements is not likely to result in integrated performance. Information technology is the focus of Chapter 6.

Challenge Questions

1. Using television receivers as an example, how could three different brands be perceived by different consumers as being the best quality brand in the market?

2. Why does the contemporary view of procurement as a strategic activity differ from the more traditional view of "purchasing"?

3. How can strategic procurement contribute to the quality of products produced by a manufacturing organization?

4. Explain the rationale underlying volume consolidation. What are the risks associated with using a single supplier for an item?

5. How does lowest TCO differ from lowest purchase price?

6. What is the underlying rationale that explains why firms should segment their purchase requirements?

7. Explain how constraints in manufacturing are interrelated with a company's decisions regarding volume and variety.

8. Why would a company's cost of manufacturing and procurement tend to increase as the firm changes from an MTP to an MTO strategy? Why would inventory costs tend to decrease?

9. How does a firm's marketing strategy impact its decisions regarding the appropriate manufacturing strategy?

10. Explain how logistics performance is crucial to JIT.

Information Technology Framework

Supply chain information systems initiate activities and track information regarding processes, facilitate information sharing both within the firm and between supply chain partners, and assist in management decision making. This chapter describes comprehensive information systems as a combination of communication networks and transaction systems. First, the chapter begins by describing the multiple roles that supply chain information systems play in enterprise management. Second, the chapter describes the major components of an integrated supply chain information system. Third, communication technology critical for logistics and supply chain operations and integration is reviewed. Fourth, the chapter provides the logistics rationale for implementing Enterprise Resource Planning (ERP) systems and describes their major elements. Finally, the chapter describes the major components of supply chain systems, including planning/coordination, operations, and inventory deployment. All component systems must be integrated to provide comprehensive functionality for analyzing, initiating, monitoring, and reporting supply chain operations.

Information System Functionality

From its inception, logistics focused on product storage and flow through the supply chain. Information flow and accuracy was often overlooked because it was not viewed as being critical to customers. In addition, information transfer rates were limited to manual processes. There are four reasons why timely and accurate information has become more critical in logistics system design and operations. First, customers perceive information about order status, product availability, delivery tracking, and invoices as a necessary dimension of customer accommodation. Customers demand real-time information. Second, with the goal of reducing total supply chain assets, managers realize that information can be used to reduce inventory and human resource requirements. In particular, requirements planning based on current information can reduce inventory by minimizing demand uncertainty. Third, information increases flexibility with regard to how, when, and where resources may be utilized to gain strategic advantage. Fourth, enhanced information transfer and exchange utilizing the Internet is facilitating collaboration and redefining supply chain relationships.

Supply chain information systems (SCIS) are the thread that links logistics activities into an integrated process. The integration builds on four levels of functionality: (1) transaction systems, (2) management control, (3) decision analysis, and (4) strategic planning. Figure 5.1 illustrates logistics activities and decisions at each level of information functionality. As the pyramid shape suggests, management control, decision analysis, and strategic planning enhancements require a strong transaction system foundation.

A **transaction system** is characterized by formalized rules, procedures, and standardized communications; a large volume of transactions; and an operational, day-to-day focus. The combination of structured processes and large transaction volume places a major emphasis on information system efficiency. At the most basic level, transaction systems initiate and record individual logistics activities and functions. Typical transaction functionality includes order entry, inventory assignment, order selection, shipping, pricing, invoicing, and customer inquiry. For example, the customer order entry transaction enters a customer request for products into the information system. The order entry transaction initiates a second transaction as inventory is assigned to the order. A third transaction is then generated to direct warehouse operations to accumulate the order. A fourth transaction initiates order shipment to the customer. The final transaction creates the invoice and a corresponding account receivable. Throughout the process, the firm and customer expect real-time information to be available concerning order status. Thus, the customer order performance cycle is completed through a series of information system transactions.[1]

The second SCIS level, **management control,** focuses on performance measurement and reporting. Performance measurement is necessary to provide feedback regarding supply chain performance and resource utilization. Common performance dimensions include cost, customer service, productivity, quality, and asset management measures. As an example, specific performance measures include transportation and warehousing cost per

---

[1] For a review of performance cycle structure and dynamics, see Chapter 2.

FIGURE 5.1 Information Functionality

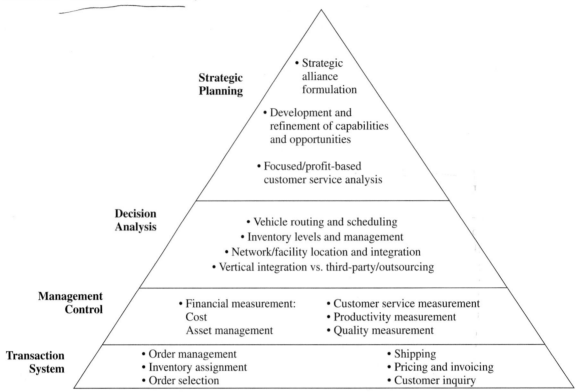

hundredweight, inventory turnover, case fill rate, cases per labor hour, and customer service perception.

While it is necessary that SCIS report historical system performance, it is also necessary for the system to identify operational exceptions. Exception information is useful to highlight potential customer or operational problems. For example, proactive SCIS should be capable of identifying future inventory shortages based on forecast requirements and planned inventory. Exception reporting should also identify potential transportation, warehouse, or labor constraints. While some control measures, such as cost, are well defined, other measures, such as service and quality, are less specific. For example, customer service can be measured internally, from the enterprise's perspective, or externally, from the customer's perspective. While internal measures are relatively easy to track, information concerning external measures is more difficult to obtain, since it involves the customer.

The third SCIS level, **decision analysis,** focuses on software tools to assist managers in identifying, evaluating, and comparing strategic and tactical alternatives to improve effectiveness. Typical analyses include supply chain design, inventory management, resource allocation, routing, and segmental profitability. Decision analysis SCIS should ideally include database maintenance, modeling, analysis, and reporting. Like management control, decision analysis may include operational considerations such as vehicle routing and warehouse planning. Decision analysis is also being used to manage customer relationships by determining the trade-offs associated with having satisfied and successful customers.

Strategic planning, the final SCIS level, organizes and synthesizes transaction data into a relational database that assists in evaluating various strategies. Essentially, strategic planning focuses on information to evaluate and refine supply chain and logistics strategy.

FIGURE 5.2 SCIS Usage, Decision Characteristics, and Justification

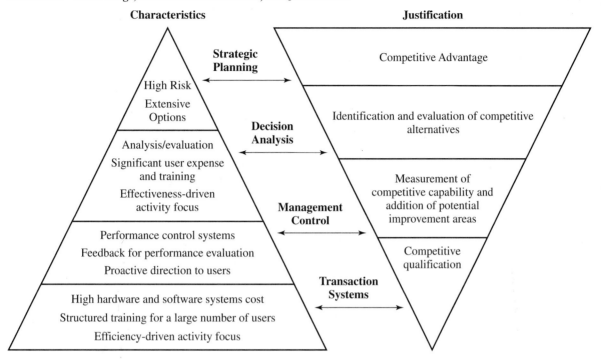

Examples of strategic planning include the desirability of strategic alliances, development and refinement of manufacturing capabilities, and opportunities related to customer responsiveness.

The relative shape of Figure 5.2 illustrates SCIS development characteristics and justification. Development and maintenance costs include hardware, software, communications, and human resources. In the past, most systems development focused on improving transaction system efficiency. While these investments originally offered returns in terms of speed and lower operating costs, there are currently fewer improvement opportunities. Most SCIS development and implementation is now focused on enhanced supply chain system integration and more effective decision making.

Comprehensive Information System Integration

A comprehensive SCIS initiates, monitors, assists in decision making, and reports on activities required to complete logistics operations and planning. The major system components are: (1) Enterprise Resource Planning (ERP) or legacy systems, (2) communication systems, (3) execution systems, and (4) planning systems. Figure 5.3 illustrates these components and their typical interfaces.

ERP or Legacy Systems

The **ERP** or **legacy systems** in Figure 5.3 are the backbone of most firms' logistics information system. This backbone maintains current and historical data and processes transactions to initiate and monitor performance. During the 1990s, many firms began to replace legacy systems with ERP systems designed as integrated transaction modules with a common and consistent database. ERP systems facilitated integrated operations and

FIGURE 5.3
SCIS: Integrated
Modules

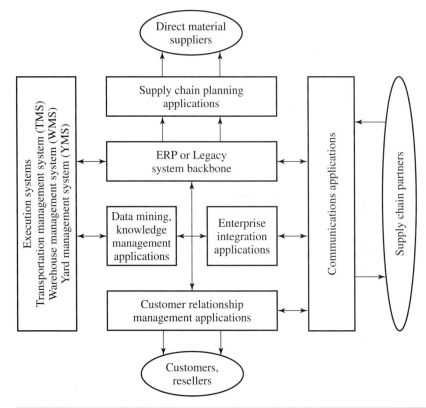

TABLE 5.1
ERP System
Capability

Typical	Advanced
Accounts payable and receivable	Collaborative planning, forecasting, and replenishment
General ledger	Customer relationship management
Human resource management	Supply chain event management
Bill of materials	Web-enabled applications
Inventory control	Advanced planning and scheduling
Routings	
Order management	
Project requirements planning	
Execution systems	

reporting to initiate, monitor, and track critical activities such as order fulfillment and replenishment. ERP systems also incorporate an integrated corporate-wide database, sometime referred to as a data warehouse, along with appropriate transactions to facilitate logistics and supply chain planning and operations. Supply chain transactions facilitated by ERP systems include order entry and management, inventory assignment, and shipping. Beyond these supply chain applications, ERP systems typically include financial, accounting, and human resource capability. Table 5.1 lists the traditional and emerging capabilities characteristic of ERP systems. Data Mining, General Decision Support, and other Enterprise Integration applications operate using the ERP backbone to develop and organize insight regarding customer, products, and operations.

To facilitate integration, ERP systems are beginning to include two additional system components, Supply Chain Planning (SCP) and Customer Relationship Management (CRM), as illustrated in Figure 5.3. Supply Chain Planning systems support operations by developing forecasts and determining production and movement requirements. The CRM system is a newer application designed to facilitate information sharing between customers, sales force, and operations management. CRM provides sales representatives and customers with current information regarding sales history, shipment history, order status, promotional summary, and shipment information. The history and current status information, combined with product development, pricing, and promotion information, allows CRM to better manage customer orders. Such timely and accurate information exchange between a firm and its customers increases the likelihood that product sales and promotion plans will be supported with required product.

Communication Systems

Communication systems facilitate information flow across the supply chain. Figure 5.3 illustrates the major communication components required for supply chain operations. Logistics information consists of real-time data on company operations and inbound material, production, inventory, customer shipment, and new customer orders. From a supply chain perspective, firms need to make order, shipment, and billing information available to suppliers, financial institutions, carriers, and customers. Communication systems are discussed in greater detail in the next major chapter section.

Execution Systems

Enterprise execution systems work in conjunction with the firm's ERP to provide specific functionality to support logistics operations. While some ERP systems support required logistics functionality, others lack functionality to facilitate warehouse and transportation operations. Selected execution system modules include Transportation Management System (TMS), Warehouse Management System (WMS), and Yard Management System (YMS). Most execution systems are "bolted-on" or integrated into the ERP system to facilitate data exchange. In addition to facilitating standard warehouse management functionality such as receiving, storage, shipping, and warehouse automation, the WMS typically includes management reporting, support for value-added services, and decision support capability. The TMS typically includes routing, load building, consolidation, and management of reverse logistics activities as well as scheduling and documentation. The YMS tracks inventory in vehicles stored in facility yards. A more detailed discussion of logistics execution systems is provided in the transportation and warehousing chapters (Chapters 7 to 11).

Planning Systems

ERP systems in general don't evaluate alternative strategies or assist with decision making. Supply chain planning systems, often termed **Advanced Planning and Scheduling (APS)** systems, are designed to assist in evaluating supply chain alternatives and advise in supply chain decision making. Sophisticated supply chain planning systems are available that permit evaluation of complex alternatives under tight decision time constraints. Typical supply chain planning applications include production scheduling, inventory resource planning, and transportation planning. Using historical and current data, APS software systematically identifies and evaluates alternative courses of action and recommends a solution within the constraints imposed. Typical constraints involve production, facility, transportation, inventory, or raw material limitations.

Planning systems can generally be grouped into two categories, strategic and tactical. Strategic planning systems are designed to assist in analyses where there are a large number of alternatives and data outside the range of current history is required. Examples of strategic planning applications include supply chain network design and structural analyses.

Tactical planning focuses on operational issues as constrained by short-term resource constraints such as production, facility, or vehicle capacity. The information support for tactical planning is typically available from a firm's data warehouse. Tactical planning processes evaluate customer requirements and identify an operational combination of production, inventory, facilities, and equipment that can be utilized within capacity constraints.

Communication Technology

Information sharing technology is critical to facilitate logistics and supply chain planning and operations. Historically, logistics coordination has been difficult since essential work is typically performed at locations remote from information technology hardware. As a result, information was not available at the work location in terms of both time and content. The past decade has witnessed remarkable advances in logistical communication systems capability, including bar code and scanning, global data synchronization, the Internet, extensible markup language, satellite technology, and image processing.

Bar Code and Scanning

Auto identification (ID) systems such as bar coding and electronic scanning were developed to facilitate logistics information collection and exchange. Typical applications include tracking warehouse receipts and retail sales. These ID systems require significant capital investment but replace error-prone and time-consuming paper-based information collection and exchange processes. In fact, increased domestic and international competition is driving shippers, carriers, warehouses, wholesalers, and retailers to develop and utilize auto ID capability to compete in today's marketplace.

Auto ID allows supply chain members to quickly track and communicate movement details with high accuracy and timeliness, so it is fast becoming a fundamental service requirement for freight tracking by carriers. Both consumers and B2B customers expect to be able to track the progress of their shipment using the Web-based system offered by carriers such as United Parcel Service and FedEx.

Bar coding is the placement of computer-readable codes on items, cartons, containers, pallets, and even rail cars. Bar code development and applications are increasing at a very rapid rate. Table 5.2 summarizes the benefits and opportunities available through auto ID

TABLE 5.2
Benefits of Automatic Identification Technologies

Shippers	Warehousing
Improve order preparation and processing	Improved order preparation, processing, and shipment
Eliminate shipping errors	Provide accurate inventory control
Reduce labor time	Customer access to real-time information
Improve record keeping	Access considerations of information security
Reduce physical inventory time	Reduced labor costs
Carriers	**Wholesalers/Retailers**
Freight bill information integrity	Unit inventory precision
Customer access to real time information	Price accuracy at point-of-sale
Improved record keeping of customer shipment activity	Improved register checkout productivity
Shipment traceability	Reduced physical inventory time
Simplified container processing	Increased system flexibility
Monitor incompatible products in vehicles	
Reduced information transfer time	

technologies. While the benefits are obvious, it is not clear which symbologies will be adopted as industry standards. Standardization and flexibility are desirable to accommodate the needs of a wide range of industries, but they also increase cost, making it more difficult for small- and medium-size shippers, carriers, and receivers to implement standardized technologies. Finally, while continued convergence to common standards is likely, surveys indicate that select industries and major shippers will continue to use proprietary codes to maximize their competitive position.[2]

Another key component of auto ID technology is the scanning process, which represents the eyes of a bar code system. A scanner optically collects bar code data and converts it to usable information. There are two types of scanners: handheld and fixed position. Each type can utilize contact or noncontact technology. Handheld scanners are either laser guns (noncontact) or wands (contact). Fixed-position scanners are either automatic scanners (noncontact) or card readers (contact). Contact technologies require the reading device to actually touch the bar code. A contact technology reduces scanning errors but decreases flexibility. Laser gun technology is the most popular scanner technology currently in use, outpacing wands as the most widely installed technology.

Scanner technology has two major applications in logistics. The first is point-of-sale (POS) in retail stores. In addition to ringing up receipts for consumers, retail POS applications provide accurate inventory control at the store level. POS allows precise tracking of each stockkeeping unit (SKU) sold and can be used to facilitate inventory replenishment. In addition to providing accurate resupply and marketing research data, POS can provide more timely strategic benefits to all channel members.

The second logistics scanner application is for materials handling and tracking. Through the use of scanner guns, materials handlers can track product movement, storage location, shipments, and receipts. While this information can be tracked manually, it is very time-consuming and subject to error. Wider usage of scanners in logistical applications will increase productivity and reduce errors. The demand for faster and less-error-prone scanning technology drives rapid changes in the marketplace for applications and technology.

Global Data Synchronization

While the phone, fax, and direct computer connection have enabled information exchange in the past, EDI and the Internet are quickly becoming the standards for effective, accurate, and low-cost information exchange. EDI is defined as direct computer-to-computer exchange of business documents in standard formats to facilitate high-volume transactions. It involves both the capability and practice of communicating information between two organizations electronically instead of via the traditional forms of mail, courier, or even fax.

Communication and information standards are essential for EDI. Communication standards specify technical characteristics necessary for the computer hardware to correctly accomplish the interchange. Communication standards deal with character sets, transmission priority, and speed. Information standards dictate the structure and content of the message. Standards organizations have developed and refined two general standards as well as numerous industry-specific standards in an effort to standardize both communication and information interchange.

EDI Transaction Sets

Communication standards are implemented using transaction sets. A transaction set provides a common standard to facilitate information interchange between partners in a specific

---

[2] For a more detailed discussion regarding current bar code applications, see Helen Richardson, "Bar Codes are Still Getting the Job Done." *Logistics Today* (December 2004), pp. 38–39.

TABLE 5.3
Primary Logistics Industry EDI Standards

UCS (Uniform Communication Standards): grocery
VICS (Voluntary Interindustry Communication Standards Committee): mass merchandisers
WINS (Warehouse Information Network Standards): warehouse operators
TDCC (Transportation Data Coordinating Committee): transportation operators
AIAG (Automotive Industry Action Group): automotive industry

FIGURE 5.4
Value-Added Networks (VANs)
The VAN collects transaction messages and information from a manufacturer and then translates those messages and information into appropriate industry-specific communication standards.

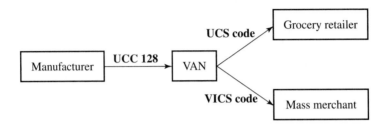

industry and country. Table 5.3 lists the common logistics-related industry transaction standards. For each industry, the transaction set defines the documents that can be transmitted. Documents typically cover common logistics activities such as ordering, warehouse operations, and transportation. Table 5.4 lists the transaction set usage matrix. The transaction set consists of a transaction code (or ID) and is followed by the data. The transaction code, for example, indicates whether the electronic communication is a warehouse shipping order (code 940) or a warehouse stock transfer receipt (code 944). In addition to the transaction code, a transaction contains warehouse number, item number, and quantity.

While applications are migrating toward common standards, there is still conflict regarding the ultimate goal. A single common standard facilitates information interchange between partners in any industry and country, but many firms believe that strategic advantage can be achieved only with proprietary EDI capabilities. Proprietary capabilities allow a firm to offer customized transactions that efficiently meet their unique information requirements.

Many firms resolve this dilemma through the use of value-added networks (VANs). A VAN, illustrated in Figure 5.4, is a common interface between sending and receiving systems. The VAN adds value by managing transactions, translating communication standards, and reducing the number of communication linkages. Transaction management includes broadcast of messages to subsets of suppliers, carriers, or customers and receipt of messages from customers using different communication standards.

The Uniform Code Council (UCC), in partnership with **European Article Numbering (EAN)** International, is the organization responsible for international numbering standards and is committed to developing common global standards for products and transaction sets. Information regarding the status of the council's current initiatives can be found on its website at **www.uc-council.org.** Another source documenting the evolving commercial standards is the Voluntary Interindustry Commerce Standards (VICS) at **www.vics.org.**

Electronic Product Code

EPC (electronic product coding) is an emerging form of product identification. The Auto-ID Center at Massachusetts Institute of Technology, with support from both manufacturers and retailers, collaborated to develop an "intelligent tracking infrastructure" for supply

TABLE 5.4
Transaction Set
Usage Matrix

Source: Adapted from materials provided by Deborah Faragher, Uniform Code Council, Inc.

TS ID	Transaction Set Name	UCS	VICS EDI
102	Associated Data		✓
180	Return Merchandise Authorization and Notification	✓	✓
204	Motor Carrier Load Tender	✓	
210	Motor Carrier Freight Details and Invoice	✓	
214	Transportation Carrier Shipment Status Message	✓	
753	Request for Routing Instructions		✓
754	Routing Instructions		✓
810	Invoice	✓	✓
812	Credit/Debit Adjustment	✓	✓
816	Organizational Relationships	✓	✓
818	Commission Sales Report	✓	
820	Payment Order/Remittance Advice	✓	✓
824	Application Advice	✓	✓
830	Planning Schedule with Release Capability	✓	✓
831	Application Control Totals	✓	✓
832	Price/Sales Catalog		✓
846	Inventory Inquiry/Advice	✓	✓
850	Purchase Order	✓	✓
852	Product Activity Data	✓	✓
853	Routing and Carrier Instructions		✓
855	Purchase Order Acknowledgment	✓	✓
856	Ship Notice/Manifest	✓	✓
857	Shipment and Billing Notice	✓	
860	Purchase Order Change Request—Buyer Initiated		✓
861	Receiving Advice/Acceptance Certificate		✓
864	Text Message	✓	✓
867	Product Transfer and Resale Report	✓	
869	Order Status Inquiry		✓
870	Order Status Report		✓
875	Grocery Products Purchase Order	✓	
876	Grocery Products Purchase Order Change	✓	
877	Manufacturer Coupon Family Code Structure	✓	
878	Product Authorization/De-Authorization	✓	
879	Price Information	✓	
880	Grocery Products Invoice	✓	
881	Manufacturer Coupon Redemption Detail	✓	
882	Direct Store Delivery Summary Information	✓	✓
883	Market Development Fund Allocation	✓	
884	Market Development Fund Settlement	✓	
885	Store Characteristics	✓	
886	Customer Call Reporting	✓	
887	Coupon Notification	✓	
888	Item Maintenance	✓	
889	Promotion Announcement	✓	✓
891	Deduction Research Report	✓	
893	Item Information Request	✓	✓
894	Delivery/Return Base Record	✓	
895	Delivery/Return Acknowledgment and/or Adjustment	✓	
896	Product Dimension Maintenance	✓	
940	Warehouse Shipping Order	✓	✓
944	Warehouse Stock Transfer Receipt Advice	✓	
945	Warehouse Shipping Advice	✓	
947	Warehouse Inventory Adjustment Advice	✓	✓
997	Functional Acknowledgment	✓	✓

chains. The two standards organizations EAN (European Article Number) and UCC (Uniform Code Council), which were developers of previous bar code standards, formed an organization called EPCglobal Inc., which is driving the adoption and implementation of the "EPCglobal Network."

As opposed to the widely used UPC bar codes, which contain only the product make (manufacturer) and model, the EPC contains a number that can be linked to an individual SKU. Each EPC is 96 bits in length and has the capability to represent all products now and into the reasonable future. In addition, EPC accommodates all existing EAN.UCC keys such Serial Shipping Container Code (SSCC) and GTIN (Global Trade Identification Number).

Radio-Frequency Exchange

Radio-frequency data communication (RFDC) technology is used within relatively small areas, such as distribution centers, to facilitate two-way information exchange. A major application is real-time communication with mobile operators such as forklift drivers and order selectors. RFDC allows drivers to have instructions and priorities updated on a real-time basis instead of using a hard copy of instructions printed hours earlier. Real-time or Wi-Fi transmissions guide work flow, offer increased flexibility and responsiveness, and can improve service using fewer resources.[3] Logistics RFDC applications also include two-way communication for warehouse picking, cycle counts, verification, and label printing.

Advanced RFDC capabilities in the form of two-way voice communication are finding their way into logistics warehouse applications. Instead of requiring warehouse operations personnel to interface with a mobile or handheld computer, voice RFDC prompts operators through tasks with audible commands and waits for verbal responses or requests. United Parcel Service uses speech-based RFDC to read zip codes from incoming packages and print routing tickets to guide packages through their sortation facilities. The voice recognition systems are based on keywords and voice patterns of each operator. The primary benefit of voice-based RFDC is an easier operator interface; since keyboard data entry is not required, two hands are available for order picking.[4]

Radio-frequency identification (RFID) is a second form of radio-frequency technology. RFID can be used to identify a container or its contents as it moves through facilities or on transportation equipment. RFID places a coded electronic chip in the container or box. RFID chips can be either active or passive. Active chips continuously emanate radio waves so that product can be located in a warehouse or a retail store, using receivers located throughout the store. Active chip technology is good for locating product in a facility as well as for identifying when it is moving in and out of the facility. Passive chips respond only when they are electronically stimulated by having the product pass through a relatively small gateway or portal that has scanners built in. Since the product must be passed through a gateway for passive chips to operate, these can be used only for tracking product movement in, out, and around a facility. With current technology, the cost of active chips (GEN II) is approximately 10 times that of passive chips because of the need for a battery and larger antenna. As the container or box moves through the supply chain, it can be scanned for an identifying code or even for the list of contents. Retailers are beginning to use RFID to allow entire cartloads of merchandise to be scanned simultaneously. Wal★Mart and other major retailers are requiring that their major suppliers place RFID tags on their cases to facilitate processing in distribution warehouses, receipt at stores, and shelf restocking. While it is too early to assess the impact of RFID applications at the retail level, it is anticipated that placing RFID tags on cases should reduce distribution warehouse and retail handling expense

---

[3] The application of Wi-Fi technology in warehouse operations is further discussed in Chapter 9.

[4] Patti Satterfied, "Voice-Directed Systems Boost Warehouse Picking," *Parcel Shipping & Distribution,* September 1999, pp. 22–4.

and reduce stockouts. The U.S. Department of Defense uses RFID to list the contents of pallets so that they can be tracked as they are loaded on transportation equipment or move through facilities.

Typically, information on a bar code is captured via a fixed or handheld scanner device. The EPC-based identification system, on the other hand, will use RFID tags in conjunction with readers in order to collect product information. The RFID tags are miniature circuits that contain the EPC code. A reader can transmit a request for product identification that will stimulate the tag on a responding item to transmit the identification number on the tag back to the reader. The identification number on the reader can then be transmitted to a computer, which can identify both the specific item as well as physical location. Information about a product in a warehouse, store, or any place within transmission range can then be shared and updated in real time across a network. EPC read speed and lack of requiring line-of-sight reading are major advantages over bar code scanners.

Internet

Widespread availability of the Internet and standardized communication interfaces offered through browsers such as Netscape and Internet Explorer have substantially expanded the opportunities and capability to exchange information between firms of all sizes. The Internet is quickly becoming the supply chain information transmission device of choice for exchanging forecasts, orders, inventory status, product updates, and shipment information. In conjunction with a server and a browser, the Internet offers a standard approach for order entry, order status inquiry, and shipment tracking. An Ohio State University survey predicts the Internet will carry 20 percent of customer orders by the year 2010.[5]

The availability of the Internet has also enabled the development of the exchange portal, a communication medium that has significant supply chain implications. An exchange portal is an infomediary that facilitates horizontal and vertical information exchange between supply chain partners. Figure 5.5 illustrates an exchange portal designed to facilitate communication between supply chain participants. The facilitating firm can provide information regarding raw material requirements, product availability, and price changes and allow the marketplace to react by placing bids or orders.

[5] The Ohio State University, "Careers Patterns Survey," 2004; available under "careers" at the Council of Supply Chain Management Professionals website, **www.cscmp.org**.

FIGURE 5.5
Single-Firm
Exchange Portal

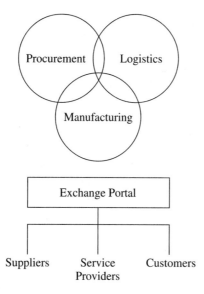

FIGURE 5.6 **Electronics Industry Exchange Portal**

Source: Reprinted with permission from e2Open.

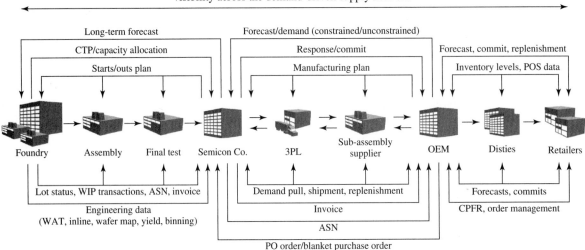

Integrating critical information from each tier and providing exception visibility across the demand-driven supply network

A second type of exchange portal is industry based. It facilitates communication between all participants within an industry and can substantially reduce transaction costs. Figure 5.6 illustrates the exchange portal that the electronics industry has developed to facilitate communication between the original equipment manufacturers and their multiple tiers of suppliers. This portal offers a common framework for exchanging information, including design information, proposal requests, commodity availability, bids, and schedules. While the information can be made available to all interested parties, it is also possible to restrict information availability. There is increasing fear that industry portal collaborations might increase the potential of monopolistic practices and trade restraints. The Federal Trade Commission (FTC) can be expected to play an increasing role in the evolution of the exchange portals, particularly for B2B activities.[6]

A third type of exchange portal is cross-industry-based and is designed to facilitate communication between firms that have common interests in commodities and services. Figure 5.7 illustrates a cross-industry exchange portal for manufacturers, suppliers, service providers, and customers. When one of the member firms has a need for raw material, product, or service, it can access the exchange portal to determine availability and potential price. Similarly, when one of the member firms has excess product or service capacity, such availability can be posted on the portal to solicit interest or a possible bid by one of the exchange members.

The Internet and the exchange portal have advanced supply chain communication from one-to-one or limited capability to a one-to-many environment capable of being extended to a many-to-many capability. The result is that extended Internet communication is a reality that offers substantial challenge in terms of exploiting widely available information.

One of the major challenges to the wide adoption of exchange portals is the definition and acceptance of online catalogs. Much like the paper version, an online catalog contains a listing of the products and services offered along with their descriptions and specifications. A catalog that is consistent across participating firms is critical to facilitate effective comparison of products and services across firms. For example, a firm desiring to purchase

---

[6] Kim S. Nash, "Really Check," *Computerworld,* June 5, 2000, pp. 58–59.

FIGURE 5.7
Cross-Industry
Exchange Portal

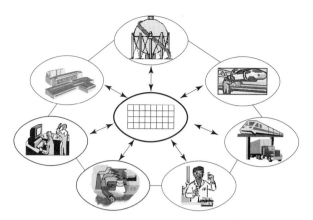

a simple T-shirt from a portal would like all the T-shirt suppliers on that portal to have a similarly formatted entry describing the shirt, its coloring, its contents, as well as other minute details so that the customer can make an effective comparison. While customers prefer consistent catalogs, suppliers prefer to use a catalog as a differentiator and are thus reluctant to deviate from their proprietary format. To facilitate information sharing and exchange, the Voluntary Interindustry Commerce Standards (VICS) and Collaborative Planning, Forecasting, and Replenishment (CPFR) are actively promoting common and consistent catalog definitions and standards.

Extensible Markup Language

Extensible Markup Language (XML) is a flexible computer language that facilitates information transfer between a wide range of applications and is readily interpretable by humans. It was published in 1998 by the World Wide Web Consortium to facilitate information transfer between systems, databases, and Web browsers. Since EDI is very structured, the setup cost and required expertise are relatively high, limiting applications to situations involving high transaction volumes. XML is emerging as the information transfer medium between firms and service providers that do not have transaction volumes to justify EDI. XML facilitates communication by breaking down many information technology barriers that have constrained EDI adoption.

A basic XML message consists of three components: the actual information being transmitted, data tags, and a document type definition (DTD). The data tag is a key feature, as it defines the data being transmitted. For example, in a shipment XML, the tag for address would be address and might appear <address>123 Main St.</address>. The tags tell computers what the data between the brackets are and where the data should go in a database or Web page. The use of common terms and the lack of sequencing requirements make XML transactions much easier to use than EDI. The XML DTD tells the computer what document format to refer to when decoding a message. A DTD is essentially a template that maps out a standard form, its tags, and their relation in a database. For example, there would be separate schema for customer orders, advanced shipping notifications, or transportation documentation.

In situations characterized by low volume, XML is superior to EDI for three reasons. First, it is not expensive to install. It is easy to design an application and requires much less time to implement. Second, XML is easy to maintain because it can be easily converted to HyperText Markup Language (HTML), the language of Web browsers. This makes it much easier to modify and share data between applications. Finally, XML is more flexible, allowing for broad applications and quick definition and extension of standards.[7]

---

[7] For more detail, see Gordon Forsyth, "XML: Breaking Down IT Barriers in Logistics," *American Shipper,* June 2000, pp. 20–6.

FIGURE 5.8
Logistics Satellite
Communication
Applications

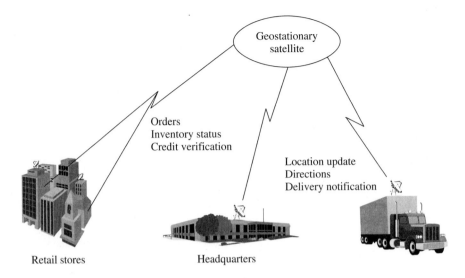

Satellite

Satellite technology allows communication across an expansive geographic area such as a region or even the world. The technology is similar to that of microwave dishes used for home television in areas outside the reach of cable. Figure 5.8 illustrates two-way communication between corporate headquarters, vehicles, and remote operational locations.

Satellite communication provides a fast and high-volume channel for information movement. Schneider National, a nationwide truckload carrier, uses communication dishes mounted on its trucks to enable two-way communication between drivers and their dispatchers. Such real-time interaction provides up-to-date information regarding location and delivery information, allowing dispatchers to redirect trucks according to need or congestion. Retail chains also use satellite communication to quickly transmit sales information back to headquarters. Wal★Mart uses daily sales figures to drive store replenishment and to provide input to marketing regarding local sales patterns.

Image Processing

Image processing utilizes facsimile (fax) and optical-scanning technology to transmit and store freight bill information, as well as other supporting documents such as proof of delivery receipts (POD) or bills of lading (BOL). The rationale for this service is that timely customer shipment information is almost as important as delivering the goods on time. As freight is delivered to customers, support documentation is sent to image processing locations, electronically scanned, and logged into the system.

Electronic images of the documents are then transmitted to a central data base where they are stored. By the next day, customers can access the documents through computer linkages or a phone call to their service representative. Customer requests for a hard copy of a document can be filled within minutes by a facsimile transmission. Customer benefits include more accurate billing, faster response from carrier personnel, and easy access to documentation. The carrier also benefits because the system eliminates the need to file paper documents, reduces the chance of loss, and provides improved credibility with customers.

Satellite technology, RF, and image processing require substantial capital investment prior to achieving significant returns. Experience has shown, however, the primary benefit of these communication technologies is not always lower cost but improved customer service. Improved service is provided in the form of more timely and accurate order entry, quicker shipment tracing, and faster transfer of sales and inventory information. There will be increased demand for these communication technology applications as customers observe the competitive benefits of real-time information transfer.

Rationale for ERP Implementation

Enterprise Resource Planning (ERP) and enterprise execution systems are the major software components of logistics information systems. ERP provides the database and the transaction capability to initiate, track, monitor, and report on customer and replenishment orders. ERP systems provide firms with information consistency, economies of scale, and integration. ERP system design includes the central database and application modules to facilitate supply chain, financial, and human resource management. Supply chain system design includes components for planning/coordination, operations, and inventory deployment. The planning/coordination component manages firm and supply chain resources, including production, storage, and transportation resources. The operations component controls transaction processing to initiate, manage, fulfill, and ship both customer and replenishment orders. Inventory deployment manages firm and, increasingly, supply chain inventory resources.

Enterprise execution systems provide the interface between the ERP and the day-to-day operations with the customer, transportation, and the warehouse. Customer relationship management systems offer information regarding the firm's activity level and performance with key customers. Transportation management systems initiate shipments and record movements to monitor the firm's transportation performance and cost. Warehouse management systems initiate warehouse activities, control material handling equipment, monitor labor performance, and report warehouse performance levels and cost.

When firms introduced extensive computing to control and monitor operations and financials in the early 1970s, most of the development was completed with minimal consideration for integration. The financial and accounting systems were typically introduced first, followed by some type of sales and order management system. When additional functionality was needed, other applications were developed or purchased. These added modules frequently used inconsistent processes, conflicting assumptions, and redundant data. In some cases functional systems were developed internally by the firm to fit internal work processes. Because of the need for increased integration and to take advantage of relatively inexpensive advanced information technology, many firms began to reinvest in their enterprise systems during the 1990s. At this point, most if not all of the Fortune 1000 firms either have implemented or are in the process of implementing an ERP system and there is substantial growth potential in the market for ERP systems for small and midlevel firms. Regardless of the size of the firm, such investments are typically rationalized through three factors: consistency, economies of scale, and integration.

Consistency

As discussed earlier, many firms or divisions developed legacy systems to meet their own specific requirements and processes. This was also true for international divisions as the firm extended markets and operations globally. Similarly, the many acquisitions and mergers that occurred over the last three decades brought together firms with incompatible legacy systems. The result was many different systems that offered different and, in many cases, inconsistent processing. One manager from a consumer products multinational reported that he had to look into 15 different computer systems to determine the sales and inventory situation for the company's South American subsidiaries![8] Table 5.5 illustrates a

---

[8] Discussion with a Johnson & Johnson logistics manager.

TABLE 5.5
Typical Legacy
System Status

	Region/Division A	Region/Division B	Region/Division C	Region/Division D
Financial	FS1	FS2	FS3	FS4
Human Resource	HR1	HR2	HR3	HR4
Order Management	OM1	OM2	OM2	OM3
Warehouse Management	WM1	WM1	WM2	WM3
Materials Planning	MP1	MP1	MP2	MP2

situation in which each division or region has a different financial (FS), human resource (HR), order management (OM), warehouse management (WM), and materials planning (MP) system. The table indicates how each region or division might have a different software or hardware platform for various supply chain and other applications. Region A has implemented Financial System 1 while Region B has implemented Financial System 2 because of its currency capabilities. Similarly divergent systems decisions are often made for other regions or divisions. The table illustrates the situation in many firms where some system components are common across multiple divisions while others, such as order management, are unique for each division. The result is inconsistent and conflicting information and multiple systems that are difficult to maintain and complex to interpret as the timing and processes may be different for each.

Thus, the first major ERP objective is to create a system that utilizes consistent data and processes for firm regions and divisions globally. In the typical application, the data is resident in a common data warehouse that can be accessed globally. In addition, the data can be modified with appropriate security and controls using transactions available in multiple languages. The transactions to initiate a specific supply chain activity are implemented using common assumptions and timing. Likewise, consistent processes allow global customers to use the same order entry procedure, for example, regardless of where they enter the order. Such a unified perspective offers senior management a consistent integrated view of the firm and operating management and ease of use by customers.

Economies of Scale

As firms merged and expanded globally, management made increasing demands to take advantage of global scale economies through resource rationalization. Similarly, customers began looking for suppliers that could provide product globally using consistent system capabilities and interfaces to take advantage of scale economies. ERP offers firms potential economies of scale in several ways. First, a single centralized processor or network of decentralized processors with common configured hardware offers the potential for substantial procurement and maintenance scale economies.

Second, the centralized ERP approach offers significant software scale economies since only a limited number of software licenses are necessary with all divisions and regions using the same application. While the initial software license cost might be substantial, the license and maintenance fees for the single ERP application should be less than the multiple copies required for each division or region. However, the real scale economy benefits result from the reduced personnel required to implement and maintain a common ERP system. Multiple divisional or regional systems require many individuals with varying hardware and software expertise to implement, maintain, and modify each application. Since some knowledge has limited transferability across hardware and software platforms, the expertise of the individuals typically cannot be used effectively. While potential scale economies for ERP expertise do exist, they may not be apparent today as a relatively limited number of individuals have developed extensive skills.

Finally, the centralized ERP approach increases the potential for a multidivisional firm to implement shared resources and services across divisions or even regions. The ability to review production, storage, or transportation resource requirements of multiple divisions in the common system increases the potential for sharing critical resources. The integrated information facilitates effective use of common suppliers, production facilities, storage facilities, or transportation equipment, resulting in substantial potential for negotiating and operating economies. While there is limited evidence that current ERP implementations are yielding these scale economies, the benefits will likely begin to accrue as the relatively recent implementations stabilize.

Integration

The final ERP benefit is enhanced system integration both within the firm and enterprise and between suppliers and customers. Internal integration results from a common integrated database and implementation of common processes across divisions and regions. Common ERP components include supply chain, financial, service, human resources, and reporting. Such commonality offers the capability to merge processes and provide major customers with a common and consistent interface with the firm. Such integration also results in standard financial practices across business units. The standardized interfaces offered by many ERP systems also facilitate external communication with supply chain partners. For example, many firms in the automobile and chemical industries are standardizing on the ERP system offered by SAP. The major manufacturers are then asking their suppliers to interface with their SAP database to obtain requirements data and to provide release schedules. Such information and process integration substantially enhances supply chain information sharing, which reduces uncertainty within the firm and between supply chain partners.

Most industry analysts believe that an ERP system should be thought of as a necessary cost of doing business. One ERP provider noted:

> I think most people would have a hard time providing an ROI number for an ERP system. A fact of business is that you might be able to run a $10 million company on a PC, but if you want to grow to be a $50 million company, you need an ERP. The trick is to purchase a system that will scale up as you grow.[9]

The number of ERP implementations has slowed among large firms as most absorb and refine what they have implemented. In contrast, smaller firms are just beginning their investment and implementation.

A new generation of ERP systems is evolving to provide additional integration, particularly with customers. These systems combine traditional ERP with Customer Relationship Management (CRM) systems to better integrate the requirements of key customers with the firm's supply chain plans and operations. The major improvement offered through these ERP advancements is the external connectivity so critical for supply chain collaboration. It is also becoming more common for these integrated applications to be accessed via the Internet, thus providing a common global interface.[10]

ERP System Design

Figure 5.9 illustrates an ERP system's major modules. The system core is the central database or information warehouse where all information is maintained to facilitate access to common and consistent data by all modules. Surrounding the database are the functional

---

[9] Anonymous, "Who's Using ERP," *Modern Materials Handling* 54, no. 13 (November 1999), pp. 14–18.

[10] Michel Roberto, "ERP Gets Redefined," *Information Technology for Manufacturing,* February 2001, pp. 36–44.

FIGURE 5.9
ERP Architecture

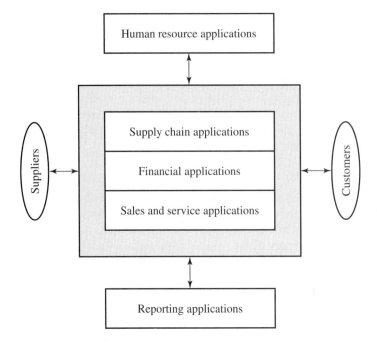

modules that initiate and coordinate business activities. Although total ERP benefits can best be achieved when all functions are integrated into a common application, many firms elect to implement systems using a modular approach to spread resource requirements and minimize risk, as a limited number of firm functions are in transition at any time.

The **central database** is the relational information repository for the entire ERP system. The central database is described as **relational** because it relates or links information regarding operational entities so that there is minimal information redundancy. Over time, information redundancy usually leads to inaccuracy because one reference to a data item is eventually changed without a comparable change in the other reference. For example, if a customer address is contained in two different locations in the database, it is likely that eventually one reference will be changed if the customer moves but the second reference may be forgotten. At that point, the database would no longer be consistent and all references to the second address would be incorrect. Although the central database is extensive and can contain millions of data items in numerous files, eight major data files are critical to logistics operations: (1) customer file, (2) product-price file, (3) supplier file, (4) order file, (5) bill-of-materials file, (6) purchase order file, (7) inventory file, and (8) history file.

The **customer file** contains information describing the firm's customers. Each entry defines one customer, including name, address, billing information, ship-to location, company contact, price list, terms of sale, and special instructions. A common customer file is helpful particularly when multiple divisions of the firm serve the same customer.

The **product-price file** contains the information describing the products and services offered by the firm. Specific entries include product number, description, physical characteristics, purchase source or manufacturing location, references to equivalent products or updates, and standard cost data. The product-price file or related file also contains information regarding prices and quantity breaks. Product-price file maintenance is increasingly challenging because of shorter product life cycles and more frequent price changes.

The **supplier file** lists the firm's suppliers for materials and services. Specific entries include supplier number, supplier name, address, transportation and receiving information, and payables instructions. A common supplier file is critical to achieve purchasing economies through supplier rationalization and consolidation.

The **order file** contains the information regarding all open orders in some stage of processing or fulfillment by the firm. Each order represents a current or potential request by a customer to ship product. The order file contains the customer number and name, requested receipt date, and the list of products and quantities that are being ordered. The order file is increasingly being required to include special shipping and packaging requests for unique customers. The system must also increasingly accept orders from multiple sources, including EDI and the Internet, as well as by internal order entry.

The **bill-of-materials file** describes how raw materials are combined for finished products. For example, a simple bill-of-materials for an automobile would indicate that one car requires one body, one chassis, four seats, one engine, one transaxle, and four tires. Although these product relationships are typically used in manufacturing, it is becoming increasingly important for logistics as well. Logistics operations are beginning to use bills of materials to facilitate packaging, customization, and kitting in distribution center operations.

The **purchase order (PO) file** is similar to the order file except that it contains the records of purchase orders that have been placed on suppliers. The purchase order may be for raw material to support product or for MRO (Maintenance, Repair, and Operating) supplies necessary to support operations and administration. MRO items are not directly included as finished products sold by the firm. Specific purchase order file information includes purchase order number, supplier number and name, request date, ship-to location, transportation mode and carrier, and a list of the items to be purchased and the corresponding quantity. Other critical requirements of the PO file are the product specifications, delivery requirements, and contracted price.

The **inventory file** records the physical inventory or quantity of product that the firm has available or may be available in the future according to current production schedules. The file also documents the physical location of the product within the material storage and facility; the product status in terms of available to ship, damaged, quality hold, or on-hold for a key customer; and lot numbers for products that must be tracked. Specific inventory file information includes product number, facility location, storage location, and inventory quantity for each product status.

The **history file** documents the firm's order and purchase order history to facilitate management reporting, budget and decision analyses, and forecasting. In essence, this file contains summaries of the customer orders that have been filled and the purchase orders that have been received.

Supply Chain Information System Design

The supply chain information system is the backbone of modern logistics operations. In the past, this infrastructure focused on initiating and controlling activities required to take, process, and ship customer orders. For today's enterprises to remain competitive, the role of information infrastructure must be extended to include requirements planning, management control, decision analysis, and integration with other members of the supply chain. While Figure 5.9 illustrated the supply chain applications relative to the other ERP applications, it did not describe the detailed flow of supply chain information and product through the process modules. Figure 5.10 illustrates the information flow and the relationship between key process modules. The key processes initiate, monitor, and measure activities

FIGURE 5-10
Supply Chain System Architecture

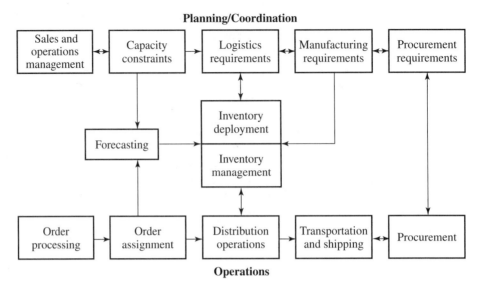

required to fulfill customer and replenishment orders. These processes take two forms. The first are the planning and coordination processes to produce and deploy inventory. The second are the operating processes to receive, process, ship, and invoice customer orders.

Planning and coordination include the processes necessary to schedule and coordinate procurement, production, and logistics resource allocation throughout the enterprise. Specific components include definition of sales and operations objectives, rationalization of capacity constraints, and determination of logistics allocation, manufacturing, and procurement requirements.

Operations include the processes necessary to manage customer order fulfillment, including order processing, inventory assignment, warehouse operations, transportation operations, and procurement coordination. These processes are required for both customer and replenishment orders. Customer orders reflect demands placed by enterprise customers. Replenishment orders initiate finished goods movement between manufacturing and distribution facilities.

Inventory deployment and management is the interface between planning/coordination and operations that controls the cycle and safety inventory stock whenever a make-to-order (MTO) or assemble-to-order (ATO) strategy is not possible. When an enterprise is able to utilize an MTO manufacturing strategy, the planning/coordination and operations processes essentially mirror each other. For example, when an MTO strategy is possible, it may not be necessary to schedule anticipatory raw materials and production or maintain buffer inventory.

Planning/Coordination

Supply chain system **planning/coordination components** form the information system foundation for manufacturers and merchandisers. These components define core activities that guide enterprise resource allocation and performance from procurement to product delivery.

As illustrated in Figure 5.10, planning/coordination includes materials planning processes both within the enterprise and between supply chain partners. The specific components are (1) sales and operations management, (2) capacity constraints, (3) logistics requirements, (4) manufacturing requirements, and (5) procurement requirements.

Sales and Operations Plans (S&OP)

S&OP represents one of the major enterprise integrators of sales, marketing, and financial goals. These strategic objectives are typically developed for a multiyear planning horizon that often includes quarterly updates. Sales and marketing's strategic objectives define target markets, product development, promotions, other marketing mix plans, and the role of logistics value-added activities such as service levels or capabilities. The objectives include customer scope, breadth of products and services, planned promotions, and desired performance levels. Sales and marketing goals are the customer service policies and objectives that define logistics and supply chain activity and performance targets. The performance targets include service availability, capability, and quality elements discussed earlier. Financial strategic objectives define revenue, financial and activity levels, and corresponding expenses, as well as capital and human resource constraints.

The combination of sales, marketing, and financial objectives defines the scope of markets, products, services, and activity levels that logistics and supply chain managers must accommodate during the planning horizon. Specific goals include projected annual or quarterly activity levels such as revenue, shipments, and case volume. Events that must be considered include product promotions, new product introductions, market rollouts, and acquisitions. Ideally, the marketing and financial plans should be integrated and consistent, as inconsistencies result in poor service, excess inventory, or failure to meet financial goals.

The S&OP process must include both long- and short-term elements. The long-term element focuses on annual and quarterly plans with the objective of coordinating the marketing and financial plans to achieve enterprise goals. While supply chain and logistics operations are not the major focus, they do merit some consideration, as planners must ensure that there is enough aggregate production, storage, and movement capacity available. The short-term element focuses on weekly and daily plans with the objective of coordination supply chain and logistics resources to ensure that specific customer requests can be satisfied. While the orientation of this process in Figure 5.10 suggests that the S&OP provides one-way input into the capacity constraint process, it is actually iterative as the plan and capacity must be jointly resolved so that the plan results can be maximized within the firm's internal or contracted constraints.

The combination of sales, marketing, and financial objectives provides direction for other enterprise plans that are operationalized in the form of an S&OP. While the process of establishing strategic objectives is, by nature, unstructured and wide-ranging, it must develop and communicate a plan detailed enough to be coordinated and operationalized through the S&OP. This process is more fully discussed in Chapter 11.

Capacity Constraints

Capacity constraints are logistics and manufacturing capacity limitations imposed by internal and external manufacturing, warehousing, and transportation resource constraints. On the basis of the activity levels defined by S&OP, these constraints determine material bottlenecks and guide resource allocation to meet market demands. For each product, capacity constraints influence the where, when, and how much for production, storage, and movement. The constraints consider aggregate limitations such as periodic production, movement, and storage capacities.

Capacity problems can be resolved by resource acquisition or speculation/postponement of production or delivery. Capacity adjustments can be made by acquisition or alliances such as contract manufacturing or facility leasing. Speculation reduces bottlenecks by anticipating production capacity requirements through prior scheduling or contract manufacturing. Postponement delays production and shipment until specific requirements are known and capacity can be allocated. It may be necessary to offer customer incentives such as discounts or allowances to postpone customer delivery. The capacity limitations time-phase the enterprise's S&OP by taking into account facility, financial, and human resource limitations. These constraints have a major influence on logistics, manufacturing, and procurement schedules.

Capacity limitations decompose the enterprise's aggregate operating plan to weekly or daily logistics requirements and determine the level of monthly or weekly production for each manufacturing location. Capacity flexibility depends on the nature of the product and leadtime. For the long term, there is usually substantial flexibility since a full range of postponement, speculation, outsourcing, and acquisition strategies may be used. In the short term, however, such as within the current week, there is limited flexibility since resources are generally committed. The ability to jointly consider the enterprise requirements and constraints is critical to effective supply chain planning and coordination. The best enterprises typically demonstrate a high level of integration across all planning/coordination components. APS systems, discussed in detail in Chapter 11, offer the information support to effectively consider these integrated demand and capacity constraints.

Logistics Requirements

Logistics requirements include time-phased facility, equipment, labor, and inventory resources necessary to accomplish the logistics mission. For example, the logistics requirement component schedules shipments of finished product from manufacturing plants to warehouses and ultimately to retailers. The shipment quantity is calculated as the difference between customer requirements and inventory level. Logistics requirements are often implemented using **Distribution Requirements Planning (DRP)** as an inventory management and process control tool. Future requirements are based on forecasts, customer orders, and promotions. Forecasts are based on sales and marketing input in conjunction with historical activity levels. Customer orders include current orders, future committed orders, and contracts. Consideration of promotional activity is particularly important in planning logistics requirements, since it often represents a large percentage of variation in volume and has a large impact on capacity. Current inventory status is product available to ship. Figure 5.11 illustrates the computation for determining periodic logistics requirements.

Specifically, for each planning period, day, week, or month, the sum of forecast plus future customer orders plus promotional volume represents period demand. It is not easy to determine the percentage of the forecasted volume that is accounted for by known customer orders, so some judgment is necessary. Typically, period demand is actually a combination of the three, since current forecasts may incorporate some future orders and promotional volume. In determining period demand, it is important that the overlap between forecast, future customer orders, and promotions be considered. Period logistics requirements are then determined as the period demand less inventory-on-hand plus planned receipts. Using this form, each period would ideally end with zero inventory available, so planned receipts would exactly equal period demand. While perfect coordination of

FIGURE 5.11
Logistics
Requirements

+   Forecasts (sales, marketing, input, histories, accounts)

+   Customer orders (current orders, future committed orders, contracts)

+   Promotions (promotion, advertising plans)

=   Period demand

−   Inventory-on-hand

−   Planned receipts

Period logistics requirements

demand and supply is ideal from an inventory management perspective, it may not be possible or the best strategy for the firm.

Logistics requirements must be synchronized within both capacity constraints and manufacturing capabilities to achieve optimal system performance; otherwise, finished goods inventory accumulates at the end of the production line.

Manufacturing Requirements

Manufacturing requirements schedule production resources and attempt to resolve day-to-day capacity bottlenecks within the materials management system. Primary bottlenecks result from raw material shortages or daily capacity limitations. Manufacturing requirements determine the Master Production Schedule (MPS) and Materials Requirements Plan (MRP II). The MPS defines weekly or daily production and machine schedules. Given the MPS, MRP II time-phases the requisition and arrival of materials and components to support the desired manufacturing plan. Although this discussion presents S&OP, capacity constraints, logistics requirements, and manufacturing requirements serially, they often must operate iteratively. This is particularly true for enterprises utilizing demand flow or market-paced manufacturing strategies. These strategies coordinate production schedules directly with market demands or orders and reduce the need for extended forecasts or planning. In a sense, demand flow or market-paced manufacturing strategies design all production as make-to-order and thus totally integrate logistics and manufacturing requirements.

Within limits, the Dell model of MTO computers illustrates a process that matches manufacturing with demand. However, even the Dell model must operate within capacity constraints within short time horizons.

Procurement Requirements

Procurement requirement modules schedule material purchase order releases, shipments, and receipts. Procurement requirements build on capacity constraints, logistics requirements, and manufacturing requirements to determine long-term material requirements and release schedules. The requirement and release schedule is then used for purchasing negotiation, contracting, coordination of transportation equipment, and arrival scheduling.

While each planning/coordination component can and frequently does operate independently, such independence often leads to inconsistencies that result in excess manufacturing and logistics inventory as well as operating inefficiencies. It was not uncommon for enterprises to have different forecasts for each functional module since each was controlled by a separate organizational function. For example, sales and marketing may develop high forecasts to drive the S&OP process to motivate the sales force, while logistics may plan on more conservative forecasts. Similarly, differences between logistics, manufacturing, and procurement forecasts resulted in inconsistencies between product acquisition, production scheduling, and logistics deployment, which in turn gave rise to unnecessary safety stocks to buffer independent operations. Integrated consideration of S&OP with capacity constraints, logistics requirements, manufacturing requirements, and procurement facilitates the firm's ability to meet specific customer requirements while minimizing the required resources.

Historically, the individual planning/coordination processes had limited ability to plan within overall capacity constraints. Each planning process was essentially uncapacitated. In essence, the initial planning process did not hold requirements, production, distribution, and transportation resources to any capacity constraints. Once the uncapacitated process was complete, heuristic processes were used to attempt to fit the demands within existing supply chain capacity constraints. Eventually, more sophisticated planning tools were developed for each of the planning/coordination processes, resulting in a more direct consideration of resource capacity. However, capacity consideration seldom extended beyond the individual functional processes. For example, manufacturing developed a plan that was generally within its resource constraints and logistics did the same. But the resulting integrated plan seldom reflected the appropriate trade-offs between the two functional areas.

Enterprises are improving requirements and capacity coordination by enhancing forecast consistency and more integrated capacity consideration, resulting in lower inventories and better resource utilization. Increased coordination can be achieved through the use of common databases and forecasts, more frequent information exchange, and more sophisticated analysis tools. High-achieving logistics enterprises use planning/coordination integration as a major source of improved effectiveness.

Operations

Coordinated, integrated **operations information systems** are also essential for supply chain competitiveness. Coordination and integration facilitate smooth and consistent customer and replenishment order information flow throughout the enterprise and offer current order status visibility. Integrated information sharing reduces delays, errors, and resource requirements. The operations processes required for customer order fulfillment and to coordinate the receipt of purchase orders are (1) order processing, (2) order assignment, (3) warehouse operations, (4) transportation, and (5) procurement.

Order Processing

Order processing is the entry point for customer orders and inquiries. It allows entry and maintenance of customer orders by using communication technologies such as mail, phone, fax, EDI, and the Internet. As orders or inquiries are received, order processing enters and retrieves required information, edits for appropriate values, and retains acceptable orders for assignment. Order processing can also offer information regarding inventory availability and delivery dates to establish and confirm customer expectations. Order processing, in conjunction with customer service representatives, forms the primary interface between the customer and the ERP or legacy system.

Table 5.6 lists primary order processing functionality. It includes entry for blanket, electronic, and manual orders. Blanket orders are large orders that reflect demand over an extended time period such as a quarter or year. Future shipments against blanket orders are triggered by individual order releases. Order processing creates and maintains the customer and replenishment order base that initiates remaining operations components.

Order Assignment

Order assignment allocates available inventory to open customer and replenishment orders. Assignment may take place in real time, as orders are received, or in a batch mode. Batch mode means that orders are grouped for periodic processing such as by day or shift. While real-time allocation is more responsive, a batch process provides the firm with more control over situations when inventory is low. For example, in a batch process, order assignment can be designed to allocate stock from current inventory only or from scheduled production capacity. The operational system is more responsive if it allows inventory assignment from scheduled production quantities or capacity. Assignment of production quantities is referred to as using available-to-promise (ATP) inventory, while assignment of production capacity refers to capable-to-promise (CTP) inventory. However, there is a trade-off, since assigning scheduled production capacity reduces the firm's ability to reschedule production. The best order assignment applications operate interactively in conjunction with order processing to generate an order solution that satisfies customer

TABLE 5.6 Operations System Functionality

Order Processing	Order Assignment	Inventory Management	Warehouse Operations	Transportation and Shipping	Procurement
Order entry (manual, electronic, blanket)	Create blanket order	Forecast analysis and modeling	Assign and track storage locations	Carrier selection	Match and pay
Credit check	Generate invoice	Forecast data maintenance and updates	Inventory cycle counting	Carrier scheduling	Open order review
Inventory availability	Generate order selection documents	Forecast parameter selection	Labor scheduling	Dispatching	Purchase order entry
Order acknowledgement	Inventory allocation	Forecast technique selection	Equipment scheduling	Document preparation	Purchase order maintenance
Order modification	Process blanket order	Inventory parameter selection	Lot control	Freight payment	Purchase order receipt
Order pricing	Release reserved inventory	Inventory simulation and testing	Order selection, location, replenishment	Performance measurement	Purchase order status
Order status inquiry	Reassign order source	Inventory requirements planning	Receiving	Shipment consolidation and routing	Quote request
Price and discount extension	Release blanket order	Promotion data integration	Putaway	Shipment rating	Requirements communication
Promotion check	Verify shipment	Replenishment order build, release, and scheduling	Storage	Shipment scheduling	Schedule receipt appointment
Returns processing		Define service objectives	Performance measurement	Shipment tracing and expediting	Supplier history
Service management				Vehicle loading	

requirements within enterprise resource constraints. In this type of operational environment, the customer service representative and the customer interact to determine the combination of products, quantities, and performance cycle length that is acceptable for both parties. Possible solutions when there is conflict in order assignment include delivery date adjustments, product substitutions, or shipment from an alternative source.

Table 5.6 lists typical order assignment functionality, which includes inventory allocation, back-order creation and processing, order selection document generation, and order verification. Order selection documents, in paper or electronic form, direct distribution operations to select an order from the distribution center or warehouse and pack it for shipment. The customer or replenishment order, with its allocated inventory and corresponding order selection material, links order assignment with distribution center physical operations.

Warehouse Operations

Warehouse operations incorporate processes to guide physical activities, including product receipt, material movement and storage, and order selection. For this reason, they are often termed inventory control or warehouse management systems and sometimes warehouse locator systems, referring to the capability to track inventory storage locations in warehouses. Warehouse operations direct all material handling activities using a combination of batch and real-time assignments. In a batch environment, the warehouse operations system develops a "to do" list of instructions or tasks to guide each material handler in the warehouse. Material handlers are the individuals who operate equipment such as forklifts. In a real-time environment, information-directed technologies such as bar coding, radio-frequency communication, and automated handling equipment operate interactively to reduce the elapsed time between decision and action. The real-time information-directed materials handling technologies, discussed in detail in Chapter 10, also must interface directly with the warehouse operations process to provide operational flexibility and reduce internal performance cycle time requirements.

Table 5.6 lists typical warehouse operation functionality. In addition to directing warehouse operations and activities, the functionality must also plan operating requirements and measure performance. Operations planning includes personnel and resource scheduling, including staff, equipment, and facility. Performance measurement includes developing personnel and equipment productivity reports.

Transportation and Shipping

A Transportation Management System (TMS) plans, executes, and manages transport and movement functions. The TMS includes shipment planning and scheduling, shipment consolidation, shipment notification, transport documentation generation, and carrier management. These processes facilitate efficient transport resource utilization as well as effective carrier management.

A unique characteristic of the TMS is that it often involves three parties—shipper, carrier, and consignee (recipient). To effectively manage the process, a basic level of information integration must exist. Information sharing requires standardized data formats for transport documents. In the United States, the Transportation Data Coordinating Committee (TDCC) and VICS have initiated and refined the standardization of transport document formats.

Table 5.6 lists transportation and shipping functionality. The TMS generates the documentation to release the order for shipment and measures the firm's ability to satisfactorily deliver the order. Historically, the TMS focused on document generation and rate tracking. Transport documents include manifests and bills of lading, specifically discussed in Chapter 8; rates are the carrier charges incurred for product movement. The large numbers of shipments made by most enterprises require an automated and exception-driven TMS that can reduce errors and report performance. With the increased opportunity to enhance performance through better transport management, contemporary TMS functionality emphasizes performance monitoring, rate auditing, routing and scheduling, invoicing, reporting, and decision analyses. Advanced TMS applications incorporate increased planning and performance measurement capability and are being termed enterprise execution systems.

Procurement

Procurement manages purchase order (PO) preparation, modification, and release and tracks vendor performance and compliance as well. Although procurement systems have not traditionally been considered part of logistics systems, the importance of integrating procurement with logistics schedules is critical to facilitate the coordination of material receipt, facility capacity, and transportation backhaul.

For integrated supply chain management, procurement must track and coordinate receiving and shipping activities to optimize facility, transport, and personnel scheduling. For example, since loading and unloading docks are often a critical facility resource, an effective procurement system should coordinate the use of the same carrier for both deliveries and shipments. This capability requires the enterprise system to have both receipt and shipment visibility. Supply chain system integration can be further enhanced through electronic integration with suppliers. Table 5.6 lists procurement functionality. A state-of-the-art procurement system provides plans, directs activities, and measures performance, coordinating inbound and outbound activity movement.

Operational systems, typically, are well integrated, but it is necessary to continuously review systems to remove bottlenecks and enhance flexibility. An effective and efficient operations ERP system is essential for high-level firm performance, yet it alone will not move the firm into the high-performance category.

Inventory Deployment and Management

The inventory deployment and management module serves as the primary interface between planning/coordination and operations by planning requirements and managing finished inventory from production until customer shipment. Specifically, where should finished inventory be moved through the supply chain? When should replenishment orders be placed? How much should be ordered? Firms with MTO materials systems have essentially integrated their planning/coordination and operations so there is minimal need for inventory deployment and management.

The first component of the inventory deployment and management system is the forecast process. The forecast process predicts product requirements by customer and distribution center to support enterprise planning.

The second module of inventory deployment and management is inventory allocation decision support ranging from simple reactive models to complex planning tools. The decision aids are necessary to guide inventory planners in deciding when and how much to order. Reactive models respond to current demand and inventory situations using reorder point and order quantity parameters. In other words, they make replenishment decisions by reacting to current inventory levels. Planning tools anticipate future requirements on the basis of forecasts and cycle time projections. The planning tools allow managers to identify potential problems while they can still be resolved using proactive management.

Inventory deployment and management systems also differ in the amount of human interaction required. Some applications require inventory planners to manually place or approve all replenishment orders. Such systems are not exception-based since all replenishment orders require explicit planner approval. Manual approval-based systems require substantially more human resources but may incorporate better judgment. More sophisticated applications automatically place replenishment orders and monitor their progress through the replenishment cycle. The sophisticated applications illustrate a more exception-based philosophy since planners are required to intervene only for exceptional replenishment orders.

Primary drivers of inventory deployment and management are customer service objectives established by management. Service objectives define target fill rates for customers and products. The combination of service objectives, demand characteristics, replenishment characteristics, and operating policies determines the where, when, and how discussed above. Effective inventory deployment and management can significantly reduce the level of inventory assets required to meet specific service objectives.

In addition to initiating basic inventory decisions, inventory deployment and management must measure inventory performance by monitoring inventory level, turns, and productivity. Table 5.6 lists inventory deployment and management functionality for a relatively sophisticated logistics application. Note that the functionality includes a number of forecasting-related activities. Inventory deployment and management requires estimates of future demand in the form of implicit or explicit forecasts. Implicit, or default, forecasts assume that next month's sales will be the same as last month's sales. Explicit forecasts as discussed in Chapter 3 are more scientific, using information about enterprise, customer, and competitor actions. The basic proposition is that more integrated forecast information facilitates inventory deployment and management and results in lower inventory requirements. The inventory management and allocation module is increasingly being required to integrate and coordinate supply chain plans with operating requirements. These technologies, which are further discussed in Chapter 11, are becoming known as Supply Chain Management or Supply Chain Planning systems.[11]

Since information technology is evolving much faster than most other logistics capabilities such as transportation and materials handling, new technologies must be constantly reviewed to determine potential logistics applications. It is impossible for a textbook to offer timely information regarding the status of all information technologies that may have logistics applications.

Summary

Supply chain information systems link logistics activities in an integrated process based on four levels of functionality. The transaction system provides the foundation by electronically taking the order, initiating order selection and shipment, and completing appropriate financial transactions. Management control systems record functional and firm operating performance and provide appropriate management reporting. Decision analysis systems assist management in the identification and evaluation of logistics alternatives. Strategic planning systems provide top management with insight regarding the impact of strategic changes such as mergers, acquisitions, and competitive actions. While the transaction system provides the foundation, management control, decision analysis, and strategic planning systems are becoming critical for high-performance supply chain management.

ERP or legacy systems are the backbone of most SCIS because of their integrated database capabilities and modular transactions. The communication systems facilitate information exchange internally within the firm's functions as well as externally across global sites and with other supply chain partners. The execution systems are becoming more critical for controlling warehouse and transportation operations. Supply chain planning systems will likely become the critical competitive differentiator for the future as firms strive to improve their asset productivity through reduced inventory and physical assets.

Remarkable advances have been made to facilitate logistical communication both within a given firm and among its supply chain partners. EDI, satellite, and more recently XML continue to enable quicker and more consistent communication between supply chain partners. Other technologies, such as bar coding, scanning, and radio frequency, are substantially enhancing the communication effectiveness between logistics information systems and the physical environment in which they must operate.

The increasing accessibility and capabilities of these information and communication systems substantially increase the availability and accuracy of supply chain information. Communication technology advances have dramatically reduced the uncertainty between large firms, but substantial opportunities remain for improved communications between smaller firms, which make up the majority of supply chain participants. While further communication system improvement will continue to reduce uncertainty, it is likely that major opportunities for future performance enhancers will be through supply chain analysis and strategic planning systems.

The foundation of any firm's supply chain information system is the ERP and execution systems that provide the database and transaction systems to initiate and track supply chain activities. Firms continue to place a strong emphasis on ERP system implementation to

---

[11] For a detailed discussion regarding the differences between ERP and Supply Chain Planning Systems, see Fiona Nah, "Supply Chain and Enterprise Systems Management and Solutions," *Information Resources Management Journal* 17, no. 3 (July–September 2004), pp. 1–4.

achieve information consistency, economies of scale, and integration. These characteristics are becoming basic requirements for global commerce. A broad-based ERP system design includes an integrated database along with modules to support supply chain, service, and financial operations, and for human resource management.

Supply chain system design includes components for planning/coordination, operations, and inventory deployment. On the basis of the firm's strategic and marketing plans, the planning/coordination component manages the firm's production, storage, and movement capacities. The operations component provides the information transactions to initiate orders, assign inventory, select orders in the warehouse, transport, and invoice customer and replenishment orders. On the basis of sales and forecast levels, the inventory deployment component manages supply chain inventory to meet required service levels while minimizing inventory.

Challenge Questions

1. Compare and contrast the role of ERP systems and planning systems in enhancing firm performance and competitiveness.
2. Compare and contrast the role of ERP systems and logistics execution systems.
3. Discuss the rationalization for ERP implementation by firms involved in supply chain management.
4. Discuss the major challenges a firm should expect when implementing an integrated ERP system, including financial, supply chain, service, and human resource applications.
5. Discuss the applications, benefits, and challenges related to the use of RFID to enhance supply chain performance.
6. Discuss how the planning/coordination and operation flow differs for MTO and MTP firms.
7. Compare and contrast the role of planning/coordination and operations in improving firm competitiveness.
8. Discuss the rationale and risks associated with using a common forecast to drive the firm's planning/coordination flow.
9. Discuss the role of the CRM system in enhancing the firm's competitiveness.
10. Describe the trade-offs that S&OP is designed to consider and discuss the challenges to implement a S&OP system.

PART TWO

Supply Chain Logistics Operations

Part 2 consists of six chapters describing detailed logistics activities and functions. Chapter 6 focuses on inventory management, including the rationale for inventory, costs associated with carrying inventory, procedures for setting and monitoring appropriate inventory levels, and a framework for managing overall inventory resources. Chapter 7 describes the transportation infrastructure, including role, functionality, and principles. The chapter continues with a description of the transportation regulatory environment, characteristics of transportation modes and the range of services provided. Chapter 8 focuses on the more managerial aspects of transportation operations such as economics, pricing, and administration. Together, costs related to inventory and transportation represent a significant majority of total logistics expense. Chapter 9 discusses the economic and service justification for warehousing and the activities required for facility design and operations. Chapter 10 focuses inside the four walls of a warehouse by reviewing packaging and materials handling technologies. The chapter discusses requirements for packaging materials and efficiency followed by a discussion of materials handling equipment capabilities and trade-offs. Chapter 11 is devoted to operational integration. It is from the integrated performance of individual activities that the power of supply chain logistics is realized.

Inventory

Inventory decisions are both high risk and high impact throughout the supply chain. Inventory committed to support future sales drives a number of anticipatory supply chain activities. Without the proper inventory assortment, lost sales and customer dissatisfaction may occur. Likewise, inventory planning is critical to manufacturing. Material or component shortages can shut down a manufacturing line or force production schedule modification, added cost and potential finished goods shortages. Just as shortages can disrupt marketing and manufacturing plans, inventory overstocks also create operating problems. Overstocks increase cost and reduce profitability as a result of added warehousing, working capital, insurance, taxes, and obsolescence. Management of inventory resources requires an understanding of functionality, principles, cost, impact, and dynamics.

Inventory Functionality and Definitions

Inventory management is risky, and risk varies depending upon a firm's position in the distribution channel. The typical measures of inventory exposure are time duration, depth, and width of commitment.

For a manufacturer, inventory risk is long-term. The manufacturer's inventory commitment begins with raw material and component parts purchase, includes work-in-process, and ends with finished goods. In addition, finished goods are often positioned in warehouses in anticipation of customer demand. In some situations, manufacturers are required to consign inventory to customer facilities. In effect, this practice shifts all inventory risk to the manufacturer. Although a manufacturer typically has a narrower product line than a retailer or wholesaler, the manufacturer's inventory commitment is deep and of long duration.

A wholesaler purchases large quantities from manufacturers and sells smaller quantities to retailers. The economic justification of a wholesaler is the capability to provide customers an assortment of merchandise from different manufacturers in specific quantities. When products are seasonal, the wholesaler may be required to take an inventory position far in advance of the selling season, thus increasing depth and duration of risk. One of the greatest challenges of wholesaling is product-line expansion to the point where the width of inventory risk approaches that of the retailer while depth and duration of risk remain characteristic of traditional wholesaling. In recent years, powerful retailers have driven a substantial increase in depth and duration by shifting inventory responsibility back to wholesalers.

For a retailer, inventory management is about the velocity of buying and selling. Retailers purchase a wide variety of products and assume substantial risk in the marketing process. Retail inventory risk can be viewed as wide but not deep. Because of the high cost of store location, retailers place prime emphasis on inventory turnover. Inventory turnover is a measure of inventory velocity and is calculated as the ratio of sales for a time period divided by average inventory.

Although retailers assume a position of risk on a wide variety of products, their position on any one product is not deep. Risk is spread across more than 30,000 stockkeeping units (SKUs) in a typical supermarket. A mass retailer offering general merchandise and food often exceeds 50,000 SKUs. Faced with this width of inventory, retailers attempt to reduce risk by pressing manufacturers and wholesalers to assume greater and greater inventory responsibility. Pushing inventory back up the channel has resulted in retailer demand for fast delivery of mixed-product shipments from wholesalers and manufacturers. Specialty retailers, in contrast to mass merchandisers, normally experience less width of inventory risk as a result of handling narrower assortments. However, they must assume greater risk with respect to depth and duration of inventory holding.

If a business plans to operate at more than one level of the distribution channel, it must be prepared to assume the associated inventory risk. For example, a food chain that operates a regional warehouse assumes risk related to wholesale functionality over and above normal retail operations. To the extent that an enterprise becomes vertically integrated, inventory must be managed at multiple levels of the supply chain.

Inventory Functionality

From an inventory perspective, the ideal situation would be a response-based supply chain. At various points in early chapters, the practicality of implementing a fully response-based supply chain was discussed in terms of the total costs and timeliness of customer support.[1]

[1] See Chapters 1 and 3.

TABLE 6.1
Inventory
Functionality

Geographical Specialization	Allows geographical positioning across multiple manufacturing and distributive units of an enterprise. Inventory maintained at different locations and stages of the value-creation process allows specialization.
Decoupling	Allows economy of scale within a single facility and permits each process to operate at maximum efficiency rather than having the speed of the entire process constrained by the slowest.
Supply/Demand Balancing	Accommodates elapsed time between inventory availability (manufacturing, growing, or extraction) and consumption.
Buffering Uncertainty	Accommodates uncertainty related to demand in excess of forecast or unexpected delays in order receipt and order processing in delivery and is typically referred to as safety stock.

While a zero-inventory supply chain is typically not attainable, it is important to remember that each dollar invested in inventory is a trade-off to an alternative use of assets.

Inventory is a current asset that should provide return on the capital invested. The return on inventory investments is the marginal profit on sales that would not occur without inventory. Accounting experts have long recognized that measuring the true cost and benefits of inventory on the corporate profit-and-loss is difficult.[2] Lack of measurement sophistication makes it difficult to evaluate the trade-offs between service levels, operating efficiencies, and inventory levels. While aggregate inventory levels throughout sectors of the economy have decreased, many enterprises still carry an average inventory that exceeds their actual business requirements. The forces driving this generalization are understood better through a review of the four prime functions of inventory. Table 6.1 summarizes inventory functionality.

These four functions, **geographical specialization, decoupling, balancing supply and demand,** and **buffering uncertainty,** require inventory investment to achieve operating objectives. While logistics, as discussed in Chapter 2, has made significant progress in reducing overall supply chain inventory, inventory properly deployed creates value and reduces total cost. Given a specific manufacturing/marketing strategy, inventories planned and committed to operations can only be reduced to a level consistent with performing the four inventory functions. All inventories exceeding the minimum level represent excess commitments.

At the minimum level, inventory invested to achieve geographical specialization and decoupling can be modified only by changes in network facility location and operational processes of the enterprise. The minimum level of inventory required to balance supply and demand depends on ability to estimate seasonal requirements. With accumulated experience over a number of seasonal periods, the inventory required to achieve marginal sales during periods of high demand can be projected fairly well. A seasonal inventory plan can be formulated on the basis of this experience.

Inventories committed to safety stocks represent the greatest potential for improved logistical performance. These commitments are operational in nature and can be adjusted rapidly in the event of an error or policy change. A variety of techniques are available to assist management in planning safety stock commitments. The focus of this chapter is the analysis of safety stock relationships and policy formulation.

---

[2] Douglas M. Lambert, *The Development of an Inventory Costing Methodology* (Chicago: National Council of Physical Distribution Management, 1976), p. 3; and *Inventory Carrying Cost, Memorandum 611* (Chicago: Drake Sheahan/Stewart Dougall, Inc., 1974).

Inventory Definitions

In formulating inventory policy, specific inventory relationships must be considered. Management must understand these relationships to determine inventory policy with respect to when and how much to order. The inventory policy drives desired inventory performance. The two key indicators of inventory performance are **service level** and **average inventory.**

Inventory Policy

Inventory policy consists of guidelines concerning what to purchase or manufacture, when to take action, and in what quantity. It also includes decisions regarding geographical inventory positioning. For example, some firms may decide to postpone inventory positioning by maintaining stock at the plant. Other firms may use a more speculative strategy of positioning product in local markets or regional warehouses. The development of sound inventory policy is the most difficult dimension of inventory management.

A second aspect of policy concerns inventory management practice. One approach is to independently manage inventory at each stocking facility. At the other extreme is central inventory management of all stocking locations. Centralized inventory management requires effective communication and coordination. The increased availability of affordable information technology and integrated planning systems allows more firms to implement centralized inventory planning.

Service Level

The service level is a performance target specified by management. It defines inventory performance objectives. Service level is often measured in terms of an order cycle time, case fill rate, line fill rate, order fill rate, or any combination of these. The **performance cycle** is the elapsed time between the release of a purchase order by a buyer to the receipt of shipment. A **case fill rate** is the percent of cases or units ordered that are shipped as requested. For example, a 95 percent case fill rate indicates that, on average, 95 cases out of 100 are filled from available stock. The remaining five cases are back-ordered or deleted. The **line fill rate** is the percent of order lines filled completely. **Order fill** is the percent of customer orders filled completely.

Inventory management is a major element of supply chain logistics strategy that must be integrated to achieve overall service objectives. While one strategy to achieve a high service level is to increase inventory, an alternative approach may be the use of fast transportation and collaboration with customers and service providers to reduce uncertainty.

Average Inventory

The materials, components, work-in-process, and finished product typically stocked in the logistical system are referred to as **average inventory.** From a policy viewpoint, target inventory levels must be planned for each facility. Figure 6.1 illustrates the performance cycles for one item at one location. At the maximum, the facility has in stock and during the normal performance cycle $70,000 and a minimum of $30,000. The difference between these two levels, $40,000 ($70,000 − $30,000), is the order quantity, resulting in a cycle inventory of $20,000. Cycle inventory or base stock is the portion of average inventory that results from replenishment. Stock level is at a maximum following stock receipt from the supplier. Customers deplete inventory until the stock level reaches its minimum. Prior to the stock level reaching the minimum, a replenishment order is initiated so that inventory will arrive before an out-of-stock occurs. The replenishment order must be initiated when the available inventory is less than or equal to forecasted demand during the performance cycle time. The amount ordered for replenishment is termed the **order quantity.** Given this basic order formulation, average cycle inventory or base stock equals one-half order quantity.

FIGURE 6.1
Inventory Cycle for Typical Product

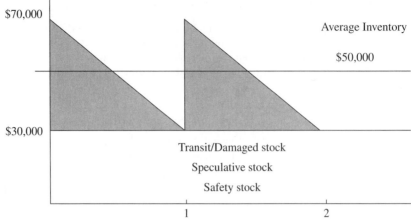

FIGURE 6.2
Inventory Relationship for Constant Sales and Performance Cycle

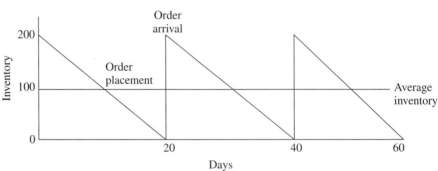

The majority of inventory in the typical logistics system is **safety stock.** Safety stock is maintained in a logistical system to protect against demand and performance cycle uncertainty. Safety stock is used only near the end of replenishment cycles when uncertainty has caused higher-than-expected demand or longer-than-expected performance cycle times. Thus, average inventory is **one-half order quantity plus safety stock.**

Average Inventory across Multiple Performance Cycles

In initial policy formulation, it is necessary to determine how much inventory to order at a specified time. To illustrate, assume the replenishment performance cycle is a constant 10 days and daily sales rate is 10 units per day. Also assume the order quantity is 200 units.

Figure 6.2 illustrates this relationship. This type of chart is referred to as a **sawtooth diagram** because of the series of right triangles. Since complete certainty exists with respect to usage and performance cycle, orders are scheduled to arrive just as the last unit is sold. Thus, no safety stock is included. Since the rate of sale in the example is 10 units per day and it takes 10 days to complete inventory replenishment, a sound reorder policy might be to order 200 units every 20 days. Given these conditions, common terminology related to policy formulation can be specified.

First, the **reorder point** is specified as 100 units on hand. The reorder point defines when a replenishment order is initiated. In this example, whenever the quantity on hand drops below 100, an additional order for 200 units is placed. The result of this policy is that daily inventory level ranges from a maximum of 200 to a minimum of zero over the performance cycle.

Second, average inventory is 100 units, since stock on hand exceeds 100 units one-half of the time, or for 10 days, and is less than 100 units one-half of the time. In fact, average inventory is equal to one-half the 200-unit order quantity.

FIGURE 6.3   **Alternative Order Quantity and Average Inventory**

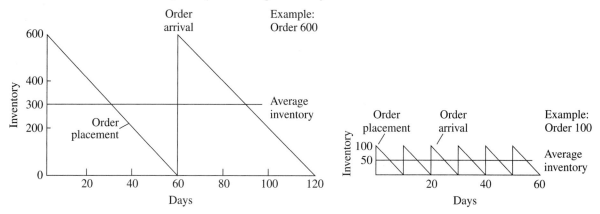

Third, assuming a work year of 240 days, 12 purchases will be required during the year. Therefore, over a period of 1 year, 200 units will be purchased 12 times for a total of 2400 units. Sales are expected to equal 10 units per/day over 240 days for a total of 2400 units. As discussed above, average inventory is 100 units. Thus, **inventory turns** will be 24 (2400 total sales/100 units of average inventory).

In time, the sheer boredom of such routine operations would lead management to ask some questions concerning the arrangement. What would happen if orders were placed more frequently than once every 20 days? Why not order 100 units every 10 days? Why order as frequently as every 20 days? Why not reorder 600 units once every 60 days? Assuming that the inventory performance cycle remains a constant 10 days, what would be the impact of each of these alternative ordering policies on reorder point, average base inventory, and inventory turnover?

The policy of ordering a smaller volume of 100 units every 10 days means that two orders would always be outstanding. Thus, the reorder point would remain 100 units on hand or on order to service average daily sales of 10 units over the 20-day inventory cycle. However, average inventory on hand would drop to 50 units, and inventory turnover would increase to 48 times per year. The policy of ordering 600 units every 60 days would result in an average base inventory of 300 units and a turnover of approximately eight times per year. These alternative ordering policies are illustrated in Figure 6.3.

The figure illustrates that average inventory is a function of the reorder quantity. Smaller replenishment order quantities do result in lower average inventory, but there are other factors such as performance cycle uncertainty, purchasing discounts, and transportation economies that are important when determining order quantity.

An exact order quantity policy can be determined by balancing the cost of ordering and the cost of maintaining average inventory. The **Economic Order Quantity (EOQ)** model provides a specific quantity balancing of these two critical cost components. By determining the EOQ and dividing it into annual demand, the frequency and size of replenishment orders minimizing the total cost of cycle inventory are identified. Prior to reviewing EOQ, it is necessary to identify costs typically associated with ordering and maintaining inventory.

Inventory Carrying Cost

Inventory carrying cost is the expense associated with maintaining inventory. Inventory expense is calculated by multiplying annual inventory carrying cost percent by average inventory value. Standard accounting practice is to value inventory at purchase or standard manufacturing cost rather than at selling price.

Assuming an annual inventory carrying cost percentage of 20 percent, the annual inventory expense for an enterprise with $1 million in average inventory would be $200,000 (20% × $1,000,000). While the calculation of inventory carrying expense is basic, determining the appropriate carrying cost percent is less obvious.

Determining carrying cost percent requires assignment of inventory-related costs. Financial accounts relevant to inventory carrying cost percent are capital, insurance, obsolescence, storage, and taxes. While cost of capital is typically based on managerial policy, expense related taxes, insurance, obsolescence, and storage varies depending on the specific attributes of individual products.

Capital

The appropriate charge to place on capital invested in inventory varies widely. Capital assessments range from the prime interest rate to a higher managerially determined percent. The logic for using the prime interest rate or a specified rate pegged to the prime rate is that cash to replace capital invested in inventory can be obtained in the money markets at that rate. Higher managerially specified capital costs are based on expected or target return on investment for capital deployed. Such target rates are typically termed **hurdle** rates.

Confusion often results from the fact that senior management frequently does not establish a clear-cut capital cost policy. For supply chain logistics planning, the cost of capital must be clearly specified since it has significant impact on system design and performance.

Taxes

Local taxing authorities in many areas assess taxes on inventory held in warehouses. The tax rate and means of assessment vary by location. The tax expense is usually a direct levy based on inventory level on a specific day of the year or average inventory level over a period of time.

Insurance

Insurance cost is an expense based upon estimated risk or loss over time. Loss risk depends on the product and the facility storing the product. For example, high-value products that are easily stolen and hazardous products result in high insurance cost. Insurance cost is also impacted by facility characteristics such as security cameras and sprinkler systems that might help reduce risk. Since September 11, 2001, issues related to terrorist risk have become of greater concern in supply chain design.

Obsolescence

Obsolescence cost results from deterioration of product during storage. A prime example of obsolescence is product that ages beyond recommended sell-by date, such as food and pharmaceuticals. Obsolescence also includes financial loss when a product no longer has fashion appeal. Obsolescence costs are typically estimated on the basis of past experience concerning markdowns, donations, or quantity destroyed. This expense is the percent of average inventory value declared obsolete each year.

Storage

Storage cost is facility expense related to product holding rather than product handling. Storage cost must be allocated on the requirements of specific products since it is not related directly to inventory value. In public or contract warehouses, storage charges are billed on an individual basis. The cost of total annual occupancy for a given product can

TABLE 6.2
**Inventory Carrying
Cost Components**

Element	Average Percent	Percent Ranges
Cost of capital	10.00%	4–40%
Taxes	1.00	.5–2
Insurance	.05	0–2
Obsolescence	1.20	.5–2
Storage	2.00	0–4
Totals	14.25%	5–50%

then be assigned by multiplying the average daily physical space occupied by the standard cost factor for a specified time. This figure can then be divided by the total number of units of merchandise processed through the facility to determine average storage cost per merchandise unit.

Table 6.2 illustrates the components of annual inventory carrying cost and typical range of component costs. It should be clear that the final carrying cost percent used by a firm is a matter of managerial policy. Decisions regarding inventory cost are important because they trade off against other logistics cost components in system design and operating decisions.

Planning Inventory

Inventory planning consists of determining when and how much to order. When to order is determined by average and variation in demand and replenishment. How much to order is determined by the order quantity. Inventory control is the process of monitoring inventory status.

When to Order

As discussed earlier, the reorder point defines when a replenishment shipment should be initiated. A reorder point can be specified in terms of units or days' supply. This discussion focuses on determining reorder points under conditions of demand and performance cycle certainty.

The basic reorder point formula is:

$$R = D \times T,$$

where

R = Reorder point in units;

D = Average daily demand in units; and

T = Average performance cycle length in days.

To illustrate this calculation, assume demand of 20 units/day and a 10-day performance cycle. In this case,

$$R = D \times T$$
$$= 20 \text{ units/day} \times 10 \text{ days}$$
$$= 200 \text{ units}.$$

An alternative form is to define reorder point in terms of days of supply. For the above example, the days of supply reorder point is 10 days.

The use of reorder point formulations implies that the replenishment shipment will arrive as scheduled. When uncertainty exists in either demand or performance cycle length, safety stock is required. When safety stock is necessary to accommodate uncertainty, the reorder point formula is:

$$R = D \times T + \text{SS},$$

where

$R =$ Reorder point in units;

$D =$ Average daily demand in units;

$T =$ Average performance cycle length in days; and

$\text{SS} =$ Safety stock in units.

Computation of safety stock under conditions of uncertainty is discussed later in this chapter.

How Much to Order

Lot sizing balances inventory carrying cost with the cost of ordering. The key to understanding the relationship is to remember that average inventory is equal to one-half the order quantity. Therefore, the greater the order quantity, the larger the average inventory and, consequently, the greater the annual carrying cost. However, the larger the order quantity, the fewer orders required per planning period and, consequently, the lower the total ordering cost. Lot quantity formulations identify the precise quantities at which the annual combined total inventory carrying and ordering cost is lowest for a given sales volume. Figure 6.4 illustrates the relationships. The point at which the sum of ordering and carrying cost is minimized represents the lowest total cost. The objective is to identify the ordering quantity that minimizes the total inventory carrying and ordering cost.

Economic Order Quantity

The EOQ is the replenishment practice that minimizes the combined inventory carrying and ordering cost. Identification of such a quantity assumes that demand and costs are relatively stable throughout the year. Since EOQ is calculated on an individual product basis, the basic formulation does not consider the impact of joint ordering of multiple products.

FIGURE 6.4
Economic Order Quantity

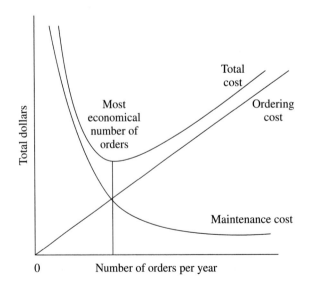

TABLE 6.3
Factors for
Determining EOQ

Annual demand volume	2400 units
Unit value at cost	$5.00
Inventory carrying cost percent	20% annually
Ordering cost	$19.00 per order

The most efficient method for calculating EOQ is mathematical. Earlier in this chapter a policy dilemma regarding whether to order 100, 200, or 600 units was presented. The answer can be found by calculating the applicable EOQ for the situation. Table 6.3 contains the necessary information.

To make the appropriate calculations, the standard formulation for EOQ is:

$$EOQ = \sqrt{\frac{2C_oD}{C_iU}}$$

where

EOQ = Economic order quantity;

C_o = Cost per order;

C_i = Annual inventory carrying cost;

D = Annual sales volume, units; and

U = Cost per unit.

Substituting from Table 6.3,

$$EOQ = \sqrt{\frac{2 \times 19 \times 2400}{0.20 \times 5.00}}$$
$$= \sqrt{91,200}$$
$$= 302 \text{ (round to 300)}.$$

Total ordering cost would amount to $152 (2400/300 × $19.00), and inventory carrying cost to $150 [300/2 × (5 × 0.20)]. Thus, rounding to allow ordering in multiples of 100 units, annual reordering, and inventory carrying cost have been equated.

To benefit from the most economical purchase arrangement, orders should be placed in the quantity of 300 units rather than 100, 200, or 600. Thus, over the year, eight orders would be placed and average base inventory would be 150 units. Referring back to Figure 6.4, we can observe the impact of ordering in quantities of 300 rather than 200. An EOQ of 300 implies that additional inventory in the form of base stock has been introduced into the system. Average inventory has been increased from 100 to 150 units on hand.

While the EOQ model determines the optimal replenishment quantity, it does require some rather stringent assumptions. The major assumptions of the simple EOQ model are: (1) all demand is satisfied; (2) rate of demand is continuous, constant, and known; (3) replenishment performance cycle time is constant and known; (4) there is a constant price of product that is independent of order quantity or time; (5) there is an infinite planning horizon; (6) there is no interaction between multiple items of inventory; (7) no inventory is in transit; and (8) no limit is placed on capital availability. The constraints imposed by some of these assumptions can be overcome through computational extensions; however, the EOQ concept illustrates the importance of the trade-offs associated with inventory carrying and replenishment ordering cost.

Relationships involving the inventory performance cycle, inventory cost, and economic order formulations are useful for guiding inventory planning. First, the EOQ is found at the point where annualized order cost and inventory carrying cost are equal. Second, average

TABLE 6.4
EOQ Data
Requirements for
Consideration of
Transportation
Economies

Annual demand volume	2400 units
Unit value at cost	$5.00
Inventory carrying cost percentage	20% annually
Ordering cost	$19.00 per order
Small shipment rate	$1.00 per unit
Large shipment rate	$0.75 per unit

base inventory equals one-half order quantity. Third, the value of the inventory unit, all other things being equal, will have a direct relationship with replenishment order frequency. In effect, the higher the product value, the more frequently it will be ordered.

While the EOQ formulation is relatively straightforward, there are other factors that must be considered in actual application. These factors refer to various adjustments necessary to take advantage of special purchase situations and unitization characteristics. Three typical adjustments are volume transportation rates, quantity discounts, and other EOQ adjustments.

Volume Transportation Rates

In the EOQ formulation, no consideration was given to the impact of transportation cost upon order quantity. Regardless of whether product is sold on a delivered basis or ownership is transferred at origin, the cost of transportation must be paid by supply chain participants. Collaborative efforts to order in quantities that minimize total cost are essential to sound logistical arrangements.

As a general rule, the greater the weight of an order, the lower the cost per pound of transportation from any origin to destination.[3] A freight-rate discount for larger shipments is common across all transportation modes. Thus, all other things being equal, supply chain arrangements should facilitate quantities that offer maximum transportation economies. Such quantities may be larger than the EOQ purchase quantity. Increasing order size has a twofold impact upon inventory cost. Assume for purposes of illustration that the most desirable transportation rate is obtained when a quantity of 480 is ordered, as compared to the EOQ-recommended order of 300 calculated earlier. The first impact of the larger order is to increase the average base inventory from 150 to 240 units. Thus, ordering in larger quantities increases inventory carrying cost.

The second impact is a decrease in the number of orders required to satisfy annual requirements. Decreased number of orders increases the shipment size facilitating lower per-unit transportation cost.

To complete the analysis it is necessary to formulate the total cost with and without transportation savings. While this calculation can be directly made by modification of the EOQ formulation, direct comparison provides a more insightful answer. The only additional data required are the applicable freight rate for ordering in quantities of 300 and 480. Table 6.4 provides the data necessary to complete the analysis.

Table 6.5 illustrates total cost analysis. Reducing total annual cost by purchasing 480 units five times per year rather than the original EOQ solution of 300 units eight times per year results in approximately a $570 savings.

The impact of volume transportation rates upon total cost of procurement cannot be neglected. In the example above, the equivalent rate per unit dropped from $1 to $0.75, or by 25 percent. Thus, any EOQ must be tested for transportation cost sensitivity across a range of weight breaks.

---

[3] To determine transportation rates, the unit quantity must be converted to weight.

TABLE 6.5
Volume
Transportation Rate
Modified EOQ

	Alternative 1: $EOQ_1 = 300$	Alternative 2: $EOQ_2 = 480$
Inventory Carrying Cost	$150	$240
Ordering Cost	$152	$95
Transportation Cost	$2,400	$1,800
Total Cost	$2,702	$2,135

TABLE 6.6
Example of Quantity
Discounts

Cost	Quantity Purchased
$5.00	1–99
4.50	100–200
4.00	201–300
3.50	301–400
3.00	401–500

Another point illustrated in the data in Table 6.5 is the fact that rather substantial changes in the size of an order and the number of orders placed per year result in only a modest change in the total ordering and inventory carrying cost. The EOQ quantity of 300 had a total annual cost of $302, whereas the revised order quantity had a comparative cost of $335.

EOQ formulations are much more sensitive to significant changes in order cycle or frequency. Likewise, substantial changes in cost factors are necessary to significantly change the economic order quantity.

Finally, two factors regarding inventory cost under conditions of origin purchase are noteworthy. FOB (Free On Board) origin purchase means that the buyer is responsible for freight cost and risk while the product is in transit. It follows that any change in weight break leading to a shipment method with a different transit time should be considered, using the added cost or savings as appropriate in a total cost analysis.

Second, the transportation cost must be added to the purchase price to determine the value of goods tied up in inventory. Once the inventory has been received, the cost of the product must be increased to reflect the inbound transportation.

Quantity Discounts

Purchase quantity discounts represent an EOQ extension analogous to volume transportation rates. Table 6.6 illustrates a sample schedule of discounts. Quantity discounts can be handled directly with the basic EOQ formulation by calculating total cost at any given volume-related purchase price, as in the process used in calculating transportation rate impact, to determine associated EOQs. If the discount at any associated quantity is sufficient to offset the added inventory carrying cost less the reduced cost of ordering, then the quantity discount is a viable choice. It should be noted that quantity discounts and volume transportation rates each drive larger purchase quantities. This does not necessarily mean that the lowest total cost purchase will always be a larger quantity than would otherwise be the case under basic EOQ.

Other EOQ Adjustments

A variety of other special situations may justify adjustments to the basic EOQ. Examples are (1) production lot size, (2) multiple-item purchase, (3) limited capital, (4) dedicated trucking, and (5) unitization. Production lot size refers to the most economical quantities from a manufacturing perspective. Multiple-item purchase refers to situations when more than one product is bought concurrently, so quantity and transportation discounts must consider the impact of product combinations. Limited capital describes situations with budget limitations for total inventory investment. Since the multiple product order must be made within the budget limitations, order quantities must recognize the need to allocate the inventory investment across the product line. Dedicated trucking can influence order quantity since the truck has a fixed cost consideration.[4] Once it is decided to use a dedicated fleet to transport replenishment product, the enterprise should try to purchase in quantities that fully use available capacity. Back haul capacity availability may justify purchasing products earlier than otherwise determined by EOQ considerations.

Another consideration when determining replenishment order quantity is unitization. Many products are stored and moved in standard units such as cases or pallets. Since these standardized units are often designed to fit transportation vehicles, there may be significant diseconomies when the EOQ does not reflect standard units. As an example, suppose that a full pallet quantity is 200 units of a specified product. Using an EOQ of 300 units would require shipments of 1.5 pallets. From a handling or transportation utilization perspective, it is probably more effective to order either one or two pallets alternately or permanently.

Managing Uncertainty

To understand basic principles, it is useful to understand inventory relationships under conditions of certainty. Formulation of inventory policy must consider uncertainty. Two types of uncertainty directly impact inventory policy. **Demand uncertainty** is rate of sale during inventory replenishment. **Performance cycle uncertainty** involves inventory replenishment time variation.

Demand Uncertainty

Sales forecasting estimates unit demand during the inventory replenishment cycle. Even with good forecasting, demand during replenishment cycle typically exceeds or falls short of what is planned. To protect against a stockout when demand exceeds forecast, safety stock is added to base inventory. Under conditions of demand uncertainty, average inventory represents one-half order quantity plus safety stock. Figure 6.5 illustrates the inventory performance cycle under conditions of demand uncertainty. The dashed line represents the

[4] See Chapter 8. In such situations, the cost of money invested in inventory should be appropriately charged when the goods are paid for at the origin.

FIGURE 6.5
Inventory Relationship, Demand Uncertainty, and Constant Performance Cycle

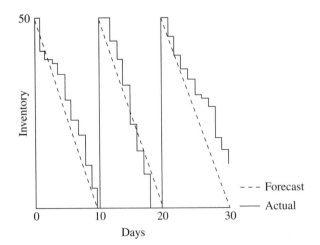

TABLE 6.7
Typical Demand
Experience during
Three Replenishment
Cycles

Day	Forecast Cycle 1		Stockout Cycle 2		Overstock Cycle 3	
	Demand	Accumulated	Demand	Accumulated	Demand	Accumulated
1	9	9	0	0	5	5
2	2	11	6	6	5	10
3	1	12	5	11	4	14
4	3	15	7	18	3	17
5	7	22	10	28	4	21
6	5	27	7	35	1	22
7	4	31	6	41	2	24
8	8	39	9	50	8	32
9	6	45	Stockout	50	3	35
10	5	50	Stockout	50	4	39

forecast. The solid line illustrates inventory on hand across multiple performance cycles. The task of planning safety stock requires three steps. First, the likelihood of stockout must be gauged. Second, demand during a stockout period must be estimated. Finally, a policy decision is required concerning the desired level of stockout protection.

Assume for purposes of illustration that the inventory performance cycle is 10 days. History indicates daily sales range from 0 to 10 units with average daily sales of 5 units. The economic order is assumed to be 50, the reorder point is 50, the planned average inventory is 25, and sales during the performance cycle are forecasted to be 50 units.

During the first cycle, although daily demand experienced variation, the average of 5 units per day was maintained. Total demand during cycle 1 was 50 units, as expected. During cycle 2, demand totaled 50 units in the first 8 days, resulting in a stockout. Thus, no sales were possible on days 9 and 10. During cycle 3, demand reached a total of 39 units. The third performance cycle ended with 11 units remaining in stock. Over the 30-day period total sales were 139 units, for average daily sale of 4.6 units.

From the history recorded in Table 6.7, it is observed that stockouts occurred on 2 of 30 total days. Since sales never exceed 10 units per day, no possibility of stockout exists on the first 5 days of the replenishment cycle. Stockouts were possible on days 6 through 10 on the remote possibility that demand during the first 5 days of the cycle averaged 10 units per day and no inventory was carried over from the previous period. Since during the three performance cycles 10 units were sold on only one occasion, it is apparent that the real risk of stockout occurs only during the last few days of the performance cycle, and then only when sales exceed the average by a substantial margin.[5] Some approximation is possible concerning sales potential for days 9 and 10 of cycle 2. A maximum of 20 units might have been sold if inventory had been available. On the other hand, it is remotely possible that even if stock had been available, no demand would have occurred on days 9 and 10. For average demand of 4 to 5 units per day, a reasonable appraisal of lost sales is 8 to 10 units.

It should be apparent that the risk of stockouts created by variations in sales is limited to a short time and includes a small percentage of total sales. Although the sales analysis presented in Table 6.7 helps achieve an understanding of the opportunity, the appropriate course of action is still not clear. Statistical probability can be used to assist management in planning safety stock.

---

[5] In this example, daily statistics are used. An alternative, which is technically more correct from a statistical viewpoint, is to utilize demand over multiple performance cycles. The major limitation of order cycles is the length of time and difficulty required to collect the necessary data.

The sales history over the 30-day period has been aggregated in Table 6.8 as a frequency distribution. The main purpose of a frequency distribution is to observe variations around the average daily demand. Given an expected average of 5 units per day, demand exceeded average on 11 days and was less than average on 12 days. An alternative way of illustrating a frequency distribution is by a bar chart, as in Figure 6.6.

Given the historical frequency of demand, it is possible to calculate the safety stock necessary to provide a specified degree of stockout protection. Probability theory is based on the random chance of a specific occurrence within a large number of occurrences. The situation illustrated uses a 28 day sample. In actual application, a larger sample size would be desirable.

The probability of occurrences assumes a pattern around a measure of central tendency, which is the average value of all occurrences. While a number of frequency distributions can be used in inventory management, the most basic is the **normal distribution.**

A normal distribution is characterized by a symmetrical bell-shaped curve, illustrated in Figure 6.7. The essential characteristic of a normal distribution is that the three measures of central tendency have equal value. The **mean** (average) value, the **median** (middle) observation, and the **mode** (most frequently observed) all have the same value. When these three measures are nearly identical, the frequency distribution is **normal.**

The basis for predicting demand during a performance cycle using a normal distribution is the **standard deviation** of observations around the three measures of central tendency.

TABLE 6.8
Frequency of Demand

Daily Demand (in units)	Frequency (days)
Stockout	2
0	1
1	2
2	2
3	3
4	4
5	5
6	3
7	3
8	2
9	2
10	1

FIGURE 6.6
Historical Analysis of Demand History

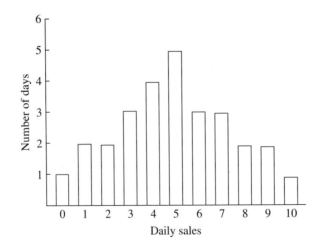

FIGURE 6.7
Normal Distribution

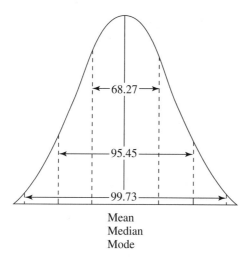

Mean
Median
Mode

The standard deviation is the dispersion of events within specified areas under the normal curve. For the inventory management application, the event is unit sales per day and the dispersion is the variation in daily sales. Within 1 standard deviation, 68.27 percent of all events occur. This means that 68.27 percent of the days during a performance cycle will experience daily sales within ±1 standard deviation of the average daily sales. Within ±2 standard deviations, 95.45 percent of all events occur. At ±3 standard deviations, 99.73 percent of all events are included. In terms of inventory policy, the standard deviation provides a method of estimating the safety stock required to achieve a specified degree of out-of-stock protection.

The first step in setting safety stocks is to calculate the standard deviation. Most calculators and spreadsheets calculate standard deviation, but if one of these aids is not available, another method to compute the standard deviation is:

$$\sigma = \sqrt{\frac{\sum F_i D_i^2}{n}}$$

where

σ = Standard deviation;

F_i = Frequency of event i;

D_i = Deviation of event from mean for event i; and

n = Total observations available.

The necessary data to determine standard deviation are contained in Table 6.9.

The standard deviation of the data in Table 6.9 is rounded to 3 units. When setting safety stocks, 2 standard deviations of protection, or 6 units, would protect against 95.45 percent of all events included in the distribution. However, the only situations of concern in determining safety stock requirements are events that exceed the mean value. No problem exists concerning inventory to satisfy demand equal to or below the average. Thus, on 50 percent of the days, no safety stock will be required. Safety stock protection at the 95 percent level will, in fact, protect against 97.72 percent of all possible events. The 95 percent coverage will cover all situations when daily demand is ±2 standard deviations of the average plus the 2.72 percent of the time when demand is more than 2 standard deviations below the mean. This added benefit results from what is typically called a **one-tail** statistical application.

TABLE 6.9
Calculation of
Standard Deviation
of Daily Demand

Units	Frequency (F_i)	Deviation from Mean (D_i)	Deviation Squared (D_i^2)	$F_i D_i^2$
0	1	−5	25	25
1	2	−4	16	32
2	2	−3	9	18
3	3	−2	4	12
4	4	−1	1	4
5	5	0	0	0
6	3	+1	1	3
7	3	+2	4	12
8	2	+3	9	18
9	2	+4	16	32
10	1	+5	25	25
$n = 28$	$\bar{s} = 5$			$\Sigma F_i D_i^2 = 181$

TABLE 6.10
Calculation of
Standard Deviation
of Replenishment
Cycle Duration

Performance Cycle (days)	Frequency (F_i)	Deviation from Mean (D_i)	Deviation Squared (D_i^2)	$F_i D_i^2$
6	2	−4	16	32
7	4	−3	9	36
8	6	−2	4	24
9	8	−1	1	8
10	10	0	0	0
11	8	+1	1	8
12	6	+2	4	24
13	4	+3	9	36
14	2	+4	16	32
				$\Sigma F_i D_i^2 = 200$

$$N = 50 \quad t = 10$$

$$\sigma = \sqrt{\frac{F_i D_i^2}{N}} = \sqrt{\frac{200}{50}} = \sqrt{2} = 2 \text{ days}$$

The above example illustrates how statistical probability can assist with the quantification of demand uncertainty, but demand conditions are not the only source of uncertainty. Performance cycles can also vary.

Performance Cycle Uncertainty

Performance cycle uncertainty means purchasing cannot assume consistent delivery. The planner should expect that actual performance cycle experience will cluster near the expected value and be skewed toward delayed delivery.

Table 6.10 presents a sample frequency distribution across multiple performance cycles. Although 10 days is the most frequent, replenishment experience ranges from 6 to 14 days. If the performance cycle follows a normal distribution, an individual performance cycle would be expected to fall between 8 and 12 days 68.27 percent of the time.

From a practical viewpoint, when cycle days drop below 10, no immediate problem exists with safety stock. If the performance cycle were consistently below the planned performance cycle, then adjustment of expected duration would be in order. The situation of most immediate concern occurs when the duration of the performance cycle exceeds 10 days.

From the viewpoint of the probability of exceeding 10 days, the frequency of such occurrences, from the data in Table 6.10, can be restated in terms of performance cycles greater than 10 days and equal to or less than 10 days. In the example data, the standard deviation would not change because the distribution is normal. However, if the actual experience has been skewed in excess of the expected cycle duration, then a **Poisson distribution** may have been more appropriate. In Poisson frequency distributions, the standard deviation is equal to the square root of the mean. As a general rule, the smaller the mean, the greater the degree of skewness.

Safety Stock with Combined Uncertainty

The typical situation confronting the inventory planner is illustrated in Figure 6.8, where both demand and performance cycle uncertainties exist. Planning for both demand and performance cycle uncertainty requires combining two independent variables. The duration of the cycle is, at least in the short run, independent of the daily demand. However, in setting safety stocks, the joint impact of the probability of both demand and performance cycle variation must be determined. Table 6.11 presents a summary of sales and replenishment cycle performance. The key to understanding the potential relationships of the data in Table 6.11 is the 10-day performance cycle. Total demand during the 10 days potentially ranges from 0 to 100 units. On each day of the cycle, the demand probability is independent of the previous day for the entire 10-day duration. Assuming the full range of potential

FIGURE 6.8
Combined Demand and Performance Cycle Uncertainty

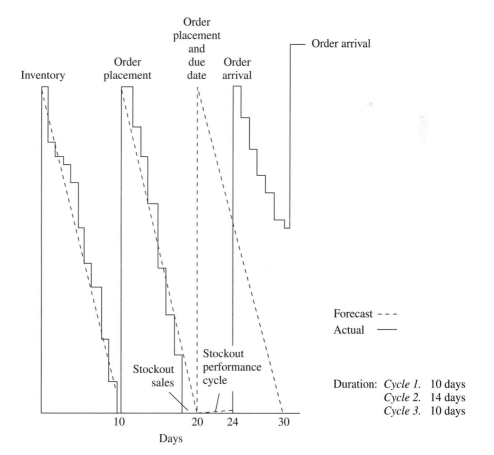

Forecast - - -
Actual ———

Duration: *Cycle 1.* 10 days
Cycle 2. 14 days
Cycle 3. 10 days

TABLE 6.11
Frequency
Distribution—
Demand and
Replenishment
Uncertainty

	Demand Distribution		Replenishment Cycle Distribution	
Daily Sales	Frequency		Days	Frequency
0	1		6	2
1	2		7	4
2	2		8	6
3	3		9	8
4	4		10	10
5	5		11	8
6	3		12	6
7	3		13	4
8	2		14	2
9	2			
10	1			
	$n = 28$		$n = 50$	
	$D = 5$		$T = 10$	
	$S_s = 2.54$		$S_t = 2$	

situations illustrated in Table 6.11, total sales during a performance cycle could range from 0 to 140 units. With this basic relationship between the two types of uncertainty in mind, safety stock requirements can be determined by either numerical or convolution procedures.

The **numerical compounding** of two independent variables involves multinominal expansion. This type of procedure requires extensive calculation. A direct method is to determine the standard deviations of demand and performance cycle uncertainty and then to approximate the combined standard deviation using the convolution formula:

$$\sigma_c = \sqrt{TS_s^2 + D^2 S_t^2},$$

where

σ_c = Standard deviation of combined probabilities;

T = Average performance cycle time;

S_t = Standard deviation of the performance cycle;

D = Average daily sales; and

S_s = Standard deviation of daily sales.

Substituting from Table 6.11,

$$\sigma_c = \sqrt{10.00(2.54)^2 + (5.00)^2(2)^2}$$
$$= \sqrt{64.52 + 100} = \sqrt{164.52}$$
$$= 12.83 \text{ (round to 13)}.$$

This formulation estimates the convoluted or combined standard deviation of T days with an average demand of D per day when the individual standard deviations are S_t and S_s, respectively. The average for the combined distribution is the product of T and D, or 50.00 (10.00 × 5.00).

Thus, given a frequency distribution of daily sales from 0 to 10 units per day and a range in replenishment cycle duration of 6 to 14 days, 13 units (1 standard deviation multiplied by 13 units) of safety stock is required to protect 84.14 percent of all performance cycles. To protect at the 97.72 percent level, a 26-unit safety stock is necessary. These levels assume a one-tail distribution since it is not necessary to protect against leadtime demand below average.

It is important to note that the specific event being protected against is a stockout during the performance cycle. The 68.27 and 97.72 percent levels are not product availability levels. These percentages reflect the probability of a stockout during a given order cycle. For example, with a 13-unit safety stock, stockouts would be expected to occur during 31.73 (100 − 68.27) percent of the performance cycles. Although this percentage provides the probability of a stockout, it does not estimate magnitude. The relative stockout magnitude indicates the percentage of units stocked out relative to demand.

Average inventory requirements would be 25 units if no safety stock were desired. The average inventory with 2 standard deviations of safety stock is 51 units [25 + (2 × 13)]. This inventory level would protect against a stockout during 97.72 percent of the performance cycles. Table 6.12 summarizes the alternatives confronting the planner in terms of assumptions and corresponding impact on average inventory.

Estimating Fill Rate

The fill rate is the magnitude of a stockout rather than the probability. The case fill rate is the percentage of units that can be filled when requested from available inventory. Figure 6.9 graphically illustrates the difference between stockout probability and stockout magnitude. Both illustrations in Figure 6.9 have a safety stock of 1 standard deviation or 13 units. For both situations, given any performance cycle, the probability of a stockout is 31.73 percent. However, during a 20-day period, the figure illustrates two instances where the stock may be depleted. These instances are at the ends of the cycle. If the order quantity is doubled, the system has the possibility of stocking out only once during the 20-day

TABLE 6.12
Average Inventory Impact Resulting from Changes in EOQ

	Order Quantity	Safety Stock	Average Inventory
Assume constant S sales and constant T performance cycle	50	0	25
Assume demand protection $+2\sigma$ and constant T performance cycle	50	6	31
Assume constant S demand and $+2\sigma$ performance cycle protection	50	20	45
Assume joint $+2\sigma$ for demand and performance cycle	50	26	51

FIGURE 6.9   **Impact of Order Quantity on Stockout Magnitude**

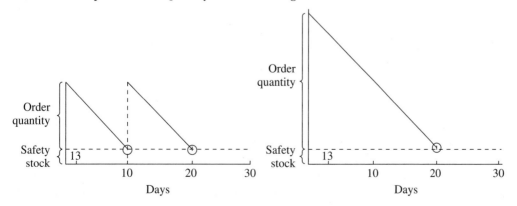

cycle. So, while both situations face the same demand pattern, the first one has more stock-out opportunities and potential. In general, for a given safety stock level, increasing the replenishment order quantity decreases the relative magnitude of potential stockouts and conversely increases customer service availability.

The mathematical formulation of the relationship is:

$$SL = 1 - \frac{f(k)\sigma_c}{Q},$$

where

SL = The stockout magnitude (the product availability level);

$f(k)$ = A function of the normal loss curve which provides the area in a right tail of a normal distribution;

σ_c = The combined standard deviation considering both demand and replenishment cycle uncertainty; and

Q = The replenishment order quantity.

TABLE 6.13
Information for Determining Required Safety Stock

Desired Service Level	99%
σ_c	13
Q	300

To complete the example, suppose a firm desired 99 percent product availability or case fill rate. Assume the Q was calculated to be 300 units. Table 6.13 summarizes the required information.

Since $f(k)$ is the term used to calculate safety stock requirements, the above equation must be solved for $f(k)$ using algebraic manipulation. The result is:

$$f(k) = (1 - SL) \times (Q/\sigma_c).$$

Substituting from Table 6.13,

$$f(k) = (1 - 0.99) \times (300/13)$$
$$= 0.01 \times 23.08 = .2308.$$

The calculated value of $f(k)$ is then compared against the values in Table 6.14 to find the one that most closely approximates the calculated value. For this example, the value of k that fits the condition is 0.4. The required safety stock level is:

$$SS = k \times \sigma_c,$$

where

SS = Safety stock in units;

k = The k factor that corresponds with $f(k)$;

σ_c = The combined standard deviation.

So, substituting in for the example,

$$SS = k \times \sigma_c$$
$$= .04 \times 13 = 5.2 \text{ units.}$$

The safety stock required to provide a 99 percent product fill rate when the order quantity is 300 units is approximately 5 units. Table 6.15 shows how the calculated safety stock and

TABLE 6.14
Loss Integral for
Standardized Normal
Distribution

k	f(k)	k	f(k)
0.0	.3989	1.6	.0232
0.1	.3509	1.7	.0182
0.2	.3068	1.8	.0143
0.3	.2667	1.9	.0111
0.4	.2304	2.0	.0085
0.5	.1977	2.1	.0065
0.6	.1686	2.2	.0049
0.7	.1428	2.3	.0037
0.8	.1202	2.4	.0027
0.9	.1004	2.5	.0020
1.0	.0833	2.6	.0015
1.1	.0686	2.7	.0011
1.2	.0561	2.8	.0008
1.3	.0455	2.9	.0005
1.4	.0366	3.0	.0004
1.5	.0293	3.1	.0003

TABLE 6.15
Impact of Order
Quantity on Safety
Stock

Order Quantity (Q)	k	Safety Stock	Average Inventory
300	0.40	5	155
200	0.70	8	108
100	1.05	14	64
50	1.40	18	43
25	1.70	22	34

average inventory levels vary for other order quantities. An increased order size can be used to compensate for decreasing the safety stock levels, or vice versa. The existence of such a trade-off implies that there is a combination of replenishment order quantities that will result in desired customer service at the minimum cost.

Dependent Demand Replenishment

With respect to dependent demand replenishment, inventory requirements are a function of known events that are not generally random. Therefore, dependent demand does not require forecasting because there is no uncertainty. It follows that no specific safety stock should be necessary to support a time-phased procurement program such as DRP.[6] The basic notion of time phasing is that parts and subassemblies need not be carried in inventory as long as they arrive when needed or just-in-time.

The case for carrying no safety stocks under conditions of dependent demand rests on two assumptions. First, procurement replenishment to support planning is predictable and constant. Second, vendors and suppliers maintain adequate inventories to satisfy 100 percent of purchase requirements. The second assumption may be operationally attained by use of volume-oriented purchase contracts that assure vendors and suppliers of eventual purchase. In such cases the safety stock requirement still exists for the overall supply chain, although the primary responsibility rests with the supplier.

---

[6] These concepts are discussed later in this chapter under Requirements Planning.

The assumption of performance cycle certainty is more difficult to achieve. Even in situations where dedicated transportation is used, an element of uncertainty is always present. The practical result is that safety stocks do exist in most dependent demand situations.

Three basic approaches have been used to introduce safety stocks into dependent demand situations. First, a common practice is to put **safety time** into the requirements plan. For example, a component is ordered earlier than needed to assure timely arrival. A second approach is to increase the requisition by a quantity specified by some estimate of expected plan error. For example, assume that plan error will not exceed 5 percent. This procedure is referred to as **overplanning top-level demand.** The net result is to increase procurement of all components in a ratio to their expected usage plus a cushion to cover plan error. Components common to different end products or subassemblies covered by the overplanning will naturally experience greater quantity buildups than single-purpose components and parts. The third method is to utilize the previously discussed statistical techniques for setting safety stocks directly to the component rather than to the item of top-level demand.

Inventory Management Policies

Inventory management implements inventory policy. The reactive or pull inventory approach uses customer demand to pull product through the distribution channel. An alternative philosophy is a planning approach that proactively allocates inventory on the basis of forecasted demand and product availability. A third, or hybrid, logic uses a combination of push and pull.

Inventory Control

The managerial procedure for implementing an inventory policy is **inventory control.** The accountability of control measures units on hand at a specific location and tracks additions and deletions. Accountability and tracking can be performed on a manual or computerized basis.

Inventory control defines how often inventory levels are reviewed to determine when and how much to order. It is performed on either a perpetual or a periodic basis.

Perpetual Review

A perpetual inventory control process continuously reviews inventory status to determine inventory replenishment needs. To utilize perpetual review, accurate tracking of all SKUs is necessary. Perpetual review is implemented through a reorder point and order quantity.

As discussed earlier,

$$\text{ROP} = D \times T + \text{SS},$$

where

ROP = Reorder point in units;

D = Average daily demand in units;

T = Average performance cycle length in days; and

SS = Safety or buffer stock in units.

The order quantity is determined using the EOQ.

TABLE 6.16

Sample Demand, Performance Cycle, and Order Quantity Characteristics

Average daily demand	20 units
Performance cycle	10 days
Order quantity	200 units

For purposes of illustration, assume no uncertainty so no safety stock is necessary. Table 6.16 summarizes demand, performance cycle, and order quantity characteristics. For this example,

$$\text{ROP} = D \times T + \text{SS}$$

$$= 20 \text{ units/day} \times 10 \text{ days} + 0 = 200 \text{ units.}$$

The perpetual review compares on-hand and on-order inventory to the item's reorder point. If the on-hand plus on-order quantity is less than the established reorder point, a replenishment order is initiated.

Mathematically, the process is:

$$\text{If } I + Q_O \leq \text{ROP, then order } Q,$$

where

$I = $ Inventory on hand;

$Q_O = $ Inventory on order from suppliers;

$\text{ROP} = $ Reorder point in units; and

$Q = $ Order quantity in units.

For the previous example, a replenishment order of 200 is placed whenever the sum of on-hand and on-order inventory is less than or equal to 200 units. Since the reorder point equals the order quantity, the previous replenishment shipment would arrive just as the next replenishment is initiated. The average inventory level for a perpetual review system is:

$$I_{avg} = Q/2 + \text{SS,}$$

where

$I_{avg} = $ Average inventory in units;

$Q = $ Order quantity units; and

$\text{SS} = $ Safety stock units.

Average inventory for the previous example is calculated as:

$$I_{avg} = Q/2 + \text{SS}$$

$$= 300/2 + 0 = 150 \text{ units.}$$

Most illustrations throughout this text are based on a perpetual review system with a fixed reorder point. The reorder formulation assumes purchase orders will be placed when the reorder point is reached, and the method of control provides a perpetual monitoring of inventory status. If these two assumptions are not satisfied, the control parameters (ROP and Q) determining the perpetual review must be refined.

Periodic Review

Periodic inventory control reviews the inventory status of an item at regular intervals such as weekly or monthly. For periodic review, the basic reorder point must be adjusted to consider the intervals between review. The formula for calculating the periodic review reorder point is:

$$ROP = D(T + P/2) + SS,$$

where

ROP = Reorder point;

$\quad$ D = Average daily demand;

$\quad\quad$ T = Average performance cycle length;

$\quad\quad$ P = Review period in days; and

$\quad$ SS = Safety stock.

Since inventory counts occur periodically, any item could fall below the desired reorder point prior to the review period. Therefore, the assumption is made that the inventory will fall below ideal reorder status prior to the periodic count approximately one-half of the review times. Assuming a review period of 7 days and using conditions similar to those of the perpetual example, the ROP then would be as follows:

$$\begin{aligned} ROP &= D(T + P/2) + SS \\ &= 20(10 + 7/2) + 0 = 20(10 + 3.5) = 270 \text{ units.} \end{aligned}$$

The average inventory formulation for the case of periodic review is:

$$I_{avg} = Q/2 + (P \times D)/2 + SS,$$

where

I_{avg} = Average inventory in units;

$\quad$ Q = Order quantity in units;

$\quad$ P = Review period in days;

$\quad$ D = Average daily demand in units;

$\quad$ SS = Safety stock in units.

For the preceding example, the average inventory is calculated as:

$$\begin{aligned} I_{avg} &= Q/2 + (P \times D)/2 + SS \\ &= 300/2 + (7 \times 10)/2 + 0 = 150 + 35 = 185 \text{ units.} \end{aligned}$$

Because of the time interval introduced by periodic review, periodic control systems generally require larger average inventories than perpetual systems.

Reactive Methods

The **reactive** or **pull inventory system,** as the name implies, responds to a channel member's inventory needs by drawing the product through the distribution channel. Replenishment shipments are initiated when available warehouse stock levels fall below a predetermined minimum or order point. The amount ordered is usually based on some lot-sizing formulation, although it may be some variable quantity that is a function of current stock levels and a predetermined maximum level.

FIGURE 6.10

A Reactive Inventory Environment

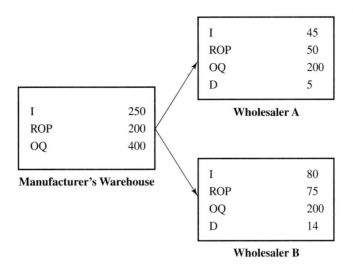

I	45
ROP	50
OQ	200
D	5

Wholesaler A

I	250
ROP	200
OQ	400

Manufacturer's Warehouse

I	80
ROP	75
OQ	200
D	14

Wholesaler B

The basic perpetual or periodic review process discussed earlier exemplifies a typical reactive system. Figure 6.10 illustrates a reactive inventory environment for a warehouse serving two wholesalers. The figure shows the current inventory (*I*), reorder point (ROP), order quantity (*Q*), and average daily demand (*D*) for each wholesaler. A review of the wholesaler inventory indicates that a resupply order for 200 units should be placed by wholesaler A from the warehouse. Since current inventory is above ROP for wholesaler B, no resupply action is necessary at this time. However, more thorough analysis illustrates that the independent actions by wholesaler A will likely cause a stockout at wholesaler B within a few days. Wholesaler B will likely stock out because inventory level is close to the reorder point and the supplying warehouse center will not have enough inventory to replenish wholesaler B.

Classical reactive inventory logic is rooted in the following assumptions. First, the system is founded on the basic assumption that all customers, market areas, and products contribute equally to profits.

Second, a reactive system assumes infinite capacity at the source. This assumption implies that product can be produced as desired and stored at the production facility until required throughout the supply chain.

Third, reactive inventory logic assumes infinite inventory availability at the supply location. The combination of assumptions 2 and 3 implies relative replenishment certainty. The reactive inventory logic provides for no back orders or stockouts in processing replenishment orders.

Fourth, reactive decision rules assume that performance cycle time can be predicted and that cycle lengths are independent. This means that each performance cycle is a random event and that extended cycles don't generally occur for subsequent replenishment orders. Although reactive logic assumes no control over cycle times, many managers are, in fact, able to influence performance cycle length through expediting and alternative sourcing strategies.

Fifth, reactive inventory logic operates best when customer demand patterns are relatively stable and consistent. Ideally, demand patterns should be stable over the relevant planning cycle for statistically developed inventory parameters to operate correctly. Most reactive system decision rules assume demand patterns based on standard normal, gamma, or Poisson distributions. When the actual demand function does not resemble one of the above functions, the statistical inventory decision rules based on these assumptions will not operate correctly.

Sixth, reactive inventory systems determine each distribution warehouse's timing and quantity of replenishment orders independently of all other sites, including the supply source. Thus, there is little potential to effectively coordinate inventory requirements across multiple distribution warehouses. The ability to take advantage of inventory information is not utilized—a serious defect when information and its communication are among the few resources that are decreasing in cost in the supply chain.

The final assumption characteristic of reactive inventory systems is that performance cycle length cannot be correlated with demand. The assumption is necessary to develop an accurate approximation of the variance of the demand over the performance cycle. For many situations higher demand levels create longer replenishment performance cycles since they also increase the demands on inventory and transportation resources. This implies that periods of high demand should not necessarily correspond to extended performance cycles caused by stockouts or limited product availability.

Operationally, most inventory managers constrain the impact of such limitations through the skillful use of manual overrides. However, these overrides often lead to ineffective inventory decisions since the resulting plan is based on inconsistent rules and managerial policy.

Planning Methods

Inventory planning methods use a shared database to coordinate inventory requirements across multiple locations or stages in the supply chain. Planning activities may occur at the plant warehouse level to coordinate inventory allocation and delivery to multiple destinations. Planning may also coordinate inventory requirements across multiple channel partners such as manufacturers and retailers. The Advanced Planning and Scheduling (APS) systems discussed in Chapters 5 and 11 illustrate the capability of planning applications. While APS systems computerize the process, it is important for logistics managers to understand the underlying logic and assumptions. Two inventory planning methods are fair share allocation and Distribution Requirements Planning (DRP).

Fair Share Allocation

A simplified inventory management planning method that provides each distribution facility with an equitable distributor of available inventory is called **fair share allocation.** Figure 6.11 illustrates the network structure, current inventory level, and daily requirements for three warehouses served by a single plant warehouse.

Using fair share allocation, the inventory planner determines the amount of inventory that can be allocated to each warehouse from the available inventory at the plant. For this

FIGURE 6.11
Fair Share Allocation Example

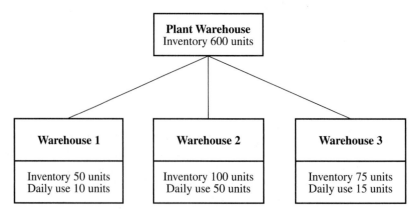

example, assume that it is desirable to retain 100 units at the plant warehouse; therefore, 500 units are available for allocation. The calculation to determine the common days supply is:

$$DS = \frac{AQ + \sum\limits_{j=1}^{n} I_j}{\sum\limits_{j=1}^{n} D_j},$$

where

DS = Common days supply for warehouse inventories;

AQ = Inventory units to be allocated from plant warehouse;

I_j = Inventory in units for warehouse j; and

D_j = Daily demand for warehouse j.

In this example,

$$DS = \frac{500 + (50 + 100 + 75)}{10 + 50 + 15}$$

$$= \frac{500 + 225}{75} = 9.67 \text{ days}.$$

The fair share allocation dictates that each warehouse should be stocked to 9.67 days of inventory. The amount to be allocated to each warehouse is determined by:

$$A_j = (DS - I_j/D_j) \times D_j,$$

where

A_j = Amount allocated to warehouse j;

DS = Days supply that each warehouse is brought up to;

I_j = Inventory in units for warehouse j; and

D_j = Daily demand for warehouse j.

The amount allocated to warehouse 1 for this example is:

$$A_1 = (9.67 - 50/10) \times 10$$

$$= (9.67 - 5) \times 10$$

$$= 4.67 \times 10 = 46.7 \text{ (round to 47 units)}.$$

The allocation for warehouses 2 and 3 can be determined similarly and is 383 and 70 units, respectively.

While fair share allocation coordinates inventory levels across multiple sites, it does not consider specific factors such as differences in performance cycle time, EOQ, or safety stock requirements. Fair share allocation methods are therefore limited in their ability to manage multistage inventories.

Requirements Planning

Requirements planning is an approach that integrates across the supply chain, taking into consideration unique requirements. Requirements planning is typically classified as Materials Requirements Planning (MRP) or Distribution Requirements Planning (DRP). There is one fundamental difference between the two techniques. MRP is driven by a production schedule. In contrast, DRP is driven by supply chain demand. So, while MRP generally

FIGURE 6.12
Conceptual Design of Integrated MRP/DRP System

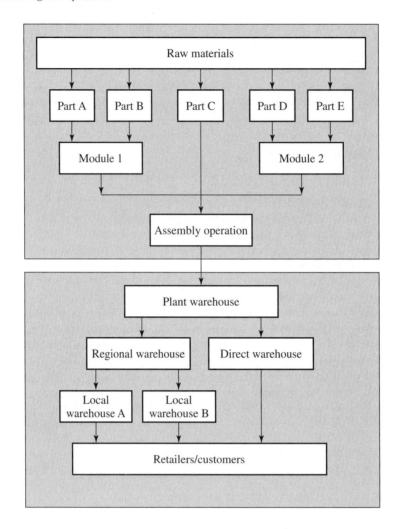

operates in a dependent demand situation, DRP is applicable to an independent demand environment where uncertain customer requirements drive inventory requirements. MRP coordinates scheduling and integration of materials into finished goods, and so controls inventory until manufacturing or assembly is completed. DRP takes coordination responsibility once finished goods are received in the plant warehouse.

Figure 6.12 illustrates the conceptual design of a combined MRP/DRP system that integrates finished goods, work-in-process, and materials planning. The top half of the figure illustrates an MRP system that time-phases raw material arrivals to support the production schedule. The result of MRP execution is finished goods inventory at the manufacturing site. The bottom half of the figure illustrates the DRP system that allocates finished inventory from the manufacturing site to distribution warehouses and ultimately to customers. DRP time-phases the movements to coordinate inventory arrivals to meet customer requirements and commitments. The MRP and DRP systems interface at the manufacturing site. Close coordination between the two systems results in minimal need for safety stock. DRP coordinates inventory levels, schedules, and when necessary, reschedules inventory movement between levels.

The fundamental DRP planning tool is the schedule, which coordinates requirements across the planning horizon. There is a schedule for each SKU at each warehouse.

FIGURE 6.13 **Distribution Requirements Planning Example**

Eastern Warehouse

	Past due	1	2	3	4	5	6	7	8
					Weeks				
Gross requirements		100	120	150	130	100	80	70	90
Scheduled receipts		0	0	400	0	0	0	400	0
Projected on hand	400	300	180	430	300	200	120	450	360
Planned orders		400	0	0	0	400	0	0	0

Safety stock: 100
Order quantity: 400
Leadtime: 2 weeks

Plant Warehouse

Safety stock: 100
Batch size: 600
Leadtime: 1 week

	Past due	1	2	3	4	5	6	7	8
					Weeks				
Gross requirements		400	150	0	150	550	0	0	0
Scheduled receipts		0	600	0	600	0	0	0	0
Projected on hand	600	200	650	650	1100	550	550	550	550
Planned production		600	0	600	0	0	0	0	0

Western Warehouse

	Past due	1	2	3	4	5	6	7	8
					Weeks				
Gross requirements		40	50	60	90	70	100	40	30
Scheduled receipts		0	0	150	0	150	150	0	0
Projected on hand	200	160	110	200	110	190	240	200	170
Planned orders		0	150	0	150	150	0	0	0

Safety stock: 50
Order quantity: 150
Leadtime: 1 week

Requirement - - - - - ►

Shipment ————►

Schedules for the same SKU are integrated to determine the overall requirements for replenishment facilities such as a plant warehouse.

Figure 6.13 illustrates DRP planning schedules for two warehouses and a central supply facility. The schedules are developed using weekly time increments known as **time buckets.** Each bucket projects one period of activity. Although weekly increments are most common, daily or monthly increments can be used. For each site and SKU, the schedule reports current on-hand balance, safety stock, performance cycle length, and order quantity. In addition, for each planning period, the schedule reports gross requirements, scheduled receipts, and projected inventory on hand. Using the combination of requirements and projected availability, DRP determines the planned orders necessary to meet anticipated requirements. Gross requirements reflect customer demand and other distribution facilities supplied by the site under review. For Figure 6.13, the gross requirements of the central supply facility reflect the cascading demands of the Eastern and Western warehouses. Scheduled receipts are the replenishment shipments planned for arrival at the distribution warehouse. Projected on-hand inventory refers to the anticipated week-ending level. It is equal to the prior week's on-hand inventory level less the current week's gross requirements plus any scheduled receipts. While planning approaches to inventory management offer significant benefits, they have some constraints.

First, inventory planning systems require accurate and coordinated forecasts for each warehouse. The forecast is necessary to direct the flow of goods through the supply chain. Ideally, the system does not maintain excess inventory at any location, so little room for error exists in a lean inventory system. To the extent this level of forecast accuracy is possible, inventory planning systems operate well.

Second, inventory planning requires consistent and reliable product for movement between warehouse facilities. While variable performance cycles can be accommodated through safety leadtimes, such uncertainty reduces planning system effectiveness.

Third, integrated planning systems are subject to system nervousness, or frequent rescheduling, because of production breakdowns or delivery delays. System nervousness leads to fluctuation in capacity utilization, rescheduling cost, and confusion in deliveries. This is intensified by the volatile operating environment characteristic of supply chain logistics. Uncertainties such as transportation and vendor delivery reliability can cause an extreme DRP nervousness.

Collaborative Inventory Replenishment

In Chapter 3 CPFR was introduced and discussed as a major collaborative effort between supply chain trading partners. Several collaborative initiatives focus only on inventory replenishment. Replenishment programs are designed to streamline the flow of goods within the supply chain. There are several specific techniques for collaborative replenishment, all of which build on supply chain relationships to rapidly replenish inventory on the basis of joint planning or actual sales experience. The intent is to reduce reliance on forecasting when and where inventory will need to be positioned to demand on a just-in-time basis. Effective collaborative replenishment programs require extensive cooperation and information sharing among supply chain partners. Specific techniques for collaborative inventory replenishment are quick response, vendor-managed inventory, and profile replenishment.

Quick Response

A technology-driven cooperative effort between retailers and suppliers to improve inventory velocity while providing merchandise supply closely matched to consumer buying patterns is quick response (QR). QR is implemented by sharing retail sales for specific products across supply chain participants to facilitate right product assortment availability when and where it is required. Instead of operating on 15- to 30-day order cycle, QR arrangements can replenish retail inventories in a few days. Continuous information exchange regarding availability and delivery reduces uncertainty for the total supply chain and creates the opportunity for maximum flexibility. With fast, dependable order response, inventory can be committed as required, resulting in increased turnover and improved availability. Wal★Mart's system is a prime example of the power of sharing sales to facilitate QR.

Vendor-Managed Inventory

Vendor-managed inventory (VMI) is a modification of quick response that eliminates the need for replenishment orders. The goal is to establish a supply chain arrangement so flexible and efficient that retail inventory is continuously replenished. The distinguishing factor between QR and VMI is who takes responsibility for setting target inventory levels and making restocking decisions. In QR, the retailer makes the decisions. In VMI, the supplier assumes more responsibility and actually manages a catagory of inventory for the retailer. By receiving daily transmission of retail sales or warehouse shipments, the supplier assumes responsibility for replenishing retail inventory in the required quantities, colors, sizes, and styles. The supplier commits to keeping the retailer in stock and to maintaining inventory velocity. In some situations, replenishment involves cross-docking or direct store delivery (DSD) designed to eliminate the need for warehousing between the factory and retail store.

Profile Replenishment

Some manufacturers, wholesalers, and retailers are experimenting with an even more sophisticated collaboration known as profile replenishment (PR). The PR strategy extends QR and VMI by giving suppliers the right to anticipate future requirements according to their overall knowledge of a merchandise category. A category profile details the combination of sizes, colors, and associated products that usually sell in a particular type of retail outlet. Given PR responsibility, the supplier can simplify retailer involvement by eliminating the need to track unit sales and inventory level for fast-moving products.

Many firms, particularly manufacturers, are using DRP and even APS logic to coordinate inventory planning with major customers. The manufacturers are extending their planning framework to include customer warehouses and, in some cases, their retail stores. Such integrated planning capabilities facilitate manufacturer coordination and management of customer inventories.

Collaborative planning effectively shares inventory requirements and availability between supply chain partners, thus reducing uncertainty. Table 6.17 illustrates the service and inventory impact in a simulated environment under conditions of low and high uncertainty.[7] Table 6.18 illustrates managerial considerations that drive adaptations of control logic.

[7] David J. Closs et al., "An Empirical Comparison of Anticipatory and Response-Based Supply Chain Strategies," *The International Journal of Logistics Management* 9, no. 2 (1998), pp. 21–34.

TABLE 6.17
Comparative Service and Inventory Characteristics for Anticipatory versus Responsive Inventory Systems

Source: Adapted from David J. Closs et al., "An Empirical Comparison of Anticipatory and Response-Based Supply Chain Strategies," *The International Journal of Logistics Management* 9, no. 2 (1998), pp. 21–34. Used with permission.

	Low Uncertainty Anticipatory	Low Uncertainty Responsive	High Uncertainty Anticipatory	High Uncertainty Responsive
Customer Service				
Fill rate percent	97.69	99.66	96.44	99.29
Inventories				
Supplier inventory	12.88	13.24	14.82	13.61
Manufacturer inventory	6.05	6.12	7.03	6.09
Distributor inventory	5.38	5.86	5.04	5.63
Retailer inventory	30.84	15.79	32.86	20.30
System inventory	55.15	41.01	59.76	45.83

TABLE 6.18
Suggested Inventory Management Logic

Use Planning Logic under Conditions Of	Use Reactive Logic under Conditions Of
Highly profitable segments	Cycle time uncertainty
Dependent demand	Demand uncertainty
Economies of scale	Destination capacity limitations
Supply uncertainty	
Source capacity limitations	
Seasonal supply buildup	

Inventory Management Practices

An integrated inventory management strategy defines the policies and process used to determine where to place inventory and when to initiate replenishment shipments, as well as how much to allocate. The strategy development process employs three steps to classify products and markets, define segment strategies, and operationalize policies and parameters.

Product/Market Classification

The objective of product/market classification is to focus and refine inventory management efforts. Product/market classification, which is also called **fine-line** or **ABC classification,** groups products, markets, or customers with similar characteristics to facilitate inventory management. The classification process recognizes that not all products and markets have the same characteristics or degree of importance. Sound inventory management requires that classification be consistent with enterprise strategy and service objectives.

Classification can be based on a variety of measures. The most common are sales, profit contribution, inventory value, usage rate, and nature of the item. The typical classification process sequences products or markets so that entries with similar characteristics are grouped together. Table 6.19 illustrates product classification using sales. The products are classified in descending order by sales volume so that the high-volume products are listed first, followed by slower movers. Classification by sales volume is one of the oldest methods used to establish selective inventory policies. For most marketing or logistics applications, a small percentage of the entities account for a large percentage of the

TABLE 6.19
Product Market Classification (Sales)

Product Identification	Annual Sales (in 000s)	Percent Total Sales	Accumulated Sales (%)	Products (%)	Classification Category
1	$45,000	30.0%	30.0%	5%	A
2	35,000	23.3	53.3	10	A
3	25,000	16.7	70.0	15	A
4	15,000	10.0	80.0	20	A
5	8,000	5.3	85.3	25	B
6	5,000	3.3	88.6	30	B
7	4,000	2.7	91.3	35	B
8	3,000	2.0	93.3	40	B
9	2,000	1.3	94.6	45	B
10	1,000	0.7	95.3	50	B
11	1,000	0.7	96.0	55	C
12	1,000	0.7	96.7	60	C
13	1,000	0.7	97.4	65	C
14	750	0.5	97.9	70	C
15	750	0.5	98.4	75	C
16	750	0.5	98.9	80	C
17	500	0.3	99.2	85	C
18	500	0.3	99.5	90	C
19	500	0.3	99.8	95	C
20	250	0.2	100.0	100	C
	$150,000				

volume. This operationalization is often called the **80/20 rule** or **Pareto's law.** The 80/20 rule, which is based on widespread observations, states that for a typical enterprise 80 percent of the sales volume is typically accounted for by 20 percent of the products. A corollary to the rule is that 80 percent of enterprise sales are accounted for by 20 percent of the customers. The reverse perspective of the rule would state that the remaining 20 percent of sales are obtained from 80 percent of the products, customers, etc. In general terms, the 80/20 rule implies that a majority of sales results from a relatively few products or customers.

Once items are classified or grouped, it is common to label each category with a character or description. High-volume, fast-moving products are often described as A items. The moderate volume items are termed the B items, and the low-volume or slow movers are known as Cs. These character labels indicate why this process is often termed ABC analysis. While fine-line classification often uses three categories, some firms use four or five categories to further refine classifications. Grouping of similar products facilitates management efforts to establish focused inventory strategies for specific product segments. For example, high-volume or fast-moving products are typically targeted for higher service levels. This often requires that fast-moving items have relatively more safety stock. Conversely, to reduce overall inventory levels, slower-moving items may be allowed relatively less safety stock, resulting in lower service levels.

In special situations, classification systems may be based on multiple factors. For example, item gross margin and importance to customers can be weighted to develop a combined index instead of simply using sales volume. The weighted rank would then group items that have similar profitability and importance characteristics. The inventory policy, including safety stock levels, is then established using the weighted rank.

The classification array defines product or market groups to be assigned similar inventory strategies. The use of item groups facilitates the identification and specification of inventory strategies without requiring tedious development of individual item strategies. It is much easier to track and manage 3 to 10 groups instead of hundreds of individual items.

Segment Strategy Definition

The second step is to define the inventory strategy for each product/market group or segment. The strategy includes specification for all aspects of the inventory management process, including service objectives, forecasting method, management technique, and review cycle.

The key to establishing selective management strategies is the realization that product segments have different degrees of importance with respect to achieving the enterprise mission. Important differences in inventory responsiveness should be designed into the policies and procedures used for inventory management.

Table 6.20 illustrates a sample integrated strategy for four item categories. In this case, the items are grouped by ABC sales volume and as a promotional or regular stock item.

TABLE 6.20
Integrated Strategy

Fine-Line Classification	Service Objective	Forecasting Procedure	Review Period	Inventory Management	Replenishment Monitoring
A (Promotional)	99%	CPFR	Perpetual	Planning—DRP	Daily
A (Regular)	98	Sales history	Perpetual	Planning—DRP	Daily
B	95	Sales history	Weekly	Planning—DRP	Weekly
C	90	Sales history	Biweekly	Reorder point	Biweekly

Promotional items are those commonly sold in special marketing efforts that result in considerable demand lumpiness. Lumpy demand patterns are characteristic of promotional periods with high volume followed by postpromotion periods with relatively low demand.

Table 6.20 illustrates a management segmentation scheme based on service objectives, forecasting process, review period, inventory management approach, and replenishment monitoring frequency. Additional or fewer characteristics of the inventory management process may be appropriate for some enterprises. Although this table is not presented as a comprehensive inventory strategy framework, it illustrates the issues that must be considered. The rationale behind each element is presented on the basis of the full-line classification.

Policies and Parameters

The final step in implementing a focused inventory management strategy is to define detailed procedures and parameters. The procedures define data requirements, software applications, performance objectives, and decision guidelines. The parameters delineate values such as review period length, service objectives, inventory carrying cost percentage, order quantities, and reorder points. The combination of parameters either determines or can be used to calculate the precise quantities necessary to make inventory management decisions.

Summary

Inventory typically represents the second largest component of logistics cost next to transportation. The risks associated with holding inventory increase as products move down the supply chain closer to the customer because the potential of having the product in the wrong place or form increases and costs have been incurred to distribute the product. In addition to the risk of lost sales due to stockouts because adequate inventory is not available, other risks include obsolescence, pilferage, and damage. Further, the cost of carrying inventory is significantly influenced by the cost of the capital tied up in the inventory. Geographic specialization, decoupling, supply/demand balancing, and buffering uncertainty provide the basic rationale for maintaining inventory. While there is substantial interest in reducing overall supply chain inventory, inventory does add value and can result in lower overall supply chain costs with appropriate trade-offs.

From a supply chain logistics perspective, the major controllable inventory elements are replenishment cycle stock, safety stock, and in-transit stock. The appropriate replenishment cycle stock can be determined using an EOQ formula to reflect the trade-off between storage and ordering cost. Safety stock depends on the mean and variance of demand and the replenishment cycle. In-transit stock depends on the transport mode.

Inventory management uses a combination of reactive and planning logics. Reactive logic is most appropriate for items with low volume, high demand, and high performance cycle uncertainty because it postpones the risk of inventory speculation. Inventory planning logic is appropriate for high-volume items with relatively stable demand. Inventory planning methods offer the potential for effective inventory management because they take advantage of improved information and economies of scale. Adaptive logic combines the two alternatives depending on product and market conditions. Collaboration offers a way for parties in the supply chain to jointly gain inventory efficiency and effectiveness.

Challenge Questions

1. How does the cost of carrying inventory impact the traditional earnings statement of the enterprise?

2. Discuss the relationship between service level, uncertainty, safety stock, and order quantity. How can trade-offs between these elements be made?

3. Discuss the disproportionate risk of holding inventory by retailers, wholesalers, and manufacturers. Why has there been a trend to push inventory back up the channel of distribution?

4. What is the difference between the probability of a stockout and the magnitude of a stockout?

5. Data suggest that while overall average inventory levels are declining, the relative percentage being held by manufacturers is increasing. Explain why you think this observation is either true or false. Describe how such a shift could benefit the operations of the entire channel and how manufacturers could take advantage of the shift.

6. Discuss the differences between reactive and planning inventory logics. What are the advantages of each? What are the major implications of each?

7. Illustrate how fine-line inventory classification can be used with product and market segments. What are the benefits and considerations when classifying inventory by product, market, and product/market?

8. What advantage does DRP have over a fair share method of inventory deployment?

9. Discuss the importance of collaboration in the developing of supply chain inventory strategies. Provide an example.

10. Customer-based inventory management strategies allow the use of different availability levels for specific customers. Discuss the rationale for such a strategy. Are such strategies discriminatory? Justify your position.

Transportation Infrastructure

The role of transportation in logistics has changed dramatically over the last three decades. Prior to transportation deregulation, the purchase of transportation could be likened to buying a commodity such as coal or grain. There was very little difference between transport suppliers in terms of product, service, or price. Transportation deregulation in 1980 introduced pricing flexibility and significantly increased the range of services transportation companies could provide customers.

Today a wide range of transportation alternatives are available to support supply chain logistics. For example, logistics managers may integrate private with for-hire transportation to reduce total logistics costs. Many for-hire carriers offer a wide variety of value-added services such as product sortation, sequencing, and customized freight delivery and presentation. Technology has enhanced real-time visibility of the location of freight throughout the supply chain and advanced information concerning delivery. Precise product delivery reduces inventory, storage, and materials handling. As a result, the value of transportation has become greater than simply moving product from one location to another. This chapter provides an overview of the transportation infrastructure and its current regulatory framework.[1]

Transport Functionality, Principles, and Participants

Transportation is a very visible element of logistics. Consumers are accustomed to seeing trucks and trains transporting product or parked at business facilities. Few consumers fully understand just how dependent our economic system is upon economical and dependable transportation. This section provides a foundation by reviewing transportation functionality and the underlying principles of transport operation.

Transport Functionality

Transportation enterprises provide two major services: product movement and product storage.

Product Movement

Whether in the form of materials, components, work-in-process, or finished goods, the basic value provided by transportation is to move inventory to specified destinations. The primary transportation value proposition is product movement throughout the supply chain. The performance of transportation is vital to procurement, manufacturing, and customer accommodation. Transportation also plays a key role in the performance of reverse logistics. Without reliable transportation, most commercial activity could not function. Transportation consumes time, financial, and environmental resources.

Transportation has a restrictive element because inventory is generally inaccessible during the transportation process. Inventory captive in the transport system is referred to as **in-transit inventory.** Naturally, when designing logistical systems, managers strive to reduce in-transit inventory to a minimum. Advancements in information technology have significantly improved access to in-transit inventory and arrival status of shipments by providing exact location and arrival times.

Transportation also uses financial resources. In the United States more than 60 percent of total logistics cost is related to transportation services.[2] Transportation cost results from driver labor, vehicle operation, capital invested in equipment, and administration. In addition, product loss and damage are significant costs.

Transportation impacts environmental resources both directly and indirectly. In direct terms, transportation represents one of the largest consumers of fuel and oil in the United States economy. Although the level of fuel and oil consumption has improved as a result of more fuel-efficient vehicles, total consumption remains high. Indirectly, transportation impacts the environment through congestion, air pollution, and noise pollution.

Product Storage

A less visible aspect of transportation is the performance of product storage. While a product is in a transportation vehicle, it is being stored. Transport vehicles can also be used for product storage at shipment origin or destination, but they are comparatively expensive storage facilities. Since the main value proposition of transportation is movement, a vehicle committed to storage is not otherwise available for transport. A trade-off exists between using a transportation vehicle versus temporarily placing products in a warehouse. If the inventory involved is scheduled to be shipped within a few days to a different location, the

---

[1] Transportation operations are discussed in Chapter 8.

[2] For a component breakdown of total logistics cost see Chapter 2.

cost of unloading, warehousing, and reloading the product may exceed the temporary cost of using the transportation vehicle for storage.[3]

Another transport service having storage implications is **diversion.** Diversion occurs when a shipment destination is changed after a product is in transit. For example, the destination of a product initially shipped from Chicago to Los Angeles may be changed to Seattle while in transit. Traditionally, the telephone was used to implement diversion strategies. Today, Internet communication between shippers, carriers' headquarters, and vehicles facilitates more efficient diversion. While diversion is primarily used to improve logistical responsiveness, it also impacts the duration of in-transit storage.

So although costly, product storage in transportation vehicles may be justified from a total cost or performance perspective when loading or unloading costs, capacity constraints, and ability to extend lead times are taken into consideration.

Transport Principles

There are two fundamental economic principles that impact transportation efficiency: **economy of scale** and **economy of distance.**

Economy of scale in transportation is the cost per unit of weight decreases as the size of a shipment increases. For example, truckload shipments utilizing an entire trailer's capacity have a lower cost per pound than smaller shipments that utilize a limited portion of vehicle capacity. It is also generally true that larger-capacity transportation vehicles, such as rail and water vehicles, are less costly per unit of weight than smaller-capacity vehicles such as trucks and airplanes. Transportation economies of scale exist because fixed cost associated with transporting a load is allocated over the increased weight. Fixed costs include administration related to scheduling, cost of equipment, time to position vehicles for loading or unloading, and invoicing. Such costs are considered fixed because they do not vary with shipment size. In other words, it costs as much to administer a 100-pound shipment as one weighing 1000-pounds.

Economy of distance refers to decreased transportation cost per unit of weight as distance increases. For example, a shipment of 800 miles will cost less to perform than two shipments of the same weight each moving 400 miles. Transportation economy of distance is often referred to as the **tapering principle.** The rationale for distance economies is similar to economies of scale. Specifically, longer distances allow fixed cost to be spread over more miles, resulting in lower per mile charges.

These principles are important when evaluating transportation alternatives. The goal from a transportation perspective is to maximize the size of the load and the distance being shipped while still meeting customer service expectations.[4]

Transport Participants

The transportation environment impacts the range of decisions that can be implemented in a logistical system. Unlike most commercial transactions, transportation decisions are influenced by six parties: (1) shipper, sometimes referred to as the **consignor;** (2) destination party, traditionally called the **consignee**; (3) carriers and agents; (4) government; (5) Internet; and (6) the public. Figure 7.1 illustrates the relationship among the involved parties. To understand the complexity of the transportation environment it is useful to review the role and perspective of each party.

---

[3] The technical terms for charges related to using transportation vehicles for storage are *demurrage* for rail cars and *detention* for trucks. See Chapter 8.

[4] For more detailed discussion, see Chapter 8.

FIGURE 7.1
Relationship among Transportation Participants

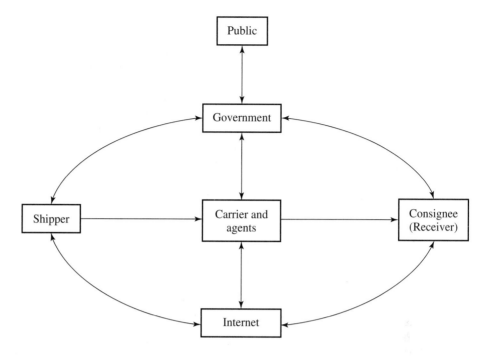

Shipper and Consignee

The shipper and consignee have a common interest in moving goods from origin to destination within a given time at the lowest cost. Services related to transportation include specified pickup and delivery times, predictable transit time, and zero loss and damage, as well as accurate and timely exchange of information and invoicing.

Carrier and Agents

The carrier, a business that performs a transportation service, desires to maximize its revenue for movement while minimizing associated costs. As a service business, carriers want to charge their customers the highest rate possible while minimizing labor, fuel, and vehicle costs required to complete the movement. To achieve this objective, the carrier seeks to coordinate pickup and delivery times to group or consolidate many different shippers' freight into movements that achieve economy of scale and distance. Brokers and freight forwarders are transport agents that facilitate carrier and customer matching. A recent development has been the emergence of Internet or online brokers that match carrier capacity and shipper requirements.

Government

The government has a vested interest in transportation because of the critical importance of reliable service to economic and social well-being. Government desires a stable and efficient transportation environment to support economic growth.

A stable and efficient transportation environment requires that carriers provide essential services at reasonable cost. Because of the direct impact of transportation on economic success, governments have traditionally been very involved in oversight of carrier practices. In some situations, such as the United States Postal Service, government is directly involved in providing the transportation service. Government historically regulated carriers by restricting markets they could service and approving prices they could charge. Governments also promote carrier development by supporting research and providing right-of-way such as roadways and airports. In some countries government maintains absolute control over markets, services, and rates. Such control allows government to have a major influence on the economic success of regions, industries, or firms.

The overall nature of transportation regulation has changed significantly over the past three decades. A later section of this chapter provides an overview of this regulatory change.

Internet

A recent development in the transportation industry is a wide assortment of Internet-based services. The primary advantage of Internet-based communication is the ability of carriers to share real-time information with customers and suppliers. In addition to direct Internet communication between businesses engaged in logistical operations, a wide variety of Web-based enterprises have been launched in recent years. Such Web-based enterprises typically provide three types of marketplaces. The first is a marketplace to exchange information for matching carrier freight capacity with available shipments. These Web-based services may also provide a marketplace to facilitate transactions.

Beyond freight matching, a second form of Internet-based information exchange relates to the purchase of fuel, equipment, parts, and supplies. Information exchanges operating over the Internet provide carriers the opportunity to aggregate their purchasing and identify opportunities across a wide range of potential vendors. The third form of information exchange facilitated by the Internet is shipment tracking and tracing capability.

The primary reason that B2B Internet usage has grown rapidly in motor carrier transport is because the U.S. freight market is highly fragmented. While in excess of 585,000 truckload carriers exist, 81 percent operate six or fewer trucks.[5] The use of Internet services to share information is attractive for both carriers and shippers.

Finally, the use of the Internet as a communication backbone is rapidly changing the nature of transportation operations. The availability of real-time information is improving shipment visibility to the point where tracing and tracking are no longer a major challenge. In addition to real-time visibility, the Internet can be used to share information concerning scheduling and capacity planning.

Public

The final transportation system participant, the public, is concerned with transportation accessibility, expense, and effectiveness as well as environmental and safety standards. The public indirectly creates transportation demand by purchasing goods. While minimizing transportation cost is important to consumers, concerns also involve environmental impact and safety. The effect of air pollution and oil spillage is a significant transportation-related social issue. The cost of environmental impact and safety is ultimately paid by consumers.

Transportation policy formation is complex because of interaction between these six participants. Such complexity results in frequent conflict between shippers, consignees, and carriers. The concern to protect public interest served as the historical justification for government involvement in economic and social regulation. The next section provides a brief review of how government regulation has changed over the years.

Transportation Regulation

Since transportation has a major impact on both domestic and international commerce, government has historically taken special interest in both controlling and promoting transportation. Control takes the form of federal and state government regulation as well as a

---

[5] American Trucking Association, *American Trucking Trends* (Alexandra, VA: American Trucking Association Inc., 2003), pp. 2–3.

wide range of administration and judicial administration. With the passage of the Act to Regulate Interstate Commerce on February 4, 1887, the federal government became active in protecting the public interest with respect to performance and provision of transportation services.

Types of Regulation

Government transportation regulation can be grouped into two categories: economic regulation and social regulation. Regulatory initiatives have historically focused on economic issues; however, recent regulatory initiatives have increasingly been directed toward safety and social issues.

Economic

Regulation of business practices is the oldest form of government control. To provide dependable transportation service and to foster economic development, both federal and state governments have actively engaged in economic regulation. For over 100 years, government regulation sought to make transportation equally accessible and economical to all without discrimination. To encourage economical and widespread transportation supply, government invested in public infrastructure such as highways, airports, waterways, and deepwater ports. However, to actually provide transportation service, the government supported and regulated a system of privately owned for-hire carriers.

Because of transportation's importance to economic growth, government believed that carriers needed to be regulated to ensure service availability, stability, and fair prices. Availability means that carrier services would be accessible to all business enterprises. Stability means that carriers would be guaranteed sufficient profits to ensure viable long-term operation. Fair prices mean that carriers could not take advantage of shippers by controlling or restricting supply.

Economic regulation generally sought to achieve its goals by controlling entry, rates, and services. In addition, economic regulatory practice treated each type of transport independently. This practice limited carrier ability to develop intermodal relationships and offerings. By 1970, federal economic regulation had reached the point where it provided oversight on 100 percent of rail and air ton-miles, 80 percent of pipeline, 43.1 percent of trucking, and 6.7 percent of domestic water carriers.[6] The degree of direct government economic regulation began to decline during the 1970s and took a dramatic turn in 1980 with the passage of major deregulatory legislation. The contemporary economic regulatory environment is dominated by free market competition more or less regulated by antitrust laws.

Social

In direct contrast to reduced transportation regulation, another trend in the 1970s and 1980s was expanded safety and social regulation. Since its inception in 1966, the federal Department of Transportation (DOT) has taken an active role in controlling the transport and handling of hazardous material and rules related to maximum driver hours and safety. The form of regulation was institutionalized by the passage of the Transportation Safety Act of 1974, which formally established safety and social regulation as a governmental initiative. Substantial legislation impacting logistical performance was passed during the next three decades. The Hazardous Materials Transportation Uniform Safety Act of 1990, which provided federal government control over equipment design, hazardous material classification, packaging, and handling, took precedence over state and local environmental regulations.

---

[6] Derived from Department of Transportation, *1972 National Transportation Report* (Washington, DC: U.S. Government Printing Office, 1972), pp. 2–44.

Additional emphasis on transportation safety has increased as a result of environmental and related liability lawsuits.

History of Regulation

The following discussion is divided into time periods reflecting dominant regulatory posture. The early period regulation discussion serves to provide future logistics managers insight into the legislative, administrative, and judicial foundations of today's transportation industry.

Pre-1920: Establishing Government Control

The original purpose of interstate regulation was to scrutinize the activities of for-hire carriers for the public interest. Railroads dominated early transportation, enjoying a near monopoly. Individual states maintained the legal right to regulate discriminatory practices within their borders, but no federal regulation existed to provide consistent interstate controls. In 1887, the Act to Regulate Commerce was passed by Congress and became the foundation of U.S. transportation regulation.[7] The act also created the Interstate Commerce Commission (ICC).

Federal regulatory power over carriers evolved from legislation and judicial decisions from 1900 through 1920. At the turn of the century, destructive competitive practices were common as a result of independent pricing by carriers. Although the ICC had the authority to review groups of rates with respect to their just and reasonable nature once published by individual carriers, no regulation existed over rate making. Attempts at joint rate making by railroads had been declared illegal. In 1903, the railroads supported the passage of the Elkins Act. This legislation eliminated secret rebates and special concessions while increasing the penalty for secret agreements to charge different from published rates. It did not, however, eliminate—independent and nonregulated pricing which was the primary cause of discrimination.

The passage of the Hepburn Act of 1906 began to establish federal regulatory power over pricing. The just-and-reasonable-review authorization of the 1887 act was expanded to include examination of maximum rates. However, the regulatory posture remained **expost,** or after the fact, until passage of the Mann-Elkins Act in 1910. This act permitted the ICC to rule on the reasonableness of proposed rates **prior** to their effective date and to suspend rates when they appeared discriminatory.

The framework for rate regulation was completed with the passage of the Transportation Act of 1920. The review power of the ICC was expanded to prescribe reasonableness of minimum as well as maximum rates. The ICC was instructed to assume a more aggressive nature concerning proposed rates. The original Act to Regulate Commerce was modified to instruct the commission to initiate, modify, and adjust rates as necessary in the public interest. The 1920 act also changed the name of the 1887 act to the Interstate Commerce Act.

1920–1940: Regulatory Formalization

Several additional transportation laws were enacted during these two decades. With some exceptions, their primary objective was to clarify issues related to the basic acts of 1887 and 1920. In 1935 the Emergency Transportation Act further instructed the ICC to set standards with respect to reasonable rate levels. By the 1930s motor carriers had become important transportation providers. In 1935 the Motor-Carrier Act placed regulation of common carrier highway transportation under the jurisdiction of the ICC. This act, which

[7] For an early history of legislative attempts prior to 1887, see L. H. Hanley, *A Congressional History of Railroads in the United States, 1850–1887,* Bulletin 342 (Madison: University of Wisconsin, 1910).

became Part II of the Interstate Commerce Act, defined the basic nature of the legal forms of for-hire and motor carriers.

In 1938 the Civil Aeronautics Act established the Civil Aeronautics Authority (CAA) as the ICC's counterpart for regulating air transport. The powers and charges of the CAA were somewhat different from those of the ICC, in that the act specified that the CAA would promote and actively develop the growth and safety of the airline industry. In 1940 the functions of the original CAA were reorganized into the Civil Aeronautics Board (CAB) and the Civil Aeronautics Administration, later known as the Federal Aeronautics Administration (FAA). In addition, the National Advisory Committee on Aeronautics was formed in the mid-1930s and in 1951 became known as the National Aeronautics and Space Administration (NASA). Starting in the 1960s, NASA concentrated attention on exploration of outer space. However, NASA was specifically charged with the responsibility for increasing aviation safety, utility, and basic knowledge through the deployment of science and technology. Thus, in the regulatory structure that resulted, the CAB regulated rate making; the FAA administered the airway system; and NASA was concerned with scientific development of aerospace, commercial, and private aviation.

The regulation of pipelines was not as clear-cut as that of railroads, motor carriers, and air transport. In 1906 the Hepburn Act declared that oil pipelines were common carriers. The need for regulation developed from the early market dominance that the Standard Oil Company gained by developing crude oil pipelines to compete with rail transport. In 1912 the ICC ruled, subsequently upheld by the Supreme Court, that private pipelines could be regulated as common carriers. While there are substantial differences between pipeline and other forms of regulation, for all effective purposes the ICC regulated pipeline traffic. Interestingly, a significant difference regarding pipeline regulation is that this type of common carrier was allowed to transport goods owned by the carrier.

1940–1970: Status Quo

Regulation of water transport prior to 1940 was extremely fragmented. Some standards existed under both the ICC and the Federal Maritime Commission (FMC). In addition, a series of acts placed regulation of various aspects of the domestic water transport under specific agencies. For example, the Transportation Act of 1940 put domestic water transport under ICC jurisdiction and gave the FMC authority over water transport in foreign commerce and between Alaska and Hawaii and other United States ports.

It is important to understand that the ICC did not actually set or establish carrier prices. Rather, the ICC reviewed and either approved or disapproved rates. Carriers under federal regulation were allowed to jointly set prices because they were exempt from the antitrust provisions of the Sherman, Clayton, and Robinson-Patman acts. This exemption was provided by the Reed-Bulwinkle Act of 1948, which permitted carriers to collaborate in rate-making bureaus. Collaborative pricing was a common feature among for-hire carriers. In particular, for-hire transportation carriers in motor and rail organized freight bureaus that standardized prices and published price lists, called tariffs, for specific geographical areas.

From 1970 until 1973 several acts were passed to aid the rapidly deteriorating rail industry of the United States. In 1970 the Rail Passenger Service Act established the National Railroad Passenger Cooperation (AMTRAK). The Regional Rail Reorganization Act of 1973 (3-R) was passed to provide economic aid to seven major northeastern railroads facing bankruptcy. As a result of 3-R Act provisions, the Consolidated Rail Corporation (CONRAIL) began to operate portions of the seven lines on April 1, 1976.

The establishment of AMTRAK and CONRAIL represented the first modern attempt of the federal government to own and operate transportation. While the subsequent passage of the Railroad Revitalization and Regulatory Reform Act of 1976 (4-R) and the Rail Transportation Improvement Act of 1976 provided financial support for AMTRAK and

CONRAIL, these acts also began to reverse the trend of regulatory expansion that had prevailed for nine decades.

1970–1980: Prelude to Deregulation

In the early 1970s, a movement was gaining momentum to review and modify economic regulation to better meet the requirements of contemporary society. A Presidential Advisory Committee recommended that increased transportation competition would be in the general public's interest. The committee's recommendations were published in a 1960 report issued by the Commerce Department.[8] A Senate Committee in 1961 produced a revised National Transportation Policy. Among other recommendations the 1961 report advocated formation of a Department of Transportation (DOT).[9] After its formation in 1966, DOT became a dominant force seeking regulatory modification. From 1972 to 1980 DOT introduced or significantly influenced legislation at 2-year intervals to modify the regulatory scope of for-hire carriers.

The initial success in regulatory reform was administrative in nature. From 1977 to 1978 CAB Chairman Alfred Kahn forced de facto deregulation of the Civil Aeronautics Board by virtue of administrative rulings that encouraged air carrier price competition and eased the establishment of new airlines. In 1977, the Federal Aviation Act was amended to deregulate domestic cargo airlines, freight forwarders, and shipper's associations with respect to pricing and entry. The standard for entry into the air cargo industry was modified to require that a new competitor be judged **fit, willing,** and **able** to carry out the proposed service. The traditional regulatory criteria of judging entry applications on the basis of **public convenience necessity** were eliminated. On October 24, 1978, the Airline Deregulation Act was passed, extending free market competition to all forms of passenger air transport. The CAB was closed November 30, 1984.

1980–2000: Deregulation

The drive for economic regulatory change in trucking and the railroads became official with the passage of the Motor Carrier Act of 1980 (MC 80) and the Staggers Rail Act (Staggers Act).[10]

MC 80 was a formal effort to stimulate competition and promote efficiency in trucking. Entry restrictions or right to conduct operations were relaxed, allowing firms to offer trucking services if they were judged fit, willing, and able. Restrictions relating to the types of freight carriers could legally haul and the range of services carriers could provide were abolished. While the ICC retained the right to protect the public against discriminatory practices and predatory pricing, individual carriers were given the right to price their services. The trucking industry's collective rate-making practices were restricted and soon would be abolished. The structural impact of MC 80 on the for-hire motor carrier industry was dramatic. Overnight the industry was transformed from a highly regulated to a highly competitive structure.

On October 14, 1980, the railroad industry was deregulated by enactment of the Staggers Rail Act. This act was a continuation of a trend initiated in the 3-R and 4-R acts and supplemented the Rail Transportation Improvement Act of 1976. The dominant philosophy

---

[8] Department of Commerce, *Federal Transportation Policy and Program* (Washington, DC: U.S. Government Printing Office, 1960).

[9] Senate Committee on Commerce, 87th Congress, *National Transportation Policy* (Washington, DC: U.S. Government Printing Office, 1961). The Department of Transportation was established by Public Law 86-670 in 1966 and initiated operation on April 1, 1967.

[10] Motor Carrier Act of 1980 (Public Law 96-296) and the Staggers Rail Act of 1980 (Public Law 96-488).

of the Staggers Act was to provide railroad management with the freedom necessary to revitalize the industry. In that respect, the most significant provision of the Staggers Act was increased pricing freedom. Railroads were authorized to selectively reduce rates to meet competition while increasing other rates to cover operating cost. Carriers were also given increased flexibility with respect to surcharges. Contract rate agreements between individual shippers and carriers were specifically legalized. In addition to price flexibility, railroad management was given liberalized authority to proceed with abandonment of poorly performing rail service. The act also provided the framework for a liberalized attitude toward mergers and increased the ability of railroads to be involved in motor carrier service.

Since the passage of the landmark legislation of 1980, several major legislative acts have further defined pricing practice and structure. The trend toward a competitive transportation marketplace was reinforced by key administrative and judicial rulings. For instance, until the passage of the 1993 Negotiated Rate Act (NRA), a regulatory loophole interfered with competitive pricing. Competition led many motor carriers to negotiate lower rates with shippers than those filed with the ICC. Eventually, the motor carrier trustees sued shippers for the difference between the ICC filed rate and the lower negotiated rate—a total of $27 billion in claims.[11] In Maislin Industries versus Primary Steel (1990), the Supreme Court found that the undercharge claims were generally valid. In response, the 1993 NRA act provided a framework for motor carriers to settle undercharge claims. However, in the final undercharge case, 2001 Willig Freight Lines Incorporated versus Shuford Mills Incorporated, the Court found that seeking undercharge restitution was an unreasonable practice.

The authority of the ICC to regulate transportation was generally weakened following passage of the Trucking Industry Reform Act of 1994.[12] This act eliminated the need for motor carriers to file rates with the ICC and consequently eliminated undercharges. Effective January 1, 1996, the ICC was abolished by passage of the ICC Termination Act of 1995. This act further deregulated transportation and established a three-person Surface Transportation Board (STB) within the DOT to administer remaining economic regulation issues across the industry.[13] The authority of the STB includes all transportation modes and incorporates freight forwarders and brokers.

Over the decades, considerable conflict existed between the federal government and state governments concerning legal right to regulate interstate commerce. Both levels of government claimed inherent rights to regulate. State government clearly had the right to regulate intrastate shipments in terms of vehicle size, entry, rates, and routes. At the height of the regulatory era, 42 states were actively engaged in some form of regulation.[14] The issues of the state's right to regulate were not as clear-cut with respect to freight moving in interstate commerce.

In an effort to increase intrastate regulatory consistency across states, the ICC attempted to clarify and expand interstate transportation. Interstate commerce was traditionally defined as product movement across state lines. In a 1993 ruling, the ICC concluded that shipments from warehouses to markets in the same state could be deemed interstate movements if the commodity had originally been shipped from out of state. The ICC argued that such shipments are part of a continuing movement and that interstate regulation should apply. In an effort to gain more direct control over intrastate regulation, the Federal Aviation Administration Authorization Act and the Reauthorization Act of 1996 essentially preempted

---

[11] Thomas Gale Moore, "Clearing the Track, The Remaining Transportation Regulations" The CATO Review of Business and Movement, 1995.

[12] Trucking Industry Reform Act of 1994 (Public Law S.B. 2275).

[13] ICC Termination Act of 1995.

[14] Cassandra Chrones Moore, "Interstate Trucking: Stronghold of the Regulations," *Policy Analysis 204*, February 16, 1994, p. 6.

economic regulation of intrastate transportation.[15] The preemption was placed in the act because Congress found that state regulation of intrastate transport had (1) imposed an unreasonable cost on interstate commerce; (2) impeded the free flow of trade, traffic, and transportation of interstate commerce; and (3) placed unreasonable cost on consumers.

This legislation preempted state regulation of prices, routes, and services for direct air carriers and related motor carrier pickup and delivery. The purpose was to level the playing field between air and motor carriers with respect to intrastate economic trucking regulation. The net effect was to remove intrastate regulation of transportation.

In 1998 the Ocean Shipping Reform Act revised and updated a previous act passed in 1984. This act served to greatly reduce the regulatory authority of the Federal Maritime Commission. While the FMC continues to regulate ocean liner shipping, carriers no longer are required to file tariffs with the FMC. The act gave carriers substantially more freedom to negotiate rates and contracts with shippers.

2000–Present: Technology, Safety and Security

The new millennium delivered some significant changes to transportation industry. Technology adoption stimulated many of these changes. The Electronic Signatures in Global and National Commerce Act of 2000 gave electronic documents signed by digital signature the same legal status as paper documents. In addition, in July 2004 the U.S. Department of Defense mandated that its 45,000 suppliers attach Radio Frequency Identification Tags to any goods sold to the military. Safety regulations also dominated in the 2000s as significant changes were made to limit truck drivers' hours of service. The most significant changes, however, were due to terrorism and the heightened transportation security of the United States following 9–11. The USA PATRIOT Act, signed into law October 26, 2001, increased inspections at ports, regulated airport screening, and heightened security at land-based border crossings. This act resulted in a widespread implementation of voluntary initiatives between the U.S. customs and private industry known as Customs-Trade Partnership against Terrorism (C-TPAT).

Other legislation in the new millenium has been the result of globalization. The Continued Dumping and Subsidy Act of 2000, known as the Byrd Amendment, was passed in response to artificial underpricing and dumping of foreign goods in U.S. markets. The law gives fines collected from foreign companies involved in dumping to United States companies filing the dumping complaints. Customs authorities have distributed more than $550 million in proceeds to United States companies, with another $240 million expected in 2004.[16] Critics of this law contend that the law has discouraged world trade and violated World Trade Organization (WTO) rules. In fact, other nations have retaliated by imposing duties as high as 100% on U.S. goods.[17]

Another example of the impact of globalization on regulation is recent efforts to reframe the Jones Act.[18] The Jones Act mandates that only United States–built ships operating under a U.S. flag and with a U.S. crew can ship goods directly from a U.S. port to another U.S. port. Similar regulations are frequently called cabotage laws. Opponents of this law argued that the Jones Act unfairly limited global competition in U.S. domestic shipping. However, because of the need to enforce laws regarding domestic trade, most countries continue to have cabotage laws.

---

[15] Federal Aviation Administration Authorization Act of 1994 (H.R. 103–2739) and Federal Aviation Reauthorization Act of 1996 (USCS 40101).

[16] "WTO Oks Byrd Amendment Sanctions," *American Shipper*, October 2004, p. 40.

[17] "Byrd Amendment Repeal Urged," The National Industrial Transportation League, December 3, 2004.

[18] Maritime Act of 1920, Section 27.

Transportation Structure

The freight transportation structure consists of the rights-of-way, vehicles, and carriers that operate within five basic transportation modes. A **mode** identifies a basic transportation method or form. The five basic transportation modes are rail, highway, water, pipeline, and air.

The relative importance of each transportation mode in the United States is measured in terms of system mileage, traffic volume, revenue, and nature of freight transported. Table 7.1 provides a summary of transportation expenditure by mode from 1960 to 2004. Tables 7.2 and 7.3 provide tonnage and revenue share by mode in 2003 and as projected to 2015. These data confirm that the truck share of the domestic freight market far exceeds

TABLE 7.1
The Nations' Freight Bill ($ billions)

Source: Adapted from Rosalyn Wilson, *16th Annual State of Logistics Report*, Council of Supply Chain Management Professionals. Oak Brook, IL, 2005.

	1960	1970	1980	1990	2000	2004
Truck	32.3	62.5	155.3	270.1	481.0	509.0
Railroad	9.0	11.9	27.9	30.0	36.0	42.0
Water	3.4	5.3	15.3	20.1	26.0	27.0
Pipeline	0.9	1.4	7.6	8.3	9.0	9.0
Air	0.4	1.2	4.0	13.7	27.0	31.0
Other carriers	0.4	0.4	1.1	4.0	10.0	18.0
Other shipper costs	1.3	1.4	2.4	3.7	5.0	8.0
Grand total	47.8	83.9	213.7	350.8	594.0	644.0
GNP (trillions)	0.5	1,046	2,831	5,832	9,960	11,740
Grand total of GNP	9.00%	8.03%	7.55%	6.02%	5.92%	5.50%

TABLE 7.2
Domestic Shipments by Mode and Volume

Source: Adapted from *United States Freight Transportation Forecast to 2015*, American Transportation Association.

	Freight Volumes (millions of tons)		Mode Share Percent		2003–2015
	2003	2015	2003	2015	Percent Change
Truck	9,062	12,141	68.9%	69.8%	34.0%
Rail	1,700	2,166	12.9%	12.5%	27.4%
Rail intermodal	122	205	0.9%	1.2%	67.7%
Air	18	31	0.1%	0.2%	70.4%
Water	1,018	1,296	7.7%	7.4%	27.2%
Pipeline	1,238	1,556	9.4%	8.9%	25.7%

TABLE 7.3
Domestic Shipments by Mode and Revenue

Source: Adapted from *United States Freight Transportation Forecast to 2015*, American Transportation Association.

	Freight revenue ($ billions)		Mode share percent		2003–2015
	2003	2015	2003	2015	percent change
Truck	610.1	1,049.1	86.9%	87.3%	72.0%
Rail	36.0	51.5	5.1%	4.3%	43.1%
Rail intermodal	7.6	15.7	1.1%	1.3%	106.6%
Air	13.1	27.8	1.9%	2.3%	112.2%
Water	7.8	12.5	1.1%	1.0%	60.3%
Pipeline	27.3	44.9	3.9%	3.7%	64.5%

that of all other modes combined. The 2003 tonnage share was 68.9 percent, and revenue share of truck transportation was 86.9 percent. While all transport modes are vital to a sound national transportation structure, it is clear that the U.S. economy, current and projected, depends on trucks. The following discussion provides a brief overview of the essential operating characteristics of each mode.

Rail

Historically, railroads have handled the largest number of ton-miles within the continental United States. A ton-mile is a standard measure of freight activity that combines weight and distance. As a result of early development of a comprehensive rail network connecting almost all cities and towns, railroads dominated intercity freight tonnage until after World War II. This early superiority resulted from the capability to economically transport large shipments and to offer frequent service, which gave railroads a near monopolistic position. However, with technology advancements, serious motor carrier competition began to develop following World War II and railroads' share of revenues and ton-miles began to decline.

Railroads once ranked first among all modes in terms of the number of miles in service. The extensive development of roads and highways to support the growth of automobiles and trucks after World War II soon changed this ranking. In 1970 there were 206,265 miles of rail track in the United States. By 2003, track mileage had declined to 98,944 miles as a result of significant abandonment.[19]

The capability to efficiently transport large tonnage over long distances is the main reason railroads continue to handle significant intercity tonnage. Railroad operations have high fixed costs because of expensive equipment, right-of-way and tracks, switching yards, and terminals. However, rail enjoys relatively low variable operating costs. The development of diesel power reduced railroad variable cost per ton-mile, and electrification has provided further cost reductions. Modified labor agreements have reduced human resource requirements, resulting in variable cost reductions.

As a result of deregulation and focused business development, rail traffic has shifted from transporting a broad range of commodities to hauling specific freight. Core railroad tonnage comes from material-extractive industries located a considerable distance from improved waterways and heavy items such as automobiles, farm equipment, and machinery. The rail fixed-variable cost structure offers competitive advantages for long-haul moves. Starting in the mid-1970s, railroads began to segment their transportation market by focusing on carload, intermodal, and container traffic. Marketing emphasis became even more segmented following passage of the Staggers Rail Act. Railroads became more responsive to specific customer needs by emphasizing bulk industries and heavy manufacturing, as contrasted to freight boxcar service. Intermodal operations were expanded by forming alliances with motor carriers. For example, United Parcel Service, primarily a multifaceted motor carrier, is the largest user of rail service to transport trailers in the United States.

To provide improved service to major customers, progressive railroads have concentrated on the development of specialized equipment, such as enclosed trilevel automotive railcars, cushioned appliance railcars, unit trains, articulated cars, and double-stack container flatcars. These technologies are being applied by railroads to reduce weight, increase carrying capacity, and facilitate interchange. The last three innovations are explained in greater detail.

---

[19] U.S. Department of Transportation, Bureau of Transportation Statistics, *Pocket Guide to Transportation* (Washington, DC: U.S. Government Printing Office, 2005).

On a unit train, all capacity is committed to transporting a single product. Typically, the product is a bulk commodity such as coal or grain. Unit trains have also been used to support assembly operations for the automobile industry. The unit train is faster and less expensive to operate than traditional trains, since it can be routed direct and nonstop from origin to destination.

Articulated cars have an extended rail chassis that can haul up to 10 containers on a single flexible unit. The concept is to reduce time required to formulate trains at railyards.

Double-stack railcars, as the name implies, are designed to transport two levels of containers on a single flatcar, thereby doubling the capacity of each railcar. Containers, discussed later in this chapter, are essentially truck trailers without wheels.

The above examples are by no means a comprehensive review of recent railroad innovations. They are representative of attempts to retain and grow railroad market share. It is clear that significant change continues to occur in traditional railroading. The 1970s challenges of survival and potential nationalization have been replaced by a revitalized rail network. Railroads currently perform a highly focused and important role in the transportation structure as the intermodal leaders of the 21st century.

Truck

Highway transportation has expanded rapidly since the end of World War II. To a significant degree the rapid growth of the motor carrier industry has resulted from speed coupled with the ability to operate door-to-door.

Trucks have flexibility because they are able to operate on a variety of roadways. Nearly one million miles of highway are available to trucks, which is more mileage than all other surface modes combined. The national fleet of over-the-road trucks exceeds 1.7 million tractors and 4.9 million trailers.[20]

In comparison to railroads, trucks have relatively small fixed investment in terminal facilities and operate on publicly financed and maintained roads. Although the cost of license fees, user fees, and tolls is considerable, these expenses are directly related to the number of trucks and miles operated. The variable cost per mile for motor carriers is high because a separate power unit and driver are required for each trailer or combination of tandem trailers. Labor requirements are also high because of driver safety restrictions and need for substantial dock labor. Truck operations are characterized by low fixed and high variable costs. In comparison to railroads, motor carriers more efficiently handle small shipments moving short distances.

Truck capabilities favor manufacturing and distributive trades, at distances up to 500 miles for high-value products. Trucks have made significant inroads into rail for medium and light manufacturing. As a result of delivery flexibility, motor carriers dominate freight moving from wholesalers and warehouses to retail stores. The future prospect for trucking is bright. Today, with the exception of small package goods moving in premium air service, almost all less-than-15,000-pound intercity shipments are transported by truck.

The trucking industry is not without problems. The primary difficulties relate to increasing cost to replace equipment, maintenance, safety, driver shortages, driver hours-of-service regulations, and dock wages. Although accelerating labor rates influence all modes of transport, trucking is labor-intensive, causing high wages to be a major concern. To counteract this trend, carriers have placed a great deal of attention on improved line-haul scheduling, computerized billing systems, mechanized terminals, tandem operations that haul two or three trailers with a single power unit, and participation in coordinated intermodal transport systems.

[20] U.S. Department of Transportation, Bureau of Transportation Statistics, "Highway Statistics, 2003, Tables MV-9 and MV-11," Washington, DC, 2003.

An alternative to for-hire truck service is shipper-owned trucks or trucks operated by integrated logistics service providers (ISPs) that are under contract to perform transport services for specific shippers.

Approximately 55 percent of all intercity truck tonnage is hauled by shipper-owned or shipper-controlled trucks. Following deregulation, this ratio reached a high of 66 percent by 1987.[21] The decline to 55 percent resulted from shippers realizing the numerous complexities and problems of operating a private fleet. The growth of ISP-operated trucking offers a service that combines the flexibility of private with the consolidation potential of for-hire operators. An ISP may perform services for multiple shippers and thus gain both economies of scale and distance.

Since 1980, deregulation has dramatically changed the nature of the for-hire trucking. The industry segments, which have become more defined since deregulation, include truckload (TL), less-than-truckload (LTL), and specialty. The dramatic change is related to the type of carriers operating in each category.

The TL segment includes loads over 15,000 pounds that generally do not require intermediate stops between origin and destination. Although large firms such as Schneider National and J. B. Hunt provide nationwide TL service, the segment is characterized by a large number of relatively small carriers and is generally very price competitive.

The LTL segment involves shipments less than 15,000 pounds that generally must be consolidated to achieve trailer capacity. As a result of origin and destination terminal costs and relatively higher marketing expenses, LTL experiences a higher percentage of fixed costs than TL. The operating characteristics of the LTL freight segment have caused extensive industry consolidation, resulting in a few relatively large national carriers and a strong regional network of smaller carriers. Some major nationwide LTL carriers are Yellow Roadway, USF Corp., FedEx Freight, Con Way Transportation, and Arkansas Best. The market shares of the top 10 LTL carriers are presented in Figure 7.2. In 2005 Yellow Roadway and USF Corp. proposed merging, suggesting continued consolidation of the nationwide LTL industry.

---

[21] U.S. Department of Transportation, Bureau of Transportation Statistics, "National Transportation Statistics, 2004," Table 1-46, Washington, DC, 2004.

FIGURE 7.2
2004 Revenue of Top 10 LTL Motor Carriers

Source: Data are from *Transport Topics,* March 7, 2005, p. 1.

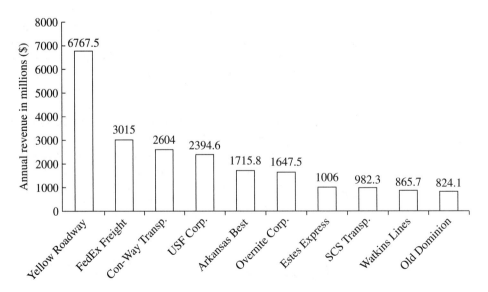

Specialty carriers include bulk and package haulers such as Waste Management and United Parcel Service. Specialty firms focus on specific transport requirements of a market or product. Specialty carriers are not generally direct competitors with the other two segments.

On the basis of the sheer size of the trucking industry and the services provided, it is quite apparent that highway transportation will continue to function as the backbone of logistical operations for the foreseeable future.

Water

Water is the oldest mode of transport. The original sailing vessels were replaced by steam-powered boats in the early 1800s and by diesel in the 1920s. A distinction is generally made between deepwater and navigable inland water transport.

Domestic water transport, which involves the Great Lakes, canals, and intracoastal waterways, has maintained a relatively constant annual ton-mile share of between 19 and 30 percent over the past four decades. While the share has remained relatively constant, the mix has changed dramatically. The percentage of river and canal ton-miles has increased by more than 183 million ton-miles between 1965 and 2002, while the Great Lakes ton-miles decreased by more than 22 million ton-miles during this same period. These figures reflect both a shift of bulk product transportation from rail and highway to lower-cost water movements on rivers and coastal canals as well as a shift from lakeside shipping to motor carrier transport.

In 2002, 26,000 miles of inland waterways were available, not including the Great Lakes or coastal shipping.[22] This network size has been stable over the past decade and is expected to remain for the foreseeable future. Fewer system miles exist for inland water than for any other transportation mode.

The main advantage of water transport is the capacity to transport extremely large shipments. Water transport employs two types of vessels for movement: Deepwater vessels are generally designed for coastal, ocean, and Great Lakes transport; diesel-towed barges generally operate on rivers and canals and have considerably more flexibility.

Water transport ranks between rail and motor carrier in terms of fixed cost. Although water carriers must develop and operate their own terminals, the right-of-way is developed and maintained by the government and results in moderate fixed costs compared to rail. The main disadvantages of water transport are the limited range of operation and slow speed. Unless the origin and destination of the movement are adjacent to a waterway, supplemental haul by rail or truck is required. The capability of water to transport large tonnage at low variable cost places this mode of transport in demand when low freight rates are desired and speed of transit is a secondary consideration.

Water transport will continue to be a viable transportation option in future supply chain logistics. The slow transit time of river transport provides a form of product storage in transit that can benefit logistics system design. In addition, the North American Free Trade Agreement (NAFTA) continues to offer the potential for increased utilization of the St. Lawrence Seaway to link new producer and consumer markets in Mexico, the Midwest, and the Canadian port cities. The passage of the Central America Free Trade Act (CAFTA) in 2005 will also have a significant impact on the use of water transport. Finally, water remains the primary transport for global logistics.

---

[22] U.S. Department of Transportation, Bureau of Transportation Statistics, "National Transportation Statistics, 2004," Table 2-7, Washington, DC, 2004.

Pipeline

Pipelines are a significant part of the U.S. transportation system. Pipelines accounted for approximately 67.8 percent of all crude and petroleum ton-mile movements. In 1998, 200,500 miles of pipeline were operational in the United States.[23]

In addition to petroleum products, the other important product transported by pipeline is natural gas. Like petroleum pipelines, natural gas pipelines in the United States are privately owned and operated, and many gas companies act as both gas distribution and contract transportation providers.

The basic nature of a pipeline is unique in comparison to any other mode of transport. Pipelines operate on a 24-hour basis, 7 days per week, and are limited only by commodity changeover and maintenance. Unlike other modes, there is no empty container or vehicle that must be returned. Pipelines have the highest fixed cost and lowest variable cost among transport modes. High fixed costs result from the right-of-way for pipeline, construction and requirements for control stations, and pumping capacity. Since pipelines are not labor-intensive, the variable operating cost is extremely low once the pipeline has been constructed. An obvious disadvantage is that pipelines are not flexible and are limited with respect to commodities that can be transported, as only products in the forms of gas, liquid, or slurry can be handled.

Experiments regarding potential movement of solid products in the form of slurry or hydraulic suspension continue. Coal slurry pipelines have proved to be an efficient and economical mode of transporting coal over long distances. Coal slurry lines require massive quantities of water, which is a significant concern among environmentalists.

Air

The newest but least utilized mode of transportation is airfreight. The significant advantage of airfreight lies in the speed with which a shipment can be transported. A coast-to-coast shipment via air requires only hours contrasted to days with other modes of transport. While costly, the speed of air transport allows other aspects of logistics such as warehousing and inventory to be reduced or eliminated.

Air transport, despite its high profile, still remains more of a potential than a reality. Although air routes exceed 4.21 billion ton-miles, airfreight accounts for 1 percent of intercity ton-miles.[24] Air transport capability is limited by load size, weight lift capacity, and aircraft availability. Traditionally, intercity airfreight was transported on scheduled passenger flights. While the practice was economical, it resulted in a limited capacity and flexibility of freight operations. The high cost of jet aircraft, coupled with the erratic nature of freight demand, served to limit the economic commitment of dedicated aircraft to all-freight operations.

However, the advent of premium air carriers such as Federal Express, United Parcel Air, and DHL Express introduced scheduled global airfreight service. While such premium service was originally targeted at high-priority documents, it has expanded to include package freight. For example, premium carriers have integrated their service to include overnight parts delivery from centralized distribution centers located at their air hubs. Overnight air delivery from a centralized warehouse is attractive to firms with a large number of high-value products and time-sensitive service requirements.

The fixed cost of air transport is low compared to rail, water, and pipeline. In fact, air transport ranks second only to highway with respect to low fixed cost. Airways and airports

---

[23] Association of Oil Pipelines, "Annual Report Comparisons from 1982–2002," Washington, DC, June 2004.

[24] U.S. Department of Transportation, Bureau of Transportation Statistics, "National Transportation Statistics 2004," Washington, DC, 2004.

are generally developed and maintained by government. The fixed costs of airfreight are associated with aircraft purchase and the requirement for specialized handling systems and cargo containers. On the other hand, air freight variable cost is extremely high as a result of fuel, user fees, maintenance, and the labor intensity of both in-flight and ground crews.

Since airports require significant real estate, they are generally limited with respect to integration with other transport modes. However, there is substantial interest in integrating air transport with other modes and developing all-freight airports to eliminate conflict with passenger service. For example, Alliance Airport, located near Fort Worth, Texas, was designed to integrate air, rail, and truck distribution from a single location.

No particular commodity dominates the traffic carried by airfreight operations. Perhaps the best distinction is that most freight has high value and priority. Businesses tend to utilize scheduled or nonscheduled air cargo movements when the service proposition justifies high cost. Products with the greatest potential for regular air movement are those having high value or extreme perishability. When the marketing period for a product is extremely limited, such as Christmas gifts, high-fashion clothing, fresh fish, or cut flowers, air may be the only practical transportation method to support national operations. Routine logistics of products such as computers, repair parts, and consumer catalogs also utilize airfreight.

Modal Classification

Table 7.4 compares the fixed-variable cost structure of each mode. Table 7.5 ranks modal operating characteristics with respect to speed, availability, dependability, capability, and frequency.

Speed refers to elapsed movement time. Airfreight is the fastest of all modes. **Availability** refers to the ability of a mode to service any given pair of locations. Highway carriers have the greatest availability since they can drive directly to origin and destination points. **Dependability** refers to potential variance from expected or published delivery schedules. Pipelines, because of their continuous service and limited interference due to weather and congestion, rank highest in dependability. **Capability** is the ability of a mode to handle any transport requirement, such as load size. Water transport is the most capable.

TABLE 7.4
Cost Structure for Each Mode

- *Rail.* High fixed cost in equipment, terminals, tracks, etc. Low variable cost.
- *Truck.* Low fixed cost (highways in place and provided by public support). Medium variable cost (fuel, maintenance, etc.).
- *Water.* Medium fixed cost (ships and equipment). Low variable cost (capability to transport large amount of tonnage).
- *Pipeline.* Highest fixed cost (rights-of-way, construction, requirements for control stations, and pumping capacity). Lowest variable cost (no labor cost of any significance).
- *Air.* Low fixed cost (aircraft and handling and cargo systems). High variable cost (fuel, labor, maintenance, etc.).

TABLE 7.5
Relative Operating Characteristics by Mode*

*Lowest rank is best.

Operating Characteristics	Rail	Truck	Water	Pipeline	Air
Speed	3	2	4	5	1
Availability	2	1	4	5	3
Dependability	3	2	4	1	5
Capability	2	3	1	5	4
Frequency	4	2	5	1	3
Composite Score	14	10	18	17	16

The final classification is **frequency,** which relates to the quantity of scheduled movements. Pipelines, again because of their continuous service between two points, lead all modes in frequency.

As Table 7.5 illustrates, the appeal of highway transport is in part explained by its high relative ranking across the five operating characteristics. Motor carriers rank first or second in all categories except capability. Although substantial improvements in motor capability resulted from relaxed size and weight limitations on interstate highways and approval to use tandem trailers, it is not realistic to assume motor transport will surpass rail or water capability.

Transportation Service

Transportation service is achieved by combining modes. Prior to deregulation, government policy limited carriers to operating in a single mode. Such restrictive ownership sought to promote competition between modes and limit the potential for monopoly practices. Following deregulation carriers were free to develop integrated modal services in efforts to more efficiently and effectively meet the needs of customers. The following section reviews the current range of services offered by different carriers. The description also includes examples of carriers representative of each category.

Traditional Carriers

The most basic carrier type is a transportation firm that provides service utilizing only one of the five basic transport modes. Focus on a single operational mode permits a carrier to become highly specialized.

Although single-mode operators are able to offer extremely efficient transport, such specialization creates difficulties for a shipper who desires intermodal transport solutions because it requires negotiation and business planning with multiple carriers. Airlines are an example of a single-mode carrier for both freight and passenger service that traditionally limits service from airport to airport. Since deregulation most carriers are developing services that facilitate multimodal integration.

Package Service

Over the past several decades a serious problem existed in the availability of small-shipment transportation. It was difficult for common carriers to provide reasonably priced small-shipment service because of overhead cost associated with terminal and line-haul operations. This overhead forced motor carriers to implement a **minimum charge.** The minimum applies to all shipments regardless of shipment size or distance. As a result of the minimum charge and lack of alternatives, an opportunity existed for companies offering specialized service to enter the small-shipment or package-service market.

Package services represent an important part of logistics, and the influence of carriers in this segment is increasing because of their size and intermodal capabilities. The advent of e-commerce and the need for consumer-direct fulfillment have significantly increased demand for package delivery. While package services are expanding, the services required do not fall neatly into the traditional modal classification scheme. Packages are regularly transported by using the line-haul services of rail, motor, and air. Package service provides both regular and premium services.

Ground Package Service

Numerous carriers offer delivery services within metropolitan areas. Other carriers offer package delivery service on a national and global basis. The most recognizable carriers are

United Parcel Service (UPS), the United States Postal Service (USPS), Federal Express Ground, and DHL Express.

The original service offered by UPS was contract delivery of local shipments for department stores. Today, UPS offers a diverse range of package services. In fact, UPS has expanded its scope of overall operating authority by shipping packages that conform to specialized size and weight restrictions nationwide and globally for consumers and business enterprises. While UPS provides logistical services related to all types of products, specialization in small packages enables a cost-effective overnight service between most cities within 300 miles.

UPS has various capabilities and offers a range of services, including ground and premium air. Table 7.6, based on UPS promotional materials, summarizes the integrated services offered by package carriers. It is interesting to note that ground service frequently involves intermodal movement by a combination of truck and train capacity.

The United States Postal Service (USPS) operates ground and air parcel service. Charges for parcel post are based on weight and distance. Generally, parcels must be

TABLE 7.6
2004—Examples of Integrated Parcel Carrier Services

Source: Modified and condensed from United Parcel Service website, www.ups.com.

Freight Services	
Same Day Air	Guaranteed same day delivery for letters and packages.
Next Day Delivery	Guaranteed weekday (Saturday available), next day delivery. Ranges from early morning (8:00 A.M.) delivery to air saver (3:00–4:30 P.M.) delivery.
Second Day Delivery	Guaranteed delivery on the second business day. Services offered range from noon delivery to end of business day delivery.
3 Day Select	Guaranteed 3 day delivery to and from every U.S. address.
Ground	Low-cost ground delivery with guaranteed delivery date.
Worldwide Express	Guaranteed delivery to and from the U.S., Canada, and Europe with next day, 2 day, and time-definite deliveries.
Standard to/from Canada	Guaranteed, fully tracked, door-to-door ground delivery from the 48 contiguous states to/from all addresses in the 10 Canadian provinces. Many time-definite delivery options available.
World Ease	A worldwide consolidated clearance service that groups several shipments destined for one country into a single shipment.
Optional, Value-Added Services	
Collect on Delivery (COD)	Payment collected immediately upon delivery and delivered promptly to customer. Will exchange international monies.
Delivery Confirmation	Confirms delivery with the recipient's signature. Additional service shows digital signature of person receiving package, proof of delivery, and telephone confirmation of delivery.
Hazardous Materials	Transport hazardous materials and international dangerous goods within the continental U.S.
Hold for Pickup	Packages are delivered to the facility of choice and carrier calls the consignee by telephone for pickup.
Saturday Pickup/Delivery	Packages shipped and picked up on Saturdays.
10KG and 23KG Boxes	A fixed-rate shipping solution for express shipments up to 10 kg (22 lb) and 25 kg (55 lb).
Hundredweight Service	Contract service for multipackage shipments less than 1000 lb that are less than a pallet load sent to a single address.
Returns	Includes labels (preprinted, on demand, and mailed), and authorized return services.
Excess Value Insurance	Third-party insurance provides protection for shipments valued between $100 and $50,000.

delivered to a post office for shipment origination. However, in the case of large users and when it is convenient for the Postal Service, pickup is provided at the shipper's location. Intercity transport is accomplished by purchasing air, highway, rail, and even water service from for-hire carriers. Delivery is provided to the destination by the Postal Service.

In 2002 DHL invested $1.2 billion for infrastructure investment in North America to expand into the domestic, package-service market.[25] A value-added service that DHL offers is a reverse logistics Smartlabel® included in original packages from multichannel vendors to consumers. Customers can conveniently return merchandise by affixing the prepaid and preaddressed Smartlabel to the original package and dropping the package into a USPS box or a DHL box. The label eases the return for the consumer and routes both return information and packages for companies.

The importance of parcel service to the logistical system cannot be overemphasized. One of the expanding forms of marketing in the United States is nonstore retailing, in which orders are placed via the Internet, telephone, or mail for subsequent home delivery. Firms that specialize in consumer fulfillment are one of the fastest growing forms of logistics service providers.

Air Package Service

Several carriers, such as Federal Express, UPS, and DHL, have entered the package or premium transportation market over the past two decades. Most organizations that provide routine package service also offer premium service. UPS, for example, offers next-day and second-day service, while the United States Postal Service provides a variety of priority services.

The first widely recognized premium package service was initiated by Federal Express (FedEx) in 1973. FedEx provides overnight service, utilizing a fleet of dedicated cargo aircraft. The original FedEx service attracted attention because of the innovative line-haul plan in which all packages were flown overnight to a terminal hub located in Memphis, Tennessee, for sorting and redistribution. Federal Express original service has been considerably expanded by offering larger package size and weight restrictions and adding global connectivity.

The demand for parcel delivery service has attracted many competitors into overnight premium package service. In addition to specialized firms like FedEx, UPS, and DHL, major motor carriers and airlines have begun to offer competitive service. Many services appeal to commercial business because they satisfy demand for rapid delivery.

Intermodal Transportation

Intermodal transportation combines two or more modes to take advantage of the inherent economies of each and thus provide an integrated service at lower total cost. Many efforts have been made over the years to integrate different transportation modes. Initial attempts at modal coordination trace back to the early 1920s, but during the regulatory years, cooperation was restrained by restrictions designed to limit monopoly practices. Intermodal offerings began to develop more successfully during the 1950s with the advent of integrated rail and motor service commonly termed **piggyback service.** This common intermodal arrangement combines the flexibility of motor for short distances with the low line-haul cost associated with rail for longer distances. The popularity of such offerings has increased significantly as a means to achieve more efficient and effective transportation.[26]

---

[25] *DHL Online Newsletter,* Issue 450, September 14, 2004.

[26] For a comprehensive discussion of contemporary intermodel operations, see John C. Taylor and George C. Jackson, "Conflict, Power and Evolution in the Intermodal Transportation Industry's Channel of Distribution," *Transportation Journal,* Spring 2000, pp. 5–17.

Technically, coordinated or intermodal transportation could be arranged among all basic modes. Descriptive jargon such as fishyback, trainship, and airtruck have become standard transportation terms.

Piggyback/TOFC/COFC

The best known and most widely used intermodal systems are the trailer on a flatcar (TOFC) and container on a flatcar (COFC). Containers are the boxes utilized for intermodal product storage and movement between motor freight, railroads, and water transportation. Containers are typically 8 feet wide, 8 feet high, and 20 or 40 feet long, and do not have highway wheels. Trailers, on the other hand, are of similar width and height but can be as long as 53 feet and have highway wheels. As the name implies, a trailer or container is placed on a railroad flatcar for some portion of the intercity line-haul and pulled by a truck at origin and destination. Line-haul cost is the expense to move railcars or trucks between cities. Since the original development of TOFC, various combinations of trailer or container on flatcar—double-stack, for instance—have increased significantly.

A variety of coordinated service plans have been developed. Each plan defines the railroad or motor carrier responsibility. Table 7.7 illustrates the most common operating plans. The plans differ by responsibility for equipment, pickup, and delivery.

While the TOFC concept facilitates direct transfer between rail and motor carriage, it also has several technical limitations. The placement of a trailer with highway wheels attached, transferred to a railcar, can lead to wind resistance, damage, and weight problems. The use of containers reduces these potential problems, as they can be double stacked and are easily transferred to water carriers. However, they require special equipment for over-the-road delivery or pickup.

TABLE 7.7
Summary of Basic Rail–Truck Coordination Plans

- *Plan 250.* Rail transportation of a shipment loaded in a carrier vehicle from terminal at origin to terminal at destination. Shipper is responsible for pickup and delivery services beyond the terminal.
- *Plan 300.* Rail transportation of a shipment loaded in a shipper vehicle from terminal at origin to terminal at destination. Shipper is responsible for pickup and delivery beyond the terminal.
- *Plan 310.* Rail transportation of an empty shipper vehicle having an immediate prior or subsequent loaded domestic movement via mail. Shipper is responsible for pickup and delivery beyond the terminal.
- *Plans 400 to 470.* These services apply only to domestic container shipments involving carrier containers or the repositioning of international containers owned or controlled by steamship companies. They include, where indicated, truck pickup at origin and/or delivery at destination.
  Plan 400: Door at origin, door at destination.
  Plan 420: Door at origin, ramp at destination.
  Plan 450: Ramp at origin, ramp at destination.
  Plan 470: Ramp at origin, door at destination.
- *Plans 600 to 625 or Service Code 20 to 67.* Their services apply to shipments involving carrier vehicles and shipper vehicles. They include truck pickup at origin and/or delivery at destination.
  Plan 600: Door at origin, door at destination (carrier vehicle).
  Plan 605: Door at origin, door at destination (shipper vehicle).
  Plan 610: Door at origin, ramp at destination (carrier vehicle).
  Plan 615: Door at origin, ramp at destination (shipper vehicle).
  Plan 620: Ramp at origin, door at destination (carrier vehicle).
  Plan 625: Ramp at origin, door at destination (shipper vehicle).
- *Plan 800.* Rail transportation of a loaded shipper vehicle from the terminal at origin to the terminal at destination where the shipment has had/will have an immediate prior or subsequent movement via water transport in international commerce without transfer of cargo. Shipper is responsible for pickup and delivery beyond the terminal.
- *Plan 810.* Rail transportation of an empty shipper vehicle from the terminal at origin to the terminal at destination having an immediate prior or subsequent loaded movement via rail in conjunction with water transport in international commerce. Shipper is responsible for pickup and delivery beyond the terminal.

Containerships

Fishyback, trainship, and containership are examples of the oldest form of intermodal transport. They utilize waterways, which are one of the least expensive modes for line-haul movement. A 2004 comparison done by the Maritime Adminstration (MARAD) showed that one 15-barge tow has the equivalent capacity of 225 railcars or 900 trucks.[27]

The fishyback, trainship, and containership concept loads a truck trailer, railcar, or container onto a barge or ship for the line-haul movement on inland navigable waterways. Such services are provided in coastal waters between Atlantic and Gulf ports, and between the Great Lakes and coastal points. Because of the low costs and efficiency of coastal barges, MARAD is advocating expanding **short sea shipping** to ease traffic congestion and alleviate air pollution.

A variant of this intermodal option is the **land bridge** concept that moves containers in a combination of sea and rail transport. The land bridge is commonly used for containers moving between Europe and the Pacific Rim to reduce the time and expense of all-water transport. For example, containers are shipped to the West Coast of North America from the Pacific Rim, loaded onto railcars for movement to the East Coast, and then reloaded onto ships for movement to Europe. The land bridge concept is based on the benefit of ocean and rail combinations that utilize a single tariff, which is lower than the combined total cost of two separate rates.

The transfer of freight between modes often requires the handling of containers and the imposition of duties. Ports are used to make this transfer as seamless and as fast as possible. Water ports on the coasts and inland waterways provide 3,214 berths for deep draft ships and transfer cargo and passengers through 1,941 public and private marine terminals.[28]

Port throughput is a big concern to supply chain managers and although there are many ports in the United States, three ocean ports, Los Angeles, Long Beach and New York account for almost half of all imports and exports in the United States. In 2002, striking terminal workers at Long Beach and Los Angeles ports caused long delays in the transfer of freight. In 2004, the continued increase in the volume of imported containers again congested West Coast ports, causing some logistics companies to inform companies to expect 7-day delays in clearing ports. In July 2005 the ports of Los Angeles and Long Beach implemented a program called PierPass. Designed to reduce prime-time congestion PierPass introduced a Traffic Mitigation Fee during peak hours of $40 per 20-foot equivalent container and for all larger than 20 foot a fee of $80. Firms willing to move freight in off-peak hours were able to register to be exempt from the fee.

Coordinated Air-Truck

Another form of intermodal transport combines air and truck. Local cartage is a vital part of every air movement because airfreight must eventually move from the airport to the final delivery destination. Air-truck movements usually provide service and flexibility comparable to straight motor freight.

Air-truck is commonly used to provide premium package services, such as those offered by UPS, FedEx, and DHL, but can also be used for more standard freight applications for several reasons. First, there is a lack of airfreight service to smaller cities in the United States. Smaller cities are often served by narrow-body aircraft and commuter planes that are not equipped to handle freight. Thus, motor carriage into small cities from metropolitan

---

[27] U.S. Waterborne Foreign Trade Containerized Cargo, Top 25 U.S. Ports, January–June 2004, Port Import Export Reporting Services. MARAD waterborne traffic statistics, http://www.marad.dot.gov/MARAD.

[28] American Association of Port Authorities 2004, www.aapa-ports.org.

airports provides a needed service at a competitive cost. Second, package carriers, while suited to serve small cities, have limited ability to handle heavy freight. Package carriers that are focused on smaller parcels and materials handling systems are limited in ability to handle heavy freight. As a result, many air carriers have extended their motor freight range to provide service to expanded geographical areas.

The concept of intermodalism appeals to both shippers and carriers because of the economic leverage of linking two modes. In fact, many authorities believe the only way to maintain a strong national transportation network is to encourage and foster intermodalism. Efforts to increase intermodalism are of prime interest to logistical planners because such development expands options available in logistical system design.

Nonoperating Intermediaries

The overall transportation industry also includes several business types that do not own or operate equipment. These nonoperating intermediaries broker services of other firms. A transportation broker is somewhat analogous to a wholesaler in a marketing channel.

Nonoperating intermediaries find economic justification by offering shippers lower rates for movement between two locations than would be possible by direct shipment via common carrier. Because of peculiarities in the common-carrier rate structure, such as minimum freight charges, surcharges, and less-than-volume rates, conditions exist whereby nonoperating intermediaries can facilitate savings for shippers. Interestingly, there are cases where nonoperating intermediaries charge higher rates than those offered by carriers. The justification for the higher charges is based on ability to arrange faster delivery and/or more value-added services. The primary intermediaries are freight forwarders, shipper associations, and brokers.

Freight Forwarders

Freight forwarders are for-profit businesses that consolidate small shipments from various customers into a bulk shipment and then utilize a common surface or air carrier for transport. At destination, the freight forwarder splits the consolidated shipment into the original smaller shipments. Local delivery may or may not be arranged by the forwarder. The main advantage of the forwarder is a lower rate per hundredweight obtained from large shipment and, in most cases, faster transport of small shipments than would be experienced if the individual customer dealt directly with the common carrier. Freight forwarders accept full responsibility for shipment performance.

Shipper Association/Cooperatives and Agents

Shipper associations are operationally similar to freight forwarders in that they consolidate small shipments into large movements to gain cost economies. Shipper associations are voluntary nonprofit entities where members, operating in a specific industry, collaborate to gain economies related to small-shipment purchases. Typically, members purchase product from common vendors or from sources of supply located in one area. A common practice is to order small quantities at frequent intervals to minimize retail inventory. Participation in a shipper association typically means improved speed of delivery, since a large number of different products may be purchased at one location, such as the garment district in New York City.

The association requires a group of shippers to establish an administrative office or arrange an agent at the location of frequent merchandise purchase. The agent arranges for individual purchases to be delivered to a local facility. When sufficient volume is accumulated, a consolidated shipment is arranged for local delivery. Some associations operate their own intercity transportation. Each member is billed a proportionate share for transportation plus a prorated share of the association's fixed cost.

Brokers

Brokers are intermediaries that coordinate transportation arrangements for shippers, consignees, and carriers. They also arrange shipments for exempt carriers and drivers who own their trucks. Brokers typically operate on a commission basis. Prior to deregulation, brokers played a minor role in logistics because of service restrictions. Today, brokers provide more extensive services such as shipment matching, rate negotiation, billing, and tracing. The entire area of brokerage operations is highly adaptable to Internet-based transactions and is increasing in importance as a result of increased globalization.

Summary

Transportation is a key activity in logistics because it moves product through the various stages of production and ultimately to consumers. This chapter introduced major principles of transportation economies and provided a brief historical summary of government regulation. It is important that logistics managers have appreciation and understanding of regulation history to fully appreciate the logic underlying today's transport system.

The transportation system contains five modes of operation: rail, motor, water, pipeline, and air. Each mode has specific attributes that render it the transportation choice appropriate for a specific freight movement. Traditional transport supply consisted of a large number of specialized carriers, each limiting operations to one specific mode. The original lack of coordinated transportation resulted in inefficiencies and high cost. Deregulation introduced competitive pricing and carrier flexibility. It became common for carriers to combine multimodal services and offer specialized services to individual customers. As a result, a wide range of specialized transport service is now available to satisfy specific customer requirements. Attention in Chapter 8 is focused on transportation operations, followed by a discussion of carrier economics, pricing, and documentation.

Challenge Questions

1. Compare and contrast the transport principles of economy of scale and economy of distance. Illustrate how they combine to create efficient transportation.
2. Describe the five modes of transportation, identifying the most significant characteristic of each.
3. Why is motor carrier freight transportation the most used method of product shipment?
4. What is the economic justification for the rapid growth of premium package services?
5. Why is it important for a logistics manager to have a degree of understanding of transportation regulatory history?
6. Why have railroad miles declined during a period of national growth?
7. Railroads have the largest percentage of intercity freight ton-miles, but motor carriers have the largest revenue. How do you explain this relationship?
8. Discuss the fundamental difference between TOFC and COFC. Why was double stacking considered a major innovation in multimodal transportation?
9. Explain the value proposition offered by freight forwarding. Provide an example that illustrates why shippers would be attracted to using the services of a freight forwarder as contrasted to arranging their own transportation.
10. The five basic modes of transportation have been available for well over 50 years. Is this the way it will always be, or can you identify a sixth mode that may become economically feasible in the foreseeable future.

Transportation Operations

Transportation is the single largest element of logistics cost. The historical view of traffic departments being staffed with individuals wearing green eyeshades and sitting amid bookshelves filled with tariffs and rate tables is a scenario far from reality in today's competitive environment. Traffic departments commit and manage over 60 percent of a typical firm's logistics expenditures. Transportation managers are responsible for arranging for inventory to be positioned in a timely and economical manner. A fundamental responsibility is to determine whether transportation services should be performed by using private or for-hire capacity. Decisions related to internal performance versus outsourcing are not totally different from those faced in many other enterprise areas. What is different about transportation is the critical impact that operations have on logistical performance. As operational expectations become more precise, order-to-delivery performance cycles more compact, and margins for error reduced near zero, successful firms have come to realize that **there is no such thing as cheap transportation.** Unless transportation is managed in an effective and efficient manner, procurement, manufacturing, and customer accommodation performance will not meet expectations. This chapter provides an overview of how transportation is managed within the logistical process.

Transportation Economics and Pricing

Transportation economics and pricing are concerned with factors and characteristics that drive cost. To develop effective logistics strategy, it is necessary to understand such factors and characteristics. Successful negotiation requires a full understanding of transportation economics. An overview of transportation economics and pricing consists of four interrelated topics: (1) economic drivers, (2) costing, (3) carrier pricing strategy, and (4) transportation rates and ratings.

Economic Drivers

Transportation economics are driven by seven factors. While not direct components of transport tariffs, each factor influences rates. The factors are: (1) distance, (2) weight, (3) density, (4) stowability, (5) handling, (6) liability, and (7) market. The following discusses the relative importance of each factor from a shipper's perspective. Keep in mind that the precise impact of each factor varies, depending on specific market and product characteristics.

Distance

Distance is a major influence on transportation cost since it directly contributes to variable expense, such as labor, fuel, and maintenance. Figure 8.1 illustrates the general relationship between distance and transportation cost. Two important points are illustrated. First, the cost curve does not begin at zero because there are fixed costs associated with shipment pickup and delivery regardless of distance. Second, the cost curve increases at a decreasing rate as a function of distance. This characteristic is known as the **tapering principle.**[1]

Weight

The second factor is load weight. As with other logistics activities, scale economies exist for most transportation movements. This relationship, illustrated in Figure 8.2, indicates that transport cost per unit of weight decreases as load size increases. This occurs because the fixed costs of pickup, delivery, and administration are spread over incremental

[1] The principles of economy of scale and economy of distance were introduced in Chapter 7.

FIGURE 8.1
Generalized Relationship between Distance and Transportation Cost

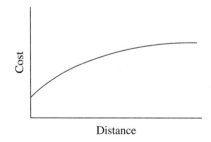

Distance

FIGURE 8.2
Generalized Relationship between Weight and Transportation Cost/Pound

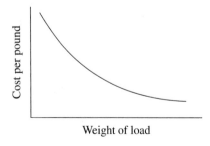

Weight of load

FIGURE 8.3
Generalized
Relationship between
Density and
Transportation
Cost/Pound

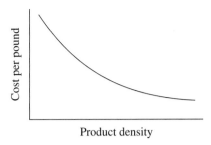

weight. This relationship is limited by the size of the transportation vehicle. Once the vehicle is full, the relationship begins again with each additional vehicle. The managerial implication is that small loads should be consolidated into larger loads to maximize scale economies.

Density

A third factor is product density. Density is the combination of weight and volume. Weight and volume are important since transportation cost for any movement is usually quoted in dollars per unit of weight. Transport charges are commonly quoted per hundredweight (CWT). In terms of weight and volume, vehicles are typically more constrained by cubic capacity than by weight. Since actual vehicle, labor, and fuel expenses are not dramatically influenced by weight, higher-density products allow fixed transport cost to be spread across more weight. As a result, higher density products are typically assessed lower transport cost per unit of weight. Figure 8.3 illustrates the relationship of declining transportation cost per unit of weight as product density increases. In general, traffic managers seek to improve product density so that trailer cubic capacity can be fully utilized.

Stowability

Stowability refers to how product dimensions fit into transportation equipment. Odd package sizes and shapes, as well as excessive size or length, may not fit well in transportation equipment, resulting in wasted cubic capacity. Although density and stowability are similar, it is possible to have items with similar densities that stow very differently. Items having rectangular shapes are much easier to stow than odd-shaped items. For example, while steel blocks and rods may have the same physical density, rods are more difficult to stow than blocks because of their length and shape. Stowability is also influenced by other aspects of size, since large numbers of items may be **nested** in shipments whereas they may be difficult to stow in small quantities. For example, it is possible to accomplish significant nesting for a truckload of trash cans while a single can is difficult to stow.

Handling

Special handling equipment may be required to load and unload trucks, railcars, or ships. In addition to special handling equipment, the manner in which products are physically grouped together in boxes or on pallets for transport and storage will impact handling cost. Chapters 9 and 10 specifically address handling issues related to packaging and storage.

Liability

Liability includes product characteristics that can result in damage. Carriers must either have insurance to protect against potential damage or accept financial responsibility. Shippers can reduce their risk, and ultimately transportation cost, by improved packaging or reducing susceptibility to loss or damage.

Market

Finally, market factors such as lane volume and balance influence transportation cost. A **transport lane** refers to movements between origin and destination points. Since transportation vehicles and drivers typically return to their origin, either they must find a **back-haul** load or the vehicle is returned or **deadheaded** empty. When empty return movements occur, labor, fuel, and maintenance costs must be charged against the original front-haul movement. Thus, the ideal situation is to achieve two-way or balanced movement of loads. However, this is rarely the case, because of demand imbalances in manufacturing and consumption locations. For example, many goods are manufactured and processed in the eastern United States and then shipped to consumer markets in the western portion of the country. This results in an imbalance in volume moving between the two geographical areas. Such imbalance causes rates to be generally lower for eastbound moves. Movement balance is also influenced by seasonality, such as the movement of fruits and vegetables to coincide with growing seasons. Demand location and seasonality result in transport rates that change with direction and season. Logistics system design must take such factors into account to achieved back-haul economies whenever possible.

Costing

The second dimension of transport economics and pricing concerns the criteria used to allocate cost. Cost allocation is primarily a carrier concern, but since cost structure influences negotiating ability, the shipper's perspective is important as well. Transportation costs are classified into a number of categories.

Variable

Costs that change in a predictable, direct manner in relation to some level of activity are labeled **variable costs.** Variable costs in transportation can be avoided only by not operating the vehicle. Aside from exceptional circumstances, transport rates must at least cover variable cost. The variable category includes direct carrier cost associated with movement of each load. These expenses are generally measured as a cost per mile or per unit of weight. Typical variable cost components include labor, fuel, and maintenance. The variable cost of operations represents the minimum amount a carrier must charge to pay daily expenses. It is not possible for any carrier to charge customers a rate below its variable cost and expect to remain in business long.

Fixed

Expenses that do not change in the short run and must be paid even when a company is not operating, such as during a holiday or a strike, are **fixed costs.** The fixed category includes costs not directly influenced by shipment volume. For transportation firms, fixed components include vehicles, terminals, rights-of-way, information systems, and support equipment. In the short term, expenses associated with fixed assets must be covered by contribution above variable costs on a per shipment basis.

Joint

Expenses created by the decision to provide a particular service are called **joint costs.** For example, when a carrier elects to haul a truckload from point A to point B, there is an implicit decision to incur a **joint** cost for the back-haul from point B to point A. Either the joint cost must be covered by the original shipper from A to B or a back-haul shipper must be found. Joint costs have significant impact on transportation charges because carrier quotations must include implied joint costs based on assessment of back-haul recovery.

Common

This category includes carrier costs that are incurred on behalf of all or selected shippers. **Common costs,** such as terminal or management expenses, are characterized as overhead. These are often allocated to a shipper according to a level of activity like the number of shipments or delivery appointments handled. However, allocating overhead in this manner may incorrectly assign costs. For example, a shipper may be charged for delivery appointments when not actually using the service.

Carrier Pricing Strategy

When setting rates, carriers typically follow one or a combination of two strategies. Although it is possible to employ a single strategy, the combination approach considers trade-offs between cost of service incurred by the carrier and value of service to the shipper.

Cost-of-Service

The **cost-of-service** strategy is a buildup approach where the carrier establishes a rate based on the cost of providing the service plus a profit margin. For example, if the cost of providing a transportation service is $200 and the profit markup is 10 percent, the carrier would charge the shipper $220. The cost-of-service approach, which represents the base or minimum for transportation charges, is most commonly used as a pricing approach for low-value goods or in highly competitive situations.

Value-of-Service

An alternative strategy that charges a price based on value as perceived by the shipper rather than the carrier cost of actually providing the service is called **value-of-service.** For example, a shipper perceives transporting 1000 pounds of electronics equipment as more critical or valuable than 1000 pounds of coal, since electronics are worth substantially more than the coal. Therefore, a shipper is probably willing to pay more for transportation. Carriers tend to utilize value-of-service pricing for high-value goods or when limited competition exists.

Value-of-service pricing is illustrated in the premium overnight freight market. When FedEx first introduced overnight delivery, there were few competitors that could provide comparable service, so it was perceived by shippers as a high-value alternative. They were willing to pay a premium for overnight delivery of a single package. Once competitors such as UPS, DHL, and the United States Postal Service entered the market, overnight rates were discounted to levels reflecting the value and cost of this service.

Combination

A **combination** pricing strategy establishes the transport price at an intermediate level between the cost-of-service minimum and the value-of-service maximum. In practice, most transportation firms use managerially determined midrange pricing. Logistics managers must understand the range of prices and the alternative strategies so they can negotiate appropriately.

Net-Rate

By taking advantage of regulatory freedom generated by the Trucking Industry Regulatory Reform Act (TIRRA) of 1994 and the reduced applicability of the filed rate doctrine, a number of common carriers are experimenting with a simplified pricing format termed **net-rate pricing.**[2] Since TIRRA eliminated tariff filing requirements for motor carriers that set

---

[2] See Chapter 7.

rates individually with customers, carriers are now, in effect, able to simplify pricing to fit an individual customer's circumstance and need. Specifically, carriers can replace individual discount sheets and class tariffs with a simplified price sheet. The net-rate pricing approach does away with the complex and administratively burdensome discount pricing structures that became common practice following initial deregulation.

Established discounts and accessorial charges are built into **net rates.** In other words, the net rate is an all-inclusive price. The goal is to drastically reduce a carrier's administrative cost and directly respond to customer demand to simplify the pricing process. Shippers are attracted to such simplification because it promotes billing accuracy and provides a clear understanding of how to generate savings in transportation.

Rates and Rating

The previous discussion introduced key strategies used by carriers to set prices. This section presents the pricing mechanics used by carriers. This discussion applies specifically to common carriers, although contract carriers follow a similar approach.

Class Rates

In transportation terminology, the price in dollars and cents per hundredweight to move a specific product between two locations is referred to as the **rate.** The rate is listed on pricing sheets or on computer files known as **tariffs.** The term **class rate** evolved from the fact that all products transported by common carriers are classified for pricing purposes. All product legally transported in interstate commerce can be shipped via class rates.

Determination of common carrier class rates is a two-step process. The first step is to determine the classification or grouping of the product being transported. The second step is the determination of the precise rate or price based on the classification of the product and the origin/destination points of the shipment.

Classification

All products transported are typically grouped together into uniform classifications. The classification takes into consideration the characteristics of a product or commodity that will influence the cost of handling or transport. Products with similar density, stowability, handling, liability, and value characteristics are grouped together into a class, thereby reducing the need to deal with each product on an individual basis. The particular class that a given product or commodity is assigned is its **rating,** which is used to determine the freight rate. It is important to understand that the classification does not identify the price or rate charged for movement of a product. Rating refers to a product's transportation characteristics in comparison to other commodities.

Truck and rail carriers each have independent classification systems. The trucking system uses the *National Motor Freight Classification,* while rail classifications are published in the *Uniform Freight Classification.* The truck classification system has 23 classes of freight, and the rail system has 31. In local or regional areas, individual groups of carriers may publish additional classification lists. Since deregulation, considerable attention has been directed to simplification of the traditional classification scheme.

Classification of individual products is based on a relative index of 100. Class 100 is considered the class of an average product, while other classes run as high as 500 and as low as 35. Each product is assigned an item number for listing purposes and then given a classification rating. As a general rule, the higher a class rating, the higher the transportation cost for the product. Historically, a product classified as 200 would be approximately twice as expensive to transport as a product rated 100. While the actual current multiple may not be two, a class 200 rating will still result in substantially higher freight costs than a class 100 rating. Products are also assigned classifications on the basis of the quantity

TABLE 8.1 **National Motor Freight Classification 100-S**

Source: Reprinted with permission from the American Trucking Association.

Item	Articles	Classes	
		LTL	TL
86750	Glass, leaded, see Note, item 86752:		
Sub 1	With landscape, pictorial, or religious designs, packed in boxes.	200.	70.
Sub 2	With curved, angled, or straight-line patterns, or with designs other than landscape, pictorial, or religious, in boxes.	100.	70.
86752	*Note:* The term "lended glass" means glass either colored or clear, set in lead or in other metal.		
86770	Glass, microscopical slide or cover, in boxes.	70.	40.
86830	Glass, rolled, overlaid with aluminum strips with metal terminals attached, in boxes, crates, or Package 1339.	77.5	45.
86840	Glass, rolled, overlaid with aluminum strips, NOI, in boxes, crates, or Package 1339.	70.	37.5
86900	Glass, silvered for mirrors, not framed, backed, or equipped with hangers or fastening devices:		
Sub 1	Shock (window glass, silvered), in boxes, see Note, item 86902; also TL., in Packages 227 or 300.	86.	40.
Sub 2	Other than shock glass; also TL, in Packages 227 or 300: Bent:		
Sub 3	Not exceeding 15 feet in length or 9 feet in breadth, in boxes.	100.	70.
Sub 4	Exceeding 15 feet in length or 9 feet in breadth, in boxes.	250.	70.
Sub 5	Not bent, see Package 785:		
Sub 6	120 united inches or less, in boxes, crates, or Packages 198,	70.	40.
Sub 7	235, or 1339.		
sub 8	Exceeding 120 united inches but not exceeding 15 feet in length or 9 feet in breadth, in boxes or crates.	100.	40.
Sub 9	Exceeding 15 feet in length or 9 feet in breadth, in boxes or crates.	200.	45.
86902	*Note:* Glass, silvered for mirrors, which has been framed or backed, or equipped with large hangers or fastening devices, is subject to the classes for mirrors, NOI.		
85940	Glass, window, other than plate, with metal edging other than sash or frames, in boxes.	77.5	45.
86960	Glazing units, glass, not in sash, see Note, item 86966, in boxes, crates, or Packages 2133, 2149, or 2281.	70.	45.
86966	*Note:* Applies on units consisting of sheets of glass separated by air or vacuum, sealed at all edges with same or other materials.		
87040	Skylight, roofing, or sidewall construction material consisting of rough rolled glass, wired or not wired, and installation accessories, see Note, item 87042, in boxes or crates.	65.	35.

shipped. Less-than-truckload (LTL) shipments of identical products will have higher ratings than truckload (TL) shipments.

Table 8.1 illustrates a page from the *National Motor Freight Classification*. It contains general product grouping 86750, which is **glass, leaded.** Notice that the leaded glass category is further subdivided into specific types of glass such as *glass, microscopical slide or cover, in boxes* (item 86770). For LTL shipments, item 86770 is assigned a 70 rating. TL shipments of leaded glass are assigned a class 40 rating, provided a minimum of 360 hundredweight is shipped.

Products are also assigned different ratings on the basis of packaging. Glass may be rated differently when shipped loose, in crates, or in boxes than when shipped in wrapped protective packing. It should be noted that packaging differences influence product density, stowability, and damage, illustrating that cost factors discussed earlier enter into the rate-determined process. Thus, a number of different classifications may apply to the same product depending on shipment size, transport mode, and product packaging.

One of the major responsibilities of transportation managers is to obtain the best possible rating for all goods shipped, so it is useful for members of a traffic department to have a thorough understanding of the classification systems. Although there are differences in rail and truck classifications, each system is guided by similar rules.

It is possible to have a product reclassified by written application to the appropriate classification board. The classification board reviews proposals for change or additions with respect to minimum weights, commodity descriptions, packaging requirements, and general rules and regulations. An alert traffic department will take an active role in classification. Significant savings may be realized by finding the correct classification for a product or by recommending a change in packaging or shipment quantity that will reduce a product's rating.

Rate Determination

Once a classification rating is obtained for a product, the rate must be determined. The rate per hundredweight is usually based on the shipment origin and destination, although the actual price charged for a particular shipment is normally subject to a minimum charge and may also be subject to surcharges. Historically, the origin and destination rates were manually maintained in notebooks that had to be updated and revised regularly. Then rates were provided on diskettes by carriers. Today, options for selecting carriers range from Internet software that examines carrier websites and determines the best rates to participation in online auctions.

Origin and destination rates are organized by zip codes. Table 8.2 illustrates rates for all freight classes from Atlanta, Georgia (zip 303), to Lansing, Michigan (zip 489). The table lists rates for shipments ranging in size from the smallest LTL (less than 500 pounds; listed

TABLE 8.2   **Example of Rates from Atlanta, Georgia (zip 303), to Lansing, Michigan (zip 489)**

Origin 303: Destination 489: MC: 81.00: RBNO 00775E								
Rate Class	**L5C**	**M5C**	**M1M**	**M2M**	**M5M**	**M10M**	**M20M**	**M30M**	**M40M**
500	233.58	193.89	147.14	119.10	84.05	65.37	40.32	32.25	28.24
400	188.24	156.25	118.58	95.98	67.73	52.69	32.55	26.03	22.79
300	144.11	119.63	90.78	73.48	51.86	40.34	24.94	19.95	17.45
250	126.30	104.84	79.56	64.40	45.45	35.34	21.86	17.48	15.31
200	98.37	81.66	61.97	50.16	35.40	27.53	17.00	13.60	11.91
175	88.65	73.58	55.84	45.20	31.90	24.81	15.30	12.24	10.72
150	76.11	63.18	47.94	38.81	27.38	21.30	13.20	10.56	9.24
125	64.76	53.76	40.80	33.03	23.31	18.12	11.25	9.00	7.88
110	56.27	46.71	35.43	28.69	20.25	15.75	9.88	7.90	6.92
100	52.62	43.68	33.15	26.83	18.94	14.73	9.22	7.38	6.46
92	49.79	41.33	31.37	25.39	17.92	13.94	8.91	7.12	6.24
85	46.15	38.31	29.07	23.53	16.61	12.92	8.58	6.86	6.01
77	42.91	35.62	27.03	21.88	15.44	12.01	8.34	6.67	5.84
70	40.48	33.59	25.50	20.64	14.57	11.33	8.10	6.48	5.67
65	38.46	31.92	24.22	19.61	13.84	10.76	8.02	6.41	5.61
60	36.84	30.58	23.21	18.78	13.26	10.31	7.94	6.35	5.56
55	34.81	28.90	21.93	17.75	12.53	9.74	7.85	6.28	5.50
50	32.79	27.22	20.66	16.71	11.80	9.18	7.77	6.22	5.44
Weight Limits (lb)	Under 500	500– 1000	1000– 2000	2000– 5000	5000– 10,000	10,000– 20,000	20,000– 30,000	30,000– 40,000	Over 40,000

as L5C) to the largest TL (greater than 40,000 pounds; listed as M40M). The rate is quoted in cents per hundredweight. Assuming a shipment of 10,000 pounds, the rate for class 85 between Atlanta and Lansing, using this example tariff, is $12.92 per hundredweight.

Historically, the published rate had to be charged for all shipments of a specific class and origin/destination combination. This required frequent review and maintenance to keep rates current. Following deregulation, carriers offered more flexibility through rate discounts. Now instead of developing an individual rate table to meet the needs of customer segments, carriers apply a discount from class rates for specific customers. The discount, generally in the range of 30 to 50 percent, depends on the shipper's volume and market competition.

An alternative to the per hundredweight charge is a per mile charge, which is common in TL shipments. As discussed previously, TL shipments are designed to reduce handling and transfer costs. Since the entire vehicle is used in a TL movement and there is no requirement to transfer the shipment at a terminal, a per mile basis offers a more appropriate pricing approach. For a one-way move, charges may range from $1.50 to over $3.00 per mile, depending on the market, the equipment, and the product involved. Although it is negotiable, this charge typically includes loading, unloading, and liability.

In addition to the variable shipment charge applied on either a per hundredweight or per mile basis, two additional charges are common for transportation: **minimum charges** and **surcharges.** The minimum charge represents the amount a shipper must pay to make a shipment, regardless of weight. To illustrate, assume that the applicable class rate is $25/CWT and the shipper wants to transport 100 pounds to a specific location. If no minimum charge exists, the shipper would pay $25. However, if the minimum charge were $250 per shipment, the shipper would be required to pay the minimum. Minimum charges cover fixed costs associated with a shipment.

A surcharge represents an additional charge designed to cover specific carrier costs. Surcharges are used to protect carriers from situations not anticipated when publishing a general rate. The surcharge may be assessed as a flat charge, a percentage, or a sliding scale based on shipment size. A common use of surcharges is to compensate carriers for dramatic changes in fuel cost. For example, the United States Information Agency reported that diesel prices jumped 48 percent in 2004 from $1.49 a gallon to $2.21. The standard fuel surcharge for one company increased from 5 cents to 20 cents per mile. The surcharge approach provides a means of immediate relief for the carrier to recover unexpected costs while not including such costs in the long-term rate structure.

Class rates, minimum charges, arbitrary charges, and surcharges form a pricing structure that, in various combinations, is applicable within the continental United States. The tariff indicates the class rate for any rating group between specified origins and destinations. In combination, the classification framework and class rate structure form a generalized pricing mechanism for all participating carriers. Each mode has specific characteristics applicable to its tariffs. In water, specific tariff provisions are made for cargo location within the ship or on the deck. In addition, provisions are made to charter entire vessels. Similar specialized provisions are found in air cargo and pipeline tariffs. Nonoperating intermediaries and package services also publish tariffs specialized to their service.

Commodity Rates

When a large quantity of a product moves between two locations on a regular basis, it is common practice for carriers to publish a **commodity rate.** Commodity rates are special or specific rates published without regard to classification. The terms and conditions of a commodity rate are usually indicated in a contract between the carrier and shipper. Commodity rates are published on a point-to-point basis and apply only on specified products. Today, most rail freight moves under commodity rates. They are less prevalent in motor carriage. Whenever a commodity rate exists, it supersedes the corresponding class or exception rate.

Exception Rates

Special rates published to provide prices lower than the prevailing class rates are called **exception rates.** The original purpose of the exception rate was to provide a special rate for a specific area, origin/destination, or commodity when justified by either competitive or high-volume movements. Rather than publish a new tariff, an exception to the classification or class rate was established.

Just as the name implies, when an exception rate is published, the classification that normally applies to the product is changed. Such changes may involve assignment of a new class or may be based on a percentage of the original class. Technically, exceptions may be higher or lower, although most are less than original class rates. Unless otherwise noted, all services provided under the class rate remain under an exception rate.

Since deregulation, several new types of exception rates have gained popularity. For example, an **aggregate tender** rate is utilized when a shipper agrees to provide multiple shipments to a carrier in exchange for a discount or exception from the prevailing class rate. The primary objective is to reduce carrier cost by permitting multiple shipment pickup during one stop at a shipper's facility or to reduce the rate for the shipper because of the carrier's reduced cost. To illustrate, UPS offers customers that tender multiple small package shipments at one time a discount based on aggregate weight and/or cubic volume. Since deregulation, numerous pricing innovations have been introduced by common carriers, based on various aggregation principles.

A **limited service** rate is utilized when a shipper agrees to perform selected services typically performed by the carrier, such as trailer loading, in exchange for a discount. A common example is a **shipper load and count** rate, where the shipper takes responsibility for loading and counting the cases. Not only does this remove the responsibility for loading the shipment from the carrier, but it also implies that the carrier, once the trailer is sealed, is not responsible for guaranteeing case count. Another example of limited service is a **released value rate,** which limits carrier liability in case of loss or damage. Normally, the carrier is responsible for full product value if loss or damage occurs in transit. The quoted rate must include adequate insurance to cover the risk. Often it is more effective for manufacturers of high-value product to self-insure to realize the lowest possible rate. Limited service is used when shippers have confidence in the carrier's capability. Cost can be reduced by eliminating duplication of effort or responsibility.

Under aggregate tender and limited service rates, as well as other innovative exception rates, the basic economic justification is the reduction of carrier cost and subsequent sharing of benefits based on shipper/carrier cooperation.

Special Rates and Services

A number of special rates and services provided by carriers are available for use in logistical operations. Several common examples are discussed.

As indicated earlier, **freight-all-kind (FAK) rates** are important to logistics operations. Under FAK rates, a mixture of different products is transported under a negotiated rating. Rather than determine the classification and applicable freight rate of individual products, an average rating is applied for the total shipment. In essence, FAK rates are line-haul rates since they replace class, exception, or commodity rates. Their purpose is to simplify the paperwork associated with the movement of mixed commodities.

Numerous special rates exist that may offer transportation savings on specific freight movements. When a commodity moves under the tariff of a single carrier, it is referred to as a **local rate** or single-line rate. If more than one carrier is involved in the freight movement, a **joint rate** may be applicable even though multiple carriers are involved in the actual transportation process. Because some motor and rail carriers operate in restricted territory, it may be necessary to utilize the services of more than one carrier to complete a shipment. Utilization of a joint rate can offer substantial savings over the use of two or more local rates.

Special price incentives to utilize a published tariff that applies to only part of the desired route are called **proportional rates.** Proportional provisions of a tariff are most often applicable to origin or destination points outside the normal geographical area of a single-line tariff. If a joint rate does not exist and proportional provisions do, the strategy of moving a shipment under proportional rates provides a discount on the single-line part of the movement, thereby resulting in a lower overall freight charge.

Transit services permit a shipment to be stopped at an intermediate point between initial origin and destination for unloading, storage, and/or processing. The shipment is then reloaded for delivery to the destination. Typical examples of transit services are milling for grain products and processing for sugar beets. When transit privileges exist, the shipment is charged a through rate from origin to destination plus a transit privilege charge.

For a variety of reasons, a shipper or consignee may desire to change routing, destination, or even the consignee after a shipment is in transit. This process is called **diversion and reconsignment.** This flexibility can be extremely important, particularly with regard to food and other perishable products where market demand can quickly change. It is a normal practice among certain types of marketing intermediaries to purchase commodities with the full intention of selling them while they are in transit. **Diversion** consists of changing the destination of a shipment prior to its arrival at the original destination. **Reconsignment** is a change in consignee prior to delivery. Both services are provided by railroads and truck carriers for a specified charge.

A **split delivery** is desired when portions of a shipment need to be delivered to different destinations. Under specified tariff conditions, delivery can involve multiple destinations. The payment is typically structured to reflect a rate as if the shipment were going to the most distant destination. In addition, there typically is a charge for each delivery.

Demurrage and detention are charges assessed for retaining freight cars or truck trailers beyond specified loading or unloading time. The term **demurrage** is used by railroads for holding a railcar beyond 48 hours before unloading the shipment. Trucks use the term **detention** to cover similar delays. In the case of motor carriers, the permitted time is specified in the tariff and is normally limited to a few hours.

In addition to basic transportation, truck and rail carriers offer a wide variety of **special** or **accessorial** services. Table 8.3 provides a list of frequently utilized ancillary services.

Carriers may also offer environmental services and special equipment. **Environmental services** refer to special control of freight while in transit, such as refrigeration, ventilation,

TABLE 8.3
Typical Carrier Ancillary Services

- *COD.* Collect payment on delivery.
- *Change COD.* Change COD recipient.
- *Inside delivery.* Deliver product inside the building.
- *Marking or tagging.* Mark or tag product as it is transported.
- *Notify before delivery.* Make appointment prior to delivery.
- *Reconsignment of delivery.* Redirect shipment to a new destination while in transit.
- *Redeliver.* Attempt second delivery.
- *Residential delivery.* Deliver at a residence without a truck dock.
- *Sorting and segregating.* Sort commodity prior to delivery.
- *Storage.* Store commodity prior to delivery.

and heating. For example, in the summer, Hershey typically transports chocolate confectionery products in refrigerated trailers to protect them from high temperature levels. **Special equipment charges** refer to the use of equipment that the carrier has purchased for a shipper's convenience. For example, specialized sanitation equipment is necessary to clean and prepare trailers for food storage and transit if the trailer has been previously utilized for nonfood products or commodities.

Although the brief coverage of special services is not all-inclusive, it does offer several examples of the range and type of services carriers offer. A carrier's role in a logistical system is most often far greater than providing line-haul transportation.

Transport Administration

Traffic managers administer a wide variety of different activities. Among the most common are: (1) operational management, (2) consolidation, (3) negotiation, (4) control, (5) auditing and claims administration, and (6) logistical integration.

Operational Management

The fundamental responsibility of a traffic department is to oversee day-to-day transportation operations. In large-scale organizations, traffic management involves a wide variety of administrative responsibilities. Firms are increasingly implementing Transportation Management Systems (TMS) as integral parts of their integration information technology strategies.[3]

In general, a TMS must proactively identify and evaluate alternative transportation strategies and tactics to determine the best methods to move product within the existing constraints. As shown in Table 8.4, this includes capabilities to select modes, plan loads, consolidate loads with other shippers, take advantage of current unbalances in traffic movement, route vehicles, and optimize use of transportation equipment. The principal deliverables of TMS are cost savings and increased functionality to provide credible delivery times.

From an operational perspective, key elements of transportation management are equipment scheduling and yard management, load planning, routing, and carrier administration.

Equipment Scheduling and Yard Management

One major responsibility of the traffic department is equipment scheduling and yard management. Scheduling is an important process in both common carrier and private transportation. A serious and costly operational bottleneck can result from transportation equipment waiting to be loaded or unloaded. Proper yard management requires careful load planning,

---

[3] The relationship of TMS to overall logistical technology is discussed in Chapter 5.

TABLE 8.4
Typical Transportation Management System Functionality

- Order consolidation
- Route optimization
- Carrier rate management
- EDI links with carriers
- Internet-based shipment tracking
- Integrated claims management
- Identify most economical mode: parcel, less-than-truckload, truckload, pool distribution, stops in transit
- Calculate best route
- Carrier selection based on cost and service including performance
- Yard management

equipment utilization, and driver scheduling. Additionally, equipment preventive maintenance must be planned, coordinated, and monitored. Finally, any specialized equipment
requirements must be planned and implemented.

Closely related to equipment scheduling is the arrangement of delivery and pickup appointments. To avoid extensive waiting time and improve equipment utilization, it is important to preschedule dock positions or slots. It is becoming common practice to establish
standing appointments for regular shipments to facilitate loading and unloading. Some
firms are implementing the practice of establishing advanced appointments at the time of
order commitment. Increasingly, the effective scheduling of equipment is key to implementing time-based logistical arrangements. For example, cross-dock arrangements are
totally dependent on precise scheduling of equipment arrival and departure.

Load Planning

How loads are planned directly impacts transportation efficiency. In the case of trucks, capacity is limited in terms of weight and cube. Planning the load sequence of a trailer must
consider product physical characteristics and the size of individual shipments, as well as
delivery sequence if multiple shipments are loaded on a single trailer. As noted earlier,
TMS software is available to help facilitate load planning.

How effectively load planning is performed will directly impact overall logistical efficiency. For example, the load plan drives the work sequence at warehouses. Transportation
equipment must be available to maintain an orderly flow of product and material from
warehouse or factory to shipment destination.

Routing and Advanced Shipment Notification (ASN)

An important part of achieving transportation efficiency is shipment **routing.** Routing pre-
determines the geographical path a vehicle will travel. Once again, routing software is an
integral part of TMS.

From an administrative viewpoint, the traffic department is responsible for assuring that
routing is performed in an efficient manner while meeting key customer service requirements. It is common practice for shippers to electronically provide consignees advanced shipment notification (ASN). While the specifics of ASN documents vary, their primary purpose
is to allow adequate time to plan arrival, arrange delivery appointments, and plan to redeploy
the shipment's content. How deliveries are planned must take into consideration special
requirements of customers in terms of time, location, and special unloading services.

Movement Administration

Traffic managers have the basic responsibility of administering the performance of for-hire
and private transportation. Effective administration requires continuous carrier performance measurement and evaluation. Until recently, efforts to measure actual carrier service
were sporadic and unreliable. A typical procedure was to include postcards with shipments
requesting consignees to record time and condition of arrival. The development of information technology has significantly improved shipment information reliability. The fact
that most shippers have reduced their carrier base has greatly simplified administration.
Effective administration requires carrier selection, integration, and evaluation.

A basic responsibility of the traffic department is to select carriers to perform for-hire
transport. To some degree all firms use the services of for-hire carriers. Even those with
commitment to private fleets regularly require the supplemented services of common, contract, and specialized carriers to complete transportation requirements. Most firms that use
for-hire transportation have implemented a **core carrier strategy.**

The concept of a core carrier is to build a working relationship with a small number of
transportation providers. Historically, shippers followed the practice of spreading their

transportation purchases across a wide variety of carriers to assure competitive rates and adequate equipment supply. During the regulated era, few differences in price existed between carriers. As a result, shippers often conducted business with hundreds of different carriers. The concentration of volume in a few core carriers creates a business relationship that standardizes operational and administrative processes. Mutual planning and acknowledged dependency between a shipper and carrier result in dependable equipment supply, customized services, improved scheduling, and more efficient overall administration.

In a number of situations, the core carrier relationships are directly between the shipper and the transportation provider. A recent development is the use of integrated service providers (ISPs) to establish and maintain business relationships with core carriers. In such situations, the ISP facilitates administration and consolidates freight across a wide variety of shippers.

The range of relationship models is ever-changing as service providers devise new and better methods of identifying and integrating transportation requirements. However, at the end of the day, it remains a fundamental responsibility of transportation management to assure a firm is supported by reliable and economical transportation. This fundamental responsibility cannot be delegated.

Consolidation

At several different points throughout this text the importance of freight consolidation is discussed. The fact that freight costs are directly related to size of shipment and length of haul places a premium upon freight consolidation. In terms made famous by the late President Truman, *the buck stops here,* meaning traffic management is the business function responsible for achieving freight consolidation.

The traditional approach to freight consolidation was to combine LTL or parcel shipment moving to a general location. The objective of outbound consolidation was straightforward. The transportation savings in moving a single consolidated shipment versus multiple individual, small shipments were typically sufficient to pay for handling and local delivery while achieving total cost reduction.

The shift to response-based logistics has introduced new challenges regarding consolidation. Time-based logistics tends to transpose the impact of unpredictable demand from inventory safety stock to creation of small shipments. All members of the supply chain are seeking to reduce inventory dwell time by more closely synchronizing replenishment with demand. The result is more frequent, small orders. Not only does the increase in small shipments result in higher transportation cost, it also translates to more handling and dock congestion.

To control transportation cost when a time-based strategy is used, managerial attention must be directed to the development of ingenious ways to realize benefits of transportation consolidation. To plan freight consolidation, it is necessary to have reliable information concerning both current and planned inventory status. It is also desirable to be able to reserve or promise scheduled production to achieve planned consolidations. To the extent practical, consolidations should be planned prior to order processing and warehouse order selection to avoid delay. All aspects of consolidation require timely and relevant information concerning planned activity.

From an operational viewpoint, freight consolidation techniques can be grouped as **reactive** and **proactive.** Each type of consolidation is important to achieving transportation efficiency.

Reactive Consolidation

A reactive approach to consolidation does not attempt to influence the composition and timing of transportation movements. The consolidation effort reacts to shipments as they come and seeks to combine individual orders into larger shipments for line-haul movement. Perhaps the most visible example of effective reactive line-haul is United Parcel Service's nightly sortation and consolidation of package freight for intercity movement.

From an operational viewpoint, there are three ways to achieve effective reactive consolidation: (1) market area, (2) scheduled delivery, and (3) pooled delivery.

The most basic method of consolidation is to combine small shipments going to different customers within a geographical **market area.** This procedure does not interrupt the natural freight flow by changing the timing of shipments. Rather, the overall quantity of shipments to a market area provides the consolidation basis.

The difficulty of developing either inbound or outbound market area consolidations is the variation in daily volume. To offset the volume deficiency, three operating arrangements are commonly used. First, consolidated shipments may be sent to an intermediate break-bulk point for purposes of line-haul transportation savings. There, individual shipments are separated and forwarded to their destination. Second, firms may elect to hold consolidated shipments for scheduled delivery on specific days to given destination markets. Third, consolidation of small shipments may be achieved by utilizing the services of a third-party logistics firm to pool delivery. The last two methods require special arrangements, which are discussed in greater detail below.

The limiting of shipments to specific markets to selected days each week is referred to as **scheduled area delivery.** The scheduled delivery plan is normally communicated to customers in a way that highlights the mutual benefits of consolidation. The shipping firm commits to the customer that all orders received prior to a specified cutoff time will be guaranteed for delivery on the scheduled day.

Participation in **pooled delivery** typically means that a freight forwarder, public warehouse, or transportation company arranges consolidation for multiple shippers serving the same geographical market area. Integrated service providers that arrange pooled consolidation services typically have standing delivery appointments at high-volume delivery destinations. It is common, under such arrangements, for the consolidation company to also perform value-added service such as sorting, sequencing, or segregation of inbound freight to accommodate customer requirements.

Proactive Consolidation

While reactive efforts to develop transportation consolidations have been successful, two forces are driving a more proactive approach. First, the impact of response-based logistical systems is creating a larger number of small shipments. This trend toward increased smaller shipments has been intensified by the growth of e-commerce. Second, proactive consolidation reflects the desire for shippers, carriers, and consignees to participate in consolidation savings.

An important step toward achieving proactive consolidation is **preorder planning** of quantity and timing to facilitate consolidated freight movement. Simply stated, the creation of orders should not be restricted to standard buying times or inventory replenishment rules. Buyer participation in order creation can greatly facilitate proactive freight consolidation.[4]

Significant freight consolidation opportunities also may exist if nonrelated firms can be coordinated. Commonly referred to as **multivendor consolidation,** the general idea of grouping different shippers' freight has always been integral to line-haul operations of LTL carriers. The new initiative is jointly planning warehousing and order processing across different companies to facilitate such consolidation. Creating such multivendor consolidation is a value-added service offered by a growing number of ISPs. Likewise,

---

[4] Carol Casper, "Multi-Vendor Consolidation," *Food Logistics,* January/February 1999, pp. 37–48.

firms are increasingly endorsing pooling arrangements with competitors to achieve logistical efficiency.[5]

Negotiation

Chapter 7 presented a description of basic transportation and associated rate regulation. For any given shipment, it is the responsibility of the traffic department to obtain the lowest possible rate consistent with service required.

The prevailing tariff represents the starting point in transportation negotiation. The key to effective negotiation is to seek win-win agreements wherein both carriers and shippers share productivity gains. As indicated several times throughout this text, the lowest possible cost for transportation may not be the lowest total cost of logistics. The traffic department must seek the lowest rate consistent with service standards. For example, if 2-day delivery is required, the traffic department seeks to select the method of transport that will consistently meet this standard at the lowest possible cost. Given the special considerations of transportation, several factors discussed throughout this section must guide rate negotiation. However, in the context of building solid carrier relationships, traffic managers must seek fair and equitable rates.

Control

Other important responsibilities under the control of transportation management are tracing, expediting, and driver hours administration. **Tracing** is a procedure to locate lost or late shipments. Shipments committed across a transportation network are bound to be misplaced or delayed from time to time. Most large carriers maintain online tracing to aid shippers in locating a shipment. The tracing action must be initiated by the shipper's traffic department, but once initiated, it is the carrier's responsibility to provide the desired information. **Expediting** involves the shipper notifying a carrier that it needs to have a specific shipment move through the carrier's system as quickly as possible and with no delays.

Driver fatigue concerns prompted the Department of Transportation's Federal Motor Carrier Safety Administration (FMCSA) in 2004 to alter the **hours of service** (HOS) that interstate truck drivers could operate. The changes were developed to ensure drivers were getting sufficient off-duty time to rest while at the same time increasing daily driving time for trucking companies. The changes significantly restructured working conditions for truckers. Under the new rules all breaks were counted as on-duty time. Although total driving hours were extended, the impact of the new regulation was to reduce the productive workday.

The new regulations lengthened daily driving time; counted rest, unloading and breaks as driving time; extended the required time off between shifts; and maintained a weekly maximum for on-duty hours. An overview of the rule changes are presented in Table 8.5.

[5] Helen L. Richardson, "Pooling with Competitors," *Transportation and Distribution*, November 1998, pp. 105–10.

TABLE 8.5
Hours of Drivers' Service

Source: United States Department of Transportation.

Old Hours of Service Rules	New Hours of Service Rules
10 hours' driving	11 hours' driving

15 hours on duty
  Breaks do not count as duty time, and extend the day.
	14 consecutive hours on duty
	  Breaks count as on-duty time.

8 cumulative hours off duty	10 consecutive and uninterrupted hours off duty
60/70 hours in 7/8 days	60/70 hours in 7/8 days Drivers must take 34 hours off duty before restarting an on-duty period.

However, there were additional reasons beyond safety for the change; reducing costs for shippers was an HOS goal. The added hour of driving time would help decrease shipping costs. United States Transportation Secretary Norman Mineta said, "If we can lower the cost of moving freight by 1 percent, the additional benefit to the economy would be more than $98 billion annually."[6]

The District of Columbia Court of Appeals vacated the new HOS rules on July 16, 2004, citing that the new rules may increase driver fatigue rather than alleviate tiredness. The new rules reflected in Table 8.5 were implemented in 2005.

HOS regulation is a good example of how government policy can influence transportation. In cases of private transportation, HOS administration is the direct responsibility of the traffic department. In for-hire carriers, oversight is the responsibility of carrier management.

Auditing and Claim Administration

When transportation service or charges are not performed as promised, shippers can make claims for restitution. Claims are typically classified as **loss and damage** or **overcharge/ undercharge.** Loss and damage claims occur when a shipper demands the carrier pay for partial or total financial loss resulting from poor performance. As the name implies, loss and damage claims usually occur when product is lost or damaged while in transit. Overcharge/undercharge claims result when the amount billed is different from that expected and are typically resolved through freight bill audit procedures.

Agreements stipulate the proper procedure for filing claims and help define which parties are responsible. Two factors regarding claim administration are of primary importance. First, detailed attention should be given to claim administration because recoveries are achieved only by aggressive audit programs. Second, large volumes of claims are indicative of carriers that are not performing their service obligations. Regardless of the dollars recovered by claim administration, the breakdown in customer service performance resulting from loss and damage claims impacts a shipper's reputation with its customers.

Auditing freight bills is an important responsibility of the traffic department. The purpose of auditing is to ensure freight bill accuracy. Transport rate complexity results in a higher error probability than in most other purchasing decisions. There are two types of freight audits. A **preaudit** determines proper charges prior to payment of a freight bill. A **postaudit** makes the same determination after payment has been made. Auditing may be either external or internal. If external, specialized freight-auditing companies are employed, utilizing personnel who are experts in specific commodity groupings. This is generally more efficient than the use of internal personnel who may not have the same level of expertise. Payment for external audit is usually based on a percentage of recovered overcharges. It is crucial that a highly ethical firm be employed for this purpose, because valuable marketing and customer information is contained in the freight bill and corporate activities may be adversely affected if sensitive information is not held in confidence.

A combination of internal and external auditing is frequently employed, depending on the value of the freight bill. For example, a bill of $600 with a 10 percent error results in a $60 recovery, but a $50 bill with a 10 percent error results in only a $5 recovery. Therefore, bills with larger recovery potential may be audited internally.

It is common practice for firms to determine and pay freight at the time a shipment is tendered to a carrier. This shifts the audit responsibility to the carrier, which must then file an undercharge claim for recovery from the shipper.

---

[6] U.S. Department of Transportation, "FMCSA 4-03, Revised Hours-of-Service Rule to Help Ensure Truck Drivers Get Adequate Rest," Washington, DC, April 24, 2003.

Logistical Integration

For any given operating period, traffic management is expected to provide the required transportation services at budgeted cost. It is also traffic management's responsibility to search for alternative ways to deploy transportation to reduce total logistics cost. For example, a slight change in packaging may create an opportunity for negotiation of a lower freight classification for a product. Although packaging costs may increase, this added expense may be offset by a substantial reduction in transportation cost. Unless such proposals originate from the traffic department, they will likely go undetected in the average firm. As indicated earlier, transportation is the highest single cost area in most logistical systems. This expenditure level combined with the dependence of logistical operations on effective transportation means that the traffic departments must play an active role in supply chain logistics planning.

Documentation

Well-defined documentation is required to perform a transportation service. With the exception of private transfer within the confines of a single firm, products are typically being sold when being transported. Thus, legal title to ownership occurs during the time the transport service is performed. When for-hire carriers are engaged to perform the transportation, the transaction must establish clear legal responsibility for all parties involved. The primary purpose of transportation documentation is to protect all parties involved in the performance of the transaction. Three primary types of transport documentation are bills of lading, freight bills, and shipment manifests.

Bill of Lading

The **bill of lading** is the basic document utilized in purchasing transport services. It serves as a receipt and documents products and quantities shipped. For this reason, accurate product description and count are essential. In case of loss, damage, or delay, the bill of lading is the basis for damage claims. The designated individual or buyer on a bill of lading is the only bona fide recipient of goods. A carrier is responsible for proper delivery according to instructions contained in the document. The information contained on the bill of lading determines all responsibilities related to timing and ownership.

The bill of lading specifies terms and conditions of carrier liability and documents responsibilities for all possible causes of loss or damage except those defined as acts of God. Figure 8.4 provides an example of a Uniform Straight Bill of Lading. Government regulations permit uniform bills of lading to be computerized and electronically transmitted between shippers and carriers.

In addition to the **uniform** bill of lading, other commonly used types are **order-notified, export,** and **government.** It is important to select the correct bill of lading for a specific shipment.

An order-notified or negotiable bill of lading is a credit instrument. It provides that delivery not be made unless the original bill of lading is surrendered to the carrier. The usual procedure is for the seller to send the order-notified bill of lading to a third party, usually a bank or credit institution. Upon customer payment for the product the credit institution releases the bill of lading. The buyer then presents it to the common carrier, which in turn releases the goods. This facilitates international transport where cross-border payment for goods may be a major consideration. An export bill of lading permits a shipper to use export rates, which may be lower than domestic rates. Export rates may reduce total cost when applied to domestic origin or destination line-haul transport. Government bills of lading may be used when the product is owned by the United States government.

FIGURE 8.4 **Uniform Straight Bill of Lading**

UNIFORM STRAIGHT BILL OF LADING

Original—Not Negotiable

(To be Printed on "White" Paper)

Shipper's No. . . . .

Agent's No. . . . .

Company

RECEIVED, subject to the classifications and tariffs in effect on the date of the issue of this Bill of Lading,

at . . . . , 19 . . .

from . . . .

the property described below, in apparent good order, except as noted (contents and condition of contents of packages unknown), marked, consigned, and destined as indicated below, which said company (the word company being understood throughout this contract as meaning any person of corporation in possession of the property under the contract) agrees to carry to its usual place (of delivery at mid destination, if on its own road or its own water line, otherwise to deliver to another carrier on the route to said destination. It is mutually agreed, as to each carrier of all or any of said property over all or any portion of said route to destination, and as to each party at any time interested in all or any of said property, that every service to be performed hereunder shall be subject to all the conditions not prohibited by law, whether printed or written, herein contained, including the conditions on back hereof, which are hereby agreed to by the shipper and accepted for himself and his assigns.

(Mail or street address of consignee—For purposes of notification only.)

Consigned to . . . .

Destination . . . . State of . . . . County of . . . .

Route . . . .

Delivering Carrier . . . . Car Initial . . . . Car No. . . . .

No. Pack-ages	Description of Articles, Special Marks, and Exceptions	*Weight (Subject to Correction)	Class or Rate	Check Column	Subject to Section 7 of conditions, if this ship-ment is to be delivered to the consignee without recourse on the consign-or, the consignor shall sign the following state-ment:
. . . .		. . . .		. . . . . .	
. . . .		. . . .		. . . . . .	The carrier shall not make delivery of this shipment without pay-ment of freight and all other lawful charges.
. . . .		. . . .		. . . . . .	
. . . .		. . . .		. . . . . .	. . . . (Signature of consignor.)
. . . .		. . . .		. . . . . .	If charges are to be pre-paid, write or stamp here, "To be Prepaid."
. . . .		. . . .		. . . . . .	. . . .
. . . .		. . . .		. . . . . .	Received $ . . . . to apply in prepayment of the charges on the property described hereon.
. . . .		. . . .		. . . . . .	Agent or Cashier.
. . . .		. . . .		. . . . . .	Per . . . . (The signature here acknowl-edges only the amount prepaid.)

* If the shipment moves between two ports by a carrier by water, the law requires that the bill of lading shall state whether it is "carrier's or shipper's weight."

Note.—Where the rate is dependent on value, shippers are required to state specifically in writing the agreed or declared value of the property.

The agreed or declared value of the property is hereby specifically stated by the shipper to be not exceeding

Charges advanced:

$ . . . .

. . . . per . . . .

. . . . Shipper. . . . . Agent.

Per . . . . Per . . . .

Permanent postoffice address of shipper . . . .

Freight Bill

The **freight bill** represents a carrier's method of charging for transportation services performed. It is developed by using information contained in the bill of lading. The freight bill may be either **prepaid** or **collect.** A prepaid bill means that transport cost is paid by the shipper prior to performance, whereas a collect shipment shifts payment responsibility to the consignee.

Considerable administration is involved in preparing bills of lading and freight bills. There has been significant effort to automate freight bills and bills of lading through EDI or Internet transactions. Some firms elect to pay their freight bills at the time the bill of lading is created, thereby combining the two documents. Such arrangements are based upon the financial benefits of reduced paperwork cost, and as noted earlier shift the audit responsibility to the carrier.

Shipment Manifest

The **shipment manifest** lists individual stops or consignees when multiple shipments are placed on a single vehicle. Each shipment requires a bill of lading. The manifest lists the stop, bill of lading, weight, and case count for each shipment. The objective of the manifest is to provide a single document that defines the overall contents of the load without requiring review of individual bills of lading. For single-stop shipments, the manifest is the same as the bill of lading.

Summary

Transportation is usually the largest single cost expenditure in most logistics operations. Prior to deregulation, transportation services were standardized and inflexible, resulting in limited ability to develop a competitive advantage. As a result of deregulation, service offerings have been expanded and restrictions relaxed, allowing transportation resources to be effectively integrated into overall supply chain logistics.

Knowledge of transportation economics and pricing is essential for effective logistics management. The primary drivers of transportation costs are distance, volume, density, stowability, handling, liability, and market factors. These drivers determine transportation prices that are presented to buyers as rates for performing specific services. Logistics managers need to have a working familiarity with the basic rate structure for line-haul and specialized transport-related services.

The fundamental responsibilities of traffic administration are operational management, consolidation, negotiation, control, auditing and claims administration, and logistical integration. All aspects of administration are essential for effective transportation management. The extent to which the administrative responsibilities discussed are performed by an internal traffic department or are provided by an integrated service provider is a matter of managerial preference.

Challenge Questions

1. Seven economic drivers that influence transportation cost were presented. Select a specific product and discuss how each factor impacts determination of a freight rate.
2. Compare and contrast variable, fixed, and joint costs.
3. Compare and contrast cost-of-service with value-of-service as alternative rate-making strategies.
4. Discuss the concept of net pricing. What advantage does net pricing provide for carriers and shippers?

5. What is the purpose of freight classification? Does the concept of classification have relevancy given deregulation of transportation?

6. Describe the difference between a rate and a rating. How do they relate to classification?

7. What is the role of the freight bill and the bill of lading in a transportation transaction?

8. What is the basic concept of multivendor consolidation? How do ISPs help achieve such consolidation?

9. Compare and contrast reactive and proactive consolidation. Provide an example of each.

10. Four aspects of transportation operations management were identified as: (1) equipment scheduling and yard management, (2) load planning, (3) routing and advanced shipment notification, and (4) movement administration. Identify a commercial transportation shipment you are aware of and discuss how each managerial aspect was involved.

Warehousing

Warehousing incorporates many different aspects of logistics operations. Because of the many types of warehouses, the presentation does not fit the neat classification schemes used in areas such as order management, inventory, and transportation. A warehouse has traditionally been viewed as a place to hold or store inventory. However, in contemporary logistical systems, warehouse functionality is more properly viewed as mixing inventory assortments to meet customer requirements. Storage of products is ideally held to a minimum. This chapter provides a foundation for understanding the value warehousing contributes in the logistics process. The discussion is relevant for all types of warehouses, including distribution centers, consolidation terminals, break-bulk facilities, and cross-docks. The objective is to introduce general managerial considerations related to warehousing.

Strategic Warehousing

While effective logistics systems should not be designed to hold inventory for extended times, there are occasions when inventory storage is justified on the basis of cost and service.

Storage has always been an important aspect of economic development. In the preindustrial era, storage was performed by individual households forced to function as self-sufficient economic units. Consumers performed warehousing and accepted the attendant risks.

As transportation capability developed, it became possible to engage in specialization. Product storage shifted from households to retailers, wholesalers, and manufacturers. Warehouses stored inventory in the logistics pipeline, serving to coordinate product supply and consumer demand. Because the value of strategic storage was not well understood, warehouses were often considered necessary evils that added cost to the distribution process. The concept that middlemen simply increase cost follows from that belief. During earlier times the need to deliver product assortments was limited. Labor productivity, materials handling efficiency, and inventory turnover were not major concerns. Because labor was relatively inexpensive, human resources were used freely. Little consideration was given to efficiency in space utilization, work methods, or materials handling. Despite such shortcomings, these initial warehouses provided a necessary bridge between production and marketing.

Following World War II, managerial attention shifted toward strategic storage. Management began to question the need for vast warehouse networks. In the distributive industries such as wholesaling and retailing, it was traditionally considered best practice to dedicate a warehouse containing a full assortment of inventory to every sales territory. As forecasting and production scheduling techniques improved, management questioned such risky inventory deployment. Production planning became more dependable as disruptions and time delays during manufacturing decreased. Seasonal production and consumption still required warehousing, but the overall need for storage to support stable manufacturing and consumption patterns was reduced.

Changing requirements in retailing more than offset any reduction in warehousing obtained as a result of these manufacturing improvements. Retail stores, faced with the challenge of providing consumers an increasing assortment of products, found it more difficult to maintain purchasing and transportation economics when buying direct from suppliers. The cost of transporting small shipments made direct ordering prohibitive. This created an opportunity to establish strategically located warehouses to provide timely and economical inventory replenishment for retailers. Progressive wholesalers and integrated retailers developed state-of-the-art warehouse systems to logistically support retail replenishment. Thus, the focus on warehousing shifted from passive storage to strategic assortment. The term **distribution center** became widely used throughout industry to capture this dynamic aspect of traditional warehousing.

Improvements in retail warehousing efficiency soon were adopted by manufacturing. For manufacturers, strategic warehousing offered a way to reduce holding or dwell time of materials and parts. Warehousing became integral to Just-in-Time (JIT) and stockless production strategies. While the basic notion of JIT is to reduce work-in-process inventory, such manufacturing strategies need dependable logistics. Achieving such logistical support across a global market typically requires strategically located warehouses. Utilizing centralized parts inventory at a central warehouse reduces the need for inventory at each assembly plant. Products can be purchased and shipped to the strategically located central warehouse, taking advantage of consolidated transportation. At the warehouse, products are sorted, sequenced, and shipped to specific manufacturing plants as needed. Where fully integrated, sortation and sequencing facilities become a vital extension of manufacturing.

On the outbound, or market-facing, side of manufacturing, warehouses can be used to create product assortments for customer shipment. The capability to receive mixed product shipments offers customers two specific advantages. First, logistical cost is reduced because an assortment of products can be delivered while taking advantage of consolidated transportation. Second, inventory of slow-moving products can be reduced because of the capability to receive smaller quantities as part of a larger consolidated shipment. Manufacturers that provide sorted and sequenced product shipments on a timely basis are positioned to achieve a competitive advantage.

An important goal in warehousing is to maximize flexibility. Flexibility is facilitated by information technology. Technology has influenced almost every aspect of warehouse operations by creating new and better ways to perform storage and handling. Flexibility is also an essential part of being able to respond to ever-changing customer demand in terms of product assortments, value-added services, and the way shipments are sequenced and presented. Information technology facilitates flexibility by allowing warehouse operators to quickly react to changing customer requirements.[1]

Strategic warehousing serves to satisfy requirements related to **local presence.** While benefits of local presence may not be as obvious as other service benefits, it is often cited by executives as a major advantage of local warehouses. The underlying belief is that a local warehouse can respond faster to customer needs than can a more distant warehouse. It is anticipated that local warehouse presence will increase market share and potentially profitability. While the local-presence factor is a frequently discussed strategy, little solid research exists to confirm or refute its existence. In addition, more reliable transportation and technology-based order processing are closing the response time gap regardless of distance. Unless a warehouse is economically or service justified, it is unlikely that local presence will favorably influence operational results. The fact remains that a network of strategically located warehouses does provide key customers the perception they will be logistically supported.

Benefits realized from strategic warehousing are classified as economic and service. No warehousing should be included in a logistical system unless it is fully justified on some combination of cost and service. Ideally, a warehouse will simultaneously provide both economic and service benefits.

Economic Benefits

Economic benefits of warehousing occur when overall logistics costs are reduced. For example, if adding a warehouse in a logistical system reduces overall transportation cost by an amount greater than required investment and operational cost, then total cost will be reduced. When total cost reductions are achievable, the warehouse is economically justified. Four basic economic benefits are: (1) consolidation and break-bulk, (2) sorting, (3) seasonal storage, and (4) reverse logistics.

Consolidation and Break-Bulk

The economic benefits of consolidation and break-bulk are to reduce transportation cost by using warehouse capability to group shipments.

In consolidation, the warehouse receives materials, from a number of sources, that are combined in exact quantities into a large single shipment to a specific destination. The benefits of consolidations are the realization of the lowest possible freight rate, timely and

---

[1] Arnold Maltz and Nicole De Horatuis, "Warehousing: The Evolution Continues," *WERC* (2004), pp. 1–58.

FIGURE 9.1
Consolidation and
Break-Bulk
Arrangements

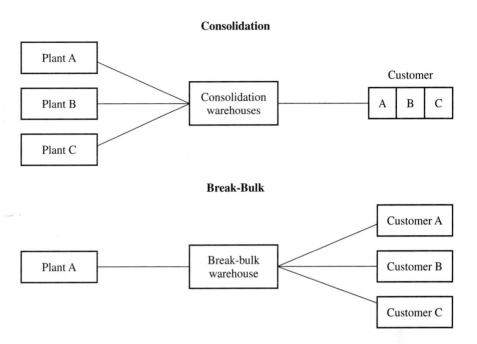

controlled delivery, and reduced congestion at a customer's receiving dock. The warehouse enables both the inbound movement from origin and the outbound movement to destination to be consolidated into a larger size shipment, which generally results in lower transportation charges per unit and most often quicker delivery.

A break-bulk operation receives a single large shipment and arranges for delivery to multiple destinations. Economy of scale is achieved by transporting the larger consolidated shipment. The break-bulk warehouse or terminal sorts or splits out individual orders and arranges local delivery.

Both consolidation and break-bulk arrangements use warehouse capacity to improve transportation efficiency. Many logistical arrangements involve both consolidation and break-bulk. Figure 9.1 illustrates each activity.

Sorting

The basic benefit of sorting is to reconfigure freight as it flows from origin to destination. Three types of assortment—cross-docking, mixing, and assembly—are widely performed in logistical systems.

The objective of **cross-docking** is to combine inventory from multiple origins into a prespecified assortment for a specific customer. Retailers make extensive use of cross-dock operations to replenish fast-moving store inventories. Cross-docking requires precise on-time delivery from each manufacturer. As product is received and unloaded at the warehouse, it is sorted by destination. In most instances, the customer has communicated precise volume requirements of each product for each destination. The manufacturers, in turn, may have sorted, loaded, and labeled the appropriate quantity by destination. Product is then literally moved across the dock from receiving into a truck dedicated to the delivery destination. Once trucks are loaded with mixed product from multiple manufacturers, they are released for transport to destination. The high degree of precision required for effective cross-docking makes successful operation highly dependent on information technology.

An end result similar to cross-docking is achieved in **mixing.** However, mixing is usually performed at an intermediate location between shipment origin and destination. In a typical mixing operation, carloads or truckloads of products are shipped from origin to mixing warehouses. These inbound shipments are planned to minimize inbound transportation cost. Upon arrival at the mixing warehouse, shipments are unloaded and sorted into the combination desired by each customer. In-transit mixing has been traditionally supported by special transportation rates that provide financial incentives to facilitate the process.[2] During the mixing process, inbound products can be combined with others regularly stocked at a warehouse. Warehouses that perform in-transit mixing have the net effect of reducing overall product storage in a logistical system while achieving customer-specific assortments and minimizing transportation cost.

The objective of **assembly** is to support manufacturing operations. Products and components are assembled from a variety of second-tier suppliers by a warehouse, often referred to as **lead suppliers** or **tier one** suppliers, located in close proximity to the manufacturing plant. While manufacturing organizations have traditionally performed assembly, it has become common to utilize value-added services performed by a lead or tier one supplier or an **integrated service provider** (ISP) to sort, sequence, and deliver components when needed in manufacturing. Like cross-docking and mixing, assembly serves to achieve a process grouping of inventory at a precise time and location. Figure 9.2 illustrates these three sorting arrangements.

Seasonal Storage

The direct economic benefit of storage is to accommodate seasonal production or demand. For example, lawn furniture and toys are typically produced year-round but are sold only during a very short marketing period. In contrast, agricultural products are harvested at specific times, with subsequent consumption occurring throughout the year. Both situations require inventory storage to support marketing efforts. Storage provides an inventory buffer, which allows production efficiencies within the constraints imposed by material sources and consumers.

Reverse Logistics Processing

A great deal of the physical work related to reverse logistics is performed at warehouses. Reverse logistics includes the activities to support: (1) returns management, (2) remanufacturing, (3) remarketing, (4) recycling, and (5) disposal. Returns management is designed to facilitate the reverse flow of product that did not sell or to accommodate recalls. Remanufacturing facilitates the reverse flow of product following its useful life. The product itself or components are then updated for sale at a discounted price. Many computer and electronics manufacturers use remanufacturing to enhance their profits after initial leases are over. Remarketers use coordination and reverse flow to position and resell product when the original user no longer needs it. The Defense Logistics Agency has a comprehensive remarketing process to facilitate transfer and sale of used equipment to other military services or governmental agencies. Recycling returns product following its useful life with the objective of decomposing it to its component materials so that they can be effectively reused. Metals, plastics, and precious commodities are often the focus of recycling activities. When material cannot be effectively reused, it still may require reverse logistics to dispose of it in the appropriate landfill.[3]

Many firms are generating significant cash flow from returns management, remanufacturing, remarketing, and recycling. Reverse logistics is concerned with both controlled and regular inventory.[4]

[2] See Chapter 8.

[3] For a broader discussion of closed loop logistics, see Chapter 11.

[4] Dale S. Rogers and Ronald Tibben-Lembke, "An Examination of Reverse Logistics Practices," *Journal of Business Logistics* 22 (2001), pp. 129–48; and Diane A. Mollenkopf and Howard Weathersby, "Creating Value through Reverse Logistics," *Logistics Quarterly* (2003/2004), pp. 20–24.

FIGURE 9.2
Sorting
Arrangements

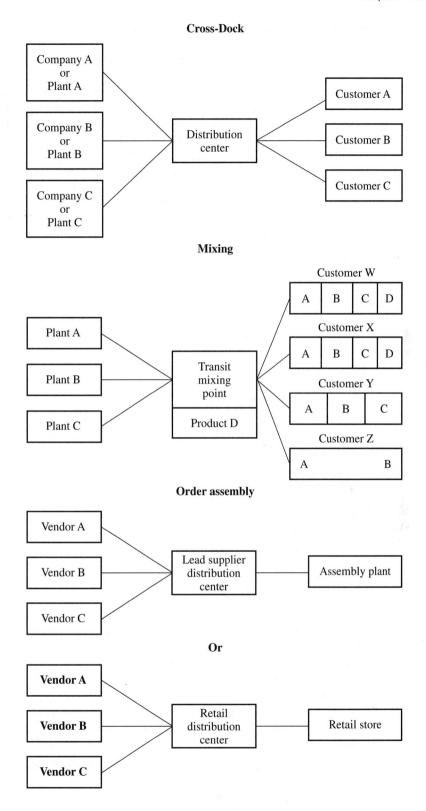

Controlled inventory consists of hazardous materials and product recalls that have potential consumer health or environmental considerations. The reclamation of controlled inventory must be performed under strict operating scrutiny that prevents improper disposal. As one might expect, varied governmental agencies, such as the Consumer Product Safety Commission, Department of Transportation (DOT), the Environmental Protection Agency (EPA), Food and Drug Administration (FDA), and the Occupational Safety and Health Administration (OSHA), are directly involved in disposal of controlled inventory.

Less attention has traditionally focused on reclamation of regular inventory. The product involved in regular inventory reclamation is typically damaged or aged beyond the recommended sell-by date. While some unsalable product results from warehouse damage, most is returned from retail inventory or direct from consumers.

While reclamation is difficult for regular inventory, it is far more challenging for controlled inventory. In both return situations, product flow lacks the orderly process characteristic of outbound movement. Reverse movement typically consists of nonuniform individual packages and cartons as contrasted to outbound movement of cases and pallets. Packages are often broken, and product is not packaged correctly. Return products typically require significant manual sortation and inspection to determine appropriate disposal. However, the opportunity to recover cost by reimbursement and recycling is significant.

Service Benefits

Warehouses can provide services that enhance top line revenue growth. When a warehouse is primarily justified on service, the supporting rationale is that sales improvements will more than offset added cost. It is a difficult assignment to quantify service return-on-investment because it's hard to measure. For example, establishing a warehouse to service a specific market may increase cost but should also increase market sales, revenue, and potentially gross margin. Warehouses can provide service as a result of (1) spot-stocking, (2) full line stocking, and (3) value-added services.

Spot-Stocking

Spot-stocking is typically used to support customer accommodation. Manufacturers of highly seasonal products often spot-stock. Instead of maintaining inventory in a warehouse year-round, or shipping to customers direct from manufacturing plants, responsiveness in peak selling periods can be enhanced through temporary inventory positioning in strategic markets. Under this concept, select inventory is positioned or **spot-stocked** in a local market warehouse in anticipation of responding to customer need during the critical sales period. Utilizing warehouse facilities for spot-stocking allows inventories to be placed in a variety of markets adjacent to key customers just prior to a maximum period of seasonal sales. For example, agricultural fertilizer companies sometimes spot-stock near farmers in anticipation of the growing season. After the growing season, such spot-stocking would likely be reduced or eliminated.

Full Line Stocking

The traditional use of warehouses by manufacturers, wholesalers, and retailers is to stock product inventory combinations in anticipation of customer orders. Typical retailers and wholesalers provide assortments representing multiple products from different manufacturers. In effect, these warehouses can provide one-stop shopping capability for goods from multiple manufacturers.

The difference between spot-stocking and full line stocking is the degree and duration of warehouse utilization. A firm following a spot-stocking strategy would temporarily warehouse a narrow product assortment in a large number of warehouses for a limited time

TABLE 9.1
Value-Added Services

• Cross-dock/transloading	• Order fulfillment
• Customer returns	• Pick/pack
• Home delivery	• Pool distribution
• In-transit merge	• Repair/refurbish
• Kan Ban	• Returnable container management
• Kitting	• Reverse logistics
• Labeling/preticketing	• RFID tag application
• Lot control	• Sequencing/metering
• Mass customization/postponement	• Specialty packaging
• Manufacturing support	• Store support/direct store delivery (DSD)

period. The full line stocking warehouse is more often restricted to a few strategic locations and operates year-round. Full line stocking warehouses improve service by reducing the number of suppliers that a customer must logistically deal with. The combined assortments also make economical larger shipments possible.

Value-Added Services

The demand for highly customized service has transformed modern distribution warehouses into facilities that specialize in performing **value-added services.** A value-added service is any work that creates a greater value for customers. Value-added services typically change the physical features or configuration of products so they are presented to customers in a unique or customized manner. Table 9.1 provides a list of typical value-added services.

Warehouses can postpone final product configuration by completing packaging, labeling, and even light manufacturing. For example, vegetables can be processed and canned in **brights** at the processing plants. Brights are cans without labels. Holding inventory as brights means that product is not committed to specific customers or carton configuration during processing. Once a specific customer order is received, the warehouse can complete labeling and finalize packaging. Examples of postponement range from packaging pharmaceuticals to customizing appliances.

Postponement provides two economic benefits. First, risk is minimized because customized packaging is not performed in anticipation of customer orders or to accommodate a forecast. Second, total inventory can be reduced by using inventory of the base product to support multiple customers' labeling and package requirements. The combination of reduced risk and lower inventory can result in reduced total cost to service even if packaging performed at the warehouse is more expensive per unit than if it were completed during manufacturing.

Warehouse Operations

Once a warehouse mission is determined, managerial attention focuses on establishing the operation. A typical warehouse contains materials, parts, and finished goods on the move. Warehouse operations consist of handling and storage. The objective is to efficiently receive inventory, store it as required, assemble it into complete orders, and make customer shipment. This emphasis on product flow renders a modern warehouse as a product mixing facility. As such, a great deal of managerial attention concerns how to design operations to facilitate efficient handling.

Handling

A first consideration is movement continuity and efficiency throughout the warehouse. Movement continuity means that it is better for an employee using handling equipment to perform longer moves than to undertake a number of short handlings to accomplish the same overall inventory move. Exchanging products between handlers or moving goods from one piece of equipment to another wastes time and increases the potential for product damage. Thus, as a general rule, longer warehouse handling movements are preferred. Goods, once in motion, should be continuously moved until arrival at their final destination.

Scale economies justify moving the largest quantities or loads possible. Instead of moving individual cases, handling procedures should be designed to move cases grouped on pallets, slipsheets, or containers.[5] The overall objective of materials handling is to eventually sort inbound shipments into unique customer assortments. The three primary handling activities are receiving, in-storage handling or transfer, and shipping.

Receiving

The majority of products and materials arrive at warehouses in large-quantity truck shipments. The first handling activity is unloading. At most warehouses, unloading is performed mechanically, using a combination of a lift truck, conveyors, and manual processes. When freight is floor stacked in the trailer, the typical procedure is to manually place products on pallets or a conveyor. When inbound product arrives unitized on pallets or in containers, lift trucks are used to move products from the vehicle to the dock. A primary benefit of receiving unitized loads is the ability to rapidly unload and release inbound transportation equipment.

In-Storage Handling

In-storage handling consists of movements that are performed within the warehouse. Following receipt and movement to a staging location, product is often moved within the facility for storage or order selection. Finally, when an order is processed it is necessary to select the required products and move them to a shipping area. These two types of in-storage handling are typically referred to as **transfer** and **selection.**

There are at least two and sometimes three transfer movements in a typical warehouse. The merchandise is initially moved from the receiving area to a storage location. This movement is typically handled by a lift truck when pallets or slipsheets are used or by other mechanical means for other types of unit loads. A second internal movement may be required prior to order assembly, depending upon warehouse operating procedures. When unit loads have to be broken down for order selection, they are usually transferred from storage to an order selection or picking area. When products are large or bulky, such as appliances, this intermediate movement to a picking area may not be necessary. Such product is often selected from the storage area and moved directly to the shipment staging area. The staging area is adjacent to the shipping dock. In order selection warehouses, the assembled customer order is transferred from the selection area to the shipping staging area. Characteristically, in-storage handling involves lower volume movements than receiving, but still relatively similar products.

Order selection is one of the major handling activities within warehouses. The selection process requires that materials, parts, and products be grouped to facilitate order assembly. It is typical for one area of a warehouse to be designated as a selection or picking area to assemble orders. For each order, the combination of products must be selected and packaged to meet specific customer order requirements.

---

[5] Specific types of handling equipment, pallets, and unitization are discussed in Chapter 10.

Shipping

Shipping consists of order verification and transportation equipment loading. As in receiving, firms may use conveyors or unit load materials handling equipment such as lift trucks to move products from the staging area into the truck trailer or container. In comparison to receiving, warehouse shipping must accommodate relatively low-volume movements of a mixture of products, thus reducing the potential for economies of scale. Shipping unit loads is becoming increasingly popular because considerable time can be saved in vehicle loading. A unit load consists of unitized or palletized product. To facilitate this loading and subsequent unloading upon delivery, many customers are requesting that suppliers provide mixed combinations of product within a trailer or on a pallet. The alternative is to floor-stack cases in the transportation vehicle. Shipment content verification is typically required when product changes ownership. Verification may be limited to a simple carton count or a piece-by-piece check for proper brand, size, and in some cases serial number to assure shipment accuracy. Over-the-road trailers are typically sealed at the time they are fully loaded and ready for shipment. The seal serves to verify that the content has not been altered during transit. Certification that seals have not been tampered with has become a critical factor in post 9-11 security.[6]

Storage

In planning warehouse layout, it is essential that products be assigned specific locations, called **slots,** on the basis of individual characteristics. The most important product variables to consider in a slotting plan are product velocity, weight, and special storage requirements.

Product velocity is the major factor driving warehouse layout. High-volume product should be positioned in the warehouse to minimize movement distance. For example, high-velocity products should be positioned near doors, primary aisles, and at lower levels in storage racks. Such positioning minimizes warehouse handling and reduces the need for frequent lifting. Conversely, products with low volume are typically assigned locations more distant from primary aisles or higher up in storage racks. Figure 9.3 illustrates a storage plan based on product movement velocity.

[6] See Chapter 12.

FIGURE 9.3
Storage Plan Based on Product Movement Velocity

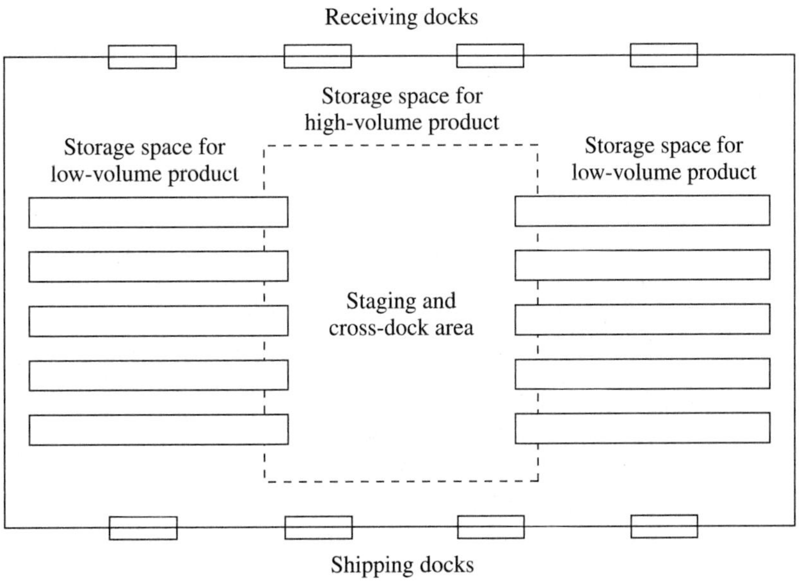

Similarly, the storage plan should take into consideration product weight and special characteristics. Relatively heavy items should be assigned storage locations low to the ground to minimize lifting. Bulky or low-density product requires cubic space. Floor space along outside walls is ideal for such items. On the other hand, smaller items may require storage shelves, bins, or drawers. The integrated storage plan must consider individual product characteristics.

A typical warehouse is engaged in a combination of **active** and **extended** product storage alternatives. Warehouses that directly serve customers typically focus on active short-term storage. In contrast, other warehouses may use extended storage for speculative, seasonal, or obsolete inventory. In controlling and measuring warehouse operations, it is important to differentiate the relative requirements and performance capabilities of active and extended storage.

Active Storage

Regardless of inventory velocity, most goods must be stored for at least a short time. Storage for basic inventory replenishment is referred to as active storage. Active storage must provide sufficient inventory to meet the periodic demands of the service area. The need for active storage is usually related to the capability to achieve transportation or handling economies of scale. For active storage, materials handling processes and technologies need to focus on quick movement and flexibility with minimal consideration for extended and dense storage.

The active storage concept includes **flow-through** or **cross-dock distribution,** which uses warehouses for consolidation and assortment while maintaining minimal or no inventory in storage. The resulting need for reduced inventory favors flow-through and cross-docking techniques that emphasize movement and de-emphasize storage. Flow-through distribution is most appropriate for high-volume, fast-moving products where quantities are reasonably predictable. While flow-through distribution places minimal demands on storage requirements, it does require that product be quickly unloaded, de-unitized, grouped and sequenced into customer assortments, and reloaded into transportation equipment. As a result, the materials handling emphasis is on accurate information-directed quick movement.

Extended Storage

When inventory is held for periods in excess of that required for normal replenishment of customer stocks, it is referred to as **extended storage.** In some special situations, storage may be required for several months prior to customer shipment. Extended storage uses materials handling processes and technologies that focus on maximum space utilization with minimal need for quick access.

A warehouse may be used for extended storage for a variety of reasons. Some products, such as seasonal items, require storage to await demand or to spread supply across time. Other reasons for extended storage include erratic demand items, product conditioning, speculative purchases, and discounts.

Product conditioning sometimes requires extended storage, such as to ripen bananas. Food warehouses typically have ripening rooms to hold products until they reach peak quality. Storage may also be necessary for extended quality checks.

Warehouses may also retain products for an extended basis when they are purchased on a speculative basis. The magnitude of speculative buying depends upon the specific materials and industries involved, but it is very common in marketing of commodities and seasonal items. For example, if a price increase for an item is expected, it is not uncommon for a firm to buy ahead at the current price and warehouse the product for later use. In this case, the discount or savings has to be traded off against extended storage and inventory carrying cost. Commodities such as grains, oil, and lumber may be purchased and stored for speculative reasons.

The warehouse may also be used to realize special discounts. Early purchase or forward-buy discounts may justify extended storage. The purchasing manager may be able to realize a substantial price reduction during a specific time of the year. Under such conditions the warehouse is expected to hold inventory in excess of active storage. Manufacturers of fertilizer, toys, and lawn furniture often attempt to shift the warehousing burden to customers by offering off-season warehouse storage allowances.

Warehouse Ownership Arrangements

Warehouses are typically classified based on ownership. A **private** warehouse is operated by the enterprise that owns the merchandise handled and stored in the facility. A **public** warehouse, in contrast, is operated as an independent business offering a range of for-hire services, such as storage, handling, and transportation. Public warehouse operators generally offer a menu of relatively standardized services to customers. **Contract warehousing,** which is a customized extension of public warehousing, combines the benefits of private and for-hire warehousing. Contract warehousing is a long-term business arrangement that provides unique or tailored logistics services for a limited number of customers. The client and the warehouse operator typically share the risks associated with the operation. The important differences between contract and public warehouse operators are the anticipated length of the relationship, degree of exclusive or customized services, and shared incorporation of benefits and risks.

Private

A private warehouse is typically operated by the firm owning the product. The building, however, may be owned or leased. The decision concerning ownership or lease is essentially financial. Sometimes it is not possible to find a warehouse for lease that fits specialized logistical requirements; for example, the physical nature of an available building may not be conducive for efficient materials handling, such as buildings with inappropriate storage racks or with shipping/receiving dock or support column constraints. The only suitable course of action may then be to design and arrange for new construction.

The major benefits of private warehousing are control, flexibility, cost, and a range of intangibles. Private warehouses offer substantial control since management has authority to prioritize activities. Such control should facilitate integration of warehouse operations with the balance of a firm's logistics operations.

Private warehouses generally offer more flexibility since operating policies, hours, and procedures can be adjusted to meet specific customer and product requirements. Firms with very specialized customers or products are often motivated to own and operate warehouses.

Private warehousing is usually considered less costly than public warehousing because private facilities are not operated for a profit. As a result, both the fixed and variable cost components of a private warehouse may be lower than for-hire counterparts.

Finally, private warehousing may offer intangible benefits. A private warehouse, with the firm's name on its sign, may stimulate customer perceptions of responsiveness and stability. This perception may provide marketing image in comparison to competitors.

Despite the above-noted benefits, the use of private warehousing is declining because of an increasing managerial interest in reducing capital invested in logistical assets. Also, the perceived cost benefit of private warehousing is potentially offset by a public warehouse's ability to gain operational economies of scale and scope as a result of the combined throughput of multiple clients.

Public

Public warehouses are used extensively in logistical systems. Almost any combination of services can be arranged on a for-hire basis for either short or long term. Public warehouses have traditionally been classified based on operational specialization such as (1) general merchandise, (2) refrigerated, (3) special commodity, (4) bonded, and (5) household goods and furniture.

General merchandise warehouses are designed to handle package products such as electronics, paper, food, small appliances, and household supplies. Refrigerated warehouses typically offer frozen or chilled capacity designed to protect food, medical, photographic, and chemical products requiring special temperatures. Special commodity warehouses are designed to handle bulk material or items requiring special handling, such as tires or clothing. Bonded warehouses are licensed by the government to store goods prior to payment of taxes or import/export duties. They exert tight control over movements in and out of the facility, since documents must accompany each move. Finally, household goods or furniture warehouses specialize in handling and storing large, bulky items such as appliances and furniture. Of course, many public warehouses offer a combination of services. Public warehouses provide flexibility and shared services benefits. They have the potential to offer operating and management expertise since warehousing is their core business.

From a financial perspective, public warehousing may be able to achieve lower operating cost than private facilities. Such variable cost differential may result from lower wage scales, better productivity, and shared overhead among clients. Public warehouses typically do not require capital investment on the part of their customers. When management performance is judged according to return on investment, the use of public warehousing can be an attractive alternative. Public warehousing offers flexibility concerning size and number of warehouses, thus allowing users to respond to supplier, customer, and seasonal demands. In comparison, private warehouses are relatively fixed and difficult to change because buildings have to be constructed, expanded, or sold.

Public warehousing can also have the potential to share scale economies since the combined requirements of users can be leveraged. Such leverage spreads fixed costs and may justify investment in state-of-the-art handling equipment. A public warehouse may also leverage transportation by providing consolidation of multiple-client freight. For example, rather than require both supplier A and supplier B to deliver to a retail store from its own warehouse, a public warehouse serving both clients could arrange combined delivery, thus providing reduced transportation cost for the customer.

A great many firms utilize public warehouses for customer accommodation because of the variable cost, scalability, range of services, and flexibility. A public warehouse charges clients a basic fee for in and out handling plus storage. In the case of handling, the charge is assessed on the cases or pounds moved. For storage, the charge is assessed on the cases or weight in storage over a time. Special or value-added services provided by public warehouses are typically priced on a negotiated basis.

Contract

Contract warehousing combines characteristics of private and public operations. A long-term contractual relationship will typically result in lower total cost than a public warehouse. At the same time, contract warehouse operations can provide benefits of expertise, flexibility, scalability, and economies of scale by sharing management, labor, equipment, and information resources across multiple clients.

Contract warehouses typically offer a range of logistical services such as transportation management, inventory control, order processing, customer service, and return merchandise processing. Contract logistics firms, typically called integrated service providers (ISPs), are capable of performing the total logistics responsibility for an enterprise.

For example, Kraft Foods has increasingly utilized contract warehousing as a replacement for private and public frozen and dry grocery facilities. Since the late 1990s, Kraft has used AmeriCold Logistics, an integrated warehousing and distribution services company, to perform storage, handling, and distribution services. The arrangement has multiple benefits for both parties. The long-term contractual arrangement allows Kraft to expand its distribution network without incurring the time or cost of building expansion. Kraft is assured that there will always be space for new products, so its distribution network is protected. AmeriCold doesn't have to be concerned with selling space to Kraft. Moreover, the longer Kraft utilizes AmeriCold's services, the better the contract warehousing firm's capability to understand business needs and provide customized services.

Network Deployment

As would be expected, many firms utilize a combination of private, public, and contract facilities.[7] Full warehouse utilization throughout a year is rare. As a managerial guideline, a typical warehouse will be fully utilized between 75 and 85 percent of the time; so from 15 to 25 percent of the time, space needed to satisfy peak requirements will not be used. In such situations, a deployment strategy may be the use of private or contract warehouses to cover the 75 percent requirement while public facilities are used to accommodate peak demand.

Developing a warehouse network strategy requires answers to two key questions. The first is how many warehouses should be established.[8] The second question focuses on which warehouse ownership types should be used in specific markets. For many firms, the answer is a combination of warehouse alternatives, differentiated by customer and product. Specifically, some customer groups may be served best from a private warehouse, while public or contract warehouses may be appropriate for others. This warehouse segmentation is increasingly popular as key customers are requiring more customized value-added services and capabilities.

Warehouse Decisions

The basic concept that warehouses provide as an enclosure for material storage and handling requires detailed analysis before the size, type, and shape of the facility can be determined. This section reviews planning issues that establish the character of the warehouse, which in turn determines attainable handling efficiency.

Site Selection

The first task is to identify both the general and then the specific warehouse location. The general area concerns the broad geography where an active warehouse makes sense from a service, economic, and strategic perspective. The general question focuses on the broader geographic area as illustrated by the need to place a warehouse in the Midwest, which generally implies having a facility in Illinois, Indiana, or Wisconsin. In contrast, a retailer such as Target or Home Depot typically selects a warehouse location that is central to a prerequisite number of retail store locations. Thus, the selection and number of retail outlets drive the support warehouse location.

---

[7] For a comprehensive discussion of the strategic use of warehousing, see Ken Ackerman, *Warehousing Profitability: A Manager's Guide* (Columbus, OH: Ackerman Publications, 2000).

[8] The general process is discussed further in Chapter 11.

Once the general warehouse location is determined, a specific building site must be identified. Typical areas in a community for locating warehouses are commercial developments and outlying or suburban areas. The factors driving site selection are service availability and cost. Land cost is the most important factor. A warehouse need not be located in a major industrial area. In many cities, warehouses are among industrial plants and in areas zoned for light or heavy industry. Most warehouses can operate legally under the restrictions placed upon general commercial property.

Beyond procurement cost, setup, and operating expenses such as transport access, utility hookups, taxes, and insurance rates require evaluation. The cost of essential services may vary extensively between sites. For example, a food-distribution firm recently rejected what otherwise appeared to be a totally satisfactory warehouse site because of projected insurance rates. The site was located near the end of a water main. During most of the day, adequate water pressure was available to handle operational and emergency requirements. However, a water problem was possible during two short periods each day. From 6:30 A.M. to 8:30 A.M. and from 5:00 P.M. to 7:00 P.M. the overall demand for water along the line was so great that a sufficient pressure was not available to handle emergencies. Because of this deficiency, abnormally high insurance rates were required and the site was rejected.

Several other requirements must be satisfied before a site is purchased. The site must offer adequate room for expansion. Necessary utilities must be available. The soil must be capable of supporting the structure. The site must be sufficiently high to afford proper water drainage. Additional requirements may be situationally necessary, depending upon the structure to be constructed. For these reasons and others, the final selection of the site should be preceded by extensive analysis.[9]

Design

Warehouse design must consider product movement characteristics. Three factors to be determined during the design process are the number of floors to include in the facility, a cube utilization plan, and product flow.

The ideal warehouse design is a one-floor building that eliminates the need to move product vertically. The use of vertical handling devices, such as elevators and conveyors, to move product from one floor to the next requires time, energy, and typically creates handling bottlenecks. So, while it is not always possible, particularly in business districts where land is restricted or expensive, as a general rule distribution warehouses should be designed as one-floor operations to facilitate materials handling.

Warehouse design must maximize cubic utilization. Most warehouses are designed with 20- to 30-foot clear ceilings, although selected automated and high-rise handling equipment can effectively use heights over 100 feet. Maximum effective warehouse height is limited by the safe lifting capabilities of materials handling equipment, such as lift trucks, rack design, and fire safety regulations imposed by sprinkler systems.

Warehouse design should facilitate continuous straight product flow through the building. This is true whether the product is moving into storage or is being cross-docked. In general, this means that product should be received at one end of a building, stored as necessary in the middle, and shipped from the other end. Figure 9.4 illustrates straight line product flow that facilitates velocity while minimizing congestion and redundant handling.

[9] Perry A. Trunlick, "All the Right Moves," *Logistics Today* (November 2003), pp. 38–40.

FIGURE 9.4
Basic Warehouse Design

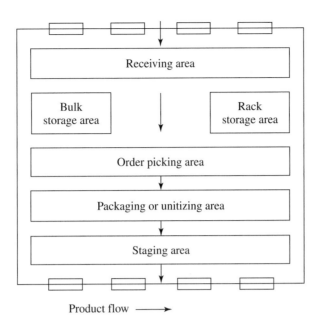

Product flow ⟶

Product-Mix Analysis

An important area of analysis is analysis of products that will be distributed through the warehouse. The design and operation of a warehouse are both dependent on the product mix. Each product should be analyzed in terms of annual sales, demand, weight, cube, and packaging. It is also important to determine the total size, cube, and weight of the average order to be processed through the warehouse. These data provide necessary information for determining warehouse space, design and layout, materials handling equipment, operating procedures, and controls.

Expansion

Because warehouses are increasingly important in supply chain networks, their future expansion should be considered during the initial planning phase. It is common to establish 5- to 10-year expansion plans. Potential expansion may justify purchase or option of a site three to five times larger than required to support initial construction.

Building design should also accommodate future expansion. Some walls may be constructed of semipermanent materials to allow quick removal. Floor areas, designed to support heavy movements, can be extended during initial construction to facilitate expansion.

Materials Handling

A materials handling system is the basic driver of warehouse design. As noted previously, product movement and assortment are the main functions of a warehouse. Consequently, the warehouse is viewed as a structure designed to facilitate efficient product flow. It is important to stress that the materials handling system must be selected early in the warehouse development process. Material handling equipment and technology are discussed in Chapter 10.

Layout

The layout or storage areas of a warehouse should be planned to facilitate product flow. The layout and the material handling system are integral. In addition, special attention must be given to location, number, and design of receiving and loading docks.

It is difficult to generalize warehouse layouts since they are usually customized to accommodate specific product handling requirements. If pallets are utilized, an early step is to determine the appropriate size. A pallet of nonstandard size may be desirable for specialized products. The most common pallet sizes are 40 × 48 inches and 32 × 40 inches. In general, the larger the pallet load, the lower the movement cost per pound or package over a given distance. One lift truck operator can move a large load in the same time and with the same effort required to move a smaller load. Analysis of product cases, stacking patterns, and industry practices will determine the size of pallet best suited to the operation. Regardless of the size finally selected, management should adopt one pallet size for use throughout the warehouse.

The second step in planning warehouse layout involves pallet positioning. The most common practice in positioning pallets is at 90 degree, or square, placement. Square positioning is widely used because of layout ease. Square placement means that the pallet is positioned perpendicular to the aisle. The placement of specific products in selected pallet locations is called **slotting.** Naturally, key to an efficient layout is a well developed slotting plan.[10]

Finally, the handling equipment must be integrated to finalize layout. The path and tempo of product flow depend upon the materials handling system. To illustrate the relationship between materials handling and layout, two systems and their respective layouts are illustrated in Figure 9.5. These examples represent two of many possible layouts.

Layout A illustrates a materials handling system and layout utilizing lift trucks for inbound and inventory transfer movements and tow tractors with trailer for order selection. This scenario assumes that products can be palletized. This layout is greatly simplified because offices, special areas, and other details are omitted.

[10] Helen L. Richardson, "Getting Your Warehouse in Order," *Logistics Today* (October 2003), pp. 38–42.

FIGURE 9.5   **Layouts A and B**

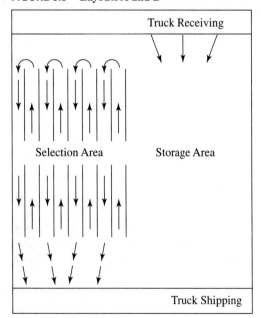

Layout A.

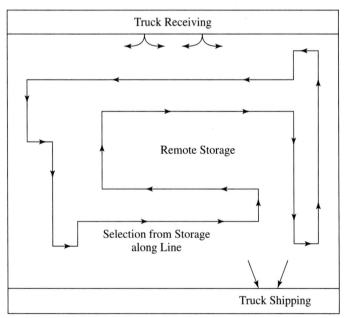

Layout B.

The floor plan of layout A is approximately square. The advocates of square design feel that it provides the best framework for overall operating efficiency. As indicated earlier in this chapter, products should be positioned in a specific area of the warehouse for order selection. Such is the case in layout A. This area is labeled the **selection, or picking, area.** Its primary purpose is to minimize the distance order pickers must travel when assembling an order.

The selection area is supported by a **storage area.** When products are received they are palletized and moved to the storage area. The selection area is replenished from storage as required. Within the selection area, products are positioned according to weight, bulk, and replenishment velocity to minimize outbound movement. Customer orders are assembled by an order selector using a tow tractor pulling trailers through the selection area. The arrows in layout A indicate product selection flow.

Layout B illustrates a materials handling system utilizing lift trucks to move product inbound and for transfer movements. A continuous towline is used for order selection. The floor plan in layout B is rectangular. In a system using a continuous-movement towline, the compact selection area is replaced by order selection directly from storage. Products are moved from receiving areas into storage positions adjacent to the towline. The orders are then selected directly from storage and loaded onto carts, which are pulled around the warehouse by the towline. Merchandise is stored or positioned to minimize inbound movement. The weakness of the fixed towline is that it facilitates selection of all products at an equal speed and frequency and does not consider special needs of high-velocity products. The arrows in layout B indicate major product movements. The line in the center of the layout illustrates the path of the towline.

As indicated, both layouts A and B are greatly simplified. The purpose is to illustrate the extremely different approaches managers have developed to reconcile the relationship between materials handling and warehouse layout.

Sizing

Several techniques are available to help estimate warehouse size. Each method begins with a projection of the total volume expected to move through the warehouse during a given period. The projection is used to estimate base and safety stocks for each product to be stocked in the warehouse. Some techniques consider both normal and peak inventory. Failure to consider utilization rates can result in overbuilding. It is important to note, however, that a major complaint of warehouse managers is underestimation of warehouse size requirements. A good rule of thumb is to allow 10 percent additional space to account for increased volume, new products, and new business opportunities.

Warehouse Management Systems (WMS)

The development of work procedures goes hard in hand with training warehouse personnel. Most firms depend upon a Warehouse Management System (WMS) to standardize work procedures and encourage best practice.[11] It is management's responsibility to see that all personnel understand and use these procedures.[12]

One of the main uses of a WMS is to coordinate order selection. Two basic methods of order selection are **discrete selection** and **wave selection,** also known as **batch selection.** In discrete selection, a specific customer's order is selected and prepared for shipment as a specific work assignment. Discrete order selection is often used when order content and handling selection are critical.

[11] Christopher R. Barnes, "Warehouse Management," *WERC* (2004), pp. 1–58.

[12] "WMS and Warehouse Productivity," *WERC Watch* (December 2003), pp. 1–7.

Wave selection can be designed and operationalized in a variety of ways. A wave can be coordinated by an area of the warehouse wherein all quantities of all products required to complete all customer orders are selected at one time. Using this type of wave selection, employees are typically assigned responsibility for a specific portion of the warehouse. Waves can also be planned around a specific shipment destination and/or carrier, for example, all UPS shipments to the East Coast. Because each employee has a thorough knowledge of a specific warehouse selection area or shipping procedure, fewer selection errors typically result using wave picking.

WMS also coordinates work procedures that are important for receiving and shipping. Established procedures for receiving and ensuring product entry into inventory records are critical. If pallets are used, the merchandise must be stacked in appropriate patterns to ensure maximum load stability and consistent case counts. Personnel working in shipping must have knowledge of trailer loading practices. In specific types of operations, particularly when merchandise changes ownership, items must be checked during loading.

Work procedures are not restricted to floor personnel. Procedures must be established for administration and maintenance. Replenishment of warehouse inventory can cause operational problems if proper ordering procedures are lacking. Normally, there is limited interaction between buyers and warehouse personnel, although such communication is improving within integrated supply chain management organizations. Buyers tend to purchase in quantities that afford the best price, and little attention is given to pallet compatible quantities or available warehouse space.

Ideally buyers should coordinate with warehouse personnel before commissioning large orders or introducing new products. The experience of some companies has forced management to require buyers to predetermine warehouse space assignment prior to ordering. Another potential problem is the quantity of cases ordered. The goal is to purchase in pallet-multiple quantities. For example, if a product is ideally stacked on pallets in a 50-case pattern, the buyer should order in multiples of 50. If an order is placed for 120 cases, upon arrival the cases will fill two pallets plus 20 on a third pallet. The extra 20 cases will require the warehouse cubic space typically used for a pallet of 50 and will require the same amount of materials handling capacity to move.

Figure 9.6 illustrates the range of activities coordinated by an advanced WMS. Historical warehouse system functionality focused on receiving replenishment shipments, stock putaway, and order picking. Figure 9.6 illustrates other traditionally standard activities under the category labeled *core functionality*. Warehouses today must offer a broader range of services as they are frequently performing form postponement. They are also required to manage more inventory on a just-in-time basis. Figure 9.6 illustrates some of these activities indicated as *advanced functionality*. Yard management, sometimes a functionality of a firm's Transportation Management System (TMS), refers to the process of managing the vehicles and the inventory within vehicles while in the warehouse yard. Faster inventory turnover requires better visibility of inventory, even when in transportation vehicles. Labor management refers to maximizing the use of warehouse labor. Historically, warehouse labor has been quite specialized, allowing for relatively easy planning. Today, however, warehouse labor is expected to perform a wider range of activities to minimize the number of employees necessary at any given point in time. Warehouse optimization refers to selection of the best location within the warehouse for the storage and retrieval of product to minimize time and movement. *Value-added services* refer to the coordination of warehouse activities to customize product, such as packaging, labeling, kitting, and setting up displays. Planned cross-docking and merging is the integration of two or more parts of a customer order that have been supplied from a different source without maintaining inventory. This strategy is sometimes used in the personal computer industry to merge a processing unit and the display monitor in a warehouse just prior to delivery to the ultimate customer.

FIGURE 9.6
Warehouse
Management System
Functionality

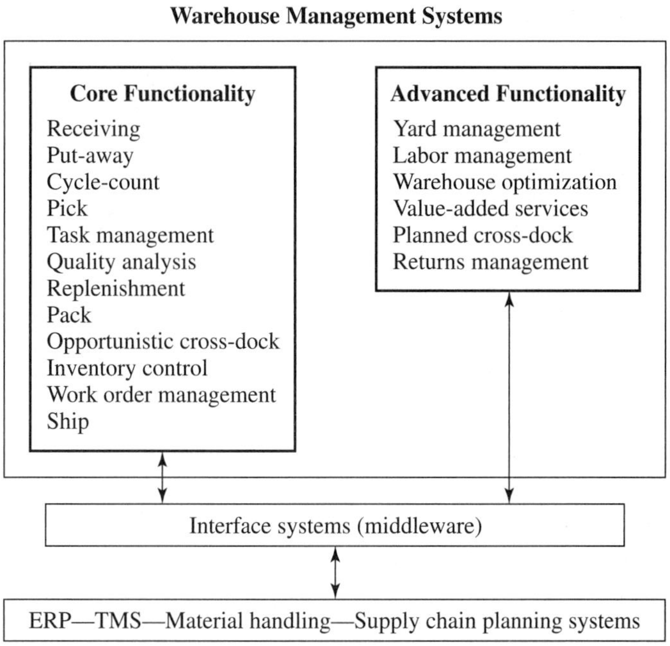

Warehouse Management Systems

Core Functionality
Receiving
Put-away
Cycle-count
Pick
Task management
Quality analysis
Replenishment
Pack
Opportunistic cross-dock
Inventory control
Work order management
Ship

Advanced Functionality
Yard management
Labor management
Warehouse optimization
Value-added services
Planned cross-dock
Returns management

Interface systems (middleware)

ERP—TMS—Material handling—Supply chain planning systems

TABLE 9.2
**WMS Functionality
and Decision Support**

Source: Reproduced with
permission from Bowersox et al.,
"RFID Applications Within
The Four Walls of a Consumer
Package Goods Warehouse,"
from Marketing and Supply
Chain Working Paper, Michigan
State University, 2005.

Selected Functionality	Decision Support Benefits
Put-away	Improved productivity and cube utilization.
Task interleaving	Routing of fork trucks on demand as contrasted to predetermined assigned tasks, areas, or sequences.
Pick/replenishment	Direct picking from single or multiple locations including pick to assure expiration date compliance. Facilitates replenishment of pick location inventories when appropriate.
Slotting	Variable slot or product placement locator assignment to enhance space utilization.
Cross-docking	Facilitate direct receipt to shipment flow.
Inventory visibility	Tracking specific inventory lots by warehouse location as well as daily visibility of receipts. Date specific lot control.
Work queue resolution	Identification of alternative ways to rapidly or efficiently resolve work constraints or queues.
Picking strategy	Routines to perform selected picking strategies.
Error correction	Ability to identify, resolve, and correct data errors in real time. Ability to identify and resolve differences in purchase orders or advanced shipment notifications (ASN) and actual quantities or product received.
Simulations	Performance of real-time decision support scenarios to assist in operational decision-making.
Return goods	Facilitate processing and audit compliance for reverse logistics programs.
Cycle counts	Ability to conduct and resolve real-time inventory counts.

Since there is no inventory of either part in the warehouse, the merging activity requires precise timing and coordination. A final execution function is the capability to manage reverse logistics activities such as returns, repair, and recycling. Both customers and environmental interests are increasing their demands that supply chains can accommodate reverse logistics. Table 9.2 summarizes WMS functionality and decision support benefits.

Accuracy and Audits

WMS functionality requires verification of inventory accuracy to maintain operational effectiveness. Inventory accuracy is typically maintained by annual physical inventory counts or by counting specific portions of the inventory on a planned basis. **Cycle counting** is the audit of selected inventory on a cyclic schedule.[13] Selection of individual items to be counted and verified can be based on a specific area of the warehouse, frequency of movement, or turnover. Once counted, discrepancies between physical and WMS inventories are reconciled to assure continued system validity.

Audits related to inventory accuracy are only one type of audit that is typically used to maintain and improve warehouse operating efficiency. Audits are also common to maintain safety, assure compliance to security regulations, drive procedural improvement, and facilitate work changes.[14]

Security

In a broad sense, security in a warehouse involves protection against merchandise pilferage, deterioration, and any form of operational disruption. Each form of security requires management attention.

Pilferage

In warehouse operations it is necessary to protect against theft by employees and thieves as well as from riots and terrorist-related disturbances. Typical security procedures should be strictly enforced at each warehouse. Security begins at the fence. As standard procedure, only authorized personnel should be permitted into the facility and on surrounding grounds. Entry to the warehouse yard should be controlled through a single gate. Without exception, no private automobile, regardless of management rank or customer status, should be allowed to enter the yard or park adjacent to the warehouse.

To illustrate the importance of security guidelines, the following experience may be helpful. A firm adopted the rule that no private vehicles would be permitted in the warehouse yard. Exceptions were made for two office employees with special needs. One night after work, one of these employees discovered a bundle taped under one fender of his car. Subsequent checking revealed that the car was literally a loaded delivery truck. The matter was promptly reported to security, who informed the employee not to alter any packages taped to the car and to continue parking inside the yard. Over the next several days, the situation was fully uncovered, with the ultimate arrest and conviction of seven warehouse employees who confessed to stealing thousands of dollars worth of company merchandise. The firm would have been far better off had it provided transportation for the two special-needs employees from the regular parking lots to their work locations.

Shortages are always a major concern in warehouse operations. Many are honest mistakes that occur during order selection and shipment, but the purpose of security is to restrict theft from all angles. A majority of thefts occur during normal working hours.

Inventory control and order processing systems help protect merchandise from being carried out of the warehouse unless accompanied by a computer release document. If

---

[13] Bill Latham, "Cycle Counting: The Best Way to Improve Inventory Accuracy," *Warehousing Forum* 19, no. 12 (November 2004), pp. 1–2.

[14] "The DC Audit," *WERC Sheet* (January 2004), pp. 1–3.

samples are authorized for salesperson use, such merchandise should be maintained in a separate inventory. Not all pilferage occurs on an individual basis. Organized efforts between warehouse personnel and truck drivers can result in deliberate overpicking or high-for-low-value product substitution in order to move unauthorized merchandise out of the warehouse. Employee work assignment rotation, total case counts, and occasional complete line-item checks can reduce vulnerability to such collaboration.

A final concern is the increased incidence of hijacking over-the-road trailer loads from yards or while in transit. Hijacking is a major logistical concern. Over-the-road hijack prevention is primarily a law-enforcement matter, but in-yard theft can be eliminated by tight security provisions. Such over-the-road theft is a significant problem in developing countries. One beverage company manager reported that he budgeted to lose one truck a week to theft for his South American operation. He instructed his drivers to simply turn over the keys and walk away rather than risk their lives. Procedures and technology related to terrorist-initiated security are discussed in Chapter 12.

Damage

Within the warehouse, a number of factors can reduce a product or material to nonsalable status. The most obvious form of product deterioration is damage from careless materials handling. For example, when pallets of merchandise are stacked in great heights, a marked change in humidity or temperature can cause packages supporting the stack to collapse. The warehouse environment must be carefully controlled and measured to provide proper product protection. Of major concern is warehouse employee carelessness. In this respect, the lift truck may well be management's worst enemy. Regardless of how often lift truck operators are warned against carrying overloads, some still attempt such shortcuts when not properly supervised. In one situation, a stack of four pallets was dropped off a lift truck at the receiving dock of a food warehouse. Standard procedure was to move two pallets per load. The dollar cost of the damaged merchandise exceeded the average daily profit of two retail supermarkets. Product deterioration from careless handling within the warehouse is a form of loss that cannot be insured against or offset with compensating revenue.

Another major form of deterioration is incompatibility of products stored or transported together. For example, care must be taken when storing or shipping chocolate to make sure that it does not absorb odors from products it is being transported with, such as household chemicals.

Safety and Maintenance

Accident prevention is a concern of warehouse management. A comprehensive safety program requires constant examination of work procedures and equipment to locate and take corrective action to eliminate unsafe conditions before accidents result. Accidents occur when workers become careless or are exposed to mechanical or physical hazards. The floors of a warehouse may cause accidents if not properly cleaned. During normal operation, rubber and glass deposits collect on aisles and, from time to time, broken cases will result in product seepage onto the floor. Proper cleaning procedures can reduce the accident risk of such hazards. Environmental safety has become a major concern of government agencies such as OSHA and cannot be neglected by management.

A preventive maintenance program is necessary for materials handling equipment. Unlike production machines, movement equipment is not stationary, so it is more difficult to properly maintain. A preventive maintenance program scheduling periodic checks of all handling equipment should be applied in every warehouse.

Summary

Warehousing exists to contribute to manufacturing and distribution efficiency. While the role of the warehouse has traditionally been to stock inventory, contemporary warehousing provides a broader value proposition in terms of economic and service benefits. Economic benefits include consolidation and break-bulk, sorting, seasonal storage, and reverse logistics. Service benefits include spot-stocking, full line stocking, and value-added services. The perspective of warehousing is changing from a traditional storage mission to one characterized by customization, velocity, and movement.

Distribution centers and warehouses are designed to accommodate the primary activities of inventory handling and storage. Handling includes receiving inbound shipments; instorage handling to move between different types of storage such as long-term, bulk, and picking; and packing and staging shipments to customers. Active storage facilitates crossdocking, consolidation, break-bulk, and postponement. Extended storage activities facilitate balancing supply and demand and speculation.

Warehouses are usually classified on the basis of ownership. A private warehouse is operated by the enterprise that owns the merchandise in the facility. A public warehouse is operated independently and offers various for-hire value-added services. A contract warehouse is a long-term business arrangement that provides tailored services for a limited number of customers. An integrated warehousing strategy often incorporates a combination of warehouse ownership options.

There are numerous managerial decisions in planning and initiating warehouse operations, including site selection, design, product-mix analysis, expansion, materials handling, layout, sizing, WMS, accuracy and audits, security, safety, and maintenance. Each of these activities requires considerable managerial effort to ensure facilities start up and run smoothly on a day-to-day basis and are able to accommodate change rapidly and successfully, as necessary to meet current business demands.

Challenge Questions

1. Provide a definition and an example of strategic storage from a logistical system you are familiar with.

2. Discuss and illustrate the economic justification for establishing a warehouse.

3. Why could a warehouse be described as a "necessary evil"?

4. How do warehouses perform order sorting?

5. Under what conditions could it make sense to combine private and public warehouses in a logistical system?

6. What role are warehouse operators playing in postponement strategies?

7. What is the concept of local presence? Is local presence growing or declining in importance?

8. Discuss and illustrate the role of warehouses in reverse logistics.

9. Illustrate the relationship between the size and shape of a distribution warehouse and the materials handling system. Why do some warehouses have square design while others are rectangular?

10. Explain the following statement: "A warehouse should merely consist of walls enclosing an efficient handling system."

Packaging and Materials Handling

Within a warehouse and while being transported throughout a logistics system, the package serves to identify and protect products. The package, containing a product, is the entity that must be moved by a firm's materials handling system. For this reason packaging and materials handling are jointly discussed.

Packaging Perspectives[1]

Packaging is typically viewed as being either **consumer,** focused primarily on marketing, or **industrial,** focused on logistics. The primary concern of logistics operations is industrial package design. Individual products or parts are typically grouped into cartons, bags, bins, or barrels for damage protection and handling efficiency. Containers used to group individual products are called **master cartons.** When master cartons are grouped into larger units for handling, the combination is referred to as **containerization** or **unitization.**

Master cartons and unit loads are the basic handling units for logistical operations. The weight, cube, and damage potential of the master carton determines transportation and materials handling requirements. If the package is not designed for efficient logistical processing, overall system performance suffers.

[1] The authors express their appreciation to Professor Diana Tweede from the Michigan State University School of Packaging for assistance provided in preparing this section.

Retail sale quantity or presentation should not be the prime determinant of master carton size. For example, beer, often sold at retail in units of 6, is normally packed in master cartons containing 24 units. The master carton should be large enough to provide handling economies of scale but light enough to facilitate handling by an individual without mechanical assistance. A prime objective in logistics is to design operations to handle a limited assortment of standardized master cartons. Master carton standardization facilitates materials handling and transportation. The importance of standardization can be illustrated by an example adapted from a shoe retailer.

The initial logistical system employed by the retailer to ship shoes from the warehouse to retail stores consisted of reusing vendor cartons. Individual pairs of shoes were grouped as best as possible into available repack cartons. The result was a variety of carton sizes going to each retail store. The method of order selection used to assemble a retail store's order was to work from warehouse-sequenced picking lists that grouped shoes by style and quantity. Shoes were selected in the warehouse, packed into cartons, and then manually stacked on a four-wheel truck for transfer to the shipping dock. The cartons were then loaded into trucks for delivery to stores. While the order picking list provided a summary of all shoes in the total shipment, it was impossible for the retail stores to determine the contents of any given carton.

Viewing materials handling delivery and store operations as an integrated system resulted in a decision to discontinue reusing vendor cartons. The new procedure used a standardized master carton that facilitated order picking and materials handling. The new logistics practice was designed around two concepts. First, standardized master cartons were adopted to permit continuous conveyor movement from point of warehouse order selection to truck loading. Second, the integrated system used a computer process to assure that each standardized master carton was packed to maximum practical cube utilization. Under the new system a picking list was generated for each carton. After the individual pairs of shoes were placed into the carton, the pick list was attached to the carton, providing a summary of contents for retail store personnel.

The advantages of a standardized master carton extended to the retail store's stockroom. Because the contents of each master carton were easily determined, it was not necessary to search through multiple cartons to find a specific style or size of shoe while a customer was waiting. Standard master cartons could be more efficiently stacked, resulting in less backroom congestion. Finally, complete identification of master carton contents facilitated retail inventory management and replenishment.

The new integrated system required purchase of master cartons, since each could be reused only about three times. However, this added cost was more than justified by reduced order picking labor, continuous movement of cartons into over-the-road trailers, and more efficient utilization of transportation trailer capacity. Since each master carton was filled to near cubic capacity, dead space in cartons was reduced. The standardized master carton size was selected to achieve maximum conformity with a high-cube over-the-road trailer, thereby eliminating dead space in stacking. The end result of standardized master carton usage was a substantial reduction in total cost combined with a far more effective materials handling system at both the warehouse and the retail shoe store.

This packaging example illustrates the importance of integrated logistical planning and the principle of lowest total cost. However, the most important point is that master carton standardization facilitated supply chain integration.

Naturally, few organizations can reduce their master carton requirements to a one size fits all. When master cartons of more than one size are required, extreme care should be taken to arrive at an assortment of compatible units. Figure 10.1 illustrates one such concept, utilizing four standard master carton sizes, that achieves modular compatibility.

FIGURE 10.1   Example and Benefits of Modular Packaging

Source: Adapted from materials provided by Walter Frederick Freedman and Company.

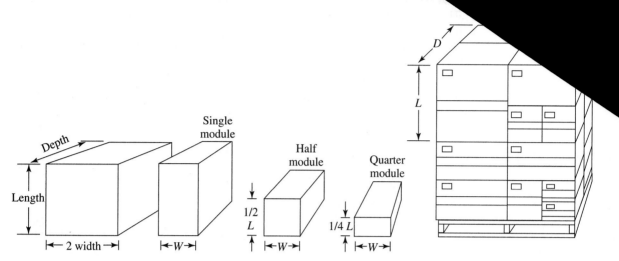

Of course, logistical considerations cannot fully dominate packaging design. The ideal package for materials handling and transportation would be a perfect cube having equal length, depth, and width while achieving maximum possible density. Seldom will such a package exist. The important point is that logistical requirements should be evaluated along with manufacturing, marketing, and product design considerations in finalizing master carton selection.

Another logistical packaging concern is the degree of desired protection. Package design and material must combine to achieve the desired level of protection without incurring the expense of overprotection. It is possible to design a package that has the correct material content but does not provide the necessary protection. Arriving at a satisfactory packaging solution involves defining the degree of allowable damage in terms of expected overall conditions and then isolating a combination of design and materials capable of meeting those specifications. For package design, there are two key principles. First, the cost of absolute protection will, in most cases, be prohibitive. Second, package construction is properly a blend of design and material.

A final logistics packaging concern is the relationship between the master carton size, order quantity, and retail display quantity. From a materials handling perspective, master cartons should be standardized and reasonably large to minimize the number of units handled at the warehouse. For ease of warehouse handling, it is desirable to have retailers purchase in master carton quantities. However, for a slow-moving product, a master carton could contain a substantial overstock for an item that sells only one unit per week but is packed in a case containing 48. Finally, in order to minimize labor, retailers often place trays from master cartons on the retail shelf so that individual products do not have to be unloaded and placed on the store shelf. Master cartons or trays meeting retail requirements for shelf space are preferred.

The determination of final package design requires a great deal of testing to assure that both marketing and logistics concerns are satisfied. While the marketing aspects are generally the focus of consumer research, logistics packaging research is determined from laboratory or experimental testing. Laboratory analysis offers a reliable way to evaluate package design as a result of advancements in testing equipment and measurement techniques.

...nt is available to measure shock severity and characteris-
...t. To a large degree, care in design has been further encour-
...ilation regarding hazardous materials.

...auses of product damage in a logistical system are vibration,
...pression. Combinations of damage can be experienced whenever
...orted or handled. Test shipment monitoring is expensive and diffi-
...entific basis. To obtain increased accuracy, computerized environ-
...be used to replicate typical conditions that a package will experience
...m. Laboratory test equipment is available to evaluate the impact of
...action of product fragility and packaging materials and design.

...andling Efficiency

...y concerns how packaging impacts logistical productivity and efficiency. All
...erations are affected by packaging—from truck loading and warehouse pick-
...ivity to transportation vehicle and storage cube utilization. Materials handling
en... in all of these situations is significantly influenced by package design, unitization, and communication characteristics.

Package Design

Product packaging in standard configurations and order quantities facilitates logistical efficiency. For example, cube utilization can be improved through reduced package size by
concentrating products such as orange juice or fabric softener, by eliminating air inside
packages, and by shipping items unassembled, nested, and with minimal dunnage. In most
cases, dunnage materials, like polystyrene foam peanuts, can be minimized simply by reducing box size. IKEA, the Swedish retailer of unassembled furniture, emphasizes cube
minimization to the point that it ships pillows vacuum-packed. IKEA uses a cube minimization packaging strategy to successfully compete in the United States even though the
company ships furniture from Sweden. Hewlett-Packard ships computer printers from the
United States to Europe using airfreight and minimal packaging.[2] H-P shrink-wraps unit
loads of printers to provide stability and reduce damage. In addition to lowering transportation cost, the overall practice reduces import duties since substantial value-added is
postponed until the product is finally assembled and sold in Europe.

Cube minimization is most important for lightweight products such as assembled lawn
furniture that **cubes out** a transport vehicle before weight limits are reached. On the other
hand, heavy products like steel ball bearings or liquid in glass bottles **weigh out** a transport
vehicle before its cube capacity is filled. When a vehicle or container weighs out, the firm
ends up shipping air in space that can't be filled with product. Total weight can sometimes
be reduced by product or package changes. For example, substituting plastic bottles for
glass significantly increases the number of bottles that can be loaded in a trailer. The move
by Gerber Baby Food toward plastic bottles is partially designed to reduce transportation
expenses.

Cube and weight minimization represent a special challenge for mail order and
e-commerce operations. These operations tend to use standardized packaging for both
purchasing and operating efficiencies. The result is often oversized packages that require
excessive dunnage and increased shipping cost. The nature of the products and the breadth
of e-commerce product lines often require multiple packages to be combined in a single

[2] Edward Feitzinger and Hau L. Lee, "Mass Customization at Hewlett-Packard: The Power of Postponement," *Harvard Business Review* (January/February 1999), pp. 116–20.

order. This is of great concern for consumers who are becoming more aware of the cost of shipping and handling direct shipments as well as for environmental concerns related to packaging disposal.

Unitization

The process of grouping master cartons into one physical unit for materials handling or transport is referred to as **unitization** or **containerization**. The concept includes all forms of product grouping, from taping two master cartons together to the use of specialized transportation equipment. All types of unitization have the basic objective of increasing handling and transport efficiency. Unit loads provide many benefits over handling individual master cartons. First, unloading time and congestion at destination are minimized. Second, product shipped in unit load quantities facilitates materials handling. Unit loads utilize approximately one-fifth the time required for manual loading or unloading. Inbound shipment verification is also simplified as receipts can be bar coded. Inventory can be positioned rapidly for order selection. Finally, in-transit damage is reduced by unit load shipping and specialized transportation equipment. All these factors reduce logistical cost. The following discussion is limited to unitization methods up to the capacity of transportation equipment.

Rigid Containers

Rigid containers provide a device within which master cartons or loose products are unitized. The premise is that placing products inside a sealed container will both protect them and facilitate handling. The use of containers handled and transported by special equipment and ships is common practice in air and water transport. In domestic distribution, containerization offers substantial transport efficiency and reduced product handling. Approximately one-half the total cost of transporting domestic goods is occurred in shuffling products between vehicles, handling across docks and platforms, packaging, and filing loss and damage claims for pilferage and for insurance. The airlines use rigid containerization both for freight and for passenger baggage. The containers, which are designed to fit in the cargo area of aircraft, facilitate loading and unloading while reducing product damage and pilferage. Table 10.1 summarizes the benefits of rigid containerization.

Returnable containers have traditionally been used to distribute some products. Most reusable packages are steel or plastic, although some firms, as noted earlier, reuse corrugated boxes. Automobile manufacturers use returnable racks for interplant shipment of body parts, and chemical companies reuse steel drums. There is an increasing trend, however, to reusable packaging applications for many small items and parts such as ingredients, grocery perishables, interplant shipments, and retail warehouse-to-store totes.

Returnable containers are particularly appropriate for integrated environments where there is reasonable container security between shippers and customers. The automobile industry uses returnable racking and packaging extensively between component suppliers and assembly plants. In a returnable package system, the parties must explicitly cooperate

TABLE 10.1
Benefits of Rigid Containerization

- Improves overall material movement efficiency.
- Reduces damage in handling and transit.
- Reduces pilferage.
- Reduces protective packaging requirements.
- Provides greater protection from element environment.
- Provides a shipment unit that can be reused a substantial number of times, thereby reducing waste and the need to dispose of the container.

to maximize container usage; otherwise, containers may be lost, misplaced, or forgotten. Alternatively, deposit systems may be necessary in more free-flow supply chains, where members are linked by occasional or nonrepetitive transactions. Deposit systems are frequently used for beverage bottles, kegs, pallets, and steel drums.

The decision to invest in a returnable package system involves explicit consideration of the number of shipment cycles and return transportation costs versus the purchase and disposal cost of expendable containers. Benefits of improved handling and reduced damage should be taken into account, as well as the future costs of sorting, tracking, and cleaning the reusable containers.

Flexible Containers

As the name implies, flexible containers do not protect a product by complete enclosure. The most common type of nonrigid containerization is stacked master cartons on either **pallets** or **slipsheets**. A hardwood pallet is illustrated in Figure 10.2. A slipsheet, which is similar to a pallet in size and purpose, is a flat stocking surface generally made of cardboard or plastic. Because slipsheets lie flat on the floor, special lift trucks are required to handle slipsheet unit loads. The primary advantage of slipsheets in comparison to pallets is cost and weight. Slipsheets are less costly than pallets and are insignificant from a weight and cube perspective.

Most industry associations recommend that a standardized pallet or slipsheet size be used as a unit load platform. The Grocery Manufacturers of America have adopted the 40 × 48-inch pallet with four-way entry and similar size slipsheets for food distribution. The beverage industry, on the other hand, has standardized on 32 × 36-inch pallets. Throughout industry, the sizes most frequently used are 40 × 48, 32 × 40, and 32 × 36. It is common practice to first identify the dimension of most frequent entry by handling equipment.

Generally, the larger a platform, the more efficient for materials handling. For instance, the 40 × 48-inch pallet provides 768 more square inches per stacking tier than the 32 × 36-inch size. Assuming that master cartons can be stacked as high as 10 tiers, the total added unitization space of the 40 × 48-inch pallet is 7680 square inches. This is 60 percent larger than the 32 × 36-inch size. The final determination of size should be based upon load, compatibility with the handling and transport equipment used throughout the logistical system, and standardized industry practice. With modern handling equipment, few restrictions are encountered in weight limitations.

While a variety of different approaches can be used to tier master cartons on slipsheets and pallets, the four most common are block, brick, row, and pinwheel. The block method

FIGURE 10.2
Example of a
Hardwood Pallet

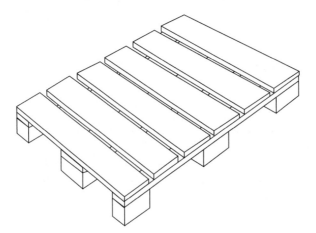

FIGURE 10.3   **Basic Pallet Master Carton Stacking Patterns**

Source: Adapted from palletization guides of the National Wooden Pallet & Container Association, Arlington, VA.

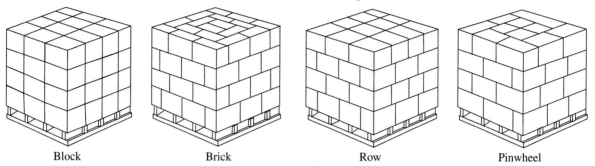

Block   Brick   Row   Pinwheel

is used with cartons of equal width and length. With differential widths and lengths, the brick, row, or pinwheel pattern is employed. Figure 10.3 illustrates these four basic patterns. Except for the block method, cartons are placed in the unit load arranged in an interlocking pattern with adjoining tiers placed at 90-degree angles to each other. Load stability is enhanced with interlocking. The block pattern does not have this benefit. While these patterns provide a good starting point when there are limited master carton sizes, most pallet patterns are determined by using computer programs.

The use of flexible unitization can increase damage potential if it is not properly restrained during handling or transport. In most situations, the stability of stacking is insufficient to secure a unit load. Standard methods of improving stability include rope tie, corner posts, steel strapping, taping and antiskid treatment, adhesives, and wrapping. These methods essentially tie the master cartons into the pallet stacking pattern. Increasingly popular methods for securing unit loads are shrink-wrap and stretch-wrap. Both wraps use film similar to that used in a kitchen for food preservation.

Pallet exchange pools have been organized as a way to overcome traditional problems of return and exchange. High-quality pallets are expensive and are difficult to retrieve once they leave the owner's control. When transfer to an external organization occurs, warehouses routinely exchange poor quality pallets and keep the higher quality ones. Pallet pools are third-party suppliers that maintain and lease high-quality pallets throughout the country for a variable fee per single cycle. A cycle might be defined as loading of pallets at a manufacturer and transporting to a retailer's warehouse. Pallet pool firms such as CHEP, which is one of the largest, assume responsibility for developing, purchasing, and maintaining pallets as well as providing control and management systems.[3]

Communication

The final logistical packaging functionality is communication or information transfer. This function is becoming increasingly critical to provide content identification, tracking, and handling instructions.

The most obvious communications role is identifying package contents for all channel members. Typical information includes manufacturer, product, container global type, count, and Universal Product Code (UPC), Electronic Product Code (EPC) and may be communicated using a bar code or RFID technology. The carton information is used to identify product for receiving, order selection, and shipment verification. Visibility is the

---

[3] For information regarding the products and services offered by a pallet pool organization such as CHEP, see www.chep.com.

major content identification consideration as material handlers should be able to observe or electronically read the label from reasonable distances in all directions. The exception for high-visibility packaging are high-value products that often have small or minimal labels to minimize the potential for pilferage.

Ease of package tracking is also important. Effective internal operation and increasingly customers require that product be tracked as it moves through the supply chain. Positive control of all movement reduces product loss and pilferage.

The final role of logistics packaging is to provide handling and damage instruction to materials handlers. The information should note any special product handling considerations such as glass containers, temperature restrictions, stacking considerations, or potential environmental concerns. If the product is potentially dangerous, such as some chemicals, the packaging or accompanying material should provide instructions for dealing with spills and container damage.

Materials Handling

Advancements in materials handling technology and equipment offer the potential to substantially improve logistics productivity. Materials handling processes and technologies impact productivity by influencing personnel, space, and capital equipment requirements. Material handling is a key logistics activity that can't be overlooked. While the technical details of materials handling technology are extensive and beyond the scope of this treatment, the following section introduces basic handling considerations and alternative system solutions.

Basic Handling Considerations

Logistical materials handling occurs throughout the supply chain. A fundamental difference exists in the handling of bulk materials and master cartons. Bulk handling includes situations wherein the product is handled without master cartons. Specialized equipment is required for handling bulk products such as solids and pellets. Bulk handling of such fluids and gaseous materials is generally completed by using pipelines or conveyors. The following discussion focuses on the nonbulk handling wherein products are shipped in master cartons.

There are several basic principles to guide the selection of materials handling processes and technologies. The principles summarized in Table 10.2 offer an initial foundation for evaluating materials handling alternatives.

Handling systems can be classified as **mechanized, semiautomated, automated,** and **information-directed.** A combination of labor and handling equipment is utilized in mechanized systems to facilitate receiving, processing, and/or shipping. Generally, labor constitutes a high percentage of overall cost in mechanized handling. Automated systems, in contrast, attempt to minimize labor as much as possible by substituting equipment capital investment. When a combination of mechanical and automated systems is used to handle material, the system is referred to as semiautomated. An information-directed system

TABLE 10.2 **Principles of Materials Handling**	• Equipment for handling and storage should be as standardized as possible. • When in motion, the system should be designed to provide maximum continuous product flow. • Investment should be in handling rather than stationary equipment. • Handling equipment should be utilized to the maximum extent possible. • In handling equipment selection the ratio of dead weight to payload should be minimized. • Whenever practical, gravity flow should be incorporated in system design.

applies information technology to direct mechanized handling equipment and work effort. Mechanized handling systems are most common, but the use of semiautomated, automated, and information-directed systems is increasing. Each approach to handling is discussed in greater detail.

Mechanized Systems

Mechanized systems employ a wide range of handling equipment. The types of equipment most commonly used are lift trucks, walkie-rider pallet trucks, towlines, tractor-trailer devices, conveyors, and carousels.

Lift Trucks

Lift trucks, also called forklifts, can move loads of master cartons both horizontally and vertically but are limited to handling unit loads. Skids, boxes, or containers may also be transported, depending upon the nature of the product.

Many types of lift trucks are available. High-stacking trucks are capable of up to 40 feet of vertical movement. Palletless or clamp trucks are available for handling products without pallets or slipsheets. Other lift truck variations are available for narrow aisle and side-loading operations. Particular attention to narrow-aisle lift trucks has increased in recent years, as warehouse designers seek to increase rack density and overall storage capacity. The lift truck is not economical for long-distance horizontal movement because of the high ratio of labor per unit of transfer. It is most effectively utilized in shipping and receiving operations and to place merchandise in high cube storage. The two most common power sources for lift trucks are propane gas and battery.

Rider Trucks

Rider trucks provide a low-cost, effective method of general materials handling utility. Typical applications include loading and unloading of transportation equipment, order selection and accumulation, and shuttling loads throughout the warehouse. Rider trucks are widely used in consumer package goods warehouses.

Towlines

Towlines consist of either in-floor or overhead-mounted cable or drag devices. They are utilized to provide continuous power to four-wheel trailers. The main advantage of a towline is continuous movement. However, such handling devices have far less flexibility than lift trucks. The most common application of towlines is for case goods order selection. Order selectors place merchandise on four-wheel trailers that are then towed to the shipping dock. A number of automated decoupling devices are available to route trailers from the main towline to specified shipping docks.

A point of debate is the relative merit of in-floor versus overhead towline installation. In-floor installation is costly to modify and difficult to maintain from a housekeeping viewpoint. Overhead installation is more flexible, but unless the warehouse floor is absolutely level, the line may jerk the front wheels of the trailers off the ground and risk product damage. The overhead line also represents a potential danger to fork truck operations.

Tractor Trailers

Tractor trailers consist of a driver-guided power unit towing a number of individual four-wheel trailers. The typical size of the trailers is 4×8 feet. The tractor in combination with trailer, like a towline, is used during order selection. The main advantage of a tow tractor with trailers is flexibility. It is not as economical as the towline because each tow unit requires a driver.

Conveyors

Conveyors are used widely in shipping and receiving operations and serve as the basic handling device for a number of order selection systems. Conveyors are classified according to power, gravity, and roller or belt movement.[4] In power configurations, the conveyor is driven by a chain. Considerable conveyor flexibility is sacrificed in power configurations. Gravity and roller driven applications permit rearrangement with minimum difficulty. Portable gravity-style roller conveyors are often used for loading and unloading and, in some cases, are transported in over-the-road trailers to assist in unloading vehicles. Conveyors are effective in that only the product is moved, eliminating the need for equipment return movements.

Carousels

A carousel operates on a different concept than most other mechanized handling equipment. Rather than require the order selector to go to the inventory storage location, the carousel moves inventory to the order selector. A carousel consists of a series of bins mounted on an oval track or rack. There may be multiple track levels, allowing for very high-density carousel storage. The entire carousel rotates, moving the selection bin to a stationary operator. The typical carousel application is for the selection of packages in such items as pack, repack, and service parts. The rationale behind carousel systems is to shrink order selection labor requirements by reducing walking length and time. Carousels, particularly modern stackable or multitiered systems, also significantly reduce storage space requirements. Some carousel systems also utilize computer-generated pick lists and computer-directed carousel rotation to further increase order selector productivity. These systems are referred to as **paperless picking** because no paperwork exists to slow down employee efforts. A variation of the carousel system is movable racks. Such racks move horizontally to eliminate the permanent aisle between the racks. This system, often used in libraries, provides more storage density but reduces picking efficiency since the racks must be moved to access specific products.

The mechanized materials handling equipment discussion is representative of a wide range of alternatives. Most systems combine different handling devices. For example, lift trucks may be used for vertical movements while tow tractor with trailers or rider trucks are the primary methods of horizontal transfer.

Semiautomated Systems

Mechanized handling is often supplemented by semiautomatic equipment. Typical equipment utilized in semiautomated handling includes automated guided vehicle systems, computerized sortation, robotics, and various forms of live racks.

Automated Guided Vehicles (AGV)

An AGVs system typically replaces mechanized tow tractors and trailers. The essential difference is that AGVs are automatically routed and positioned and activated without a driver.

AGV equipment typically relies on an optical, magnetic, or wireless radio guidance system. In the optical application directional lines are placed on the warehouse floor. The AGV is then guided by a light beam focused on the guidepath. Magnetic AGVs follow an energized wire installed within the floor. Wireless radio (Wi-Fi) direction is guided by high-frequency transmission. The primary advantage of an AGV is direct labor reduction. AGVs using wireless guidance systems are not limited to predetermined warehouse flow

---

[4] For a more detailed discussion of conveyor alternatives and characteristics, see David Maloney, "Conveyors," *Modern Materials Handling* 55, no. 1 (January 2000), pp. 490–553.

routes. Lower cost and increased flexibility have enhanced the applicability of AGVs for warehouse movements that are repetitive and frequent or are in very congested areas.

Sortation

Automated sortation devices are typically used in combination with conveyors. As products are selected in the warehouse and placed on a conveyor for movement to the shipping dock, they must be sorted into specific combinations. For example, inventory to satisfy multiple orders may be selected in batches, creating the need for sortation and sequencing into individual shipments. Most sortation controllers can be programmed to permit customized flow and decision logic to meet changing requirements.

Automated sortation provides two primary benefits. The first is a reduction in labor. The second is a significant increase in speed and accuracy of order selection. High-speed sortation systems, such as those used by United Parcel Service, can sort and align packages at rates exceeding one per second.

Robotics

The robot is a machine that can be programmed to perform one or a series of functions. The appeal of robotics lies in the ability to program functionality and decision logic to direct the handling process. The popularity of robotics resulted from its widespread adoption in the automotive industry during the early 1980s in an effort to automate select manual tasks. However, a warehouse provides a far different challenge. In warehousing, the goal is to efficiently accumulate the unique inventory requirements of a customer's order. Thus, requirements can vary extensively from one order to the next, resulting in far less routine than is typical of manufacturing.

A successful application of robotics in warehousing is to build and break down unit loads. In the breakdown process, the robot is programmed to recognize product stacking patterns in unitized loads and place products in a predetermined position on a conveyor belt. The use of robots to build unit loads is essentially the reverse of breakdown. Another use of robotics in warehousing occurs in environments where it is difficult for humans to function. Examples include materials handling in high-noise areas, hazardous materials, and extreme temperature operations, such as frozen foods or heat treatment areas.

Significant potential exists to integrate robots in mechanized warehouses to perform select functions. The capability to incorporate program logic, in addition to robots' speed, dependability, and accuracy, makes robotics an attractive alternative to traditional manual handling in situations that are highly repetitive or unfriendly to humans.

Live Racks

A device commonly used to reduce manual labor in warehouses is storage rack design in which product automatically flows to the desired selection position. The typical live rack contains roller conveyors and is constructed for rear loading. The rear of the rack is elevated higher than the front, causing a gravity flow toward the front. When cartons or unit loads are removed from the front, all other cartons or loads in that specific rack flow forward.

The use of the live rack reduces the need to use lift trucks to transfer unit loads. A significant advantage of live rack storage is the potential for automatic rotation of product as a result of rear loading. Rear loading facilitates **first-in, first-out (FIFO)** inventory management. Applications of gravity flow racks are varied. For example, live racks are utilized to sequence palletized fresh bread for shipping from bakeries.

Automated Systems

For several decades the concept of automated handling has offered great potential and limited accomplishment. Initial automated handling efforts focused on master carton order selection systems. Recently, emphasis has shifted to automated high-rise storage and retrieval systems. While the basic concepts of automation remain valid, the primary barriers are high capital investment and low degree of flexibility.

Potential to Automate

The appeal of automation is that it substitutes capital equipment for labor. In addition to requiring less direct labor, an automated system has the potential to operate faster and more accurately than its mechanized counterpart.

To date, most automated systems have been designed and constructed for specific applications. The guidelines previously noted for selection of mechanized handling systems (Table 10.2) are not applicable to automated systems. For example, storage equipment in an automated system is an integral part of the handling capability and can represent as much as 50 percent of the total investment. The ratio of dead weight to payload has little relevance when handling is automated.

Although information technology plays an important part in all handling systems, it is essential in automated systems. Information technology controls the automated selection equipment and interfaces with the WMS. A major disadvantage of automation is its dependency on proprietary information technology networks. To reduce such dependency, newer automated systems are being linked to the Internet and use standard browsers as the network for controlling warehouse operations. Automated warehouses require integration between the WMS and the material handling operating systems.

Order Selection

Initially, automation was applied to master carton selection or order assembly in the warehouse. Because of high labor intensity in order selection, the basic objective was to integrate mechanized, semiautomated, and automated handling into a system that offers the advantages of high productivity and accuracy while using minimal labor.

The general process begins with an automated order selection device preloaded with product. The device itself consists of a series of flow racks stacked vertically. Merchandise is loaded from the rear and permitted to flow forward in the live rack on gravity conveyors until stopped by a rack door. Between or down the middle of the racks, power conveyors create a merchandise flow line, with several flow lines positioned vertical to each other, one to service each level or height of rack doors.

Upon receipt of an order, the warehouse control system generates sequenced instructions to trip the rack doors and allow merchandise, as required, to flow forward onto the powered conveyors. The conveyors in turn transport merchandise to an order packing area for placement in shipment containers or unitization prior to transfer of products to the shipment staging area. Product is, ideally, selected and loaded sequentially so it can be unloaded in the sequence desired by the customer.

When compared to modern automation, these initial attempts at automated package handling were highly inefficient. A great deal of labor was required to perform merchandise preselection loading into the racks, and the automated selection equipment used was expensive. Early applications were limited to merchandise of extremely high value, with common or standardized master carton size, or situations where working conditions justify such investment. For example, these initial systems were widely tested for frozen food order selection.

Substantial advancements have been made in automated selection of case goods. The handling of fast-moving products in master cartons, typical of cross-docking, can be fully automated from the point of merchandise receipt to placement in over-the-road trailers. Such systems use an integrated network of power and gravity conveyors linking power-motivated live storage. The entire process is computer controlled and coupled with the order and WMS. Upon arrival, merchandise is automatically routed to the live storage position and inventory records are updated. When orders are received, merchandise is pre-cubed to package or vehicle size and scheduled for selection. At the appropriate time, all merchandise is routed in loading sequence and automatically transported by conveyor to the loading dock. In some situations, the first manual handling of the merchandise within the warehouse occurs when it is stacked into the outbound transport vehicle.

Automated Storage/Retrieval

An automated unit-load handling system, or **Automated Storage and Retrieval System (AS/RS),** that uses high-rise storage is a popular form of automation. Figure 10.4 illustrates the concept of a high-rise AS/RS. AS/RSs are particularly appropriate for items such as heavy boxes or those products in controlled environments such as bakeries or frozen food. The high-rise concept of handling is typically automated from receiving to shipping. The four primary AS/RS components include storage racks, storage and retrieval equipment, input/output system, and control system.

The name high-rise derives from the physical appearance of the storage rack. The rack is structured-steel vertical storage, which can be as high as 120 feet. The typical stacking height of palletized cartons in a mechanized handling system is 20 feet, so the potential of high-rise storage is clear. Because humans are not an integral part of AS/RSs, they are often referred to as **lights-out** facilities.

The typical high-rise facility consists of rows of storage racks. The rows of racks are separated by aisles ranging from 120 to over 800 feet in length. Primary storage and retrieval activities occur within these aisles. A storage and retrieval crane travels up and down the aisle alternatively storing and selecting product. A variety of storage and retrieval equipment is available. Most machines require guidance at the top and bottom to provide the vertical stability necessary for high-speed horizontal movement and vertical hoisting. Horizontal speeds range from 300 to 400 feet per minute (fpm) with hoisting speeds of up to 100 fpm or more.

FIGURE 10.4
AS/RS High-Rise Warehouse

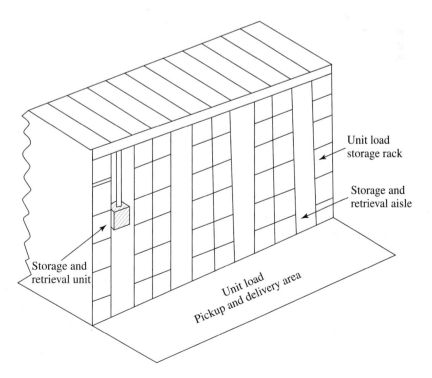

Unit load storage rack

Storage and retrieval aisle

Storage and retrieval unit

Unit load Pickup and delivery area

The initial function of the storage and retrieval equipment is to reach the desired storage location rapidly. A second function is to insert or remove merchandise from the rack. For the most part, load insertion and removal are achieved by shuttle tables, which can enter and exit from the rack at speeds up to 100 fpm. Since the shuttle table moves only a few feet, it must accelerate and stop rapidly.

The storage and retrieval machine is essentially a combined lift truck and pallet holder built into a movable crane. The machine moves up and down the aisle to insert or remove a unit load from a storage bin. When the AS/RS operates with unit loads, the process is typically automated. However, the AS/RS often incorporates manual picking when the system selects cases or master cartons. In some installations, the storage and retrieval machine is positioned to service different aisles by transfer cars. Numerous transfer arrangements and layouts are available. Transfer units may be **dedicated** or **nondedicated.** The dedicated transfer car is always stationed at the end of the aisle in which the storage and retrieval equipment is working. The nondedicated transfer car works a number of aisles and retrieval machines on a scheduled basis to achieve maximum equipment utilization. The decision as to whether to include aisle-to-aisle transfer in a high-rise storage system rests with the economics of throughput rate and number of aisles included in the overall system.

The input/output system in high-rise storage is concerned with moving loads to and from the rack area. Two types of movement are involved. First, loads must be transported from receiving docks or production lines to the storage area. Second, within the immediate peripheral area of the racks, loads must be positioned for entry or exit. The greatest potential handling problem is in the peripheral area. A common practice assigns separate stations for pickup and removal capable of staging an adequate supply of loads to each aisle to fully utilize the storage and retrieval equipment. For maximum input/output performance, the normal procedure requires different stations for transfer of inbound and outbound loads assigned to the same aisle. The pickup and discharge (P/D) stations are linked to the handling systems that transfer merchandise to and from the high-rise storage area. The control system in high-rise storage is similar to the automated order selection systems described earlier. In addition to scheduling arrivals and location assignments, the control system handles inventory control and stock rotation. The control system also tracks product location within the AS/RS, storage bin utilization, and crane operations. In the case of high-rise storage, system reliability and integrity are critical to achieving productivity and maximum equipment utilization.

In manufacturing applications, product flowing from production is automatically formed into unit loads. The unit load is then transported to the high-rise storage area by power conveyor. When the load arrives, it is assigned to a storage bin and transferred by power conveyor to the appropriate pickup station. At this point, the storage and retrieval equipment takes over and moves the unit load to its planned storage location. When orders are received, the control system directs the retrieval of specified unit loads. From the outbound delivery station, the unit load flows by power and gravity conveyor to the appropriate shipping dock. While retrieval and outbound delivery are being accomplished, all paperwork necessary to initiate product shipment is completed.

AS/RSs seek to increase materials handling productivity by providing maximum storage density per square foot of floor space and to minimize direct labor required in handling. The highly controlled nature of an AS/RS achieves reliable pilferage-free and damage-free handling with extremely accurate control. However, high-rise AS/RSs are generally better as storage than as handling devices, thus reducing their appeal in situations where fast inventory turns are more important than inexpensive storage. The loss of flexibility has caused some firms to rethink the use of automated systems.

Information-Directed Systems

The concept of information-directed handling is relatively new and the subject of a great deal of research and development. The concept is appealing because it combines the control typical of automated handling with the flexibility of mechanized systems. Information-directed systems use mechanized handling controlled by information technology. Two common examples of information-directed materials handling systems are RF wireless (Wi-Fi) and light-directed operations.

RF Wireless (Wi-Fi)

RF wireless handling uses standard mechanized materials handling equipment coordinated by information technology to provide operator directions and control in real time. Typical Wi-Fi systems utilize lift trucks. However, the basic use of Wi-Fi to instruct movement of lift trucks is expanded in an information-directed application to become a highly integrated materials handling system. In terms of layout and design, the warehouse facility is often essentially the same as any mechanized facility. The difference is that all lift truck movements are directed and monitored by some combination of computer mounted on the lift truck, handheld computer, or voice-activated communication. The real-time information interchange is designed to achieve flexibility and better utilization.

The main advantage of RF is to improve speed and flexibility of lift truck operations. Instead of following handwritten instructions or computer listings generated in batches, drivers receive work assignments through either handheld or vehicle-mounted RF terminals. Use of RF technology provides real-time communication to central data processing systems. In operation, the WMS in conjunction with the operations control computer plans and initiates all movements, communicates the requirements to the material handlers, and tracks the completion of all tasks. Decision support systems analyze all movement requirements to assign equipment in such a way that direct movement is maximized and deadhead movement is minimized. This process of assigning lift trucks to continuous assignments is called **task interleaving.** In task interleaving, lift trucks are assigned independent of traditional work areas to specific jobs or work areas that need resources such as receiving or shipping.

Information-directed handling offers great potential because selected benefits of automation can be achieved without substantial capital investment. Information-directed systems can also substantially increase productivity by tracking lift truck performance, thereby allowing compensation to be based on performance. The main drawback of information-directed handling is accountability regarding work assignment. As a specific lift truck proceeds during a work period, it may be involved in loading or unloading several different vehicles, selecting items for many orders, and completing several nonrelated handling assignments. The wide variety of work assignments increases the complexity of work direction and can decrease performance accountability. This complexity increases the demands placed on driver capabilities.

Substantial research is being conducted to explore new concepts of warehouse design and layout to fully exploit the potential of information-directed material handling. One concept, referred to as **chatoic design,** builds on the flexibility of using information technology to allow a warehouse to be stocked and operated to maximize inbound and outbound movement efficiency. A warehouse operated under chaotic principles would place all merchandise in location as directed by the WMS in an effort to minimize total handling.[5]

---

[5] Duncan McFarlane and Yossi Sheffi, "The Impact of Automatic Identification on Supply Chain Operations," *International Journal of Logistics Management* 14, no. 1 (2003), pp. 1–17.

Pick-to-Light

A technology referred to as **pick-to-light** is a carousel system variation that is becoming increasingly common. In these systems, order selectors pick designated items directly into cartons or onto conveyors from **lighted** carousel locations or storage bins. A series of lights or a **light tree** in front of each pick location indicates the number of items to pick from each location. A variation of the pick-to-light system is **put-to-light,** where order selectors place product in lighted containers. Each container or tote is assigned to a specific order or customer, so the light is telling which customers are to receive a specific product.

Special Handling Considerations

The primary mission of materials handling is to facilitate merchandise flow in an orderly and efficient manner from manufacturer to point of sale. This section identifies and discusses special considerations important to selection and operation of materials handling equipment.

E-Fulfillment

Satisfaction of Internet fulfillment places some special demands on a firm's warehousing and materials handling. Both e-tailers and brick-and-mortar retailers moving into the e-tail environment have been forced to adapt their processes to meet the specific needs of this marketplace. Four specific considerations that influence warehousing and materials handling in an e-fulfillment environment are order volume, products, people, and tracking.[6] First, to serve end consumers, an e-fulfillment facility typically must process a large number of very small orders. This means that it is difficult to achieve any substantial economies of scale for picking operations. Second, e-fulfillment facilities must generally deal with a wide range of product, which translates to large inventories and the use of flow-through practices to consolidate orders for shipment. Firms electing to consolidate orders must have the capability to effectively receive and merge a large number of very small orders rapidly. Third, an e-fulfillment facility is people-intensive because the required flexibility in picking reduces order selection to manual or limited application of pick-to-light technology. In many cases, e-fulfillment operations are seasonal, increasing the need for ongoing training for new and seasonal employees. Fourth, increased consumer expectations regarding tracking require that many activities within the warehouse and interfacing with the carrier be electronically scanned and tracked. Despite rapid growth in e-tailing, many firms are still trying to resolve the warehousing and materials handling processes most appropriate to support this activity. In many cases, these e-tailers are outsourcing fulfillment to integrated service providers (ISPs). In any case, the e-tailing environment will continue to place increasing demands on a more timely, responsive, and integrated warehouse and materials handling operation.

Environmental Concerns

There is increased concern regarding environmental impact of warehouse operations. In particular, attention has been directed to the impact of materials handling equipment such as lift trucks. Pollution of nonelectric lift trucks is similar to that of automobile engines. There is also increasing interest regarding the handling and disposal of hazardous materials used or stored in warehouse operations. Firms have to ensure that such materials are disposed of properly to avoid pollution liability.

Regulatory Environment

The distribution warehouse is one of the most labor-intensive operations for most firms. It is also one of the most dangerous as approximately 100 deaths and 95,000 injuries occur

[6] Amy Hardgrove, "Fulfillment: The Last Step in the E-Tail Process," *Grocery Distribution* (July/August 2000), pp. 27–30.

annually.[7] To reduce these numbers, OSHA is extending its regulatory influence over warehouse operations and technology. In March 1999, OSHA established the Powered Industrial Truck Operator Training (PITOT) regulation requiring the training and reevaluation of all lift truck drivers. Drivers failing evaluation and those involved in accidents must undergo refresher training. Another evolving regulation focuses on lift and angle weight. Many of the injuries identified above are back and spinal injuries caused by improper lifting of master cartons or of unitizing equipment. OSHA now places limits on the weight an individual can lift, the angle of lift, and the number of repetitive actions. The recommended weight is calculated, starting at 51 pounds and subtracting for factors relating to how far, how much, and how many. For most repetitive materials handling jobs, the approved weight limits range from 20 to 30 pounds. A third OSHA focus is warehouse cleanliness, particularly for facilities dealing with food and pharmaceuticals. Floors and work areas must be clean to inhibit rodents and to guarantee worker safety from slippage or tripping. Designing warehouse operations to consider these limits is critical, since fines can be substantial and legal liability can result in excessive judgments.

Returns Processing

For a variety of reasons, merchandise may be recalled by or returned to a manufacturer. This is particularly true in an e-tailing environment where up to 30 percent of orders are returned. Normally such reverse logistics is not of sufficient quantity or regularity to justify unitized movement, so the only convenient method for processing reverse flows of merchandise is manual handling. To the degree practical, materials handling design should consider the cost and service impact of reverse logistics. Such flows often involve pallets, cartons, and packaging materials in addition to damaged, dated, or excess merchandise. Many firms are choosing to have returns processed by an integrated service provider to separate flows and reduce the chance for error or contamination.[8]

Summary

Packaging has a significant impact on the cost and productivity of logistics. Purchasing of packaging materials, packaging design, and the subsequent need for material disposal represent the most obvious costs of packaging. Packaging affects the cost of every logistical activity. Inventory control depends upon the accuracy of manual or automatic identification systems keyed by product packaging. Order selection speed, accuracy, and efficiency are influenced by package identification, configuration, and handling ease. Handling cost depends upon unitization capability and techniques. Transportation and storage costs are driven by package size and density. Customer service depends upon packaging to achieve quality control during distribution, to provide customer education and convenience, and to comply with environmental regulations. The concept of packaging postponement to achieve strategic flexibility is particularly important, given the increasing length and complexity of global supply chains and the costs of locating new facilities.

High-performance materials handling is a key to warehouse productivity for several important reasons. First, a significant number of labor hours are devoted to materials handling. Second, materials handling capabilities limit the direct benefits that can be gained by improved information technology. While information technology has introduced new technologies and capabilities, the preponderance of materials handling involves labor. Third, until recently, materials handling has not been managed on an integrated basis with other logistical activities, nor has it received a great deal of senior management attention. Finally,

---

[7] Alison Paddock, "Operator Training: Setting the Goals," *Grocery Distribution* (July/August 2000), p. 34.

[8] For an expanded discussion of reverse logistics see Chapter 11.

automation technology capable of reducing materials handling labor is only now beginning to reach full potential.

Although discussed separately, packaging, containerization, and materials handling represent integral parts of the logistical operating system. All three must be considered when designing an integrated supply chain.

Challenge Questions

1. Provide an illustration that highlights the differences between consumer and industrial packaging.
2. What is the primary purpose of bar codes or RFID in packaging? Is the role different in materials handling?
3. Discuss the differences between rigid and nonrigid containers. Discuss the importance of load securing in unitization.
4. What benefits do flexible unit-load materials have in contrast to rigid containers?
5. What trade-offs are involved in the use of returnable equipment?
6. In terms of basic materials handling, what is the role of a unit load?
7. Why have automated handling systems failed to meet their expected potential?
8. Compare and contrast order selection and unit load automation.
9. What is the logic of "live racks"?
10. What type of product and logistical applications are most suitable to AS/RS applications?

Operational Integration

The dominant theme of supply chain collaboration is the advancement of operational integration. The benefits attainable from collaboration are directly related to capturing efficiencies between functions within an enterprise as well as across enterprises that constitute a domestic or international supply chain. This chapter focuses on the challenges of integrative management by examining why integration creates value and by detailing the challenges of both enterprise integration and supply chain integration. Essential supply chain processes are identified. Attention is then directed to information technology available to facilitate integrated supply chain planning. The chapter concludes with a review of pricing. In final analysis, pricing practices and administration are critical to supply chain continuity.

Why Integration Creates Value

The basic benefits and challenges of integrated management were introduced in Chapter 1. To further explain the importance of integrated management, it is useful to point out that customers have at least three perspectives of value.

The traditional perspective of value is **economic value.** Economic value builds on economy of scale in operations as the source of efficiency. Economy of scale seeks to fully utilize fixed assets to achieve the lowest, total landed cost. The focus of economic value is efficiency of product/service creation. Economic value is all about doing things as well as possible. The customer take-away of economic value is high quality at a low price.

A second value perspective is **market value.** Market value is about presenting an attractive assortment of products at the right time and place to realize effectiveness. Market value focuses on achieving economy of scope in product/service presentation. The creation of multimerchant shopping malls, large-scale mass-merchandising retail stores and multivendor e-commerce fulfillment operations are all initiatives to achieve **market value.** The customer's take-away in terms of market value is **convenient product/service assortment and choice.**

Realization of both economic and market value is important to customers. However, increasingly firms are recognizing that business success also depends upon a third perspective of value, referred to as **relevancy.** Relevancy involves customization of value-adding services, over and above product and positioning, that make a real difference to customers. Relevancy value means the right products and services, as reflected by market value, at the right price, as reflected by economic value, modified, sequenced, synchronized, and otherwise positioned in a manner that creates valuable segmental diversity. In a consumer context, for example, relevancy means transforming ingredients into ready-to-eat meals. In general merchandise retailing, relevancy means transforming products into fashionable apparel. In manufacturing and assembly, relevancy is achieved by integrating specific components into products to increase functionality desired by a specific customer. The customer's take-away in terms of relevancy is a unique product/service bundle.

The simultaneous achievement of economic value, market value, and relevancy value requires total integration of the overall business process and is known as the integrative management value proposition, as illustrated in Table 11.1.

Systems Concept and Analysis

The **systems concept** is an analytical framework that seeks **total** integration of components essential to achieving stated objectives. The components of a logistics system are typically called functions. The logistical functions, as discussed in Chapter 2, were identified as order processing, inventory, transportation, warehousing, materials handling and packaging, and facility network design. **Systems analysis,** applied to logistics, seeks to quantify trade-offs between these five functions. The goal of systems analysis methodology

TABLE 11.1
Integrative Management Value Proposition

Economic Value	Market Value	Relevancy Value
• Lowest total cost	• Attractive assortment	• Customization
• Economy-of-scale efficiency	• Economy-of-scope effectiveness	• Segmental diversity
• Product/service creation	• Product/service presentation	• Product/service positioning
Procurement/Manufacturing Strategy	**Market/Distribution Strategy**	**Supply Chain Strategy**

is to create a whole or integrated effort, which is greater than the sum of the individual parts or functions. Such integration creates a synergistic interrelationship between functions in pursuit of higher overall achievement. In systems terminology, functional excellence is defined in terms of contributions a function makes to the overall process as contrasted to isolated performance in a specific area. Until the last few decades of the 20th century, process integration was generally neglected by managers who were trained to pursue functional excellence. Rapid advancement in information technology has increased the ability to identify and understand trade-offs to enhance logistics and supply chain initiatives.

When analyzed from a process perspective, the goal is balanced performance between functional areas within an enterprise and across the supply chain. For example, manufacturing economics are typically minimized by long production runs and low procurement costs. In contrast, integrated process management raises questions concerning the total cost and customer impact of such practices. A traditional financial orientation typically seeks to minimize inventories. While inventory should always be maintained as low as practical, arbitrary reductions below a level required to facilitate integrated operations typically increase total cost. Marketing's basic desire is to have finished goods inventory available in local markets. Inventory stocked in close geographical proximity to customers is believed to facilitate sales. Such anticipatory deployment of inventory is risky and may be in direct conflict with the least total cost process. In fact, e-commerce connectivity and fulfillment strategies are driving entirely different inventory stocking and logistics strategies.

In systems analysis, attention is focused on the interaction between components. Each component contributes a specific functionality essential to achieving system objectives. To illustrate, consider a high-fidelity stereo system. Many components are integrated for the single purpose of sound reproduction. The speakers, transistors, amplifier, and other components have purpose only if they contribute to quality sound. However, failure of any component will cause the output of the stereo system to fail.

Some principles can be stated concerning general systems theory. First, the performance of the total system or process is of singular importance. Components are important only if they enhance total system performance. For example, if the stereo system can achieve superior sound with two speakers, then it is unnecessary to include additional speakers. Second, individual components need not have best or optimum design. Emphasis is on the integrated relationship between components that constitute the system. Transistors, as an example, are hidden from view inside the stereo system. As such, they do not need to be aesthetically pleasing. To spend money and time designing an appealing transistor is not necessary in terms of system integration. Third, a functional relationship, called **trade-off,** exists between components that serve to stimulate or hinder total system performance. Suppose a trade-off allows a lower-quality amplifier to be used if an extra transistor is added to the system. The cost of the extra transistor must be justified in terms of savings in amplifier cost. Finally, components linked together as an integrated system may produce end results greater than possible through individual performance. In fact, the desired result may be unattainable without such integrated performance. A stereo system will technically operate without speakers, but audible sound is impossible.

The principles of systems analysis are basic and logically consistent. An integrated process with cross-functional integration can be expected to achieve greater results than one deficient in coordinated performance. In logistical systems, synergistic performance is targeted customer service at the lowest possible total cost. Although logical and indisputable in concept, effective application of systems integration is operationally difficult. In the final analysis, it matters little how much a firm spends to perform any specific function, such as transportation, as long as overall performance goals are realized at the lowest total cost expenditure.

Logistical Integration Objectives

To achieve logistical integration within a supply chain context, six operational objectives must be simultaneously achieved: (1) responsiveness, (2) variance reduction, (3) inventory reduction, (4) shipment consolidation, (5) quality, and (6) life cycle support. The relative importance of each is directly related to a firm's logistical strategy.

Responsiveness

A firm's ability to satisfy customer requirements in a timely manner is referred to as **responsiveness.** As noted repeatedly, information technology is facilitating response-based strategies that permit operational commitment to be postponed to the last possible time, followed by accelerated delivery. The implementation of responsive strategies serves to reduce inventories committed or deployed in anticipation of customer requirements. Responsiveness serves to shift operational emphasis from forecasting future requirements to accommodating customers on a rapid order-to-shipment basis. Ideally, in a responsive system, inventory is not deployed until a customer commits. To support such commitment, a firm must have the logistical attributes of inventory availability and timely delivery once a customer order is received.

Variance Reduction

All operating areas of a logistical system are susceptible to variance. Variance results from failure to perform any expected facet of logistical operations as anticipated. For example, delay in customer order processing, an unexpected disruption in order selection, goods arriving damaged at a customer's location, and/or failure to deliver at the right location on time all create unplanned variance in the order-to-delivery cycle. A common solution to safeguard against detrimental variance is to use inventory safety stocks to buffer operations. It is also common to use premium transportation to overcome unexpected variance that delays planned delivery. Such practices, given their associated high cost, can be minimized by using information technology to maintain positive logistics control. To the extent that variance is minimized, logistical productivity will improve. Thus, **variance reduction,** the elimination of system disruptions, is one basic objective of integrated logistics management.

Inventory Reduction

To achieve the objective of **inventory reduction,** an integrated logistics system must control asset commitment and turn velocity. Asset commitment is the financial value of deployed inventory. Turn velocity reflects the rate at which inventory is replenished over time. High turn rates, coupled with desired inventory availability, mean assets devoted to inventory are being efficiently and effectively utilized; that is, overall assets committed to support an integrated operation are minimized.

It is important to keep in mind that inventory can and does facilitate desirable benefits. Inventories are critical to achieving economies of scale in manufacturing and procurement. The objective is to reduce and manage inventory to the lowest possible level while simultaneously achieving overall supply chain performance objectives.

Shipment Consolidation

One of the most significant logistical costs is transportation. Over 60 cents of each logistics dollar is expended for transportation. Transportation cost is directly related to the type of product, size of shipment, and movement distance. Many logistical systems that feature direct fulfillment depend on high-speed, small-shipment transportation, which is costly. A system objective is to achieve **shipment consolidation** in an effort to reduce transportation cost. As a general rule, the larger a shipment and the longer the distance it is transported, the lower is the cost per unit. Consolidation requires innovative programs to combine small shipments for timely consolidated movement. Such programs require multifirm coordination because they transcend the supply chain. Successful e-commerce fulfillment direct-to-consumers requires innovative ways to achieve effective consolidation.

Quality

A fundamental operational objective is continuous **quality** improvement. Total Quality Management (TQM) is a major initiative throughout most facets of industry. Aspects of quality were discussed in Chapters 3 and 4. If a product becomes defective or if service promises are not kept, little if any value can be added by the logistics process. Logistical costs, once expended, cannot be reversed or recovered. In fact, when product quality fails after customer delivery and replacement is necessary, logistical costs rapidly accumulate. In addition to the initial logistics cost, products must be returned and replaced. Such unplanned movements typically cost more than original distribution. For this reason, commitment to zero-defect order-to-delivery performance is a major goal of leading-edge logistics.

Logistics itself is performed under challenging conditions. The difficulty of achieving zero-defect logistics is magnified by the fact that logistical operations typically are performed across a vast geographical area during all times of day and night and without direct supervision.

Life Cycle Support

The final integration design objective is **life cycle support.** Few items are sold without some guarantee that the product will perform as advertised. In some situations, the initial value-added inventory flow to customers must be reversed. Product return is common as a result of increasingly rigid quality standards, product expiration dating, and responsibility for hazardous consequences. Reverse logistics also results from the increasing number of laws encouraging recycling of beverage containers and packaging materials. The significant point concerning reverse logistics is the need to maintain maximum control when a potential health liability exists, such as a contaminated product. The operational requirements for reverse logistics range from lowest total cost, such as returning bottles for recycling, to maximum control in situations involving defective products. Firms that design efficient reverse logistics often are able to reclaim value by reducing the quantity of products that might otherwise be scrapped or sold at a discount. Sound integrative strategy cannot be formulated without careful review of reverse logistical requirements.

For some products, such as copying equipment, primary profit lies in the sale of supplies and aftermarket service to maintain the product. The importance of life cycle support is significantly different in situations wherein a majority of profits are achieved in the aftermarket. For firms marketing consumer durables or industrial equipment, the commitment to life cycle support constitutes a versatile and demanding marketing opportunity as well as one of the largest costs of logistical operations. Life cycle support requires **cradle-to-cradle** logistics. Cradle-to-cradle logistical support goes beyond reverse logistics and recycling to include the possibility of aftermarket service, product recall, and product disposal.

Enterprise Integration

The basic level of integration is the internal operations of individual firms. To inexperienced managers, the integration of functions under the managerial control of one enterprise might appear easy to achieve. In actual practice, some of the most challenging integration issues involve cross-functional trade-offs within a specific company. As noted earlier in the discussion of systems analysis, functional management is deeply embedded as best practice within most firms.

Internal Integration Barriers

Managers do not attempt to integrate operations in a vacuum. It is important to recognize barriers that serve to inhibit process integration. Barriers to internal integration find their origins in traditional functional practices related to organization, measurement and reward systems, inventory leverage, infocratic structure, and knowledge hoarding.

Organization

The organization structure of a business can serve to stifle cross-functional processes. Most business organizations seek to align authority and responsibility on the basis of functional work. In essence, both structure and financial budget closely follow work responsibility. The traditional practice has been to group all persons involved in performing specific work into functional departments such as inventory control, warehousing operations, or transportation. Each of these organizations has an operational responsibility, which is reflected in its functional goals.

To illustrate, transportation and inventory have traditionally been managed by separate organizational units. Created in isolation, goals for managing transportation and inventory can be contradictory. Transportation decisions aimed at reducing freight cost require shipment consolidation, but transportation consolidation might cause inventory to increase.

Popular terms to describe such function myopia are a **sandbox** or **silo** mentality. The traditional managerial belief was that functional excellence would automatically equate to superior performance. In integrated process management, it matters little how much is spent to perform a specific function as long as process performance goals are achieved at the lowest total cost expenditure. Successful integration of processes, such as logistics, requires that managers look beyond their organizational structure and achieve cross-functional integration. This may or may not require organizational change. Regardless, successful process integration requires significant traditional management behavioral modification.

Measurement and Reward Systems

Traditional measurement and reward systems serve to make cross-functional coordination difficult. Measurement systems typically mirror organization structure. Most reward systems are based on functional achievement. To facilitate internal process integration, new measures, increasingly called **balanced scorecards,** must be developed. Managers must be encouraged to view specific functions as contributing to a process rather than their stand-alone performance. A function may, at times, have to absorb increased costs for the sake of achieving lower total process cost. Unless a measurement and reward system is in place that does not penalize managers who absorb cost, integration will remain more theory than practice.

Inventory Leverage

It is a proven fact that inventory can be leveraged to facilitate functional performance. The traditional position is to maintain sufficient inventory to protect against demand and operational uncertainty. Stockpiling both materials and finished inventory leverages maximum manufacturing economy of scale. Such economy of scale can result in low per unit cost of manufacturing. Forward commitment of inventory to local markets can leverage sales. While such practices create benefits, they may be achieved at a cost, which is not typically allocated to that function. The integrative challenge is the cost/benefit balance of such leveraging and risks associated with potential inventory obsolescence.

Infocratic Structure

Information technology is a key enabler of process integration. A significant problem results from the fact that structure and availability of information have traditionally been based on functional organization relationships. As a result, information is typically formatted in terms of functional requirements and accountability. This early practice in formatting information has developed what is referred to as infocratic structure. The content and flow of available information follows long-standing functional organization lines of command and control. When managers attempt to reorganize to enable cross-functional processes, the infocratic structure serves as an invisible force to retain traditional functional information flows. The impact of infocratic structure is one of the driving reasons why Enterprise Resource Planning (ERP) systems have great general management appeal. The infocratic structure also helps explain why ERP implementations are so difficult.[1]

Knowledge Hoarding

In most business situations, knowledge is power, so unwillingness to share and a general lack of understanding regarding how to share knowledge are not uncommon. By enforcing functional specialization and by developing a workforce composed of experts, organizations inherently doom process integration. Consider, for example, the case when an experienced employee retires or for some other reason departs a firm. Replacement personnel must be given sufficient time to learn, but if information is restricted, all the time in the world may not help bring the new employee up to speed.

A more serious situation occurs when managers fail or are unable to develop procedures and systems for transferring cross-functional knowledge. Much process work is shared between jobs and is not restricted to a specific functional area, so transfer of knowledge and experience is vital.

The Great Divide

Clearly many obstacles make functional integration difficult. To some extent, the five barriers discussed above have contributed to a common situation in business referred to as the **great divide.** The great divide reflects an organizational condition wherein achieved integration is partial but not complete on an end-to-end basis, as illustrated in Figure 11.1. The most common situation is when a firm achieves only partial integration of distribution/ marketing on the outbound side of the enterprise and procurement/manufacturing on the inbound side. The paradox is that firms seem to be capable of achieving highly integrated operations with suppliers from whom they purchase materials and components. Firms also join operations in customer accommodation to service customers. Such initiatives reflect cross-functional integration that, in fact, extends beyond a single business enterprise. Despite these accomplishments, managers report considerable difficulty in linking these two types of external collaboration into an enterprise-wide integrative process. In short, managers seem to achieve more successful integration with external business partners than they do with managers and departments within their own firm.[2]

The phenomenon of the great divide is interesting and challenging. The fact that such operational discontinuity is common among firms in many different industries supports generalization. First, integration appears to be easier with groups external to a firm, such as

[1] See Chapter 5 for a detailed discussion of Enterprise Resource Systems.

[2] Donald J. Bowersox, David J. Closs, and Theodore P. Stank, *21st Century Logistics: Making Supply Chain Integration a Reality* (Oak Brook, IL: Council of Logistics Management, 1999).

FIGURE 11.1
The Great Divide: The Challenge of Managing across Functional Boundaries

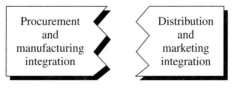

suppliers and customers, at least in part because the balance of power is typically clear and integrative objectives such as sales and costs can be quantified. Second, senior managers in most organizations do not have a sufficiently clear vision of internal process requirements and related measures to drive across-the-enterprise integration. Finally, the barriers outlined earlier serve to render end-to-end integration a difficult-to-achieve end state in most organizations.

Several authors writing on the challenges of implementing integrative processes have concluded that the typical traditional organization cannot accommodate sufficient change to transform from a functional to process orientation. This group advocates that successful implementation of integrative process management requires a major structural and philosophical shift in traditional command and control practice. Some go so far as to advocate the need to fully disintegrate traditional organizational structure.[3]

Most observers of current logistics practice feel significant inroads into improved process performance are being realized as a result of modifying and repositioning functional capabilities. The key is to align, focus, and measure functional performance in terms of process contribution. The goal is to close the great divide by achieving a single strategy, facilitated by well-defined processes, relevant measurement, common forecasting and planning, and a supportive reward system.

How Much Integration Is Enough?

The critical question concerning a firm's ability to participate in supply chain collaboration is: How much internal integration within a participating firm is necessary to achieve across-the-supply-chain collaborative success? This is a difficult question to answer. Any assessment must acknowledge two facts.

First, few, if any, existing supply chain arrangements are, in fact, end-to-end integrations. The more common examples reflect integration of cross-organizational processes involving either procurement and manufacturing or marketing and distribution. In other words, the separation of these cross-organizational processes serves to disrupt a firm's continuous supply chain operations. However, even limited integration appears to create value for the participating organizations. Therefore, one could conclude that limited collaboration offers sufficient benefits to justify supply chain initiatives.

Second, the number one reason given by executives to explain the limited scope of and high failure rate of supply chain collaboration is the inability of participating partners to perform as promised. For example, collaborations fail because a firm's manufacturing cannot or does not produce the products marketing promised to customers. Likewise, collaborations fail because marketing does not provide manufacturing with timely and detailed promotional plans for market distribution partners. Of course collaborations also fail because logistics is not able to perform to the expectations of manufacturing and/or marketing. This second assessment point serves to support the insight that comprehensive across-the-supply-chain collaborations will not occur until participating firms achieve high levels of credible internal integration. In short, long-term supply chain success requires that participating firms resolve their internal great divides. Attention is focused on supply chain collaboration in Chapter 15.

Supply Chain Processes

Excellence in supply chain logistics requires the simultaneous achievement of eight key processes. Table 11.2 identifies the eight key processes and provides a brief description of each. These eight processes have been discussed at various points throughout the first

---

[3] Christopher Meyer and David Power, "Enterprise Disintegration: The Storm Before the Calm," *Commentary* (Lexington, MA: Barker and Sloane, 1999).

TABLE 11.2
Eight Supply Chain Processes

Process	Description
Demand planning responsiveness	The assessment of demand and strategic design to achieve maximum responsiveness to customer requirements.
Customer relationship collaboration	The development and administration of relationships with customers to facilitate strategic information sharing, joint planning, and integrated operations.
Order fulfillment/service delivery	The ability to execute superior and sustainable order-to-delivery performance and related essential services.
Product/service development launch	The participation in product service development and lean launch.
Manufacturing customization	The support of manufacturing strategy and facilitation of postponement throughout the supply chain.
Supplier relationship collaboration	The development and administration of relationships with suppliers to facilitate strategic information sharing, joint planning, and integrated operations.
Life cycle support	The repair and support of products during their life cycle, including warranty, maintenance, and repair.
Reverse logistics	The return and disposition of inventories in a cost-effective and secure manner.

10 chapters. Although these integrative processes are not the exclusive domain of logistics, some critical elements of logistical performance are integral to a firm achieving high-level operational performance. Therefore, logistics structure, strategy, and continuous operational execution must be focused on achieving and continuously improving these essential eight processes. Simultaneous operational achievement of these eight processes forms the essence of achieving operational integration and performance excellence.

Supply chain operational planning requires the coordination of a number of the processes identified in Table 11.2. Specifically, demand planning responsiveness, customer relationship collaboration, order fulfillment/service delivery, manufacturing customization, and supplier relationship collaboration must be coordinated to satisfy customers and effectively use resources. The system to provide this coordination is the supply chain planning system.

The supply chain planning system and the related information systems seek to integrate information and coordinate overall logistics and supply chain decisions while recognizing the dynamics between other firm functions and processes. The three factors driving planning system development and implementation are (1) supply chain visibility, (2) simultaneous resource consideration, and (3) resource utilization.

Supply Chain Visibility

The first reason for planning system development is the need for **visibility** regarding location and status of supply chain inventory and resources. Visibility implies not only being able to track supply chain inventory and resources but also that information regarding available resources can be effectively evaluated and managed. For example, at any given point in time, manufacturers may have thousands of shipments in-transit and inventory stored in hundreds of locations around the globe. Simply being able to identify shipments and inventory is not sufficient; supply chain visibility requires exception management to highlight the need for resource or activity plans to minimize or prevent potential problems.

While the United States and its allies demonstrated the benefits of effective military planning and technology during the Persian Gulf War during the early 1990s, the Defense Department learned that its logistics and supply chain systems did not perform to the same standard. A major reason cited for poor logistical performance was lack of supply chain visibility. For security and other reasons, the Defense Department and its service suppliers did not have integrated information systems capable of documenting or identifying inventory status or location. There was minimal integration between each military service (Army, Navy, and Air Force) and the logistics service providers, such as the Defense Logistics Agency. Such logistics integration had not historically received a major focus. This lack of integration coupled with the fear that potential foes could gain an advantage by breaking into the tracking system or monitoring movements, resulted in performance that was not reflective of what should have been possible in 1991.

Limited visibility regarding inventory in-transit and expected arrival times resulted in significant uncertainty regarding product availability. The lack of certainty in a situation where product availability is critical resulted in additional inventory and requisitions to reduce the chance of stockouts. While it is clear that no military force can tolerate short supply, excessive inventories both are expensive and may be wasteful of critical resources.

Simultaneous Resource Consideration

Once the planning system determines resource status and availability through visibility, the second reason for a planning system is the need to consider combined supply chain demand, capacity, material requirements, and constraints. Supply chain requirements reflect the customer demand for product quantity, delivery timing, and location. While some of these customer requirements may be negotiable, logistics must execute to the agreed-to requirements and standards.

The constraints to meeting customer requirements are materials, production, storage, and transportation capacity, which represent the physical limitations of processes and facilities. Prior planning methods have typically considered these capacity constraints in a sequential manner. For example, an initial plan is made that operates within production constraints. The initial plan is then adjusted to reflect material and sourcing constraints. The second plan is then revised again to consider storage and transportation constraints. While the processes and sequences may be different, sequential decision making results in suboptimal and inferior planning and capacity utilization.

Achieving optimum supply chain performance requires simultaneous consideration of relevant supply chain requirements and capacity constraints to identify trade-offs where increased functional costs, such as in manufacturing or storage, might lead to lower overall system costs. A planning system needs to quantitatively evaluate the trade-offs and suggest plans that can optimize overall performance.

Resource Utilization

Logistics and supply chain management decisions have major influences on many enterprise resources, including production, distribution facilities and equipment, transportation equipment, and inventories. These resources consume a substantial proportion of a typical firm's fixed and working assets. Just as was the case with planning systems, functional management focused on the resource utilization within its scope of responsibility. For example, production management focused on minimizing plant and equipment required for manufacturing. The typical result was long production runs and minimum setups and changeovers. However, longer production runs invariably result in more finished inventory, as substantial quantities are manufactured in anticipation of projected demand. The excess inventory increases working capital requirements and space requirements. Extended production runs also requires longer-term and more accurate forecasts.

With functional resource trade-offs in mind, the final reason driving planning system development is the need for a coordinated approach that considers service requirements while minimizing combined supply chain resources. This is a critical capability when supply chain and firm performance place a strong emphasis on overall asset utilization.

Effective planning requires a combination of information systems to provide the data and managers to make decisions. The blend of technology and management processes is increasingly being termed Sales and Operations Planning (S&OP). The following section illustrates some of the specific conflicts associated with S&OP and describes the major process and system components.

Sales and Operations Planning (S&OP)

An integrated S&OP process is increasingly necessary for effective supply chain operations. As illustrated in Chapter 5, the S&OP process collaboratively establishes a coordinated plan for responding to customer requirements within the resource constraints of the enterprise. Traditionally, firms have sequentially and often independently developed financial, sales, and operations plans. First, finance develops revenue plans often designed to meet the expectations of Wall Street. Second, sales develops marketing plans and tactics that meet the revenue targets for the firm's product groups. This includes establishing specific product innovation, pricing, and promotion plans to achieve the desired results. Finally, supply chain operations develop materials, manufacturing, and logistics plans that can meet customer demands within the operating constraints of the firm and its supply chain partners. Figure 11.2 illustrates some of the conflicts involved. Sales would like to sell a wide variation of products, rapidly responding to customers, and with short lead times. In effect, the sales goal is to maximize the revenue by providing the customers whatever they want and when they want it. Supply chain operations would prefer to minimize the product variations and production changeovers, constrain schedule variations, and extend lead times to take advantage of economies of scale. In effect, a major focus of supply chain operations is to take advantage of manufacturing, transportation, and handling economies of scale. Since there is significant potential for conflict in these objectives, meeting unique customer requests versus operations economies of scale, it is necessary to systematically consider the trade-offs and collaboratively create consistent plans. This includes developing and agreeing to forecasts, product introduction, marketing tactics, and operating plans that can meet financial and customer commitments within the constraints of the enterprise.

FIGURE 11.2
Planning Process Conflicts

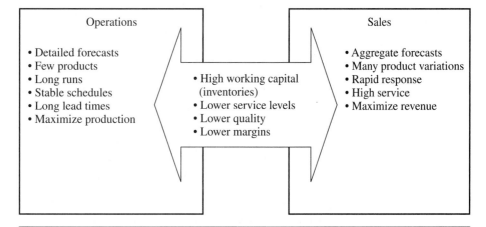

Balancing Objectives

Operations	High working capital (inventories)	Sales
• Detailed forecasts	• High working capital (inventories)	• Aggregate forecasts
• Few products	• Lower service levels	• Many product variations
• Long runs	• Lower quality	• Rapid response
• Stable schedules	• Lower margins	• High service
• Long lead times		• Maximize revenue
• Maximize production		

Traditional functional approach to planning leads to differing interests, suboptimal actions, and slower improvement

FIGURE 11.3 S&OP Process

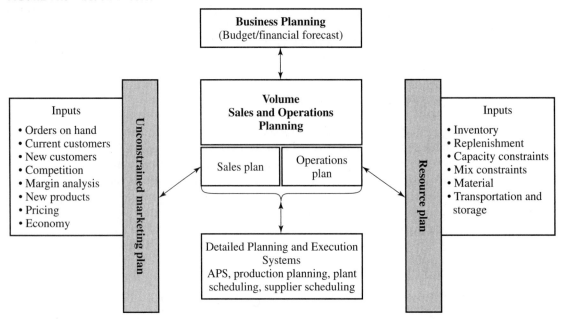

While S&OP has significant information technology considerations, it is not just an information technology application. It is a combination of information systems, with significant elements of financial, marketing, and supply chain planning elements, integrated with organizational processes, responsibility, and accountability to develop consensus and execute collaborative plans. Thus, an effective S&OP requires a blending of process and technology within a collaborative organization. Figure 11.3 illustrates the S&OP process. The first component of the S&OP process is a business plan in terms of a financial forecast and a corresponding budget. This plan is used to guide activity levels and determine aggregate volume and resource requirements. The second component of the S&OP is the sales plan, which is developed from the unconstrained marketing plan. The unconstrained marketing plan determines the maximum sales and profitability level that could be achieved if there were no supply chain operating constraints. As Figure 11.3 indicates, the unconstrained marketing plan synthesizes the information regarding orders on hand, current customers, new customers, competition, selling margins, new product potential, pricing, and the overall economy to project what sales could be if there were no supply chain or operations constraints. The final component of the S&OP is the resource plan, which is developed from the firm's internal and partner resource constraints. The operations plan synthesizes the resource demands and constraints to identify and evaluate potential trade-offs.

The business, unconstrained marketing, and resource plans are integrated and synchronized through the S&OP process. The process requires a combination of technology to identify and evaluate the binding constraints as well as managerial input to determine which constraints might be released in the form of prioritizing customer shipments, changes in marketing plans, overtime operations, or outsourcing production. Once the S&OP process is completed for current and future time periods, the result is a common and consistent plan that synthesizes the firm's financial and marketing plans with its resource capabilities. Once this aggregate plan is approved, it becomes the basis of more detailed supply chain planning application systems. The next section discusses some of these applications in detail.

While not every firm uses an integrated and coordinated S&OP process, virtually all firms develop business, marketing, and operational plans. When the S&OP process is not integrated and collaborative, there are no feedback loops or synchronization. The result is a high probability that they will not be consistent and conflicts will arise. As indicated in Figure 11.2, such conflicts will often result in unsatisfied customer and/or poor resource utilization. It is important to note that the arrows in Figure 11.3 are bidirectional, indicating that an effective S&OP process requires two-way information flow and collaboration. Firms are becoming increasingly interested in a more formal and collaborative S&OP process to facilitate meeting the precise requirements of increasingly demanding customers within the constraints that are being imposed by firms that increasingly asset conscious.

Supply Chain Planning Applications

Supply chain planning applications are increasing in both number and scope. Such applications are evolving to facilitate consideration of a broader range of activities and resources within the scope of supply chain plans. There are, however, some applications that are typical for many planning environments. These include demand management, production planning, requirements planning, and transportation planning.

Demand Management

The increasing complexity of product offerings and marketing tactics in conjunction with shorter product life cycles requires more accuracy, flexibility, and consistency in determining inventory requirements. Demand management systems attempt to provide such capabilities.

Demand management develops the forecast that drives anticipatory supply chain processes. The forecasts are the projections of monthly, weekly, or daily demand that determine production and inventory requirements. Each projected quantity might include some portion of future orders placed in anticipation of customer demand along with some portion of forecasted demand based on history. Essentially, the demand management process integrates historically based forecasts with other information regarding events that could influence future sales activity, such as promotional plans, pricing changes, and new product introductions, to obtain the best possible integrated statement of requirements.

Another aspect of the demand management process focuses on creating forecast consistency across multiple products and warehouse facilities. Effective integrated management requires a single accurate forecast for each item and facility. The aggregate and combined requirements must reflect a plan that is consistent with divisional and overall firm sales and financial projections. The demand management system is the information technology component of the S&OP process to develop the unconstrained marketing plan. The demand management system begins with a base forecast and then incorporates such factors as product life cycle, changes in distribution channels, pricing and promotional tactics, and product mix variations. The demand management system also rationalizes the detailed logistics plans, unique forecasts for each warehouse and product, with the aggregate product group and national plans. For example, the sum of individual warehouse facility sales should be consistent with national sales projections. Similarly, item level requirements need to be adjusted to reflect the activity level for related items. For instance, requirements for existing products may have to be reduced to reflect the market's reaction to a new product introduction or one item's requirements may need to be adjusted during the promotion of a substitutable item.

Production Planning

Production planning uses the statement of requirements obtained from demand management in conjunction with manufacturing resources and constraints to develop a workable manufacturing plan. The statement of requirements defines what items are needed and when. Although there has been a definite trend toward make-to-order (MTO) and assemble-to-order (ATO) manufacturing, such response-based practices are not always possible because of production capacity or resource constraints. The limitations occur in the form of facility, equipment, and labor availability.

Production planning systems match the requirements plan with the production constraints. The objective is to satisfy the necessary requirements at the minimum total production cost while not violating any constraints. Effective production planning results in a time-sequenced plan to manufacture the correct items in a timely manner while operating within facility, equipment, and labor constraints. Production planning identifies the items that should be produced in anticipation of need to remain within production constraints and yet minimize inventory.

Requirements Planning

Requirements planning extends the planning process beyond the plant walls. While it is important to achieve economical plant performance, effective supply chain management requires consideration of the impact production decisions have on downstream performance. For example, production plans may suggest a long run of a single item. This will build up finished inventory, requiring storage and transport capacity. While such long manufacturing runs might minimize manufacturing cost, overall system performance might be better served with shorter runs resulting in reduced inventory storage and risk. The requirements planning process uses evaluative techniques to trade off the costs of production, inventory, storage, and transportation. The analysis attempts to satisfy customer demand, minimize overall cost, and remain within the supply chain's physical constraints.

Transportation Planning

Transportation planning coordinates transportation resources within the firm and between supply chain partners. Historically, purchasing and finished goods transportation both attempted to minimize their freight cost individually. Procurement minimized the expense of raw material movements by working with suppliers and inbound carriers. Logistics focused on minimizing outbound freight expense by working with customers and their transportation carriers. There was also often a third managerial focus on international and expedited shipments. The individual perspectives of transportation often results in limited economies of scale, limited information sharing, and excessive transportation expense.

Transportation planning integrates movement demands, vehicle resources, and relevant costs into a common tactical decision support system that seeks to minimize overall freight expense. The analysis suggests ways that freight can be shifted among carriers or consolidated to achieve scale economies. It also facilitates information sharing with carriers and other service providers to enable better asset utilization.

Logistics and supply chain planning are essential for effective resource utilization. Lack of accurate and comprehensive logistics and supply chain planning tools historically resulted in poor utilization of production, storage, and transportation capacity. The increasingly strong focus on improved asset utilization in conjunction with improved information management and decision analysis capabilities and techniques has brought comprehensive planning systems to reality. The following section describes the major components of a supply chain planning system. While the components for supply chain planning application are similar, the discussion is presented in the context of a requirements planning system. The current terminology for the information systems that perform requirements planning is advanced planning and scheduling (APS) system.

APS System Overview

To correspond with the planning and execution of effective logistics and supply chain strategies, supply chain planning systems incorporate both spatial and temporal considerations. The spatial considerations include movement between raw material providers, manufacturing plants, warehouses, distributors, retailers, and the end customer. The temporal considerations include the timing and scheduling of the movements.

The APS system in Figure 11.4 is a network including plants, warehouses, and customers as well as transportation flows. This network reflects the resource status and allocation at a point in time, for example, on the first day of the month. Effective planning requires a process that can time-phase and coordinate resource requirements and constraints through time. For example, if product X is needed by the customer in period 3, its movement through the supply chain must be time-phased for arrival by period 3. Assuming a one-period performance cycle between each stage in the supply chain, this means that the APS must plan for the shipment of X from the plant during period 1 and shipment from the distribution center during period 2.

More specifically, suppose a firm is facing the situation summarized in Table 11.3. Customers require 200 units of product during each of the next five periods with the exception of period 4, when a special promotion increases demand to 600 units. The firm's production capacity is 300 units per week. On the extremes, the firm can select between two

FIGURE 11.4
Advanced Planning and Scheduling Overview

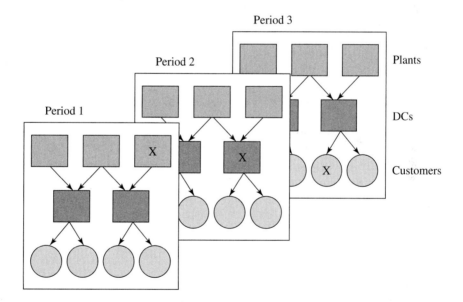

TABLE 11.3
Sample APS Planning Situation

	Time Period				
	1	**2**	**3**	**4**	**5**
Requirement	200	200	200	600	200
Production Capacity	300	300	300	300	300
Alternative 1 (overtime):					
Production	200	200	200	600	200
Inventory Carryover	—	—	—	—	—
Alternative 2 (build ahead):					
Production	300	300	300	300	200
Inventory Carryover	100	200	300	—	—

approaches to satisfy customer requirements given the production constraints. Alternative 1 is to wait until the fourth time period and then run production overtime to meet customer requirements. This alternative results in higher production cost but no cost to carry or store inventory. Alternative 2 is to build ahead using the extra 100-unit capacity in the time prior to period 4. With this alternative, an extra 100 units is built and added to inventory each period until it is required during period 4. This alternative does not require overtime production but does require increased inventory carrying and storage costs. There are, of course, intermediate alternatives to these two extremes. The ideal option is to select the combination resulting in the lowest combined cost of manufacturing and storage.[4] Using linear optimization techniques, APS identifies the most cost-effective trade-offs considering all relevant costs. While firms have wanted to consider these trade-offs previously, analysis capabilities only allowed for evaluation of two or three major trade-offs to minimize problem complexity. Supply chain planning tools like APS offer the ability to thoroughly evaluate complex trade-offs involving a large number of alternatives.

APS System Components

While there are many conceptual approaches to designing supply chain planning applications like APS, the major components are fundamentally the same: demand management, resource management, resource optimization, and resource allocation. Figure 11.5 illustrates how these modules relate to each other and to the corporate ERP or legacy system.

The **demand management** module develops the requirement projections for the planning horizon. In effect, it generates sales forecasts based on sales history, currently scheduled orders, scheduled marketing activities, and customer information. In the case of requirements planning, the forecasts are in terms of orders while it would be shipments in the case of transportation planning. Ideally, demand management works collaboratively and interactively both internally across the firm's functional components and externally with supply chain partners to develop a common and consistent forecast for each time period, location, and item. The forecast must also incorporate feedback from customers to integrate the influence of combined demand generation activities such as advertising and promotion.

The **resource management** component defines and coordinates supply chain system resources and constraints. Since APS systems use the resource and constraint information to evaluate the trade-offs associated with supply chain decisions, information accuracy and integrity are critical to provide optimal decisions and enhance planning system credibility. Obviously, incorrect planning decisions not only suboptimize supply chain performance but also severely reduce management credibility in the planning system itself. In addition

---

[4] Bowersox, Closs, and Stank, *21st Century Logistics.*

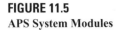

FIGURE 11.5
APS System Modules

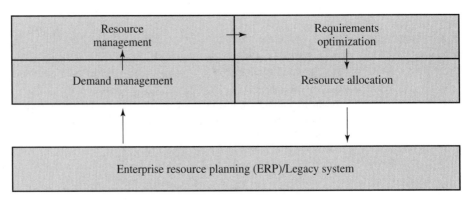

to the requirements definition developed by the demand management module, APS requires four other types of information: product and customer definitions, resource definitions and costs, system limitations, and planning objective function.

The product and customer definitions provide constants regarding the firm's products and customers to support the planning process. The product definitions provide the product descriptions and physical characteristics, such as weight and cube, standard costs, and bill of material. The customer definitions provide the ship-to location and distribution assignments, along with special service requirements. The combination of both defines what is being manufactured, distributed, where it is being delivered, and the performance cycles involved in distribution.

The resource definitions specify the physical resources used to accomplish supply chain activities such as manufacturing, storage, and movement. The resources include manufacturing equipment and process rates, storage facilities, and transportation equipment and availability. In addition to defining the existence of specific resources, the database must include the cost and performance characteristics and costs associated with resource usage.

System limitations define major supply chain activity constraints. These include the capacity limitations associated with production, storage, and movement. Production capacity defines how much product can be produced within a specific time period and what are the trade-offs associated with making various mixes of products. Storage capacity defines the amount of product that can be stored in a specific facility. Movement capacity defines the volume of product that can be transported between facilities or to customers within a given time frame.

The planning function defines criteria for developing a solution. Typical objective functions include minimizing total cost or any of its subcomponents, meeting all customer requirements, or minimizing the number of instances when capacity is exceeded.

This combination of demand management and resource management information provides the basis for the APS evaluation of alternative supply chain strategies. The module includes the databases to store the definitions, resources, constraints, and objectives as well as the processes to validate and maintain it. Users are finding that one of the major challenges to effective supply chain planning systems is the ability to develop and maintain accurate and consistent data.

The **resource optimization** module is the computational engine or "black box" of the supply chain planning system. Using the requirements from the demand management module and the definitions, resources, limitations, and objectives from the resource management module, resource optimization uses a combination of mathematical programming and heuristics to determine how to most effectively meet customer requirements while optimizing resource utilization. Mathematical programming is a combination of linear programming and mixed-integer programming, which is used to minimize the specified objective function; heuristics are computational rules of thumb or shortcuts that reduce the time or computational resources required to develop an integrated plan. In effect, the resource optimization module evaluates multiple planning alternatives and systematically completes the trade-offs to identify the best alternatives until a near-optimal result is achieved. The resource optimization module also determines when requirements cannot be met and which resources are the most constraining on supply chain performance. The resource optimization module results are supply chain plans projected into future time periods that minimize overall costs while attempting to operate within major resource constraints. The plan specifies which products should be produced when and determines movement and storage requirements across the supply chain.

The resource optimization module can also be used to conduct sensitivity or what-if analyses to determine the impact of changes in market requirements or constraints. These analyses allow the supply chain planner to isolate the impact of demand and performance uncertainty on supply chain capabilities and operations. Using the insight regarding the trade-offs and the impact of uncertainty, the supply chain planning resource optimization module guides the planner in establishing the most effective sourcing, production, movement, and storage strategy.

Following planner review and evaluation of the resource optimization module results, the **resource allocation** module specifies the resource assignments and communicates them to the ERP system to initiate appropriate transactions. The results include requirements for procurement, production, storage, and transport. The specific requests can be communicated to the ERP system in the form of transactions or instructions to complete a specific activity. Each transaction includes detailed instructions regarding type of supply chain activity, suppliers, customer, products involved, and required timing, along with a list of relevant products and quantities. The resource allocation module also provides information regarding when product is available to promise (ATP) or capable to promise (CTP). ATP is used to designate that even though actual inventory is not currently available, it will be available for shipment or promise at a specific date in the future. In effect, the ATP designation allows firms to commit scheduled production to customers. CTP is used to designate when requested product can be promised for future delivery. CTP requires a much broader analysis, as it determines whether there is future specific capacity or capability, given current and projected supply chain demands. ATP and CTP can dramatically enhance supply chain performance and effectiveness by allowing commitments against future production and capacity. The result is more rapid commitments to customers, fewer customer surprises, and enhanced resource utilization.

Supply Chain Planning Benefits

While some supply chain planning system benefits were discussed earlier, there are three broad benefits that accrue from planning system utilization. These are responsiveness to changes, comprehensive perspective, and resource utilization.

First, logistics and supply chain managers have used extended lead times and schedule freezes to plan for future supply chain activity. For example, production would be scheduled 3 to 4 weeks into the future and then frozen to minimize uncertainty and allow for effective resource utilization. Long lead times and freeze periods were necessary since the planning process was complex and required substantial analyses. While this approach reduced uncertainty, it also substantially reduced flexibility and responsiveness. Today's customer requires more responsiveness to market needs, and demand for lower inventory levels rules out long cycle times. Marketplace and firm changes can be quickly made in the demand management and resource management modules, allowing for the planning process to use the most current and accurate information. The requirements optimization module then solves the allocation, allowing daily and single week planning cycles rather than multiple weeks or months. Supply chain planning thus results in a process that can be much more responsive to marketplace or firm changes.

Second, effective supply chain management requires planning and coordination across firm functions and between supply chain partners. The process must consider the trade-offs associated with shifting activities and resources across functions and organizations. Such a comprehensive perspective increases planning process complexity substantially. The complexity follows from the number of organizations, facilities, products, and assets that must be considered when coordinating activities and resources across an entire supply chain. Supply chain planning systems offer the capability to consider the extended supply chain and make the appropriate trade-offs to achieve optimal performance.

Third, supply chain planning typically results in substantial performance improvements. While more comprehensive planning and reduced uncertainty usually result in improved customer service, another major planning system benefit is enhanced resource utilization.

More effective and responsive planning allows a more level assignment of resources for existing sourcing, production, storage, and transportation capacity. The result is that existing capacity is used more effectively. Firms also report that supply chain planning systems have significantly reduced asset requirements by smoothing resource demands. The decreases include estimates of 20 to 25 percent reductions in plant, equipment, facilities, and inventory.

While comprehensive supply chain planning is a relatively new capability, the future outlook is bright as the technology and capacity to effectively evaluate and manage integrated supply chains are developed. Supply chain planning can take a comprehensive and dynamic perspective of the entire supply chain and focus on reducing the supply chain asset requirements as demanded by financial markets.

Supply Chain Planning Considerations

Prior to the actual implementation, there are many considerations for supply chain planning system adoption. Managers cite their major considerations to be (1) integrated versus bolt-on application, (2) data integrity, and (3) application education.

The first consideration concerns the level of integration with other supply chain applications. Technically, there are three options for acquiring and implementing planning applications. The first is development using internal firm resources. This is not very common, as planning system development requires substantial expertise and most firms without substantial software competency could not effectively design, develop, or maintain such complex planning systems. In addition, the planning process of individual industries or firms is not usually different enough to be able to achieve any significant competitive advantage. Options two and three are to use a supply chain planning application that is integrated with the firm's ERP system or one from a third-party that **bolts on** to the firm's ERP system. Some ERP providers, such as SAP, offer an APS that is designed to be closely integrated with their ERP system. The obvious benefits of such integration include data consistency and integrity, as well as reduced need to transfer data between applications, which results in delays and potential errors. The alternative is to use a **bolt-on** or **best-of-breed** approach that seeks to identify the best supply chain planning system for the firm on the basis of features and functionality and then attach it to the firm's ERP system. The result is a planning system that better meets the firm's specific requirements or offers improved performance but at a probable cost of reduced integration. While providers of both integrated and bolt-on supply chain planning applications are attempting to enhance their integration with ERP system providers, operational integration between execution and planning systems remains a challenge.

Data integrity is a second major consideration for supply chain planning system implementation. Planning systems rely on absolute data integrity for effective decision making. While data integrity has always been important, it is more critical for planning systems since missing and inaccurate data can dramatically impact decision reliability and stability. One often-cited data integrity problem concerns product level detail such as cube and weight. While this is basic data, accuracy is not easy to maintain when there are a large number of products with constant changes and new product introductions. Managers cite that in the process of implementing supply chain planning applications, it is not uncommon to find a few hundred products with incorrect or missing physical characteristics. While it may not be a large percentage of products in number, the inaccuracy can substantially impact planning system decision making. For example, missing or inaccurate cube can result in a transportation planning system making a recommendation to overload a transportation vehicle. Specifically, the planning system will think that a large amount of product can be loaded into a truck when the product data contains an incorrect or zero cube. While the decision errors resulting from data integrity problems can be significant, the larger problem is that such errors substantially reduce the credibility of planning systems in general. A few highly visible errors such as overloading transportation vehicles or storage facilities cause management and planners to question the integrity of the entire planning system and process. The result is that management and operations personnel don't trust the results and prefer to return to the old tried and true methods of planning and scheduling. Thus, the potential for improved planning is reduced until the trust can be redeveloped. A strong focus on developing and maintaining data integrity is critical to effective planning system implementation.

Education regarding planning system application is a third major consideration. User training for supply chain execution and planning systems has usually focused on the mechanics to initiate the transactions. So, the user would be trained in data or parameter entry where the system would provide quick feedback regarding the acceptability of the entry. Supply chain planning systems are relatively more complex, as the feedback is not immediate and the impact may be extensive. For example, changing the requirements or forecast for one item in a time period may shift production schedules for related items on the other side of the world. Understanding planning system dynamics is critical to successful application. Such understanding requires thorough knowledge of APS system mechanics and system interactions. Although such knowledge can be initiated through training, it must be refined and extended through education and experience. Planning system education must focus on the characteristics and relationships between supply chain management activities and processes both internal and external to the firm. The education process must be much broader than existing training approaches. Planning system experience can be developed by using job shadowing experience and simulations. The shadowing environment provides actual on-the-job experience in a real-time environment. The simulated environment provides a laboratory where inexperienced planners can see or observe the results of their planning environment at low risk to the firm. The combination of these two educational experiences provides a solid foundation for implementing successful supply chain planning applications.

Pricing

Pricing is an important aspect of marketing strategy that directly impacts logistical operations. The terms and conditions of pricing determine which party has responsibility for performing logistics activities. A major trend in price strategy has been to **debundle** the price of products and materials so that services such as transportation, which were traditionally included in price, become separate and visible items. Pricing practices have a direct impact on the timing and stability of logistical operations. In this section, several basic pricing structures are reviewed, followed by a discussion of pricing impact areas. No attempt is made to review the broad range of economic and psychological issues related to price strategy. The focus is on the relationship between pricing and logistical operations.

Pricing Fundamentals

Pricing decisions directly determine which party in the transaction is responsible for performing logistics activities, passage of title, and liability. F.O.B. origin and delivered pricing are the two most common methods.

F.O.B. Pricing

The term **F.O.B.** technically means **free on board** or **freight on board.** A number of variations of FOB pricing are used in practice. **F.O.B. origin** is the simplest way to quote price.

FIGURE 11.6

Terms of Sales and Responsibilities

Source: Reprinted with permission from *The Purchasing Handbook*, McGraw-Hill Publishing Company.

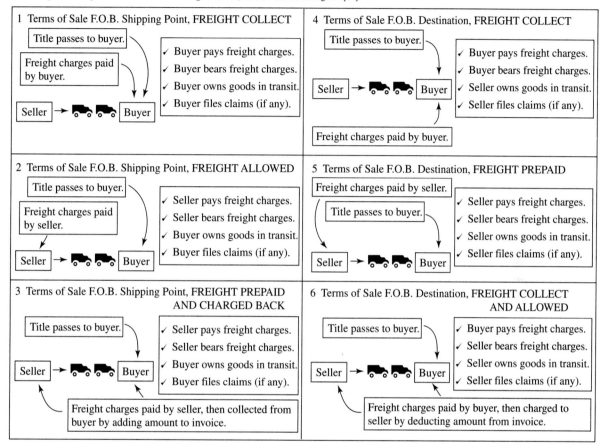

Under F.O.B. origin the seller indicates the price at point of origin and agrees to tender a shipment for transportation loading, but assumes no further responsibility. The buyer selects the mode of transportation, chooses a carrier, pays transportation charges, and takes risk of in-transit loss and/or damage. In **F.O.B. destination pricing,** title does not pass to the buyer until delivery is completed. Under F.O.B. destination pricing, the seller arranges for transportation and the charges are added to the sales invoice.

The range of terms and corresponding responsibilities for pricing are illustrated in Figure 11.6. Review of the various sales terms makes it clear that the firm paying the freight bill does not necessarily assume responsibility for ownership of goods in transit, for the freight burden, or for filing of freight claims. These are issues of negotiation that are critical to supply chain collaboration.

Delivered Pricing

The primary difference between F.O.B. and **delivered pricing** is that in delivered pricing the seller establishes a price that includes transportation. In other words, the transportation cost is not specified as a separate item. There are several variations of delivered pricing.

Under **single-zone delivered pricing,** buyers pay a single price regardless of where they are located. Delivered prices typically reflect the seller's average transportation cost.

In actual practice, some customers pay more than their fair share for transportation while others are subsidized. The United States Postal Service uses a single-zone pricing policy throughout the United States for first-class letters. The same fee or postage rate is charged for a given size and weight regardless of distance traveled to the destination.

Single-zone delivered pricing is typically used when transportation costs are a relatively small percentage of selling price. The main advantage to the seller is the high degree of logistical control. For the buyer, despite being based on averages, such pricing systems have the advantage of simplicity.

The practice of **multiple-zone pricing** establishes different prices for specific geographic areas. The underlying idea is that logistics cost differentials can be more fairly assigned when two or more zones—typically based on distance—are used to quote delivered pricing. Parcel carriers such as United Parcel Service use multiple-zone pricing.

The most complicated and controversial form of delivered pricing is the use of a **base-point pricing system** in which the final delivered price is determined by the product's list price plus transportation cost from a designated base point, usually the manufacturing location. This designated point is used for computing the delivered price whether or not the shipment actually originates from the base location. Base-point pricing is common in shipping assembled automobile from manufacturing plants to dealers.

Figure 11.7 illustrates how a base-point pricing system typically generates different net returns to a seller. The customer is quoted a delivered price of $100 per unit. Plant A is the base point. Actual transportation cost from plant A to the customer is $25 per unit. Plant A's base product price is $85 per unit. Transportation costs from plants B and C are $20 and $35 per unit, respectively.

When shipments are made from plant A, the company's net return is $75 per unit, the $100 delivered price minus the $25 transportation cost. The net return to the company varies if shipments are made from plant B or C. With a delivered price of $100, plant B collects $5 in **phantom freight** on shipments to a customer. Phantom freight occurs when a buyer pays transportation costs greater than those actually incurred to move the shipment. If plant C is the shipment origin, the company must absorb $10 of the transportation costs. **Freight absorption** occurs when a seller pays all or a portion of the actual transportation cost and does not recover the full expenditure from the buyer. In other words, the seller decides to absorb transportation cost to be competitive.

FIGURE 11.7
Base-Point Pricing

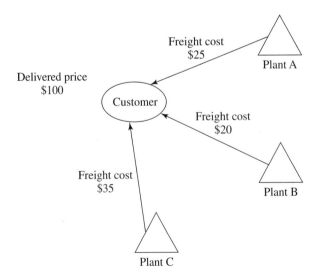

Base-point pricing simplifies price quotations but can have a negative impact on customers and supply chain collaboration. For example, dissatisfaction may result if customers discover they are being charged more for transportation than actual freight costs. Such pricing practices may also result in a large amount of freight absorption for sellers.

Pricing Issues

Pricing practices are also integral to logistics operations in at least four other ways: potential discrimination, quantity discounts, pickup allowances, and promotional pricing.

Potential Discrimination

The legality of transportation pricing is an important consideration and must be carefully reviewed and administered to protect against potential discrimination. The Clayton Act of 1914 as amended by the Robinson-Patman Act of 1936 prohibits price discrimination among buyers when the practices **substantially lessen competition.**

Zone pricing has the potential to be discriminatory because some buyers pay more than actual transportation cost while others pay less. Zone pricing systems are illegal when the net result is to charge different delivered prices for identical products to direct competitors. In recent years, determination of the legality of delivered zone pricing systems has centered around the issue of whether **a seller acts independently and not in collusion with competitors.** The Federal Trade Commission is unlikely to take action unless there is clear-cut evidence of such conspiracy.

In the past, selected base-point pricing has been found illegal under both the Robinson-Patman Act and the Federal Trade Commission Act. The concern is whether it results in direct competitors having differential margins. To avoid potential legal problems, a majority of firms use either F.O.B. or uniform delivered pricing policies. This strategy is generally preferable compared to defending average costing practices required in zone pricing or contending with the potential legal difficulties associated with base-point pricing. The following guidelines should be considered when establishing geographic pricing: First, a firm should not discriminate between competing buyers in the same region, especially in zone pricing for buyers on either side of a zonal boundary, because such action may violate the Robinson-Patman Act. Second, the firm's strategy should not appear to be predatory, especially in freight absorption pricing, because such a strategy would violate Section 2 of the Sherman Act. Third, in choosing the basing point or zone pricing, the firm should not attempt to fix prices among competitors because such action would violate Section 1 of the Sherman Act.

Quantity Discounts

Quantity discounts are offered by a firm as an inducement to increase order size or overall volume of business. To be nondiscriminatory, an identical discount structure must be available to all buyers. Under the Robinson-Patman Act, it is the responsibility of the seller to prove that the identical, noncumulative discounts are available to all qualified buyers. The quantity discount offered must be justifiable on the basis of direct cost saving.

The Robinson-Patman Act states that cost differences can be justified on the basis of savings in the manufacturing, delivery, or selling of goods. Quantity-related discounts based on reductions in manufacturing or selling cost are difficult to prove. Logistics-related savings are relatively easier to document since many are shipment-specific. Transportation and handling savings are often used to justify quantity discounts. Thus, lower transportation rates for volume shipments are common.

In contrast to noncumulative discounts, cumulative discounts—based on consecutive purchases over some specified time period—are more difficult to justify. Cumulative discounts, by the very nature of their calculation base, favor large-volume purchasers while discriminating against smaller buyers. However, price discrimination can be substantiated only when potential or real injury to competition is determined.

Pickup Allowances

Pickup allowances are equivalent to purchasing merchandise on an F.O.B. origin basis. Buyers are given a reduction from the standard delivered price if they or a representative picks up shipments at the seller's location and performs transportation. A buyer may also use a for-hire carrier or an ISP to perform merchandise pickup. In the food and grocery industry, which traditionally practiced delivered pricing, firms have realized significant savings by using private and for-hire carriers to pick up rather than purchase merchandise on a delivered basis.

While some confusion exists concerning how to best establish a pickup allowance, a safe rule is that a seller should provide the same allowance to all directly competitive buyers. A uniform pickup allowance is often the price incentive offered to the customer closest to the shipping point. Other common policies offer pickup allowances equivalent to the applicable common carrier rate for the shipment.

Pickup allowances offer potential benefits for both the seller and the buyer. Shippers are required to deal with fewer small shipments, thereby reducing the need for extensive outbound consolidation. Buyers gain control over the merchandise earlier and are in a position to achieve greater utilization of captive transportation equipment and drivers.

Promotional Pricing

An additional aspect of pricing that impacts logistical operations is the use of short-term promotions to provide purchase incentives. Firms that pursue aggressive promotional strategies have a choice of designing their budgets to encourage consumers, via coupons, or wholesalers and retailers, via trade allowances, to purchase their products. For example, Procter & Gamble has an annual advertising and promotional budget that exceeds $2 billion. Marketing management must allocate these funds between media advertising focused on consumers and a combination of coupons and trade promotions. Budget dollars allocated to trade promotion push the purchase of P&G products and cause two results. First, the logistics systems of Procter & Gamble and its customers must handle increased product volume just before, during, and oftentimes immediately after a promotional period. Second, trade promotion spending alters the effective price at which product is being sold. From a logistical perspective, the short-term increase in volume is of primary concern. Thus, while ultimate consumption may not demonstrate seasonal characteristics, logistical operations may have to deal with seasonal-like surges caused by promotional pushes.

The widespread practice of promotional pricing has traditionally been the way to provide trade purchase incentives. Manufacturers establish artificially high list prices with the expectation of reducing the effective price by trade promotion, consumer coupons, and product slotting allowances. Administration of regular price changes usually involves advanced notification to customers, creating the opportunity for them to **forward-buy.** This practice stimulates volume surges, which add excessive costs, and creates practices that in final analyses do not add value. Forward buying involves customers purchasing merchandise beyond their current needs to take advantage of lower prices. Sometimes these customers resell the extra product to others, while retaining some or all of the promotional allowance. This practice is known as **diverting.** In effect, a firm is profiting by taking advantage of purchase incentives available to customers in one area of the country but not others.

In an effort to stabilize promotional pricing, some firms have begun to develop collaborative programs. Manufacturers and retailers working together agree to **net prices** that are administered over a planned time horizon. The manufacturer and retailer jointly plan the promotion and advertising strategy for a product or merchandising category. A **dead net price** takes into account quantity purchase discounts, prompt payment discounts, and any other applicable price incentives. Finally, an agreement is reached concerning the duration of the negotiated price. These agreements also specify how performance will be measured during the operating period as a basis for future agreements.

The price negotiation framework described above has resulted in what is known as **EveryDay Low Pricing** (EDLP). Wal★Mart is generally credited with having created EDLP, the strategy around which it seeks to build customer loyalty. Other firms have developed EDLP strategies in collaboration with suppliers while following a promotional pricing in consumer merchandising.

Few firms operate at the extremes of either EDLP or promotional pricing; however, most creative merchandisers develop a combination approach to stimulate consumer purchasing. While price promotion is used to generate consumer traffic and encourage in-store impulse buying, few items are consistently sold as loss leaders, thereby reducing the risk of predatory pricing allegations.

In a more general sense, business in a free market society will and should engage in a wide variety of pricing and advertising activities. The challenge is to rationalize how such promotional efforts affect logistics. The timing and magnitude of promotional pricing need to be evaluated in terms of ability to consume and the capacity to efficiently handle volume surges. To a significant degree, **trade loading** practices result from end-of-period or end-of-year earnings pressures. This so-called Wall Street effect goes hand in hand with the use of promotional pricing to stimulate product flow so that sales can be booked during a specific time period. Such practices may offer short-term earnings relief but do little, if anything, to stimulate consumption. They are, however, guaranteed to increase logistics cost. Practices related to end-of-period and end-of-year sales loading are a primary target of Section 404 of the Sarbanes-Oxley (SOX) Act, discussed in Chapter 16.

Menu Pricing

From a seller's perspective, a pricing program must be established to accurately and equitably charge customers for the cost of products and services. Menu pricing is a technique used by many firms to accomplish this objective. An effective menu pricing system has three components: platform service price, value-added service specified costs, and efficiency incentives.

Platform Service Price

The first step in menu pricing is to establish the basic service platform to be offered to all customers and an appropriate price reflecting the costs related to providing that service level. The platform service price is expected to be paid by all customers, whether or not they require or desire the specified sources. For example, the basic platform service price might be established for the following service level: "Full trailer of mixed products in unit load quantities on slip sheet from a warehouse for customer unload." The pricing quoted for this combination of delivery specifications, quantity, configuration, and unload requirements is the basis from which any additional charges or discounts are considered. Certain standard discounts may also be quoted as part of the basic service platform. For example, traditional quantity discounts and customer pickup allowances are typically considered in the basic platform price.

Value-Added Service Costs

The second aspect of menu pricing involves specifying upcharges for performing customer requested value-added services. From the example above, an upcharge would be imposed for customized unit loading requested by a customer, such as layering products on the slip sheet in a specific order or configuring retail-ready unit loads. A separate upcharge would be established for multiple stop-offs during the delivery, and a third upcharge could be charged for using pallets rather than slip sheets. This approach results in each customer paying for the specific combination of services it desires. Table 9.1 provided a listing of typical value-added services for which shippers frequently establish upcharges in their menu pricing programs. Of course, shippers may choose to offer some of these services as part of their basic service platform, in which case their basic price should include the appropriate charges.

Efficiency Incentives

The third step in a comprehensive menu pricing program is the establishment of efficiency incentives. Such incentives may be offered to encourage customers to comply with specified practices that reduce logistics costs. The incentives provide a mechanism for each of the parties to share in the benefits of such cost-reducing efforts. For example, a discount or allowance might be given to encourage EDI ordering, another incentive offered to receivers who guarantee unloading trucks in 2 hours or less, and a third incentive for using specified pallets.

To introduce costing precision into menu pricing, some industry leaders have begun using **activity-based costing** to help quantify the combined total cost impact of either the buying or selling organization performing a specific task. Armed with precise costs related to performing each aspect of the transaction, both parties are able to quantify value and cost benefits. The result is a **cost-to-serve** model, which in effect quantifies menu pricing.

Summary

Operational integration is a managerial challenge at the level of individual enterprises, across domestic supply chains, and for the conduct of international business. Operational integration creates value as a result of coordinated cross-functional efficiency. The application of systems analysis and assessment of total cost provides a methodology to integrate functions into a productive process. Integrated processes offer distinct cost and service benefits.

At the individual firm level operational integration is difficult. Barriers exist and serve as obstacles to internal operational integration. This resistance to integration can be traced to long-standing functional management practices and related information systems and reward practices. Conventional measurement practices and metrics serve to reinforce functionalism. The resistance to process integration is strong and can be universally observed. The commonly observed phenomenon referred to as the great divide reflects the common difficulty in achieving enterprise end-to-end integration.

The paradox is that many firms successfully integrate with customers and/or suppliers. Thus, firms often integrate more outside their specific enterprise than they do internally. This means that many attempts at extending the enterprise across the supply chain are, at best, partial solutions. However, many such limited supply chain engagements appear to be valuable arrangements for their participants. It remains unclear just how much internal integration is necessary for a firm to be a viable supply chain participant. Of course, the risk is that failure to achieve internal operational integration may cause a firm to be unable to meet supply chain commitments.

The reason that partial supply chain integration achieves value is directly related to the significant potential to reduce waste, duplication, and operational redundancy. In particular, collaboration offers ways to reduce inventory investments and related risk for participating firms. Successful supply chain integration requires cross-organizational programs to facilitate operations, technology and planning, and relationship management collaboration. While few, if any, across-the-supply-chain collaborations exist today, the potential benefits of such holistic integration are staggering.

Challenge Questions

1. Compare and contrast economic, market, and relevancy value.

2. Illustrate the differences in product/service creation, presentation, and positioning.

3. Explain the following statement: "The methodology is systems analysis and the theoretical framework is the systems concept."

4. Why is variance reduction important to logistical integration? Illustrate in terms of logistical operations.

5. What is the meaning of the phrase *cradle-to-cradle* logistics? Discuss the operational differences of original versus reverse logistics.

6. How do reward systems serve as barriers to enterprise integration?

7. In your words, describe and illustrate the *great divide.* Do you believe the great divide phenomenon is as widely experienced as the text indicates? Support your position with an illustration.

8. Discuss the major supply chain planning applications with particular focus on the role and anticipated benefits for each application.

9. Compare and contrast the focus of business, marketing, and operations planning. How does S&OP mediate some of the conflict?

10. What is a shipper's responsibility when terms of purchase are F.O.B. origin? F.O.B. destination? Why would a shipper prefer one over the other?

PART THREE

Supply Chain Logistics Design

One of the two primary responsibilities of a firm's logistics management, as established in Chapters 1 and 2, is to participate in supply chain logistics design. Part 3 contains three chapters devoted to various logistics design issues. Chapter 12 establishes the global perspective of today's business operations. Few companies enjoy the simplicity of conducting business within a single nation. The complexity of globalization has increased as a result of extended territory. Given the dynamic nature of contemporary business, it is not unusual for managers to conduct continuous evaluations of their logistics support structure. Chapter 13 focuses on network integration. An integrative model is developed and illustrated that combines the temporal and spatial dimensions of logistics into a single theoretical framework. The integration structure provides the basis for process development, trade-off quantification, and integrative measurement. In Chapter 14, the theoretical framework is operationalized in terms of methodology and technique to guide logistical systems design. A step-by-step design process provides a guide to deal with channel structure and strategy design and implementation. Chapter 14 also presents an overview of operational planning and analysis tools to assist managers in dealing with logistics operations.

Global Strategic Positioning

Globalization offers many opportunities and challenges for logistics and supply chain operations and strategies. The opportunities include increasing markets and a wider range of manufacturing alternatives with varying absolute and comparative human and material resource advantages. Some regions of the world can provide significant economies of scale because of their competitive wage scales, while other regions offer significant flexibility because of their expertise. The challenges related to taking advantage of these benefits include more demanding logistics operating environments, security considerations, and more complex total cost analyses. Chapter 12 discusses the stages of global supply chain integrations, the need for and the challenges of global security, and concludes with guidelines for making global sourcing decisions.

Global Supply Chain Integration

Whereas an effective logistics system is important for domestic supply chain integration, it is absolutely essential for successful global manufacturing and marketing. Domestic logistics focuses on performing movement and storage activities to support supply chain integration in a relatively controlled environment. Global logistics must support operations in a variety of different national, political, and economic settings while also dealing with increased uncertainty associated with the distance, demand, diversity, and documentation of international commerce.

The operating challenges of global logistics systems vary significantly in each major global region. The North American logistics challenge is one of an open geography with extensive and flexible transportation options and limited need for cross-border documentation. The European logistician, in contrast, is confronted by relatively compact geography involving numerous political, cultural, regulatory, and language situations. The European infrastructure is also quite congested because of population density and the fact that many of the roads date back centuries. The Pacific Rim logistical challenge is island-based, requiring extensive water and air shipment to transcend vast distances. These different characteristics require that firms having global operations develop and maintain a wide variety of capabilities and expertise.

In the past, an enterprise could survive by operating with unique North American, European, or Pacific Rim business strategies. While it was easier to create and operate unique regional strategies, the resulting duplication often resulted in loss of economies of scale and poor asset utilization. While regionalization remains viable for some firms, those desiring to grow and prosper must face the challenges of globalization. Strategic business initiatives must change as a firm and its supply chain become progressively more global.

Logistics in a Global Economy

Global operations increase logistics cost and complexity. Estimated 2002 logistics cost for industrialized nations exceeded $6.7 trillion, or 13.8 percent of estimated global Gross Domestic Product (GDP). Table 12.1 lists GDP and estimated logistics cost by country. In

TABLE 12.1
Estimated 2002 National Logistical Expenditures

Source: Reprinted with permission from Alexandre M. Rodrigues, Donald J. Bowersox, and Roger J. Calantone "Estimation of Global Logistics Expenditures: Current Update," from *Journal of Business Logistics,* Vol. 26, no. 2, 2005, pp. 1–16.

Region	Country	GDP (U.S.$ billion)	Logistics (U.S.$ billion)	Logistics (% GDP)
North America	Canada	925	110	11.9%
	Mexico	905	136	15.0%
	United States	10,308	957	9.3%
	Region	12,137	1,203	9.9%
Europe	Belgium	285	35	12.1%
	Denmark	166	23	13.6%
	France	1,601	186	11.6%
	Germany	2,236	374	16.7%
	Greece	199	26	13.0%
	Ireland	143	21	14.9%
	Italy	1,525	186	12.2%
	Netherlands	470	56	11.8%
	Portugal	186	25	13.4%
	Spain	878	124	14.1%
	United Kingdom	1,549	174	11.3%
	Region	9,238	1,229	13.3%
Pacific Rim	China	5,861	1,052	17.9%
	India	2,800	487	17.4%
	Hong Kong, China	183	24	13.2%
	Japan	3,425	390	11.4%
	Korea, Rep.	807	102	12.7%
	Singapore	100	14	14.3%
	Taiwan, China	406	57	14.1%
	Region	13,582	2,127	15.7%
South America	Brazil	1,355	204	15.0%
	Venezuela, RB	135	16	12.0%
	Argentina	413	52	12.6%
	Region	1,903	272	14.3%
Remaining other countries		11,912	1,902	16.0%
Total		48,771	6,732	13.8%

terms of complexity, global operations, in contrast to domestic operations, are characterized by increased uncertainty, increased variability, decreased control, and decreased visibility. Uncertainty results from greater distances, longer lead times, and decreased market knowledge. Increased variation results from unique customer and documentation requirements. Decreased control results from the extensive use of international service firms coupled with potential government intervention in such areas as customs requirements and trade restrictions. Decreased visibility results from longer transit and holding times with less ability to track and determine exactly where shipments are located.

These unique challenges complicate development of an efficient and effective global supply chain strategy. Fortunately, there are forces that both drive and facilitate globalization and necessitate borderless logistics operations.

Stages of International Development

The continuum of global trade development ranges from export/import to local presence to the concept of a stateless enterprise. The following discussion describes conceptual and managerial implications of strategic development. Table 12.2 lists the product, marketing, supply chain, management, information technology, and human resource strategies characteristic for each stage of globalization.

Export/Import: A National Perspective

The initial stage of international trade is characterized by exporting and importing. A participating organization typically is focused on its domestic operations and views international transactions in terms of supporting domestic business. Specifically, a firm uses an export/import strategy to increase the revenues or decrease costs associated with a domestic

TABLE 12.2 Differential Characteristics of Global Development

Three Stages of Development	Product Focus	Marketing Strategy	Supply Chain Strategy	Management	Information and Decision Support	Human Resource Development
Export/import	Domestic production and distribution	Specific customers	Agents and third-party logistics service providers	Transaction driven with integrated financials	Home country focused with limited EDI	Management with "home country" focus and limited international experience
International operations: local presence	Local market customization supported by postponement or local production	Focused specific market areas, which may cross national boundaries	Subsidiaries and local distributors with specific business charters and visible local presence	Decentralized management of local operators and strategic alliances with local profit responsibility	Independent database and decision support	Limited top management with international experience and strong "home country" decision focus
Globalization	Global brands	All economic regions	Worldwide flow of key resources to leverage global sourcing and marketing advantages	Centralized planning with locally flexible distribution supported with common systems	Integrated database and decision support	International training and experience required for all upper level management with some requirements for midlevel management

operation. As Table 12.2 indicates, an export/import strategy typically involves a standardized product manufactured in the firm's home country, focused on a limited customer base, with logistics services required for export/import provided by specialized integrated service providers (ISPs). The business context is transaction driven, with the common financial statements providing the only level of integration.

A national export/import business orientation influences logistical decisions in three ways. First, sourcing and resource choices are influenced by artificial constraints. These constraints are typically in the form of use restrictions, local content laws, or price surcharges. A **use restriction** is a limitation, usually government imposed, that restricts the level of import sales or purchase. For example, the enterprise may require that internal divisions be used for material sources even though prices or quality are not competitive. **Local content laws** specify the proportion of a product that must be sourced within the local economy. **Price surcharges** involve higher charges for foreign-sourced product imposed by governments to maintain the viability of local suppliers. In combination, use restrictions, local content laws, and price surcharges limit management's ability to select what otherwise would be the preferred supplier.

Second, logistics to support export/import operations increases planning complexity. A fundamental logistics objective is smooth product flow to facilitate efficient capacity utilization. This objective is sometimes difficult in an export/import operation because of uncertainty and government constraints.

Third, an export/import strategy extends domestic logistics systems and operating practices to global origins and destinations. While an export/import strategy doesn't introduce much complexity into domestic operations, it will likely increase operational complexity, since exceptions are numerous. Local managers must accommodate exceptions while remaining within corporate policy and procedure guidelines. For example, while bribery is both an illegal and unethical practice in most developed countries, such "facilitating" payments may be the only means of getting product moved or cleared through customs in developing countries. As a result, foreign-based logistics management must often accommodate local, cultural, language, employment, and political environments without full understanding at corporate headquarters.

International Operations: Local Presence

The second stage of international development is characterized by establishment of operations in a foreign country. Internal operations may include varied combinations of marketing, sales, production, and logistics. Establishment of local facilities and operations serves to increase market awareness and sensitivity. This is often referred to as establishing **local presence.** The local presence strategy uses local production and distribution often supported by a postponement strategy to customize products. Firms engaged in local presence often restrict their operations to a limited number of geographic areas. At the outset of a local presence strategy, foreign operations will often depend on parent company management and personnel, values; procedures, and operations. However, over time, business units operating within a foreign market area will have to adopt local business practices.

This adoption typically means developing unique management, marketing, and sales organizations and may include the use of local business systems. As local presence operations expand, the host country philosophy will increasingly emerge; however, the company headquarters' strategic vision remains dominant. Individual country operations are still measured against home country expectations and standards.

Globalization: The Stateless Enterprise

The stateless enterprise contrasts sharply to operations guided by either an export/import or international perspective. The original concept of the stateless enterprise was popularized in a *Business Week* article well over a decade ago. The article described stateless enterprises as those with senior management that effectively makes decisions with little or no regard to national boundaries.[1]

Stateless enterprises maintain regional operations and develop a headquarters structure to coordinate across area operations. Thus, the enterprise is stateless in the sense that no specific home or parent country dominates policy. Senior management likely represents a combination of nationalities. Denationalized operations function on the basis of local marketing, and sales initiatives and are typically supported by world-class manufacturing and logistics operations. Product sourcing and marketing decisions can be made across a wide range of geographical alternatives. Systems and procedures are designed to meet individual country requirements and are aggregated as necessary to share knowledge and for financial reporting. A truly global firm employs global brands with limited customization to reflect market sensitivities, operates in most global regions, employs a global resource view in terms of production and logistics, and incorporates integrated reporting systems and planning technologies to achieve global operating synergies.

Consider, for example, an enterprise that has its historical origin in Germany, Japan, or the United States, but with a high percentage of its sales, ownership, and assets maintained and managed in China. China is estimated to be the world's third largest economy, but there are many supply chain aspects, such as logistics capabilities and infrastructure that are still quite third-world. China's communications, intermodal transport systems, tracking and tracing, and limited highways outside major cities make it very difficult to employ 21st-century supply chain operating practices. For these reasons, a stateless enterprise operating in China needs a combination of local management to facilitate local operations and enterprise management that fully understands the implications of developing business systems, a rapid rate of change, and exploding but unbalanced export/import volume.

Examples of firms that fit the specification of stateless enterprises are ABB (Switzerland), Coca Cola (United States), Dow Chemical (United States), Hoechst (Germany), IBM (United States), ICI (Britain), Johnson & Johnson (United States), Nestlé (Switzerland), Novartis (Switzerland), and Philips (Netherlands). These firms are characterized by a combination of global brands produced and marketed globally with integrated systems and management that can synthesize global operations while being sensitive to regional and local considerations.

While most enterprises engaged in international business are operating in stages 1 and 2, to become a global player, a truly international firm must migrate toward global marketing and operations. Such globalization requires a significant level of management trust that transcends countries and cultures. Such trust can grow only as managers increasingly live and work across cultures.

Managing the Global Supply Chain

To meet the challenges discussed above, logistics management must consider five major differences between domestic and international operations: (1) performance cycle structure, (2) transportation, (3) operational considerations, (4) information systems integration, and (5) alliances. These considerations must then be incorporated into the firm's global operating strategy.

Performance Cycle Structure

The length of the performance cycle is a major difference between domestic and global operations. Instead of 1- to 5-day transit times and 2- to 10-day total performance cycles,

---

[1] "The Stateless Corporation," *Business Week,* May 14, 1990, p. 98.

global operational cycles often require weeks or months. For example, it is common for automotive parts from Pacific Rim suppliers to take 60 days from order release until physical delivery at a U.S. manufacturing facility. Similarly, fashion merchandise may take anywhere from 30 to 60 days from the time the manufacturer order is released until it is received at a U.S. distribution warehouse.

The reasons leading to a longer order cycle to delivery cycle are communication delays, financing requirements, special packaging requirements, ocean freight scheduling, slow transit times, and customs clearance. Communication may be delayed by time zone and language differences. Financing delays are caused by the requirements for letters of credit and currency translations. Special packaging may be required to protect products from in-transit damage due to high humidity, temperature, and weather conditions. Once a product is containerized, it must be scheduled for movement to and between ports having appropriate handling capabilities. This scheduling process can require up to 30 days if the origin and destination ports are not located on high-volume traffic lanes or the ships moving to the desired port lack the necessary equipment. Transit time, once the ship is en route, ranges from 10 to 21 days. Port delays are common as ships wait for others to clear harbor facilities. Customs clearance may further extend total time. Although it is increasingly common to utilize electronic messaging to preclear product shipments through customs prior to arrival at international ports, the elapsed performance cycle time is still lengthy. Special security issues, described later in this chapter, can create additional delays. Another problem is restricted availability of containers. Movement from Asia to the United States is generally unbalanced as more material is imported into the United States than is exported to Asia. As a result, there is strong demand for containers to move product from Asia to the United States but little motivation to ship the empty containers back. This demonstrates how unbalanced trade, either domestically or internationally, can introduce complexity into logistics operations.

These factors cause international logistics performance cycles to be longer, less consistent, and less flexible than typical in domestic operations. This lack of consistency increases planning difficulty. It is more difficult to determine shipment status and to anticipate arrival times. The longer performance cycle also results in higher asset commitment because significant inventory is in transit at any point in time.

Transportation

The U.S. initiative to deregulate transportation during the early 1980s has extended globally. Three significant global changes have occurred: (1) intermodal ownership and operation, (2) privatization, and (3) cabotage and bilateral agreements.

Historically, there have been regulatory restrictions regarding international transportation ownership and operating rights. Transport carriers were limited to operating within a single transportation mode with few, if any, joint pricing and operating agreements. Traditionally, steamship lines could not own or manage integrated land-based operations such as motor or rail carriers. Without joint ownership, operations, and pricing agreements, the performance of international shipping was complicated. International shipments typically required multiple carriers to perform a single freight movement. Specifically, government rather than market forces determined the extent of services foreign-owned carriers could perform. Although some ownership and operating restrictions remain, marketing and alliance arrangements among countries have substantially improved transportation flexibility. The removal of multimodal ownership restrictions in the United States and in most other industrialized nations served to facilitate integrated movement. In response to some of these changes in national ownership requirements, an increasing number of global service providers have been established such as DeutschePost, FedEx, TNT, and United Parcel Service.

A second transportation influence on global operations is increased carrier privatization. Historically, many international carriers were owned and operated by national governments in an effort to promote trade and provide national security. Government-owned carriers are typically subsidized and often place surcharges on foreign enterprises that use these services. Artificially high pricing and poor service often made it costly and unreliable to ship via such government-owned carriers. Inefficiencies also resulted from strong unionization and work rules. The combination of high operating cost and low efficiency caused many government-owned carriers to operate at a loss. A great many such carriers have been privatized and must operate in a competitive environment. Carrier privatization has resulted in increased availability of efficient international carriers.

Changes in cabotage and bilateral service agreements are the third transportation influence impacting international trade. Cabotage laws require passengers or goods moving between two domestic ports to utilize only domestic carriers. For example, water shipment from Los Angeles to New York was required to use a U.S. carrier. Similar cabotage laws restricted Canadian drivers from transporting a backhaul load to Detroit once a shipment originating in Canada was unloaded in Texas. Cabotage laws were designed to protect domestic transportation industries even though they also served to reduce overall transportation equipment utilization and related efficiency. The European Community has relaxed cabotage restrictions to increase trade efficiency. Such reduced cabotage restrictions will save U.S. corporations 10 to 15 percent in intra-European shipping costs. While the U.S. has not rescinded its cabotage laws relating to Canada and Mexico, some of the restrictions have been reduced to enhance equipment utilization and to reduce the environmental impact.

Operational Considerations

There are a number of unique operational considerations in a global environment. First, international operations typically require multiple languages for both product and documentation. A technical product such as a computer or a calculator must have local features such as keyboard characters and language on both the product itself and related manuals. From a logistics perspective, language differences dramatically increase complexity since a product is limited to a specific country once it is language-customized. For example, even though Western Europe is much smaller than the United States in a geographic sense, it requires relatively more inventory to support marketing efforts since separate inventories may be required to accommodate various languages. Although product proliferation due to language requirement has been reduced through multilingual packaging and postponement strategies, such practices are not always acceptable. Some consumers are reluctant to accept products not labeled in their native tongue. In addition to product language implications, international operations may require multilingual documentation for each country through which the shipment passes. Although English is the general language of commerce, some countries require that transportation and customs documentation be provided in the local language. This increases the time and effort for international operations, since complex documents must be translated prior to shipment. These communication and documentation difficulties can be somewhat overcome through standardized electronic transactions.

The second global operational consideration is unique national accommodations such as performance features, technical characteristics, environmental considerations, and safety requirements. Performance feature differences include specific product functionality such as speed or process constraints. Technical characteristics include power supplies, documentation, and metrics. Environmental considerations include chemicals that can be used or the types and amount of waste generated. Safety requirements include automatic shutoffs and specialized documentation. While they may not be substantial, the small differences between country requirements may significantly increase required SKUs and subsequent inventory levels.

TABLE 12.3
**Common Forms
of International
Logistics
Documentation**

- *Export irrevocable commercial letter of credit.* A contract between an importer and a bank that transfers liability or paying the exporter from the importer to the (supposedly more creditworthy) importer's bank.
- *Bank draft (or bill of exchange).* A means of payment for an import/export transaction. Two types exist: transaction payable on sight with proper documents (*sight draft*), and transaction payable at some fixed time after acceptance of proper documents (*time draft*). Either type of draft accompanied by instructions and other documents (*but no letter of credit*) is a documentary draft.
- *Bill of lading.* Issued by the shipping company or its agent as evidence of a contract for shipping the merchandise and as a claim to ownership of the goods.
- *Combined transport document.* May replace the bill of lading if goods are shipped by air (*airway bill*) or by more than one mode of transportation.
- *Commercial invoice.* A document written by the exporter to precisely describe the goods and the terms of sale (similar to a shipping invoice used in domestic shipments).
- *Insurance certificate.* Explains what type of coverage is utilized (fire, theft, water), the name of the insurer, and the exporter whose property is being insured.
- *Certificate of origin.* Denotes the country in which the goods were produced to assess tariffs and other government-imposed restrictions on trade.

The third operating consideration is the sheer amount of documentation required for international operations. While domestic operations can generally be completed by using only an invoice and bill of lading, international operations require substantial documentation regarding order contents, transportation, financing, and government control. Table 12.3 lists and describes common forms of international documentation.

The fourth operating consideration is the high incidence of countertrade and duty drawback found in some international situations. While most established firms prefer cash transactions, countertrade is important. Countertrade, in essence, is when a seller agrees to accept products as payment or purchase products from the buyer as part of a sales agreement. While such agreements have financial consequences, they also have major implications for logistics and marketing in terms of disposal of goods received as payment. Duty drawback describes situations when a firm pays a duty to import goods into a foreign country but the duty paid can be drawn back or returned if the items or a comparable designate are exported. For example, Pepsi supplies syrup to the Soviet government, which bottles and markets the soft drink with practically no control from Pepsi. In return, Pepsi is paid for the syrup by receiving exclusive rights to distribute Russian Stolichnaya vodka in the United States. This exclusive right requires marketing and logistics support.

Information Systems Integration

A major challenge in globalization is information systems integration. Since firms typically globalize by acquisition and merger, the integration of systems typically lags. Operational integration requires the ability to route orders and manage inventory requirements electronically throughout the world. Development of supportive technology integration represents substantial capital investment. The overall process was significantly facilitated by the global initiative to achieve Y2K compliance. As discussed in Chapter 5, two types of system integration are required to support global operations. The first is a global transaction or ERP system. The global ERP system is necessary to provide common data regarding global customers, suppliers, products, and financials. It is also necessary to provide common and consistent information regarding order and inventory status regardless of the location from which a global customer is inquiring or where the shipment is to be delivered. The second system integration requirement is a global planning system that can maximize overall manufacturing and delivery asset utilization while meeting customer service requirements. Few firms have fully integrated global information systems or capability.

Alliances

A final international operations consideration is the growing importance of third-party alliances. While alliances with carriers and specialized service suppliers are important in domestic operations, they are essential in international commerce. Without alliances, it would be necessary for an enterprise operating internationally to maintain contacts with retailers, wholesalers, manufacturers, suppliers, and service providers throughout the world. International alliances provide market access and expertise and reduce the inherent risk of global operations. The number of alternatives and the complexity of globalization require alliances.

In summary, globalization is an evolving frontier that is increasingly demanding supply chain integration. As firms expand their focus toward international markets, demand for logistical competency increases because of longer supply chains, more variation, increased uncertainty, and more documentation. While the forces of change push toward borderless operations, supply chain logistics management still confronts market, financial, and channel barriers. The barriers are exemplified by distance, demand, diversity, and documentation. The challenge is to position an enterprise to take advantage of the benefits of global marketing and manufacturing by developing world-spanning logistical competency.

Supply Chain Security[2]

As a result of the terrorist attacks of September 11, 2001, supply chain risk and security are two topics that logistics managers are increasingly concerned with. Supply chain risk management focuses on minimizing the impact of supplier operational difficulties, business failures, and unplanned production stoppages on firm operations. Managers must be concerned not only about their specific suppliers, but performance throughout their extended supply chain. This process, which is termed **business continuity planning,** must identify and evaluate suppliers with respect to their potential for failure and the risk implications for the firm. When there is substantial risk, management should take action to mitigate the risk through increased control of the supplier or identification of alternative suppliers. Mitigating supply base risk is typically the direct responsibility of procurement.

Supply chain security is the application of policies, procedures, and technology to protect assets, product, facilities, equipment, information, and personnel from theft, damage, or terrorism and to prevent the introduction of unauthorized contraband, people, or weapons of mass destruction. The supply chain security challenges posed by the threat of terrorism have significant implications for firms, suppliers, customers, carriers, terminal operators, governments, and global trading partners. Indeed, the global economy is dependent on supply chain security and resiliency. While supply chain security was defined previously, supply chain **resiliency** refers to a supply chain's ability to withstand and recover from an incident. A resilient supply chain is proactive in anticipating and establishing planned steps to prevent and respond to security incidents. Resilient supply chains quickly rebuild or reestablish alternative means of operations when they experience a security incident.

For firms, it is no longer adequate to focus on internal security procedures geared toward the prevention of theft and emergency planning for unplanned incidents at plants and warehouses. Today's managers must think and plan beyond the four walls of their facilities. The challenge of supply chain security extends beyond theft prevention to the threat of terrorism

---

[2] This section is developed from material in David J. Closs and Edmund F. McGarrell, "Enhancing Supply Chain Security" (Washington: IBM Center for the Business of Government), April 2004.

and requires the integration of security with many other enforcement units. Thus, cross-functional teams including representation from logistics, production control, procurement, tax, customs, security, government relations, internal controls, and human resources are needed to develop and implement comprehensive supply chain security initiatives and processes. Firms must not only be concerned about security procedures within their own operations and those of first-tier suppliers and shipment destinations. They also need to be concerned about the security throughout the entire supply chain.

While the need to protect a firm's customers and employees from terrorist incidents is obvious, there are other reasons that supply chain management must place a strong emphasis on ensuring security. First, a supply chain security failure can temporarily or permanently damage a firm's brand. Even the accidental importation of beef infected with **mad cow disease** from Canada had a significant negative impact on the firms involved.[3] If a firm does not take appropriate actions to ensure supply chain security, executives may be charged with the legal liability for failure to protect the firm's assets. Second, a supply chain security failure may result in serious economic impact to a region or an industry. The closure of the borders following September 11, 2001, resulted in a number of plant closures, which decreased economic activity and employment. Similarly, the mad cow disease incident resulted in an extended decline in the Washington state beef industry.

Given the global nature of supply chains, firms are similarly dependent on the procedures, laws, and regulations that may be unique in different countries across the globe. Decisions regarding suppliers are likely to increasingly depend on the trusted partner status of the supplier's firm and country. Specifically, have supply chain partners and service providers demonstrated that they can be trusted to ensure the security of product when it is within their control? Finally, supply chain managers must engage in self-appraisal of supply chain security and contingency planning, and cross-functional teams must develop crisis management plans that include planning, mitigation, detection, response, and recovery components.

In order to promote economic growth and increase international trade, governments are responsible to facilitate the movement of people and goods across borders and are ultimately responsible for the safety of people, country, and commerce. For government agencies, the traditional focus has been on the control of trade, insuring the collection of taxes and fees, restricting the flow of illegal items, with sampling inspection of imports for security.[4] The contemporary focus, however, is shifting to trade facilitation with security facilitated in earlier supply chain operations by identifying trusted partners to increase security through export inspection and information trails. The very notion of trusted partners, however, creates the need for global cooperation.

The United States and many of its trading partners have responded to the threat of terrorism by initiating efforts to build security and facilitate trade. Congress mandated that the Department of Homeland Security (DHS) Directorate of Border and Transportation Security ensure the speedy, orderly, and efficient flow of lawful traffic and commerce. United States Customs and Border Protection, now part of DHS, has attempted to facilitate trade and increase security through the Customs Trade Partnership against Terrorism (C-TPAT), Container Security Initiative (CSI), and related programs.[5] C-TPAT seeks to advance-certify selected shippers through self-appraisals of security procedures coupled with customs audits and verifications. CSI calls for prescreening of containers coupled with fast tracking when the cargo reaches the United States. The Advanced Manifest Rule (AMR)

---

[3] For a more detailed discussion, see http://www.cnn.com/2003/US/12/23/mad.cow/index.html.

[4] The level of control of imports and exports of course varies with the movement of certain tightly controlled technologies.

[5] For a more detailed and current discussion regarding these initiatives to enhance supply chain security, see the U.S. Department of Homeland Security website at www.dhs.gov.

and more recent Advance Cargo Information (ACI) require detailed cargo data before the cargo is brought into or shipped from the United States by ocean, air, rail, or truck.[6] The Free and Secure Trade (FAST) program allows low-risk goods transported by trusted carriers for trusted firms to pass rapidly through border crossings while reserving inspection resources for unknown or high-risk shipments. These provisions all require international cooperation. The next evolution in these developments will be to utilize technology to enhance the detection of tampering, increase tracking efficiency and effectiveness, and extend the scope of "trusted partners" to increase efficiency at a greater number of shipping locations.

These global efforts are not confined to initiatives of the U.S. government. The World Trade Organization (WTO) also seeks to facilitate trade by moving controls and inspection to the export stage by sharing uniform information among government agencies, firms, suppliers, carriers, and customers. The World Customs Organization (WCO), including the 161 member countries involved in the Global Standards for Supply Chain Security initiative, similarly seeks to promote trade facilitation by developing and promoting guidelines to help customs administrations work together to promote rapid clearance of low risk cross-border shipments.

The U.S. Customs programs as well as the efforts of the WTO and WCO have broadened customs verification processes to include exports, relying on declarations that include essential data for adequate cargo risk assessment. The data include commodity description, price, origin and destination, shipper and consignee, and transportation provider to be used by certifying manufacturers, carriers, and other entities. The International Organization for Standardization (ISO) is working with Strategic Council on Security Technology on a Smart and Secure Tradelanes (SST) initiative. SST is developing a technology platform to track containers globally and generate chain-of-custody audit trails.

The goal is to create global data exchange that allows all members of a supply chain to work together, creating an environment somewhat similar to that of the quality initiative collaboration of the early 1990s. At that time, consumers were demanding substantially increased product and service quality. The result was a strong organizational focus on efforts to increase product and process quality. While firms initially felt that they could increase prices to cover the cost of quality improvements, the market quickly responded that it was necessary to increase quality, but without corresponding price increases. In fact, many firms found it was possible to increase quality while reducing cost. Similarly, it is important to note that enhanced supply chain security is expected with no increase in cost. Thus, the challenge today is to review, refine, and extend existing supply chain logistics practices to provide the desired security controls while simultaneously maintaining costs.

Firms, governments, and governmental associations are only some of the institutional components of the supply chain security. The loss of a key supplier can critically disrupt a supply chain, and firms are dependent on the security procedures of suppliers in order to ensure their own security and to maintain trusted partner status with government agencies. Customers are obviously the end point of the supply chain, and thus firms are ultimately dependent on their satisfaction. Customers are also important in the sense that the information needed to allow auditing of cargo movement from supplier to customer must extend to customer operations. Food and product recalls linked to imminent danger are perhaps the best examples of this requirement.

Carriers, freight forwarders, port authorities, and terminal operators each have responsibilities for critical stages in the origin to destination supply chain process. The best

---

[6] The AMR applies to sea cargo. The Advance Electronic Presentation of Cargo Information encompasses ocean, air, rail, and truck. Similar requirements were imposed by Israel in November 2003 and will soon be enacted in India for ocean and air shipments.

procedures of a trusted trading partner are meaningless unless supported by effective carrier security procedures to secure goods while in transit. In addition to being key points for inspection, port facilities are potential targets for terrorists seeking to disrupt the supply chain either through attacks on the facility or as infiltration points for cargo tampering. Consequently, the entire supply chain is dependent on the security procedures such as access control, personnel screening, physical four-wall security, and emergency preparedness of port authorities and carriers and for effective security.

Supply chain security requires that logistics management work cross-functionally with security, quality, legal, and customs personnel. The combined team must be focused not only on theft and asset protection but also on preventing the use of shipments for the conveyance of contraband and weapons of mass destruction. The inadvertent shipment of such contraband poses threats not only to the firm but also to global trade generally. Attention must be directed to the entire supply chain, and all of these efforts, whether examined at the firm level or that of international government associations, require public-private communication, cooperation, and collaboration.

International Sourcing

One of the major challenges of business today having specific impact on logistical management is the dramatic increase in international sourcing, particularly from low-cost countries such as China and Malaysia. Firms in virtually all durable goods industries are investigating Asia, Eastern Europe, Latin America, and Africa as potential sources for finished goods or, at least, component parts. This section reviews the rationale for international sourcing from low-cost countries, identifies some of the challenges, and offers some guidelines regarding sourcing strategy.

Rationale for Low-Cost-Country Sourcing

Increased need for global competitiveness is driving many firms, particularly those in durable and fashion industries, to identify and establish relationships with suppliers in low-cost countries. There are a number of justifications for such sourcing initiatives. First, sourcing from countries with low wage rates typically reduces manufacturing cost. While such strategies may reduce manufacturing cost, some firms have not considered the total cost impact of international sourcing particularly with respect to the logistics cost components of transportation and inventory. Second, seeking out suppliers in low-cost countries can also increase the number of possible sources and thus increase the competitive pressure on domestic suppliers. Third, low-cost-country sourcing can increase the firm's exposure to state-of-the-art product and process technologies. Without pressure from global suppliers, there may be reluctance on the part of domestic suppliers to investigate or invest in new technologies because they have significant assets tied up in older technologies. Conversely, global suppliers may place significant focus on new technologies to establish a competitive position in foreign markets even given the issues discussed earlier regarding extended supply chains. A final rationale for low-cost-country sourcing is to establish a local presence to facilitate sales in the international country. For example, while the U.S. automobile industry is significantly increasing sourcing from low-cost countries to reduce component cost, it is also seeking to facilitate automobile sales in the local country. Because of political or legal constraints, it is often necessary for a firm to have local relationships and production operations to be allowed to sell their product in the local country. The combination of these make a strong case for sourcing from a low-cost country, but it is necessary to also consider the challenges.

Challenges for Low-Cost-Country Sourcing

While the rationale for low-cost-import sourcing is substantial, there is also a long list of issues and challenges related to such sourcing strategies. These issues and challenges are further complicated by the fact that the benefits and costs related to low-cost-country sourcing accrue to different organizational units. Procurement or manufacturing may receive the benefits through lower-cost materials or components. Many of the costs and the challenges to ship and guarantee delivery of the materials are the responsibility of logistics. Benefits and costs must be integrated across the full supply chain process in order to make the correct sourcing decision.

The first challenge is the identification of sources capable of producing the materials in the quality and quantity required. While it is becoming easier to achieve the quality objective, ensuring that the potential supplier has the ability to meet volume and seasonal fluctuation demands in a suitable time frame remains a challenge.

The second challenge considers the protection of a firm's intellectual property as products or components are produced and transported. The suppliers and countries involved need to have legal constraints in place to protect product designs and related trade secrets.

The third challenge relates to understanding import/export compliance issues. There may be government regulations regarding the volume of a commodity that can be imported before duties or other restrictions are enforced. The percentage of materials that are foreign-sourced may also restrict a firm's ability to sell to select customers. Government contracts may require a specific level of domestically made components. For example, if the contract requires that the product is "Made in the U.S.A.," 95 percent of the material must be of domestic origin.

The fourth challenge relates to communication with suppliers and transportation companies. While the procurement negotiation with low-cost countries is not easy, there is often a greater difficulty in dealing with carriers, freight forwarders, and government customs as a result of time zone, language, and technology differences.

The fifth challenge is the need to guarantee the security of the product while it is in transit. Not only does supply chain security require that the product is secure, the process must also secure containers and vehicles both full and empty.

The sixth challenge concerns the inventory and obsolescence risk associated with extended transit times. With the longer transit times associated with low-cost-country sourcing, it is not uncommon for the firm to have 1 or 2 months' supply of product in transit, which must be counted as an asset and incur the related inventory carrying cost. Extended lead times also increase the potential for obsolescence, as orders have longer lead times and there is generally little flexibility for change. Such extended lead times also can impact recovery when a quality issue develops. It is not unusual for firms to fly components from off-shore suppliers to recover from unexpected quality problems or delayed shipments.

The final challenge, which synthesizes the previous ones, focuses on the need to understand the difference between piece price and total cost. While the piece price may include the material as well as direct and indirect labor, the total cost perspective needs to consider other cost elements, including freight, inventory, obsolescence, duties, taxes, recovery, and other risk considerations.

Guidelines for Sourcing

The decision to source material and components domestically or from a low-cost country is a complex one. While the direct and indirect product costs represent one major factor, there are many other factors that must be considered and weighted appropriately. Products and components that have extended times between manufacturing changeovers are ideal for low-cost-country sourcing. A counterexample would be the life cycle for an electronics component, which is typically quite short and so would generally trend toward domestic

TABLE 12.4
Sourcing Guidelines

Criteria	Domestic Sourcing	Low-Cost-Country Sourcing
Product life cycle length	Short	Long
Product variations in size, color, or style	Many	Few
Labor content	Low	High
Intellectual property content	High	Low
Transport cost	High	Low
Product value	High	Low
Security or import constraints	High	Low
Transport uncertainty	High	Low

sourcing. Products and components that have numerous variations should also generally be domestically sourced because the extended lead times associated with low-cost-country sourcing makes it difficult to forecast the precise mix of product that will be demanded. Products or components with high labor content should take advantage of the typically low labor rates in low-cost counties. Products or components with high intellectual property content should be sourced domestically, as the legal systems in many of the low-cost countries do not provide adequate trade secret protection. Domestic sourcing is generally appropriate for products and components with relatively high transport cost such as those that are bulky or damage easy. Products or components with relatively low value are ideal for low-cost-country sourcing, as the inventory carrying cost while it is in transit is not significant. Products and components that are constrained for security or other types of import restrictions by a domestic government should tend toward domestic sourcing. For example, there may be customs delays in importing electronic goods when the supplier does not have the trust of the importing government because of the potential for importing contraband. Finally, products or components that have a high degree of transport uncertainty because of relatively low volumes or location on trade lanes with limited service would suggest domestic sourcing.

There is no simple answer regarding which products or components should be domestically sourced, as a number of the criteria are somewhat qualitative. Table 12.4 lists the general sourcing criteria. The final determination depends on the specific item and the firm's expertise. As firms increase their global operations and marketing efforts, logistics managers should be increasingly involved to provide a realistic assessment of the total cost and performance implications.

Summary

As a supply chain strategy becomes international, new complexities are encountered. These complexities result from longer distances, demand differentials, cultural diversity, and complex documentation. Nevertheless, firms will increasingly confront the need to expand operations into the global arena. Strategies to achieve a share of the rapidly expanding world market range from export/import to local presence to true globalization. Regardless of the strategic focus, success will, to a large extent, be dependent upon a firm's logistical capabilities.

Supply chain security has evolved from a relatively minor issue to a major consideration following the events of September 11, 2001. While the need to protect the security of consumers and the public is obvious, logistics management must also be concerned with brand and enterprise protection as well. The U.S. Department of Homeland Security initiatives to enhance supply chain security place significant demands upon logistical management to develop and maintain trusted relationships, identify potential supply chain security concerns, apply appropriate technology to enhance supply chain security, and work with domestic and international governments to define common security initiatives that can enhance security without substantially increased cost. However, this is not just a problem for the United States; many other countries are also concerned about security, so a consistent solution is desirable. These responsibilities require that logistics and supply chain managers work cross-functionally with other enterprise organizations, including security, quality, legal, and public relations, and with public sector representatives from other countries as well.

Decisions regarding global sourcing and marketing require more complex trade-off analyses than traditionally required for domestic logistics. Both the quantitative and qualitative factors are more complex. While transportation, inventory, and warehousing costs are very substantial for global operations, other cost components, including tariffs, duties, documentation, and import restrictions, can also make a substantial impact on true total cost. However, in addition to the quantitative considerations, international operations introduce a number of other variables that are much more difficult to quantify. Many of these variables relate directly to logistics operations. The major qualitative considerations include relationship management, infrastructure consistency, production and transit reliability, and security. With increased global marketing and manufacturing operations, logistics management needs to be more involved in developing and implementing global strategies.

Challenge Questions

1. Compare and contrast domestic and global logistics operations.

2. Discuss how logistics management must evolve to reflect the differing needs for each stage of international development.

3. Discuss the logistics operational considerations for operating in a global environment.

4. Compare and contrast the roles that logistics management, supply chain management, product quality, corporate security, logistics service providers, and the government need to play to enhance supply chain security.

5. Describe the role that logistics and supply chain management should take in complying with C-TPAT, CSI, AMR, and ACI security initiatives.

6. Describe the role that information technology can play in enhancing supply chain security. Focus the discussion on the following technologies: RFID, shipment tracking and tracing, and supply chain planning systems.

7. Discuss the rationale and challenges related to sourcing from low-cost countries.

8. Describe the factors that should be considered by logistical management in the total cost analysis for global sourcing and marketing

9. Discuss how product variations, security and import constraints, and transportation uncertainty should impact global sourcing and marketing decisions.

10. Compare and contrast export/import operations to local presence. What are the logistics ramifications of each stage of international development?

Network Integration

For the most part, managers confront a new and challenging assignment when they are asked to participate in logistical system reengineering. Due to the rapid rate of change in almost every facet of logistical operations, managers can expect considerable discontinuity when they try to use previous experience to guide the creation and implementation of new logistical competencies. Therefore, success or failure may depend on how well the planning team is able to quantify the forces at work and rationalize a logical and believable action plan. Having a comprehensive understanding of the theoretical constructs that serve as the foundation of logistical integration provides an important step toward developing an integrated strategy.

In earlier chapters, the essence of logistical strategy was identified as achieving least-total-cost operations while simultaneously maintaining flexibility. Flexibility is the key to providing high-level basic customer accommodation while at the same time maintaining sufficient operating capacity to meet and exceed key customer expectations. To exploit flexibility, an enterprise needs to achieve a high level of logistical process integration. Integration is required at two operating levels. First, the operating areas of logistics must be integrated across a network of warehouse facilities supportive of customer accommodation, manufacturing, and procurement requirements. Such network integration is essential if a firm is using logistical competency to gain competitive advantage. Second, integration must extend beyond a single firm by supporting relationships across the supply chain. This chapter presents a framework to assist managers in achieving such integration.[1]

Enterprise Facility Network

Prior to the availability of low-cost dependable surface transportation, most of the world's commerce relied on product and material movement by water. During this early period, commercial activity concentrated around port cities. Overland transport of goods was costly and slow. For example, the lead time to order designer clothing from across the continental United States could exceed 9 months. Although demand for fast and efficient transport existed, it was not until the invention of the steam locomotive in 1829 that the transportation technology revolution began in the United States. Today, the transportation system in this country is a highly developed network of rail, water, air, highway, and pipeline services. Each transport alternative provides a different type of service for use within a logistical system. This availability of economical transportation creates the opportunity to establish a competitively superior warehouse network to service customers.

The importance of facility location analysis has been recognized since the middle of the 19th century, when the German economist Joachim von Thünen wrote *The Isolated State*.[2] For von Thünen, the primary determinant of economic development was the price of land and the cost to transport products from farm to market. The value of land was viewed as being directly related to the cost of transportation and the ability of a product to command an adequate price to cover all cost and result in profitable operation. Von Thünen's basic principle was that the value of specific produce at the growing location decreases with distance from the primary selling market.

Following von Thünen, Alfred Weber generalized location theory from an agrarian to an industrial society.[3] Weber's theoretical system consisted of numerous consuming locations spread over a geographical area and linked together by linear transportation costs. Weber developed a scheme to classify major materials as either **ubiquitous** or **localized.** Ubiquitous materials were those available at all locations. Localized raw materials consisted of mineral deposits found only at selected areas. On the basis of his analysis, Weber developed a **material index.** The index was the ratio of the localized raw material to the total weight of the finished product. Various types of industry were assigned a **locational weight** based on the material index. Utilizing these two measures, Weber generalized that industries would locate facilities at the point of consumption when the manufacturing process was weight-gaining and near the point of raw material deposit when the manufacturing process was weight-losing. Finally, if the manufacturing process were neither weight-gaining nor weight-losing, firms would select plant locations at an intermediate point.

Several location theorists followed von Thünen and Weber. The most notable contributions toward a general theory of location were developed by August Lösch, Edgar Hoover,

---

[1] The reader is cautioned that this chapter stresses theoretical constructs that determine logistical system design. The material offers a framework to guide trade-off analysis. While theoretical discussions tend to be abstract, the principles presented are logically consistent regardless of the competitive or cultural setting within which logistical reengineering is performed.

[2] Joachim von Thünen, *The Isolated State,* Beziehung auf Landwirtschaft und Nationalökonomie. Hamburg, 1862.

[3] Alfred Weber, *Theory of the Location of Industries,* translated by Carl J. Friedrich (Chicago, IL: University of Chicago Press, 1928).

Melvin Greenhut, Walter Isard, and Michael Webber.[4] In their writings, these five authors highlighted the importance of geographical specialization in industrial location, including quantification of the importance of transportation.

Spectrum of Location Decisions

In terms of logistical planning, transportation offers the potential to link geographically dispersed manufacturing, warehousing, and market locations into an integrated system. Logistical system facilities include all locations at which materials, work-in-process, or finished inventories are handled or stored. Thus, all retail stores, finished goods warehouses, manufacturing plants, and material storage warehouses represent logistical network locations. It follows that selection of individual locations, as well as the composite locational network, represents important competitive and cost-related logistical decisions.

A manufacturing plant location may require several years to fully implement. For example, General Motors' decision to build a new Cadillac assembly plant in Lansing, Michigan, spanned over 5 years from concept to reality. In contrast, some warehouse arrangements are sufficiently flexible to be used only during specified times. The selection of retail locations is a specialized decision influenced by marketing and competitive conditions. The discussion that follows concentrates on selecting warehouse locations. Among all the location decisions faced by logistical managers, those involving warehouse networks are most frequently reviewed.

Local Presence: An Obsolete Paradigm

A long-standing belief in business is that a firm must have facilities in local markets to successfully conduct business. During economic development of North America, erratic transportation service created serious doubt about a firm's ability to promise delivery in a timely and consistent manner. In short, customers felt that unless a supplier maintained inventory within the local market area it would be difficult, if not impossible, to provide consistent delivery. This perception, commonly referred to as the **local presence paradigm,** resulted in logistical strategies committed to forward deployment of inventory. As recently as the early 1960s it was not uncommon for manufacturers to operate 20 or more warehouses to service the U.S. mainland. Some firms went so far as to have full line inventory warehouses located near all major sales markets.

When a tradition such as local warehousing is part of a successful strategy, it is difficult to change. However, for the past several decades the cost and risk associated with maintaining local presence have required reexamination. Transportation services have dramatically expanded, and reliability has increased to the point where shipment arrival times are dependable and predictable. Rapid advances in information technology have reduced the time required to identify and communicate customer requirements. Technology is available to track transportation vehicles, thereby providing accurate delivery information. Next-day delivery from a warehouse facility located as far away as 800 to 1000 miles is common practice.

Transportation, information technology, and inventory economics all favor the use of smaller rather than larger numbers of warehouses to service customers within a geographical

---

[4] August Lösch, *Die Räumliche Ordnung der Wirtschaft* (Jena: Gustav Fischer Verlag, 1940); Edgar M. Hoover, *The Location of Economic Activity* (New York: McGraw-Hill Book Company, 1938); Melvin L. Greenhut, *Plant Location in Theory and Practice* (Chapel Hill, NC: University of North Carolina Press, 1956); Walter Isard et al., *Methods of Regional Analysis: An Introduction to Regional Science* (New York: John Wiley & Sons, Inc. 1960); Walter Isard, *Location and Space Economy* (Cambridge, MA: The MIT Press, 1968); and Michael J. Webber, *Impact of Uncertainty on Location* (Cambridge, MA: The MIT Press, 1972).

area. In many situations, customer perceptions concerning local presence continue to influence decentralization of inventory. The answer to the question "How much local presence is desirable?" is best understood by carefully examining the relationships that drive logistical system design.

Warehouse Requirements

Warehouses are established in a logistical system to lower total cost or to improve customer service. In some situations, the benefits of cost reduction and improved service can be achieved simultaneously.

Warehouses create value for the processes they support. Manufacturing requires warehouses to store, sort, and sequence materials and components. Facilities used for inbound materials and components are often referred to as **supply facing warehouses.** Warehouses are also used to store, sequence, and combine inventory for consolidated shipment to next-destination customers in the supply chain. Warehouses used to support customer accommodation are often referred to as **demand facing warehouses.** Demand facing warehouse requirements are directly related to manufacturing and marketing strategies.

Due to the specialized materials handling and inventory process requirements, warehouses typically specialize in performing either supply or demand facing services. Warehouses committed to supporting manufacturing are typically located close to the factories they support; in contrast, warehouses dedicated to customer accommodation are typically strategically located throughout the geographical market area serviced.

The combinations of information technology, e-procurement fulfillment, and response-based business strategies have combined to radically alter how and why warehouses are used. The economic justification and desired functionality of a warehouse is typically distinctly different for facilities dedicated to procurement, manufacturing, or customer accommodation.

Procurement Drivers

Procurement drivers, as discussed in Chapter 4, center on using warehouses to help purchase materials and components at the lowest total inbound cost. Sophisticated purchasing executives have long realized that a combination of purchase price, quantity discount, payment terms, and logistical support is required to achieve lowest delivered cost. In an effort to develop and support dedicated and customized working relationships, most firms have reduced their overall number of suppliers. The logic is the development of a limited number of relationships with suppliers that can be operationally integrated into a firm's supply chain. The goals of relational buying are to eliminate waste, duplication, and unplanned redundancy.

In an effort to improve overall operating efficiency, life cycle considerations have become prominent in purchase decisions. This relational dynamic of working with limited suppliers is based on a cradle-to-grave philosophy, spanning from new product development to reclamation and disposal of unused materials and unsold inventory. Such a **closed-loop** focus results from buying practices that directly impact the requirements and functionality of supply faced warehousing. Value-added services related to procurement are increasingly being debundled from the purchase price. Such debundling facilitates functional absorption and spin-off between manufacturers and their suppliers. There is also a trend toward more response-based business strategies, which is redefining expectations concerning supplier support and participation in the value-added process. The result is new structural relationships, such as tier one suppliers and lead facilitators. Finally, the seasonality of selected supplies, opportunities to purchase at reduced prices, and the need to rapidly accommodate manufacturing spikes continue to make selected warehousing of materials a sound business decision.

As a result of these trends, the role of supply facing warehouses continues to change. Warehouses were traditionally used to stockpile raw materials and component parts. Today such facilities place greater emphasis on sorting and sequencing materials and components as they flow into manufacturing. The goal is to streamline flow of materials and components by eliminating duplicate handling and storage of identical inventories at multiple locations throughout the material supply network.

Manufacturing Drivers

Warehouses that support manufacturing are used to consolidate finished product for outbound customer shipment. The capability to consolidate a variety of products contrasts to individual product shipment. A primary advantage of a manufacturing demand facing warehouse is the ability to provide customers full line product assortment on a single invoice at truckload transportation rates. In fact, a manufacturer's capability to provide such consolidation may be the primary reason for selection as a preferred supplier.

Leading examples of demand facing warehouses are the networks used by such firms as General Mills, Johnson & Johnson, Kraft, and Kimberly-Clark. At Johnson & Johnson, warehouses are used to support hospital and consumer business sectors by serving as inventory consolidators for a variety of different business units. As a result, customers can purchase full assortments of products from different business units on a single invoice for shipment on one order. Kimberly-Clark produces a wide variety of individual products on specific manufacturing lines at specialized plants. Such products as Kleenex®, Scott Tissue®, and Huggies® disposable diapers are manufactured at economy-of-scale volume, then temporarily are positioned in demand facing warehouses. Customer-specific truckloads of assorted products are assembled at the warehouse. At the Nabisco Division of Kraft, branch warehouses are located adjacent to individual bakeries. Inventories of all major products are maintained at each branch to facilitate full-service shipments to customers.

The primary determinant of the warehousing required to support manufacturing is the specific production strategy being implemented. In Chapter 4, three basic manufacturing strategies—make to plan (MTP), make to order (MTO), and assemble to order (ATO)—were discussed. The extent of demand facing warehousing can be directly linked to the support requirements of each manufacturing strategy. In a general sense, MTO manufacturing strategies require supply facing warehousing support but little, if any, demand facing storage. Conversely, MTP manufacturing strategies, which focus resources to achieve maximum manufacturing economy of scale, require substantial demand facing warehouse capacity.

Customer Accommodation Drivers

Customer accommodation warehouses create value by providing customized inventory assortments to wholesalers and retailers. A warehouse located geographically close to customers seeks to minimize inbound transportation cost by maximizing consolidation and length of haul from manufacturing plants followed by relatively short outbound movement to customers. The geographic size of a market area served from a support warehouse depends on the number of suppliers, the desired service speed, size of average order, and cost per unit of local delivery. The warehouse facility exists to provide customers inventory assortment and replenishment. A warehouse is justified if it offers a way to achieve a competitive service or cost advantage.

Rapid Replenishment

Customer accommodation warehouses have traditionally provided assortments of products from varied manufacturers and various suppliers for retailers. A retail store typically does not have sufficient demand to order inventory in large quantities directly from wholesalers or manufacturers. A typical retail replenishment order is placed with a wholesaler that sells a variety of different manufacturer products.

Customer accommodation warehouses are common in the food and mass merchandise industries. The modern food warehouse usually is located geographically near the retail stores it services. From this central warehouse, consolidated product assortments can rapidly replenish retail inventories because of the close geographical proximity. Large retail stores may receive multiple truckloads from the warehouse on a daily basis. Location of the warehouse within the market served is justified as the least-cost way to rapidly replenish an assortment of inventory to either an end customer or a retailer.

Market-Based ATO

The design of a customer accommodation warehouse network is directly related to inventory deployment strategy. The establishment of a warehouse is a result of forward inventory deployment in anticipation of future demand. This assumption means that a manufacturing firm utilizing such a distributive network is to some degree dependent upon forecasting inventory requirements to offset response time to meet customer requirements. The preceding discussion indicates that inventories deployed forward after manufacturing are typical in situations where firms are manufacturing to plan or when they are engaged in decentralized assembly to order. In assemble to order (ATO) situations, common or undifferentiated components are stocked in warehouse inventory in anticipation of performing customized manufacturing or assembly at the warehouse upon receipt of customer orders.

An increasing amount of ATO operations are performed in warehouses located close to customers, as contrasted to centralized manufacturing locations. Assembly in close proximity to major markets allows the benefits of postponement while avoiding the high cost and time related to long-distance direct shipment.

Warehouse Justification

Warehouses are justified in a logistical system when a service or cost advantage results from their positioning between suppliers, manufacturers, and customers. Competitive advantage generated by establishing a warehouse network can result from lower total cost or faster delivery. From the viewpoint of transportation economies, cost advantage results from using the warehouse to achieve freight consolidation. However, freight consolidation typically requires inventory to support assembly of customized orders. Alternatively, consolidation or assortment may be achieved by establishing flow-through facilities or cross-dock sortation that operates without predetermined inventories. Such continuous movement effectively converts warehouses from inventory storage to mixing facilities. Of course some business situations will justify a combination of inventory storage and continuous flow-through or cross-dock operations to effectively and economically service customers. From the perspective of integrative management, the key logistics system design questions become: How many and what kinds of warehouses should a firm establish? Where should they be located? What services should they provide? What inventories should they stock? Which customers should they service? This sequence of interrelated questions represents the classical logistics network design challenge. For manufacturing firms, network design begins with marketing strategy and continues into manufacturing and procurement planning. In retailing and wholesaling enterprises, the framework spans from purchasing to customer accommodation strategies.

Total Cost Integration

Economic forces such as transportation and inventory should determine a firm's initial network of warehouse facilities. The following discussion identifies cost trade-offs individually related to transportation and inventory, and their integration, to identify the least-total-cost facility network.

Transportation Economics

The key to achieving economical transportation is summarized in two basic principles. The first, often called the **quantity principle,** is that individual shipments should be as large as the involved carrier can legally transport in the equipment being used. The second, often called the **tapering principle,** is that large shipments should be transported distances as long as possible. Both of these principles were developed in detail in Chapter 8. In combination they serve to spread the fixed cost related to transportation over as much weight and as many miles as possible.

Cost-Based Warehouse Justification

The basic economic principle justifying establishment of a warehouse is transportation consolidation. Manufacturers typically sell products over a broad geographical market area. If customer orders tend to be small, then the potential cost savings of consolidated transportation may provide economic justification for establishing a warehouse.

To illustrate, assume a manufacturer's average shipment size is 500 pounds and the applicable freight rate to a customer is $7.28 per hundredweight. Each shipment made direct from the manufacturing location to the market would have a transportation cost of $36.40. The quantity or volume transportation rate for shipments 20,000 pounds or greater is $2.40 per hundredweight. Finally, local delivery within the market area is $1.35 per hundredweight. Under these conditions, products shipped to the market via quantity rates and distributed locally would cost $3.75 per hundredweight, or $18.75 per 500-pound shipment. If a warehouse could be established, stocked with inventory, and operated for a total cost of less than $17.65 per 500-pound shipment ($36.40 − $18.75), or $3.53 per hundredweight, the overall cost of distributing to the market by using a warehouse would be reduced. Given these economic relationships, establishment of a warehouse offers the potential to reduce total logistics cost.

Figure 13.1 illustrates the basic economic principle of warehouse justification. *PL* is identified as the manufacturing location, and *WL* is the warehouse location within a given market area. The vertical line at point *PL* labeled P_c reflects the handling and shipping cost associated with preparation of a 500-pound LTL shipment (*C*) and a 20,000-pound truckload shipment (*A*). The slope of line *AB* reflects the truckload freight rate from the plant to *WL*, the warehouse, which is assumed for this example to be linear with distance. The vertical line labeled *WC* at point *WL* represents the cost of operating the warehouse and maintaining inventory. The lines labeled *D* reflect delivery cost from the warehouse to customers within the market area *Ma* to *Ma'*. The slope of line *CD* reflects the LTL rate from the plant to customers located between the plant and the boundary *Ma*. The shaded area represents the locations to which the total cost of a 500-pound customer shipment using a consolidation warehouse would be lower than direct shipment from the manufacturing plant.

From the perspective of cost alone, it would make no difference whether customers located exactly at points *Ma* and *Ma'* were serviced from the manufacturing plant or the warehouse.

FIGURE 13.1
Economic
Justification of a
Warehouse Facility
Based on
Transportation Cost

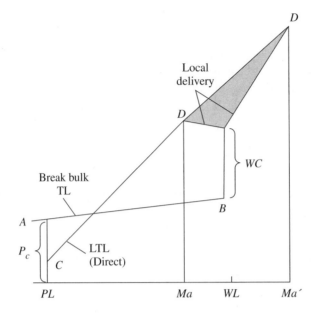

Network Transportation Cost Minimization

As a general rule, warehouses would be added to the network in situations where

$$\sum \frac{P_{\bar{v}} + T_{\bar{v}}}{N_{\bar{x}}} + W_{\bar{x}} + L_{\bar{x}} \leq \sum P_{\bar{x}} + T_{\bar{x}},$$

where

$P_{\bar{v}}$ = Processing cost of volume shipment;

$T_{\bar{v}}$ = Transportation cost of volume shipment;

$W_{\bar{x}}$ = Warehousing cost of average shipment;

$L_{\bar{x}}$ = Local delivery of average shipment;

$N_{\bar{x}}$ = Number of average shipments per volume shipment;

$P_{\bar{x}}$ = Processing cost of average shipment; and

$T_{\bar{x}}$ = Direct freight cost of average shipment.

The only limitation to this generalization is that sufficient shipment volume be available to cover the fixed cost of each warehouse facility. As long as the combined cost of warehousing and local delivery is equal to or less than the combined cost of shipping direct to customers, the establishment and operation of additional warehouse facilities would be economically justified.

The generalized relationship of transportation cost and number of warehouses in a network is illustrated in Figure 13.2. Total transportation cost will initially decline as warehouses are added to the logistical network. In actual operations, a consolidation location can be a warehouse or a cross-dock facility offering transportation break-bulk. It is not necessary to stock inventory in a warehouse to achieve the lowest transportation cost. The reduction in transport cost results from consolidated volume shipments to the break-bulk location, coupled with short-haul small shipments to final destination. The cost of shipping small orders direct from manufacturing to customers is at the extreme upper left of the cost curve illustrated in Figure 13.2. At the low point near the middle of the transportation cost curve, the number of facilities required to achieve maximum freight consolidation is identified. Transportation cost is minimized at the point of maximum freight consolidation.

FIGURE 13.2
Transportation Cost as a Function of the Number of Warehouse Locations

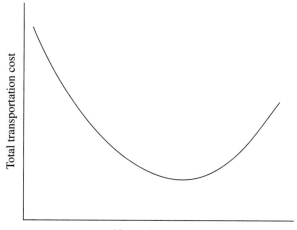

If facilities are expanded beyond the maximum consolidation point, total transportation cost will increase, because the inbound volume capable of being consolidated to each facility decreases. The increased frequency of smaller inbound shipments results in a higher cost per hundredweight for shipments inbound to the facility. In other words, as the frequency of small inbound shipments increases, total transportation cost increases.

Inventory Economics

Inventory level in a logistical system directly depends on the number of stocking locations. The framework for planning inventory deployment is the performance cycle. Although one element of the performance cycle is transportation, which provides spatial closure, the key driver of inventory economics is time. The forward deployment of inventory in a logistical system potentially improves service response time. Such deployment also increases overall system inventory, resulting in greater cost and risk.

Service-Based Warehouse Justification

The inventory related to a warehouse network consists of **base, transit,** and **safety stock.** For the total logistical network, average inventory commitment is

$$\bar{I} = \sum_{i=j}^{n} \frac{Q_s}{2} + SS_i + IT$$

where

$\bar{I}$ = Average inventory in the total network;

n = Number of performance cycles in the network;

Q_s = Order quantity for a given performance cycle identified by the appropriate subscript;

SS_i = safety stock, for a given performance cycle identified by the appropriate subscript; and

IT = In-transit inventory.

As warehouses are added to a logistics system, the number of performance cycles increases. This added complexity directly impacts the quantity of inventory required across the network.

The impact on base stock by adding warehouses is not significant. The base stock level within a logistical system is determined by manufacturing and transportation lot sizes, which do not change as a function of the number of market facing warehouses. The combination of maintenance and ordering cost, adjusted to take into consideration volume transportation rates and purchase discounts, determines the replenishment EOQ and the resultant base stock. In just-in-time procurement situations, base stock is determined by the order quantity required to support the planned manufacturing run or assembly. In either situation, the base stock determination is independent of the number of market facing warehouses in the logistical system.

Transit stock is inventory captive in transportation vehicles. While in transit, this inventory is **available to promise** but it cannot be physically accessed. Available to promise means it can be committed to customers by use of a reservation or inventory mortgaging capability in the order management system. As more performance cycles are added to a logistical network, the anticipated impact is that existing cycles will experience a reduction in transit inventory. This reduction occurs because the total network transit days and related uncertainty are reduced. To illustrate, assume a single product is being sold in markets A and B and is currently being supplied from warehouse X, as presented in Figure 13.3. Assume the forecasted average daily sales are 6 units for market A and 7 for market B. The performance cycle duration is 6 days to market A and 10 days to market B.

With other things held constant, what will happen to transit inventory if a second warehouse is added, as in Figure 13.4? Table 13.1 provides a summary of results. The main

FIGURE 13.3
Logistical Network: Two Markets, One Warehouse

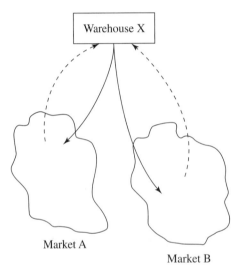

Market A

Market B

FIGURE 13.4
Logistical Network: Two Markets, Two Warehouses

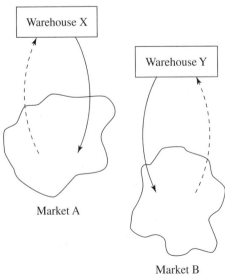

Market A

Market B

TABLE 13.1   **Transit Inventory under Different Logistical Networks**

Forecasted Average Daily Sales	Market Area	Warehouse X Only	Two-Warehouse Facilities		
			Warehouse X	Warehouse Y	Combined
6	A	36	36	—	36
7	B	70	—	28	28
	$\sum A + B$	106			64
	$\bar{I}_a$	18			18
	$\bar{I}_b$	35			14
	$\sum \bar{I}$	53			32

TABLE 13.2
Logistical Structure:
One Warehouse, Four
Plants

	Warehouse X			
Manufacturing Plant	Performance Cycle Duration	Forecasted Average Sales	Transit Inventory	$\bar{I}$
A	10	35	350	175
B	15	200	3,000	1,500
C	12	60	720	360
D	20	80	1,600	800
	57	375	5,670	2,835

change is that the performance cycle to market B has been reduced from 10 to 4 days. Thus, the second warehouse reduced average transit inventory for the network from 53 to 32 units. It should be noted that the second warehouse did not create additional performance cycles on the customer accommodation side of the logistics flow. However, on the inbound side, each product stocked in the new warehouse requires a replenishment source. Assuming a full product line at each warehouse, the number of performance cycles required to replenish the network will increase each time a new warehouse is added.

Despite the increased need for inventory replenishment, the average in-transit inventory for the total network dropped as new warehouses were added because of a reduction in days required to service customers. Assume that warehouse X is supplied by four manufacturing plants whose individual performance cycles and forecasted average usage are illustrated in Table 13.2.

For purposes of comparison, assume a unit value of $5 for all warehouse products. Utilizing only warehouse X, the average transit inventory would be 2835 units at $5 each, or $14,175.

Table 13.3 illustrates the addition of warehouse Y. Average transit inventory in the two-warehouse logistical network dropped to 2248 units or, at $5 each, $11,240. Thus, even though four new plant-to-warehouse replenishment cycles were added to the logistical network, the average transit time was reduced because of the reduction in total replenishment days.

The addition of warehouses typically will reduce total in-transit days and, thus, in-transit inventory. This result will vary in accordance with the particulars of each situation. Each network of locations must be carefully analyzed to determine average transit inventory impact. The key to understanding the general nature of the relationship is to remember that total transit days are reduced even though the number of required performance cycles increases. The qualification is that while an increase in the number of performance cycles typically reduces transit days, it may also increase overall lead time uncertainty. As the number

TABLE 13.3
Logistical Structure: Two Warehouses, Four Plants

Manufacturing Plant	Performance Cycle Duration	Forecasted Average Sales	Transit Inventory	$\bar{I}$
		Warehouse X		
A	10	20	200	100
B	15	100	1,500	750
C	12	35	420	210
D	20	30	600	300
	57	185	2,720	1,360
		Warehouse Y		
A	5	15	75	38
B	8	100	800	400
C	6	25	150	75
D	15	50	750	375
	34	190	1,775	888
	$\Sigma xy = 91$	$\Sigma xy = 375$	$\Sigma xy = 4{,}495$	$\Sigma \bar{x}xy = 2{,}248$

of performance cycles increases, the possibility of breakdowns leading to potential service failures also increases. This potential impact is accommodated by safety stock.

Safety stock is added to base and transit stock to provide protection against sales and performance cycle uncertainty. Both aspects of uncertainty are time-related. Sales uncertainty is concerned with customer demand that exceeds forecasted sales during the replenishment time. Performance cycle uncertainty is concerned with variation in the total days required to replenish warehouse inventory. From the viewpoint of safety stock, the expected result of adding warehouses will be an increase in average system inventory. The purpose of safety stock is to protect against unplanned stockouts during inventory replenishment. Thus, **if safety stock increases as a function of adding warehouses, then the overall network uncertainty must also be increasing.**

The addition of warehouses to the logistical network impacts uncertainty in two ways. First, as performance cycle days are reduced, the variability in sales during replenishment as well as cycle variability are both also reduced. Therefore, reducing the length of the performance cycle relieves, to some degree, the need for safety stock to protect against variability.

Adding locations also has a significant impact on average inventory. Each new performance cycle added to the system creates the need for an additional safety stock. The introduction of an additional warehouse to service a specific market area reduces the size of the statistical distribution used to determine safety stock requirements for each warehouse. In effect, the size of the market area being serviced by any given facility is reduced without a corresponding reduction in uncertainty. To illustrate, when the demand of several markets is combined by using a single warehouse, the variability of demand is averaged across markets. This allows peaks in demand in one market to be offset by low demand in others. In essence, the idle stock of one market can be used to meet safety stock requirements of other markets.

To illustrate, Table 13.4 provides a summary of monthly sales in three markets on a combined and separate basis. Average sales for the three markets combined is 22 units per month, with the greatest variation above the average in month 6, when sales reached 29 units, or 7 units over the average. If the goal is to provide 100 percent protection against stockout and total sales of 29 units have an equal probability of occurring in any month, a safety stock of 7 units would be required.

TABLE 13.4
Summary of Sales in One Combined and Three Separate Markets

Month	Combined Sales, All Markets	Unit Sales per Market		
		A	B	C
1	18	9	0	9
2	22	6	3	13
3	24	7	5	12
4	20	8	4	8
5	17	2	4	11
6	29	10	5	14
7	21	7	6	8
8	26	7	7	12
9	18	5	6	7
10	24	9	5	10
11	23	8	4	11
12	23	12	2	9
Total Sales	265	90	51	124
Average Monthly Sales	21.1	7.5	4.3	10.3
Value Greater Than Average	7	4	3	4

The average monthly sales for markets A, B, and C are 8, 4, and 10 units (rounded), respectively. The maximum demand in excess of forecast is in market A, with 5 units in month 12; for market B, 3 units in month 8; and for market C, 4 units in month 6. The total of each of these three extreme months equals 11 units. If safety stocks are planned for each market on a separate basis, 11 units of safety stock would be required for the total network while only 7 units of safety stock would be required to service all markets from a single warehouse. An increase in total system safety stock of 4 units is required to provide the same inventory availability when using three warehouses.

This simplified example illustrates the general safety stock impact of adding warehouses to a logistical network. The important point to understand is that increased safety stock results from an inability to aggregate uncertainty across market areas. As a consequence, unique safety stocks are required to accommodate local demand variation.

Network Inventory Cost Minimization

The overall impact upon average inventory of increasing the number of warehouses in a logistical network is generalized in Figure 13.5. A reduction in average transit inventory is assumed as illustrated by the line $\bar{I}_t$. The assumption is that a linear relationship exists between average transit inventory and the number of warehouses in the network. As noted earlier in this section, such a relationship may not be linear, depending upon the characteristics of the particular system under consideration. However, the general tendency is for a linear reduction as performance cycles are increased.

The curve labeled $\bar{I}_{ss}$ (average safety stock) increases as warehouses are added to the network. Inventory increases at a decreasing rate, since the net increase required for each new facility declines. The incremental safety stock is the sum of added inventory to accommodate uncertainty of demand minus the inventory reduction required to accommodate for less lead time uncertainty. Thus, the incremental inventory required to maintain customer service performance diminishes for each new warehouse location added to the system. The average inventory curve, $\bar{I}$, represents the combined impact of safety stock and transit inventory. The significant observation is that the safety stock dominates the impact of transit inventory. For the overall network, the average inventory is the safety stock plus half of the order quantity and transit inventory. Thus, given the same demand and customer service goals, total inventory increases at a decreasing rate as the number of warehouses in a logistical network increases.

FIGURE 13.5
Average Inventory as a Function of Number of Warehouse Locations

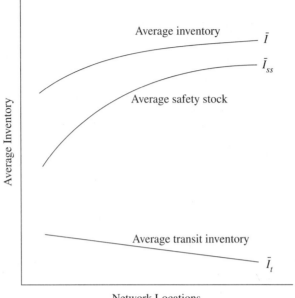

Total Cost Network

As noted earlier, the identification of the least-total-cost-network design is the goal of logistical integration. The basic concept of total cost for the overall logistical system is illustrated in Figure 13.6. The low point on the total transportation cost curve is between seven and eight facilities. Total cost related to average inventory commitment increases with each additional warehouse. For the overall system, the lowest total cost network is six locations. The point of lowest inventory cost would be a single warehouse.

FIGURE 13.6
Least-Total-Cost Network

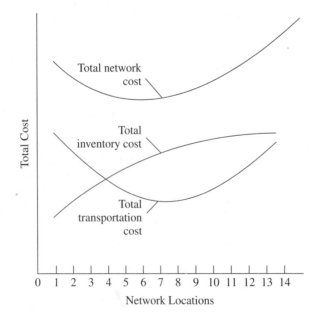

Trade-off Relationships

The identification of the least-total-cost network of six warehouses in Figure 13.6 illustrates the trade-off relationships. Note that the **minimal total cost point for the system is not at the point of least cost for either transportation or inventory.** This trade-off illustrates the hallmark of integrated logistical analysis.

Assumptions and Limitations

In actual practice, it is difficult to identify and measure all aspects of total logistical cost. Many assumptions are required to analyze logistical network analysis. An additional concern is the fact that analysis such as that illustrated in Figure 13.6 does not encompass the complexity of total cost integration.

The two-dimensional display in Figure 13.6 represents projected sales across a single planning period. Transportation requirements are represented by a single average-size shipment. In actual operations, it is likely that neither of these assumptions will represent actual circumstances. First, the nature of logistical network design is not that of a short-term planning problem. When facility decisions are involved, the planning horizon should consider a range of different sales alternatives. Second, actual shipment and order sizes will vary substantially around an average. A realistic approach to planning must incorporate a range of shipment sizes supported by alternative logistical methods to satisfy customer service requirements. In actual operation, alternative modes of transportation are employed, as necessary, to achieve the desired speed of delivery.

Significant cost trade-offs exist between inventory and transportation. Inventory cost as a function of the number of warehouses is directly related to the desired level of inventory availability. If no safety stock is maintained in the system, total inventory requirement is limited to base and transit stock. Under a no-safety-stock situation, the total least cost for the system would be at or near the point of lowest transportation cost. Thus, assumptions made with respect to the desired inventory availability and fill rate are essential to trade-off analysis and have a significant impact on the least-total-cost-design solution.

The locational selection aspect of logistical network planning is far more complex than simply deciding how many facilities to choose from a single array of locations, as illustrated in Figure 13.6. A firm engaged in nationwide logistics has a wide latitude in choice of where to locate warehouses. Within the United States there are 50 states, within which one or more distribution warehouses could be located. Assume that the total allowable warehouses for a logistical system cannot exceed 50 and locations are limited to a maximum of one in each state. Given this range of options, there still are 1.1259×10^{15} combinations of warehouses to be evaluated in the identification of the least-total-cost network.

To overcome some of these limitations, variations in shipment size and transportation alternatives need to be introduced for the analysis. Extending the analysis to a more complete treatment of variables typically requires the use of planning models and techniques discussed in Chapter 14. Three critical variables are shipment size, transportation mode, and location alternatives. The constants are level of inventory availability, performance cycle time, and the specific warehouse locations being evaluated.

In constructing a more comprehensive analysis, shipment size can be grouped in terms of frequency of occurrence and transportation mode economically justified to handle each shipment size within the specified performance cycle time constraints. For each shipment size, a total cost relationship can be identified. The result is a two-dimensional analysis for each shipment size and appropriate transportation mode. Next, the individual two-dimensional profiles can be linked by joining the points of least cost by a planning curve. In a technical sense, this is an **envelope curve** that joins the low total-cost points of individual shipment size/transport mode relationships. Figure 13.7 offers a three-dimensional picture of integrated shipment size, transportation mode, and location.

FIGURE 13.7
Three-Dimensional
Total Cost Curve

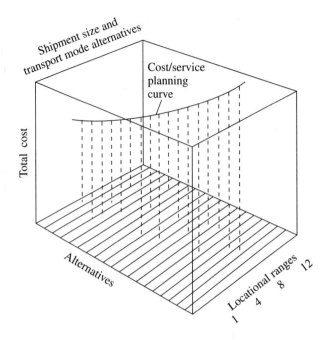

The planning curve joins the point of total least cost for each shipment size. It does not join locational points. For example, the number of locations to support least cost for one size of shipment may be more or less than for another. Further analysis is required to identify the specific locations that offer the least cost alternative for each shipment size and transport combination. Assume that the locations under consideration consist of a network ranging from 1 to 12 warehouses. Within this range, the planning curve will identify a smaller number of acceptable locations for detailed evaluation. In Figure 13.7, the points of least cost, shipment size, and transportation combinations fall within a range of four to eight locations.

Analysis is required to select the final warehouse network. Initially, the time duration of the performance cycle and inventory availability assumptions should be held constant. The service availability and performance cycle duration serve as parameters to help isolate an initial least cost approximation. At a later point in strategy formulation, these parameters can be relaxed and subjected to sensitivity analysis. The fit of the least cost planning curve requires marginal cost analysis for each shipment size/transportation mode combination for networks of four, five, six, seven, and eight warehouse locations. Provided customer service objectives are achieved within the four- to eight-warehouse range, a first-cut least-total-cost network of potential warehouses is identified.

A final refinement involves the evaluation of specific warehouse sites or facilities. In the case of Figure 13.7, which is also the situation in most complex modeling approaches, the best-fit-location network is limited to an array of warehouse locations preselected for analysis. The results may be managerially satisfactory but not cost-superior to a different group of locations. Each warehouse assortment selected for analysis will have a least cost combination. The final policy may require that the analysis be completed with several different network combinations to identify those most suitable for a given business situation. The final warehouse selection made by using such a trial-and-error methodology will never identify the mathematical optimal solution to minimize total logistical cost. It will, however, help management identify a superior network to the existing operation that will improve service and/or reduce total logistics cost.

To evaluate the wide range of variables in designing a logistical system, complex models have been developed. The assumptions required to support integrated system design are important from the viewpoint of their impact upon strategy formulation. The integrated total cost curve must take into consideration all relevant variables that are critical to logistical system design.

Formulating Logistical Strategy

To finalize logistical strategy, it is necessary to evaluate the relationships between alternative customer service levels and associated cost. While substantial difficulties exist in the measurement of revenue, the comparative evaluation of marginal service performance and related cost offers a way to approximate an ideal logistical system design. The general approach consists of (1) determining a least-total-cost network, (2) measuring service availability and capability associated with the least-total-cost-system design, (3) conducting sensitivity analysis related to incremental service and cost directly with revenue generation, and (4) finalizing the plan.

Cost Minimization

Just as a physical replication of a geographical area illustrates elevations, depressions, and contours of land surface, an economic map can highlight logistical cost differentials. Generally, peak costs for labor and essential services occur in large metropolitan areas. However, because of demand concentration, total logistics cost resulting from transportation and inventory consolidation benefits is often minimized in metropolitan areas.

A strategy of least total cost seeks a logistical system network with the lowest fixed and variable costs. A system design to achieve least total cost is driven purely by cost-to-cost trade-offs. In terms of basic relationships, a total-least-cost design was illustrated in Figure 13.6. The level of customer service that is associated with a least cost logistical design results from safety stock policy and the locational proximity of warehouses to customers. The overall level of customer service associated with the least-total-cost-system design is referred to as the **threshold service level.**

Threshold Service

To establish a threshold service level it is necessary to initiate network reengineering with policies regarding desired inventory **availability** and **capability.** It is common practice to have the customer service capability based on the existing order entry and processing system, warehouse operations based on standard order fulfillment time at existing facilities, and transportation delivery time based on capabilities of existing transportation methods. Given these assumptions, current performance provides the starting point for evaluating potential service improvement.

The typical starting point for customer service availability analysis is to assume performance at a generally acceptable fill rate. Often the prevailing industry standard is used as a first approximation. For example, if safety stock availability were established at 97.75 percent for combined probability of demand and lead time uncertainty, it would be anticipated that approximately 98 out of 100 items ordered would be delivered as specified.

Given the initial assumptions, each customer is assigned a shipment location on the basis of least total cost. In multiproduct situations, selection of service territories for each facility will depend on the products stocked at each warehouse and the degree of consolidation required by customers. Because costs have significant geographical differentials, the service area for any given facility will vary in size and configuration. Figure 13.8 provides an illustration of the assignment of warehouse service areas based upon equalized total

FIGURE 13.8
Determination of Service Territories: Three-Point, Least Cost System

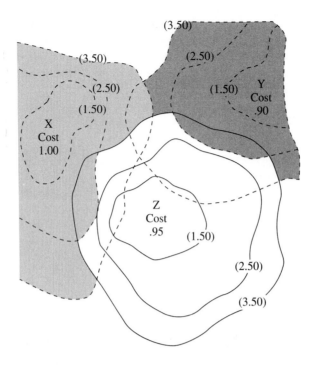

delivered cost. The irregularity of service territories results from outbound transportation cost differentials from the three warehouses.

In Figure 13.8 the warehouses are identified by the letters X, Y, and Z. The hypothetical cost associated with each facility represents all logistical cost for an average order except transportation. The differential of average order cost between facilities reflects local differentials.

Around each facility total cost lines are displayed at intervals of $1.50, $2.50, and $3.50. The cost represented by the line is the total cost of logistics, including transportation to points connected along the line. Customers located within a given area can be serviced at a cost less than that displayed on the line. The overall service area of each warehouse is determined by lowest total cost assignment. The territory boundary line represents the point of equal total cost between two warehouses. Along this line, total cost to service a customer is equal. However, a substantial difference could exist in delivery time.

Two conditions are assumed in Figure 13.8. First, the illustration is based on distribution of an average order. Thus, outbound logistics costs are equated on the average. To the degree that order size varies from the average, alternative territory boundaries would vary according to shipment size. Second, delivery time is estimated on the basis of distance. Transit inventory also is estimated based on delivery time. In accordance with this initial analysis of threshold service, it cannot be concluded that delivery times will be consistent within territories or that equal total logistics cost will be experienced within a service area.

The fact that the initial network is designed to achieve least logistics cost does not mean that threshold customer service will be low. The elapsed time from the customer's order placement to product delivery in a least-cost system is expected to be longer on average than would be experienced in alternative networks that have been modified to improve overall service performance. However, customers located near a warehouse facility in all networks have potential to receive rapid delivery. Because the least-cost location tends to favor areas of high demand concentration, a substantial number of customers will have rapid delivery potential.

Given an estimate of expected order cycle time, management is in a position to make basic customer delivery commitments. A service statement policy may be as follows: Order performance for area A will be 5 days from receipt of orders at the warehouse facility. It is our policy to be able to fill 98 percent of all orders within the 5-day period.

The actual performance of a logistical system is measured by the degree to which such service standards are consistently achieved. Given quantification of the variables involved, the threshold service related to the least-total-cost system offers the starting point of developing a firm's basic service platform. The next step in policy formulation is to test the customer suitability of the threshold service level.

Service Sensitivity Analysis

The threshold service resulting from the least-total-cost logistical design provides a basis for **service sensitivity analysis.** The basic service capabilities of a network can be increased or decreased by variation in number of warehouses, change in one or more performance cycles to increase speed or consistency of operations, and/or change in safety stock policy.

Locational Modification

The warehouse structure of the logistical system establishes the service that can be realized without changing the performance cycle or safety stock policy. To illustrate the relationship between number of warehouses and resultant service time, assume an important measure is the percentage of demand satisfied within a specified time interval. The general impact of adding warehouses to the system is presented in Table 13.5. Several points of interest are illustrated.

First, incremental service is a diminishing function. For example, the first five warehouse locations provide 24-hour performance to 42 percent of all customers. To double the percentage of 24-hour service from 42 to 84 percent, 9 additional warehouses, or a total of 14, are required.

Second, high degrees of service are achieved much faster for longer performance intervals than for the shorter intervals. For example, four warehouse locations provide 85 percent performance within the 96-hour performance cycle. Increasing the total locations

TABLE 13.5
Service Capabilities within Time Intervals as a Function of Number of Locations

Network Locations	Percentage Demand by Performance Cycle Duration (hours)			
	24	48	72	96
1	15	31	53	70
2	23	44	61	76
3	32	49	64	81
4	37	55	70	85
5	42	60	75	87
6	48	65	79	89
7	54	70	83	90
8	60	76	84	90
9	65	80	85	91
10	70	82	86	92
11	74	84	87	92
12	78	84	88	93
13	82	85	88	93
14	84	86	89	94

from 4 to 14 improves the 96-hour performance by only 9 percent. In contrast, a total of 14 warehouses cannot achieve 85 percent given a 24-hour performance cycle.

Finally, the total cost associated with each location added to the logistical network increases dramatically. Thus, while the incremental service resulting from additional locations diminishes, the incremental cost associated with each new location increases. The service payoff for each new facility is incrementally less.

Logistics managers are often asked to estimate the inventory impact of adding or deleting warehouses. This relationship between uncertainty and required inventory is called the **portfolio effect.**[5] The portfolio effect can be estimated using the **square root rule.** The square root rule, originally proposed by Maister, suggests that the safety stock increase as a result of adding a warehouse is equal to the ratio of the square root of the number of locations in the newly prepared network divided by the square root of the number of existing locations.[6]

For example, assume that a manager wants to estimate the inventory impact of shifting from a one- to a two-warehouse network. In effect, the network is being doubled. For reasons discussed earlier, demand variability will be increased. Using the square root rule, the firm's aggregate safety stock (SS_j) for a two-warehouse system can be estimated as

$$SS_j = \frac{\sqrt{N_j}}{\sqrt{N_i}} \times SS_i$$

$$= \frac{\sqrt{2}}{\sqrt{1}} \times SS_i$$

$$= 1.41 \times SS_i$$

where

SS_j = Aggregate safety stock for N_j warehouses or product variations;

N_j = Number of warehouse locations or product variations for the new configuration;

N_i = Number of warehouse locations or product variations for the existing configuration; and

SS_i = Aggregate safety stock for N_i warehouses or product variations.

The projected inventory increase resulting from adding a second warehouse is estimated as a 141 percent increase in safety stock. Table 13.6 illustrates the impact of the change for

[5] For a more detailed discussion of the portfolio effect, see Walter Zinn, Michael Levy, and Donald J. Bowersox, "Measuring the Effect of Inventory Centralization/Decentralization on Aggregate Safety Stock: The Square Root Law Revisited," *Journal of Business Logistics* 10, no. 1 (1989), pp. 1–14; and Philip T. Evers, "Expanding the Square Root Law: An Analysis of Both Safety and Cycle Stocks," *Logistics and Transportation Review* 31, no. 1 (1995), pp. 1–20.

[6] D. H. Maister, "Centralization of Inventories and the 'Square Root Law,'" *International Journal of Physical Distribution* 6, no. 3 (1976), pp. 124–134.

TABLE 13.6
Inventory Impact of Modified Warehouse Network from a Base of One Warehouse

Network Locations	Safety Stock Level
1	100
2	141
3	173
4	200
5	224

a range of one to five warehouses. Although the square root rule works reasonably well for estimating inventory impact, it requires assumptions regarding demand. The first assumption is that the stocking locations or product variations must have approximately the same level of demand. Specifically, if there are currently two stocking locations, they must have approximately the same demand level for the square root rule to work accurately. Second, the demand levels at each warehouse or for each product variation must not be correlated. This means that demand deviation for each location must be independent. Finally, the square root rule requires that demand for each warehouse approximate a normal distribution. While the appropriateness of these assumptions must be taken into consideration, the square root rule is a useful way to estimate the inventory impact of adding or deleting warehouses to a logistical network.

Performance Cycle Modification

Speed and consistency of service can be varied to a specific market or customer by a modification of some aspect of the performance cycle. To improve service, Web-based ordering and premium transportation can be used. Therefore, geographical proximity and the number of warehouses do not equate directly to fast or consistent delivery. The decision to increase service by adopting a faster performance cycle arrangement will typically increase variable cost. In contrast, service improvement, by virtue of added warehouses, involves a high degree of fixed cost and could result in less overall system flexibility.

No generalizations can be offered regarding the cost/service improvement ratio attainable from performance cycle modification. The typical relationship of premium to lowest cost transportation results in a significant incentive in favor of large shipments. Thus, if order volume is substantial, the economics of logistics can be expected to favor use of a warehouse or consolidation point to service a market area.

The impact of using premium transportation will increase total cost. Adjustments from the least-total-cost logistical system can typically be justified if the improved service results in increased profitability.

Safety Stock Modification

A direct way to change service is to increase or decrease the amount of safety stock held at one or more warehouses. The impact of increasing the safety stock across a total system will shift the average inventory cost curve upward. A goal of increasing customer service availability will result in increased safety stocks at each warehouse. As availability is increased, the safety stocks required to achieve each equal increment of availability increase at an increasing rate.

Finalizing Strategy

Management often falls into the trap of being overly optimistic in terms of service commitments to customers. The result may be excessively high customer expectations followed by erratic performance. In part, such overcommitment results from lack of understanding of the total cost required to support high, zero-defect service.

The final step in establishing a strategy is to evaluate the cost of incremental service in terms of generating offsetting revenue. To illustrate, assume that the current system is geared to service at least 90 percent of all customers at a 95 percent inventory availability within 60 hours of order receipt. Furthermore, assume that the current logistical system is meeting these objectives at lowest total cost by utilizing a network of five warehouses. Marketing, however, is not satisfied and believes that service capability should be increased to the point where 90 percent of all customers would receive 97 percent inventory availability delivered within 24 hours. Logistical management needs to estimate the cost of this strategic commitment.

FIGURE 13.9
Comparative Total Cost for 5- and 12-Distribution-Point Systems

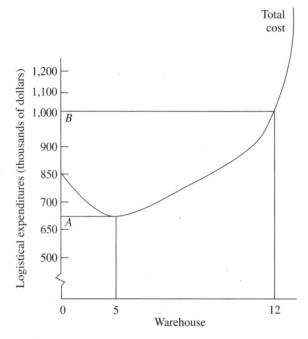

Figure 13.9 illustrates how the alternative strategies can be evaluated. Assume marketing is requesting a 2 percent improvement in inventory availability combined with a 36-hour improvement in delivery capability. Assume design analysis identifies that 12 warehouse facilities represent the lowest cost network capable of achieving the new service standards. The total cost of this expanded service capability is measured on the vertical axis of Figure 13.9 by the distance between points *A* and *B*. The total cost of achieving marketing's requested service will require approximately a $400,000 per year increase in logistical cost. Assuming an average before-tax profit margin of 10 percent of sales, it would be necessary to generate $4 million in incremental sales to break even on the cost of providing the added service.

Acceptance or rejection of marketing's proposal for increased service involves strategic positioning. Logistics can provide whichever performance the firm's overall customer service strategy requires. Policy changes, once adopted, will influence the logistical network design. To finalize logistical policy management typically requires considering a range of strategic alternatives.

Summary

The primary drivers of logistics network design are requirements resulting from integrated procurement, manufacturing, and customer accommodation strategies. Within the framework of these interlocking strategies, integrated logistics requirements are satisfied by achieving total cost and service trade-offs. These capabilities play out across a network of enterprise facilities. Important to the performance of logistics requirements are warehouse facilities. Such facilities are justified in logistical system design as a result of their contribution to cost reduction, service improvement, or a combination of both.

Transportation and inventory economics are critical network design considerations. In the least-total-cost equation, transportation reflects with the spatial aspects of logistics. The ability to consolidate transportation is a primary justification for including warehouses in a network design. Inventory introduces the temporal dimension of logistics. Average inventory increases as the number of warehouses in a system increase in a stable demand situation. Total cost integration provides a framework for simultaneous integration of logistics, manufacturing, and procurement costs. Thus, total cost analysis provides the methodology for logistical network integration.

Accurate total cost analysis is not without practical problems. Foremost is the fact that a great many important costs are not specifically measured or reported by standard accounting systems. A second problem involved in total cost analysis is the need to consider a wide variety of network design alternatives. To develop complete analysis of a planning situation, alternative shipment sizes, modes of shipment, and range of available warehouse locations must be considered.

These problems can be overcome if care is taken in network analysis. The cost format recommended for total cost analysis is to group all functional costs associated with inventory and transportation. The significant contribution of total cost integration is that it provides a simultaneous analysis of time- and space-impacted costs involved in logistical network design.

The formulation of a logistical strategy requires that total cost analysis be evaluated in terms of customer service performance. Logistical service is measured in terms of availability, capability, and quality of performance. The ultimate realization of each service attribute is directly related to logistical network design. To realize the highest level of logistical operational support within overall enterprise integration, in theory each customer should be provided service to the point where marginal cost equates to marginal revenue. Such marginal equalization is not practical to achieve; however, the relationship serves as a normative planning goal.

The formulation of a service policy starts from the identification and analysis of the least-total-cost-system design. Given a managerially specified inventory availability target, service capability associated with the least cost design can be quantified. This initial service level is referred to as the threshold service level. To evaluate potential modifications to the least cost design, sensitivity analysis is used. Service levels may be improved by modifying (1) variation in the number of facilities, (2) change in one or more aspects of the performance cycle, and/or (3) change in safety stock.

Challenge Questions

1. Describe in your words the meaning of spatial/temporal integration in logistical system integration.

2. What justification of logic can be presented to support the placement of a warehouse in a logistical system?

3. Why do transportation costs initially decrease as the number of warehouses in a system increases? Why do transportation costs eventually increase as the number of warehouses increase? Why do inventory costs increase as the number of warehouses in a system increases?

4. In your words, what is the locational impact of inventory? How does it differ for transit inventory and safety stock?

5. What is meant by the threshold service level of a least cost system?

6. Why does customer service not increase proportionately to increases in total cost when a logistical system is being designed?

7. In Table 13.5, why does customer service speed of performance increase faster for customers located greater distances from a warehouse facility? What is the implication of this relationship for system design?

8. Discuss the differences between improving customer service through faster and more consistent transportation, higher inventory levels, and/or expanded numbers of warehouses.

9. In your words describe the relationship among procurement, manufacturing, and customer accommodation in integrated logistics system design.

10. In what ways can customer service performance be improved by incorporating flexible distribution operations into a logistical system design?

Logistics Design and Operational Planning

The supply chain logistics environment is constantly evolving as a result of changes in markets, competitors, suppliers, and technology. To develop and focus the enterprise strategy to match this changing environment and effectively evaluate alternatives, a systematic planning and design methodology is required. This chapter presents a generalized methodology that includes an overview of techniques used for logistics planning.

Planning Methodology

Even for established industries, a firm's markets, demand, cost, and service requirements change rapidly in response to customer and competitor behavior. To accommodate such change, firms often face questions such as: (1) How many warehouses should our logistics system use and where should they be located? (2) What are the inventory/service trade-offs for each warehouse? (3) What types of transportation equipment should be used and how should vehicles be routed? (4) Is investment in a new materials handling technology justified?

The answers to such questions are usually complex and data-intensive. The complexity is due to the large number of factors influencing logistics total cost and the range of

FIGURE 14.1
Research Process

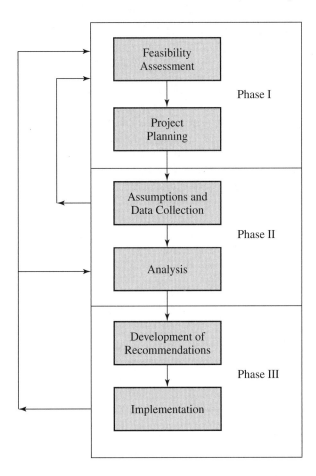

alternative solutions. The data-intensiveness is due to the large amount of information required to evaluate logistical alternatives. A typical logistics system design must evaluate a range of service alternatives, cost characteristics, and operating technologies. Such analyses require a structured process and effective analytical tools.

Just as no ideal logistical system is suitable for all enterprises, the method for identifying and evaluating alternative logistics strategies can vary extensively. However, there is a general process applicable to most logistics design and analysis situations. Figure 14.1 illustrates a generalized planning process flow. The process is segmented into three phases: problem definition and planning, data collection and analysis, and recommendation and implementation.

Phase I: Problem Definition and Planning

Phase I of logistics system design and planning provides the foundation for the overall analysis. A thorough and well-documented problem definition and plan are essential to all that follows.

Feasibility Assessment

Logistics design and planning must begin with a comprehensive evaluation of the current operating situation. The objective is to understand the environment, process, and performance characteristics of the current system and to determine what, if any, modifications appear worthy of evaluation. The process of evaluating change is referred to as a feasibility assessment, and includes situational analysis, framing the supporting logic, and cost/benefit estimation.

Situation Analysis

The collection of performance measures, characteristics, and information that describes the current logistics environment is called the situational analysis. A typical analysis requires internal operational review, a market assessment, and a technology assessment to determine existing capabilities and improvement potential.

The internal operating review focuses on developing a clear understanding of existing logistics practices and processes. It profiles historical performance, data availability, strategies, operations, and tactical policies and practices. The review usually covers the overall process as well as each logistics function. In order to fully understand how logistics supports procurement, manufacturing operations, and customer accommodation, the situational analysis should span the full functionality of the supply chain.

A complete internal review examines all major resources, such as workforce, equipment, facilities, relationships, and information. In particular, the internal review should focus on a comprehensive evaluation of the existing system's capabilities and deficiencies. Each element of the logistics system must be carefully examined with respect to its stated objectives and its capabilities to meet those objectives. For example, is the logistics management information system consistently providing and measuring the agreed-to customer service objectives? Likewise, does the material management process adequately support manufacturing requirements? Does the current network of warehouses effectively support customer service objectives? Finally, how do logistics performance capabilities and measures compare across business units and locations? These and many similar questions form the basis of the self-appraisal required for the internal analysis. The comprehensive review attempts to identify the opportunities that might motivate or justify logistics system redesign or refinement.

Table 14.1 lists some of the topics frequently covered during an internal review. The format highlights the fact that the assessment must consider the processes, decisions, and key measures for each major logistics activity. Process considerations focus on physical and information flows through the supply chain. Decision considerations focus on the logic and criteria currently used for supply chain management. Measurement considerations focus on the key performance indicators and the firm's ability to measure them. Supply chain performance metrics are further developed in Chapter 16.

The specific review content depends on the scope of the analysis. It is unusual that the information desired is readily available. The purpose of the internal review is not detailed data collection but rather a diagnostic look at current logistics processes and procedures as well as a probe to determine what type of data are available. Most significantly, the internal review is directed at the identification of areas where substantial opportunity for improvement exists.

The market assessment is a review of the trends and service demands required by customers. The market assessment objective is to document and formalize customer perceptions and desires with regard to potential changes in the firm's logistics capabilities. The assessment might include interviews with select customers or more substantive customer surveys.[1] Table 14.2 illustrates some typical market assessment topics. The assessment should focus on external relationships with suppliers, customers, and in some situations consumers. The assessment should consider trends in requirements and processes as well as enterprise and competitor capabilities.

---

[1] Francis J. Gonillart and Frederick D. Sturdivant. "Spend a Day in the Life of Your Customers," *Harvard Business Review* 72, no. 1 (January/February 1994), pp. 116–25.

TABLE 14.1 Selected Internal Review Topics

	Processes	Decisions	Measurements
Customer Service	What is the current information flow? What is the order profile and how is it changing? How are orders received?	How are order sourcing decisions made? What happens when inventory is not available to fill an order? How are manufacturing and warehouse capacity allocation decisions made?	What are the key measures of customer service? How are they measured? What is the current performance level?
Materials Management	What is the current material flow through plants and warehouses? What processes are performed at each manufacturing site and warehouse?	How are production planning and scheduling decisions made?	What are the key manufacturing and warehouse capacity limitations? What are the key measures of materials management performance? How are they measured? What is the current performance level?
Transportation	What modes are currently used? What is the weight profile of orders and shipments and how are they different? What is the flow for requesting, paying, and exchanging information with carriers? What is the information flow for shipment documentation?	How are the mode and carrier choice decisions made for each shipment? How are carriers evaluated?	What are the key transportation performance measures? How are they measured? What is the current performance level? What are the relative economic performance characteristics of each mode and carrier?
Warehousing	What storage and handling facilities are currently used and what functions do they perform? What product lines are maintained in each facility? What are the storage, handling, and other value-added functions that are or may be performed at each facility?	How are shipment consolidation decisions made at each facility? What decisions are made by material handlers and how do they make those decisions? How is product stored in the facility and how are product selection decisions made?	What is the throughput and storage volume of each facility? What are the key warehouse performance measures? How are they measured? What is the current performance level? What are the relative economic performance characteristics of each facility?
Inventory	What value-added functions do current inventory stockpiles play?	How are inventory management decisions made? Who makes them and what information is used to support the decisions?	What is the corporate inventory carrying cost? What are the key inventory performance measures? How are they measured? What is the current performance level?

Technology assessment focuses on the application and capabilities of key logistics technologies, including transportation, storage, materials handling, packaging, and information processing. The assessment considers the firm's capabilities in terms of current technology as well as the potential for applying new technologies. For example, can advanced materials handling capabilities offered through integrated service providers enhance logistics performance? What is the role of advanced information technology, communication, and decision support systems in enabling responsive logistics capabilities? Finally, what can wireless, RFID, satellite, scanning, or other communication technology contribute to improved logistics system capability? The objective of the technology assessment is to

TABLE 14.2 **Sample Market Assessment Topics**

	Market Trends	Enterprise Capabilities	Competitive Capabilities
Suppliers	What value-added services are suppliers providing? What are the major bottlenecks with current suppliers?	What are the opportunities to internalize or outsource value-added services? How can processes be changed to reduce bottlenecks?	What actions are competitors taking to refine product and information flow with suppliers? What are competitive benchmarks in terms of number of suppliers, cost characteristics, and performance measures?
Customers	What are the major constraints and bottlenecks when servicing key customers? What are the cost impacts of these constraints and bottlenecks? How are customer ordering patterns changing? What are the primary customers' criteria?	What functions or activities can be shifted to or from customers to enhance logistics system performance? How do customers evaluate our performance on their key measurement criteria?	What services are competitors providing our customers? How do competitors perform on key performance measures as identified by customers?
Consumers	How are consumer purchasing patterns changing with respect to purchase locations, times, and selection criteria? What are the consumer trends with respect to logistics activities such as purchase quantities, packaging, home delivery, and product quality?	How are we able to respond to changes in consumer purchasing patterns and selection criteria	How are our competitors responding to changes in consumer purchasing patterns and selection criteria?

identify technology advancements that facilitate effective trade-offs with other logistics resources such as transportation or inventory. Table 14.3 illustrates typical technology assessment topics across selected logistics functions. Such an assessment should be completed with respect to each component of the logistics system as well as from the perspective of overall integration.

Supporting Logic

The second feasibility assessment task is the development of a supporting logic to integrate the findings of the internal review, market assessment, and technology study. Supporting logic development often constitutes the most difficult part of the strategic planning process. The purpose of the situational analysis is to provide senior management with the best possible vision of the strengths and weaknesses of existing logistics system capabilities for both the existing and potential future logistical requirements. Supporting logic development builds on this comprehensive review in three ways.

First, it must identify the value proposition to justify detailed research and analysis. In this sense, the supporting logic development forces a critical view of potential improvement opportunities, including determination of whether the cost/benefit justification provides a solid business case. Supporting logic development utilizes logistics principles, such as the tapering principle, principle of inventory aggregation, and total landed cost principle discussed in previous chapters, to determine the feasibility of conducting a detailed analysis to quantify the potential benefits. While completing the remaining tasks in the managerial planning process does not commit a firm to implementation or even guarantee an

TABLE 14.3 Typical Technology Assessment

	Current Technology	State-of-the Art Technology
Forecasting	What are the current technologies for collecting, maintaining, and developing forecasts?	How are the best firms developing forecasts?
Order Entry	What order entry technologies are used currently? What order entry technology are customers requiring?	How are the best firms performing order entry? What new technologies are available to improve order entry effectiveness?
Order Processing	What is the process to allocate available inventory to customer orders? What are the limitations of the current approach?	How are the best firms performing order processing? What new technologies (hardware and software) are available to improve order processing effectiveness?
Requirements Planning	What decision processes are used to determine production and distribution inventory requirements? How are these processes supported with current information and decision aids?	How are the best firms making production and inventory planning decisions? What new technologies are available to improve requirements planning effectiveness?
Invoicing and EDI	How are invoices, inquiries, advanced shipment notifications, and payments currently transmitted?	How are the best firms using EDI? What new communications and data exchange technologies are available to improve invoicing and other forms of customer communication?
Warehouse Operations	How are warehouse personnel and scheduling decisions made? How are warehousing operating instructions provided to supervisors and material handlers? How do warehouse supervisors and material handlers track activities and performance?	How are the best firms using information and materials handling technologies in the warehouse? What new information and materials handling technologies are available to improve warehouse operating effectiveness?
Transportation	How are transportation consolidation, routing, and scheduling decisions made? How is transportation documentation developed and communicated with carriers and customers? How are transportation costs determined, assessed, and monitored? What packaging and loading technologies are used?	How are the best firms using information, packaging, and loading technologies with carriers? What new information, packaging, loading, and communication technologies are available to improve transportation operating effectiveness?
Decision Support	How are logistical, tactical, and strategic planning decisions made? What information is used and what analysis is completed?	How are the best companies making similar tactical or strategic decisions? What information and evaluation technologies are available to enhance decision effectiveness?

improved logistics system design, the potential benefits and risks associated with change should be clearly identified in developing the supporting logic.

Second, supporting logic development critically evaluates current procedures and practices on the basis of a comprehensive factual analysis to remove perceptual biases. Identification of areas with improvement potential, as well as those where operations are satisfactory, provides a foundation to determine the need for strategic change. For example, it may be apparent that excess inventory or obsolete stock units represent a serious problem and significant potential exists to reduce cost and improve service. While the appraisal process frequently confirms that many aspects of the existing system are more right than wrong, the decisions to consider change should be based on potential improvement. If supporting logic supports the current number and location of warehouses, subsequent analysis can focus on streamlining inventory levels without serious risk of suboptimization. The deliverables of this evaluation process include classification of planning and evaluation issues prioritized into primary and secondary categories across short- and long-range planning horizons.

Third, the process of developing supporting logic should include clear statements of potential redesign alternatives. The statement should include: (1) definition of current procedures and systems, (2) identification of the most likely system design alternatives based on leading industry competitive practices and the prevailing theories of integrated logistics, and (3) suggestion of innovative approaches based on new theory and technologies. The alternatives should challenge existing practices, but they must also be practical. The less frequently a redesign project is conducted to reevaluate current procedures and designs, the more important it is to identify a range of options for consideration. For example, evaluation of a total logistics management system or supply chain structure should consider a wider range of options if done every 5 years than if completed every 2 years.

At this point in the planning and design process, it is well worth the effort to construct flow diagrams and/or outlines illustrating the basic concepts and justification associated with each alternative. The illustrations should frame opportunities for flexible logistics practices, clearly outline value-added and information flow requirements, and provide a comprehensive overview of the options. Some refined or segmented logistics practices are difficult to illustrate in a single flow diagram. For example, regional variations, product-mix variations, and differential shipment policies are difficult to depict, although they do form the basis of design alternatives. When segmental strategies are proposed, it is easier to portray each option independently.

A recommended procedure requires the manager responsible for evaluating the logistical strategy to develop a logical statement and justification of potential benefits. Using the customer accommodation concepts (Chapter 3) and logistics integration logic and methodology (Chapter 13), the responsible manager should document and justify the most attractive strategy modifications.

Cost/Benefit Estimate

The final feasibility assessment task, the cost/benefit estimate, is an estimate of the potential benefits and risks associated with performing a logistics analysis and implementing the recommendations. Benefits should be categorized in terms of service improvements, cost reduction, and cost prevention. The categories are not mutually exclusive, given that an ideal logistics strategy might include some degree of all three benefits simultaneously. The risks represent the potential downside related to the proposed changes. Service improvement includes an estimate of the impact of enhanced availability, quality, or capability. Improved service increases loyalty of existing customers and may also attract new business.

Cost reduction benefits may be observed in two forms. First, benefits may occur as a result of a one-time reduction in financial or managerial resources required to support and operate the logistics system. For example, logistical redesign may allow the sale of warehouses, materials handling equipment, or information technology systems. Reductions in capital deployed for inventory and other logistics-related assets can significantly enhance a firm's performance if ongoing costs are eliminated and free cash spin-off is generated. Second, cost reductions may be found in the form of reduced out-of-pocket or variable expenses. For example, new technologies for materials handling and information processing often reduce variable cost by allowing more efficient processing and operations.

Cost prevention helps eliminate involvement in programs and operations experiencing cost increases. For example, many materials handling and information technology upgrades are at least partially justified through financial analysis regarding the implications of future labor availability and wage levels. Naturally, any cost-prevention justification is based on an estimate of future conditions and therefore is vulnerable to a degree of error. While logistics system redesign may not be approved entirely on the basis of cost prevention because of such uncertainty, these preventive measures are still important to consider.

No rules exist to determine when a planning situation offers adequate cost/benefit potential to justify in-depth analysis. Ideally, some review should be completed on a continuous basis at regularly specified intervals to assure the viability of current and future logistics operations. In the final analysis, the decision to undertake in-depth planning will depend on how convincing the supporting logic is, how believable estimated benefits are, and whether estimated benefits offer sufficient return on investment to justify organizational and operational change. These potential benefits must be balanced against the out-of-pocket cost required to complete the process.

Although they are not always a goal of a planning and design project, immediate improvement opportunities are frequently possible. The rapid capture of "low hanging fruit" can often increase revenue or decrease cost sufficiently to justify the remainder of an analysis. As the project team identifies these opportunities, the responsible executive should evaluate each opportunity to balance the quick return in terms of the implementation risk.

Project Planning

Project planning is the second Phase I activity. Logistics system complexity requires that any effort to identify and evaluate strategic or tactical alternatives must be planned thoroughly to provide a sound basis for implementing change. Project planning involves these specific tasks: statement of objectives, statement of constraints, measurement standards, assumptive logic, analysis techniques, and project work plan.

Statement of Objectives

The statement of objectives documents the cost and service expectations for the logistics system revisions. It is essential that they be stated specifically and in terms of measurable factors. The objectives define market or industry segments, the time frame for change, and specific performance expectations. These requirements typically define specific goals that management is seeking to achieve. For example, the following suggest a combination of measurable objectives that might be used to guide a logistics analysis:

A. Provide the 100 most profitable customers with perfect order performance on all orders.
B. For all other customers provide the following performance:
    1. Inventory availability:
       • 99% for category A products
       • 95% for category B products
       • 90% for category C products
    2. Desired delivery of 98% of all orders within 48 hours of order placement
    3. Minimize customer shipments from secondary warehouses
    4. Fill mixed commodity orders without back order on a minimum of 85 percent of all orders
    5. Hold back orders for a maximum of 5 days

Specific definition of these objectives directs system design efforts to achieve explicit customer service performance levels. Total system cost to meet the service objectives can then be determined by using an appropriate analytical method as discussed later in this chapter. To the extent that logistics total cost does not fall within management expectations, alternative customer service performance levels can be tested by using sensitivity analysis to determine impact on overall logistics cost.

Alternatively, performance objectives can establish maximum total cost constraints, and then a system that achieves maximum customer service level attainable within an acceptable logistics budget may be designed. Such cost-driven solutions are practical since recommendations are guaranteed to fit within acceptable budget ranges. Such cost-constrained design solutions lack sensitivity to service-oriented drivers.

Statement of Constraints

The second project planning consideration concerns design constraints. On the basis of the situational analysis, it is expected that senior management will place some restrictions on the scope of permissible system modifications. The nature of such restrictions depends upon the specific circumstances of individual firms. However, two typical examples are provided to illustrate how constraints can affect the overall planning process.

One restriction common to warehouse network system design concerns the existing manufacturing facilities and their product-mix assortment. To simplify the study, management often holds existing manufacturing facilities and product mix constant during logistical system redesign. Such constraints may be justified on the basis of large financial investments in existing manufacturing plants and the ability of the organization to absorb change.

A second example of constraints concerns customer accommodation activities of separate divisions. In firms with a traditional pattern of decentralized profit responsibility, management may elect to include some divisions in a centralized logistics system while omitting others. Thus, some divisions are managerially identified as candidates for change while others are not.

All design constraints serve to limit the scope of the analysis. However, as one executive stated, "Why study things we don't plan to do anything about?" Unless there is a reasonable chance that management will be inclined to accept recommendations to significantly change logistics strategy or operations, their limitations may best be treated as a study constraint.

The purpose of developing a statement of constraints is to have a well-defined starting point and overall perspective for the planning effort. If quantitative analysis techniques are used, major constraints may be reconsidered later. In contrast to the situation assessment discussed earlier, the statement of constraints defines specific organizational elements, buildings, systems, procedures, and/or practices to be retained from the existing logistical system.

Measurement Standards and Assumptive Logic

The feasibility assessment often highlights a central need for development of measurement standards. Such standards direct the analysis by identifying cost assumptions and performance objectives essential to evaluate recommendations. Management must stipulate measurement standards and objectives as a prerequisite for plan formulation. It is important that the standards adequately reflect total system performance rather than a limited, suboptimal focus on logistics functions. Once formulated, such standards must be monitored and tracked throughout system development to allow measurement of change impact. Although considerable managerial discretion exists in the formulation of standards, care must be exercised not to dilute the validity of the analysis and subsequent results by setting impractical or constantly changing goals.

An important requirement is to establish a list of assumptions that provide the logic supporting the standards. These assumptions should receive top-management approval because they can significantly shape the results of the strategic plan. For example, a relatively small variation in the standard cost and procedure for evaluating inventory can create major variations in the resulting strategic plan.[2]

Measurement standards should include definitions of how cost components such as transportation, inventory, and order processing are quantified, including detailed financial account references. The standards must also include specification of relevant customer service measures and method of calculation.

Project Work Plan

On the basis of feasibility assessment, objectives, constraints, standards, and analysis techniques, a project work plan can be developed and the resources and time required for completion identified. The alternatives and opportunities specified during the feasibility assessment provide the basis for determining the scope of the study. In turn, the scope determines the required time to complete the study.

Project management is responsible for the achievement of expected results within time and budget constraints. One of the most common errors in strategic planning is to underestimate the time required to complete a specific assignment. Overruns increase financial expenditures and reduce project credibility. Fortunately, there are a number of PC-based software project management packages available to structure projects, guide resource allocation, and measure progress. Such methodologies identify deliverables and the interrelationship between tasks.[3]

Phase II: Data Collection and Analysis

Once the feasibility assessment and project plan are completed, Phase II of a network design study focuses on data collection and analysis. This phase requires assumption definition, data collection, and analysis of alternatives.

Assumptions and Data Collection

This activity extends the feasibility assessment and project plan by developing detailed planning assumptions and identifying data collection requirements by (1) defining analysis approaches and techniques, (2) defining and reviewing assumptions, (3) identifying data sources, (4) collecting data, and (5) collecting validation data.

Defining Analysis Approaches and Techniques

An early Phase II task is the determination of the appropriate analysis technique for the planning situation under consideration. While a wide number of options are available, the most common techniques are analytical, simulation, and optimization. An analytical approach uses numerical tools such as spreadsheets to evaluate each logistical alternative. A typical example of an analytical approach is the determination of inventory/service trade-offs using the formulas discussed in Chapter 6. Spreadsheet availability and capability have increased the use of analytical tools for logistical analysis.

---

[2] For a detailed measurement discussion, see Patrick M. Byrne and William J. Markham, *Improving Quality and Productivity in the Logistics Process* (Oak Brook, IL: Council of Logistics Management, 1991), Chap. 10.

[3] An example of such planning software is *Microsoft Project* (Redmond, WA).

A simulation approach can be likened to a laboratory for testing supply chain logistics alternatives. Simulation is widely used, particularly when significant uncertainty is involved. The testing environment can be physical, such as a model materials handling system that physically illustrates product flow in a scaled-down environment, or numerical, such as a computer model. Current software makes simulation one of the most cost-effective approaches for evaluating dynamic logistics alternatives.[4] For example, a PC-based simulation can model the flows, activity levels, and performance characteristics. Many simulations have the capability to illustrate system characteristics graphically. For example, supply chain dynamic simulation can be used to illustrate the trade-off between inventory allocation strategy and supply chain performance.[5]

Optimization uses linear or mathematical programming to evaluate alternatives and select the best design or alternatives under consideration. While optimization has the benefit of being able to identify the best option, optimizations are often smaller in scope than typical simulation applications.

Defining and Reviewing Assumptions

Assumption definition and review builds on the situation analysis, project objectives, constraints, and measurement standards. For planning purposes, the assumptions define the key operating characteristics, variables, and economics of current and alternative systems. While the format will differ by project, assumptions generally fall into three classes: (1) business assumptions, (2) management assumptions, and (3) analysis assumptions.

Business assumptions define the characteristics of the general business environment, including relevant market, consumer, and product trends and competitive actions. The assumptions define the broad environment within which an alternative logistics plan must operate. Business assumptions are generally outside the ability of the firm to change.

Management assumptions define the physical and economic characteristics of the current or alternative logistics environment and are generally within management's ability to change or refine. Typical management assumptions include the alternative warehouse locations to be considered, transport modes and ownership arrangements, logistics processes, and fixed and variable cost.

Analysis assumptions define the constraints and limitations required to fit the problem to the analysis technique. These assumptions frequently focus on problem size, degree of analysis detail, and solution methodology. Table 14.4 offers more detailed descriptions for each assumption category.

Identifying Data Sources

In actual practice, the process of data collection begins with a feasibility assessment. In addition, a fairly detailed specification of data is required to formulate or fit the desired analytical technique. However, at this point in the planning procedure, detailed data must be collected and organized to support the analysis. For situations when data is extremely difficult to collect or when the necessary level of accuracy is unknown, sensitivity analysis can be used to identify data impact. For example, an initial analysis may be completed using transportation costs estimated with distance-based regressions. If analysis indicates that the

---

[4] For a comprehensive discussion of simulation alternatives, see James J. Swain, "Flexible Tools for Modeling," *OR/MS Today*, December 1993, pp. 62–78; and John D. Sterman, *Business Dynamics: Systems Thinking and Modeling for a Complex World* (Burr Ridge, IL: McGraw-Hill, 2000).

[5] For a general simulation modeling tool incorporating graphics, see W. David Kelton, Randall P. Sadowski, and David T. Sturrock, *Simulation with Arena*, 3rd ed. (New York: McGraw-Hill, 2004). For a more specialized business process modeling tool, see IBM WBI Workbench (Armonk, NY: International Business Machines, 2003).

TABLE 14.4
Assumption
Categories Elements

Assumption Classes/Categories	Description
Business Assumptions	
Scope	Definition of business units and product lines to be included.
Alternatives	Range of options that can be considered.
Market trends	Nature and magnitude of change in market preferences and buying patterns.
Product trends	Nature and magnitude of change in product buying patterns, particularly with respect to package size and packaging.
Competitive actions	Competitive logistics strengths, weaknesses, and strategies.
Management Assumptions	
Markets	Demand patterns by market area, product, and shipment size.
Distribution facilities	Locations, operating policies, economic characteristics, and performance history of current and potential distribution facilities.
Transportation	Transportation rates for movement between potential and existing distribution facilities and customers.
Inventory	Inventory levels and operating policies for each distribution facility.
Analysis Assumptions	
Product groups	Detailed product information aggregated to fit within scope of analysis technique.
Market areas	Customer demand grouped to aggregate market areas to fit the scope of analysis technique.

best answer is very sensitive to the actual freight rates, then additional effort is required to obtain more precise transport rates from carrier quotes. Once a technique is operational, sensitivity analysis can be used to identify the major solution drivers. When these sensitive drivers, such as outbound transportation expense, are identified, additional effort can be directed to increasing transportation replication accuracy.

The first major data category is sales and customer orders. The annual sales forecast and percentage of sales by month, as well as seasonality patterns, are usually necessary to determine logistics volume and activity levels. Historical samples of customer invoices are also necessary to determine shipping patterns by market and shipment size. The combination of aggregate measures of demand and shipment profiles characterizes the logistics requirements that must be met.

Specific customer data are also required to add a spatial dimension to a logistics analysis. The spatial dimension reflects the fact that effective logistics to key customers requires the cost and time associated to deliver to precise locations be quantified. In the overall analysis, customers and markets are often aggregated by location, type, size, order frequency, and growth rate to reduce analysis complexity. However, such aggregation is normally not satisfactory for evaluation of key customer service capability.

For supply chain logistics analysis, it is necessary to identify and track the costs associated with manufacturing and purchasing. While manufacturing plant locations may not be a variable component in a logistical system design, it is typically necessary to consider the number and location of plants, product mix, production schedules, and seasonality. Policies and costs associated with inventory transfer, reordering, and warehouse processing must be identified. In particular, inventory control rules and product allocation procedures are important elements. Finally, for each current and potential warehouse, it is necessary to establish operating costs, capacities, product mix, storage levels, and service capabilities.

Transportation data requirements include the number and type of modes utilized, modal selection criteria, rates and transit times, shipping rules, and policies. If private transportation is included in the analysis, then information is required concerning the private fleet.

The preceding discussion offers some perspective regarding the necessary data to evaluate a logistics network. The primary justification for placing the formal data collection process after the selection of analysis technique is to match the data to the analysis technique requirements.

It is also useful to document competitive logistical system designs and flows to provide information regarding competitor strategies and capabilities. In most cases, this information is readily available from published material, annual reports, and general knowledge of company executives. The main purpose in collecting such data is to provide competitive benchmarks that compare customer service capabilities, facility networks, and operating capabilities.

Data Collection

Once alternative data sources have been identified, the data collection process can begin. The process includes assembly of required data and conversion to appropriate formats for the analysis tool. This is often a tedious and time-consuming task, so errors are likely. Potential errors include collecting data from a misrepresentative time period and overlooking data that do not reflect major components of logistics activity, such as customer pickup volume. For this reason, the data collection process should be carefully documented to assist in identifying errors that might reduce analysis accuracy and to determine any necessary changes to achieve acceptable accuracy.

Validation Data

In addition to collecting data to support alternative analysis, base case or validation data must also be collected to verify that the results accurately reflect reality. The specific question concerns whether the chosen analytical approach accurately replicates historical logistics practices. The objective of validation is to increase credibility with management regarding the analysis process. If the process does not yield credible results, management will have little confidence in analysis results and resulting recommendations.

Analysis

Analysis involves use of the technique and data to evaluate strategic and tactical logistics alternatives. The analysis process includes: (1) analysis questions, (2) validating baseline analysis, (3) analyses of alternatives, and (4) sensitivity analysis.

Analysis Questions

The first task defines specific analysis questions concerning alternatives and the range of acceptable uncertainty. The specific questions build on research objectives and constraints by identifying specific operating policies and parameters. For example, the questions for a warehouse site analysis must identify the specific location combinations to be evaluated. In the case of an inventory analysis, questions might focus on alternative service and uncertainty levels.

Suppose that a strategic planning effort is focusing on the identification of a network of warehouses to serve the U.S. domestic market. Assume that the current network uses four warehouses located in Newark, New Jersey; Atlanta, Georgia; Chicago, Illinois; and Los Angeles, California. Table 14.5 summarizes the shipment volume, cost, and service characteristics of the existing system. Shipment volume is defined in terms of weight shipped; cost, in terms of transportation and inventory carrying expenses; and service level, in terms

TABLE 14.5 **Summary Distribution Performance**

Distribution Center	Shipment Volume (000 lbs)	Inbound Transportation	Outbound Transportation	Inventory Carrying Cost ($)	Total Cost
Newark	693,000	317,000	264,000	476,000	1,750,000
Atlanta	136,400	62,000	62,000	92,000	216,000
Chicago	455,540	208,000	284,000	303,000	795,000
Los Angeles	10,020	5,000	5,000	6,000	16,000
Total	1,294,960	592,000	615,000	877,000	2,777,000

of the percentage of sales volume serviced within 2 days' transit time from the warehouse. Likely questions for the analysis might be: (1) What is the performance impact if the Chicago warehouse is closed? (2) What is the performance impact of removing the Los Angeles warehouse? and (3) What is the performance impact of removing the Atlanta warehouse?

These questions represent but a few of the potential analysis alternatives. Other alternatives could include fewer or more warehouse locations or evaluation of different locations. It is important to recognize that care must be taken to define the analysis questions so that a wide range of possible options can be evaluated without requiring time-consuming modification of the model or additional data collection.

Validating Baseline Analysis

The second task involves a baseline analysis of the current logistics environment. Results should be compared with the validation data collected previously to determine the degree of fit between historical and analytical findings. The comparison should focus on identifying significant differences and determining sources of possible error. Potential errors may result from incorrect or inaccurate input data, inappropriate or inaccurate analysis procedures, or unrepresentative validation data. As discrepancies are encountered, errors should be identified and corrected. In some cases the error cannot be corrected but can be otherwise explained. Once discrepancies have been removed or explained to within ±2 percent, the application is generally accepted as a valid representation.

Analyses of Alternatives

Once the approach has been validated, the next step is to complete an evaluation of design alternatives. The analysis should determine the relevant performance characteristics for each alternative design or strategy. The options should quantify the impact of changes in management policies and practices involving factors such as the number of warehouses, inventory target levels, or the transportation shipment size profile.

Sensitivity Analysis

Once this analysis is completed, the best performing alternatives can be targeted for further sensitivity evaluation. Here uncontrollable factors such as demand, factor costs, and competitive actions can be varied to assess each alternative's ability to operate under a variety of conditions. For example, suppose that the alternative analysis indicates that four warehouses provide the ideal cost/service trade-off for the firm's market area assuming the base demand level. Sensitivity analysis would test the appropriateness of this solution under alternative demand or cost scenarios. In other words, would four warehouses still be the correct decision if demand increased or decreased by 10 percent? Sensitivity analysis in conjunction with an assessment of potential scenario probabilities is then used in a decision tree to identify the best alternative to meet managerial expectations.

Phase III: Recommendations and Implementation

Phase III operationalizes planning and design efforts by making specific management recommendations and developing implementation plans.

Recommendations

Alternative and sensitivity analysis results are reviewed to finalize managerial recommendations. This review process includes four tasks: (1) identifying the best alternative, (2) estimating costs and benefits, (3) developing a risk appraisal, and (4) developing a presentation.

Identifying the Best Alternative

The alternatives and sensitivity analyses should identify the best options to consider for implementation. However, multiple alternatives often yield similar or comparable results. Performance characteristics and conditions for each alternative must be compared to identify the two or three best options. Although the concept of best may have different interpretations, it will generally be the alternative that meets desired service objectives at the minimum total cost.

Estimating Costs and Benefits

In the earlier discussion of strategic planning, potential benefits were identified as service improvement, cost reduction, and cost prevention. It was noted that these benefits are not mutually exclusive and that a sound strategy might realize all benefits simultaneously. When evaluating the potential of a particular logistics strategy, an analysis comparing present cost and service capabilities with projected conditions should be completed for each alternative. The ideal cost/benefit analysis compares the alternatives for a base period and then projects comparative operations across some planning horizon. Benefits can thus be projected on the basis of both one-time savings that result from system redesign as well as recurring operating economies.

Evaluating Risk

A second type of justification necessary to support strategic planning recommendations is an assessment of the risk involved. Risk assessment considers the probability that the planning environment will match the assumptions. Additionally, it considers the potential hazards related to system changeover.

Risk related to adoption of a specific alternative can be quantified by using sensitivity analyses. For example, assumptions can be varied and the resulting impact on system performance across alternatives can be determined. To illustrate, sensitivity analysis can be used to identify the system performance for different demand and cost assumptions. If the selected alternative is still best even though demand increases or decreases by 20 percent, management can conclude that there is little risk associated with moderate errors in the demand environment. The end result of a risk appraisal provides a financial evaluation of the downside risk if planning assumptions fail to materialize.

Presentation

The final task is development of a managerial presentation that identifies, quantifies, and justifies suggested changes. The presentation and accompanying report must identify specific operating and strategic changes, provide a qualitative rationale as to why such change is appropriate, and then quantitatively justify the changes in terms of service, expense, asset utilization, and productivity improvements. The presentation should incorporate extensive use of graphs, maps, and flowcharts to illustrate changes in logistics operating practices, flows, and distribution network.

Implementation

The actual plan or design implementation is the final process activity. An adequate implementation plan is critical since putting the plan or design into action is the only means to obtain a return on the planning process. While actual implementation may require a number of events, there are four broad tasks: defining the implementation plan, scheduling implementation, defining acceptance criteria, and implementing the plan.

Defining the Plan

The first task defines the implementation plan in terms of the individual events, their sequence, and dependencies. While the initial plan may be macro level, it must ultimately be refined to provide individual assignment responsibility and accountability. Plan dependencies identify the interrelationships between events and, thus, define the completion sequence.

Scheduling

The second task schedules the implementation and time-phases the assignments identified previously. The schedule must allow adequate time for acquiring facilities and equipment, negotiating agreements, developing procedures, and training. Implementation scheduling, ideally, should employ one of the software scheduling aids discussed earlier.

Acceptance

The third task defines the acceptance criteria for evaluating the success of the plan. Acceptance criteria should focus on service improvements, cost reduction, improved asset utilization, and enhanced quality. If the primary focus is service, acceptance criteria must identify detailed components such as improved product availability or reduced performance cycle time. If the primary focus is cost, the acceptance criteria must define the expected positive and negative changes in all affected cost categories. It is important that the acceptance criteria take a broad perspective so that motivation focuses on total logistics system performance rather than performance of an individual function. It is also important that the acceptance criteria incorporate broad organizational input.

Plan Implementation

The final task is actual implementation of the plan or design. Implementation must include adequate controls to ensure that performance as scheduled and that acceptance criteria are carefully monitored. It is critical that a formalized process be used to guide logistics system design and refinement projects to ensure that the objectives are documented and understood and that the analyses are completed appropriately.

Supply Chain Analysis Methods and Techniques

High-performance supply chain management requires regular comprehensive analyses of supply chain tactics and strategies. Supply chain design analysis performs the strategic evaluation of supply chain alternatives such as sourcing, plant location, warehouse location, and market service areas, increasingly important to optimize flows for global supply chains. Dynamic simulation can be used to investigate the dynamics of multiple-stage inventories such as among suppliers, plants, and warehouses, and tactical transportation analysis assists in truck routing and scheduling. Regular freight lane analysis is necessary to respond to rate changes and balance of freight flows; tactical inventory analyses are necessary to identify items with excess inventory and to determine the appropriate inventory target levels. For this range of decisions, the following sections describe the specific questions, alternative analytical techniques, and typical data requirements.

Design Decisions

Logistics and supply chain managers are often faced with decisions regarding the strategic and operational designs of their supply chain networks. Supply chain networks include the combination of suppliers, manufacturing plants, warehouses, consolidation points, service providers, and retailers to bring product from the raw material stage to the end consumer. The broad decisions include commodity and product flow as well as where specific value-added activities should take place within the supply chain. Increased material sourcing alternatives, production economies of scale, reduced transportation, and integrated service provider alternatives have increased the need to regularly and more comprehensively evaluate supply chain design alternatives. In recent years, supply chain design analysis is extending further to include marketing channel design as a result of global sourcing and marketing considerations. For example, many firms are investigating the use of alternative channels to market such as home delivery. Supply chain design analysis can be used to determine the total costs and trade-offs in considering alternative channel strategies, activity outsourcing, or offshoring. Global operations also dramatically increase supply chain design alternative complexity and the importance of an accurate assessment of supply chain trade-offs. Thus, the importance of regular supply chain design analysis has increased substantially.

Supply chain design decisions focus on selecting the number and location of plants, warehouses, and other supply chain **nodes.** Typical management questions include:

1. Where should the manufacturing plants be located and which products should they produce?
2. How many warehouses should the firm use, and where should they be located?
3. What customers or market areas should be serviced from each warehouse?
4. Which product lines should be produced or stocked at each plant or warehouse?
5. What is the role of master or regional distribution centers relative to field or local warehouses?
6. What sourcing and marketing channels should be used to source material and serve international markets?
7. What combination of public and private warehouse facilities should be used?
8. What service providers and value-added services should be used meet market requirements?

A typical supply chain design requires analyses addressing combinations of the above questions.

Typical supply chain design problems can be characterized as very complex and data-intensive. Complexity is created by the number of sourcing, plant, warehouse, market, and product alternatives that can be considered; data intensity is created because the analysis requires detailed demand and transportation data for existing strategies as well as for potential alternatives. Sophisticated modeling and analysis techniques must be employed to effectively deal with the complexity and data intensity necessary to identify the best alternatives. The decision support systems used to evaluate supply chain design alternatives are generally some form of mathematical optimization. The general logic and data requirements are described below.

Design Logic

Supply chain design techniques typically use some form of optimization to systematically evaluate design alternatives. The design alternatives include combinations of suppliers, plants, warehouses, and product stocking strategies. Linear or mixed integer optimization are common techniques used to select from a number of available options while considering specific constraints. Mixed integer optimization is the most common, as it can force some variables to be integers, which can require warehouses to be open or closed, whereas standard linear programming could result in a "half open" warehouse. House and Karrenbauer provided a long-standing definition of optimization relevant to logistics:[6]

> An optimization model considers the aggregate set of requirements from the customers, the aggregate set of production possibilities for the producers, the potential intermediary points, the transportation alternatives and develops the optimal system. The model determines on an aggregate flow basis where the warehouses should be, where the stocking points should be, how big the warehouses should be and what kinds of transportation options should be implemented.

Supply chain design tools attempt to identify the least cost alternative among supply chain alternatives while considering relevant constraints. For the relevant problem scope, the analysis includes fixed and variable costs incurred because of facilities such as suppliers, manufacturing plants, warehouses, and consolidation points; transportation; handling; production; and inventory. Figure 14.2 illustrates the scope of a typical supply chain design analyses. The major supply chain design constraints include market region demands, plant production capacity, warehouse storage capacity, and product stocking strategy. Notwithstanding the value of optimization, linear programming confronts some major problems when dealing with complex logistical system designs. First, to format a comprehensive design, it is necessary to develop explicit functional relationships for the full range of design options. The functional relationship must consider all possible combinations for suppliers,

---

[6] Robert G. House and Jeffrey J. Karrenbauer, "Logistics System Modeling," *International Journal of Physical Distribution and Materials Management* 8, no. 4 (May 1978), pp. 189–99.

FIGURE 14.2 **Total Cost Analysis Approach**

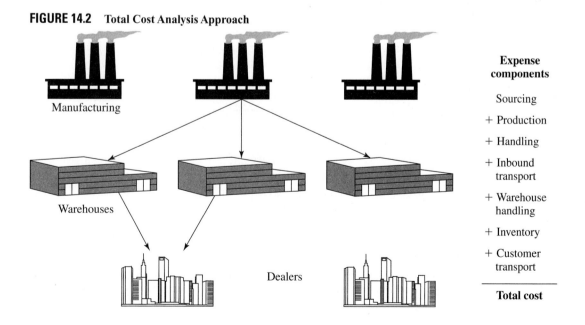

Manufacturing

Warehouses

Dealers

Expense components

Sourcing

+ Production

+ Handling

+ Inbound transport

+ Warehouse handling

+ Inventory

+ Customer transport

_____

Total cost

production locations, distribution locations, wholesalers, markets, and products. The sheer number of alternatives and the associated constraints result in a very large problem. Second, the optimality feature of the technique is relative; that is, it is only as valid as the design problem definition. Too many simplifying assumptions can render a solution mathematically optimal but useless in terms of business practice. Third, the capability of existing linear programming procedures is typically limited by the number of echelons or stages in the supply chain and by the problem size. For example, problems requiring the analysis of flows from production locations to warehouses and then to markets (i.e., three echelons) can be solved easily by most optimizers. However, the size limitations may make it difficult to perform a complete supply chain analysis.

As discussed earlier in the chapter, the analysis phase of the process includes identification of appropriate tools, data requirements, and evaluation of alternatives. Each task is discussed below.

Tool Selection

A supply chain design analysis typically begins with the selection of an appropriate modeling tool. While generalized mixed integer programming packages can be used, supply chain design is unique and common enough that it is advisable to seek out one of the customized tools. There are a number of PC-based packages that can be used to effectively evaluate supply chain alternatives. Ballou and Masters have completed a number of surveys documenting the availability of these tools.[7] These design tools typically differ in their capacity, flexibility, graphics, and solution speed. These analysis tools can be purchased or leased for limited use. In general, the tools try to determine the combination of plant and distribution center alternatives that minimizes the cost while operating within demand and capacity constraints.

Data Requirements

The primary supply chain design analysis data requirements include market product, network, customer demand, transportation rate, and variable and fixed cost definitions.

Supply chain design analysis requires that demand be classified or assigned to geographic market areas. The combination of geographic areas constitutes a logistics service area. Such an area may be a country or global region. The demand for each customer is assigned to one of the market areas. The selection of a market definition method is an extremely important element of the system design procedure. Figure 14.3 illustrates how the United States might be segmented into market areas for a supply chain analysis. Each dot represents an aggregation of demand. A number of market definition structures have been developed. The most useful structures for supply chain modeling are (1) county, (2) standard metropolitan statistical area (SMSA), and (3) zip or postal codes. Postal codes are the international equivalent of zip codes. The most common structure uses zip or postal codes since company records usually include such information. In addition, extensive government and transportation data are available by zip codes. The major issues for selecting a market definition approach concern the number of areas required to provide accurate results. While more market detail increases accuracy, it also increases analysis effort and time. Research indicates that for North America, approximately 200 markets offer an effective trade-off between accuracy and analysis effort.[8]

[7] Ronald H. Ballou and James M. Masters, "Facility Location Commercial Software Survey," *Journal of Business Logistics* 20, no. 1 (1999), pp. 215–33.

[8] For original research regarding the number of market areas, see Robert G. House and Kenneth D. Jaime, "Measuring the Impact of an Alternative Method Classification System in Distribution Planning," *Journal of Business Logistics* 2, no. 2 (1981), pp.1–31; and Ronald H. Ballou, "Information Considerations for Logistics Network Planning," *International Journal of Physical Distribution and Materials Management* 17, no. 7 (1987), pp. 3–14.

FIGURE 14.3
Supply Chain
Network

Source: Used with permission
from Logic Tools, Chicago.

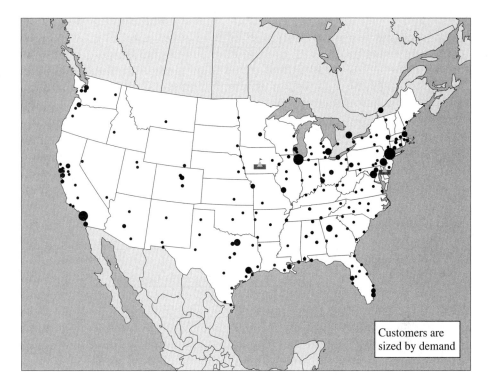

Customers are
sized by demand

Product definition refers to the number of stockkeeping units required to complete the analysis. Although individual SKU flows can be considered in performing supply chain design analysis, it is usually not necessary to use such detail. Individual items, especially those with similar distribution characteristics, production sites, and channel arrangements, can be grouped or aggregated to simplify the analysis. Typical supply chain analyses are completed at the product family level. SKU aggregation into product families reduces analysis complexity and therefore data collection and optimizer run times.

The network definition specifies the channel members, institutions, and possible locations to be included in the analysis. Specific issues concern the combinations of suppliers, manufacturers, warehouses, wholesalers, and retailers that are to be included. Network definition also includes consideration of new plants, warehouses, or channel member alternatives. Figure 14.4 illustrates a channel for industrial and retail customers. While using a more comprehensive definition reduces the chance of suboptimizing system performance, total channel and supply chain design analysis increases complexity, again resulting in more extensive data collection and longer solution times. Supply chain analysts must evaluate the trade-offs between increasing analysis complexity and improved potential for total supply chain optimization.

Market demand defines shipment volume to each geographic area identified as a market. Specifically, supply chain analysis is based on the relative product volume shipped to each market area. While the volume may pertain to the number of units or cases shipped to each market, most supply chain design analyses are based on weight, since transportation cost is strongly influenced by weight moved. Market demand utilized in the analysis may also be based on historical shipments or anticipated volume if substantial changes are expected. The market demand must be profiled into different shipment sizes, since transportation cost is significantly influenced by shipment size.

FIGURE 14.4

Channel Network Example

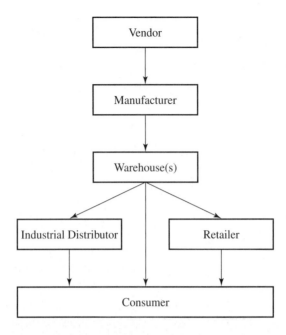

Inbound and outbound transportation rates are a major supply chain design data requirement. Rates must be provided for shipments between existing and potential supply chain members and markets. In addition, rates must be developed for each shipment size and for each potential transportation link between existing and alternative warehouses and markets. It is common for supply chain analysis to require in excess of a million individual rates. Because of the large number, rates are commonly developed by using regressions or are retrieved from carrier rate files.

Variable and fixed costs associated with operating manufacturing plants and warehouses are the final major supply chain design factor. Variable cost includes expenses related to labor, energy, utilities, and materials. In general, variable expenses are a function of facility throughput. Fixed costs include expenses related to facilities, equipment, and supervisory management. Within a relevant plant and warehouse facility operating range, fixed costs remain relatively constant. While variable and fixed cost differences by geography are typically not substantial, there are minor geographic considerations, which should be included to ensure analysis accuracy. The major differences result from geographic peculiarities in wage rates, energy cost, land values, and taxes.

Evaluation of Alternatives

Typical supply chain design analysis can lead to evaluation of a large number of alternatives, even for a relatively small analysis where the enterprise wants to consider all possible combinations of just 10 different distribution centers, for example. There are 6.2 million variations ranging from 10 different combinations of 1 distribution center to 1 combination of 10. If it took a single minute to evaluate each alternative, it would take 11 years to investigate all possible options. This emphasizes the importance of the feasibility assessment discussed earlier. This does not even include the possibility of looking at combinations of different suppliers or manufacturing plants.

The baseline analysis is typically first to validate the costs and establish the credibility of the analysis tool. Figure 14.5 illustrates the baseline results of a supply chain system

FIGURE 14.5
**Base Supply Chain
Network**

Source: Used with permission
from Logic Tools, Chicago.

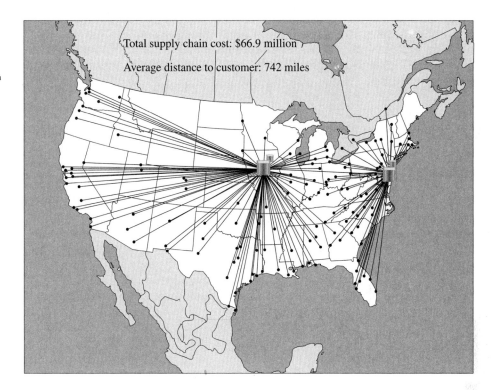

Total supply chain cost: $66.9 million

Average distance to customer: 742 miles

with two plants and two warehouses. The figure illustrates a supply chain with a plant with colocated warehouses in Pennsylvania and Iowa. As noted in the figure, the performance of this scenario is $66.9 million and an average distance of 742 miles. While supply chain design tools provide good performance data in terms of cost, service is typically reported in distance or time to market rather than a measure such as fill rate. The distance is a proxy variable representing transit time from the warehouse to the customer. Prior to investigating other scenarios, these results should be compared with the firm's historical data to determine if the model's costs provide an approximate representation of the firm's actual operation. If the historical and modeled costs are not approximately equal, any differences must be investigated to identify potential errors or provide some explanation. Reasonable accuracy is critical to build managerial credibility.

Other alternatives can be modeled to investigate other supply chain design options. In some cases, supply chain design tools can systematically evaluate a series of alternatives such as determining the optimum number of warehouses between 3 and 10. In other cases, when the number or production mix of plants is under investigation, the analyst must identify and evaluate each option separately. This again emphasizes the need to critically assess each alternative regarding its feasibility so that it is not necessary to complete a detailed evaluation of alternatives with limited feasibility.

Figure 14.6 illustrates a revised supply chain design based on the situation discussed earlier. The results demonstrate that a 3-plant and 4-warehouse supply chain yields substantially better performance than the baseline case. As the figure notes, the total cost is reduced to $61.8 million with an average distance between the warehouse and customer of 428 miles. In this case, the alternative supply chain design can both improve service, in terms of distance to the customer, and reduce the total cost. Bender provides a more

FIGURE 14.6
Alternative Supply Chain Network

Source: Used with permission from Logic Tools, Chicago.

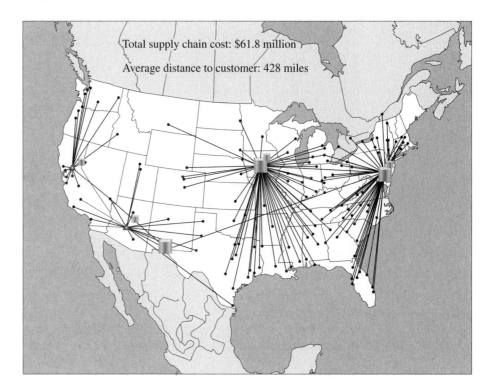

Total supply chain cost: $61.8 million

Average distance to customer: 428 miles

detailed description of the systematic process to identify and evaluate supply chain alternatives using a decision support tool.[9]

Although the supply chain design tools are increasingly sophisticated, there are a few issues that must be considered in their application. The first concerns the treatment of inventory carrying cost. As illustrated in Chapter 13, inventory carrying cost should theoretically increase at a decreasing rate as the number of distribution centers increases. While this is generally true, there may be exceptions such as when a regional distribution center is used to provide backup stock for slow-moving items at 5 warehouses. Even though the total number of warehouses is increased to 6, it likely that the total inventory to provide equivalent service would actually decrease because of the pooling of backup inventory. Similarly, many of the supply chain design tools do not have standardized processes to determine the inventory implications of different design alternatives. Since there is no standardized process, it is important to understand and make any appropriate adjustments to the inventory carrying cost computed by supply chain design tools.[10]

The second concerns changes in assumptions regarding shipment sizes. Most of the supply chain design tools use a constant shipment size for each transport lane. While this may be acceptable as long as the number of distribution centers does not change significantly, it is likely that the shipment size would change with a significant change in the number of warehouses. For example, if current shipments between a plant and four warehouses are

[9] Paul S. Bender. "How to Design an Optimum Worldwide Supply Chain." *Supply Chain Management Review* 1, no. 1 (Spring 1997), pp. 70–81.

[10] For a more detailed discussion of techniques to evaluate multiple location inventories, see Ronald H. Ballou and Apostolos Burnetas, "Planning Multiple Location Inventories," *Journal of Business Logistics* 24, no. 2 (2003), pp. 65–90; and Pablo Miranda, Rodrigo Garrido. "Incorporating Inventory Control Decisions into a Strategic Distribution Network Design Model with Stochastic Demand." *Transportation Research. Part E, Logistics & Transportation Review* 40E, no. 3 (May 2004). pp. 183–208.

a truckload, it is likely that shipments would be smaller if the number of warehouses increased to 8. The analysis must consider the impact of such change.

The third concerns the focus of the analyses. In the past, a substantial number of supply chain design analyses focused on warehouse location. Since logistics networks were relatively stable, it was unnecessary for firms to complete logistics system analyses regularly; however, the dynamics of alternative supply chain options, changing cost levels, and availability of integrated service providers requires that supply chain networks be evaluated and refined more frequently today. It is also increasingly necessary to coordinate supply chain design strategy with product and process design, which may require evaluations annually, quarterly, or even monthly.[11]

Over the past decade, there has been an increase in both the scope and focus of supply chain design analyses. In terms of scope, the analyses consider a broader range of supply chain members, including commodity providers, suppliers, manufacturers, distributors, and retailers. In terms of focus, supply chain design analyses are shifting from minimizing total cost toward maximizing profits or return on assets. Designs that maximize profitability consider revenue as well as cost and are designed to assign available product and resources to the most profitable customers. Designs that maximize return on assets identify supply chain alternatives that may result in higher variable costs but utilize fewer assets through outsourcing or use of service providers. As a result of the increasing opportunities enabled by globalization, outsourcing, organizational consolidation, shared services, and changes in relative cost, ongoing analysis of supply chain alternatives is becoming more regular.[12]

Inventory Decisions

Inventory analysis decisions focus on determining the optimum inventory management parameters to meet desired service levels with minimum investment. Inventory parameters refer to safety stock, reorder point, order quantity, and review cycles for a specific facility and product combination. This analysis can be designed to refine inventory parameters on a periodic or daily basis. Daily refinements make parameters more sensitive to environmental changes such as demand levels or performance cycle length; however, they also result in nervous inventory management systems. System nervousness causes frequent expediting and deexpediting of numerous small shipments.

Inventory analysis focuses on the decisions discussed in Chapter 6. Specific questions include: (1) How much product should be produced during the next production cycle? (2) Which warehouses should maintain inventories of each item? (3) Should slow-moving items be centralized? (4) What is the optimum size of replenishment orders (the order quantity decision)? (5) What is the necessary reorder point for replenishment orders (the safety stock decision)?

There are two types of methods to evaluate and select from inventory management options: analytic and simulation.

Analytic Inventory Techniques

Analytic inventory methods utilize functional relationships such as those discussed in Chapter 6 to determine ideal inventory stocking parameters based on the desired service

[11] For an example process for coordinating product, process, and supply chain design, see C. Forza, F. Salvador, and M. Rungtusanatham. "Coordinating Product Design, Process Design, and Supply Chain Design Decisions: Part B. Coordinating Approaches, Tradeoffs, and Future Research Direction." *Journal of Operations Management* 23, no. 3 (April 2005). pp. 319.

[12] For a more detailed discussion regarding the future of supply chain planning and tools, see David Simchi-Levi. "The Master of Design." *Supply Chain Management Review* 4, no. 5 (November/December 2000), pp. 74–81.

FIGURE 14.7 **Analytic Inventory Overview**

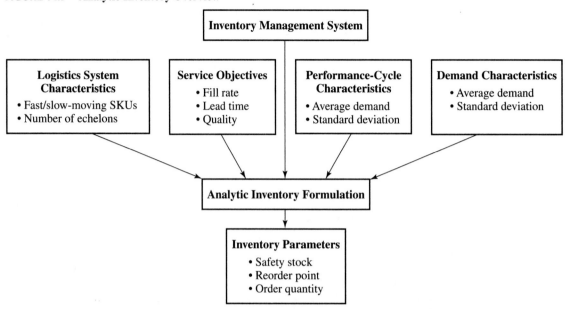

level. Figure 14.7 illustrates the analytic inventory concept. The technique uses service objectives, demand characteristics, performance cycle characteristics, and the logistics system characteristics as input to calculate optimum inventory parameters. From an inventory management perspective, service objectives are typically defined in terms of case or order fill rates. Demand characteristics describe the periodic average and standard deviation of customer demand. Performance cycle characteristics describe the average and standard deviations for replenishment performance cycles. Logistics system characteristics describe the number of distribution stages or echelons requiring inventory management decisions. The analytical inventory technique is based on assumptions describing the logistics system stocking echelons and the probabilities relating demand and performance cycle characteristics. The probability relationships, along with the service level objectives, determine the optimal inventory management parameters in terms of replenishment order quantities and reorder points. Numerous examples of software applications exist that utilize analytic techniques to determine optimum inventory management parameters.[13]

The advantage of analytic inventory techniques is the ability to directly determine optimum inventory parameters, given certain assumptions regarding operating environment. On the other hand, analytic inventory techniques are limited in terms of accuracy when assumptions are not met. For example, since most analytic inventory techniques assume normally distributed demand and performance cycles, the techniques lose accuracy when the shape of actual demand or performance cycles deviates from the normality assumption.[14] Nevertheless, analytical inventory techniques are often a good place to start when attempting to determine optimum inventory parameters.[15]

---

[13] An example of such an inventory management system is *Inventory Analyst* from Logic-Tools (Chicago), which determines the ideal inventory parameters to optimize order quantity and safety stock. Most APS applications, such as i2's *Rhythm,* SAP's *Advanced Planning Optimizer,* and *Manugistics,* incorporate analytic techniques into their advanced planning and scheduling software.

[14] These assumptions regarding normal demand and lead times can be overcome with numerical methods such as those discussed in J. Masters, "Determination of Near Optimal Stock Levels for Multi-Echelon Distribution Inventories," *Journal of Business Logistics* 14, no. 2 (1993), pp. 165–96.

[15] Spreadsheets can be used to develop and apply analytical inventory techniques. For an example, see the "Inventory Calculator" from the supporting material.

FIGURE 14.8
Inventory Simulation Overview

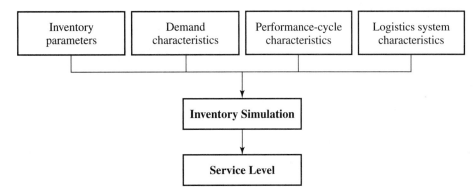

Simulation Inventory Techniques

The inventory simulation approach creates a mathematical and probabilistic model of the logistics operating environment as it actually exists. As Figure 14.8 illustrates, the simulation approach is similar to creating a laboratory testing environment for the supply chain network and operating policies. Simulation is similar to the analytic approach except that the roles of the inventory parameters and service levels are reversed.

In simulation, inventory parameters such as the order quantities and the reorder points that are to be tested become the simulation inputs. These inputs define the environment to be tested. The major simulation outputs are the service level and inventory performance characteristics of the testing environment. The simulation, in effect, evaluates the performance of a specific situation. If the reported performance does not achieve desired objectives, the inventory parameters must be changed and a new environment is simulated. It is sometimes necessary to complete a number of simulations to identify the combination of inventory parameters that yields desired performance.

The major benefit of simulation techniques is the ability to model a wide range of supply chain environments without requiring simplifying assumptions. It is possible to accurately simulate virtually any supply chain environment by incorporating network characteristics and operating policies. The major shortfall of simulation techniques is their limited ability to search for and identify optimum solutions. While there are inventory simulation examples that incorporate search algorithms, they are limited in capability and scope. There are indications that simulation is becoming more popular as firms attempt to understand inventory dynamics in the logistics channel.[16]

Inventory decision support applications are increasing in importance due to the emphasis on streamlining inventory levels to reduce the logistics asset base. The demand for more refined inventory parameters has increased the need for more sophisticated inventory analysis techniques. Software firms have responded by developing both stand-alone and integrated applications.[17]

Transportation Decisions

Transportation analyses focus on routing and scheduling of transportation equipment to improve vehicle and driver utilization while meeting customer service requirements. Transportation decisions can be characterized as strategic or tactical. Strategic transportation decisions concern long-term resource allocation, such as for extended time periods.

---

[16] D. van der Zee and J. van der Vorst. "A Modeling Framework for Supply Chain Simulation: Opportunities for Improved Decision Making." *Decision Sciences* 36, no. 1 (February 2005), pp. 65–95.

[17] Examples include James Aaron Cooke, "Simulate Before You Act," *Logistics Management and Distribution Report* 38, no. 9 (September 1999), pp.77–80; and "IBM Product Analyzes Your Supply Chain," *Industrial Distribution* 88, no. 8 (August 1999), p. 44.

FIGURE 14.9
Typical Routing or
Delivery Problem

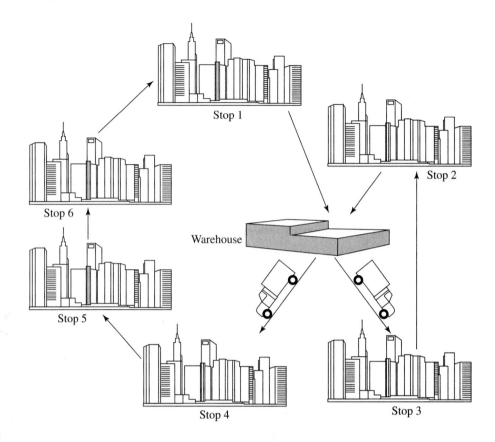

Thus, strategic routing decisions identify fixed transport routes that may be used for months or years. Tactical transportation decisions concern short-term resource allocations such as daily or weekly routes. The objective of transportation analysis is to minimize the combination of vehicles, hours, and miles required to deliver product. Typical transportation analysis questions include: (1) How should deliveries be grouped to form routes? (2) What is the best delivery sequence for servicing customers? (3) Which routes should be assigned to which vehicle types? (4) What is the best type of vehicle for servicing different customer types? (5) What delivery sequence should be used to accommodate time restrictions imposed by customers? Figure 14.9 illustrates a typical routing or delivery problem. The warehouse represents the central departure site for all delivery vehicles, and each stop represents a customer location, such as a retailer.

Transportation Analysis Techniques

Routing and scheduling analyses have been well researched for supply chain tactical and operational planning. They are particularly important for firms completing partial load delivery activities such as package or beverage distribution. The techniques can generally be classified as heuristic approaches, exact approaches, interactive approaches, and combination approaches.[18]

Heuristic approaches utilize rule-of-thumb clustering or savings techniques to develop routes by sequentially adding and deleting stops. Exact, or optimal, approaches use mathematical (linear) programming to identify the best routes. Historically, optimization solution

---

[18] For a further discussion of each of these approaches, see Kevin Bott and Ronald H. Ballou, "Research Perspectives in Vehicle Routing and Scheduling," *Transportation Research* 20A, no. 3 (1986), pp. 239–43.

methods have been too computationally complex for even the fastest computers, but recent mathematical programming advances have enhanced their capabilities. The main difficulties with most exact procedures are (1) the large number of constraints and variables needed to represent even the basic routing and scheduling problem and (2) the impact of this size on computation time and computer storage space.

Interactive approaches utilize a combination of simulation, cost calculator, or graphics capability to support an interactive decision process. The decision maker identifies the alternatives for evaluation. The interactive decision support system then determines and plots the routes and calculates the performance characteristics in terms of time and cost. The decision maker then interactively evaluates the performance characteristics of each alternative and refines the strategy until no additional improvement is likely. The obvious drawback of interactive approaches is the dependence on the skill and ability of the decision maker, particularly as the problem size and complexity increase.

Combinations of the three approaches have proved very effective. Two criteria are important in evaluating alternative solution approaches: generalizability and accuracy. Generalizability is the ability to efficiently incorporate extensions for special situations, such as pickups and deliveries, multiple depots, time windows, vehicle capacities, and legal driving times, in an actual setting. Accuracy refers to the ability to closely approximate performance characteristics and the results' proximity to an optimal solution. Accuracy determines the level of and credibility in the possible savings as a result of decreased vehicle operating expense, better customer service, and improved fleet productivity.[19] There are numerous examples of PC- and server-based routing and scheduling packages.[20]

Transportation Analysis Data Requirements

Transportation analysis requires three types of data: network, pickup or delivery demand, and operating characteristics. The network defines all possible routes and is the backbone of any transportation routing system. In some cases, a network is defined by using street maps of the delivery area. Each intersection is a node, and the streets become links. The network contains the links between each node, the road distance, the transit time, and any special constraints such as weight limits or tolls. A street-level network is very accurate and precise, particularly when there are constraints such as rivers and mountains. The deficiency of a street-level network is the high cost of development and maintenance. The other approach involves plotting customers on a grid and then computing the possible links between customers, using straight line distance. Latitude and longitude coordinates are often used. While a grid system is less costly to develop and maintain than a street-level network, it is less accurate and does not consider constraints as well.

Demand data defines periodic customer pickup and delivery requirements. For strategic or long-term analyses, demand is specified in terms of average periodic pickups or deliveries per customer. Routes are then created on the basis of the average demand with a capacity allowance for extremely high demand periods. For tactical routing analysis, demand typically represents customer orders scheduled for delivery during the period being

---

[19] For an expanded discussion of alternative analysis approaches, see Bott and Ballou, "Research Perspectives in Vehicle Routing and Scheduling"; Ronald H. Ballou and Yogesh K. Agerwal, "A Performance Comparison of Several Popular Algorithms for Vehicle Routing and Scheduling," *Journal of Business Logistics* 9, no. 1 (1988), pp. 51–64; and Ronald H. Ballou, "A Continued Comparison of Several Popular Algorithms for Vehicle Routing and Scheduling," *Journal of Business Logistics* 11, no. 2 (1990), pp. 111–26. For a discussion of a transport planning success story, see Jonathan Bridle. "Integrated Transport Planning: Supply-Chain Success." *Logistics and Transport Focus* 6, no. 5. (June 2004), pp. 50–53.

[20] Examples of transportation routing and scheduling software include CAPS RoutePro (www.CAPS.com) and Descartes Systems Routing & Scheduling (www. Descartes.com).

planned, such as daily. Tactical analysis allows the routes to be precisely designed for delivery requirements with no allowance for uncertainty.

Operating characteristics define the number of vehicles, vehicle limitations, driver constraints, and operating costs. Vehicle limitations include capacity and weight restrictions as well as unloading constraints such as dock requirements. Driver constraints include driving time and unloading restrictions. Operating costs include fixed and variable expenses associated with vehicles and drivers.

Transportation analysis for vehicle routing and scheduling is receiving increased interest because of the effectiveness and availability of low-cost software. Many firms involved in day-to-day transportation operations have reduced transportation expenses by 10 to 15 percent through the use of tactical or strategic transportation analysis. As customers continue to demand smaller orders, transportation analysis will become increasingly important to make effective routing, scheduling, and consolidation decisions.

Freight Lane Analysis

One common logistics analysis concerns transportation movements on specific freight lanes. The analysis can be completed on a very specific basis between facilities or on a broader regional basis. Freight lane analysis focuses on the balance of volume between origin and destination points. To maximize vehicle utilization, movements should be balanced, or roughly equal, in both directions. Lanes may include two or more points, as Figure 14.10 illustrates. Triangular freight lanes attempt to coordinate movement between three points by moving combinations of material and finished product between suppliers, manufacturers, and customers.

Freight lane analysis involves both movement volume and the number of shipments or trips between points. The objective is to identify imbalances that offer opportunities for enhanced logistics productivity. Once lane imbalances are identified, management attempts to identify volume that can be transported in the underutilized direction. This might be accomplished by switching carriers or modes, shifting volume to or from a private fleet, increasing back-haul of raw materials, or creating an alliance with another shipper. Conversely, volume in the overutilized direction might be diverted to other carriers or shippers or sourced from an alternative location.

Table 14.6 illustrates a lane analysis that clearly identifies shipment imbalances. The transportation manager should attempt to balance the triangular move by developing additional volume between Cincinnati and Detroit. The volume could be developed either by moving product sources to the Cincinnati area or by creating an alliance with a shipper that moves volume between Cincinnati and Detroit with no back-haul.

FIGURE 14.10
Example of Triangular Freight Lane

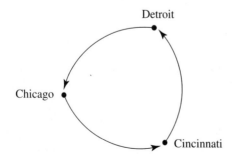

	Origin	Destination	Weight (CWT)	Shipments
TABLE 14.6 Freight Lane Analysis of Monthly Movements	Detroit	Chicago	8740	23
	Chicago	Cincinnati	5100	17
	Cincinnati	Detroit	2000	8

Inventory Analysis

Another common logistics analysis focuses on inventory performance and productivity. Typical inventory analysis considers relative product sales volume and inventory turnover and is performed on an ABC basis, as discussed in Chapter 6. For example, by listing the top 10 sales and inventory groupings in decreasing sequence, a logistics manager can quickly determine product groups that have a major influence on volume and inventory levels. As indicated in Chapter 6, 80 percent of sales are typically accounted for by 20 percent of the items. It is also typical that 80 percent of the inventory accounts for only 20 percent of the volume. Knowledge of these characteristics and the items that make up each product group is useful in targeting inventory management efforts. Items that demonstrate a large inventory commitment relative to sales can be selected for intensive management efforts to reduce inventory level and improve performance.

Table 14.7 (page 350) illustrates a typical inventory analysis report. This example is sorted by item sales, although there is some logic to sequencing the report by decreasing inventory level or inventory turns. Items with relatively high inventories or low turns should be targeted for management attention.

Summary

This chapter provides a comprehensive review of the logistics planning process, decisions, and techniques. It is designed to guide the logistics manager through the overall process of situation analysis, alternative identification, data collection, quantitative evaluation, and development of viable recommendations.

The methodology, which is generic enough for most logistics problem solving, includes three phases: problem definition and planning, data collection and analysis, and recommendations and implementation. The problem definition and planning phase is concerned with the feasibility assessment and project planning. Feasibility assessment includes situation analysis, supporting logic development, and cost/benefit estimation. Project planning requires statements of objectives, constraints, measurement standard, analysis technique specification, and project work plan development.

The data collection and analysis phase develops assumptions, collects data, and completes the quantitative and qualitative analyses. Assumptions development and data collection include tasks to define the analysis approach, formalize assumptions, identify data sources, and collect and validate data. The analysis step involves definition of analysis questions, completion of validation and baseline analyses, and completion of alternative and sensitivity analyses.

The recommendations and implementation phase develops the final plan. The recommendation development step includes identification and evaluation of the best alternatives. The implementation step defines a recommended course of action, schedules development, defines acceptance criteria, and schedules final implementation.

Regular supply chain design analysis is becoming increasingly critical to respond to changes in global material availability, market demands, and production resource

TABLE 14.7 Typical Inventory Analysis Report

Product	Total Unit Demand	Standard Cost	Sales at Standard Cost	Percent Sales	Cumulative Sales Percent	Total Inventory	Inventory at Standard Cost	Percent Inventory	Cumulative Inventory Percent	Item	Cumulative Items	Inventory Turns	Class
Part A	3,487	423.76	1,477,656.03	14.35	14.35	453	191,931.32	16.58	16.58	1	4.00	7.70	A
Part B	31,347	43.82	1,373,573.25	13.34	27.68	1,938	84,909.82	7.33	23.91	1	8.00	16.18	A
Part C	21,221	47.49	1,007,770.10	9.79	37.47	1,652	78,447.73	6.78	30.69	1	12.00	12.85	A
Part D	15,077	52.82	796,319.01	7.73	45.20	1,489	78,669.62	6.79	37.48	1	16.00	10.12	A
Part E	14,956	35.22	526,774.13	5.11	50.32	1,767	62,241.97	5.38	42.86	1	20.00	8.46	A
Part F	5,826	80.93	471,481.17	4.58	54.89	272	22,041.74	1.90	44.76	1	24.00	21.39	A
Part G	57,304	8.16	467,868.82	4.54	59.44	3,630	29,637.63	2.56	47.32	1	28.00	15.79	A
Part H	3,591	74.64	267,986.82	2.60	62.04	379	28,303.30	2.44	49.76	1	32.00	9.47	A
Part I	8,139	32.46	264,225.47	2.57	64.60	1,467	47,640.20	4.11	53.88	1	36.00	5.55	A
Part J	19,036	13.50	257,079.87	2.50	67.10	453	6,114.31	0.53	54.41	1	40.00	42.05	A
Part K	8,169	31.38	256,344.63	2.49	69.59	153	4,806.26	0.42	54.82	1	44.00	53.34	A
Part L	33,457	7.60	254,277.51	2.47	72.06	9,022	68,572.76	5.92	60.74	1	48.00	3.71	A
Part M	6,609	38.32	253,245.67	2.46	74.52	1,655	63,401.31	5.48	66.22	1	52.00	3.99	A
Part N	29,394	8.61	252,950.09	2.46	76.97	3,391	29,177.21	2.52	68.74	1	56.00	8.67	A
Part O	17,296	14.45	249,861.10	2.43	79.40	1,414	20,420.37	1.76	70.50	1	60.00	12.24	A
Part P	3,089	76.08	235,029.27	2.28	81.68	921	70,039.66	6.05	76.55	1	64.00	3.36	B
Part Q	1,579	144.08	227,520.08	2.21	83.89	340	48,916.42	4.22	80.78	1	68.00	4.65	B
Part R	6,577	34.41	226,278.06	2.20	86.09	440	15,155.23	1.31	82.09	1	72.00	14.93	B
Part S	6,326	35.02	221,551.81	2.15	88.24	201	7,032.45	0.61	82.69	1	76.00	31.50	B
Part T	5,041	43.11	217,344.77	2.11	90.35	970	41,808.09	3.61	86.30	1	80.00	5.20	B
Part U	8,906	23.74	211,432.08	2.05	92.40	1,473	34,960.94	3.02	89.32	1	84.00	6.05	B
Part V	2,106	99.55	209,613.04	2.04	94.44	314	31,234.67	2.70	92.02	1	88.00	6.71	B
Part W	10,097	19.73	199,176.93	1.93	96.37	705	13,897.74	1.20	93.22	1	92.00	14.33	C
Part X	10,031	19.85	199,145.62	1.93	98.31	2,489	49,412.08	4.27	97.49	1	96.00	4.03	C
Part Y	34,529	5.05	174,510.19	1.69	100.00	5,753	29,077.41	2.51	100.00	1	100.00	6.00	C
TOTAL	363,189		10,299.016	100.00%	100.00%	42,740	1,157,850	100.00	100.00%	25		8.89	

availability. In response to this requirement, supply chain design optimization tools are becoming more widely available to support strategic and tactical analyses. More tactical tools such as dynamic simulation and routing and scheduling algorithms can be used to investigate and evaluate inventory and transportation alternatives. The importance of such comprehensive planning and analysis methods and tools is growing as a result of the possible alternatives to and complexity of global supply chains. Ad hoc tactical analyses such as freight lane balancing and ABC inventory analysis must be completed regularly to respond to changes in transportation rates, flows, and product demands.

Challenge Questions

1. What is the basic objective in a logistics design and analysis study? Is it normally a one-time activity?

2. What is sensitivity analysis, and what is its role in systems design and analysis?

3. Why is it important to develop supporting logic to guide the logistical planning process?

4. Both internal and external review assessments must consider a number of measures. What are they and why are they important?

5. Why is a cost/benefit evaluation important to logistical systems design efforts?

6. What is the key objective in freight lane analysis?

7. In a general sense, what are the essential differences between analytic and simulation techniques?

8. What is the main advantage of the typical optimization technique in comparison to simulation?

9. At what point in the typical analysis does the technique give way to the managerial review and evaluation process?

10. Compare and contrast strategic and tactical transportation decisions.

PART FOUR

Administration

This final part deals with the second primary responsibility of a firm's logistical management—administration. Chapter 15 develops principles of organization and relationship management that are essential for realizing integrated operations. Alternative collaborative models are developed and illustrated as a means to facilitate cooperation among customers, material suppliers, service suppliers, and the enterprise orchestrating the supply chain arrangement. Attention is also directed to cross-organizational change management and concepts of human resource organization. The ubiquitous nature of logistical operations creates a unique organizational structure challenge. The dispersion of logistical operations across vast geographical areas serves to place special attention on developing effective management and control processes. Chapter 16 shifts focus to performance assessment and the development of cost measurement to support activity-based management. Particular attention is directed to the development of logistics and supply chain performance metrics.

Relationship Development and Management

Among the topics of logistics, few hold more managerial interest than developing and managing organizational relationships. For most of business history, emphasis was devoted to relationships internal to an organization, developing an appropriate organizational structure to efficiently and effectively perform the work of logistics. However, the information revolution and the focus on supply chain integration are forcing logistics executives to rethink nearly every aspect of traditional organizational logic and to extend their thinking to relationships with suppliers and customers. In fact, the essence of supply chain management lies in the ability to orchestrate collaborative relationships both internally and with supply chain partners.

Development and Management of Internal Logistics Relationships

Prior to the 1950s, functions now accepted as logistics were generally viewed as facilitating or support work. Organization responsibility for logistics was typically dispersed throughout the firm. Figure 15.1 is a hypothetical organization chart that depicts the fragmentation that was typical at that time. This fragmentation often meant that aspects of logistical work were performed without coordination, often resulting in duplication and waste. Information was frequently distorted or delayed, and lines of authority and responsibility were typically

FIGURE 15.1
Traditional
Organization of
Logistically Related
Functions

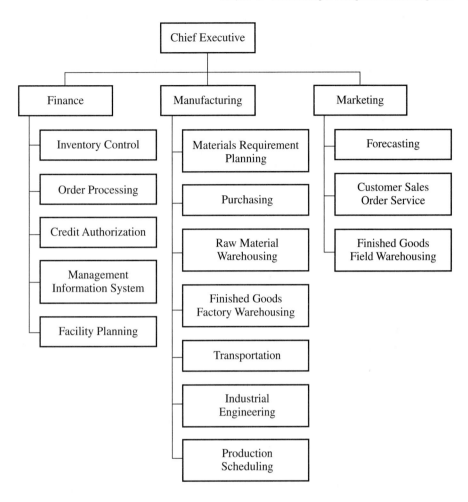

blurred. Managers, recognizing the need for total cost control, began to reorganize and combine logistics functions into a single managerial group. Structuring logistics as an integrated organization first appeared in the 1950s.[1]

Functional Aggregation

The motivation driving functional aggregation was a growing belief that grouping logistics functions into a single organization would increase the likelihood of integration and facilitate improved understanding of how decisions and procedures in one operational area impact performance in other areas. The belief was that eventually all functions would begin to work as a single group focused on total system performance. This integration paradigm, based on organizational proximity, prevailed throughout a 35-year period. Many different types and levels of functional integration appeared during this time. For many firms, the ink

[1] For early articles discussing this initial integration of logistics activities, see Donald J. Bowersox, "Emerging Patterns of Physical Distribution Organization," *Transportation and Distribution Management,* May 1968, pp. 53–59; John F. Stolle, "How to Manage Physical Distribution," *Harvard Business Review,* July/August 1967, pp. 93–100; and Robert E. Weigand, "The Management of Physical Distribution: A Dilemma," *Michigan State University Business Topics,* Summer 1962, pp. 67–72.

FIGURE 15.2   **Logistics Functional Aggregation**

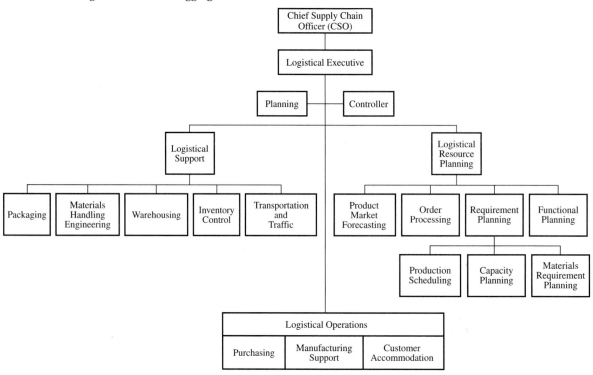

had barely dried on what appeared to be the perfect logistics organization when new and far more pervasive rethinking of what constituted the ideal structure emerged.[2]

The highest level of functional aggregation in logistics organization is depicted in Figure 15.2. This organization structure seeks to unify all logistical functions and operations under a single senior manager. Organizations having the comprehensive nature illustrated in Figure 15.2 were and continue to be rare. However, the trend was clearly to group as many logistical planning and operational functions as practical under single authority and responsibility. The goal was the strategic management of all materials and finished product movement and storage to the maximum benefit of the enterprise.

The rapid development of logistical information systems provided an impetus for functionally integrated organizations. Information technology became available to plan and operate systems that fully integrated logistical operations. Several aspects of the structure presented in Figure 15.2 justify further discussion.

---

[2] For a review of empirical research related to logistics organization evolution, see A. T. Kearney, *Measuring Productivity in Physical Distribution: The $40 Billion Gold Mine* (Oak Brook, IL: Council of Logistics Management, 1978); A. T. Kearney, "Organizing Physical Distribution to Improve Bottom Line Results," *Annual Proceedings of the Council of Logistics Management,* 1981, pp. 1–14; A. T. Kearney, *Measuring and Improving Productivity in the Logistics Process: Achieving Customer Satisfaction Breakthroughs* (Oak Brook, IL: Council of Logistics Management, 1991). A. T. Kearney completed and published studies in Europe, Asia, and North America in 1993. These studies were distributed by Kearney in captive publications. For a review of Michigan State University research on logistics organization and best practice, see: Donald J. Bowersox et al., *Leading Edge Logistics: Competitive Positioning for the 1990s* (Oak Brook, IL: Council of Logistics Management, 1989); Donald J. Bowersox et al., *Logistical Excellence: It's Not Business as Usual* (Burlington, MA: Digital Press, 1992); The Global Logistics Research Team at Michigan State University, *World Class Logistics: The Challenge of Managing Continuous Change* (Oak Brook, IL: Council of Logistics Management, 1995); Donald J. Bowersox, David J. Closs, and Theodore P. Stank, *21st Century Logistics: Making Supply Chain Integration a Reality* (Oak Brook, IL: Council of Logistics Management, 1999).

First, each area of logistics—purchasing, manufacturing support, and customer accommodation—is structured as a separate line operation. The lines of authority and responsibility directly enable each bundle of supportive services to be performed as part of an overall integrated logistical effort. Since areas of operation responsibility are well defined, it is possible to establish manufacturing support as an operation unit similar to purchasing and customer accommodation. Because each unit is operationally self-sufficient, each can maintain the flexibility to accommodate critical services required by its respective operational area. In addition, since overall logistical activities can be planned and coordinated on an integrated basis, operational synergies between areas can be exploited.

Second, five capabilities grouped under logistical support are positioned as operational services. This shared service orientation is the mechanism to integrate logistical operations. It is important to stress that logistical support is not a staff organization. Rather, the group manages day-to-day logistics work, which is structured with matrix accountability for direct liaison between customer accommodation, manufacturing support, and purchasing operations.

Third, logistical resource planning embraces the full potential of management information to plan and coordinate operations. Order processing triggers the logistical system into operation and generates the integrated database required for control. Logistical resource planning facilitates integration. Logistical resource plans are based on product/market forecasting, order processing, and inventory status to determine overall requirements for any planning period. On the basis of identified requirements, the planning unit operationalizes manufacturing by coordinating production scheduling, capacity planning, and materials requirement planning.

Finally, overall planning and controllership exist at the highest level of the organization. These initiatives serve to facilitate integration. The planning group is concerned with long-range strategic positioning and is responsible for logistical system quality improvement and reengineering. The logistical controller is concerned with measurement of cost and customer service performance and provision of information for managerial decision making. The development of procedures for logistical controllership is one of the most critical areas of integrated logistical administration. The need for accurate measurement is a direct result of increased emphasis placed on continuous improvement in customer service performance.[3] The measurement task is extremely important because of the large operating and capital dollar expenditures involved in logistics.

The functionally integrated logistical organization offers a single logic to guide the efficient application of financial and human resources from material sourcing to final product customer delivery. It therefore positions a firm to manage trade-offs among purchasing, manufacturing support, and customer accommodation.

A Shift in Emphasis from Function to Process

Almost overnight, the emphasis shifted from function to process. Firms began to examine the role logistical competency could play in the overall process of creating customer value. This ushered in new thinking regarding how to best achieve integrated logistical performance. To a significant degree, the focus on process reduced the pressure to aggregate functions into all-encompassing organizational units. The critical question became not how to organize individual functions, but rather how to best manage the overall logistical process. The challenges and opportunities of functional disaggregation and information-driven integration began to emerge.

---

[3] Performance measurement is discussed in greater detail in Chapter 16.

The mission of logistics work is to position inventory when and where it is required to facilitate profitable sales. This supportive work must be performed around the clock and typically throughout the world, which means that logistics needs to be an integral part of all processes. The ideal structure for logistics would be an organization that performs essential work as part of the processes it supports while achieving the synergism of cross-functional integration.

Information technology introduced the potential of virtual integration as contrasted to physically combining logistics functions. Using information technology to coordinate or orchestrate integrated performance allows the responsibility for performing work itself to be distributed throughout the overall organization. Integration requires that logistics combine with other areas such as marketing and manufacturing. For example, instead of focusing on how to relate transportation and inventory, the real challenge is to integrate transportation, inventory, new product development, flexible manufacturing, and customer success. To achieve overall organization integration, a firm must combine a wide variety of capabilities into new organization units. This means that traditional single-function departments must be assimilated into a process. Such assimilation often requires that traditional organizations be disaggregated and then recombined in new and unique ways. In one sense, such functional disaggregation may appear to come back full circle to the early days of fragmented single-function departments. However, the critical difference in the emerging organization model is the widespread availability of information. The new organization format is characterized by an extremely different culture concerning how information and knowledge are managed and shared.

Figure 15.3 illustrates how the process-oriented organization might be structured around the eight supply chain processes discussed in Chapter 11. Each key process is led by a process owner who manages a team of members drawn from the critical functional areas which impact process performance.

The concept of process organization is envisioned as the result of three factors: (1) the development of a highly involved work environment with self-directed work teams as a vehicle to empower employees to generate maximum performance; (2) improved productivity that results from managing processes rather than functions, a notion that has always rested at the core of integrated logistics; and (3) the rapid sharing of accurate information that allows all facets of the organization to be integrated. Information technology is viewed as the load-bearing structure of the new enterprise, replacing organizational hierarchy.

The essence of the argument for this radical restructuring is that the traditional concept of organization change through functional aggregation is not sufficient to stimulate major breakthroughs in service or productivity. Rather, traditional organization change shifts or realigns functions without serious redesign of the basic work process. Because such restructuring typically assumes that functional organizations will continue to perform basic work, little or no difference in actual practice results. In essence, companies are refocusing old business practices rather than designing new, more efficient processes.

The challenges of managing logistics as a process are threefold. First, all effort must be focused on value added to the customer. An activity exists and is justified only to the extent it contributes customer value. Therefore, a logistical commitment must be motivated by a belief that customers desire a specific activity to be performed. Logistical mangers must develop the capacity to think externally. Second, integrating logistics as part of a process requires that all skills necessary to complete the work be available regardless of their functional organization. Organizational grouping on the basis of selected function can artificially separate natural work flows and create bottlenecks. When horizontal structures are put in place, critical skills need to be positioned and made accessible to assure that required work is accomplished. Finally, work performed in a process context should stimulate synergism. With systems integration, the design of work as a process means that overall

FIGURE 15.3
Process Organization

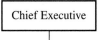

Chief Executive

Process owner: Demand planning	Process team: Marketing, sales, logistics, manufacturing, finance, information technology
Process owner: Customer relationship management	Process team: Marketing, sales, logistics, information technology
Process owner: Order fulfillment/service delivery	Process team: Sales, order processing, logistics, customer service, accounting
Process owner: Product/service development launch	Process team: New product development, marketing, procurement, manufacturing, logistics
Process owner: Manufacturing customization	Process team: Procurement, manufacturing, logistics
Process owner: Supplier relationship collaboration	Process team: Procurement, manufacturing, information technology
Process owner: Life cycle support	Process team: Procurement, logistics, customer service, finance
Process owner: Reverse logistics	Process team: Logistics, customer service

organizational trade-offs are structured to achieve maximum performance for minimum input investment.[4]

The radical changes proposed by a shift from a functional to a process orientation have mixed messages for managers involved in logistics. On the positive side, general adoption of a process orientation builds upon the basic principles of systems integration. At the core of integrated logistics is a commitment to functional excellence that contributes to process performance. A general shift to managing logistics as a process means that it will be positioned as a central contributor to all initiatives that focus on new product development and customer order generation, fulfillment, and delivery. The overall trend of process integration expands the operational potential and impact of logistics.

Less clear is a full understanding of how processes themselves will be performed and managed. The most advanced logistical solutions observed during the past decade have combined organization form and best-practice performance to manage the overall logistics process using a modified hierarchical structure. The concept of matrix organization has emerged as a common structure to facilitate horizontal management. The availability of

[4] Michael Hammer and Steven Stanton, "How Process Enterprises Really Work," *Harvard Business Review,* November/December 1999, pp. 108–17.

superior information to operationalize a matrix approach relaxes dependence on a rigid formal organization structure. In terms of architecture for a logistical organization, the critical questions are: (1) How much formal hierarchical structure can and should be retained in seeking to enable and encourage a process orientation? (2) How can an organization be structured so that it can manage a process as complex as global logistics without becoming overly bureaucratic? To address these questions, managers need to fully understand the potential of virtual organization, which advocates information-driven logistical networks that integrate across organization boundaries.

Virtuality and Organization Transparency

It is highly unlikely that the attention being given to process will end management's quest for ideal logistical organization. While several different scenarios concerning the organization of the future are technologically feasible, one of the most intriguing is speculation that formal hierarchical command and control organization structure will be replaced with an informal electronic network often referred to as a **virtual organization.**[5] The adjective **virtual** implies underlying existence without formal recognition.[6] In other words, a virtual organization, whether it is a total enterprise or a specific core competency, would exist as a provider of integrated performance but not as an identifiable unit of formal organization structure. In the case of logistics, key work teams may be electronically linked to perform critical activities in an integrated fashion. These work teams could be transparent in terms of the formal organization structure of their membership; that is, formal organization charts may not be related to actual work flow. In fact, logistics organizations of the future could be characterized by functional disaggregation throughout the organization to focus on work flow rather than structure.

The concepts of virtuality and transparency have far-reaching implications for longstanding organizational concepts such as centralization and decentralization. To meet customer requirements for speed and response, authority would need to be pushed down the organization. Strategic direction would be expected to originate at headquarters. Operational adaptations would increasingly be made on the front lines. Frontline managers would be increasingly expected to refine strategy and apply it directly to operations. Centralization and decentralization would increasingly become meaningless terms. Organizations of the future would seek to capture the best of centralization and decentralization without commitment to either concept.[7]

The idea behind disaggregation is that the power of information technology would facilitate integrated management and performance of logistics work without grouping or aggregating functions into a formal organization unit. The responsibility for performing logistics work should ideally be organizationally positioned with users. The user, in this sense, is the organization that requires transportation, warehousing, inventory, or any other

---

[5] For more detail and examples of virtual organizations, see Charles C. Snow, Raymond E. Miles, and Henry J. Coleman Jr., "Managing 21st Century Network Organizations," *Organizational Dynamics* 20, no. 3 (Winter 1992), pp. 5–20; Walter Kiechel III, "How We Will Work in the Year 2000," *Fortune* 127, no. 10 (May 17, 1993), pp. 38–52; Joan Magretta, "The Power of Virtual Integration: An Interview with Dell Computer's Michael Dell," *Harvard Business Review*, March/April 1998, pp. 73–84; Nicholas G. Carr, "Being Virtual: Character and The New Economy," *Harvard Business Review*, May/June 1999, pp. 181–86; William H. Davidrow and Michael S. Malone, *The Virtual Corporation: Structuring and Revitalizing the Corporation for the 21st Century* (New York: Harper Business, 1992); John A. Byrne, "The Virtual Corporation: The Company of the Future Will Be the Ultimate in Adaptability," *Business Week*, February 8, 1993, pp. 98–102; and Kevin P. Gayne and Renee Dye, "The Competitive Dynamics of Network-Based Businesses," *Harvard Business Review*, January/February 1998, pp. 99–109.

[6] Webster's dictionary defines *virtual* as "being such in essence or effect though not formally recognized or admitted."

[7] Donald J. Bowersox et al., *Logistical Excellence: It's Not Business as Usual* (Burlington, MA: Digital Press, 1992), pp. 173–74.

logistics service to complete its mission. Making those who perform the logistical services an integral part of the user organization has potential to increase relevancy and flexibility. In essence, ultimate empowerment would result. Each organization throughout an enterprise would perform its required logistical services. The disintegration paradigm is based on the belief that logistical functionality need not be organizationally assigned to a special command and control structure to efficiently and effectively coordinate performance.

There are many arguments counter to functional disaggregation. First and foremost is the possibility that disaggregation would create a danger of reverting to a functional fixation or myopia characteristic of fragmented logistics. A second concern is that critical scale and scope in logistical operations would be lost and result in diseconomies. Finally, standardization and simplification of work could decrease if similar types of work are spread throughout user organizations without formal feedback mechanisms.

While the above arguments are not exhaustive, they are characteristic of the concerns managers have about abandoning formal integrated organizations. The key to improved performance is the realization that relevancy and flexibility may be increased by creating an electronic network to facilitate logistical coordination as contrasted to reliance on formal organization structuring. Actually, adequate information technology to facilitate integration did not exist when the paradigm of functional organization grouping was first embraced.

The jury is out concerning if and when the functionally disaggregated information-coordinated network will become a realistic logistics organization solution. Research on best practice indicates that some firms are at the initial stages of linking disparate work electronically rather than physically or organizationally.[8]

Leading Organization Change

A final topic of concern to logistics managers is how to lead change. It is one thing to decide what should be done. It is an entirely different thing to get it done. Once again, logistics managers cannot expect to find a blueprint to guide them. As a general rule, they are involved in three primary types of change.

First, there are issues related to strategic change. Strategic change issues involve the implementation of new and improved ways to service customers. The topic of strategic change management has been dealt with in several different places throughout the text.

The second type of change concerns modifications in a firm's operational structure. On the basis of strategic considerations, logistics executives are constantly engaged in modifying where products are positioned, how customer requirements are handled, and so forth. Such network and operations reengineering represents a great deal of the change that must be managed to keep a firm's capabilities in line with its strategic requirements.

The third type of change concerns human resource structure. As the mission and scope of logistics change, managers have traditionally found it difficult to alter organization structures in a timely manner. Research clearly illustrates that organization change is frequent.

It is critical to avoid a quick-fix mentality. The prevailing command and control organization structure has survived for centuries—it need not all be dismantled overnight. The key is development of a change model that charts a meaningful and believable course of transition. As noted earlier, managers should use caution in trying to accelerate the transition of logistical organization structures. Despite the appeal of changing quickly, real success may be enhanced by proceeding with care.

---

[8] Donald J. Bowersox, David J. Closs, and Theodore P. Stank, *21st Century Logistics: Making Supply Chain Integration a Reality* (Oak Brook, IL: Council of Supply Chain Professionals, 1999).

A final consideration concerning change is an organization's capacity to absorb new and challenging operational practices. While all of the desired change is taking place, the day-to-day business still needs to be run. Though some advocate radical change, it does not appear to fit logistical organizations very well.

The notion of radical change is not new or unique. Despite the fact that knowledge expands rapidly, associated skills and accepted practices change at a much slower pace. Joseph Schumpeter envisioned a need for what he labeled **creative destruction**.[9] Most managerial experts agree that firms must develop skills for systematic abandonment and build into their fundamental structure a mechanism for managing change. The problem in part is magnified by the fact that most significant change does not result from internal initiatives. Rather, radical improvements are typically in response to external creativity. This notion of **disruptive technology** prompts the belief among some experts that massive change can be achieved only by total destruction of existing structural arrangements. In the final analysis, the tempo of change a firm can accommodate remains unique to each organization. How much change an organization can absorb requires precise calibration. Typically, it is less than most change managers gauge it to be and actual change takes longer than anticipated.

Development and Management of Supply Chain Relationships

A supply chain perspective shifts the relevant business model from a loosely linked group of independent businesses to a multienterprise coordinated effort focused on supply chain efficiency improvement and increased competitiveness. While not all supply chain collaborative arrangements involve logistics, most do. In such arrangements, attention shifts from firm-based logistical management to the coordination of supply chain performance. Two beliefs facilitate this drive for efficiency and competitiveness.

First, the fundamental belief is that cooperative behavior will reduce risk and greatly improve efficiency of the overall logistical process. To achieve a high degree of cooperation it is necessary for supply chain participants to share strategic information. Such information sharing must not be limited to transaction data. Equally or more important is a willingness to share information concerning future plans so participating firms can jointly develop the best way to satisfy customer requirements. Collaborative information is essential to positioning and coordinating participating firms to jointly do the right things faster and more efficiently.

The second belief is the opportunity to eliminate waste and duplicate effort. As a result of collaboration, substantial inventory deployed in a traditional channel can be eliminated. Supply chain collaboration can also eliminate or reduce risk associated with inventory speculation. Significant inventory can be eliminated. The notion of supply chain rationalization is not that inventory is bad and should be totally eliminated; rather, inventory deployment should be driven by economic and service necessities and not tradition and anticipatory practices.

Firms that have increased supply chain competitiveness exhibit several similarities. First, their collaborative practices are technology driven. Second, their business solutions achieve competitive superiority. Finally, most initiatives combine the experience and talents of key supply chain participants blended with a combination of third-party or integrated service providers. At the heart of these firms is a solid commitment to creating and maintaining a unique supply chain culture. Such cultures are forged on a fundamental understanding of risk, power, and leadership.

---

[9] Joseph A. Schumpeter, *Capitalism, Socialism, and Democracy,* 6th ed. (London: Urwin Paperbacks, 1987).

Risk, Power, and Leadership

Dependency is a primary driver of supply chain solidarity. To the degree that participating enterprises acknowledge mutual dependency, the potential exists to develop collaborative relationships. Dependency drives a willingness to plan functional integration, share key information, and participate in joint operations. The concepts of **risk, power,** and **leadership** are essential to understanding acknowledged dependency and how it makes supply chain integration work.

Risk

Enterprises that participate in supply chain arrangements must acknowledge they have responsibility for performing specific roles. They must also believe that their business will be better off in the long run as a result of collaboration. Each enterprise must be positioned to specialize in an operational area or function based on its unique **core competency.** The driving force behind supply chain integration is to leverage these core competencies.

As a general rule, a supply chain member whose competency is highly specialized will assume comparatively less risk with respect to overall performance. Conversely, firms that have a great deal at stake will be positioned as the prime facilitators and will confront the most risk in the supply chain arrangement. Firms with unique specialization, more often than not, will participate in multiple supply chains. For example, a wholesaler incurs risk as a result of stocking products for a specific manufacturer. The traditional practice among wholesalers is to hedge such risk by offering customers an assortment of many different manufacturers' products, thereby reducing reliance on any supplier.

In contrast, a manufacturer with a limited product line may be totally captive to a few supply chain arrangements. In essence, the manufacturer may be betting the business that the collaboration will be successful. For manufacturers, commitment to supply chain arrangements can be risky business. The **disproportionate risk** among channel members is of primary importance because it structures dependency relationships and determines how the collaboration will be managed. Some participants have a deeper dependence on supply chain success than others. Therefore, participants with the most risk can be expected to assume active roles and shoulder greater responsibility for facilitating collaboration.

Power

In a practical sense, the prerogative and even the obligation to spearhead collaboration rests with the supply chain participant who enjoys the greatest relative power. In many situations, that participant will also be the firm having the greatest risk. Over the last decade significant power shifts have occurred in business. One of the most significant is the increased power of retailers, which resulted from four somewhat independent developments.

First, the general trend of retail consolidation translated into fewer but more dominant retailers with more extensive market coverage. Second, the proliferation of point-of-sale data, frequent-shopper programs, and credit card use provides retailers with easy access to vital market information. As a result, retailers are positioned to rapidly identify and accommodate consumer trends. Many mass merchants maintain in-store computers and continuous point-of-sale transmission to keep merchandise buyers fully informed of developing market trends. A third factor favoring retailers is the increasing difficulty and high cost manufacturers confront in developing new brands. The fact is that many private-label products owned by retailers have greater market penetration than so-called national brands. For example, the Gap and The Limited almost exclusively distribute private branded merchandise. Finally, as discussed throughout the text, the process of logistical replenishment has shifted toward a response-based posture. The exact timing and sophisticated orchestration of a high-velocity market-paced logistics system are ideally driven from the point of consumer purchase. When consumers purchase products, the final or ultimate value of the supply chain is achieved.

While the above noted forces are a modern reality, not all forces are shifting power forward in the supply chain. Today's scrambled merchandising environments result in products increasingly being cross-channel-distributed to accommodate specific markets that are volatile and rapidly changing. New retail formats, both Internet-based and traditional brick and mortar, are blurring channel arrangements. The result is that manufacturers have a growing range of alternatives for distributing their products.

As a substitute for full reliance on traditional brand power, selected manufacturers have reengineered their operations to become the dominant supplier for selected consumer product or categories. The movement toward category dominance allows manufacturers to offer greater value to their prospective supply chain partners. In addition to superior brands at competitive prices, dominant category position can involve several key operational capabilities that increase a firm's attractiveness as a supply chain participant.

Because both manufacturers and distributors have repositioned traditional operations, the potential exists to leverage collaboration. **As a general rule, powerful firms tend to link together in the development of supply chain arrangements.** For the arrangement to be successful the dominant parties to the cooperative arrangement need to agree to a leadership model.

Leadership

Just as individual organizations need leaders, so do supply chains. At the present stage of supply chain maturity, no definitive generalization can be made concerning how firms gain leadership responsibility. In many situations, specific firms are thrust into a leadership position purely as a result of their size, economic power, customer patronage, or comprehensive product portfolio. In other arrangements, for less obvious reasons, there is a clear presence of leadership on the part of one enterprise, which is acknowledged in the form of mutual dependency and respect on the part of other participating supply chain members. In other situations leadership appears to gravitate to the firm that initiates the relationship.

The Range of Extended Supply Chain Relationships

There are numerous types and forms of interorganizational relationships that tend to be characterized as examples of supply chain integration and collaboration.[10] Figure 15.4 presents a classification framework for these relationships.

As discussed earlier, the driving force underlying the emergence of collaborative relationships among firms in a supply chain is the recognition of mutual dependence. When a firm acknowledges dependency with its suppliers and/or its customers, the stage is set for collaboration. The degree to which dependence is mutually recognized and acknowledged by all parties in the relationship defines the nature of the resulting relationship.

As seen in Figure 15.4, there are five basic forms of collaboration among supply chain participants. The most elementary of these are contracting and outsourcing. In these relationships, dependency is acknowledged only to a limited extent. Contracting with a supplier or customer introduces a time dimension to traditional buying and selling by framing price, service, and performance expectations over a specified period. A manufacturer may contract with a material or parts supplier to purchase a particular item or items for a specified period at a specified price. In turn, the supplier agrees to deliver the specified item(s)

---

[10] The terminology used to describe types of relations varies widely. For a discussion, see Lloyd Rinehart, James A. Eckert, Robert B. Handfield, Thomas J. Page Jr., and Thomas Atkin, "An Assessment of Supplier Customer Relationships," *Journal of Business Logistics* 25, no. 1 (2004), pp. 25–61.

FIGURE 15.4
Relationship
Classification
Framework

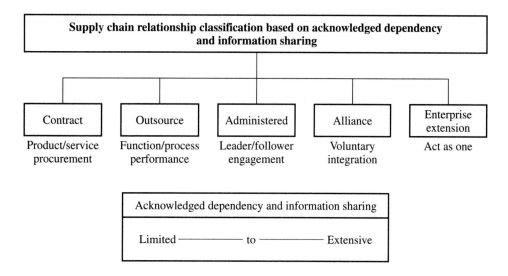

according to negotiated terms and delivery requirements. In outsourcing, the focus shifts from buying or selling a product or material to performing a specific service or activity. Typical outsourced activities range from manufacturing to logistics activities such as transportation or warehousing. It is critical to understand, however, that contracting and outsourcing do not necessarily imply that comprehensive supply chain integration and collaboration take place. The relationships involve a degree of information sharing, primarily operational information, but there is limited joint planning among the firms involved, and there are generally specific periods for rebidding or terminating the relationships. Although firms that outsource functions, or even processes, must maintain cordial relationships with the service suppliers, the service being provided is precisely specified in terms of performance and cost, and the relationship among the firms is clearly based in traditional command-and-control principles, with the buyer as the leader.

In administered relationships, a dominant firm assumes leadership responsibility and seeks collaboration with trading partners and/or service suppliers. In such relationships there is frequently sharing of not only operational information but, to a limited degree, strategic information as well. Additionally, there is limited joint planning, to the extent that independent firms have an understanding that they will be better off if they work together and follow the leader. A distinguishing feature of such relationships is that the expectation is that the relationship will be continuous and there is no specific termination or rebid time frame. However, although the leader must consider all participants' welfare, the relationship is basically governed by command and control based in the leader's power.

Although different terminology may be used, true collaborative relationships among supply chain participants can be described as alliances or, in the extreme, as enterprise extension. The distinguishing feature of these relationships is that they are governed by the participants' desire and willingness to voluntarily work together in an intellectual and operational manner. They voluntarily agree to integration of human, financial, operational, or technical resources to create greater efficiency and greater impact with consumers. Ultimately, through collaboration, participating firms create joint policies and integrate operations. The relationship includes extensive joint planning and is expected to be continuous for at least the intermediate term and potentially the very long term. Enterprise extension represents the extreme of interdependence and information sharing. In such instances, two or more firms willingly integrate to the extent that they essentially can be viewed as a single entity. Examples of alliance and enterprise extension are, in fact, relatively few. An arrangement such as Collaborative Planning, Forecasting, and Replenishment (CPFR), discussed in Chapter 3, provides an example of the potential of these forms of collaboration.

Supply Chain Integrative Framework[11]

A supply chain integrative framework is required to define the nature of collaboration required in alliances and enterprise extension. Such a framework requires that capabilities and competencies essential to integrating supply chain logistics are identified and implemented. The creation of value related to supply chain integration is best achieved by simultaneous orchestration of the four critical flows shown in Figure 15.5: product/service, market accommodation, information, and cash.

The product/service value flow represents the value-added movement of products and services from the raw material source to the end customers. Product value increases as it flows along the supply chain as a result of physical modification, packaging, market proximity, customization, service support, and related activities that enhance end-consumer desirability of the product.

While the product/service flow generally moves from the resource base to end customers, as noted earlier, supply chain arrangements must also accommodate critical reverse flows such as product recalls, reclamation, and recycling. The market accommodation flow provides a structure to achieve postsales service administration. Market accommodation also involves information exchange concerning sales patterns and product usage essential for supply chain planning. Examples are product customization requirements, point-of-sale (POS) data, end-customer consumption, and warehouse releases. This information provides supply chain members with channel visibility concerning the timing and location of product consumption. Planning and operations can be better synchronized when all participants share a common understanding of demand and consumption patterns.

The information flow is bidirectional exchange of transactional data, inventory status, and strategic plans between supply chain participants. Typical examples of this aspect of collaboration are forecasts, promotional plans, purchase orders, order acknowledgments, shipping and inventory information, invoices, payments, and replenishment requirements. Information exchange initiates, controls, and records the product/service value flow. Historically paper-based, an increasing amount of the information flow is now being exchanged via EDI and Web-based connectivity.

Cash typically flows in the reverse direction of value-added activities. However, in arrangements involving promotion and rebate, cash flows to facilitate product and service movement. Cash flow velocity and asset utilization are critical to superior supply chain performance.

[11] This section and illustrations are based on Donald J. Bowersox, David J. Closs, and Theodore P. Stank, *21st Century Logistics: Making Supply Chain Integration a Reality,* Council of Supply Chain Management Professionals, Oak Brook, IL, 1999.

FIGURE 15.5
Supply Chain Flows

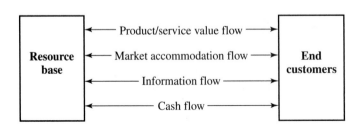

FIGURE 15.6
Supply Chain Framework

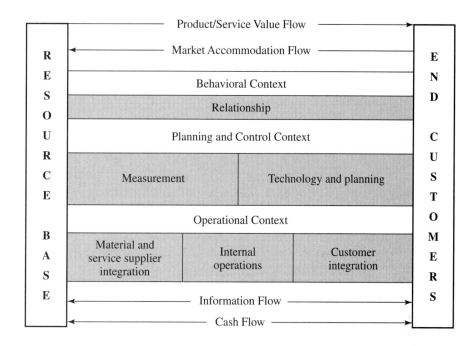

Naturally, these four flows must occur between firms even when the supply chain is not integrated. However, situations characterized by low coordination and integration between supply chain participants typically result in delay, redundancy, and inefficiency. To facilitate effective and efficient supply chain flows, competencies and their supporting capabilities must be integrated.

Framework Constructs

The supply chain integrative framework illustrated in Figure 15.6 encompasses a broad range of capabilities and competencies. The framework serves to facilitate operations into a supply chain context by integrating basic work, functions, capabilities, and competencies.

A job or basic work, such as order picking or truck driving, is the most visible part of the logistical operations. Jobs are often industry- or firm-specific in content; however, they are usually grouped into organizational units to facilitate control. For example, all the jobs related to warehousing are often grouped. Another common grouping is to organize all jobs related to transport into a transportation department. These functional groupings are significant because they are highly visible elements of an organization. Departments have traditionally been the focal point for financial budgeting, performance measurement, and operational control. Functional work arrangements constitute the drivers of logistical best practice. It is the functions or drivers that combine to create value. The critical shift in operational thinking is to view functional excellence in terms of process performance that enhances *overall* supply chain integration.

To achieve integration, functional value should be focused in terms of universal capabilities. A **capability** is the knowledge and achievement level essential to developing integrated performance. Capabilities relate to why work is being performed as contrasted to a functional perspective concerning how it is performed. The capability reflects the value contribution of the work. Inherent in a capability is the application of integrative principles that allow multiple functions to be synchronized into value-creating competencies. Whereas jobs and functions may be highly relevant to specific industries and work

TABLE 15.1 **Supply Chain Context, Competencies, and Supportive Capabilities**

	Operational Context			Planning and Control Context		Behavioral Context
Competencies	**Customer Integration**	**Internal Integration**	**Material/Service Supplier Integration**	**Technology and Planning Integration**	**Measurement Integration**	**Relationship Integration**
Supportive Capabilities	Segmental focus	Cross-functional unification	Strategic alignment	Information management	Functional assessment	Role specificity
	Relevancy	Standardization	Operational fusion	Internal communication	Activity-based and total cost methodology	Guidelines
	Responsiveness	Simplification	Financial linkage	Connectivity	Comprehensive metrics	Information sharing
	Flexibility	Compliance	Supplier management	Collaborative forecasting and planning	Financial impact	Gain/risk sharing
		Structural adaptation				

situations, capabilities are universal. Capabilities span the supply chain and are equally applicable to suppliers, manufacturers, wholesalers/distributors, and across the full range of retail formats. Capabilities reflecting best logistics practice are to some degree observable in all firms that participate in a supply chain.

Examples of capabilities include the ability to (1) identify and accommodate the needs of specific customers; (2) work with supply chain partners to achieve integrated operations; (3) effectively share operating and planning information between supply chain partners; (4) measure and understand overall supply chain performance; and (5) share benefits and risks.

The fusing of capabilities results in universal **competencies**. Table 15.1 details the capabilities related to each of the six integrative competencies grouped in terms of their supply chain context. The operational context includes traditional processes related to procurement, production, and customer accommodation. The planning and control context incorporates information technology and planning systems, as well as measurement competency. The behavioral context relates to how a firm manages internal and external relationships among supply chain entities.

The Operational Context

Operations involve the processes that facilitate order fulfillment and replenishment across the supply chain. To achieve leading performance in an operational context, firms must be customer-focused, must achieve interorganizational coordination, and must excel in functional and process performance.

Customer integration builds on the philosophies and activities that develop intimacy and is the competency that builds lasting competitive advantage. Firms have always paid attention to the needs of customers but only recently have begun to identify and consider their differences in terms of capable operational segmentation. Any firm seeking supply chain integration must also demonstrate strong commitment to the supportive capabilities of segmentation, relevancy, responsiveness, and flexibility.

Internal integration focuses on the joint activities and processes within a firm that coordinate functions related to procurement, manufacture, and customer accommodation.

Many firms have attempted to integrate internal functionality but anecdotal and quantitative evidence strongly indicates there are significant gaps. Managers often report more success in coordinating with customers than with their own manufacturing, logistical, and marketing operations. The capabilities that support internal integration are cross-functional unification, standardization, simplification, compliance, and structural adaptation.

Supplier integration focuses on capabilities that create operational linkages with material- and service-providing supply chain partners. While the customer is the overriding focal point or supply chain driver, overall success also will depend on strategic alignment, operational fusion, financial linkage, and supplier management. Competency in supplier integration results from performing the capabilities seamlessly in internal work processes. Firms that desire to excel must blend their operating processes with those of supply partners to meet increasingly broad and demanding customer expectations.

It is not insignificant that the 13 capabilities that support customer, internal, and supplier integration can be identified, quantified, and organizationally learned.

The Planning and Control Context

Operational excellence must be supported by integrated planning and measurement capabilities. This involves joining technology across the supply chain to monitor, control, and facilitate overall supply chain performance.

Planning and control integration concerns the design, application, and coordination of information to enhance purchasing, manufacturing, customer order fulfillment, and resource planning. This competency includes database access to enable sharing of appropriate information among supply chain participants. It also concerns transaction systems to initiate and process replenishment and customer orders. In addition to information management, it is essential that capabilities related to internal communication, connectivity, and collaboration be developed.

Measurement integration is the ability to monitor and benchmark functional and process performance, both within the firm and across the supply chain. Because each firm is unique, the collaborative effort must define, operationalize, and monitor standard or common measures. Competency in measurement requires the capabilities of functional assessment and activity-based methodologies, comprehensive metrics, and financial impact assessment.

The Behavioral Context

Effective relationship management is the final competency essential in supply chain engagements. Successful implementation of supply chain strategy rests on the quality of the basic business relationship between partners. In general, managers are far more experienced in competition than they are in collaboration.

Whereas guidelines exist for the development of meaningful and distinctive supply chain relationships, no two situations are identical. No shortcuts or substitutes exist for the detailed commitment necessary to build and develop successful long-term relationships. In dealing with customers, suppliers, and service providers, firms must specify roles, define guidelines, share information, share risk and gains, resolve conflict, and, when necessary, be able to dissolve an unproductive arrangement. The managerial skill sets required for successful supply chain integration require development of an interorganizational culture. This is particularly true since the dynamic environment in which firms compete requires regular review of assumptions, processes, and measures to assure those relationships remain relevant.

Finally, ample evidence suggests that managers must plan for the ultimate dismantling or renovation of supply chains. While some arrangements may encounter a natural death as a result of losing momentum, others may persevere to the point that they no longer embody leading-edge practice. Thus, like most managerial concerns, supply chain integration is a dynamic situation that must be continuously reevaluated.

Initiating Relationships

In an effort to better understand the anatomy of what makes for a successful collaborative relationship, in-depth case studies were completed with grocery manufacturing firms that are generally recognized as leaders in interorganizational arrangements.[12] The alliances investigated included relationships with material suppliers, logistical service providers, and merchandisers. Guidelines were developed concerning initiating an alliance, implementing an alliance, and maintaining alliance vitality. While the focus was specifically on alliances, the logic can be extended to any successful collaborative relationship.

The alliances studied were typically initiated by the firm that was the customer in the relationship. One potential explanation for this pattern is the exercise of buying power. In a buyer/seller relationship, the seller will often implement reasonable changes at the request of its customer to facilitate interorganizational exchange. Also, when a seller's personnel initially approach a potential customer about forming an alliance, the suggestion does not carry the same weight and impact as when the suggestion is generated within the buying firm's organization.

Some alliances do show some anomalies to this pattern. In some cases the seller actually sparked the initial deal by planting the seed as far as conceptualizing the viability of an alliance. When the customer was ready to form the alliance, it initiated more detailed discussion.

Another critical consideration during the development of a collaborative relationship is the need for the initiating firm to perform an in-depth assessment of its internal practices, policies, and culture. The initiating firm should evaluate its ability to make any necessary internal changes to implement and support a successful relationship.[13] For example, in manufacturer/material supplier alliances, the manufacturers had to examine their ability to redefine the importance of purchase price. Buyers needed a method to incorporate the intangible benefits of an alliance in competitive evaluations. The key for the buyer was the evaluation of total cost of ownership, not strictly purchase price.

Another internal assessment includes the ability to truly empower the key alliance contacts to manage the relationship. For example, manufacturers needed to honestly assess the level of operational and strategic integration they could foster with service suppliers. Integration that generated the type of competitive advantage envisioned at the alliance's initial design, such as increased productivity of rapid response to customer orders, could be achieved only through extensive information sharing. The questions to be addressed concern the level of systems capability, data collection, analysis, performance measurement, and training that was necessary to enable the information to be shared in a timely and accurate manner.

Integration capability also needs to be evaluated if the alliance involves a number of partner plants, warehouses, and/or stores that operate under different conditions, capabilities, or competitive requirements. This is especially important for firms that operate multiple warehouses and/or store locations. A key concern in this situation is the ability for

---

[12] This section is adapted from Judith M. Schmitz, Robert Frankel, and David J. Frayer, "ECR Alliances: A Best Practice Model," Joint Industry Project on Efficient Consumer Response, Grocery Manufacturers Association, Washington, DC, 1995.

[13] For an in-depth discussion of internal assessment, see Clifford F. Lynch, *Logistics Outsourcing: A Management Guide* (Oak Brook, IL: Council of Logistics Management, 2000), pp. 37–38.

internal units to utilize common operating practices and compatible information systems. The flexibility to adapt to meet specific market-based requirements is important to long-term viability.

Implementing Relationships

The key to a successful implementation is choosing a partner wisely. The partners should have compatible cultures, a common strategic vision, and supportive operating philosophies. It is not necessary that organization cultures be identical. Rather, the strategic intentions and philosophies must be compatible to ensure that core competencies and strengths are complementary.

For example, manufacturers initiated alliances with service suppliers in part to achieve improved warehousing operations, transportation reliability, and/or increased consolidation programs that support their particular strategic competitive advantage in the marketplace. Although the service suppliers are leaders, manufacturers may have a more sophisticated conceptualization and operationalization of quality, performance measurement standards, and expertise. The attraction between the partners is based, to a considerable degree, on the service suppliers' ability and willingness to provide creative, innovative operational and information-based solutions to the manufacturer's problems and on the service suppliers' desire to internalize the quality and performance measurement expertise that are the hallmark of the manufacturer. In this sense, the alliance partners' operating philosophies support and complement each other, in particular by enhancing their common strategic vision of improving systemwide logistics processes.

The alliances should start on a small scale to foster easily achievable successes or early wins. It is important that such early wins be acknowledged to motivate key contacts and build confidence concerning alliance performance. For example, in the manufacturer/material supplier alliances, starting small meant that investments were not initially made in information technology. Manual communication systems were sufficient and provided the opportunity for key contacts. A critical issue is to implement the alliance in its simplest form and then fine-tune the arrangement with technological sophistication when improvements will add substantial value.

Maintaining Relationships

Long-term continuity is dependent on three key activities: (1) mutual strategic and operational goals, (2) two-way performance measurements, and (3) formal and informal feedback mechanisms.

Strategic and operational goals must be mutually determined when the alliance is implemented. This proposition has been discussed extensively in the academic and business press and appeals to common sense. It is perhaps less well understood that these goals must be tracked, reviewed, and updated frequently to gain improvements over the long term. For example, if a manufacturer develops a new product, a mutual goal must be set with customers concerning that product's position, especially its market launch. This goal must include consideration of the merchandiser's critical role in new product introduction and acceptance.

Goals should be translated into specific performance measures that can be continually tracked. The performance measurements used and the measurement frequency should be jointly determined. Also, the measures should be two-way. Oftentimes, performance measures between manufacturers and material suppliers focus specifically on the suppliers' performance attributes, such as on-time delivery and quality. One of the alliances studied developed a joint measure of success—total systems inventory. The manufacturer acknowledged that it was important for both partners to reduce inventory, not just the manufacturer. The measure of total systems inventory includes consideration of both partners to ensure that reductions are real and benefit both parties.

Feedback on performance can be provided through formal and informal methods. Annual reviews are formal assessments of alliance performance. These reviews typically involve top managers and focus primarily on examining and updating strategic goals. Quarterly or monthly reviews are not as formal as annual assessments and usually do not include top managers. They focus on tracking and reviewing strategic goals and operational performance. When used, the reviews enable changes in operating practice to be made to achieve strategic goals and create an avenue for continuous improvement projects to be identified.

Weekly/daily reviews may also occur on an informal basis. These reviews are managed by the key contacts and are intended to solve specific problems and identify potential opportunities for improvement. They are critical to resolving or avoiding conflicts and allow key contacts to develop close working relationships. Although the process is typically informal in nature, the resolution mechanisms may be quite detailed. For example, when a partnered manufacturer and service supplier do not operate on the same physical site, the involved partners may have specific lists of contact personnel for the plant and the service supplier's customer center or warehouse facility.

Developing Trust

It is clear that no real collaboration can exist in supply chain relationships without meaningful trust. While a powerful firm may be able to influence the behavior of a less powerful organization, the change in behavior may be temporary and certainly entered into unwillingly. Research has also shown that consistent use of coercion by one organization ultimately leads the vulnerable firm to seek alternative supply chain relationships.[14] Further, the fundamental premise of collaborative relationships is that supply chain management requires firms to work together to find ways to increase the value delivered to end customers. In fact, research clearly shows that the presence of trust substantially improves the chances of successful supply chain performance.[15]

But trust is an elusive concept that means different things to different people. So two questions must be answered. First, in a supply chain context, what is trust? Second, how can organizations build trust among each other?

Reliability and Character-Based Trust

It is clear that trust has more than one dimension. While several typologies of trust exist, the most meaningful way to understand trust in supply chain collaboration is to distinguish between reliability-based trust and character-based trust.

Reliability-based trust is grounded in an organization's perception of a potential partner's actual behavior and operating performance. Essentially, it involves a perception that the partner is willing to perform and is capable of performing as promised. If supply chain participants cannot rely on partner performance as promised, all efforts to develop collaborative relationships fail. Simply put, a firm that is perceived as incapable of delivering as promised will also be perceived as being unreliable and therefore unworthy of trust in a relationship.

[14] Nirmalya Kumar, "The Power of Trust in Manufacturer-Retailer Relationships," *Harvard Business Review,* November/December 1999, p. 98.

[15] Ik-Whan G. Kwon and Taewon Suh, "Factors Affecting the Level of Trust and Commitment in Supply Chain Relationships," *Journal of Supply Chain Management* 40, no. 2, Spring 2004, p. 4.

Character-based trust is based in an organization's culture and philosophy. Essentially, it stems from perceptions that supply chain partners are interested in each other's welfare and will not act without considering the action's impact on the other.[16] When this aspect of trust is developed, participants do not feel vulnerable to the actions of one another. Trusting partners believe that each will protect the other's interest. For example, a manufacturer who shares its plans for new product introductions or promotion with a retailer trusts that the retailer will not share that information with a competitive supplier. Likewise, sharing of production schedule information with a supplier of component parts will occur only when a manufacturer has trust that the information will be used appropriately.

It is clear that reliability-based trust is necessary to the formation of collaborative relationships in supply chains, but it is not a sufficient condition. For example, a partner who frequently threatens to punish and consistently follows through with that punishment can be said to have reliability. It is not likely, however, to be trusted in character.

Trust clearly develops over time and repeated interactions among organizations. In particular, character-based trust evolves when partners perceive that each acts fairly and equitably with the others. Notions of character-based trust are especially relevant when one supply chain partner is clearly more powerful than the others are. In such situations, it is dependent upon less powerful firms' perception of justice in prior interactions. Justice, in turn, has two components of interest: distributive justice and procedural justice.

Distributive Justice

Distributive justice depends upon how the risks, benefits, and rewards of supply chain participation are shared. In effect, it has to do with how equitably supply chain participants perceive they are compensated for their functional performance. Such actions as forcing a supplier to take ownership of inventory or unilaterally reducing allowable margins in a distribution channel are likely to lead to perceptions of inequality and a lack of justice. Trust is not likely to be developed in such circumstances.

Procedural Justice

Procedural justice, on the other hand, is related to the manner in which problems and disputes among supply chain participants are resolved. When a powerful firm unilaterally imposes its will on less powerful organizations, the effect is to destroy, or at least lessen, trust. When issues are openly discussed and a mechanism exists for consideration of all parties' points of view, firms can trust their interests will be considered. Conflicts are resolved through open discussion, negotiation, and such procedures as mediation or arbitration. For example, several manufacturers like Caterpillar have developed dealer councils that oversee implementation of new dealer-related policies and are used to resolve conflicts between a specific dealer and the manufacturer. Such approaches are more likely to be perceived as procedurally just than approaches that rely purely on one party's power.

Building Trust in Relationships

To build trust first requires that a firm demonstrate reliability in its operations, consistently performing as promised and meeting expectations. As noted above, however, reliability is only one aspect of building trust.

The second key requirement for building trust is full and frank sharing of all information necessary for the effective functioning of the relationship. In fact, information sharing

[16] Nirmalya Kumar, "The Power of Trust in Manufacturer-Retailer Relationships," *Harvard Business Review,* November/December 1999, p. 95.

and communication have been stressed throughout the text as the foundation for effective collaboration. Companies that hoard information or fail to disclose vital facts are not likely to be trusted.

Related to information sharing is explanation. Sometimes a company, because of competitive pressures, may be required to undertake actions that its supply chain partners may perceive as threatening. For example, a manufacturer opening new distribution channels might threaten existing retailers. Just such a situation arose when John Deere introduced a second line of lawn tractors and recruited Home Depot and other independent dealers, bypassing its traditional network. In such situations, trust may be maintained through thorough explanation of the rationale and business case that drove such a decision.

In many ways the entire subject of supply chain management is also a discussion of relationship management. The text has focused on issues related to logistical processes in the supply chain and managing these processes across company boundaries. Unique operating relationships among supply chain participants differ significantly in their intensity and extent of real collaboration. Power, leadership, conflict, cooperation, risk, and reward are all critical issues in relationship management. Resolution of these issues, however, ultimately depends upon the development of trust among supply chain participants.

Summary

Logistics is undergoing massive change. New concepts and ideas concerning how the best organizations achieve logistical goals appear daily. The challenge is to sort through the best of time-proven practices and merge them with the most applicable new ideas and concepts.

A careful review of logistics organization development suggests that most advanced firms have evolved through many forms of functional aggregation. The evolution started from a highly fragmented structure in which logistical functions were assigned to a wide variety of different departments. For over four decades firms have been grouping an increasing number of logistical functional responsibilities into single-organization units. The typical format for aggregation was the traditional bureaucratic organization structure. The objective was to aggregate functions in an effort to improve operational integration.

The advent of management focusing on critical processes began to usher in what is referred to as horizontal organizations. Today, leading-edge firms are beginning to experiment with process management. There is increasing evidence that a new form of organization may be emerging that adopts the use of information technology to implement and manage logistics as a transparent organization structure. While such arrangements remain more conceptual than real, the required information technology is available today. The concept has particular appeal to the management of logistics, which involves substantial challenge in terms of time and geographical scope of operations.

Perhaps the most difficult job of all is managing change in the organization. Whether the change is strategic, involving fundamental new processes, operational, or only in personnel, managers must develop new skills that allow them to implement change without disrupting the focus of the organization.

In addition to managing the internal organization, supply chain executives are intimately involved in managing relationships among organizations. Collaborative relationships provide a mechanism to reduce operating expense, enhance productivity, and meet customer requirements. Successful integration requires cross-organizational programs to facilitate operations, technology and planning, and relationship management. Initiating, implementing, and maintaining relationships with suppliers and customers are highly dependent upon the existence of trust among those firms. While reliability is a critical aspect of trust, ultimate success in relationship management will depend upon evaluation of character as firms make decisions concerning which supply chains they choose to participate in.

Challenge Questions

1. What is the functional aggregation paradigm and why is it important?

2. Discuss the three challenges logistics faces as it manages on a process, rather than a functional, basis. Describe each challenge and give an example of how it may be overcome.

3. What is meant by the term "structural compression"? How does this term affect logistics?

4. What is a horizontal company and how would this type of company be organized? What are the strengths of this type of organization structure?

5. Defend a position on the following question: Does radical organization change require disintegration of existing structures?

6. What creates power in the context of supply chain collaboration? Why do many observers feel power is shifting forward or closer to consumers in many supply chain arrangements?

7. Distinguish among different types of supply chain collaborative arrangements. What drives the differences?

8. Describe the relationship between logistical capabilities and competencies.

9. What are the major considerations in initiating a logistics alliance? In implementation? In maintenance?

10. Distinguish between reliability and character-based trust. Why is character-based trust critical in collaborative relationships?

CHAPTER SIXTEEN

Operational, Financial, and Social Performance

Creating competitive advantage through high-performance logistics requires integrated measurement systems. The old adage, "If you don't measure it, you can't manage it," holds true for logistical activities both internal to an organization and externally with supply chain partners. For this reason, a framework for performance assessment must be established.

Measurement System Objectives

Effective measurement systems must be constructed to accomplish the three objectives of monitoring, controlling, and directing logistical operations.

Monitoring is accomplished by the establishment of appropriate metrics to track system performance for reporting to management. For example, typically metrics are developed and data gathered to report basic service performance related to fill rates and on-time deliveries and for logistics costs such as transportation and warehousing. **Controlling** is accomplished by having appropriate standards of performance relative to the established metrics to indicate when the logistics system requires modification or attention. For example, if fill rates fall below standards, logistics managers must identify the causes and make adjustments to bring the process back into compliance. The third objective, **directing,** is

376

FIGURE 16.1
Shareholder Value
Model

related to employee motivation and reward for performance. For example, some companies encourage warehouse personnel to achieve high levels of productivity. They must be paid for 8 hours of work, on the basis of standard measures of picking or loading. If the tasks are completed in less than 8 hours, they may be allowed personal time off.

An overriding objective of superior logistical performance is to improve **shareholder value.** A comprehensive measurement system must therefore address the critical points of impact on shareholder value. Figure 16.1 provides a framework that considers both operational excellence and asset utilization in logistical performance. On the operational excellence dimension, key metrics focus on improved accommodation of customers through increased customer success and on lowest total cost of service.

Asset utilization reflects effectiveness in managing the firm's fixed assets and working capital. Fixed capital assets include manufacturing and warehouse facilities, transportation and materials handling equipment, and information technology hardware. Working capital represents cash, the inventory investment, and differential in investments related to accounts receivable versus accounts payable. In particular, by more efficiently managing the assets related to logistics operations, the firm may be able to liberate assets from the existing base. This freed capital is known as **cash spin,** which can be used for reinvestment in other aspects of the organization. Overall asset utilization is particularly important to shareholders and to how the firm is viewed by financial investors.

Operational Assessment

A system for logistics performance assessment first requires a functional perspective. In addition to basic functional performance, improved methods for measurement of customer accommodation are receiving increased attention in many organizations. Measurement of integrated supply chain performance poses a major challenge for contemporary management. Benchmarking is a fourth concern in logistics assessment.

Functional Perspectives

Research over a period of years suggests that functional measures of logistics performance can be classified into these categories: (1) cost, (2) customer service, (3) quality,

TABLE 16.1   **Typical Performance Metrics**

Cost Management	Customer Service	Quality	Productivity	Asset Management
Total cost	Fill rate	Damage frequency	Units shipped per employee	Inventory turns
Cost per unit	Stockouts	Order entry accuracy	Units per labor dollar	Inventory levels, number of days supply
Cost as a percentage of sales	Shipping errors	Picking/shipping accuracy	Orders per sales representative	Obsolete inventory
Inbound freight	On-time delivery	Document/invoicing accuracy	Comparison to historical standard	Return on net assets
Outbound freight	Back orders	Information availability	Goal programs	Return on investment
Administrative	Cycle time	Information accuracy	Productivity index	Inventory classification (ABC)
Warehouse order processing	Delivery consistency	Number of credit claims	Equipment downtime	Economic value-added (EVA)
Direct labor	Response time to inquiries	Number of customer returns	Order entry productivity	
Comparison of actual versus budget	Response accuracy		Warehouse labor productivity	
Cost trend analysis	Complete orders		Transportation labor productivity	
Direct product profitability	Customer complaints			
Customer segment profitability	Sales force complaints			
Inventory carrying	Overall reliability			
Cost of returned goods	Overall satisfaction			
Cost of damage				
Cost of service failures				
Cost of back order				

(4) productivity, and (5) asset management.[1] Table 16.1 provides an overview of measurements related to each of these five areas of concern.

Cost

The most direct reflection of logistics performance is the actual cost incurred to accomplish specific operations. As shown in Table 16.1, **cost performance** is typically measured in terms of total dollars spent on each function. Thus, it is common to monitor and report cost data for specific logistics functions such as warehousing, outbound transportation, inbound transportation, and order processing. Such categories may be further fine-tuned and cost data reported for individual activities such as warehouse picking and order loading.

It is also common to monitor and report cost data as a percentage of sales or as a cost per unit of volume. For example, transportation cost is frequently expensed as a percentage of dollar sales volume and as the number of dollars spent per order delivered. Warehouse

---

[1] Donald J. Bowersox et al., *Leading Edge Logistics: Competitive Positioning for the 1990s* (Oak Brook, IL: Council of Logistics Management, 1989); World Class Logistics Research Team at Michigan State University, *World Class Logistics: The Challenge of Managing Continuous Change* (Oak Brook, IL: Council of Logistics Management, 1995); Donald J. Bowersox, David J. Closs, and Theodore P. Stank, *21st Century Logistics: Making Supply Chain Integration a Reality* (Oak Brook, IL: Council of Logistics Management, 1999).

cost may also be reported as a percentage of sales and cost of individual activities reported such as the picking cost per item or loading cost per order. Such measures, when compared to historical levels or performance standards, provide critical information regarding the potential need to take corrective action. When considering the number of different specific logistics activities, ranging from entering an order to picking an item to unloading a delivery vehicle, and the number of different ways in which volume can be measured, ranging from sales dollars to number of orders to pounds of product, a rather lengthy list of possible cost metrics could be generated. The key is for logistics executives to identify the most appropriate metrics for their organization and consistently apply them over time to control and direct the activities.

Table 16.1 also shows other measures related to the cost of logistical performance, such as direct product profitability, customer profitability, and cost of service failures. In fact, most firms recognize the importance of these measures but currently lack the information necessary to accurately assess these costs. Accurate measurement in these critical dimensions requires a level of sophistication in accounting data that has just recently become available. Activity-based costing is discussed later in this chapter as a means to more accurately assess the cost related directly to customers and products.

Basic Customer Service

In Chapter 3, the elements of basic customer service were identified as availability, operational performance, and service reliability. An effective basic service platform requires specific metrics for assessing performance in each dimension.

Availability is typically reflected by an organization's fill rate. It is critical to note, however, that fill rate may be measured in a variety of ways:

$$\text{Item fill rate} = \frac{\text{Number of items delivered to customers}}{\text{Number of items ordered by customers}}$$

$$\text{Line fill rate} = \frac{\text{Number of purchase order lines delivered complete to customers}}{\text{Number of purchase order lines ordered by customers}}$$

$$\text{Value fill rate} = \frac{\text{Total dollar value delivered to customers}}{\text{Total dollar value of customer orders}}$$

$$\text{Order fill rate} = \frac{\text{Number of orders delivered complete}}{\text{Number of customer orders}}$$

Clearly, the order fill rate, also known as orders shipped complete, is the most stringent measure of a firm's performance relative to product availability. In this metric, an order that is missing only one item on one line is considered to be incomplete. It is also common for companies to track specifically the number of stockouts encountered and number of back orders generated during a time period as indicators of availability.

Operational performance deals with time and is typically measured by average order cycle time, consistency of order cycle time, and/or on-time deliveries. **Average order cycle time** is typically computed as the average number of days, or other units of time, elapsed between order receipt and delivery to customers. **Order cycle consistency** is measured over a large number of order cycles and compares actual with planned performance. For example, suppose average order cycle time is 5 days. If 20 percent were completed in 2 days and 30 percent in 8 days, there is great inconsistency around the average. In situations where delivery dates or times are specified by customers, the most stringent measure of order cycle capability is **on-time delivery,** the percentage of times the customer's delivery requirements are actually met.

Quality

Performance relative to service reliability is generally reflected in an organization's measurement of **logistics quality.** As Table 16.1 shows, many of the quality metrics are designed to monitor the effectiveness of individual activities, while others are focused on the overall logistics function. Accuracy of work performance in such activities as order entry, warehouse picking, and document preparation is typically tracked by computing the ratio of the total number of times the activity is performed correctly to the total number of times it is performed. For example, picking accuracy of 99.5 percent indicates that 99.5 out of every 100 times, the correct items were picked in the warehouse.

Overall quality performance can also be measured in a variety of ways. Typical measures include damage frequency, which is computed as the ratio of the number of damaged units to the total number of units. While damage frequency can be measured at several points in the logistics process, such as warehouse damage, loading damage, and transportation damage, it frequently is not detected until customers receive shipments or even some point in time after receipt. Therefore, many organizations also monitor the number of customer returns of damaged or defective goods. It is also common to measure customer claims and refunds on adjustments.

Other important indicators of quality performance relate to information. Many organizations specifically measure their ability to provide information by noting those instances when information is not available on request. It is also common to track instances when inaccurate information is discovered. For example, when physical counts of merchandise inventory differ from the inventory status as reported in the database, the information system must be updated to reflect actual operating status. Additionally, the occurrence of information inaccuracy should be recorded for future action.

Productivity

The relationship between output of goods, work completed, and/or services produced and quantities of inputs or resources utilized to produce the output is **productivity.** If a system has clearly measurable outputs and identifiable, measurable inputs that can be matched to the appropriate outputs, productivity measurement is quite routine.

Generally, as Table 16.1 shows, logistics executives are very concerned with measuring the productivity of labor. While the labor input can be quantified in many ways, the most typical manner is by labor expense, labor hours, or number of individual employees. Thus, typical labor productivity measures in transportation include units shipped or delivered per employee, labor dollar, and labor hour. Warehouse labor productivity may be measured by units received, picked, and/or stored per employee, dollar, or hour. Similar measures can be developed for other activities, such as order entry and order processing. It is also common for managers to set goals for productivity improvement and compare actual performance to goal, or at the very least to prior year performance.

Asset Management

Utilization of capital investments in facilities and equipment as well as working capital invested in inventory is the concern of **asset management.** Logistics facilities, equipment, and inventory can represent a substantial segment of a firm's assets. For example, in the case of wholesalers, inventory frequently exceeds 80 percent of total capital. Asset management metrics focus on how well logistics managers utilize the capital invested in operations.

Facilities and equipment are frequently measured in terms of capacity utilization, or the percentage of total capacity used. For example, if a warehouse is capable of shipping 10,000 cases per day, but ships only 8,000, capacity utilization is only 80 percent. It is also common to measure equipment utilization in terms of time. Logistics managers are typically concerned with the number or percentage of hours that equipment is not utilized, which is measured as equipment **downtime.** Downtime can be applied to transportation, warehouse, and materials handling equipment. These measures indicate the effective or ineffective utilization of capital asset investment.

Asset management measurement also focuses on inventory. **Inventory turnover rate** is the most common measure of performance. Throughout the text, improved inventory turnover has been stressed as a critical focus of logistical management. It is important to understand how firms specifically measure inventory turnover rate. In fact, three specific metrics exist, each of which is used by different types of firms:

$$\text{Inventory turnover} = \frac{\text{Cost of goods sold during a time period}}{\text{Average inventory valued at cost during the time period}}$$

$$\text{Inventory turnover} = \frac{\text{Sales revenue during a time period}}{\text{Average inventory valued at selling price during time period}}$$

$$\text{Inventory turnover} = \frac{\text{Units sold during a time period}}{\text{Average unit inventory during the time period}}$$

The vast majority of firms use the first to calculate inventory turnover rate. However, some retail organizations use the second. In fact, either of the two ratios should yield approximately the same result. Any differences in the two calculations would result from changes in the amount of gross margin (the difference between sales and cost of goods sold) during the time period.

The third approach, using units rather than dollars, is particularly applicable to products whose cost or selling prices change significantly during a relatively short time. For example, inventory turnover of gasoline, which changes in cost and price almost daily, would most appropriately be measured by computing units of gasoline sold and units of inventory rather than dollars of any kind.

As a final note on computation of turnover, it is critical that average inventory be determined by using as many data points as possible. For example, suppose a company had no inventory at the beginning of the year, bought and held a large quantity for 11 months, then sold all inventory before end of year. Using only the beginning and ending inventory positions, average inventory would be zero and turnover infinite. Clearly, this would be misleading to management.

Inventory investment can also be tracked in terms of the amount that is available to meet forecasted sales volume and is expressed as the **days of supply.** For example, if sales are forecast at 100 units per day and 5,000 units are in inventory, the firm has 50 days of supply on hand.

Of major interest to senior executives is **return on assets** and **return on investment.** Rate of return is of such importance that it is discussed in considerable detail later in this chapter.

Most organizations have substantially improved their functional measurement systems over the past 10 years. The number of specific metrics has increased, and the quality of information has improved. Much of the improvement in information quality can be attributed to improved technology. Years ago measurement of on-time delivery typically did not actually monitor delivery receipt by the customer. Most firms had no mechanism to capture information concerning when customers received orders. Instead, they typically measured on-time shipment by discerning if the order was shipped on time. It was assumed that if shipments left the supplier's facility "on time," then they also arrived at customer facilities "on time." Thus, the transportation delivery aspect of the order cycle was ignored. Today, using EDI linkages, satellite, and Internet tracking, many organizations monitor whether orders actually arrive at the customer location on time.

Measuring Customer Accommodation

Chapter 3 presented the conclusion that basic logistical service performance is necessary but is not sufficient for firms that are truly committed to logistical excellence. Today, many firms have focused increased attention on alternative methods of measuring their ability to accommodate customer requirements. As a result, an additional set of metrics is required for companies that strive to move beyond measuring basic customer service. Measurement of perfect orders, absolute performance, and customer satisfaction are three such approaches. The ultimate in accommodation, customer success, has no specific metrics but remains the goal for firms committed to supply chain relationships.

Perfect Orders

The perfect order concept was discussed in Chapter 3 as an indicator of an organization's commitment to zero-defect logistics. Delivery of perfect orders is the ultimate measure of quality in logistics operations. A perfect order measures the effectiveness of the firm's overall integrated logistical performance rather than individual functions. It measures whether an order proceeds flawlessly through every step—order entry, credit clearance, inventory availability, accurate picking, on-time delivery, correct invoicing, and payment without deductions—of the order management process without fault, be it expediting, exception processing, or manual intervention. Table 16.2 expands on these dimensions of the perfect order. In fact, as many as 20 different logistic service elements may impact a perfect order. From a measurement perspective, perfect order performance is computed as the ratio of perfect orders during a given time period to the total number of orders completed during that period. Today, with some exceptions, even the best logistics organizations report achieving only 60 to 70 percent perfect order performance. There are simply so many things that can go wrong with an order!

Absolute Performance

Most basic service and quality measures, and even perfect order measures, are aggregated over many orders and over a period of time. The problem some executives report with these on-average, over-time measures is that they tend to disguise the organization's real impact on its customer base. These executives feel that such measures can actually result in a feeling of complacency within the firm and that it is more appropriate to track absolute performance as close to real time as possible. The absolute approach provides a better indication of how a firm's logistical performance really impacts customers. For example, managers may feel that 99.5 percent on-time delivery represents excellent performance. As an executive of a large delivery company said, "To us, 99.5 percent on-time delivery would mean that on a typical day, over 5000 customers received late orders. We can't feel good about having that kind of impact on that many customers." This firm, and many other companies

TABLE 16.2
Dimensions of the "Perfect Order"

Source: Reprinted with permission from Donald J. Bowersox, David J. Closs, and Theodore P. Stank, *21st Century Logistics: Making Supply Chain Integration a Reality,* Oak Brook, Illinois, Council of Supply Chain Management Professionals, 1999, p. 94.

Correct order entry	Timely arrival
Correctly formatted EDI and transaction codes	Shipment not damaged
Items are available	Correct invoice
Ship date allows delivery	Accurate overcharges
Order picked correctly	No customer deductions
Paperwork complete and accurate	No errors in payment processing

seeking to achieve maximum impact in the market, monitors absolute rates of failure and success as well as the more typical ratio and percentage metrics.

Customer Satisfaction

The ultimate judge of how well an organization accommodates customer expectations and requirements is the customer. All of the internally generated statistics related to basic service, perfect order, or absolute performance may be internal indicators of customer accommodation, but to quantify satisfaction requires monitoring, measuring, and collecting information from the customer. While a comprehensive discussion of interview and survey research methodology is beyond the scope of this text, typical satisfaction measurement requires careful investigation of customer expectations, requirements, and perceptions of firm performance related to all aspects of logistics operations. For example, the typical survey measures customer expectations and performance perceptions regarding availability, order cycle time, information availability, order accuracy, problem resolution, and other aspects of logistics quality. It is useful to gather information concerning customers' overall feelings of satisfaction in addition to their assessment of specific logistics activities. Additional questions may be included to capture customer perceptions of competitor performance. Only through collecting data from customers can real satisfaction be assessed! Further, efforts to enhance customer success can be measured only from the customer's perspective.

Supply Chain Comprehensive Metrics

The contemporary focus on overall supply chain performance and effectiveness demands metrics that provide an integrated perspective. This perspective must be comparable and consistent across both firm functions and supply chain institutions. Without integrated measures, managers in different functions and in different firms may have different perspectives concerning actual logistical performance. Specific measures to consider are cash-to-cash conversion time, supply chain inventory days of supply, dwell time, on-shelf in-stock percentage, total supply chain cost, and supply chain response time.

Cash-to-Cash Conversion

The cash-to-cash conversion concept was introduced in Chapter 1. It is a measure of an organization's effective use of cash. While inventory is typically reported as a current asset on the balance sheet, the reported dollar value may not be a valid indicator of the organization's true asset deployment. Some inventory may have been delivered to customers that, because of trade credit terms of sale, have not yet paid for related invoices. Conversely, an organization may owe its suppliers for products or components that are in its possession. Cash-to-cash cycle time is the time required to convert a dollar spent on inventory into a dollar collected from sales revenue. It can be measured by adding a firm's days of supply of inventory and its days of accounts receivable outstanding, subtracting the days of trade accounts payable outstanding. Consider a hypothetical retailer that maintains a 30-day supply of inventory, has 30 days' trade credit from suppliers, and sells to end consumers in cash-only transactions. This firm theoretically has a cash-to-cash cycle time equal to zero because it sells and collects from end customers just as its payment is due to suppliers. More importantly, the firm's actual investment of money in inventory is zero, regardless of what the balance sheet says.

Cash-to-cash cycle time is not solely impacted by logistics, although logistics is an important aspect. It is a measure of internal process because it includes a component of marketing—customer pricing and terms of sale—as well as a component from procurement—supplier pricing and terms. It offers an integrated perspective of the organization's real commitment of financial resources to inventory.

Inventory Days of Supply

Traditional measures of inventory performance, turnover, and days of supply, focus on individual firms. From a supply chain perspective, the flaw in these measures is that one firm may improve its performance by simply shifting inventory to its suppliers or to customers. Supply chain inventory days of supply is focused on total inventory at all locations and is typically defined as the total finished goods inventory at all plants, warehouses, wholesalers, and retailers expressed as the calendar days of sales available based on recent sales activity. This measure may be further extended to include raw materials and components held by manufacturing plants and suppliers. These unfinished inventories are converted to equivalent units of finished goods and included as part of the true total supply chain inventory. This measure, when adopted by all members of a supply chain, provides the focus of integrated operations.

Dwell Time

Dwell time is another metric reflecting overall supply chain performance in managing assets. Inventory dwell time is the ratio of the days inventory sits idle in the supply chain to the days it is being productively used or positioned. While it is sometimes necessary for inventory to sit idle for reasons of quality control or to buffer uncertainty, extended dwell time reflects the potential magnitude of nonproductive inventory. Dwell time can also be computed for other assets, especially transportation equipment. For example, railcar utilization can be measured by computing the number of days a rail car sits idle and empty versus the number of days it is loaded with freight. Reducing asset dwell time is a key objective for many logistics executives. Assets that sit idle are not contributing to productivity in the supply chain.

On-Shelf In-Stock Percent

Ultimately, a key objective of all participants in a supply chain is to have products available when and where end customers are ready to buy. Individual firm metrics related to fill rates at warehouses or to retail stores provide little assurance that products are available for consumer selection when a consumer is shopping. For example, a study of catalog retailers found that in-stock levels averaged less than 85 percent.[2] For this reason, in some supply chain relationships, a critical measure of overall performance is the on-shelf in-stock percent, the percentage of time that a product is available on the shelf in a store. The rationale is that consumers typically cannot or will not select and buy an item that is not easily available on the store shelf. Increasing the on-shelf in-stock percent benefits all members of the supply chain, not only the retailer. While it focuses on the retail impact, consider also the impact on suppliers when their products are not on the shelves at the time consumers want to buy.

Supply Chain Total Cost

Much of the discussion of cost thus far has focused on an individual firm's logistics costs. Figure 16.2 illustrates the fact that total supply chain cost is the aggregate of costs across all firms in the supply chain, not an individual organization. This perspective is absolutely critical to effective supply chain management. Focusing on a single firm's cost may lead to suboptimization and attempts by one company to shift cost to another. If the objective in supply chain management is to reduce total cost, it is reasonable to assume that one organization may actually experience increased cost as others in the supply chain experience reductions. As long as the total reductions in cost are larger than the cost increase for one

---

[2] John C. Taylor and Stanley E. Fawcett, "Catalog Retailer In-Stock Performance: An Assessment of Customer Service Levels," *Journal of Business Logistics* 25, no. 2 (2004), pp. 119–35.

FIGURE 16.2
**Total Supply Chain
Cost**

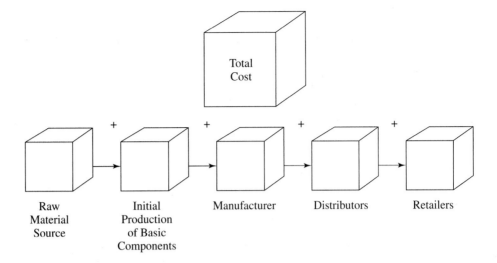

supply chain member, the supply chain as a whole is improved. It is then incumbent upon those companies whose cost is reduced to share benefits to fairly compensate those whose cost is increased. This willingness to share benefits and risks associated with changes in operational integration is the essence of true supply chain management.

Supply Chain Response Time

An interesting and extremely meaningful metric for comprehensive supply chain performance is **Supply Chain Response Time (SCRT).** SCRT is computed as the amount of time required for all firms in a supply chain to recognize a fundamental shift in marketplace demand, internalize that finding, replan, and adjust output to meet that demand. For example, in the auto industry, when it was discovered that demand for sport utility vehicles was extremely high, it took several years for the auto companies to develop sufficient production and capacity, rearrange supplier relationships, and meet consumer demand. In most instances, developing an actual metric for SCRT would be a theoretical approximation rather than a real measure. Nevertheless, it is extremely useful for supply chain executives to think in terms of how long it would take for an entire supply chain to ready all activities from raw material sourcing to final distribution when demand for a product is significantly greater (or less) that anticipated.

Benchmarking

Benchmarking is a critical aspect of performance measurement that makes management aware of state-of-the-art business practice. Many firms have adopted benchmarking as a tool to assess their operations in relation to those of leading firms, both competitors and noncompetitors, in related and nonrelated industries. While benchmarking performance metrics has become a fairly standard practice, many firms do not benchmark processes.

An important decision in benchmarking is the choice of organizations to benchmark. Many firms compare performance of internal business units involved in similar operations or located in different regions. For example, Johnson & Johnson, with over 150 different business units, has ample opportunity for internal benchmarking. Since business units in large diversified corporations are often unaware of what occurs in other units, internal benchmarking provides a way to share knowledge as well as improve performance.

Internal benchmarking, however, provides little information concerning performance relative to competition. A firm may be lagging competition and not be aware of it. Information about competitor performance can be used to identify where improvement is most

TABLE 16.3
Performance
Benchmarking
Differential

Source: Reprinted with permission from Donald J. Bowersox, David J. Closs, and Theodore P. Stank, *21st Century Logistics: Making Supply Chain Integration a Reality,* Oak Brook, IL, Council of Supply Chain Management Professionals, 1999, p. 97.

Performance Dimension	Percent of High Index Achieving Firms	Percent of Average Index Achieving Firms
Customer Service	92.5	56.0
Cost Management	80.0	47.1
Quality	70.0	31.0
Productivity	77.5	38.5
Asset Management	55.0	25.8

Note: All differentials are statistically significant at the .05 level.

needed; however, it is extremely difficult to capture information about competitors' operational processes.

Nonrestricted benchmarking involves efforts to compare both metrics and processes to best practices, regardless of where the relevant practice is found. It does not restrict sources of information to any particular company or industry. Nonrestricted benchmarking is grounded in the philosophy that is possible to learn from organizations in unrelated industries that have outstanding performance or use innovative approaches. L. L. Bean, the mail and catalog company, has been benchmarked in order fulfillment processes by firms from such diverse fields as food, personal care, and electronics.

Benchmarking is an important tool in the performance assessment system of an organization. In a study of best-practice supply chain companies referenced in Table 16.3, it was found that those firms that perform at high levels of supply chain capability are much more likely to be involved in benchmarking activity than firms that demonstrate average supply chain capability. Table 16.3 shows the results of the research related to benchmarking. In all categories, high-achieving companies are more involved in benchmarking than average-achieving firms. It is clear that benchmarking is considered an essential aspect of measurement by leading organizations.

Financial Assessment

In today's corporate environment, logistics executives must be informed and ready to demonstrate how supply chain practices and processes affect the overall financial health of their organization. Traditional performance assessment does not describe achievement in the financial language spoken at the board level. Measurement systems must enable logistics managers to link supply chain performance directly to financial results. To do so effectively, logistics managers must be well grounded in two critical tools for financial assessment: cost-revenue analysis and the strategic profit model.

Cost-Revenue Analysis

The achievement of logistical integration requires the establishment of a cost-revenue analysis framework. Traditional accounting practices make such a framework difficult for logistics executives. Contribution margin and full-costing methodologies have been supplemented by the use of **Activity-Based Costing (ABC)** as the most promising way to identify and control logistics expenses.

Public Accounting Practice

The two main financial reports of a business enterprise are the **balance sheet** and the **income statement.** The balance sheet reflects the financial position of a firm at a specific point in time. The purpose of a balance sheet is to summarize assets and liabilities and to indicate the net worth of ownership. The income statement reflects the revenues and costs associated with specific operations over a specified period of time. As the name income implies, its purpose is to determine the financial success of operations. Logistical functions are an integral part of both statements; however, the primary deficiency in logistical costing and analysis is the method by which standardized accounting costs are identified, classified, and reported. Unfortunately, the conventional methods of accounting do not fully satisfy logistical costing requirements.

The first problem results from the fact that accounting practice aggregates costs on a standard or natural account basis rather than on an activity basis. The practice of grouping expenses into natural accounts such as salaries, rent, utilities, and depreciation fails to identify or assign operations responsibility. To help overcome the natural account aggregation, it is common for statements to be subdivided by managerial or organizational areas of responsibility within an enterprise. Internal income statements generally classify and group expenses along organization budgetary lines. Thus, costs are detailed by managerial responsibility. However, many expenses associated with logistical performance cut across organization units. For example, efforts to reduce inventory will reduce inventory carrying cost, but they may also lead to more back orders, which would increase total transportation cost. The result is inadequate data for integrated performance measurement.

A somewhat overlapping deficiency of accounting involves the traditional methods of reporting transportation expenditures. It remains standard practice in accounting to deduct inbound freight expense from gross sales as part of the cost of goods to arrive at a gross margin figure. Outbound freight, on the other hand, is generally reported as an operating expense. However, the problem extends beyond where freight is accounted for and reported. In many purchasing situations, freight is not reported as a specific cost. Many products are purchased on a delivered price basis, which includes transportation cost. Most progressive procurement procedures require that expenses for all services, including transportation, be debundled from the total purchase cost for evaluative purposes.

A final deficiency in traditional accounting practice is the failure to specify and assign inventory cost. The deficiency has two aspects. First, full costs associated with the maintenance of inventory, such as insurance and taxes, are not identified, resulting in an understatement or obscurity in reporting inventory cost. Second, the financial burden for assets committed to material, work-in-process, and finished goods inventory is not identified, measured, or separated from other forms of capital expense incurred by the enterprise. In fact, if a firm deploys internal funds to support inventory requirements, it is likely that no capital expenses will be reflected by the profit and loss statement.

To remedy these shortcomings, several modifications to traditional accounting are required to track logistical costs. In particular, the two largest individual expenses in logistics—transportation and inventory—have traditionally been reported in a manner that obscures their importance instead of highlighting them. Although the situation is improving, routine isolation and reporting of logistical costs is not standard practice in most organizations.

To control cost and improve operational efficiency, it is necessary to properly identify and capture all relevant cost information in a manner that is meaningful to decision makers. Logistical costing must also provide those executives with the information to determine whether a specific segment of business such as a customer, order, product, channel, or service is profitable. This requires the matching of specific revenue with specific costs.

Effective costing requires identification of the specific expenses included in an analysis framework. Two frameworks that each have numerous proponents are the **contribution approach** and the **net profit approach.**

Contribution Approach

A pure contribution approach requires that all costs be identified as fixed or variable according to the cost behavior. Fixed costs are those that do not directly change with volume of activity. In the short term those costs would remain even if volume were reduced to zero. For example, the cost of a delivery truck is fixed. If the truck cost $40,000, the firm is charged $40,000 (or the appropriate depreciation) whether the truck is used for 1 or 1,000 deliveries. Variable costs are those costs that do change as a result of volume. The gasoline required to operate a delivery truck is variable: Total gasoline cost depends upon how frequently and how far the truck is driven.

It is also necessary in contribution analysis to specify which are direct costs and which are indirect costs. Direct costs are those that are specifically incurred because of the existence of the product, customer, or other segment under consideration. If that segment were eliminated, the direct cost would no longer exist. All variable costs can be directly traced to specific products, customers, channels, and the like. Some fixed costs may also be direct if they exist to logistically support a specific business segment. For example, a warehouse facility may be constructed specifically to support a specific product line or major customer account. Indirect costs exist because of more than one segment of business and would continue to exist even if one specific segment were eliminated. Thus, a warehouse that maintains multiple product lines would continue to operate even if one product line was discontinued. In this case, the warehouse is indirect to the products.

Income statements in the contribution method of analysis can be prepared that identify profitability for each segment by determination of fixed, variable, direct, and indirect costs. Table 16.4 provides a hypothetical example of such income statements for a firm analyzing profitability of two customers, a hospital and a retailer. Variable costs of goods sold are directly related to the product mix sold in each customer segment; it includes only direct labor, materials, and supplies. All factory overhead costs are treated as indirect costs in the contribution margin approach. Variable direct costs include such items as sales commission, discounts, certain logistics costs related to servicing each customer, and any other expenses that vary directly with volume sold to each customer. Fixed direct costs include any other costs that can be traced directly to the specific customer. Such costs might include certain aspects of sales, salaries and expenses, advertising, transportation, warehousing, order processing, and other logistical activities. The key is that these expenses must be directly attributable to those customers. Indirect fixed costs includes all expenses that cannot easily be traced to a specific segment. Many of these may also be logistics-related costs. For example, shared warehouse, transportation equipment, and other jointly used resources should be specified as indirect costs.

TABLE 16.4
Contribution Margin Income Statement for Two Customers

	Hospital	Retailer	Total
Revenue	$100,000	$150,000	$250,000
Less: Variable Cost of Goods Sold	42,000	75,000	117,000
Variable Gross Profit	58,000	75,000	133,000
Less: Variable Direct Cost	6,000	15,000	21,000
Gross Segment Contribution	52,000	60,000	112,000
Less: Fixed Direct Costs	15,000	21,000	36,000
Net Segment Contribution	$ 37,000	$ 39,000	76,000
Less: Indirect Fixed Costs			41,000
Net Profit			$ 25,000
Net Segment Contribution Ratio	37%	26%	30.4%

In Table 16.4, both customers are covering direct costs and making a substantial contribution to indirect fixed cost. The hospital, however, has a substantially higher percentage net segment contribution than does the retailer—37 percent versus 26 percent. A large portion of this difference is attributable to the difference in variable gross profit of 58 percent versus 50 percent. This difference suggests that analysis of the product mix for the retailer should be conducted to determine whether emphasis should be placed on a more profitable mix. Elimination of the retailer would be a clear mistake, however, as the hospital customer would then have to bear all of the indirect fixed cost, resulting in a net loss of $4,000.

Net Profit Approach

The net profit approach to financial assessment of segments requires that all operating costs be charged or allocated to an operating segment. Proponents of this approach argue that all of a company's activities exist to support the production and delivery of goods and services to customers. Furthermore, in many firms most costs are, in fact, joint or shared costs. To determine the true profitability of a channel, territory, or product, each segment must be allocated its fair share of these costs. In the previous example, allocating indirect fixed cost on the basis of sales volume would result in the hospital being charged with 40 percent, or $16,400, and the retailer 60 percent, or $24,600. The net profit of serving the hospital would be $20,600. The net profit from the retail customer would be $14,400.

Clearly, significant problems arise in determining how to allocate indirect costs on a fair and equitable basis. Proponents of the contribution margin approach contend that such allocations are necessarily arbitrary and result in misleading financial assessment. They point to the use of sales volume as a typical basis for allocation of expense and the inherent bias in such an approach. For example, the retailer above accounts for 60 percent of total sales volume but does not necessarily account for 60 percent of the expense of advertising, warehousing, order processing, or any other shared activity. It may account for much more or less of each expense category, depending upon circumstances that are not at all related simply to sales volume.

Net profit proponents argue, however, that the traditional notions of fixed and variable cost and direct and indirect cost are too simplistic. Many of the so-called indirect fixed costs are not, in fact, indirect or fixed at all. These expenses rise and fall, depending upon demands placed upon the business by the various operating segments.

Activity-Based Costing

As a partial solution to the problem of arbitrary allocations, **Activity-Based Costing (ABC)** suggests that costs should first be traced to activities performed and then activities should be related to specific product or customer segments of the business. Suppose, for example, the order processing expense is basically a fixed indirect cost in our hypothetical example, amounting to $5,000. Allocating this expense to the two customers on the basis of sales volume results in a charge of $2,000 to the hospital and $3,000 to the retailer. However, it is likely that the hospital places very many orders during the year, each of a small quantity, while the retailer may place only a few large orders. If the hospital placed 80 orders and the retailer placed 20 orders, an ABC approach would charge the hospital with 80 percent, or $4,000, and the retailer with 20 percent, or $1,000, of the order processing expense. Applying similar logic to other indirect fixed costs by identifying the activities and cost drivers could result in further refinement of customer profitability.

Identifying the activities, related expenses, and the drivers of expense represents the biggest challenge in an ABC approach. Order processing cost may be related to the number of orders in one company and to the number of lines on orders in another company. Warehouse picking expense may be related to the number of items picked in one company and to the number of pounds in another. Transportation might be related to number of deliveries for one firm and number of miles driven for another. According to proponents of this activity-based costing method, one cost that should be excluded from allocation to segments is the cost of excess capacity. Thus, if an order processing system could process 5 million orders per year but is only utilized for 4 million orders, the excess capacity should not be charged to any segment. Similarly, if a warehouse and its employees could handle 100,000 shipments but are only used for 80,000, the excess capacity is a cost of the time period rather than a cost attributable to an existing operating segment. All other costs, however, should be traced through an activity-based system.

Much of the distinction between the contribution margin and net profit approaches to segment cost analysis is disappearing as analysts are developing better approaches to identify expense behavior. Advocates of direct costing and contribution margin would probably go along with the tracing of costs to segments based on activities performed, as long as the basis for tracing reflects the real cost of the activity. Historically, their argument has been based on the fairness and appropriateness of the allocation method. Even the most avid proponent of full costing, on the other hand, would not argue in favor of arbitrary allocation of cost. The development of better ABC systems has the potential for ultimately resolving this controversy, which has existed in marketing and logistics for a number of years.

Strategic Profit Model

While costing and profitability assessment are important aspects of financial controllership, the most critical measure of strategic success is **Return on Investment (ROI).** There are two ways of viewing ROI. The first is **Return on Net Worth (RONW),** which measures the profitability of the funds that the owners of the firm have invested in the firm. The second is **Return on Assets (ROA),** which measures the profitability generated by managing a firm's operational assets. While owners and investors are most likely interested in RONW, ROA offers a measure of how well management is utilizing assets to earn profits.

Figure 16.3 presents the Strategic Profit Model (SPM), with hypothetical data. The SPM is a tool frequently used to analyze ROI in a business firm. In fact, the SPM is a tool that incorporates both income and balance sheet data and demonstrates how these data relate to each other to result in ROA.

One of the primary benefits of the SPM is that it shows very clearly that a key financial objective of the firm is to achieve and increase ROA. Too often, managers focus on more limited objectives. For example, sales management may focus on sales as the primary objective of the business and, therefore, will base decisions on sales volume. Logistics managers may focus on cost minimization or turnover and feel that decisions must be based on reducing expense or increasing the firm's efficient utilization of assets. The SPM demonstrates that there are two fundamental ways in which a firm can increase return on assets: managing net profit margin and/or managing asset turnover. Logistics operations have a significant impact on both.

Net Profit Margin

Expressed as a percentage, net profit margin is net profit divided by net sales. Going beyond this simple expression, however, net profit margin actually measures the proportion of each sales dollar that is kept by the firm as net profit. For example, the hypothetical firm has a net profit margin of 5 percent; this simply means that $0.05 out of every $1 represents net profit for the company. It is important to note that net profit margin is also divided into a number of specific components. These components are sales volume, cost of goods sold, and operating expenses. For a full evaluation of whether the firm's net profit margin is

FIGURE 16.3   **Strategic Profit Model**

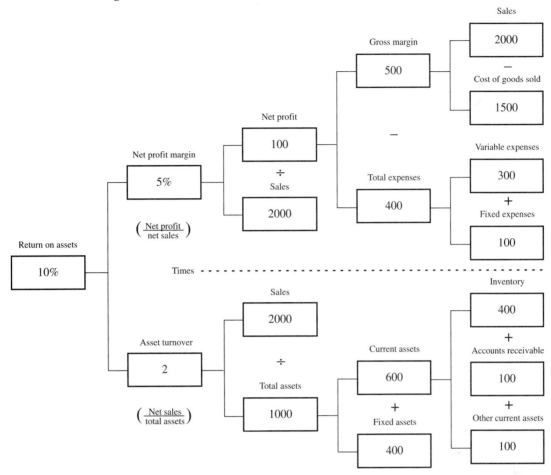

adequate, and whether it might be improved, it is necessary to investigate each component to determine whether an increase or decrease in any one component or in any combination of components might lead to improved net profit margin performance.

Asset Turnover

The ratio of total sales divided by total assets is asset turnover, which measures the efficiency of management in utilizing assets. It shows how many dollars in total sales volume are being generated by each dollar that the firm has invested in assets. For example, the hypothetical company with an asset turnover ratio of 2:1 is generating $2.00 in sales volume for each dollar it has invested in assets. As Figure 16.3 illustrates, there are a number of assets used to generate sales. The most important are inventories, accounts receivable, and fixed facilities. Inventory is a particularly important asset to many firms because it is typically one of the largest areas of asset investment. Thus, it is common in logistics to focus specifically on the management of the inventory turnover ratio.

Applications of the SPM

The SPM can be used for many different types of logistical analysis. Two of the most con mon are the impact of changes in logistical activities or processes on ROA and analysis segmental ROA.

FIGURE 16.4 **Strategic Profit Model (Inventory Reduction)**

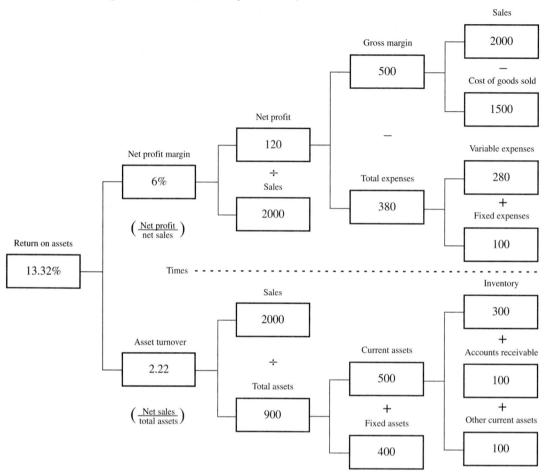

Figure 16.4 illustrates a recomputation of ROA assuming that the hypothetical firm was able to accomplish an inventory reduction of $100. The most obvious impact of this inventory reduction occurs through the reduction in the inventory asset from $400 to $300. A corresponding change in total assets results in a new asset turnover rate of 2.22 versus the base case of 2.0 times. It is assumed, for explanatory purposes, that sales volume remains the same.

However, a reduction in average inventory also has an impact on operating expenses. Inventory carrying costs, discussed in Chapter 6, should be reduced as well. In this example, assuming an inventory carrying cost of 20 percent, the expense reduction amounts to $20, increasing net profit to $120, and net profit margin to 6 percent. The combined profit margin and asset turnover impact of inventory reduction result in an increase in ROA from 10 percent to over 13.3 percent. No wonder so many organizations are focusing on methods to improve inventory management!

The simplifying assumption of no change in sales could be subjected to further examination by using the SPM. A variety of scenarios regarding potential changes in volume, expenses, and investments can be proposed and analyzed. In fact, the SPM framework is very adaptable to a spreadsheet model, which allows investigation and analysis of many different changes in logistics operations and their projected impact on ROA. Changes in facility

TABLE 16.5
CMROI for Two
Products

	Product A	Product B
Sales	$100,000	$50,000
Cost of Goods	60,000	35,000
Gross Margin	40,000 (40%)	15,000 (30%)
Direct Expense	25,000	9000
Contribution Margin	15,000 (15%)	6000 (12%)
Average Inventory	40,000	10,000
CMROI	37.5%	60%

structure or methods with projected changes in expenses, asset investment, and sales level can be analyzed to project impact on ROA.

The SPM, in conjunction with concepts discussed in the section on cost/revenue analysis, can also be used to examine the return on assets generated by various customer or product segments of a business. Table 16.5 provides a sample calculation of **Contribution Margin Return on Inventory Investment (CMROI)** for two products. Contribution margin for each product is calculated by using only those expenses directly traced to each product.

No indirect costs are allocated. Similarly, asset investments directly attributable to specific products should be identified. In this case, the only direct asset investment is inventory investment. Notice that product B has lower gross margin and contribution margin but actually provides a substantially higher return because of its low average inventory investment. In other situations, for example, analysis of customer return on assets, accounts receivable, and other direct asset investments attributable to a specific customer should be included.

Other segment profitability and ROI analyses can be conducted by using the SPM framework. It requires careful thought and identification of those costs and asset investments traceable to specific segments. With this approach, the logistics executive has a powerful and useful tool for identifying how logistics process, activities, and decisions impact the financial objectives of the organization.

One problem faced by logistics executives is that typical approaches to logistics performance assessment are not generally expressed in terms that are meaningful to other senior executives. For example, transportation expense per mile, warehouse picking expense, and cost-related metrics are extremely meaningful in terms of managing those specific activities but are somewhat obscure to executives in finance and marketing. The SPM framework is a very useful tool for relating logistics activities to the overall financial objectives of the organization. It provides a mechanism to trace specifically how changes in logistics' assets or expenses relate directly to measures that are more meaningful to other executives: measures such as profit margin, asset turnover, and return on assets.

Social Issues in Logistics Performance Measurement

Because of numerous instances of financial mismanagement by major corporations, in 2002 the U.S. Congress passed the Sarbanes-Oxley Act (SOX). Although the focus of the law is on financial reporting by corporations to their shareholders, it became apparent soo after its enactment that it also has important implications for logistics and supply cha management, especially with respect to how performance is measured and reported. B cause SOX covers any information that affects what the company must report to the Se rities and Exchange Commission (SEC), companies must have adequate controls in p to compute and report on a standardized basis all spending and revenue. In particular, two aspects of the act are highly relevant to supply chain and logistics management. The first is requirements for internal control and the second relates to issues of supply chain security.

Requirements for Internal Control

Section 404 of SOX requires that a company file an internal control report at the same time it files its corporate annual report. The SEC will evaluate the internal controls used by the firm to determine its adequacy for ensuring that the financial reports are consistent and accurate. Thus, every firm covered by the act must have internal measurement capabilities that comply with SEC requirements. It is important to note that the SEC does not specify what the internal controls and measures must be, but it does require that the controls ensure the integrity of financial information. In essence, companies must demonstrate that their measurement systems ensure that financial data such as revenue, cost of goods sold, expenses, assets, and liabilities are accurately reported. This has a direct impact on logistics performance measurement.[3]

Table 16.6 provides examples of supply chain and logistics activities, the financial elements affected, and measures that might be used to ensure the accuracy of the financial information. APICS, a professional association, and Protiviti, a consulting firm, suggest that the internal metrics shown in column 5 of the table can be used to validate the financial elements shown in columns 3 and 4. For example, measuring inventory accuracy is critical to ensure that the firm accurately reports cost of sales on its income statement and investment in inventory on the balance sheet. Likewise, other internal measures shown in the table can be linked directly to income statement and balance sheet items. Although the framework suggested in the table is only an example, it demonstrates the fact that companies are required by SOX to have a system of internal measurement that ensures the accuracy of financial information.

Supply Chain Security

Although SOX does not directly address issues of supply chain security, its indirect impact is enormous. Essentially, because corporate executives are required to guarantee the financial reporting of their firm, they must be sure that they are aware of the risks the firm faces. Many of these risks, of course, are related to supply chain operations in general and supply chain security in particular. Another federal program, the Customs-Trade Partnership against Terrorism (C-TPAT), discussed in Chapter 11, also affects the need for greater supply chain security.

Consider, for example, shipments of goods that have a long lead time and/or have the potential to be held up for a long time at an international border because of security risks or transportation delays. In many instances, the buyer may be contractually obligated to pay for the goods regardless of when they are received. Thus, the buyer owns inventory but may not receive actual possession for some time.[4] Historically, such situations were essentially unknown to senior executives, but in the current environment this financial commitment, and related risk, must be acknowledged. Basically, the requirements for supply chain security and for full disclosure of the financial status of the organization have combined to force senior executives to have a much greater understanding of the details of logistical operations. It also places a premium on having the ability to monitor the location and status of shipments in a timely and accurate manner.

Although many managers feel that the legal requirements of SOX are a burden on the organization, others view it as an opportunity for improvement. The requirements for more

---

[3] Roger Morton, "SOX and the Supply Chain," *Logistics Today* 45, no. 10 (October 2004), p. 27.

[4] Peter M. Tirshwell, "How to Avoid This," *Journal of Commerce* (November 2, 2004), p. 1.

TABLE 16.6

Supply Chain and Logistics Measures Related to Financial Reporting

Source: Reprinted with permission from Protiviti/APICS, "Capitalizing on Sarbanes-Oxley Compliance to Build Supply Chain Advantage," May 2003, p. 9.

Supply Chain Business Process	Supply Chain Transactions	Financial Reporting Elements (balance sheet)	Financial Reporting Elements (income statement)	Supply Chain Reporting Elements (some examples)
		Activity Level		
Plan	Raw materials are purchased	• Raw materials • Accounts payable • Cash and debt	• Cost of sales	• Supplier delivery performance • Cost and quality • Planned deliveries
Source	Purchase of equipment, direct and indirect material, and services	• Property and equipment (net) • Accounts payable • Cash and debt	• Depreciation • Taxes	• Supplier delivery performance • Cost and quality • Planned deliveries
Produce	Products are manufactured or raw materials are converted	• Raw materials • Work in process • Accounts payable • Accrued expenses • Wages payable • Cash	• Cost of sales • Wages • Utilities	• On-time delivery • Quality and cost • Routing accuracy • Production plan performance • Production schedule performance • Scrap rate • WIP levels • Planned production
Store	Raw materials, work in process, or finished goods are stored	• Raw materials • Work in process • Finished goods • Accounts payable • Accrued expenses • Wages payable • Cash	• Cost of sales • Wages • Utilities	• Inventory accuracy • Queue, buffer, and safety stock levels • Inventory turnover • Scrap rate
Transport	Goods are transported	• Work in process • Finished goods • Accounts payable • Wages payable • Cash	• Cost of sales • Wages	• On-time delivery • Quality and cost • Scrap rate
Sell	Products or services are sold	• Accounts receivable (net) • Finished goods • Warranty reserves • Commissions payable • Cash	• Net revenues • Cost of sales • Selling expenses • Marketing expenses • Commissions	• Sales plan performance • Customer service • Percent sales order changes • Order entry accuracy
Return	Sold goods are returned	• Accounts receivable (net) • Inventory reserves • Accounts payable • Warranty reserves • Commissions payable • Cash	• Net revenues	• Quality and customer service • Planned returns

detailed knowledge of where finished products and materials are at all times, from their point of origin to arrival at final destination, make it necessary for companies to commit more resources to providing supply chain visibility to management. In turn, by having greater visibility, the opportunity exists to improve decisions by basing them on better and more timely information.

Summary

Effective management of logistics operations and supply chain integration requires establishment of a framework for performance assessment and financial controllership. This framework provides the mechanism to monitor system performance, control activities, and direct personnel to achieve higher levels of productivity.

Comprehensive performance measurement systems include metrics for each of the logistics functions. Five critical dimensions of functional performance must be addressed: cost, customer service, quality, productivity, and asset management. Leading firms extend their functional measurement systems to include metrics focused on their ability to accommodate customer requirements. These include measures of absolute performance rather than average performance, perfect orders, consumer-focused measures, and customer satisfaction. To aid in achievement of supply chain integration, leading firms have instituted a set of across-firm metrics such as inventory days of supply, inventory dwell time, cash-to-cash cycle time, and total supply chain cost.

Effective financial assessment requires knowledge of cost-revenue analysis and the strategic profit model. Traditional accounting practices are typically inadequate for logistics costing. Effective decision making requires that management be able to match revenues with expenses incurred to service specific customers, channels, and products. Contribution and net profit approaches represent alternative formats for cost/revenue analysis. Activity-based costing provides management the ability to more specifically trace logistics expenses to the segments that generate revenue. An additional tool for controllership is the strategic profit model. This model provides managers the ability to assess the impact of logistics decisions on profitability, asset utilization, and return on assets. It also provides the ability to more accurately assess segments in terms of profit and return on investment. The chapter concludes with a discussion of the growing importances of social issues in logistics performance measurement. The importance of internal control and security is discussed in terms of Sarbanes-Oxley requirements.

Challenge Questions

1. Briefly discuss the three objectives for developing and implementing performance measurement systems.
2. Compare and contrast the various metrics for product availability. Why is the perfect order fill rate considered the most stringent metric?
3. Is the ideal of a perfect order a realistic operational goal?
4. Why is it important that a firm measure customer perception as a regular part of performance measurement?
5. Why are comprehensive measures of supply chain performance, such as total supply chain cost, so difficult to develop?
6. Compare and contrast the contribution approach with the net profit approach in cost/revenue analysis.
7. Do you believe that activity-based costing represents an equitable basis for allocating indirect expenses?
8. Suppose you have been asked by a firm to assess the impact on return on assets of outsourcing transportation. Currently the firm uses a private truck fleet and is considering a switch to a for-hire transportation company. Which aspects of the strategic profit model would be affected?
9. How can the strategic profit model be integrated with cost-revenue analysis for the purpose of analyzing the return on assets from servicing a specific customer account?
10. How does the Sarbanes-Oxley Act impact requirements for logistics performance measurement?

In the final analysis, the logistical management challenge is to rise above a traditional functional perspective to help capture and promulgate the need for managers to reinvent what they are all about. What they should be about is very simple—servicing customers. While it is sometimes hard to comprehend why, the fact is that most business firms are in need of a significant transformation to reposition resources to best accomplish this basic goal. For a host of reasons, complexity dominates the modern enterprise. Reinvention of a business is all about simplification, standardization, and integration. It is all about getting back to basics. Logistics is basic.

The logistics manager of the future will be much more of a change leader and much less of a technician. The challenge of change will be driven by the need to synchronize the speed and flexibility of logistical competency into the process of creating customer value. Technology and technique will not be limiting factors. If no new technology is invented for a decade or more, we still will not have fully exploited technology currently available. The concepts being promoted as new ways to improve productivity are for the most part old. Such concepts as activity-based costing, time-based competition, ABC inventory analysis, process integration, collaboration, quick response, segmentation, and so forth, are not new. What is new is that today's leader is supported by information technology that makes them work.

Of course, the challenge to reinvent the enterprise is not the sole responsibility of logisticians, but it is a responsibility of logistical managers to participate in the process, especially those who lead global operations, have stewardship for extensive capital and human resources, and facilitate the delivery of products and services to customers. The logistical executive of the future will not be able to neglect responsibility for contributing to and participating in the change management required to transform the enterprise to the digital information age.

To this end, authors typically collect quotations and statements that they feel capture the meaning and intensity of their message. To the logistics manager of today and tomorrow who will face the challenges of change, we offer the following quotes as a source of compassion and inspiration:

Concerning Change: Logistics Is Not an Ordinary Occupation

> Experience teaches that men are so much governed by what they are accustomed to see and practice that the simplest and most obvious improvements in the most ordinary occupations are adapted with hesitation, reluctance and by slow graduations.—*Alexander Hamilton,* 1791

Concerning Organization: It Is a Matter of Perspective

> We trained hard . . . but it seemed that every time we were beginning to form up into teams we would be reorganized. I was to learn later in life that we tend to meet any new situation by reorganizing; and a wonderful method it can be for creating the illusion of progress while producing confusion, inefficiency and demoralization.—*Petronius,* 200 B.C.

Concerning New Ideas: Some Are Not So New

> One may even dream of production so organized that no business concern or other economic unit would be obligated to carry stocks of raw materials or of finished goods . . . picture supplies of every sort flowing into factories just as machines are ready to use them; goods flowing out to freight cars and trucks just pulling up to shipping platforms;

merchandise arriving at the dealer's shelves just when space was made available . . . under such conditions the burden of expense and risk borne by society because of the stocks necessary to the production process would be at a minimum.—*Everett S. Lyon,* 1929

Concerning Appreciation: What Have You Done for Me Lately?

The Logistician

Logisticians are a sad and embittered race of men who are very much in demand in war, and who sink resentfully into obscurity in peace. They deal only in facts, but must work for men who merchant in theories. They emerge during war because war is very much a fact. They disappear in peace because peace is mostly theory. The people who merchant in theories, and who employ logisticians in war and ignore them in peace, are generals.

Generals are a happily blessed race who radiate confidence and power. They feed only on ambrosia and drink only nectar. In peace, they stride confidently and can invade a world simply sweeping their hands grandly over a map, pointing their fingers decisively up terrain corridors, and blocking defiles and obstacles with the sides of their hands. In war, they must stride more slowly because each general has a logistician riding on his back and he knows that, at any moment, the logistician may lean forward and whisper: "No, you can't do that." Generals fear logisticians in war and, in peace, generals try to forget logisticians.

Romping along beside generals are strategists and tacticians. Logisticians despise strategists and tacticians. Strategists and tacticians do not know about logisticians until they grow up to be generals—which they usually do.

Sometimes a logistician becomes a general. If he does, he must associate with generals whom he hates; he has a retinue of strategists and tacticians whom he despises; and, on his back, is a logistician whom he fears. This is why logisticians who become generals always have ulcers and cannot eat their ambrosia.—*Author unknown; made available by Major William K. Bawden, RCAF*

Name Index

Subject Index